# DICKENSIAN DRAMAS

## VOLUME I

Dickens loved the stage—he enjoyed thousands of evenings in the theatre, and longed to write for it and to perform himself, an ambition that he eventually satisfied by touring alone with his Readings. Victorian prejudice and his need to preserve his personal image kept him from openly becoming a stage professional earlier in his career, but all his work was informed by his dramatic imagination. He found ways of circumventing these taboos by seeking closer and closer contact over the staging of his work with dramatic writers, admired actors, and trusted theatre managements. This book presents, for the first time, fully edited texts of some of the plays which these tacit collaborations produced: dramatizations of Dickens's early novels (from *The Pickwick Papers* to *Barnaby Rudge*) and, especially, his Christmas books, which appeared almost annually between 1843 and 1848. Each of these, from *A Christmas Carol* onwards, was staged in London's new West End theatres simultaneously with the book publication. Dickens sent proof sheets to his friends to 'dramatize' work that was increasingly already conceived for the stage, and for the acting of his friends Bob and Mary Ann Keeley. This selection of the plays created in this way, some previously unpublished, offers the first opportunity for modern scholars to consider not only an exciting body of translations to the stage made by the first generation of Dickensian adaptors, but also the influence of their work and of the performances they enabled upon Dickens himself.

# DICKENSIAN DRAMAS

*Plays from Charles Dickens*

*VOLUME I*

EDITED BY
JACKY BRATTON

**OXFORD**
UNIVERSITY PRESS

# OXFORD
### UNIVERSITY PRESS

Great Clarendon Street, Oxford, OX2 6DP,
United Kingdom

Oxford University Press is a department of the University of Oxford.
It furthers the University's objective of excellence in research, scholarship,
and education by publishing worldwide. Oxford is a registered trade mark of
Oxford University Press in the UK and in certain other countries

First Edition published in 2017

Impression: 1

Published in the United States of America by Oxford University Press
198 Madison Avenue, New York, NY 10016, United States of America

British Library Cataloguing in Publication Data

Data available

Library of Congress Control Number: 2016938163

ISBN 978-0-19-878795-2

Printed and bound by
CPI Group (UK) Ltd, Croydon, CR0 4YY

# ACKNOWLEDGEMENTS

T HIS edition would not be possible without the use of the collection of manuscripts plays preserved by the Lord Chamberlain's office, housed by the British
Library, to whom I am grateful for permission to transcribe and reproduce them;
I would also like to thank all the library staff for their wide knowledge and unfailing
help with this project. I would also like to thank Professor Tracy C. Davis for the gift
of her transcription of *A Cricket on the Hearth*, which forms the basis of my edition
here, and which she dropped from her *Broadview Anthology of Nineteenth-Century
British Performance* when I chose to include it. Cordial thanks also to Professor Dan
Rebellato and Peter MacAllister for giving me the benefit of their opinions and some
valuable information concerning *The Battle of Life*.

The majority of the illustrations come from the Victoria and Albert Theatre
Collection, and I am grateful for their permission to reproduce them, and especially
to Kate Dorney for her help and support.

I am also grateful for the responses of colleagues before whom I presented my first
thoughts about the early Dickensian drama at a series of conferences from 2011
onwards; to my partner Gilli Bush-Bailey and to my friend Christine Webb for reading and commenting upon many drafts; and to my fellow-editor Jim Davis, who
cheerfully agreed to join this enterprise and has produced the far more editorially
complicated second volume.

# CONTENTS

# LIST OF ILLUSTRATIONS

# LIST OF ABBREVIATIONS

## EDITORIAL

| | |
|---|---|
| LC | Lord Chamberlain |
| MS | manuscript |
| sd | stage direction |

## BIBLIOGRAPHIC

| | |
|---|---|
| *Adelphi Calendar* | *The Adelphi Theatre Calendar: A Record of Dramatic Performances at a Leading Victorian Theatre* <http://www.umass.edu/AdelphiTheatreCalendar/index.htm> |
| Bolton | H. Philip Bolton, *Dickens Dramatized* (Boston, Mass.: G.K. Hall & Co., 1987) |
| Bratton, *New Readings* | Jacky Bratton, *New Readings in Theatre History* (Cambridge: Cambridge University Press, 2003) |
| Bratton, *West End* | Jacky Bratton, *The Making of the West End Stage: Marriage, Management and the Mapping of Gender in London, 1830–1870* (Cambridge: Cambridge University Press, 2011) |
| *DNB* | *The Oxford Dictionary of National Biography* <http://www.oxforddnb.com> |
| Hatton & Cleaver | Thomas Hatton and Arthur H. Cleaver, *A Bibliography of the Periodical Works of Charles Dickens* (London: Chapman and Hall, 1933) |
| *ILN* | *Illustrated London News* |
| *Letters* | *The Letters of Charles Dickens*, Pilgrim edn, ed. Madeleine House, Graham Storey, Kathleen Tillotson, and Nina Burgis, 12 vols, 1–4 (Oxford: Clarendon Press, 1965, 1969, 1974, 1977) |
| *OED* | *The Oxford English Dictionary* <http://www.oed.com> |
| *TLS* | *Times Literary Supplement* |
| Tomalin | Claire Tomalin, *Charles Dickens, a Life* (London: Viking, 2011) |

# INTRODUCTION

EDMUND WILSON asserts that Dickens was 'the greatest dramatic writer that the English have had since Shakespeare'.[1] It is the aim of this collection and its companion to make that claim good, taking it in a quite literal way, as meaning that Charles Dickens created work which is now, and always has been, seen and heard as dramas, as eagerly as it has been read in the form of novels and stories. His work has entered the dramatic canon by the back door, for reasons to do with the culture of his own times as well as with the ongoing literary preferences of English studies. This indirection, unfortunate as its impact may have been on the development of English theatre in the nineteenth century, could be argued to have had a benign after-effect on the life of his work in dramatic form. Since Dickens wrote very few plays himself, beyond his first days as one of the swarm of new writers in the 1830s, every generation, beginning with his own but continuing to this day, has made his works into plays and films for itself, inevitably working by means of contemporary conventions and resources. At the long remove at which we now stand from the middle of the nineteenth century, with all that implies about changes in literary language and tastes, modern audiences (as distinct from readers) are in this sense fortunate, because they stand in relation to Dickensian drama as non-English-speaking audiences do to Shakespeare. For us Dickens has to be dramatized, just as for non-Anglophone audiences Shakespeare has to be translated. So fresh versions of Dickens are constantly made, that have the advantage of being always in the dramatic languages of the day.

There is a huge and appreciative audience for Dickens on film, in the digital media, and in all kinds of live dramatization on the popular stage. Taking one twenty-first-century British Christmas season as an example, in the week beginning 17 December 2007, the Gielgud Theatre in Shaftesbury Avenue was playing both parts of David Edgar's protractedly faithful adaptation *The Life and Adventures of Nicholas Nickleby*, and the Young Vic had a South African company staging *Ikrismas Kherol*, set in a township gangland with a female Scrooge and billed as not suitable for children. As well as these ventures in the quality market, there was huge popular deployment of Dickensianism, or what one may call the matter of Dickens: a London gay runners' club advertised a benefit for Stonewall in the form of *A Christmas Carol—a Gay and Ghostly Pantomime*; the TV Guide for Christmas week offered no fewer than six full-length Dickens movies, namely David Lean's 1946 *Great Expectations*, the 1934 *David Copperfield*, Alastair Sim's Scrooge in a *Christmas Carol* directed by Brian Desmond Hurst in 1951, *Oliver Twist* interpreted by Roman Polanski in 2005, plus a *Christmas*

---

[1] Edmund Wilson, *The Wound and the Bow* (Cambridge: Houghton Mifflin, 1941), 3.

*Carol* financed by Hallmark films in 1999 and *Christmas Carol: The Movie* animated by Jimmy T. Murakami in 2001. TV drama also offered in this single week a *David Copperfield*, a filmed version of Edgar's *Nicholas Nickleby* repeated all week for those unable to get to Shaftesbury Avenue, a similarly marathon showing of the 2006 BBC serialization of *Bleak House*, a new *Old Curiosity Shop*, a new serialized *Oliver Twist*, and three further redeployments of *A Christmas Carol*: a documentary fronted by Griff Rhys Jones explaining that Dickens invented Christmas by writing this story, *Blackadder's Christmas Carol*, and finally a festive version of a popular game show dubbed 'Deal or No Deal: Scrooge v. Santa', shown on a loop for four consecutive hours on Christmas Day.

Self-evidently this is not a matter of the modern media offering literary treats or little-known revivals; Dickens is deployed as a matter of course, served up knowingly or reverently, in reliable and attractive new productions of well-loved Christmas fare, burlesqued, taken for granted, or just tacked on as a symbol of the season.[2] One of the striking aspects of the week in 2007 is the depth of existing material from previous decades, whether aimed at adults or children, studious readers or game-show addicts, that was available to the programmers. Philip Bolton marks out 'nine or ten epochs' in the 3,000-odd dramatizations he lists, each characterized by a different performative and mediatized engagement with the matter of Dickens, but they make up a trajectory that shows no sign of falling off. After the nineteenth-century boom eras that are represented in this book and its companion, there was an interesting period, around the beginning of the twentieth century, when Dickensian plays were the staple fare of the obscurest reaches of the stage, lovingly tended by amateurs and by actors on the lower rungs of the professional ladder who specialized in a Dickensian role as in a previous century a performer might have been a noted *commedia* pantaloon or a pantomime columbine. Then Dickensian films, Bolton notes, began in 1903,[3] and art house film makers and high-budget television dramatizers today still regularly present us with the major novels thoughtfully interpreted; but no one feels excluded from having a go: not counting small fry such as TV episodes, sixty-four versions of *A Christmas Carol* are listed on the film database IMDb, including those starring the Muppets, the Smurfs, the Flintstones, Barbie, and a company of dogs.

Perhaps this exuberant dramatic presence in the lower reaches of the entertainment industry partially accounts for the wincing distaste most twentieth-century critics displayed for the links between Dickens and the popular stage in his own lifetime.[4] Indeed, the influence of the popular theatre upon Dickens and his work has been a matter of observation and often opprobrium from the start, and is still a major topic

---

[2] *Oliver Twist* screened in parts, from 18 December 2007 onwards, BBC1; an 'all-star adaptation'; *A Christmas Carol* at the Young Vic, 3 December to 19 January, by the South African Isango/Portobello company, in a double bill with *The Magic Flute*; it was transposed to a township setting as *Ikrismas Kherol*, with Pauline Malefane playing first Scrooge, and then the Queen of the Night.

[3] Bolton, 5.

[4] With the notable exception of Paul Schlicke, who has devoted many years to exploring those links: see especially his *Dickens and Popular Entertainment* (London: Allen and Unwin, 1985).

in commentary on the novelist today.[5] To Dickens's contemporaries, their reciprocity was frequently a stick with which to beat both the theatre of the time and the outrageously popular new novelist and his stories. Thackeray, for example, reviewed *The Cricket on the Hearth* in terms replete with sly derision. He claims that it 'has the effect of a beautiful theatrical piece'; he quotes the opening at length, and enquires 'is this like nature, or like the brilliant ballet-pantomime to which I have compared it? All the properties on the little stage waken into ludicrous life as they will in the pantomime tomorrow night.'[6] As he well knew, the dramatization of the story, facilitated by Dickens, would in fact appear that same Boxing Day night on the stage of the Lyceum.[7] Often subsequent judgement has been equally negative, whether couched as regret for the coarsening effect of melodrama upon characterization in the novels or even as concern for the author's very life, jeopardized by his giving way to the regrettable impulse to perform his own work in gruelling readings. For reasons that can only be surmised, it has seemed necessary to demonstrate critically that Dickens's gifts were those of the novelist, and that his novels are wonderfully 'dramatic'—but they are not plays. The usual formulation in twentieth-century critical writing is that 'much of the Dickensian energy is lost when he writes directly for the stage or when his fiction is adapted for dramatic purposes.'[8] Thus Carol MacKay, introducing a collection of essays from a conference whose intention was to celebrate Dickens on stage, but which, in effect, flees back to the security of the printed page—'exploring the lure of the theatre for Dickens as a means of better understanding what constitutes his narrative art.' Sometimes that 'lure', the threat of the stage to the master's energy, is represented with shuddering physical directness, as in a melodrama: his readings, MacKay tells us, 'drained Dickens's life energies, bringing about his demise'.[9] Even the playwright John Glavin, an advocate of Grotowskian plunderings of the novels for performance, asserts that Dickens feared the stage, 'almost as much as he hated writing'.[10]

In this century some critics, including outstandingly Juliet John, have begun to recuperate the dramatic aspect of Dickens's writings along with a new understanding of the mode of melodrama as a response to modern life which should not be judged through the hostile critical lens of Realism. John also stresses the importance to Dickens's creative life of acting and the actors he knew and admired; but she still dismisses with a show of regret the dramatists who also took part in transmitting his creations to the huge popular audience. 'It is a pity,' she says, 'that Dickens the playwright comes no closer to representing "actual truth" on the stage than the hacks he

---

[5] For a brief recapitulation of the critical approach to his 'theatricality', see Juliet John, *Dickens's Villains: Melodrama, Character, Popular Culture* (Oxford: Oxford University Press, 2001), 1–3.

[6] *Morning Chronicle*, 25 December 1845. For a fuller consideration of the dispute between Dickens and Thackeray known as the 'dignity of literature debate', see Bratton, *West End*, 90–1. Some of the material in this introduction appeared in that book in an earlier form.

[7] See *The Cricket on the Hearth* for this dramatization.

[8] Carol Hanbery MacKay, ed., 'Before the curtain', in *Dramatic Dickens* (Basingstoke: Macmillan, 1989), 6.

[9] MacKay, 'Before the curtain', 1, 7.

[10] John Glavin, *After Dickens: Reading, Adaptation and Performance* (Cambridge: Cambridge University Press, 1999), 19.

so unrelentingly mocks.'[11] My argument is that 'Dickens the playwright' is a figure whom we should get to know afresh, not from his few original play texts but from the rest of his work, his novels and especially his novellas, as they appeared and still appear in the theatre. He continued, as he himself said, to write for the stage all his life. 'Every writer of fiction, though he may not adopt the dramatic form, writes in effect for the stage' he announced at the annual dinner of the Royal Theatrical Fund in 1858. What he was not prepared to do was write *directly* for the stage, and so to be seen as a playwright, which meant a hack. Therefore those very 'hacks', like the managers and actors of the nascent West End stage, were necessary to the process of getting his work to the stage. His dramatic genius grew and matured not in writing plays, but in writing narrative fiction that was imbricated with performance. The stage writers whose versions of Dickens's works are published here were not literary giants as he was, but that is no reason to dismiss their contribution to his creations; and, despite his mockery, Dickens himself did not do so. What follows will briefly trace to its roots the critical confusion about what the stage meant to Dickens, as a preface to the real work of the book, which is, by making a selection of the plays taken from his work early in his career available in print, to restore his collaborators to some visibility, so that future scholarship can avoid the misprision inevitable in condemning their work unseen.

## THE PROBLEMS OF PREJUDICE

An attempt to account for the feeling against the dramatization of Dickens's works that does not at the same time succumb to that prejudice begins with the universally acknowledged fact that Dickens loved the stage. He claimed[12] never to have spent an evening in a theatre—and he spent thousands of evenings there—without pleasure; in his early life he took serious steps to become a professional actor, possibly buying roles in a private theatre, certainly working hard to learn and imitate Charles Mathews's style, but ducking his audition at Covent Garden on the grounds of a sore throat. In his early writing years he delighted in writing directly for the stage. He began as a child, with burlettas for the toy theatre, and moved on to libretti and farces as soon as he counted himself a professional writer. In 1836, when Dickens was twenty-four, John Braham accepted his farce *The Strange Gentleman* for the St James's Theatre, where Madame Sala, the mother of George Augustus who was to write for *Household Words* under Dickens's direction, was in the cast. It was the first box-office success of Braham's management, and Dickens's follow-up farce, *Is She his Wife* (1837), was also well received, though his intervening libretto for *The Village Coquettes* (1836) was not so good. Then the comic actor Harley, who took the lead in both farces, got up an impersonation of Mr Pickwick for his benefit night, with Dickens's help; for the author's writing for the stage outwith dramatic form had begun, and soon eclipsed his playwriting. However, the explosive success of *The Pickwick Papers* in no small part took

---

[11]  John, *Dickens's Villains*, 78.

[12]  In addressing the annual dinner of the General Theatrical Fund Association, 6 April 1846.

the shape of stage adaptations, which ran away with the new characters Dickens created and used them freely to people modern London on the stage. Before the ninth monthly part of the novel was out, W. Leman Rede had made a play of it for the Adelphi; Edward Stirling was ready with his version at the City of London in March 1837, and W.T. Moncrieff wrote it up for the Strand in July. The parts publication was not complete until November.[13] By this time Dickens had begun, in January 1837, to publish his next popular sensation, *Oliver Twist*, and he may have tried to dramatize that for the St James's, where an unsuccessful version of the story was staged on 27 March 1838 after only twelve parts had appeared in *Bentley's Miscellany*.[14] Whether or not he was involved in this abortive effort, dramatizing the book was certainly on his mind, and that same month he wrote to Fred Yates, the manager of the Adelphi, offering to adapt it: 'your name as the Jew and mine as the author would knock any other attempts quite out of the field'.[15] Yates apparently did not see any reason to pay the already-expensive and rather self-assertive young Dickens, however, and had his Fagin written for him by one of his house dramatists—so unimportant an artisan that there is still dispute over which of them it was.[16] Characteristically aiming higher because he had failed so far, Dickens tried again, going with John Forster to Covent Garden to offer to write a stage version for Macready as a part of the grand actor-manager's second season of attempting to restore the National Drama. No doubt aware of the critical disapprobation in some circles of 'Newgate' novels, including this one, on criminal themes, Macready made an ideologically blinded misjudgement: 'I told them,' he notes primly in his diary, 'of the utter impracticability of *Oliver Twist* for any dramatic purpose.'[17] By that time it was already playing at the Pavilion and the Surrey, but these theatres, of course, did not seem to Macready to have 'dramatic' purposes. Unabashed, Dickens then offered to write him something new, adding that 'if I had as much time as I had inclination I would write on and on, farce after farce, and comedy after comedy, until I wrote you something that would run'.[18] Macready allowed him to come to Covent Garden and read his new farce, *The Lamplighter*, and remarked to himself that the surprising man 'reads as well as an experienced actor would'; but he was busy nursing Bulwer Lytton's bombastic tragedy *Richelieu* into existence, and no one in the company responded well to *The Lamplighter*.[19] It was not a great drama; but of course *Oliver Twist* is.

After this brush with literary hierarchies and prejudices at Covent Garden and the lukewarm professional reception of *The Lamplighter*, Dickens seems to have decided something very important: that his rise to the top of his profession meant he must distance himself from the mob of jobbing, semi-anonymous writers whose markets included the popular stage. The huge unforeseen success of *Pickwick* and *Oliver Twist*

---

[13] F. Dubrez Fawcett, *Dickens the Dramatist* (London: W.H. Allen, 1952), 45–52.

[14] Bolton, 110.   [15] CD to FY [mid-March 1838?], *Letters* vol. 1, 388–9.

[16] See Bolton, 113–14.

[17] J.C. Trewin, ed., *The Journal of William Charles Macready 1832–1851* (London: Longmans, 1967), 126.

[18] CD to W.C. Macready [19 November 1838?], *Letters* vol. 1, 456–7.

[19] Trewin, ed., *The Journal*, 128.

made him suddenly aware that he had overcommitted and underpriced himself in a cut-throat marketplace, and that he urgently needed to put himself on a higher, more exclusive plane—that of the gentleman novelist. He fell out with most of the large number of publishers to whom he had committed himself, calling them blackguards and robbers, and withdrew from some of his journalism and from the St James's, later trying to suppress his own apprentice stage work.[20] He histrionically lost his patience for the way in which his stories and characters were recycled back into the creative pool by other writers, and struck out at them too as pirates and thieves. Dickens thrust W.T. Moncrieff, in particular, back into the depths from which he himself was now breaking free, famously writing to John Forster 'if the *Pickwick* has been the means of putting a few shillings in the vermin-eaten pockets of so miserable a creature, and has saved him from the workhouse or a jail, let him empty out his little pot of filth and welcome'.[21] Dickens's subsequent tone in his exuberant, not to say vainglorious tirades against the dramaturgs whom he now cast as pirates to be gibbeted by his awesome revenge, visited with 'execution summary and terrible',[22] should not be accepted as the ultimate truth about them, any more than we should believe his exclamation that the publisher Bentley was 'an infernal, rich, plundering, thundering old Jew' like Fagin.[23]

Dickens's convulsive separation of himself from the level of the unsuccessful hack has been taken by many commentators as licence to repeat his attacks upon his contemporaries; but that response is not justified. To cycle and recycle prose works into plays, and vice versa, with little regard to who had first written them, was entirely normal in the on-demand writing culture to which Dickens had so far belonged.[24] When Robert Seymour, already a successful illustrator, proposed to the publishers Chapman and Hall his series of comic plates that were to become the *Pickwick Papers*, he suggested a list of writers who could provide some accompanying text. It comprised Henry Mayhew, Theodore Hook, Leigh Hunt, John Poole, Alfred Forrester, Charles Dickens, and William Moncrieff.[25] These men were all part of the 1830s world of quick, cheap, commissioned writing, and among them Dickens was not the most senior nor necessarily at that moment the most highly regarded. Moncrieff was probably the best known, and certainly he was the recognized dramatist on the list. He was as determined as Dickens to stand upon his dignity and defend his rights, and the tone of his self-justifications has contributed to the inclination of many modern Dickensians to treat his work with unnecessary scorn. His rather desperate attempts at self-defence include the prefaces and advertisements with which he surrounded the first play reprinted in this volume, his *Sam Weller, or the Pickwickians*, on the playbills at the

---

[20] See Tomalin, 69–71.    [21] To John Forster [7 September 1837], *Letters* vol. 1, 304.

[22] In the March 1838 *Sketches by Boz*, quoted in Bolton, 154.    [23] Quoted in Tomalin, 71.

[24] See Bolton, 36: he cites Charles Reade to 'epitomize the intricate, intimate involvement of popular, narrative art in the nineteenth century with popular, contemporary stagecraft' observing that Reade 'wrote both novels and plays. In permutation of the possibilities, Reade also took plays from novels by others, novels from plays by others, plays from his own novels, and novels from his own plays.'

[25] Mary Teresa McGowan, 'Pickwick and the pirates: a study of some early imitations, dramatizations and plagiarisms of *Pickwick Papers*', unpublished PhD thesis, University of London 1975, 170, n.2, quoting J. Grego, *Pictorial Pickwickiana*, 2 vols (London, 1899), vol. i, 12, 20, 279.

New Strand Theatre, where it was staged successfully from 12 June 1837 onwards, and in the printed version that he published later that year. He did not think that he had committed any kind of offence, as is clear from the inclusion in the printed volume of a 'Notice to the managers of theatres' attempting to defend his own copyrights in his plays which, he says, have been illegally claimed by the publisher John Cumberland. As far as Moncrieff is concerned, he himself is not a thief, though the publishers clearly are. His work on this text, he suggests, has been an adaptation of something not otherwise available for performance, a perfectly proper proceeding, and one which was more difficult than simply writing an original play. However disingenuously, he claims he took it up as a challenge to see what he could do, where others had failed, in bringing to the stage something which the author himself had not intended to be dramatic. He apologizes for ending the work differently from Dickens—parts publication was not complete when he wrote—but hopes that his play has assisted the popular success of the original. This last wish has always presented itself to subsequent Dickensian scholars as the acme of presumption, justifying Dickens's vile-tempered response; but in the context of the time, it was not nearly so unreasonable. Moncrieff could have been the one chosen to write the original text; even if he did not actually know that, he had no reason to see himself, at the time, as occupying an inferior position to the younger writer who was selected. Their inequality was not yet so clear; and Moncrieff's Pickwick play was, indeed, a success, playing much longer at the New Strand than any of Dickens's did at the St James's.

By considering afresh Dickens's ensuing actions in respect of writing for the stage, beginning with the ostensibly charitable efforts that he made to assist stage writers like Moncrieff, who were (or could be asserted to be) less fortunate than himself, we may approach a new understanding of his misrepresentation, even his misdirection, of his dramatic creativity. During his most successful writing years Dickens did not eschew involvement with the stage, though he did not write plays or act professionally. But he seized every opportunity to act and direct on as serious a footing as possible, creating the Amateur Company and staging plays with them to show before everyone from his own family to the Queen and Prince Albert, touring the extra-theatrical venues of the country with hugely ambitious, but not-for-profit performances. He could, instead, have realized what he eventually confessed had been his greatest unfulfilled dream: to be the writer-actor-manager to transform the Victorian stage, the man in control of 'a great theatre, in the direction of which I should hold supreme authority'.[26] He had all the talents for it, as well as the drive. Mary Cowden Clarke, whom he directed in *Every Man in His Humour*, noted that he had a professionalism surpassing anything actually practised on the stage of his own day: 'ever present, superintending, directing, suggesting [...] the essence of punctuality and methodical precision [...] He never seemed to overlook anything, but to note the very slightest point that conduced to the "going well" of the whole performance'.[27] But he did not do it. We may only conclude

---

[26] In a conversation with Charles Kent, quoted in T.E. Pemberton, *Dickens and the Stage* (London: George Redway, 1888), 99–100.

[27] Quoted in Pemberton, *Dickens and the Stage*, 103–6.

that he thought he could not go there without losing the social position of wide esteem and unblemished respectability which he greatly valued, and to which he clung even after the change in his life and career upon his separation from his wife in 1857.[28] Until then he carefully defined his stage efforts as strictly amateur, done for the love of The Drama and without personal profit, usually avowing an intention to benefit a poor writer or his family—even when, as in the case of Douglas Jerrold, the subjects angrily repudiated such charitable undertakings.[29] Others of his fellow writers also repudiated these efforts in general, Thackeray defending the gentility and dignity of literature as being positively undermined by Dickens and his Amateur Company of players with their sensational appeals. Such conspicuous amateurism was, however, the only way Dickens allowed himself to appear at the head of a theatrical company.

The sense that professional performance could fatally undermine his public estimation and position—what a modern writer would call his image—was not simply a quirk of Dickens's imagination. Theatre was still associated, when he was a young man, with vice and degradation; the fact that the art of Shakespeare was thus embroiled with prostitution and ignorant exploitation was widely lamented. Dickens's provincial tours with classic plays, and later with his own readings, brought large audiences in to see performances in public halls and lecture rooms who would have had moral and religious scruples about entering a theatre, who were indeed deeply suspicious of any kind of feigning and dressing up. The 'fireside' audience whom his periodicals and Christmas tales reached were not the pleasure-seeking, theatre-going lower middle classes, the 'gents', but a much larger and more influential percentile, the 'serious' small and larger businessmen and chapel-going mechanics and artisans, with their wives and children. For them, indeed to some extent down to them, the gentleman novelist wrote. And at the other class margin, the personal desire Dickens felt to guard his self-definition as a gentleman rather than a tradesman of the pen in the eyes of Society, the upper classes, was vindicated when Thackeray was blackballed by the members of the Athenaeum, in the year after his argument with Dickens about the dignity of literature took place.[30] So to be a theatrical amateur, at a time when amateurism in general was seen as a higher and better way of exercising any art or talent than making money from it, was Dickens's defence against falling back into the social abjection from which success as a major novelist had rescued him. However much he longed to take the theatre of his day into his hands, he could not compromise his complicated, contradictory status by entering into the unequivocally lower reaches where the theatrical profession lay.

There were, however, artistic consequences. Dickens had told Macready he would like the opportunity to develop as a dramatist by the usual means of writing many plays and learning from seeing them produced, so that he could develop his work, and

---

[28] See Tomalin, 289, for a summary of these changes, including the end of his amateur acting career for charity.

[29] See Michael Slater, *Douglas Jerrold, 1803–1857* (London: Duckworth, 2002), 199.

[30] See K.J. Fielding, 'Thackeray and the "Dignity of literature"' parts 1 and 2', *TLS*, 19 September 1958, 536, and September 1958, 552.

thereby advance the practice of the stage and change the expectations of audiences. His offer of farces and comedies was not welcomed within the rarefied circles of the National Drama, and he withdrew and thought again. Eventually he found other ways forward, shaping a new, compound form of narrative and characterization, in and beyond his novels, with the assistance of his play-writing and acting friends in the new West End. A proper understanding of those more oblique possibilities requires that we should look through the smokescreen he generated to cover his theatrical activity, and consider his next ten years of work for the stage in the form we now have it—the texts of the dramas that he anticipated would be made from his narratives, and in which he developed as a writer for the stage, even as he confined his owned compositions to print.

## THE PLAYS HE DID NOT WRITE

From 1837 onwards Dickens developed creative strategies that allowed him to be a novelist in his public persona, but also a dramatist at one remove. By their means he both extended the reach of his work beyond the middle-class reading publics, and diversified and charged the work itself by interaction with theatre-makers whom he could direct, such as Albert Smith and Mark Lemon, or whom he admired and learnt from, like Mary Ann and Robert Keeley. This volume offers a selection of the plays that were produced in London under this dispensation, beginning before the author started his active participation in preparing his work for the stage by considering the interventions of some of the earliest and most successful actors and writers who worked with his materials. The first play here is *Sam Weller, or the Pickwickians*, written by the despised Moncrieff for the actor-manager William James Hammond.

Hammond in partnership with his brother-in-law Douglas Jerrold took on, in the spring of 1836, the management of the New Strand Theatre, a little playhouse in the nascent West End with a troubled relationship with the licensing authorities. They began with a cheeky reference to the licensing situation by staging *Othello—according to the Act of Parliament*, which meant a burlesque version of the tragedy complete with the musical accompaniment required to satisfy the 'burletta' licence they held. Each of the co-managers had an agenda as well as a profit to pursue, Jerrold seeking the staging of his own plays, which were acerbically Radical and relied on words— according to the critics, far too many words for artistic effect, regardless of their legality; and Hammond wanting a stage to showcase his own one-man performances. Hammond was one of a number of late Georgian actors who, with hindsight, we may place as essentially solo performers who would have been music hall (or indeed stand-up or popular singing) stars, had they been born into a later generation. He had become a 'lion', a singing celebrity, in provincial concert rooms, and in theatres, especially on the northern circuits, playing low comedy parts and introducing his own songs; by 1836 he had 'scarcely any rival upon the stage'[31] as a comic singer. Critics,

---

[31] Obituary, *Era*, 1 October 1848; *Actors by Daylight* no. 13, 14 July 1838, 98.

however, found fault with his venture into London management for its increasing focus upon himself,[32] especially in the star part he built in his first season, Sam Weller. He finished that season with Moncrieff's *Sam Weller* as his benefit night performance on 12 October and reopened on 17 April 1838 with a new version called *The Pickwickians*, altered to bring it closer to the now-completed story. This lasted until the end of May, and by the beginning of July he was advertising a sequel, *Sam Weller's Tour or the Pickwickians in France*. He took the Liver theatre in Liverpool for the winter season 1838–9, closing with a speech in the character of Weller that Moncrieff had written for him. The growing concentration of the Strand's offerings on himself had caused comment in the trade press, such as the theatrical weekly *Actors By Gaslight*, which features a picture of Hammond as Sam and a biography in issue 13, 14 July 1838, but becomes increasingly annoyed in editorial comment over succeeding months, and by 27 October, in issue 23, is denouncing his '*exclusive* system' (223) of turning all new plays into vehicles for himself, and next season began to denounce Sam Weller and everything Pickwickian as tedious and worn out. But the character served Hammond well, and he might be argued to have returned the favour: Weller was at least partly created in the minds of many people, and not only those who did not read the original, by Hammond's impersonation, and so by Moncrieff's adaptations. The printed text of the first play he did shows how the solo performance of Sam sat somewhat loosely within the drama. It is prefaced with the statement on the first page that 'Some of the parodies in this Drama are omitted on the stage, on account of the length of the representation', which indicates that the songs, in particular, are elaborations tailored for Hammond to perform at will. Elsewhere the text shows typographic oddities that confirm that it is in parts a transcript of Hammond's performance, created collaboratively with the actor and available in print to profit from his success.[33] One may well say that it was partly Hammond who made Sam Weller a universally known cockney archetype. Moncrieff's script for him augmented Dickens's Wellerisms from the current stock, where that form of joke already existed, and added other popular material, including the hit song 'Jim Crow', which then came to be identified with Sam down the generations.[34] His work in this play can be seen as the first instance of the fruitful feedback between Dickens's popularity on stage and in print, a process that has subsequently been condemned as vulgarization of the novelist's work, but might better be regarded as one of its deep wells of creativity. Such collaborations, while no doubt coarsening the novelist's observation of Sam Weller and his father, nevertheless made Sam available as an archetype, an aid to the understanding of something previously

[32] See *Actors by Daylight* no. 28, 27 October 1838, 222–3, 'The Strand Theatre and Mr Hammond'.

[33] The scene framing the song at the end of Act 1 scene 3 is not in the licenser's MS and is annotated as 'Published with the music, and a likeness of Mr Hammond, by Limbird & Co., 143, Strand.' The song in Act 3 scene 4 within which Sam's account of the Bardell vs Pickwick trial is set as 'spoken' interjections is apparently a version of one with which the singer was already successful, by the popular songwriter Thomas Hudson, entitled 'L.A.W.!'. It is in a smaller typeface than the rest of the play and deviates markedly from the text in the manuscript, suggesting that it was another set piece which could be separately purchased, whether for imitation or as a memento of Hammond's star turn.

[34] See McGowan, 'Pickwick and the pirates', 138–9, especially n.2., and 87–9 on Wellerisms.

not defined. Weller is a crystallization of the knowing Londoner whom Dickens drew from the culture around him, and his acceptance back into common culture extended the author's impact to people outside the reading audience. It was Hammond's Sam who became known, I would suggest, to the many people whose own lives he championed, and quite closely reflected: the non-reading, even the illiterate, but often clever and streetwise 'London characters' like himself, who frequented the theatres or heard jokes and songs in the taverns and streets.

## 'I FEEL SURE ABOUT HER': DICKENS AND MARY ANN KEELEY

We have no evidence of what Dickens thought of William Hammond, but he had very clear responses to some actors' contributions to his works, both good and bad.[35] During the flurry of stagings of *Oliver Twist* in 1838 he commented on the casting of an actress he did not know, Mrs Honner, as Oliver at Sadler's Wells, saying he was sure she was bound to be much too big, and legend has it that his reaction to the version he saw at the Surrey was to lie down in the corner of his box until it was over.[36] There is no record of his response to the performance of Mary Ann (Mrs Robert) Keeley as Oliver in the production Yates eventually mounted at the Adelphi in 1839, but his known attitude to her work on his texts was always positive, beginning with his review of her in November 1834 as 'extremely good' in a character in a Buckstone farce that he found strangely familiar to him—it was quietly taken from the Boz sketch *The Bloomsbury Christening*. In the next year, 1835, he gave the Keeleys a rave review as 'a pair of innocent servants in a murdering household'[37]—their speciality double act, long polished and repeated, in an old play by John Banim, *The Sergeant's Wife* (English Opera House, 1827). Dickens liked Robert Keeley's droll, dim-witted comic style enough to take acting lessons from him when he was contemplating a stage career for himself; and the family were to become his good friends, both personal and professional. As they climbed to the top of their respective professional trees, collaboration between the writer and the actor-managers took several, often very productive, forms.

Like Dickens, in the late 1830s and early 1840s the Keeleys were working hard to find the best ways forward in a profession somewhat under a cloud. Theatre in Britain was in a state of turmoil, a kind of planning blight having been cast by the inconclusive outcome of a Parliamentary Select Committee's investigations in 1832, which pronounced the subject of its scrutiny to be in a bad state, but failed to do anything at all decisive about it.[38] The Theatres Act of 1843 would eventually provide an impulse (though hardly a blueprint) for change, but in the meantime the rules were unclear,

---

[35] This section's heading appeared in a letter to Robert Keeley, 24 June 1844. Mamie Dickens and Georgina Hogarth, eds, *The Letters of Charles Dickens* (London: Chapman and Hall, 1880), 2 vols, vol. 1, 57.
[36] Bolton, 112, 110.     [37] Bolton, 68.
[38] See the discussion in Bratton, *New Readings*, and Bratton, *West End*, 9–12.

the stakeholders uneasy, and problems like those faced by Hammond and Jerrold at the New Strand tended to stymie every initiative. In this situation the Keeleys, both highly talented and ambitious, arrived on the London stage. Mary Ann (Goward) was born in 1805 and made her debut in York, after training as a soprano, in 1823. Moving to London she moved from the concert to the theatrical stage, under the wing of Fanny Kelly at the English Opera House, which would become the Lyceum again when the Keeleys took it over in the 1840s. Meanwhile, Mary Ann launched herself in a series of soubrette parts and, since she was small, charming, and energetic, into playing as a boy in burlesques.[39] She was spectacularly successful in these roles, like many young actresses of the day, and went on to build upon them something quite individual, especially in Dickensian dramas. Her Oliver Twist, in the play Yates did not let Dickens write for the Adelphi, was admired in February 1839, but then surpassed by two contrasting boy roles next season: her Jack Sheppard in an adaptation of Ainsworth's novel, and her Smike in Edward Stirling's version of *Nicholas Nickleby*. She regarded Smike as one of her most important characterizations, a pathetic boy role to contrast with her roguish burlesque boys and her infamous, and much tougher, impersonation of Jack Sheppard. In old age she recalled the difficulties of making a first impression of the pathos and vulnerability of Smike on the audience who expected her to be funny.[40] She also recounted stories of Dickens in rehearsal, objecting to Stirling's sentimentality: 'the adapter had put into Smike's mouth a lot of stuff about "the little robins in the field"; I shall never forget Dickens's face when he heard me repeating these lines. Turning to the prompter he said, "D - n the robins; cut them out."' The interviewer who reported this conversation in 1899 (upon her death) asserts that:

The late Mrs Keeley was a close friend of Dickens, and in her time the actress played many of his characters. Dickens superintended the rehearsals of 'Nicholas Nickleby,' but Mrs Keeley said she did not think he cared much about any of his works being dramatized. The plays were mere paste and scissors, done by old Stirling, and, at rehearsal, the novelist knocked them about pretty considerably, always effecting an improvement.[41]

There is no evidence from Dickens himself that he was so closely involved in this production as to superintend rehearsals and doctor the script 'considerably', and in the definitive edition of his letters a note mentioning his damning of the robins is attached to a letter[42] about his seeing the play not at a rehearsal, but at an early performance; it seems unlikely, however, that he could have spoken to the prompter on that occasion. Stirling's text, published here, offers an intriguing suggestion that something did indeed happen before the opening night to cause the adapter to cut, and then to restore, the offending robins and the surrounding solo scene and soliloquy for Smike, at the end of Act 1 scene 3. The licensing manuscript does not include this section at all.

---

[39] For a fuller discussion of the transvestite boy role and the category crisis of the 1840s, see Bratton, *West End*, 117–44.

[40] See Walter Newman, *The Keeleys on Stage and at Home* (London: Bentley and Son, 1895), 80.

[41] *Westminster Gazette*, 13 March 1889, 3, 'Literary Notes and News'.

[42] Letter to Forster [23 November 1838?], *Letters* vol. 1, 459–60, 460 n.1.

Instead, it has a symbol in the text indicating that something is to be added; if that extra material was ever in the Lord Chamberlain's office, it has not survived. The printed texts, however, do include the robins, within a long soliloquy and some business for Smike—Mary Ann Keeley—to bring down the curtain in a storm of applause. Dickens, perhaps drawn in by friendship and success, told Forster that the production was 'excellent' in many aspects, from staging and costuming to acting. He wrote to manager Fred Yates saying his performance as a 'glorious Mantalini is beyond all praise' and that he also wanted to congratulate Mrs Keeley on her Smike, and O. Smith on Newman Noggs, and that he had no objection whatsoever to the dramatization of his work 'where the thing is so admirably done in every respect' as it was in this production.[43] He had apparently no fear that the summary ending Stirling had been obliged to add was likely to do the book any harm, especially since a member of the cast (shifting from the actor playing Nicholas in the manuscript to Mary Ann Keeley in later texts) explicitly recommended 'the future career of Nicholas Nickleby' to the audience in the tag line of the play. Yates continued to use the services of Edward Stirling as his dramatizer of Dickens, and Mary Ann Keeley as his lead, in a version of *The Old Curiosity Shop* with himself as Quilp in November 1840; it was not as successful as the plays with happy endings and her boy impersonations. Then the Keeleys left the Adelphi, and engaged in the summer of 1841 at the New Strand, where Mary Ann was trumpeted as a star on the bills. She played leg roles, wearing the tights and tunic of burlesque, Mercury in Leman Rede's *The Mission of Mercury*, and a comic devil in a second burlesque called *The Devil and Dr Faustus*, but by August she had another Dickensian role from the adapting pen of Stirling, Barnaby Rudge.

Martin Meisel suggests that 'the character in the novel is so suited to her line that it is arguable that Dickens was influenced by her Smike'[44] in creating it, though other influences on this long-incubated novel have struck less stage-conscious critics as of primary importance. But Barnaby as performed by Mary Ann seems from the text published for the first time in this volume to have been a brilliant creation, not a previously enacted type, charging the melodramatic central story with an alarming, unpredictable interest to balance the broad comedy of Simon Tappertit, played by Attwood, and the menacing frisson of the manager Henry Hall playing Hugh. These two gleaned some critical approval at the time as the best exemplars of their characters on offer, but all the critics, like Forster, preferred Louisa Fairbrother's more conventional representation elsewhere of a leggy and delicious Barnaby to Mary Ann Keeley's strange characterization.[45] Through her known stage persona—her association with Jack Sheppard—as well as through Stirling's rowdy strip-cartoon of a drama with its onstage presentation of a rioting mob, the play came into the territory of 'Newgate' fiction, already mentioned here in relation to *Oliver Twist*, that was a strong focus of middle-class

---

[43] Letter to Frederick Yates [29 November 1838?], *Letters* vol. 1, 463–4.

[44] Martin Meisel, *Realizations: Narrative, Pictorial, and Theatrical Arts in Nineteenth-Century England* (Princeton: Princeton University Press, 1983), 260–1.

[45] See Bratton, *West End*, 128 for Maclise's lascivious description of Fairbrother in the role, and further discussion.

anxieties in the period.[46] The explicit objection to *Barnaby Rudge* is the same as in the case of *Oliver Twist*, the heroicization of criminal acts, but critics also damn with faint praise Keeley's 'artful' and not necessarily pretty cross-gender performances, which are unsettling because they cannot be consumed as mere sexual display. The play was not revived after the end of August at the New Strand. Manager Hall was anxious, no doubt, to preserve the good standing his other successes had given him that year, and did not continue this piece with its 'splendid scenery, powerful cast, and startling effects'[47] when the higher classes of society returned to town in the autumn. Mary Ann Keeley stayed, however, and expanded her repertoire in a second way that was to be important in her association with Dickens, in a lower-class character role as the wife of Mr Punch, a showman. The newborn periodical *Punch* (biased no doubt by the fact that the play in question was by its editor Mark Lemon) praised her efforts in interesting terms:

Mrs Keeley played the tambourine, and the part of *Snozzle femme*. This was more than acting; it was nature enriched with humour—character broadly painted without a tinge of caricature. The solemnity of her countenance, while performing with her feet, was a correct copy of self-approbation—of the wonder-how-I-do-it-so-well—always observable during the dances of the *fair* sex; her tones when singing were unerringly brought from the street; her spangled dress was assuredly borrowed from Scrowton's caravan. As a work of dramatic art, this performance is, of its kind, most complete.[48]

This particular kind of performance, drawn from close observation of working-class women, was to prove important in the next, and most striking, development in Dickens's rapprochement with Mary Ann Keeley and the stage: the Christmas books.


## 1843 AND THE KEELEY MANAGEMENT

In 1843 the long-awaited change to the regulation of London theatres took place, in the shape of 6&7 Vict., c.68: the Theatres Act. Under its provisions the many already-built theatres and would-be managements of London were released from restrictions upon staging straight plays, and the West End immediately began to develop.[49] At Easter 1844, Mary Ann Keeley took on the lease of the Lyceum, with her husband Robert as stage manager. In an opening-night address she boldly put herself up as the 'fair lessee', as *The Morning Post* reported on 9 April 1844, declaring:

---

[46] See John, *Dickens's Villains*, chapter 5, where she discusses the reception of *Oliver Twist* as a Newgate novel and analyses the 'controversial cult status' of these books and plays as 'very much to do with anxieties about power—in particular the power of popular culture at the dawn of the "modern" age' (123).

[47] *Morning Chronicle* advertisement, 19 August 1841.

[48] *Punch*, 25 September 1841.       [49] See Bratton, *West End*.

> T'is true I might have fill'd an humble station
> In our theatrical administration
> But female influence soon gains the ascendant—
> When it begins, no one can see the end on't.
> Instead of coming to it by degrees
> I thought at once the premiership I'd seize
> To keep the place I very much incline
> Unless this house calls on me to resign

and asserting her policy, and the new freedom of her stage:

> My views with brevity I now will state
> Upon the principle legitimate.
> The drama call'd legitimate may thrive
> As well in two or three acts as in five....
> Man, by his mind, not by the height, we rate—
> Talent, not length, makes plays legitimate.

Her first hit was *Martin Chuzzlewit*, dramatized by Edward Stirling (at his own risk—the Keeleys meanly refused to commission him) but mounted with Dickens's explicit permission and indeed his direct involvement. He wrote to them saying that he would not on principle write them a prologue, though 'if I felt I could reasonably do such a thing for anyone, I could do it for you', but instead he offered to come himself and work with them: 'if you have the piece on the stage, and rehearse on Friday, I will gladly come down at any time you may appoint on that morning and go through it with you all'.[50] This was perhaps the knocking into shape of Stirling's efforts that Mary Ann recalled; and the critics and the public greatly approved. Stirling later triumphantly (and no doubt exaggeratedly) claimed[51] that it then ran for 280 nights and cleared £8,000. Certainly the play was a big success over the two seasons of the Keeley management and Stirling's version was played at other theatres around the country.

The couple had gone into management after a long period in which they developed their complementary skills, establishing themselves to a chorus of approval: 'the Keeley is perfect; she animates as it were the feigned stolidity of her spouse; what a domestic duet they must enact: take her in the amorous, sentimental, comic, or pathetic, she can alike "steal away the senses"'.[52] Dickens had expected Bob to succeed as Mrs Gamp, but assumed Mary Ann would take Ruth Pinch; knowing better, she chose to build on their double act and her own success in boy roles, by creating for the stage Bailey, the boy servant. They brought their skills, and high audience expectations, to new impersonations fuelled by Dickens's comic inventiveness. For the ecstatic critical reception of their first major hit, see the headnote to the play.

The prologue which Dickens would not write was provided by Albert Smith, his close friend at the time, who, not constrained as the author would have been, was able

[50] Letter to Bob Keeley, 24 June 1844, quoted in Malcolm Morley, '*Martin Chuzzlewit* in the theatre', *Dickensian*, vol. 47, 1950–1, 98–102, 98.
[51] Quoted in Morley, '*Martin Chuzzlewit*', 98.    [52] *Era*, 8 August 1841.

to make admirably clear what Dickens brought to the theatrical table. Mrs Keeley began:

> No ghostly legend from some mouldering page,
> And 'carefully adapted for the stage',
> No grand romantic drama, deep and dire,
> Full of 'tyerrific combat' and red fire
> Boast we tonight. No flimsy plot shall trench
> Upon our scene 'translated from the French';
> But one in deep emotions far more rife
> The powerful romance of common life.
>
> We owe this story of the present hour
> To that great master-hand—whose graphic power
> Can call up laughter—bid the tear to start,
> And find an echoing chord in every heart.
> Whom we have learn'd to deem an household friend,
> Who, 'midst his varied writings never penn'd
> One line that might his guileless pages spot,
> 'One word that, dying, he would wish to blot.'

Having thus tacitly invoked the comparison with Shakespeare, she proceeded to cite a parade of Dickensian characters already known and loved, who were indeed an important part of the foundation of her West End success. It ends sentimentally:

> And, lastly, whilst around both cot and hall
> The echoes of the 'Christmas Carol' fall,
> 'Bob Cratchit' on raised wages, spruce and trim,
> leads forward, with his crutch, poor 'Tiny Tim'

and it was the success of *A Christmas Carol* on stage, the previous year, that set the pattern for the Dickensian stage post-1843.


## 'LIKE THE BRILLIANT BALLET-PANTOMIME'

Dickens took some care to spring his short book *A Christmas Carol* as a surprise on the public at Christmas 1843, in the midst of the rather unsuccessful parts publication of *Martin Chuzzlewit*. He thought he had in hand a money-making commodity, as well as an expression of his faith, and published it beautifully presented but cheaply priced, at his own expense, hoping for a large personal profit—which did not materialize, though the book was a huge success.[53] It was also a success for the penny-publishers who issued a version at only 2d, whom he sued in vain, and for the eight London theatre managements who had mounted it by February 1844, whom he left

---

[53] Tomalin, 148–9.

alone, or in the case of the Adelphi, actively assisted.[54] Every Dickens publication was by now an eagerly awaited source of stage material; but this was special. In *A Christmas Carol* the author had provided a complete fable, published all at once, having its own shape and his particular genius for depicting what people did not, until then, know that they wanted so much to see. Knowing what would happen, Dickens not only gave Stirling exclusive permission to dramatize, for the Adelphi, but spent time with him, assisting at rehearsals—a considerable change of attitude, if Stirling's own account can be credited.[55] Stirling made a good job of the play, deploying his own talents and the by now substantial resources of the Adelphi. These included not only a strong acting company and expensive machinery and scenography, but also the composer Rodwell and his pit orchestra, from whom Stirling commissioned new and arranged 'old English' ballads. The result was what we would now recognize as a spectacular musical. But the most widely used dramatization was by one Charles Webb, which is published here for the first time. It was entirely unauthorized, and arises from the uncharted deeps of the London theatre; the little we know of Webb is to be found in the introduction to his play, *Old Scrooge*, in this volume. To judge by this play, he was a competent manager of stage materials, and his work was readily adaptable to all sorts of venues and companies. It is preferred here to Stirling's 'authorized' version as being the text more London audiences saw, illustrating the range of work inspired by Dickens, and the opportunities he gave to the creative underworld of his time.

The author took note of the possibilities he had provided, and the successive Christmas books that he published in 1844, 1845, 1846, and 1848 were differently managed in their coming to the stage. Having tried in vain to approach the Adelphi via his friendship with Yates and then capitulating in 1845 to 'collaborating' with the persistent Stirling, he turned to his friends on stage and among the lesser writers to create these next four Christmas works for simultaneous publication and opening in the West End. In this way he had some control over at least one version, some confidence in the outcome, and at least a modest share of the profit. By the end, the success of the Christmas works was widely thought to owe as much to the input of the stage, and especially the Keeleys, as to Dickens himself. *The Chimes* came first, with two versions claimed as explicitly sanctioned by Dickens, at the Adelphi and the Lyceum. He worked out that an official theatrical version could be created by sending advance proof sheets to his friends Gilbert Abbott A'Beckett and Mark Lemon, both of whom were still active in the theatre. This opened at the Adelphi on publication day, 18 December 1844, fifteen days after its triumphant first night as a private reading by Dickens himself: see the headnote to the text for *The Chimes* in this volume. It also opened in a version by Edward Stirling at the Lyceum on 26 December, part of the Keeleys' successful second season. The bills for the two productions are very similar, both using a design showing the bells entwined with Goblins derived from the standing-card bookseller's advertisement drawn by Cruickshank, and both claiming Dickens's

---

[54] Tomalin, 150; Bolton, 234.

[55] See Edward Stirling, *Old Drury Lane: Fifty Years' Recollections of Author, Actor, and Manager* (London: Chatto and Windus, 1881), 2 vols, vol. 1, 187.

permission. It seems likely that droll little Bob Keeley made a more suitable Trotty Veck than O. Smith at the Adelphi, whose presence and persona were macabre and villainous, his voice sepulchral; the Lyceum version ran longer,[56] but the present edition is of the script over which Dickens actively cooperated, the one staged at the Adelphi.

The lesser dramatizers did not, of course, give up because of the master's entry into the field by proxy, and exposure of this most Radical of the Christmas books reached far down the social scale by means of the stage. Malcolm Morley in 1950[57] mentions with characteristic contempt the 'ghouls' and 'semi-literate playwrights' of the other London theatres who took up the story. A more interesting way of thinking about their versions might be to consider whether *The Chimes* had something special to contribute to a wide audience at this particular moment in the development of the modern theatre. The social crisis of the early 1840s is not easy to find in the surviving plays of the period, where fear of censorship and a sense of their audiences' aspirations made theatre managers very chary of direct social comment. The excuse of Dickens's name made this piece, and especially the figure of Will Fern and the oppression and desperation he represents, into an opportunity for what the Chartist newspaper, *The Northern Star*, on 28 December called 'a reality that was almost startling' in its representation of the 'three-quarters starved labourer'. The critic was speaking, with approbation, of the Lyceum production, in which Emery excelled in this role. There was even greater opportunity for such 'realism' elsewhere. The passing of the Theatres Act had freed the many barely legal theatres already operating across London, some of them in exclusively working-class districts, to put on straight plays, and in 1844 several texts of *The Chimes* were submitted from these little-league theatres for licence. A version by a Miss Mellon was performed at the Queens, and one by Charles Webb was advertised but never got to the stage at the Strand. Miss Mellon's text is now incomplete, and Webb's text is not available to us; but from the lowest ranks, where soon the effort to stay within the licensing system was to prove not worthwhile, two have survived. One is by Samuel Atkyns, actor-manager at the Albert Saloon, and the other by Edward Edwards for the Apollo Saloon.[58] Both show interesting differences from the authorized texts. They are more graphic: at the Apollo Saloon, for example, a series of wordless pictures were presented in the climactic section, 'The scene Illuminated discovers—Meg sitting in a miserable Cot—alone at work very Pale and Poor as Illustration. Clouds past over and change again to picture of Richard at Door—then change again to water side with Meg and child as Picture. As it darkens Toby starts up exclaiming Meg Meg—sinks in a swoon as Act drop descends' (f1133v). One might conjecture that the messages so presented would have been more legible than they are in the A'Beckett/Lemon version. The Saloon versions were also more explicit, both in giving the Spirits or Goblins clearer lines to condemn Toby's transgression in

---

[56]  See my discussion in Bratton, *West End*, 182–4.

[57]  Malcolm Morley, 'Ring up *The Chimes*', *Dickensian*, vol. 47, 1950, 202–6.

[58]  Add. MS 42980 ff. 1089–1119r (Royal Albert), ff. 1120–50 (Apollo), and Add. MS 42981 ff. 2–32v (Queens).

trusting to 'the dull vermin of the earth—the putters down of crushed and broken natures' (Atkyns, f1105v) and in including more of Dickens's lines for Will Fern, his condemnations of patronizing arrogance and dilettantism in regard to the rural poor (Atkyns, f1101r&v).

The next step in Dickens's rapprochement with the stage over the Christmas books was conclusive, and the outcome triumphant. To put on *The Cricket on the Hearth* he brought together the dramaturg and the theatrical company of his choice and, very obviously, he wrote for them. This was the piece out of whose theatricality Thackeray made such snobbish capital. But it certainly did work best in the theatre. Contemplating its huge stage success, Philip Bolton suggests[59] that it 'may epitomize the process whereby the Yuletide brainchildren of Charles Dickens were enshrined by theatrical means in the popular imagination of two nations'. There was, he demonstrates, a 'first big burst of enthusiasm' with at least thirty separate stagings in London in the first year, 1845–6, plus provincial tours and New York openings. After this point the stage history became 'really impressive', especially with the long-lasting success of Dion Boucicault's *Dot*, which opened at the Winter Garden New York in 1859, and became a famous vehicle for the actor J.L. Toole. That text is to be found in the second volume of this collection. Here the early stagings are represented by the version Dickens planned to put upon the stage. He sold it to the Keeleys, managing at the Lyceum, and had it dramatized by Albert Smith from proof sheets sent to him in advance. Smith's was not a difficult task: the story, as Malcolm Morley puts it,[60] is 'purposely' 'patterned as near to play form as could be', needing little more than the dialogue pruning and marking out, and the stage-like effects that are imagined in the overseeing of Dot and in John's dream sequence converting into actual stage directions. The contributions of the cast, in particular Mary Ann Keeley's bustling Dot and her husband's mix of humour and pathos as Caleb Plummer, have been anticipated in the creation of their roles, which, on this occasion, they took according to the intentions of the author. Mary Ann's competence—her managing qualities—could be said to modify quite significantly Dickens's too-sweet notion of the innocent child bride in this text; and the intertheatrical resonances of the Keeley family, including their fifteen-year-old daughter making her stage debut, would add depth to the play, especially in the family scene in Chirp the Third when Bob as Caleb confesses to the blind Bertha, played by Mary, with the help of her mother playing Dot, that they have deceived her all this while about her father's circumstances. The *Illustrated London News* reviewer says:

Mrs Keeley's Dot was perfection: we never saw her in a part in which she appeared so completely at home. Her busy, bustling, affectionate manner in the first 'chirp' or act, and her anxiety in the last one—the little pantomime scene in which she comes and seats herself on her little stool at the feet of her husband, who has been sitting up all night at his dreary hearth—and the voluble and earnest haste with which she pours forth the explanation of her apparently equivocal conduct, as soon as she finds herself at liberty to do so—were inimitable.[61]

[59] Bolton, 273.
[60] Malcolm Morley, '"The Cricket" on the stage', *Dickensian*, vol. 48, 1951–2, 17–24, 17.
[61] *ILN*, 27 December 1845.

'Inimitable', of course, is the ultimate accolade in the world of Charles Dickens. Even the joke, twice repeated in the play text, that Dot is proud of her legs and doesn't mind them being seen, may suggest Mary Ann Keeley's fame in tights. The second time it occurs, at the entrance of the Peerybingle party in Chirp the Second, Dickens had referred to Tilly's legs, but Smith takes the opportunity to offer Mary Ann another intertheatrical moment. Book and performance company feed back.

Their success did not escape the notice, or the condemnation, of the cultural gate-keepers. As well as Thackeray's Christmas Day scorn and insinuations in *The Morning Post*, on 27 December *The Times* (in any case rattled because Dickens was about to launch a rival daily paper) announced that '[w]e owe it to literature to protest against this last production of Mr Dickens' which is, they claim, 'fatally inclined to the deterioration of modern taste'. This vicious tendency is proven by the fact that 'whatever may be its defects, criticism is disarmed by the somewhat startling announcement that it was concocted chiefly with a view to its production at the Lyceum theatre'. Such contamination is obviously a sufficient explanation for its unnatural dialogue, outrageous sentiments, and generally repulsive staginess. And its enormous success.[62] Besides the Lyceum, it played at the Adelphi, adapted by Stirling, at many more of the saloon theatres than even *The Chimes*, and also, this time, at the grand legitimate house, the Haymarket, made over by the manager Webster.

The popular success of the joint Christmas venture between author and dramatizers might be regarded as peaking with *The Cricket on the Hearth* in 1845. The next Christmas book was *The Battle of Life* in 1846, damned by the *Theatrical Times* in advance simply for existing upon the stage, and while Bolton's count reveals that the popular audience was prepared to like it, and all the minor houses took it up with enthusiasm—at least nineteen of them by February—its success waned abruptly thereafter.[63] Whether this was simply because it had been created for the Keeleys and could not do without them, or was something to do with innovation in the play itself that was not understood—that it was a dramatic development that Dickens had begun because he had worked with the professional company and thought closely about what he might do next—is a matter of conjecture.

Dickens was unequivocally involved with the dramatization in 1846: under what the hostile *Morning Post* dubs a 'new-fangled arrangement' he sold the rights to pre-publication access to the Keeley management at the Lyceum, and himself worked with them at the late rehearsals, energetically sorting out the miscopied dialogue and fumbled business on his first visit and then reading the whole story to the company on the morning of the first night.[64] Malcolm Morley sees this read-through as 'better late than never', rescuing the production, which became 'easily the best' in London;[65] but it is worth wondering whether one might see the reading as not so much a last-ditch attempt to correct errors, as Morley's phrase suggests, but rather as a move by the

---

[62] *Morning Chronicle*, 25 December 1845; *Times*, 27 December 1845.      [63] Bolton, 296.

[64] See letter to Mrs Charles Dickens, 19 December 1846, *Letters* vol. 4, 680–1.

[65] Malcolm Morley, '*The Battle of Life* in the theatre', *Dickensian*, vol. 48, 1951–5, 76–81, 77.

writer to give the company a feeling of the unusual tempo and mood of the piece. The play is very odd, in mid-century terms: as the hostile *Morning Post* review declared, 'we are forcibly struck with the barrenness of the outline [...] the characters are mere *silhouettes*—misty and undefined [...] the plot flows on in calm insipidity'. The prejudiced reviewer skewers this oddity as showing Dickens's weakness as a dramatic writer, but it might be read as exactly the opposite. Perhaps he was moving, in a piece so fundamentally conceived for the stage, in the direction of developing drama in a new direction—not a move that his side-long approach to playwriting would allow him to follow through. If he had been willing openly to write his own plays, and so forge a new style, this texts hints that the development of dramatic writing in the later nineteenth century could have been quite different. *The Battle of Life* displays a kind of embodied and visual poeticism, an independence of plot, and an attitude to character as psychological mirroring, that is and is not Realism: it suggests a kind of play-writing that was not to surface decisively for another fifty years, on the other side of the Naturalist revolution. It is worth noting, perhaps, as a clue to a path not taken, that *Bitva Zhizni* (*The Battle of Life*) became part of the Moscow Art Theatre repertoire in 1924.[66]

Whatever its hints about Dickens the lost dramatic writer, the inspiration of *The Battle of Life* by its immediate theatrical situation is quite clear. It is written to the strengths of the Lyceum company. It is easy to argue that the characters of Clemency Newcome and Benjamin Britain, in the story as well as on stage, owed much to Mary Ann and Bob Keeley: *The Illustrated London News* declared that the character of Britain seemed to have been written for Bob Keeley, and Mary Ann excelled even her brilliance in Dot. We know Dickens was a great admirer of the double act they made famous, the characters of Robin and Margot in John Banim's *The Sergeant's Wife* (English Opera House, 1827). They played this pair of servants, who constituted the comic dimension of a confection from the French about murderous banditti, before they were married, backing Fanny Kelly, who did a famous melodramatic-mime in the title role of the piece. Robin is very young and very stupid, and Margot, also young but brave and resourceful, is continually frustrated by his cowardly and feeble efforts with ladders, hidden passages, and the apparatus of comic-man heroism as she strives to help the heroine, exclaiming at one point, 'For a woman—a friendless one, in such need of help—I will do all a friend or woman can',[67] and presenting her with some very business-like assistance in the form of a loaded pistol. Ten years on, married, successful, and in charge of their own theatre, Dickens knew the resourceful Mary Ann and the glum clown Bob well enough to allow 'all the weight of the plot' and 'nearly the whole sympathies of the audience' to ride on her realization of Clemency Newcome, with Britain as her stooge. Their work together in the supper scene was 'the purest comedy', the *Era* reviewer asserted,[68] but:

---

[66] My thanks to Peter McAllister for this information.

[67] John Banim, *The Sergeant's Wife*, Lacy 335 (London, n.d.), 28.   [68] *Era*, 27 December 1846.

Mrs Keeley's Clemency Newcome was, without exception, one of the finest pieces of acting we ever witnessed on any stage [ … ] she carried the portraiture almost beyond the quaint sketch Mr Dickens has given of the simple awkward maid-servant. But glorious as was her comedy— her very ludicrous appearance, and shuffling gait, and hapless elbows—her ludicrous way of signing her name was more so—it was in the serious portion of the part that she produced the strongest effect upon the audience [ … ] through the intensity of her acting alone, did Marion chiefly become an object of interest to the audience.

Thus Mary Ann Keeley was provided with a role in which she could combine her comic powers with the kind of affective melodramatic performance Fanny Kelly had given in the earlier play. It is a new form of mutually inspired creation, generated between author, dramatizer (Albert Smith again), and actress. *The Illustrated London News* portioned out the praise unequally: the reviewer perhaps did not understand what Dickens might have been doing, in developing the play as he did and leaving space within it for the creativity of the actors, when he declared that it was:

a most unqualified success. For this, however, be it understood, the author and dramatist were mainly endebted to the unequalled acting of Mrs Keeley as Clemency Newcombe … otherwise the piece was somewhat wearisome.[69]

There was no Christmas book in 1847, and by 1848 the Keeleys had also moved on, ending their Lyceum management. Mark Lemon, the weakest and most sentimental of Dickens's friendly dramaturgs, produced a version of *The Haunted Man* for Madame Celeste at the Adelphi, but the work there was no substitute for the old team, and the difficulties of Dickens's arm's-length theatrical creativity perhaps overwhelmed the enterprise. It is the last play in this volume of early work, the breaking of the wave of the writings of the young Charles Dickens. There are wonderful dramatic possibilities in his later work, and some of the mature novels offered purchase to his contemporaries—Celeste was well served by *A Tale of Two Cities*, for example—but this early run of writing that was partly inspired by, and rapidly returned to, the stage of the 1840s came to a natural conclusion. The author eventually went on to make his own supercharged dramatic productions in the 'inimitable' travelling one-man show, and he returned to work with other theatre-makers, admiring and emulating the French actor Charles Fechter in particular, and finding Wilkie Collins a good writing partner. That later work is part of the second volume in this collection.

[69] *ILN*, 26 December 1846.

# THE CONTENTS OF THIS VOLUME

The plays published in the first volume are:

W.T. Moncrieff, *Sam Weller, or the Pickwickians*, New Strand
    Theatre, June 1837;
Edward Stirling, *Nicholas Nickleby*, Adelphi, November 1838;
Edward Stirling, *Barnaby Rudge*, New Strand Theatre, August 1841;
Charles Webb, *Old Scrooge*, Sadler's Wells and New Strand Theatre, February 1844;
Edward Stirling, *Martin Chuzzlewit*, Lyceum, July 1844;
Gilbert Abbott A'Beckett and Mark Lemon, *The Chimes*, Adelphi, December 1844;
Albert Smith, *The Cricket on the Hearth*, Lyceum, December 1845;
Albert Smith, *The Battle of Life*, Lyceum, December 1846;
Mark Lemon, *The Haunted Man*, Adelphi, December 1848.

The copy text preferred in most cases is the manuscript submitted to the Lord Chamberlain's office for licensing, collated with printed early versions where they exist. In this way I have sought to represent the earliest stage state of each piece, bearing in mind the problems each of these sources presents. There is, on the one hand, the problem that any manuscript sent for licence was a more or less perfunctory copy of an original still not finalized, or not kept up to date as rehearsals progressed, and on the other the desire on the part of some of the authors, when publishing for their own profit and good name, to embellish the text with more stage descriptions and directions and perhaps to restore or work up material previously discarded in the staging. The Lord Chamberlain's copies, however, especially where they were written out by the author, sometimes seem to offer clues to performance intention. Punctuation and spelling indicate rhythm and timing in delivery. Where this seems to be a possibility, I have reproduced these peculiarities, with non-standard spellings such as the omission of the final 'e', replaced by an apostrophe, in the past tense of a verb and the use of the termination 'or' instead of 'our' in for example 'favour', as well as attempts to indicate dialect like the v/w transposition in cockney speech. The punctuation of some texts is even more deliberately performative, especially the use of dashes and, in the case of Albert Smith, colons, to indicate breaths and pauses within a speech. These often occur where orthodox punctuation would use a full stop, but can be scattered liberally across the dialogue. These peculiarities have been retained to give the modern reader as full an impression of the performance conventions and usages of the mid-nineteenth century as possible. Apart from this endeavour to represent any features that might relate to performance, I have regularized and to an extent modernized the presentation of the plays, to facilitate reading. I have silently supplied much missing punctuation, such as apostrophes, capital letters at the beginning and full stops at the end of sentences. The form of stage directions, which differs between and often within the plays, has been standardized. Speech ascriptions and the layout of speeches on the page have been similarly regularized. The texts have some individual peculiarities which I have retained, and details about each text are included in the headnotes, together with more information about each of the dramatic authors.

# ONE

## W.T. Moncrieff, *Sam Weller, or the Pickwickians*, New Strand Theatre, from 12 June 1837

### INTRODUCTION

WILLIAM THOMAS MONCRIEFF (1794–1857) was one of the writers suggested by the originator Robert Seymour as a suitable man to write the letterpress to accompany his series of pictures that Dickens made into *The Pickwick Papers*. He was more experienced and more eminent, at the time, than the young Dickens. A cockney tradesman's son, he had been writing, first songs and theatre criticism, and then plays, since early in the century, with several major successes including *Giovanni in London* (1817), the satirical take on *Don Giovanni* which brought Vestris her first major success in London, and then *Tom and Jerry* (Adelphi, 1821), a truly epoch-making hit which converted Pierce Egan's shapeless saga of flash London and the world of the Regency buck into a defining moment in the development of modern metropolitan language and culture.[1] But by 1837, though aged only forty-three, he was in a rapid decline, having attempted the management of Vauxhall Gardens and opened a music shop in Regent's Street, and consequently twice been arrested for debt. He wrote more than 200 plays, but he was losing his sight; in the 1840s he began to apply for charitable help to institutions like the Literary Fund where Dickens was, by that stage, a leader, and in 1844 he entered the Charterhouse as a pensioner, only to make trouble by leading the old men in rebellion against the peculations of the management and their own degradation.

Dickens famously branded Moncrieff a miserable thief[2] when his stage versions of *Pickwick* proved successful, and his scornful portrait of a dramatic hack in *Nicholas Nickleby* is taken to be a further thrust at the older man. Their complicated attacks and counterclaims made as they jockeyed for the high moral and creative ground are discussed in the Introduction, as is the contribution made by the actor-manager of the New Strand Theatre, William Hammond, to the creation of Sam Weller in the public mind. The provisional and malleable nature of these dramatizations is illustrated by the evolution of this text, which was written to catch a moment—when *Pickwick* became an overnight success, long before its parts publication was complete—and to provide a vehicle for an actor who saw an opportunity for himself. It was then adapted to reflect his input, before it was printed, then changed to include material from Dickens's further episodes, and eventually provided with a sequel, the dramatist using a new plot, Dickens's characters, and also some of his own[3]—overall, very like a modern television serialization.

---

[1] See Bratton, *New Readings*, 155–68.    [2] See Introduction, 'The Problems of Prejudice'.
[3] See Introduction, 'The Plays He Did Not Write'.

*The Pickwick Papers* were a fertile source of stage materials: Volume 2 includes two texts taken from the novel at later dates, James Albery's *Jingle* and *Bardell versus Pickwick* by John Hollingshead.

## THE TEXT

This text is a collation of the version printed in London in 1837 'for the author', which is used as the copy text ('1837'), with the MS in the Lord Chamberlain's collection, Add. MS 42942 ff. 478–552v. From indications in the text, and the detailed discussion offered by Mary McGowan,[4] it appears that both these versions stem from a manuscript or possibly even multiple manuscripts no longer extant, presumably used in the theatre. The extant texts have been altered in different ways. The printed text is much longer, and gives significantly more lines and business and several songs for the women in the play, which may have been cut from the licensing version by way of self-censorship, or may have developed in rehearsal or performance. The solo riffs in which Hammond elaborates his characterization of Sam Weller are also often longer in the printed version. There is a note on p. 1 of 1837 saying 'Some of the parodies in this Drama are omitted on the stage, on account of the length of the representation', but there are no indications in the text; we may conjecture that Hammond's songs are meant. The printed text is preferred for completeness: this material was created for performance, and may all have been seen at one time or another. On the other hand the printed copy also includes aids for the reader, not only more elaborate stage directions, which have been included here (apart from the technical details of entrances, 'R1E' etc.), but also in places an attempt at phonetic representation of cockney pronunciation, and a mechanical application of the v/w transposition, sometimes in impossible instances. This is not helpful, and I have preferred the indications of the speech of the Wellers and other cockney characters as given in the manuscript.

---

[4] Mary Teresa McGowan, 'Pickwick and the pirates: a study of some early imitations, dramatizations and plagiarisms of *Pickwick Papers*', unpublished PhD thesis, University of London 1975, 214–20. She suggests that the MS derives from the printed text, but I think it more likely that both come from a lost source.

## Characters and cast of the first production

| | |
|---|---|
| Mr Pickwick | Mr A. Younge |
| Augustus Snodgrass, Esq. | Mr Melville |
| Tracy Tupman, Esq. | Mr E. Burton |
| Nathaniel Winkle, Esq. | Mr Roberts |
| Mr Wardle | Mr G. Cooke |
| G. Nupkins, Esq. (Mayor of Ipswich) | Mr Chicheley |
| Mr Leo Hunter | Mr Nicholson |
| Alfred Jingle, Esq. | Mr J. Lee |
| Mr Samuel Weller | Mr W.J. Hammond |
| Mr Weller, sen. | Mr H. Hall |
| Job Trotter | Mr Attwood |
| Master Joseph Dumpling (the Fat Boy) | Mr A. Richardson |

Honourable Simon Slumkey; Horatio Fizkin, Esq.; Rackstraw; Dogsflesh; Canteen; Alleycampain; Drunken Liberal; Ballad Singer; Match Seller: Turnkey; Grummer; and numerous other characters, by Messrs Dearlove, Burton, Searle, Chapman, etc., etc.

| | |
|---|---|
| Miss Rachel Wardle | Mrs Johnson |
| Miss Isabella Wardle | Mrs Hammond |
| Miss Emily Wardle | Miss Daly |
| Mrs Bardell | Mrs Melville |
| Mrs Leo Hunter | Miss E. Hamilton |
| Miss Tabby | Mrs H. Hall |
| Mary Summers | Miss Petifer |
| Miss Lucretia Kitchener | Miss Brookes |

Mrs Barclay, Boarders, Visitors, Servants, etc., etc.

1. William Hammond as Sam Weller.

# ACT I

## SCENE 1

*Entrance to Coach Yard of the White Hart Inn—Bar and Coffee-Room on one side—Staircase, leading to a range of bedrooms, on the other.*

SAM WELLER, *in an old white hat, red striped waistcoat, with sleeves, yellow velveteen smalls, coloured stockings, and highlows, discovered cleaning boots.*

SAM. (*singing*)  Vith von boot here, and t'other boot there,  1
  Every kipple vill make a pair!

*Enter* SALLY CHAMBERMAID.

CHAM.  Why, Sam—Sam, I say; No. 22 wants his boots.
SAM.  Ask No. 22 vether he'll have 'em now, or vait till he gets 'em?
CHAM.  Come, come, don't be a fool, Sam—the gentleman wants 'em directly.  5
SAM.  Vell—you *are* a nice young ooman, for a musical party, you are. Look at these here boots—eleven pair of boots and von shoe, as b'longs to No. 6, with the vooden leg—the eleven boots to be call'd at half-past eight, and the shoe at nine. Who's No. 22, that he's to put all the others out? No—no, reg'lar rotation—as Jack Ketch said, vhen he tied up the malefactors.  10
CHAM.  Ah! I shall never make my money of you—you are the most lazy, idle, imperent thing as never was—but never mind—I've told you the gentleman wants his boots—and you'd better do 'em—and that's all about it. (*Exit* CHAMBERMAID)
SAM.  Well, we sha'n't be bankrupts this here term, at all events; though we mayn't quite make our fortins. No matter for that—we can manage to eat our biled mutton  15
  vithout capers, and sha'n't care much for horse-radish vhile ve can get roast beef. We've got a reg'lar inn full. Let me see vhat customers we have—there is a pair of Bluchers in 13—two pair of halves in the commercial—there is these here painted tops in the snuggery, inside the bar—five more tops and a pair of Vellingtons, very much worn, that looks as if they belongs to King Dick, in the coffee-room—one  20
  vooden leg, as I said afore, in No. 6—and a pair of hessians—ditto lady's shoes, in private sitting-room, No. 5—I think there's a love affair between these here hessians and the female kids—if so, and the hessians is anything of a gen'lman, he is worth a shilling a day, let alone the errands—I must go and see arter 'em. (*Exit* SAM)

*Enter* PICKWICK, *with* JACK RACKSTRAW, *a cabman.*

---

12 *never*: MS omits 'never'.  16 *vhile ve can get*: MS replaces 'vhile ve can get' with 'with our'.

25  RACK.    Now, sir! here you are—all the vay from Gosvell-street.

PICK.    You've come very quick, cabman!

RACK.    Yes, sir! wery quick—alvays does!

PICK.    How old is that horse of yours?

RACK.    Forty-two, sir! come next Doncaster!

30  PICK.    Bless me! forty-two!—I must note that down—and how long do you keep him out at a time?

RACK.    Vot's he taking down my number for? Is he von of the Cruelty to Animals chaps I vonder? (*aside*) Vy, we keeps him out two or three veeks at a time. He lives at Pentonville, vhen he's at home—but we seldom takes him home, on account of

35      his veakness.

PICK.    Astonishing!

RACK.    He always falls down vhen he's took out of the cab—but vhen he's in it, ve bears him up wery tight, and takes him in wery short, so as he can't wery vell fall down—and then we've got a pair of precious large wheels on, so when he does

40      move, they run after him, and he must go on, he can't help it.

PICK.    Wonderful! the tenacity of life in animals. Here'll be information for the club!—Here's your money, friend! (*offering money to* RACKSTRAW)

RACK.    Wants me to take more than my fare. I know'd he was an informer. There's Tommy Dogsflesh, the hackney, on the stand—and Bill Mudlark, the waterman on

45      the crossing—so I'm blow'd if I don't have a touch at him, if I get six months for it. (*aside*)

PICK.    Here's your money, my good man!

RACK.    You be damned, and your money too!—I'll have a turn-up vith you, for it—and give you a pint to boot—old ogles. (*squares up to him*)

*Enter* WINKLE, TUPMAN, *and* SNODGRASS, L.

50  SNOD.    Eh! what alarm?—what dire confusion?

RACK.    Ulloa, who are you?—pals! Here, Tommy Dogsflesh—Bill Mudlark (*calling off*). Now, then, for all four of you—one down t'other come on—or all at once if you likes it better.

*Enter* TOMMY DOGSFLESH *and* BILL MUDLARK.

29  *Doncaster*: September—the time of the long-established St Leger meeting at Doncaster racecourse. The joke, that the speedy cab horse marks his birthday from a race meeting, is Moncrieff's.

33  *I vonder*: MS omits 'I vonder'.

48  *damned*: This is the first of many instances where 'damned' or its equivalents have been substituted in the MS. In this instance 'hang'd' is used instead. This is a common kind of self-censorship in MSS submitted to the Lord Chamberlain's office.

49  *old ogles*: The cabbie's defiances are drawn from the slang of the streets and, possibly, the prize ring, with which Moncrieff was familiar from his famous dramatization of Egan's work in *Tom and Jerry*. So the insulting name 'ogles' might well mean 'spectacles'—Dickens has him knocking off Pickwick's glasses at this moment, and 'to ogle' is to look closely or intently, with pejorative overtones. His offer to 'give you a pint to boot' is possibly boxing slang: the offer of a handicap, he will give Pickwick a point, and still beat him.

DOG.   Here's a lark—vot's the row—go to vork, Jack—tip it him, 942—give him one
in his bread-basket.                                                                                  55

SNOD.   Are you mad, man?

WIN.   Or drunk?

TUP.   Or both?

RACK.   Neither, my coveys—(*sparring*)—Vot did you take my number for, and put
down all as I said, on purpose to aggrawate me to commit an assault—but I'll take   60
the shine out of ye. There's one for your nob. (*sparring at* PICKWICK, *etc.*)

SNOD.   Police!—Police! (*calling off*)

DOG.   (*knocking his hat over his eyes*) I think you said Pelisse—does your mother
know you're out?

MUD.   Go it, Tommy—never say die—sarve 'em out—put 'em under the pump—I   65
hates all hinformers—hurrah! (*a general scuffle*)

*Enter* JINGLE, *from coffee-room, and* SAM *from opposite side.*

JIN.   Ulloa, ulloa!—what's the fun here?

RACK.   Only giving an informer his gruel—that's all.

PICK.   I am no informer!—I deny the imputation!

JIN.   An't you—an't ye—I may profit by this—(*aside*) I see it all—take yourself off,   70
Patent Safety—it is entirely a mistake—very respectable gentleman—so none of
your nonsense. Don't be down, sir—these little accidents will happen in the best
regulated families—pull 'em up for it—five pounds and costs—or three months
tread-mill—put that in your pipe and smoke it—like the flavour, eh!—damned
rascals!                                                                                              75

SAM.   Aye, aye!—cut your lucky—be off, young eightpenny.

RACK.   Vell, I've knock'd a double rat-tat on their mugs, to let 'em know who vas
coming—that's von satisfaction—so now I'll be going, this way, Tommy—ve'll take a
drain at the Blue Posts. (*Exit* RACKSTRAW *followed by* DOGSFLESH *and* MUDLARK)

JIN.   Eccentric rogues—but we've got rid of them—run Boots, tell the waiter to get   80
glasses round—brandy and water—hot and strong—sweet and plenty—raw beef
steak for the gentleman's damaged eye—nothing like raw beef steak, sir—cold
pump handle, very good—not always convenient—damn'd awkward—standing
two hours in the street, with eye against pump handle—very—eh!

59 *Vot did you*: MS inserts 'vant to'.

64 *does…out?*: The ubiquitous street cry of the day, 'does your mother know you're out?', implied the
juvenility, and therefore the naivety and general incapacity, of the person addressed.

71 *Patent Safety*: The Patent Safety Cab was registered in 1834. It was so called because fitted with a
device to prevent it overturning.

74 *damned*: 'damned' deleted in MS.

76 *cut your lucky*: Current slang in the 1830s for to make one's escape. Dickens gives the alternative
phrase, to 'make' one's lucky, to Sam, in chapter 10.

76 *eightpenny*: Sam names the cabman from his fare, reckoned to be eightpence per mile (Peter
Cunningham, *Hand-Book of London*, 1850).

83 *damn'd*: 'damn'd' omitted in MS.

85 SAM.   I'll order 'em directly, sir!—glasses round—then in course they'll order one for me—queer chap, that—like nothing on earth but a suspicious character—as the papers say! (*Exit* SAM)

PICK.   You've rendered us a great service, sir—we must know each other better—my name is Pickwick, these are Messrs Snodgrass, Tupman, and Winkle, my friends,
90 members of the Corresponding Society of the Pickwick Club, of which I have the honour to be founder and president. We have just formed ourselves into an association in pursuit of knowledge—with liberty to pay our own expenses—and having a friend living in the neighbourhood of Rochester—our first excursion will be directed in that quarter.

95 JIN.   Something may come of this (*aside*). Rochester—how odd—going there myself—accompany you—lots of information!

PICK.   Most happy, sir—this will, indeed, be a most valuable acquisition!

JIN.   Say no more—settled thing—all set off together—smart fellow, that cabman— handled his fives cleverly—but if I'd been your friend, in the green jemmy, here—I'd
100 have punched his head in a pig's whisper—hackney too—'gad I would—no gammon—damn me.

*Enter* SAM.

SAM.   Now, sir, brandy and vater's all ready, I've had my glass; and I can assure you it's very good—I speaks from experience.

JIN.   This way then—now for it—all right in no time.

(*Exit* JINGLE *followed by* PICKWICK, SNODGRASS, TUPMAN, *and* WINKLE, *into coffee-room*)

105 SAM.   Rum blades, them ere—but we sees all sorts here—worst of being a Boots is, it puts a stop to hambition—you can't rise no higher, and the human mind naturally aspires; as the pick-pocket said to the gallows—I'm summat like a fly in a treacle-can—I should uncommonly like to change my situation, although the folks does call me a shining character—I emulates the great Vauxhall balloon—I'm for rising in
110 the world—a Boots is sich a sort of amphibious profession, it ha'n't any regular standing in the list of trades. Well, I must look for'ards, as the telescopes do—that 'ere chap with the shabby Vellingtons, 'as got into a good thing vith these ere new comers—he looked like vanting to join a company, and so he's joined them—ah, he's up to snuff, and a pinch or two over, he is!—Oh! here comes the gemman as had
115 the turn up with that illegitimate jarvey—he's vhat I should call, statistically speaking, comfortable.

*Enter* PICKWICK *from coffee-room.*

85 *they'll order one*: MS has 'they mean one' for 'they'll order one' and omits 'as the papers say'.
101 *damn*: MS substitutes 'hang'.
113 *although...joined them*: MS omits 'although...character' and 'he looked like...joined them'.
116 *statistically speaking, comfortable*: MS omits 'speaking'.

PICK.    A very comprehensive character, our new friend—he must be an honorary associate in our peregrinations—but there's one thing we've totally forgotten, that is, an assistant companion—in my knowledge of human nature, it struck me, that the Boots, here, is a very intelligent fellow; besides which, these Boots are very eli- 120 gible for travelling, so with the sanction of my three companions—Oh! here he is—a word with you my good fellow.

SAM.    Sir, to you—I'll just take off my lilly shallow, 't'ant a wery good 'un to look at, but it's an astonishing 'un to wear—and afore the brim went, it was a very handsome tile—however, it's lighter without it, that's von thing—and every hole lets in some 125 air, that's another—Wentillation gossamer, I calls it!

PICK.    It does indeed look light—but now to my business with you!

SAM.    Eh! that's the pint, sir!—out with it—as the father said to the child when it swallowed the farden!

PICK.    I want to know, in the first place, whether you've any reason to be discon- 130 tented with your present situation?

SAM.    Afore I answer that ere question, sir, I should like to know vhether you're a-going to perwide me with a better?

PICK.    I've half made up my mind to engage you myself!

SAM.    Have you, though—                                                                        135

PICK.    I have!

SAM.    Wages?

PICK.    Twelve pounds a year!

SAM.    Clothes?

PICK.    Two suits—                                                                              140

SAM.    Vork?

PICK.    To attend upon me, and my three companions, in the coffee-room, there.

SAM.    Take the bill down! I'm let to a single gentleman—and the terms is agreed upon, if the clothes fit me half as well as the place, they'll do.

PICK.    You accept the situation?                                                               145

SAM.    Certainly.

PICK.    You can get a character, of course.

SAM.    Ax the landlady about that.

PICK.    Can you engage at once?

SAM.    I'll get into the clothes immediately, if they're here.                                 150

PICK.    You can call at my tailor's in Piccadilly, who will fit you directly—I am inclined to be satisfied with the inquiries I have already made about you—Oh! here come our friends.

---

121  *besides...companions*: MS omits 'besides...companions'.
123  *lilly shallow*: Low-crowned white hat.
125  *that's von thing*: MS omits 'that's von thing'.
129  *Eh!...farden*: This speech and Sam's next both omitted in MS.
145  *You accept the situation?*: MS omits this speech and Sam's 'Certainly'.
152  *You can call...inclined to be*: MS omits Pickwick's reference to his tailor and 'inclined to be'.

*Enter* SNODGRASS, TUPMAN, WINKLE, *and* JINGLE, *from coffee-room.*

PICK.    Brother Pickwickians, I have the pleasure to inform you that I've engaged—
155 SAM.    Samuel Veller, at your service—
PICK.    To accompany us in our peregrinations—so now then, Mr—
JIN.    Jingle, Alfred Jingle, Esq., a gentleman of small property—very—(*aside*) and
good character—I may say characters, for I sustained the first line of business in the
Kent Circuit; (*aside*) therefore we can start at once—mail coach—eh! ya, hip, that's
160    the way. (*Sings*)

Now then, Mr Samuel Weller,
Let's haste to the White Horse Cellar—
Get a snack before we go.

SAM.    With all my heart, sir—I've just to take leave of the maids—mustn't go without
165    leave, you know, sir—any luggage sir? (*to* JINGLE)
JIN.    Who, I?—only brown paper parcel, here, that's all—other luggage gone by
water—large trunks—packing cases, nail'd up, big as houses—heavy—heavy—
damned heavy—very!
SAM.    Hadn't I better call a truck to take this for you, mister?
170 JIN.    Funny—very funny!—low comedy—never mind, will joke—come, gents, we
must go.—You'll pay for the brandy and water.—You must mind when you pass
through the gateway at Charing Cross—take care of your heads—terrible place—
dangerous work—very!—t'other day—five children—mother—tall lady eating
sandwiches—forgot the arch—crash—knock—children look'd round—mother's
175    head gone—sandwich in her hand—no mouth to put it in—head of a family
off—shocking—shocking!—very!
PICK.    We'll take care—now then, brother Pickwickians—now then to commence
our memorable peregrinations.

CHORUS, OMNES.

AIR 'Vive le Roi.'

Pickwicks on, o'er hill and dale;
180      We'll from all, knowledge draw!
Far and near, spread the tale—
Boys hurrah! boys hurrah!

Hearts that fame, like ours, inspires,
Critic frowns ne'er shall awe,

185      *mustn't go…know, sir*: MS omits 'mustn't go…know, sir'.
168      *other luggage…heavy—very!*: MS omits 'other luggage…heavy—very!' Sam's riposte about the
light paper parcel needing a truck would work better in performance without Jingle's elaboration.
176      *terrible place…family off*: MS omits 'terrible place…very!', 'knock', 'sandwich in her hand', and
'head of a family off'.
178.2      *AIR 'Vive le Roi.'*: From Balfe's *Siege of Rochelle* (Drury Lane, 1835).

Till our Club's last name expires—　　　　　　　　185
Boys hurrah! boys hurrah!

(*Exeunt Omnes*)


# SCENE 2

*Apartment in* MR WARDLE'S *Mansion, Manor Farm, Dingley Dell.*

*Enter* ISABELLA, EMILY, *and* AUNT RACHEL, R.

TRIO, OMNES.

AIR 'Nice young maidens.'

Fond and faithful, pure and fair,　　　　　　　　1
Nice young maidens!
Why should we pine in despair,
Born for loving, as we are;
Make us, God of Love, thy care,　　　　　　　　5
Nice young maidens!

Why are we doom'd apes to lead,
Nice young maidens!
Men were better, far, indeed,
For young maidens!　　　　　　　　10
Bachelors—not to be named,—
We to mend, should be asham'd;
Can we by any one be blam'd,
Nice young maidens!

ISA.　Ah! Nice young maidens, indeed; but what's the use of our being such nice 15
young maidens, if no nice young men ever comes here to see how *very nice* we are.

EM.　Right, Isabella, dear!—Heigho! papa grows almost everything at Dingley
Dell—his own hogs—his own vegetables—his own mutton—his own poultry—
what a pity it is, he can't grow a few young men as well.

---

0.2 RACHEL: Spelt 'Rachael' throughout MS.

0.4 '*Nice young maidens.*': 'Nice young maidens' was collected as a Northumbrian folk song, and was
available to Moncrieff on broadside and in songsters, a copy of one of which, printed in Dublin *c.*1840,
survives in the British Library.

14 *Why are we doom'd … Nice young maidens!*: Second stanza of the song not present in MS.

18 *vegetables*: MS abbreviates this list of produce here, inserting 'etc.' to end it, which is suggestive
of a copyist shortening the task, rather than a note of performance, where the actress would be unlikely
to say 'etc.' The MS is markedly prone to abbreviating the scenes between the women: see this play's
Introduction.

20 RACH.    It is, indeed, Emily, love!

ISA.    Ah, poor Rachel, I feel for you, with all my heart! if it's annoying for us, who have not waited so *very* long for lovers—we have neither of us arrived at years of discretion, yet, what must it be for you, that have waited the time you have—it's terrible to think of.

25 RACH.    Time, indeed! but certainly time does seem long, when one's waiting—not, but it's partly my own fault, such chances as I have had; such offers as have been made to me; there was my dear Lothario, at Stoke Pogis, bitterly do I resent my cruelty to him—heigho!

ISA.    Let me see, that was in the year one, I believe, aunt, wasn't it?

30 RACH.    Pert chit! No miss, it was not two years ago—it was when you was in your pinafore at school, eating bread and butter.

ISA.    And a little sugar—poor aunt.

*Enter* WARDLE, *with letter.*

WAR.    Good news, girls!—good news!—here Joe—Joe, I say—(*calling*)—damn that boy, he's asleep again.

*Enter* FAT BOY, *drowsily.*

35 F. BOY    Yes, sir—yaw, aw. (*snores and closes his eyes*)

WAR.    Confound you—you must be awake now—we must all be awake.

ISA.    Eh! why? What's the matter, Pa?

EM.    Oh, pray tell us, pa. I'm all anxiety to know.

WAR.    Matter, girl! This is the matter: a letter from my old friend, Pickwick!—he's in
40    the neighbourhood, with three young fellows—three members of his celebrated club.

RACH.    Young men! Oh my susceptible heart!

ISA.    Three young club-ites, glorious! Papa—you know I make war, in common with my sex, against all clubs, as anti-matrimonial and useless!—hearts and diamonds
45    for me—but where are they, papa?

EM.    Aye, where are they?—a thousand romantic visions flit across my mind.

WAR.    They are coming here; Pickwick has promised me a visit.

RACH.    But when? brother?

ISA. *and* EM.    Ah, when?—when, papa?

50 WAR.    There's the rub—they have come to inspect all that is worth seeing in the neighbourhood—no doubt we shall find them at the Review!

---

23   *if it's ... yet*: MS omits 'if it's ... yet'.

28   *Time ... cruelty to him*: MS omits 'Time', 'not, but ... chances' and 'there was my dear ... cruelty to him'.

29   *I believe, aunt?*: MS omits 'I believe, aunt?' and in Rachel's response 'No miss', and 'in your pinafore'.

33   *damn*: 'hang' in MS. MS omits the second 'good news', the Fat Boy's speech, and Wardle's 'Confound you'.

38   *Eh! why? ... anxiety to know*: MS omits both girls' speeches and begins Wardle's at 'a letter' then omits 'young fellows—three' and 'celebrated', Rachel's 'Young men!' and both girls' speeches, and Wardle's answer.

48   *But when?*: MS inserts 'are they coming?' to clarify the subject after its omissions.

50   *the rub ... worth seeing*: MS omits 'the rub ... worth seeing'.

ISA.    No doubt—no doubt—don't let us wait for them, papa, but set out in search of them; nothing like securing beaus to our bosoms when we can.

RACH.    So I say—thank heaven! we shall, at last have somebody else to visit us, besides the old clergyman and the justice of the peace.                                    55

WAR.    A very good idea, girls—we'll go and bring them here forthwith, I long to see my old friend, Pickwick, once again; we shall have something to cheer us up now. Joe—Joe—damn that boy, he's asleep again.

F. BOY    (*waking*) Yes, sir—yaw—aw.

WAR.    Order the barouche, directly; we can go to the Review and the rook-shooting,  60 both under one—kill two birds with one stone, as the doctors say—there—there— away with you, he's good for nothing, but to play the Somnambulist—he'll make a capital sleep-walker.

F. BOY.    Yes, sir—yaw—aw. (*snores, stumbles, knocks his head against edge of scene, and exits*)

WAR.    There's no time to waste, so on with your bonnets, and let's start directly,—  65 this way—this way.

ISA., EM., *and* RACH.    Delightful—charming—exquisitely agitating!

(*Exeunt Omnes*)


# SCENE 3

*Itinerant Suttling Booth, and Romantic Landscape, near the Lines, Chatham.*

CANTEEN, ALLYCAMPAIGN, PIEMEN, COUNTRYMEN, *etc. discovered.*


CHORUS, OMNES
AIR 'Follow the Drum.'

Though 'tis not now the month of May,                                                      1
When bees from flower to flower hum,
The soldiers through the town march gay,
And the people flock to the sound of the drum;

53 *No doubt ... when we can*: MS simplifies this speech to 'Let us set out papa in search of them.'

57 *we'll go ... once again*: MS omits 'we'll go ... once again'.

58 *damn*: 'where's' in MS, which omits Fat Boy's speech.

63 *sleep-walker*: MS ends the speech at 'kill two birds' thus omitting Wardle's reference to the stage— Bellini's opera *La sonnambula* was first heard in 1831, and versions were very popular on London stages; the original title role was the preserve of famous divas Pasta and Malibran. Grisi sang it at the King's Theatre in June 1837, two weeks before this play was staged at the Strand.

67 *Yes, sir ... agitating*: MS omits the Fat Boy's answer and exit, and the women's response.

0.4 *AIR 'Follow the Drum.'*: A broadside ballad of this name was in circulation; the British Library dates two different printings as around 1840.

5       Yes, men and women, girls and boys,
         All jump up as they hear the noise,
         And from their houses, out they come,
         To see the soldiers, and hear the drum.
         Though 'tis not now, etc.

(*Distant noise of artillery heard without*)

10  CAN.    There they go it—there they go it—they're hard at it—now then, Allycampaign, have you got the ginger pop, and the brandy balls ready, for these military, after they've gone through their manoeuvres; for they'll be here to bivouac, you know.

ALLY.    Aye—aye—they'll have their whack, I know that, well enough, master.

CAN.    And have you got the chine, that we made, ready for the light horse and
15      cavalry, to cut into; and the double stout, for the artillery. (*artillery heard without*) There they go again, they'll be as hungry as sharp shooters, soon.

ALLY.    Everything is ready, so they may come and perform their manoeuvres as soon as they like; the sham fight must be nearly over by this time. I can't see, for my part, what's the use of a sham fight, it all ends in smoke—if they kill'd one another
20      in real arnest, there would be something worth looking at—summat to amuse the ladies! This make belief is only wasting powder and shot.

CAN.    Talking of shot, mind you look sharp after the *shot*—but eh! here's the gentry a-coming, I must go in and get the sandwiches and bottled porter ready—ah, there is nothing like a review, and we has one *quarterly* here, though they never gives any
25      quarter—Come boys.

(*Exit Canteen, Allycampaign, etc. into booth*)
*Enter* WARDLE, AUNT RACHEL, EMILY, ISABELLA, *and* FAT BOY.

WAR.    No signs of my friend, Pickwick, and I have look'd all among the heavy dragoons.

ISA.    And not a stranger to be seen among the light infantry—how provoking!

EM.    I hope we haven't missed them, heigho!

30  WAR.    Joe—Joe—I say—damn that boy, he's asleep again—fell asleep while they were firing off the cannon—why, Joe—I say—

F. BOY.    Yes, sir, I am up—yaw, aw.

---

12 *and the brandy balls…you know*: MS omits 'and the brandy balls' and 'for they'll…you know'.

16 *light horse…sharp shooters, soon*: MS omits sd and last sentence, and substitutes 'infantry' for 'horse'.

17 *ready*: MS adds 'master'.

21 *Everything is ready…powder and shot*: MS trims this speech throughout, omitting 'so they…like', 'it all ends in smoke', 'another', 'worth looking at—summat', and substituting 'It's' for 'This make belief is'.

22 *shot*: 'shot' meaning bill, the reckoning.

25 *quarter*: The first pun here is on the periodical *The Quarterly Review*, published by Murray since 1809. The MS omits the pun on 'giving quarter'.

27 *all…dragoons*: MS substitutes 'everywhere' for 'all…dragoons'.

30 *And not a stranger…damn*: MS omits the girls' speeches and Wardle's 'damn'.

32 *Yes, sir…yaw, aw*: MS omits Fat Boy's speech.

WAR.    Up! confound you—look out, and see if you can discover any strangers.

F. BOY.    I will, sir! (*yawns, shuts his eyes, and snores*)

WAR.    Was there ever such a fellow.—Is that the way you look out? Shutting your  35
eyes, sirrah!

F. BOY.    Yes, sir! (*snores*) I'm going. (*yawns*)

WAR.    Ah! to the land of Nod! There never was such a rascal!

ISA.    It certainly has been a grand sight—and does honour to the troops.

SONG, ISABELLA

AIR 'Oh they marched through the Town.'

> They marched o'er the plain, with their banners so gay,                40
> And then march'd back again, while their bands they did play;
> The troops were the finest that e'er I did see,
> And the officers, all smil'd most sweetly on me!

> Though they fired not with ball, yet they hit me outright,
> Though I knew that the fight, was but, still, a sham fight        45
> But of all sights—I'd at a review soonest be,
> For the officers all smil'd most sweetly on me!

*Enter* PICKWICK, SNODGRASS, TUPMAN, WINKLE, *and* SAM.

WAR.    Eh! what do I see? here they are!—Welcome—my dear friend, Pickwick—
welcome gentlemen—happy to see you all—haven't forgotten you since I met you,
last winter, at the club. Allow me to introduce you to my family—my daughters—  50
my girls!—my sister, too, Miss Rachel Wardle. She's a Miss, though she'd not amiss!

RACH.    Lor! Brother—

WAR.    True—true! Nobody can deny it—very glad to see you all. You must go with us
to Manor Farm—I sha'n't lose sight of you now I've once got you—we must have a
jollification of it—Pickwick, my boy! I'll put the ladies under the charge of your  55
friends—I've a world of things to say to you, that will take up all your attention.
We'll just walk as far as Muggleton, to meet a party that I've promised to join in
rook-shooting.

PICK.    Rook-shooting! my dear friend, Wardle, that will be the very thing—my
young friend, Winkle, here, is an excellent rook-shooter—a most capital shot!        60

---

36 *Shutting…sirrah!*: MS omits 'Shutting…sirrah!'

39.2 *AIR 'Oh they marched through the Town.'*: A song by Nelson introduced by Vestris in *The Grenadier* (Olympic, 1831).

50 *Welcome…at the club*: MS omits 'Welcome…at the club' and abbreviates to 'welcome gentlemen'.

51 *She's a Miss…not amiss*: MS garbles this pun by leaving out 'though she'd not amiss' and also Rachel's protest and his affirmation of the truth of his description.

55 *lose sight of you…of it*: MS omits 'lose sight of you…of it'.

56 *that…attention*: MS omits 'that…attention'.

60 *excellent…shot*: MS omits 'rook-shooter—a most capital', Winkle's protest and Pickwick's insistence, and Wardle's 'Well, we'll try him'.

WIN.    No! No!

PICK.    You know you are—it's only modesty.

WAR.    Well, we'll try him—Joe shall drive the women home to prepare tea for us—while we bag a score or two. Joe—Joe! Damn that boy—he's gone to sleep again!

65   PICK.    Very extraordinary boy, that!—does he always sleep in this way?

WAR.    Sleep—he's never awake! Goes on errands fast asleep—dreams as he eats his dinner—and snores as he waits at table!

PICK.    How very odd!

WAR.    Ah! Odd indeed!—I'm proud of that boy—wouldn't part with him on any

70   account—he is a natural curiosity. Have the goodness somebody to pinch him in the leg—nothing else wakes him.

SAM.    Do it directly, sir!—not a morsel of trouble. (*pinches* FAT BOY)

F. BOY    Oh! Lord!

SAM.    Don't mention it—quite velcome—I can assure you.

75   WAR.    Look after the barouche, Joe—come Pickwick—pair your friends and the girls.

PICK.    With pleasure—allow me—Miss Rachel Wardle—Mr Tracy Tupman, an ardent admirer of the sex—a perfect Abelard. (*introduces them*)

RACH.    Oh! the dear man! Heigho! (*aside*) Oh! sir! (*as he takes her hand, amatorily*)

80   TUP.    Enchanting creature! (*they retire up the stage toying*)

PICK.    Miss Isabella Wardle—Mr Nathaniel Winkle! (*introducing them*)

ISA.    (*aside*) A very *natty* beau—a sportsman too. Well, I must have some sport with him!

WIN.    Happy to be introduced to so beautiful a preserve! (*they retire, making a set at each other*)

85   EM.    Now comes my turn—I'm all in a twitter. (*aside*)

PICK.    Miss Emily Wardle—Mr Augustus Snodgrass—a very celebrated poet, Miss Emily, I can assure you. (*introducing them*)

SNOD.    Aetherial vision of some brighter sphere!—I joy in this fair greeting.

---

64   *while … two*: MS omits 'while we bag a score or two'.

64   *Damn that boy*: MS has 'very strange' rather than 'Damn that boy'.

74   *Oh! Lord! … assure you*: MS omits exchange between Fat Boy and Sam.

78   *Abelard*: MS inserts 'an ardent admirer' to 'Abelard', which is not derived from the novel. The ensuing scene, like all those involving the women, is much changed and normally abbreviated in the MS.

79.1   *as he … amatorily*: MS omits sd.        80   *they … toying*: MS omits sd.

81   *introducing them*: MS omits sd.

82   *natty*: MS has 'pretty'. The slang term 'natty' for smart and neat had not yet entirely left behind overtones of the street.

84.1   *they retire … each other*: MS omits sd.

85   *Now … twitter*: MS omits this speech.

87   *I can … introducing them*: MS omits 'I can assure you' and sd.

88   *Aetherial … greeting*: MS omits this speech.

EM.     (*aside*) How Byronish and romantic he looks—there is poetry in his very shirt
collar. (*they retire, enthusiastically*)        90

PICK.     Sam and my fat friend—you have been introduced to each other.

SAM.     Oh yes—I gripp'd his calf—so we are on intimate terms—as the gnat said to
the cow's tail.

F. BOY     (*snores*)

WAR.     Well, now then, you all know one another—so that's as it should be. (*loud
explosion heard without—all the ladies scream, and throw themselves into the gentlemen's arms*)

SNOD.     (*to* EM.) I'll with my life preserve you!        95

WIN.     I certainly smell powder!

TUP.     What, in heaven's name, was that?

PICK.     Don't be alarmed—they've only been springing the mine in the battery!—
now the review is all over—

ISA. *and* EM.     (*recovering from their confusion, and laughing at their alarm*) How        100
very ridiculous! Ha—ha!

RACH.     I beg your pardon, Mr Tupman, but, my nerves are so weak. Bless me! How
forward those girls are—there's dear Emily flirting with the coarse-hair-looking gentleman, already. What spirits young people have. Do you think my nieces pretty?
(*to* TUPMAN)

TUP.     I should, if their aunt wasn't here!        105

RACH.     Oh! you naughty man!—but, really, if their complexions were a *little* better,
don't you think they would be nice-looking girls—by candlelight? don't you think
so?

TUP.     (*embarrassed*) Yes, I—I think they would!—but

RACH.     Oh! You quiz! I know what you are going to say. You are going to say—that        110
Isabella stoops—I know you are—well, she *does* stoop! and that Emily's a little too
bold—well, she *is* bold—but my dear brother *don't* see it—it would break his heart
if he did. Heighho! I hope the guns won't fire again—for I'm so timid—I always
require some one to support me, on the slightest alarm! (*languishingly*)

TUP.     I will support you, enchanting creature!        115

EM.     (*aside to Isabella*) I'm sure aunt is talking about us—she looks so maliciously—

ISA.     Does she?—I'll soon spoil her. Aunt!—hem—aunt!

90 *looks…enthusiastically*: MS omits everything after 'looks'.

91 *you*: MS substitutes 'we' for 'you', apparently mistakenly.

93 *cow's tail*: Another Wellerism that is not in the MS. MS then cuts next exchange, down to Rachel's 'I
beg your pardon'.

102 *nerves*: MS has 'knees' for 'nerves'.

104 *Bless me!…already*: MS abbreviates to 'Bless my soul there's those girls flirting'. And includes the sd
'*to* TUPMAN' twice.

108 *really, if…think so?*: MS cuts from 'really, if' to 'don't you think' but inserts 'don't you think so?'

109 *embarrassed…but*: MS cuts the sd but inserts the final 'but'.

114 *well, she does stoop!…languishingly*: MS omits final sd and trims this speech, omitting 'well she does
stoop', substituting 'can't for 'don't', and omitting 'it would break his heart if he did! Heighho!' and 'I'm so
timid'.

RACH.    Yes, my dear love!—

ISA.    I'm *so* afraid you'll catch cold, aunt—have a silk handkerchief to tie round your
120    dear old head—consider your age!

RACH.    The spiteful puss!—before this gentleman too—I could bite my tongue off
    with vexation. (*aside*)

WAR.    Come, let us be off—the rooks will be waiting for us—besides we shall get a
    peep at the grand Cricket Match that's playing on the common, behind the Blue
125    Lion all Muggleton against the Dingley Dell-ers.

WIN.    Bravo! I dote on a cricket match!

ISA.    And I'm no bad hand at a ball!—nor foot either, Mr Winkle.

WAR.    Well, then, you're very appropriate partners—Eh! Girl!—Come, I think that's
    a notch. Ha!—ha! So let's away. Joe!—damn that boy—he's asleep again. You'll fol-
130    low with—what's the name of your man, Pickwick?

PICK.    Weller—Samuel Weller!

WAR.    You'll follow with Mr Weller. Pinch him, when you want to wake him,
    Mr Weller!

SAM.    I'll take care, sir!

135    WAR.    Well, now then!

SNOD.    Allow me fairest of created creatures! (*offering his arm, affectedly*)

EM.    Quite Milton-ish and sublime, I declare—(*aside*) Oh! Augustus! Heigho!

RACH.    (*taking Tupman's arm, affectedly*) Heigho!

ISA.    The little god has certainly started some game today—(*aside*)—heigho! (*tak-
    ing Winkle's arm sportively*)

(*Exeunt* WARDLE, PICKWICK, AUNT RACHEL *and* TUPMAN, EMILY *and*
SNODGRASS, ISABELLA *and* WINKLE)

140    SAM.    Vell, this is a queer start—this is—now young twenty stun! are you avake?

F. BOY.    Yes. (*snores*)

SAM.    You are as nice a specimen of a prize boy, as ever I seed.

F. BOY.    Thank'ye. (*snores*)

SAM.    You aint got nothin' on your mind as makes you fret yourself, has you?

145    F. BOY.    Not as I knows on—yaw—aw!

SAM.    I should *ray*ther ha' thought, to look at you, that you vas labourin under an
    unreqvited attachment to some young ooman.

F. BOY.    Not as I knows on—yaw—aw!

SAM.    Glad to hear it—do you ever drink anything?

---

122    *Does she…vexation*: MS omits the whole exchange between the girls and Rachel.

125    *behind the Blue Lion*: MS omits 'behind the Blue Lion'.

129    *notch*: OED cites *Pickwick Papers* as its first example of the use of the term 'notch' as a verb meaning
'to keep score' in cricket, which Moncrieff here and below transmutes into a noun to mean that which is
scored, a run or in this instance a hit.

129    *let's away*: MS cuts Winkle and Isabella's exchange and Wardle's speech to this point.

129    *damn*: MS substitutes 'where's'.

135    *Well, now then!*: MS ends the scene here with a general exit.

F. BOY.    I likes eating better—not but what I'm fond of a drop of something, when  150
    it's good.
SAM.    Vell, ve'll try vhat the next tap is made on, as the cooper said to the bung! and
    arter that, ve'll see vhat ve can do to frighten the rooks, and astonish the crows, a bit!

SONG, SAM.

AIR 'Jim Crow.'

Rooks and daws must look out, when
Rook-shooting, Cockneys go,          155
For those who shoot at pigeons
Wery often kills a crow!
Hop about, and skip about,
And jump jist so,
Keep for rooks, a sharp look out—      160
Nor kill the Crow!

Of all the birds that make a noise,
There's no one like the crow,
He's mock'd by all the little boys,
Still as he does, they do!          165
Vheel about, and turn about,
And jump jist so,
Laughing at their silly rout,
He jumps Jim Crow!

Though he knows nothin of the laws,     170
My blessings on the crow,
He never speaks vithout some *cause*,
All counsel can't say so!
Vheel about, and turn about, etc.

The daw's a rogue, most pliant,      175
As vell, the rooks they know;
The pigeon is the client,
Vile the lawyer is the crow!
Vheel about, turn about, etc.

The crows they glean the cornfields now;    180
Fly, valk, and ride, they do.
There's Jackey Crow, and old Jim Crow,
And Astley's famed Du-Crow!
Vheel about, turn about, etc.

Those who to blame me wenture,     185
Let them to the play-house go,
They'll find the doves they censure,

> Vhile they always spares the crow!
> Vheel about, turn about, etc.

190    'Tis true I can't sing younger,
> But 'tis time that I should go,
> For my friends, if I stay longer,
> Vith me may pick a crow!
> Vheel about, turn about, etc.


## SCENE 4

*Room in the Blue Lion Inn, Muggleton.*

*Enter* JINGLE, *in flannel jacket and straw hat, followed by* JOB TROTTER.

1  JIN.    Yes—introduced myself—you know my way—joined all Muggleton—spoil'd
Dingley Dell—second innings—thirty notches—floor'd best batsman—capital long
bowler—very!

TROT.    Yes, you can draw the long bow well enough! but what's your purpose in
5  coming here?

JIN.    Tell ye directly—twinkling of an eye—Party of Pickwickians—rare fellows—
short memories—long purses—met 'em in London—joined company—rode to
Rochester—stood Sam—Crown Inn—grand ball—fond of dancing—Winkle
drunk—borrowed his coat—Tupman paid ticket—sweet on old widow—Doctor
10  Slammer, Army Surgeon—pills like bullets—got jealous—challenge, poor Winkle,
next morning—P. C. coat—knew nothing of the matter—went out instead of me—
Pitt Fort—nearly shot—mistake discovered—found me out—laugh-huff—
acquaintance interrupted—unlucky—very!

194 *Vheel about, turn about, etc.*: The end of this scene, between Sam and the Fat Boy, is not present in
the MS and is entirely unnecessary to the plot. The printed text has a note (p. 21) with the information that
'This song is Published with the Music, and a Likeness of Mr Hammond, by Limbird et Co., 143, Strand.'
One might conjecture that its absence is not in this case an expedient abbreviation of the copy text, but
rather represents a passage introduced or built up after the first night, elaborating Hammond's role as Sam,
which he subsequently performed separately and in other plays. 'Jim Crow' was a huge hit in the 1830s,
introduced by T.D. Rice and adopted by many singers, having a catchy tune easily adapted, as here, to new
sets of words. Hammond's use of it in his Sam Weller performances fixed it to the character of Sam in the
popular memory (see Introduction, 'The Plays He Did Not Write').

8 *stood Sam*: to 'stand Sam' is London 'fast' slang for to pay the expenses for food or drink; *OED* cites
Moncrieff's own stage version of *Tom and Jerry* in 1823 as its first instance. The impecunious Jingle presumably means to say the Pickwickians 'stood Sam' for him.

11 *P. C. coat*: Winkle's newly invented, bright blue Pickwick Club 'uniform' coat had 'PC' on its buttons.
Jingle's shorthand would not have been intelligible here to any audience member who had not read the
original text.

13 *joined company…unlucky—very!*: MS omits 'joined company', 'grand ball', 'pills like bullets', 'knew
nothing of the matter', 'Pitt Fort', and 'unlucky—very!'

TROT.    Well, but I can't see your drift now.

JIN.    Buzzard—muff—stupid—Too good to part with—pluck 'em a little more—fall   15
in with 'em here—go where they go—meet rich heiress—get married—take circuit—engage you!—'Dismal Jimmy,' low comedy make your fortune—capital
spec!—very!

TROT.    I begin to perceive now, you'll want me, as usual, to be your confederate. Play
Archer, to your Aimwell?                                                          20

JIN.    Mulberry livery—stock dress—pious face—hymn book—'collection, number
four'—begets confidence—all right—done thing—we'll swim yet, damme!

TROT.    You are the very prince of gaggers! if you only acted as well on the stage, as
off, you'd make an honest fortune, but as it is—

JIN.    No moralizing, all twaddle, Job Trotter—beg pardon, Dismal Jimmy!—low   25
comedian Hookem Snivey—Babe of Grace—Ebenezer meeting—My friend—great
rascal—very!

TROT.    Thank ye—ulloa! Here's company coming.

JIN.    Eh! My pigeons—mustn't be seen together—Exit hastily—take tizzey—(*gives
money*) pipe and pint—find you in the tap—wait till call'd for—                  30

TROT.    Aye—aye!—I know my cue,—wait for the word—there's the Shepherd
there—so we can both get pious!  (*Exit*)

*Enter* PICKWICK, SNODGRASS, WINKLE, WARDLE, *and* SAM WELLER.

PICK.    Mr Winkle, as my disciple and associate, I must say, that any man who pretends to a knowledge of that, which he don't understand, to the danger and detri-
ment of human life, is wrong—decidedly wrong!                                     35

---

17  *take circuit*: A theatrical circuit, the round of regional playhouses served by a travelling company. MS
omits much of the theatrical reference here, including all of Trotter's response, which draws on the lead
characters in *She Stoops to Conquer*, and most of Jingle's evocation of stage piety in the next speech.

17  *'Dismal Jimmy'*: 'Dismal Jimmy' began as a name suggesting a character given to spoiling the enjoyment of others by religiose gloom, possibly from a nickname given to Admiral James, later Lord, Gambier,
a pious man and a supporter of William Wilberforce and the missionary activities of the early nineteenth
century, who insisted upon religious observances aboard the ships he commanded.

18  *Buzzard...capital spec!—very!*: MS omits 'Buzzard...stupid', 'fall in with 'em here' and 'low comedy...fortune' and ends the speech with 'capital spec!'. Jingle glosses 'buzzard' in his next words: it means a
stupid or worthless person, a usage going back to *Piers Plowman* (*OED*).

23  *You are...gaggers!*: MS omits 'You are...gaggers!' A 'gagger' in this context ironically implies the
lowest level of the acting profession, where the performers improvised their lines in a stock scenario.

26  *Hookem Snivey*: He turns a slang phrase for an imposture, 'hookum-snivey', recorded by *OED* from
1781 onwards, into a name, and then elaborates with phrases drawn from Protestant-sectarian language to
imply Trotter's assuming the character of a religious hypocrite. Moncrieff perhaps picks up 'Ebenezer' from
Dickens's characterization of Sam Weller's mother-in-law and her Temperance association.

30  *Eh!...find you*: MS substitutes 'But they're coming' for 'Eh!' and 'go' for 'Exit hastily...find you'. A
tizzey is a six-penny piece. MS omits Job's response.

35  *pretends to...human life*: MS substitutes 'pretends to' with 'know' and omits 'of that, which' and 'to
the danger...human life.'

SAM.   Only a slight mistake in the genl'man, sir! Though it vas very unfortinate, certainly; he only shot at the crow and wing'd a pigeon!

PICK.   Wing'd a pigeon! Sam? nonsense, he had nearly kill'd my dear friend, Tupman—forty-five sparrow shots in the fleshy part of his arm—luck they warn't
40    swan-shot!—while the cursed rook or the crow, whichever you call it, got off scot free—cawing—cawing—cawing! As if he was laughing at us for our pains.

SAM.   Yes, he didn't go vithout *caws*, sir, certainly; but I gave Mr Vinkle to the care of young Daniel Lambert, to take him to the ladies; so he'll soon be all right again.

45    WAR.   Aye—aye!—therefore let's think no more about it—the success of the Cricket Match makes full amends, for our failure in the Rook shooting! though I certainly did expect your friend to have turned out a better shot.

JIN.   (*coming forward*) Now for it. (*aside*) Ah! capital game—Cricket, sir—smart sport—fine exercise—very!—

50    WAR.   Eh! who's this?

PICK.   (*recognizing him*) What, my friend, Mr Jingle!

JIN.   Ah, Pickwick! how are you?—glad to see you—Capital fun—lots of beer— hogsheads!—rounds of beef—bullocks!—mustard—cart loads! glorious day— make yourself at home—glad to see you—very!

55    PICK.   Allow me to introduce you to Mr Wardle, a friend of mine.

JIN.   Friend of yours! My dear sir, how are you? friend of *my* friend—give me your hand, sir, shall be delighted to visit you! must dine together—and—

PICK.   But how come you here, Mr Jingle?

JIN.   Came?—stopping at Crown, here, Muggleton—met a party—flannel jackets—
60    white trousers—anchovy sandwiches—devill'd kidneys—splendid fellows—glori- ous!—capital game, certainly—well play'd—well play'd—admirable strokes—very—

WAR.   You've play'd it sir?

JIN.   I think I have,—thousands of times! not here—West Indies—exciting sport— warm work—red hot—scorching!—play'd a match once—friend, the Colonel,—Sir
65    Thomas Blazo!—single wicket—who should get most runs.—Won the toss—first innings—seven o'clock, A.M.—six Natives to look out—went in—kept in—heat intense—Natives all fainted—taken away—fresh half dozen ordered—fainted also—Blazo bowling—supported by two Sepoys—couldn't bowl me out—fainted too—clear'd away the Colonel—wouldn't give in—faithful attendant, Quanko
70    Sambo, last man left—sun so hot—bat in blisters—ball scorch'd brown—five hundred and fifty runs—rather exhausted—Quanko mustered up last remaining strength— bowled me out—had a bath, and went home to dinner!

PICK.   And what became of, what's his name?—sir!

36 *SAM*: The manuscript garbles this section in the process of abbreviation, swapping 'crow' and 'pigeon' and making nonsense of the exchange between Sam and Pickwick, before omitting Wardle's speech from 'Aye—aye!' and cutting the entire scene between Pickwick and Jingle, including the story of Quanko Sambo, down to Jingle's 'But come, let's in'.

43 The Fat Boy is called 'the infant Lambert' by Dickens in the equivalent chapter (7), a reference to the famous Daniel Lambert, who died in 1806 weighing more than 52 stone.

JIN.   Blazo?

WAR.   No, the other gentleman!                                                               75

JIN.   Quanko Sambo. Poor Quanko—never recovered it—bowled on, on his own account—and bowled off on mine—died, sir!—died.

SAM.   Yes, I think I attended his funeral.

JIN.   But, come, let's in to dining-room—Dingley Dell, treats all Muggleton—Devilish good dinner. Cold—but capital!—peep'd into the room this morning—   80 fowls—pies—and all that sort of thing.—Pleasant fellows—well-behaved—very!

WAR.   Aye—aye! and then we'll off to Manor Farm. We'll take your friend with us, Pickwick!

JIN.   Shall be delighted—very!—but must dine first—drink Dumkin's health—return  thanks  to  Luffey!—Demosthenes—Diogenes—Alexander—damme—  85
(*sings*)

> We won't go home till morning,
> We won't go home till morning,
> We won't go home till morning,
> Till day-light does appear!

WAR.   Wonderful man!                                                                         90

SAM.   Yes—I vonder vhether his mother had any more on 'em—it vasn't in natur for her to have had twins of the same sort—they vould have been shown as a phenomena, if she had!

WAR.   Well, now then for dinner—and then for Manor Farm—for Rural Sports and the Pleasures of the Chase!—                                                               95

SNOD.   For Native Solitude and high Poetic Musing!

COMIC GLEE, OMNES
AIR 'Old Norfolk Melody.'

> Come my jolly boys, come, come with me,
> And visit Manor Farm;
> With a clodpole here, and a clodpole there,
> And here a lad, and there a lad,                                                           100
>         And every where a lad!
> And Oh, my jolly boys, will you come with me,
> All o'er the hills so green, oh!

85  *damme*: 'damme' not in MS.

89  *We won't go . . . does appear!*: Another of the sets of words to the traditional French tune 'Marlbrook'.

96.2  *AIR 'Old Norfolk Melody.'*: 1837 has a note 'Adapted by Alexander Lee to the words "Come, come my Merry Men" etc and sung at Vauxhall Gardens.' It seems to be one of the many variations on a traditional song first published by Playford in *Wit and Mirth: or Pills to Purge Melancholy* in 1720, and transmitted to the twentieth century as 'Old Macdonald had a farm.'

105

> Come my jolly boys, will you come with me,
> To see my cocks and hens;
> With a tuck, tuck, here, etc.

> Come my merry men, will you come with me,
> To see my Suffolk pigs;
> With a week, week, here, etc.

(*Exeunt Omnes*)

## SCENE 5

*Arbour and Garden of Manor Farm.*

*Enter* AUNT RACHEL, ISABELLA, *and* EMILY, R.

SNATCH, OMNES

AIR 'Here in Cool Grot and Mossy Cell.'

1

> Here, in cool shades, in Dingley Dell,
> We single maids and spinsters dwell!
> Here from man's dominion free,
> We rove and sigh in liberty!

*Enter* FAT BOY *staring very strangely.*

5   ISA.    Eh! bless me! what's the matter—Joe seems agitated—something very extra-ordinary and alarming must have happened, to move him. For heaven's sake! Joe—what horrid event?—

F. BOY   (*yawns*)

ISA.    No—no!—speak—tell us—

EM.    Good heavens—I hope no accident?

10   RACH.    Surely the dear man—tell me, Joe, I conjure you—what fatal—

F. BOY.    Oh! Mistress—mistress—dreadful news—he's kill'd—yaw—aw!

RACH. ISA., *and* EM.   (*severally*) Mercy on us! who?—speak—speak!

F. BOY.    Mr—yaw—aw—aw!—

RACH., ISA., *and* EM.   (*severally pulling* FAT BOY) Who? my dear Augustus?—Poor

15   Natty?—Mr Tupman?—tell us instantly—who?

F. BOY.    That's what I'm going to do. Mr—yaw—aw!—

---

0.4 *AIR 'Here in Cool Grot and Mossy Cell.'*: Garret Wesley won the Catch Club prize medal at Trinity College Dublin in 1779 with this glee. The MS substitutes 'for liberty' for 'in liberty' in the last line, which seems to alter the sense rather radically.

    6 *something very...to move him*: MS omits 'something very...to move him', the Fat Boy's yawn, and Isabella's exclamation.

RACH., ISA., *and* EM. (*severally pulling* FAT BOY) This suspense—this anxiety—this alarm—it must be—in mercy—pity—Joe!—

F. BOY. Yes, it is Mr—yaw—aw—aw!—

RACH., ISA., *and* EM. (*severally pulling and shaking* FAT BOY) Distraction—agony—despair. 20

*Enter* TUPMAN, *his arm in a sling.*

RACH. Ah! there's blood upon his arm—he's killed. (*screams, faints, and is caught by* FAT BOY, *who, falling asleep, almost lets her down*)

ISA. Aunt! aunt! throw some water over her Joe.

F. BOY. (*snores*)

ISA. Bless me, he's asleep again! how provoking.

RACH. No, no, I am better—is he wounded—is he dead—is he? Ha! Ha! (*hysterically*) tell me—are you dead? (*to* TUPMAN) 25

TUP. Touching sensibility—no—no, compose yourself, dearest madam—I pledge you my honour, I am not dead, only shot—

RACH. Through the heart?

ISA. With an arrow?—oh Cupid! Cupid!

TUP. No, no, in the arm, with a gun! Mr Winkle, mistook me for a rook, that was all. 30

ISA. Mercy on me, I hope he will take aim better with me. (*aside*)

RACH. 'Tis his voice, he yet may be recovered, dear man, go for a surgeon.

TUP. Matchless affection—no, no, I'm only a little faint—a glass of negus and a sandwich, with a little diaculum plaister, is all I shall require to restore me.

ISA. We will go and see it prepared for you instantly—come Emily—let us leave the 35 doves together, for a short time—poor things—follow us, Joe. (*Exeunt* ISABELLA *and* EMILY)

F. BOY. (*yawning*) I'm a coming—they're always a saying I'm asleep—I'll show them I can be awake sometimes! (*aside*) I'm only going to shut the hot-house windows. (*Exit* FAT BOY *on one side, yawning and snoring*)

TUP. Oh, Miss Rachel, dear, enchanting, Miss Rachel! how can I repay you for the 40 generous sympathy you've evinced in my behalf! All powerful deity of Love!

RACH. Love!

TUP. Yes, angel of a woman!

RACH. Angel!

TUP. I repeat the term—I die for you! 45

RACH. Is your wound, then, worse?

32 *No, no . . . 'Tis his voice*: MS inserts 'Joe' after 'No, no' and omits her laugh, and then cuts Tupman's 'Touching sensibility' and the next four speeches, resuming with Rachel's ''Tis his voice'.

34 *diaculum plaister*: A form of wound dressing, once a vegetable ointment, later the forerunner of modern sticking plasters, made with lead oxide. OED

36 *Matchless affection . . . poor things*: MS omits 'Matchless affection . . . a little faint', and Isabella's 'for you instantly', and 'let us leave . . . poor things'.

39 *they're always . . . hot-house windows*: MS omits 'they're always . . . asleep', substitutes 'when I chooses' for 'sometimes' and transposes the final phrase to 'the windows in the hot-house'.

TUP.    No—no—say but you love me.

RACH.    What will my mother say?

TUP.    The deaf old lady, I met on entering! does she know you're out? if not, she need
50    know nothing of the matter—she might talk of youth, of inexperience else, and
blight our happiness—let us only consult ourselves—a post chaise at midnight—an
elopement—the Blue Lion, Muggleton!

RACH.    An elopement!—no—no, it is too rash a step; what will the world—

TUP.    We are our own world, Divinity! Enchantress!

55    RACH.    Seductive man, I can't resist you—all-powerful passion must excuse me.
(TUPMAN *kneels, takes* RACHEL's *hand, and kisses it passionately*)

*Enter* FAT BOY, R., *unseen—gazes at them, and gives a loud snore—they both start—
Rachel screams.*

RACH.    Mercy on me, what's that?

TUP.    Discovered.

F. BOY.    I'm only dreaming—there's young missus's are quite awake, though—yaw—
aw! (*loud laugh heard without*)

*Enter* ISABELLA *and* EMILY *on each side—Isabella with negus, and Emily with
plaister.*

60    ISA.    Don't let us disturb you, aunt, I beg.

EM.    We've only brought the plaister and negus.

ISA.    Hope you find yourself better; but I see you are—ah, there's nothing like
sympathy.

TUP.    Curse that Fat Boy—but he can't have overheard our assignation. (*aside*)

65    ISA.    We won't mention anything if Joe don't.

EM.    And I'm sure he won't; that is, if he knows it—only, unfortunately, he's a habit
of talking in his sleep.

F. BOY.    Yes—I talks in my sleep. (*snores*)

TUP.    What's to be done? I must burke or smother him. (*aside*)

70    ISA.    What can detain papa and poor Mr Winkle?

EM.    Is my Augustus unfaithful? (*noise without*)

*Enter* PICKWICK, WARDLE, SNODGRASS, *and* WINKLE, *intoxicated; attended by*
JINGLE *and* SAM—*the latter supporting Pickwick—*JINGLE *leading* WARDLE—*and*
SNODGRASS *and* WINKLE *supporting one another.*

---

52 *The deaf old lady…Muggleton*: MS abbreviates this scene to the bones of the action, and in doing so
removes the joke in Tupman's speech about the common phrase 'does your mother know you're out?' which
was normally a mere taunt, suggesting the naivety of the person being ragged, but which Moncrieff here
builds into the absurd proposition of elopement.

53 *what will the world*: MS cuts Rachel's speech and the exchange to the entry of the Fat Boy.

64 TUP: MS cuts to Isabella's speech, 'What can detain papa?' leaving out Tupman's worries about being
discovered by the Fat Boy.

WAR. (*singing*)

> We are nae fou yet, we are nae fou yet,
> But just a wee drap in the ee;
> The cock may craw, the day may daw,
> But aye, we'll take the Barley bree! 75

SAM. Hold up, sir!—hold up, sir!

ISA. Good heavens! is anything the matter?

PICK. (*hiccupping*) Nothing's the matter—we—we're all right!—I say, Wardle, ain't we?

WAR. I should think so—My dears, here's Mr Pickwick's friend, Mr Jingle, come 80 'pon a little visit.

RACH. (*aside*) Amazement! who do I see?—my long lost, loved Lothario?—Be still my heart!

JIN. (*aside*) What the devil—my Lucretia Mactab, of Hookem Snivey—Here's a turn up—mum! 85

EM. Dear me—how very queer my Augustus looks. (*aside*) Is there anything the matter with Mr Snodgrass?

JIN. Nothing the matter, ma'am—Cricket Dinner—Glorious Party—Capital Songs— Eloquent Speeches—Old Port—Claret—good—very good—wine ma'am—wine. (*Sings*)

> Bacchus! Bacchus! I adore thee! 90

SNOD. It wasn't the wine—Celestial creature!—it was the salmon.

SAM. It's wery odd—but when a gentl'man gets drunk, it somehow never is the vine as makes him so!—Mr Snodgrass is only a little elewated, ma'am—Mr Vinkle, here, has bin a bit in the sun, too, vhile your papa and the governor has bin makin themselves comfortable—they only vants forty vinks to be all right agin—young Kitchen- 95 stuff, here, can shew 'em the way to a sophy.

WIN. I won't go to any sophy—I'll go out a tiger-shooting—where's some young buffaloes?

SAM. (*pointing to* FAT BOY) Here's von, sir.

F. BOY. (*snores*)

ISA. My admirer has been out sporting for something—they must have a nap and 100 some soda-water, or they'll miss our Christmas Eve festivities.

WIN. Let's have another bottle, Wardle—lend me a dog, and I'll go out bat-shooting— didn't half shoot that Tupman, this morning.

---

75 *We are nae...Barley bree!*: The chorus of Robert Burns's drinking song 'Willie Brewed a Peck o' Maut,' written in 1783.

78 *Nothing's...we're*: MS omits 'Nothing's...we're'.

86 *aside*: MS omits the aside.

100 *Capital Songs...My admirer*: MS omits 'Capital Songs...very good...wine' and the entire following exchange about the fault being with the salmon, from Snodgrass's speech, to resume with Isabella's 'My admirer'.

RACH.    Sanguinary monster!

105 JIN.    Dog—Bat-shooting! Dogs, fine animals—sagacious creatures—Dog of my own once.—Pointer—surprizing instinct!!—out shooting one day—entering enclosure—whistled—no go!—stock still—call'd him—'Ponto!—Ponto!'—wouldn't move—stood transfixed—staring at a board—looked up—saw an inscription—'Gamekeeper ordered to shoot all dogs found in this enclosure.' Wouldn't pass it—
110    wonderful dog—valuable Canis—that—very!

ISA.    You'd better lie down, Mr Winkle.

WIN.    I'll never lie down. (*falls down*)

WAR.    Hurrah! Joe, attend to Mr Winkle—damn that boy—he's—yaw—aw!— asleep—asleep. (*sleeps, snores*)

115 F. BOY.    I'll accompany you, sir! (*snores, leads his master off, both snoring*)

TUP.    I'll be magnanimous; though he shot me in the morning—as he seems a dead man now—I'll take care of him.

ISA.    Do, pray, sir! It's only the fresh air!

TUP.    (*picks Winkle up, and leads him off, R., he exclaiming, weeping*) Oh! if my
120    mother did but know I was out!

SNOD.    (*hiccupping*) It wasn't the hare, 'twas the pickled salmon—it's got into my head—I must have some brandy to keep it down—more salmon—a little cold punch—nobody shall lead me—I feel the inspiration of the muse—oh, let me quaff the Heliconian fount—pickled salmon, a cock salmon! (*reels off, R.*)

125 EM.    Dear Mr Snodgrass, how particularly shocking!

SAM.    How werry happy they all are—and vhat's the odds, so long as you're happy!— now governor, sir!

PICK.    Hurrah! (*throws his spectacles down and dances*)

SAM.    How wery vell he does it—now, sir! if you please—for Bedfordshire!

130 PICK.    I shall go only by the coach!

SAM.    (*taking him on his back*) Here you are, sir! outside place—all right behind, sir! (*carries off* PICKWICK, *on his back—he exclaiming*—Take care of my luggage!)

RACH.    What a terribly shocking scene!

EM.    Young men are so soon led away, my papa, and Mr Pickwick, should have
135    known better.

ISA.    (*to Jingle*) Very disgusting, aint it, sir?

JIN.    Dreadful, dreadful—horrid spectacle—quite boys—haven't drunk so much as I have by a bottle and a half—(*aside*)—better go and look after 'em—must speak to old woman, here (*aside*)—do themselves a mischief, perhaps.

---

104 *Sanguinary monster*: MS omits Rachel's interjection and much abbreviates Jingle's dog story.

110 *valuable Canis*: Moncrieff, rearranging the episodes from the novel to locate Jingle's story here as part of an elaborate drunken scene which Dickens had only sketched, has him use the word 'canis', Latin for dog, to show off his genteel schooling. Much of the ensuing detail of the Pickwickians' drunkenness is cut from the MS, presumably for brevity, since such a scene would not normally provoke censorship.

112 *lie*: MS has 'lay' for 'lie'.

117 *care of him*: From this point to the end of the scene, the MS abbreviates the drunken exits of the Pickwickians and the following encounter between Jingle and Rachel to the bare bones of the plot, reducing it to less than 25 per cent of its length.

EM.    Heaven forbid! I mustn't lose a moment, come, Bella!                    140

(*Exeunt Isabella and Emily*)

JIN.    Hem! coast clear—good opportunity, very! (*aside*) Calista!
RACH.    Lothario! Ha! (*they rush into each other's arms*) How is it I see you—after so
long an absence?
JIN.    Faithless woman—driven to despair—left Hookem Snivey—English Legion—
Queen of Spain—Major General—Spanish Donna—Old Bolero Fizgig's only    145
daughter, Christina—Grandee—splendid creature—loved me to distraction—
Jealous father—high-soul'd daughter—handsome Englishman—Donna Christina,
in despair—Prussic Acid—Stomach pump in portmanteau—Operation per-
formed—Old Bolero in ecstasies—Consent to our union—join hands, floods of
tears—Romantic story!—very!                                                    150
RACH.    Oh, then you've proved false to your vows, as well as me—she lives?
JIN.    No—no!—dead—never recovered the stomach pump—undermined the con-
stitution—fell a victim—I am now free—take prussic acid myself—Perfidious, false
Calista!
RACH.    Oh, Lothario! never should I have yielded to Mr Tupman, but for your absence.  155
JIN.    (*aside*) Oh—oh!—the cat jumps that way—Tupman—the horrid reprobate—
Giovanni the Sixteenth—only wants your money—seven trials for bigamy—Poor-
Law Commissioners after him now—
RACH.    Gracious heavens!—and I've promised to elope with him, tonight. Oh,
Lothario!—Lothario!—terrible situation—what shall I do?                         160
JIN.    Leave all to me—I'll save you yet—elope!
RACH.    Elope!
JIN.    Yes—a post chaise from the Blue Lion—my tiger shall manage all—Dismal
Jimmy is in the kitchen—have got Bleeding Nun's dress—make assignation—meet
him in the garden—Joe there instead—lead him into horse-pond—pop you, mean-   165
time, in the chaise—off to London—get married—forgive—never do so any
more!—Come, say it is to be—it is—see it all—yielding eye. (*sings*)

> In hurry post haste for a licence,
> In hurry, ding dong, I'll come back.

It's all settled—we shall be happy—very—very! one kiss!                        170
RACH.    I can refuse you nothing.
JIN.    Rum old girl—have her at last. (*aside, as he's embracing*)

*Enter* FAT BOY.

F. BOY.    Why, she was kissing t'other gentleman just now—master will whop me for
telling lies—swear I was dreaming. (*aside*) You are wanted in the kitchen, Mister, for
the revels! they've hung up the mistletoe.                                      175

---

172.1 *Enter* FAT BOY: Among the many omissions in the MS cutting this scene to the bone, the Fat Boy's
entry is completely removed.

JIN.    I wish you was hung up. (*aside*) Coming directly—kiss 'em all—practising for it now.

F. BOY.    (*grinning*) Yes, I see!

JIN.    Go to the devil with you. (*kicks* FAT BOY *off*) Now for Tupman—borrow ten
180    pounds—arrange plan—carry off old girl!—glorious idea—very—very! This way—this way!

(*Exeunt Ambo*)


# SCENE 6

*Old English Servants' Hall—Manor Farm—Large Fire—Mistletoe in the centre, etc.*

*Enter* SAM WELLER, *surrounded by* MARY SUMMERS, *and a group of* SERVANT MAIDS, COUNTRY BUMPKINS, etc.

CHORUS, OMNES.
AIR 'Old Christmas Carol.'

1
> Now rest ye, merry gentlemen,
>     Let nothing you dismay,
> Old Christmas it is come again,
>     Therefore we should be gay—
5
> Should sport and laugh, and sing and quaff,
>     To hail this happy day,
> Which brings tidings of comfort and joy!

SAM.    Now then, young vimmen, as Christmas comes but vonce a year, it's wery meritorious that ve should make the most of it, so ve'll go to vork impromtu!—
10    Quite a proper contrivance, this here mistletoe—I vonder who inwented it—there certainly is nothing that substitutes so vell for eating and drinking, as kissing does—he must ha' bin wery hungry who first thought on't, vich fully accounts for it, for hunger sharpens vit, they say, so he must ha' bin wery sharp set, almost as sharp set as I am—so here goes. (*is about to kiss maids, they scream*)
15 MARY.    Oh, lor! Mr Weller, there must be no kissing before master and the young ladies.

---

9 *impromtu*: 'impromtu': thus in 1837; the word is not included in the MS text, which cuts Sam's speech to 'Now then, young vimmen, it's quite a proper contrivance, this here mistletoe—he must ha' bin wery hungry who first thought on't, and as I'm ready, vy here.' The whole scene is shortened by about 75 per cent of its length, including cutting both songs ('Old English Gentleman' and 'Mistletoe Bough'). The substance is unchanged in tone and intent, and the purpose would appear to be abbreviation of the copy, rather than exclusion of any element. Only the longer cuts will be signalled here.

SAM.    You are the wery moral of prudence and propriety, my dear! jist vhat I say, so I shall take the extreme small liberty of kissing you all behind their backs.

MARY.    Oh, fie! Mr Weller, that ain't it—master and the young ladies always sets the example and kisses first.

SAM.    Vy, you quite deals in paradoxes here—as the charity boy said to his A B C, vhen 20 he couldn't make it out. Vell, I must keep my appetite, I suppose, and take double allowance vhen I does get it, on account of having fasted. Oh, here comes master and the gentlefolks, they have voke up as fresh as daisies—ah, there's nothing like getting intoxicated in fine veather, you does recover so wery soon, and this here has bin quvite a September day—so wery mild and clear—I shouldn't mind, for my part, if there vas 25 to come a trifle of snow—it don't look like Christmas vithout it—I likes everything as is seasonable, as the man said vhen he cried over the mustard-pot.

*Enter* WARDLE, PICKWICK, SNODGRASS, TUPMAN, WINKLE, JINGLE, AUNT RACHEL, ISABELLA, *and* EMILY, *followed by* FAT BOY.

WAR.    The wine was rather strong, faith; but thanks to sleep and soda water, we're now all right again—now my boys we are all ready for the revels.

ISA.    Hope you feel no further ill effects from the salmon, Mr Snodgrass?    30

EM.    Or the sauce, eh! sister!

SNOD.    'twas all a wild phantasma, lovely creature—imagination's airy trickery!

SAM.    I could ha' sworn now, as it vas the cold punch—vhat a thing it is to be poetical. (*aside*)

ISA.    Do you usually do such execution, as to bring down your man, when you fire 35 with *grape* shot, Mr Winkle?

WIN.    Quarter—quarter! Miss Isabella—don't make game of me—I should have shot better only I'm not quite used to the guns, yet.

JIN.    (*aside to* TUPMAN) Mind what I've said—word to the wise!—True Friend— very!—    40

TUP.    You are—you are!—borrowed ten pounds of me, just now—Noble confi- dence—I trust all to you!

JIN.    You can't do better—got your order for the post chaise—all right—settled everything—got all in readiness.—In the midst of the dance, I'll steal out—prepare matters—old girl will follow—you wait a few moments—then steal after her—find 45 her waiting at door.—Off with you—she knows private outlet—mind, not a word to your Venus, before company—Fat Boy has seen you—spoil everything.—

TUP.    My dear friend—I'll take care—I burn with all the impatience of ardour and passion!

JIN.    Mum!    50

WAR.    What are we waiting for?—'tis time our revelry commenc'd—are all the serv- ants assembled?

24 *getting intoxicated*: Reference to intoxication is cut in MS, as is Wardle's first speech on the strength of the wine, below, and the girls' teasing of Snodgrass about the salmon.

37 *Miss Isabella*: MS has him address Emily, not Isabella.

52 *assembled*: MS cuts from here to Wardle's 'where's Joe?' leaving out the naming of Christmas customs.

SAM.    Ve are all here, sir!—as the Pensioners say, on pay day.

WAR.    According to the good old custom, in our family, from time immemorial,
55    every one must enjoy themselves to-night, high and low—rich and poor—Master
and servants.

JIN.    Capital custom—very!—Christmas Carols—waiting for waits—Elder Wine for
the young folks—Mince Pies—Wassail Bowl—Ale and Apples—Blindman's Buff—
Forfeits—Country Dance—Hunt the Slipper—Kiss in the Ring—Snap-dragon—
60    pleasant—very!

WAR.    Talking of snap-dragon—where's Joe? Joe,—damn that boy, he's asleep again!
No matter—the snap-dragon will wake him—he'll burn his fingers if he sleeps over
that. Why Joe,—Joe!

F. BOY.    (*snores*)

WAR.    Oh, there you are! bring in the wassail bowl!—

65 F. BOY.    I aint forgot that—I'm not asleep—here it is!

(*Wassail bowl brought in by two* SERVANTS)

PICK.    A noble sight—why should such generous customs—the fount of hospitality—the glory of Old England—ever be suffered to decay?

WAR.    Bravo! bravo!—let it go round—and to encourage you to drink deeply,
friends, I'll give you 'A Merry Christmas and a Happy New Year!'

70 SAM.    And wery proper—now then, boys,—three cheers—good ones—take 'em
from me.

OMNES.    (*led by* SAM) Hurrah!—Hurrah!—Hurrah!—

SAM.    A little von in—as Vellington said when he sprung the mine in the town, aud
blow'd up the citadel.—'Von cheer more!'

75 OMNES.    Hurrah! (*the wassail bowl is passed round, all drink, Sam, à la Jobson, gets
double allowance*)

F. BOY.    (*nearly chokes himself with roasted apple getting into his mouth*) I must keep
watch to-night—for I've got to keep watch in the garden—young mistresses has
promised me a double share of mince pies—besides some of the turkey—I must
mind nobody don't see me—Constable Dick and his man are all ready, behind the
80    pales—yaw—aw.

SAM.    Vhat's young opium-eater about, that he looks so lively—he ain't choked himself, has he? (*aside*)

WAR.    Eh! the conviviality stopping—I must volunteer a song—you must all bear
chorus.

85 SAM.    I'll bear chorus, sir; follow me, girls!

---

67 *A noble... decay?*: MS cuts Pickwick's speech.

75 *Jobson*: Jobson is the drunken cobbler in Charles Coffrey and John Mottley's ballad opera *The Devil
to Pay* (Drury Lane, 1731), still playing as a farce in the 1830s. In the second scene Jobson arrives at a party
intent upon getting drunk, and a punch bowl is handed round; there was presumably some traditional business whereby he got his lips to the bowl more frequently than others did.

83 *WAR*: MS cuts from here, removing the song, to Wardle's next speech.

F. BOY.    Singing always sets me asleep—I'll take my post while I can. (*steals off unperceived*)

SONG AND CHORUS, WARDLE *and* OMNES.

AIR 'Old English Gentleman.'

I love the good old customs, and the good old times revere,
When the good old hospitality, at Christmas time, would cheer,
With good plum pudding and roast beef, and humming nut-brown beer,
The hearts of all the poor around for more than half a year;—                    90
    Like a Good Old English Gentleman, all of the olden time!
    Like a Good Old English, etc.

I love the good old Christmas fires, round which, still pass'd the joke;
The good old Christmas carols, that of peace and joy still spoke;
The good old Christmas boxes, that still lightened labour's yoke;              95
And the good old Christmas garnish, too, the holly and the oak!—
    Like a Good Old English Gentleman, all of the olden time!
    Like a Good Old English, etc.

My good old ancestors still kept them up, for many a day;
Old England's boast and comfort, too, oh! ne'er may they decay!                100
But, cheering young and old, be by their sons preserved for aye,
And, glad their children's hearts, long after they have pass'd away!—
    Like a Good Old English Gentleman, all of the olden time!
    Like a Good Old English, etc.

(*Storm begins to rise without, wind, etc.*)

WAR.    Eh! what's that? the wind rising!—a drift of snow, falling, too?—this is as it   105
    should be—give the fire another poke, Mr Weller—let the wassail bowl go round—
    'To the girls we love!'—and then, hey for the mistletoe!
SAM.    Hear! hear! hear!—I'll poke the fire, sir!—and send the vassail bowl round.
    A reg'lar gen'l'man that—independent of his breeding—such wery nice pork!
SNOD.    Mystic branch!—devoted to love's chaste salutes!—I shall perform thy Druid   110
    rites, with all the purity of high poetic feeling!
EM.    (*aside*) There's no occasion for his being too particular about his poetic purity.
    I shall be quite satisfied with his kissing like ordinary men!
RACH.    I'm all in a tremble—this mistletoe is so very awful! It does put such thoughts
    into one's head, especially when one's on the very eve of an elopement—innocence   115

86.3 *AIR 'Old English Gentleman.'*: An 'excellent old song' according to Bishop Percy, found in many broadside collections, but rewritten and published in 1833 by Purday who was unsuccessfully sued for plagiarism by Murray, the Edinburgh theatre manager.

110 *chaste salutes*: MS curtails his speech here and omits Emily's response.

114 *very awful*: MS cuts from here to 'innocence,' removing any suggestion that Aunt Rachel has impure thoughts or memories, rather than simply fears. Isabella's exchange with Emily is also cut, so that she says nothing but just drops her handkerchief.

preserve me! I dare not look at Mr Tupman. Oh, Lothario—Lothario! (*aside*)

ISA.    My poor swain, Mr Winkle, looks as if he was going sporting without a certificate—he seems to be afraid of trespassing. I must give him a little encouragement, or we shall have no sport at all. Harkye, girls! (*to* EMILY *etc.*) Mr Pickwick—(*whispers*)

120 EM.    (*aside to* ISABELLA) But how are we to get him under the mistletoe?

ISA.    I'll drop my handkerchief—you know his gallantry. (ISABELLA *walks under the mistletoe and drops her handkerchief*)

PICK.    You've dropped something, Miss Bella—permit me—(*advancing under mistletoe,* ISABELLA, EMILY, *and* MAIDS *suddenly surround him, and begin kissing him under the mistletoe, one after the other—he struggles—all laugh*)

WAR.    The baggages! fairly caught, by Jove, Pickwick!

SNOD.    Orpheus with the Thracian maids.

125 TUP.    Titillating situation!—I hope they won't serve me so! nature could not support it!

WIN.    (*aside*) Never saw buck-hunting before.

SAM.    I shouldn't mind being sarved in that vay, every day in the veek, Sundays included; as the sick man said vhen he took the treacle posset.

RACH.    That is not fair, my dear nieces; no person should be kiss'd by more than six

130 at once.

WAR.    Very well, sister Rachel! but come—come—that there may be no partiality, and that every one may be kiss'd in their turn—Isabella, girl, start off the mistletoe dance.

JIN.    (*aside to* RACHEL) Calista, love, watch opportunity—follow my leader. (*aside to* TUPMAN) Tupman, look out—nothing can be better—capital chance—very!

135 RACH.    (*aside*) Excruciating agitation—oh, my virgin heart—oh, Lothario!

WAR.    Now then, are you all ready? Now, Isabella!

SAM.    I'm alvays ready—not at all partic'lar about turns—takes 'em as I can catch 'em—and thank'ee, too, as the old ooman said to the fleas.

PICK.    Wait till I can get my breath. These young devils—angels, I mean, have nearly

140 suffocated me with sweets.

WAR.    Now Isabella!


SONG. ISABELLA.

AIR 'Oh, the Mistletoe Bough.'

The Mistletoe Bough hangs in the hall,
The holly branch, shines on the old oak wall;
The squire's retainers are blithe and gay,
145    Keeping their Christmas holiday.

---

124 SNOD: The three club members' comments are cut in the MS.

134 *aside to Rachel…capital chance—very!*: Jingle's exchanges aside with Rachel and Tupman are cut in the MS.

139 PICK: Pickwick's speech, Isabella's song and Winkle's following speech are cut in the MS.

141.2 *AIR 'Oh, the Mistletoe Bough.'*: Air by Sir Henry Bishop to a text by T.H. Bayley, current in the 1830s and subsequently passing into oral tradition.

The mystic kiss must soon be given,
Will raise our thoughts from earth to heaven!
For, ah! that kiss, with rapture rife,
Will soon make many a maid a wife!
Oh, the Mistletoe Bough! etc. 150

WIN. (*aside*) The ladies breaking cover—then it's clearly the first of September. So hey for partridge shooting!

### MISTLETOE KISSING DANCE
AIR 'Petticoat Loose.'

(WARDLE *and* AUNT RACHEL *lead off, kiss under the mistletoe, followed by* WINKLE *and* ISABELLA—SNODGRASS *and* EMILY—PICKWICK *and* JINGLE—SAM *and the other* MEN, *with the* MAIDS, *etc. During the progress of the dance,* JINGLE *slips away, followed by* RACHEL, *and afterwards by* TUPMAN. *The dance is finished by* SAM, *in the enthusiasm of the moment, kissing the* MAIDS *all round, amidst general shrieks*)

MARY. Imperent feller!
PICK. Sam—Sam!
SAM. Natur, sir!—natur, sir!—as the cat said vhen she eat the gold fish—if they 155
hadn't kiss'd you all round, you'd ha' done jist the same.
PICK. (*tickled*) Egad, I don't know but I should, Sam.
WAR. Very good, Mr Weller. But, hey! where's Rachel?—where's Tupman?
ISA. (*maliciously*) Oh, they'll be heard of all in good time, papa!—

*Enter* FAT BOY, *yawning, followed by* CONSTABLES, *with* TUPMAN, *and* JOB TROTTER, *in female dress, covered with large mantle.*

F. BOY. I've kotch'd 'em—the lovyers were jist getting over the garden wall. 160
WAR. Caught, who?
F. BOY. The old gentleman, here, and Miss Rachel—you can't say I'm not awake
now, master? (*snores and falls asleep*)
WAR. What the devil! Tupman and my sister?—Why, you hussey! at your age—well
may you hide your face. Uncloak the brazen baggage. 165
SAM. I'll do that, sir!—Now, ma'am, you must diskiver yourself, if you please—as
the telescope said to the dog star. (*pulls off mantle and discovers* JOB TROTTER)
WAR. What the devil! Mr Jingle's servant? Damn that Fat Boy—let me get at him—
I'll murder him, the villain!
F. BOY. No, don't—I aint no willin—let me go to bed—hide in the blankets—yaw— 170
aw! (WOMEN *screen* FAT BOY—PICKWICK *holds* WARDLE—JOB TROTTER *sneaks
off, getting a kick from* SAM *as he goes*—TUPMAN *stands stupefied with horror*—
ISABELLA *and* EMILY *look on with malicious expectation*)

---

157 *Egad…Sam*: MS cuts Pickwick's response.

WAR.   I won't be held—but, ulloa! where's my dear friend, Jingle?—and where the
devil, I say again, is Rachel, the old fool?

*Enter* LANDLORD *of the Blue Lion, Muggleton, L.*

LAND.   Bad news, Squire—but it warn't my fault—tried to stop 'em, but couldn't—
175    strange gentleman came from your house, to the Lion—got t'other strange gentle-
man's post-chaise, that he'd order'd, and rode off with Miss Rachel.
WAR.   Damn me if it ain't Jingle!
F. BOY.   (*waking*) Now am I a willin?
TUP.   Treacherous, faithless woman!
180  SAM.   Wery bad, sir!—carrying off your sweetheart.
TUP.   That's not all—he's carried off my ten pounds, too. But I'll be revenged—I'll
pursue him—serve him with a copy of a writ.
ISA. *and* EM.   Love will have its way, papa!—Young folks!
WAR.   Love, the devil!—the old tabby. Give orders for post horses—will no one go
185  with me?
PICK.   I will, for the honour of the Pickwickians!
SAM.   And I vill, 'cause it's my duty—as the soldier said, vhen he vent to be shot at,
for six-pence a-day!
WAR.   Thanks!—thanks!—let's be off at once, then—I'll not sleep till I have over-
190  taken them.

FINALE OMNES

AIR 'Tramp Chorus.'

Scamp—scamp—scamp, o'er hill and plain,
Scour all around,
Till he is found;
And we the fugitive regain!
195                    Be this the cry—restore or die!
Scamp—scamp—scamp, etc.

(*While this is singing,* SAM *equips* MR PICKWICK, *with shawl, etc., for travelling.*
FAT BOY *brings* WARDLE *his gun, and drop falls on*
*Tableau, to end the First Act.*)

178  *F. BOY.* (*waking*): MS cuts from here to Wardle's response 'the devil!'
190.2  *AIR* 'Tramp Chorus.': By Sir Henry Bishop, in Thomas Morton's *Knight of Snowdoun*
(Covent Garden, 1811).

# ACT II

## SCENE 1

*Apartment in* MR PICKWICK'S *lodgings, at Mrs Bardell's, Goswell Street Road.* SAM *discovered putting the room to rights.*

SAM. (*singing*)   Home, home—I'm glad we're at home,    1
         Be it ever so humble, there's no place like home!

Not but what this is a comfortable crib, enough—now the Governor's in it—as the spider said of his web, vhen the blue-bottle took his first floor. I dare say old Mother Bardell is glad enough he's returned. (*continues singing*)   5

     For there's no luck about the house,
       No luck by night or day;
     There is no luck about the house,
       When the Governor's avay!

*Enter* PICKWICK.

PICK. You are merry, Sam.                10
SAM. It's only a propensity I have, sir—as the cricket said when he chirruped—born with me.
PICK. I am not at all displeased, Sam, to find myself once more at home, after all our fatigues and anxiety—that vagabond, Jingle—
SAM. Wery rum start, sir! His running away vith the old maid. Certainly I thought 15 it vas nigh a being all up vith us, vhen that ere vehicle let us all down so coolly—he got clean out of sight of us then.
PICK. True—true, Sam! I never expected we should have discovered them till the mischief was all done.
SAM. Nor more ve shouldn't, sir—if I hadn't happened to have a little knowledge of 20 the human understanding—I know'd, directly I seed vhat leather that was in the blacking hole, at the Goose and Gridiron, that they were there—see vhat it is to ha' bin a boots, sir—vhat insight it gives von into things. Your search vou'd ha' bin quite bootless without me.

---

9 *For there's…Governor's avay*: Sam sings snatches of well-known songs, 'Home Sweet Home' from Payne and Bishop's *Clari, or the Maid of Milan* (Covent Garden, 1823) and a ballad probably by the working-class Scotswoman Jean Adams, which was referred to in print as early as *c.*1745, as 'A Song to the Tune of, The Abbot of Canterbury, etc.' [Edinburgh?], [1745?], ESTC Number T011381. (from *Examining the OED*, project headed by Charlotte Brewer: <http://oed.hertford.ox.ac.uk/main/content/view/390/436/index. html> accessed 16 September 2014).

25  PICK.    You're a wag, Sam.

  SAM.    Yes, sir—it runs in the family—my eldest brother vas troubled vith the same complaint, it may be catching—I us'd to sleep vith him—that ere chap, in the green coat, bargan'd for the old gal jist for all the vorld as if she'd bin a joint o' meat, though von can't scarcely wonder at it, considering she's all bone.

30  PICK.    The mercenary rascal extorted one hundred and fifty pounds, before he'd resign the foolish infatuated woman; but I'll expose the villain wherever I meet him.

  SAM.    She vas certainly wery fatuated vith him, sir—for sich a thin un, sir!

  PICK.    You must have seen a great deal of the world, Sam, from the sharpness of your remarks. You are quite a philosopher, Sam.

35  SAM.    Yes—I vorn't alvays a boots, sir—I vas a wagginer's boy, vonce.

  PICK.    When was that, Sam?—

  SAM.    Vhen I was first pitch'd neck and crop into the vorld, to play at leap-frog vith its troubles. I was a carrier's boy at startin'—then a vagginer's—then a helper—then a boots—now I'm a gentl'man's servant—I shall be a gentl'man myself, von of these

40    days—vith my pipe in my mouth, and a summer-house, in the back garden—who knows—I shouldn't be surprized, for vonce.

  PICK.    You are quite a philosopher, Sam.

  SAM.    Yes, sir—all my generation were—my father's wery much in that line, now! If my mother-in-law blows him up, he vhistles—vhen she flies into a passion and

45    breaks his pipe—he goes out and fetches another—then she screams wery loud and falls into 'sterics—and he smokes wery comfortable till she comes too agin.—That's philosophy, sir, aint it?

  PICK.    A very good substitute for it, at all events. It must have been of great service to you, in the course of your rambling life, Sam.

50  SAM.    Service, sir—you may say that—arter I run away from the carrier, and afore I took up with the vagginer, I had unfurnish'd lodgings for a fortnight!

  PICK.    Unfurnished lodgings, Sam?

  SAM.    Yes—under the dry arches of Waterloo Bridge—fine sleeping places, those, within ten minutes walk of all the public offices—only if there's any objection to

55    'em, it is that the sitevation is *ray*ther too airy—I seed some quveer sights there—sights as ud penetrate your benevolent heart, and come out on the other side of it, sir!—you don't see the reg'lar wagrants there—trust 'em, they knows better than that—only the starvin' houseless creatures as rolls themselves up in the dark corners of them lonesom places—poor wretches! as aint up to the twopenny rope!

60  PICK.    Twopenny rope, Sam!—I must make a note of that. What's the twopenny rope?

  SAM.    The twopenny rope, sir—is jist a cheap lodgin house, vhere the beds is twopence a night!—vhen the lady or gen'lman as keeps the hotel, first begun bis'ness—they us'd to make the beds on the floor—but instead of takin twopenny vorth of

65    sleep, the lodgers staid there all day—so now they makes the beds of slips of coarse sacking, fasten'd to two ropes across the room—and ev'ry mornin, at six o'clock,

---

66  *across the room*: 'across the room' not in 1837.

they cuts the ropes, and down they all comes, vide avake—takes up their togs—and toddles quvietly off.

PICK.    Very remarkable, indeed—I must communicate it to the Club. But now to business—I have a great deal in hand—you must go to the George and Vulture, and 70 summon my associates here, directly—then I'll instruct you further.

SAM.    I'll be off directly, sir—as the coach vheel said to the axle-tree—if I only suit my place, as vell as my place suits me, ve'll be like the tailor's scissors, ve'll only part to meet again—as the billy doos say!—I don't know vhether I'm to be a footman or a groom—or a game-keeper—or a seedsman—I looks like a sort of compo of ev'ry 75 von on 'em. Never mind—there's change of air—plenty to see—and little to do— and all this suits my complaint, uncommon—so long life to the Pickvickians, say I! (*Exit* SAM)

PICK.    A very honest fellow, that—but apropos—I have never told my landlady, Mrs Bardell, that I have taken him into my service—she may have some objection to his 80 being in the house—I must break it to her, by degrees. Let me do it at once. Mrs Bardell!—Mrs Bardell!—(*ringing bell and calling*)

*Enter* MRS BARDELL.

MRS B.    (*curtseying*) Yes, sir! Oh, if my lonely widowhood was but cheer'd by such a comforter—his income would be so very convenient. (*aside*)

PICK.    Ahem!—ahem!—I've a question to ask you, my dear Mrs Bardell.                    85

MRS B.    A question! La, sir! What can he mean? How my heart bumps.

PICK.    Do you think it's a much greater expense to keep two people than to keep one?

MRS B.    Bless his dear spectacles! why, he's surely never going to—(*aside*)—La, sir! what an idea!

PICK.    Well—but do you—Mrs Bardell?                    90

MRS B.    He's certainly going to pop the question—mercy on me! (*aside*) Ahem!—that depends a great deal upon whether the person's a careful and saving person—you know, sir!

PICK.    That's very true—but the person I have in my eye—(*looks very hard at* MRS BARDELL)—I think possesses these qualities, and has, moreover, a considerable 95 knowledge of the world, and a great deal of sharpness, Mrs Bardell, which may be of material use to me.

MRS B.    La! Mr Pickwick—He certainly means to propose. (*aside*)

PICK.    'Tis fact, I assure you—and to tell you the truth—I've made up my mind!

MRS B.    You don't say so, sir?                    100

PICK.    You'll think it very strange that I never consulted you about this matter—but tell me, what is your opinion?

---

67 *takes up their togs*: MS, which has not deviated a great deal so far in this opening scene, abbreviates this speech and removes some slang here, substituting 'and the lodgers pick up their clothes' for 'takes up their togs'.

72 MS cuts all the rest of Sam's exit speech, which has the marks of the direct address to the audience by a solo artist. See Introduction.

102 *tell me . . . your opinion?*: MS has 'candidly now?' in place of 'tell me . . . your opinion?'

MRS B.   Unhop'd for happiness!—I certainly must faint, presently—it will be but
proper—(*aside*)—Oh! Mr Pickwick, you're very kind, sir!

105 PICK.   It will save you a great deal of trouble, won't it?

MRS B.   Angel of a man!—Oh! I never thought anything of the trouble, sir!—though,
of course, I shall take more trouble to please you, than ever now—it is so kind of
you, Mr Pickwick, to have so much consideration for my loneliness.

PICK.   I'm glad she didn't make any objection—(*aside*)—That is a consideration I
110 never thought about—but you're right when I am in town, you'll always have somebody to sit with you—so you will.

MRS B.   I could worship his very gaiters, I'm sure I ought to be a very happy
woman. (*aside*)

PICK.   And your little boy—he, too, will have a companion, Mrs Bardell—a lively
115 one, who'll teach him, I'll be bound, more tricks in a week, than he would ever learn
in a year, else.

MRS B.   Oh, you duck!—(PICKWICK *starts*)—Oh, you kind, good, playful dear!—I
can resist no longer!—(*throws her arms round* PICKWICK's *neck*)

PICK.   Bless my soul! Mrs Bardell—my good woman—dear me, what a situation—
120 pray consider, Mrs Bardell—don't—if any body should come!

MRS B.   (*passionately*) Oh, let them come!—now will be a good time to faint—this
will repay me all my Alfred's treachery. (*aside*)

PICK.   Mercy on me! I hear somebody coming up the stairs—don't—don't—there's
a good creature, don't.

125 MRS B.   Ha! (*faints in* PICKWICK's *arms*)

*Enter* SAM, *followed by* SNODGRASS, TUPMAN, *and* WINKLE, L.—*they all stand amazed.*

SAM.   Eh! master settling for his lodgings with his landlady—I beg pardon, sir, wery
sorry to disturb you—didn't know you vas engaged.

TUP.   Susceptible situation.

WIN.   Wouldn't have spoilt sport, by any means, if I had known.

130 SNOD.   What, in the name of all created mysteries, means this?

PICK.   Ah, what indeed! Sam, lead this woman down stairs.

SAM.   Anything but carry her, sir!—now ma'am.

MRS B.   Oh, I'm better now—I'm very much obliged to you—bashful creature—he
doesn't want his friends to know. (*aside*)

135 SAM.   Lean on my arm, ma'am,—as light as you can, if you please, and I'll see you
down stairs.

MRS B.   Thank you, sir—thank you—I shall have the happiness of being a wife once
more after all! beloved Pickwick. (*aside*) Adieu, love! (*Exit* MRS BARDELL, *led off
by* SAM, R.)

PICK.   I cannot conceive what has been the matter with that woman—I merely
140 announced to her my intention of keeping a man servant, when she fell into the
singular paroxysm in which you found her—very extraordinary thing!

SNOD.   (*sarcastically*) Very.

PICK.   Placed me in such an extremely awkward situation.

WIN.    (*pointedly*) Oh, very.

PICK.    I understand your insinuations, friends, but I can assure you they are  145
unfounded.

TUP.    Don't deny it, it's very natural—man must love—Oh, Rachel! Heighho!

*Re-enter* SAM.

SAM.    I've got her safe down stairs, sir, she's had a powerful pull at her own private
brandy bottle, and is all right now—I vas so wery much affected, I declare I vas
obliged to take a dose of the same physic.          150

PICK.    Enough—enough, Sam! I've summoned you here, my dear friends and colleagues, to attend me in an expedition to the Borough of Eatanswill—the popular
candidate for which is my friend—I've promised to nominate him, we should not do
our duty if we miss'd being present at a scene so animating to every Englishman.

SNOD.    We will go with you—are you not our leader—our illustrious leader?          155

PICK.    Independent of patriotism, it will cheer the dark misanthropy and disgust of
life, which you, my dear Tupman, express'd over the buttock of beef, at the Leather
Bottle, yesterday afternoon, for the loss of the perfidious Rachel—you too, my dear
coadjutors—Snodgrass and Winkle will meet the girls of your hearts—Wardle is a
freeholder, he'll attend to give his vote, and no doubt he will treat his daughters with  160
a view of the proceedings.

SNOD.    Oh, my adorable Emily! We'll all of us go—let us set out this very moment.

PICK.    Well said—Sam, step down to the Belle Sauvage, and secure four places for
Eatanswill.

SAM.    Go directly, sir! my father drives the Dorking Coach, as goes through the  165
wery place.

PICK.    Your father!

SAM.    Yes, sir, of the Markiss of Granby—but I'll tell you how it came about.—My
father, sir, was a coachman—a vidover he vas—and fat enough for anything—uncommon fat to be sure—his Missus dies, and leaves him four hundred pound—down he  170
goes to Doctors' Commons, to see the Lawyer, and draw the blunt; wery smart—
top boots on, nosegay in his button-hole—broad-brim'd tile—green shawl—quite
the gen'lman. Touter gets hold on him, and axes him if he vants a licence. Dash
my vestkit, says my father, I newer thought of that, my father says—but ain't I too
fat. Not a bit of it, sir, says the Touter, ve married a genl'man twice your size last  175
veek,—you're but a babby to him. Well, avay he follows the Touter, like a tame mon-
key arter a organ. What's the lady's name, says the Lawyer.—Blest if I knows, says
my father,—put down Mrs Clarke—Susan Clarke, Markiss of Granby, Dorking,

---

153 *nominate him*: MS cuts the explanation that Pickwick is to nominate a friend and substitutes 'there
is an election there'.

160 *vote*: MS cuts the information that Wardle is to be a voter.

173 *he vants a*: MS inserts 'wedding', presumably for clarity.

174 *newer*: In this instance both 1837 and MS have the v/w transposition, 'never' to 'newer', which might
have been as spoken, but looks very confusing in print.

she'll have me, I knows, if I axes her. Vell, the licence was made out—and she did
180   have him—and vat's more—she's got him now—and I ha'nt never had any of the four
hundred pounds—beg pardon, sir! but ven I gets on this ere grievance, I runs on
like a new greas'd wheel-barrow—I'll go and book the places, directly. (*Exit* SAM.)
PICK.   Ha! ha! Now then, for Britons' Birth-right—our Country—our Charter—
Eatanswill and Freedom! Onwards, Pickwickians—'tis Liberty invites you!

QUARTETTE, OMNES.

AIR 'Hurrah! for the Road.'

185          Hurrah! hurrah! for Eatanswill,
Hurrah! for the cause of Reform;
And the voters who be honest will,
And brave corruption's storm.
Then let us for freedom, mount our steeds,
190          And lighten taxation's load;
For Eatanswill to Liberty leads,
Then hurrah! hurrah! for the road!

(*Exit* OMNES)

# SCENE 2

*Hustings and Polling Booths, at Eatanswill,* FIZKIN's *division, P. S. ornamented with
Orange Ribbons—Buff Flags, with inscriptions,* 'Fizkin for Ever,' 'Church and State,'
*etc.* SLUMKEY's *Division, O. P. ornamented with Blue Ribbons, and Flags, inscribed,*
'Slumkey for Ever,' 'Liberty of the Press,' *etc. Place in Centre for* MAYOR. DRUNKEN
LIBERAL, MATCH SELLER, BALLAD SINGER, *and* VOTERS, Blue and Buff VOTERS,
*with their Colours, discovered—Shouting and Huzzaing—some crying,* 'Slumkey for
Ever,' *others* 'Fizkin for Ever,' 'No Slumkey,' 'No Fizkin,' *etc.*

1 D. LIB.   I'm for uniwersal suffering—Slumkey for ever—Fizkin for ever—Blue for
ever—Buff for ever—Everybody for ever!
B. SIN.   That's jist my politics—I'm all for Armony—triangular Parleyments—and
Wotes by ballad—though I does sing songs agin the hopposition.

---

192 *for the road*: MS has a space left for this song, but it is blank. This is not uncommon in submitted
MSS, where songs are often indicated but not included; however, the ironic political tone of this one might
not have pleased the LC's officers, had they seen it. 'Hurrah for the Road' is the title of a broadside ballad
printed by Catnach in the 1820s.

0.7 *Hustings and Polling Booths...No Fizkin,' etc.*: The MS has no descriptive stage setting here, only
'Voters and mob discovered shouting'.
3 *Parleyments*: MS omits the reference here to, presumably, annual parliamentary elections, perhaps
avoiding anything suggestive of the Chartist demands.

M. SEL.    Vell, so long as our member does but bring in a bill to put down them ere 5
lucifers, as has been the ruin of matches, vhy I don't care.
VOTERS.    (*tumultuously and severally*) 'Slumkey for ever!' 'Fizkin for ever!' 'No
Slumkey,' etc.

*Enter* JOB TROTTER, *with Buff favours.*

TROT.    Patriotic rogues—but what are you wasting your time, waiting here for?
Don't you know that the election won't begin this half hour—and that the generous 10
Fizkin, our noble Buff candidate, has just opened all the public-houses, free, gratis,
and for nothing?
OMNES.    Hurrah! All the public-houses opened—this way—this way—Fizkin for
ever! (*Exeunt* DRUNKEN LIBERAL, BALLAD SINGER, MATCH SELLER, VOTERS,
etc., *tumultuously*)
TROT.    Oh! the depravity of mankind—as that worthy shepherd, Stiggings, piously 15
remarks,—a public-house is the devil's own mousetrap—Gin is his toasted cheese—
and human mortals his varmints—and he no sooner sets his bait than he catches
the *rats* like winking—there certainly never was such a clever rogue as that Jingle—
he ought to play Iago—Stukely—Joseph Surface, and all the first-rate melodramatic
villains, by patent. One hundred and fifty pounds! for not keeping an old harridan, 20
that any one else would have given a hundred and fifty pounds to get rid of—he has
set up gentleman with the plunder—Captain Fitztory!—has turned Conservative—
advocates Aristocratic principles—and has managed to become head Committee-
man to Horatio Fizkin, Esq., of Fizkin Lodge. Eh! talk of the devil and he'll appear,
they say.                                                                                                              25

*Enter* JINGLE, *decorated with large orange favours.*

Well, Jingle, how do you get on?
JIN.    Capital—very!—opened public-houses—Goat in Boots—Cat in Pattens—Hog
in Armour—only left Slumkey beer shops!—famous move that—very!—not all
though—last night, got up tea-party—voters' wives, forty-five—served up green
parasols, seven and sixpence each—one a-piece—parting present—great effect— 30
got votes—all their husbands—half their brothers—beats flannel—ribbons—stockings!—wet or dry—can't go out—High Street—green parasols—half a dozen—
politic—warn't it—very!
TROT.    It was, indeed!—but what do you intend next?

---

9 *waiting*: MS has 'bawling' for 'waiting'.

17 *varmints*: Vermin. 1837 has 'warmints,' which is one of several instances of the v/w transposition
being used in speeches by someone other than the Wellers, in the play.

20 *Stukely... by patent*: Stukely is the villain in Moore's *The Gamester* (Drury Lane, 1753). The MS omits
the theatrical references, which are not derived from Dickens.

33 *Capital—very!... warn't it—very!*: The description of the bribing of electors with drink and green
parasols is transferred to Jingle from an anonymous agent in Dickens's chapter 13; the comic names of the
pubs, not included in the MS, seem to be Moncrieff's invention.

35 JIN.   Red Book—Pension List—Sinecure!—Government—valuable services—
Home Department—Privy Council—who knows—pleasant—'ent it—very!—right
too—very!

TROT.   Why, I dare say you'll have done as much to deserve a pension, as most of the
people that have one.

40 JIN.   Sharp remark—very!—can't applaud—Havn't time—Fizkin waiting—Rose
and Crown—going for him—nominee—famous speech—short-hand writers sadly
puzzled—can't remember—great advantage—follow me—Master Fizkin, damn'd
good fellow—purse immense—large as fishnet—must be lightened—proper—
needful—'ent it—very—very!

45 TROT.   Oh, very proper—I'll be off with you, directly—capital gag, our calling
Slumkey's party Destructives—volunteering to preserve the people's property—
gad, if it once comes into our hands, we'll take care of it, with a witness to it—this
way—this way—Captain—

JIN.   Fitztory!—travelling name—just the thing—imposing—'ent it—very—very—
50 very!—(*Exeunt* JINGLE *and* TROTTER)

*Enter* WARDLE, ISABELLA, *and* EMILY.

WAR.   Come along, girls—come along—rare bustling scene, faith!—never saw so
great a party spirit, in so small a place, in my life. Buff and Blue—they'll buffet one
another, till they're black and blue, before they're done, or I'm very much mistaken—one half of them will really be in buff, and the other half, look very blue
55 indeed. Well, I shall vote for the liberal party.

ISA.   You know I'm for freedom of speech, pa. Right of election!—purity of choice!—
choosing one's own representative!—and every thing of that kind!

WAR.   You're a Radical, you madcap, you are. What are your principles, Emily?

EM.   I would be more exclusive, sir!—as Mr Snodgrass says—the institutions of our
60 forefathers should be preserved inviolate—I disclaim innovation, and would have
no changes in the state—everything should remain just as it is!

ISA.   Mercy on me, Emily! I'd change *my* state directly, if I could—I don't want to
remain as I am by any means—nor does Mr Winkle—or I'm very much mistaken—
True Blue for ever!

65 EM.   Orange—the peerless Orange, for me!

DUET, ISABELLA *and* EMILY.

AIR 'Hurrah! for the Red and the Blue.'

Hurrah! for the Buff and the Blue,
May they both to their Monarch prove true,

42 *damn'd*: 'damn'd' omitted in MS.

52 *in my life*: MS cut from here to Wardle's remark 'never quarrel about politics, girls!', removing, as it
generally does, a sequence between the female characters, and also avoiding possibly contentious responses
to political remarks.

65.2 *AIR 'Hurrah! for the Red and the Blue.'*: This song does not surface in the record until it (or one of
the same title) is published in 1854 as written by Edward Farmer and composed by Charles Coote.

> Be staunch to the cause,
> Of our Charter and Laws,
> And while raising the glories, 70
> Of Whigs and of Tories,
> Still keep England's welfare in view!

WAR.    Well said—never quarrel about politics, girls!—Hey! here's two of our friends coming.

ISA.    Mr Winkle—then I may promise myself some sport. 75

EM.    Augustus—the high, imaginative Snodgrass—oh! what transport!

*Enter* WINKLE *and* SNODGRASS, *the former with Blue—the latter with Orange favours.*

ISA.    Welcome, gentlemen—welcome, Mr Winkle—you must join *us*, for I see by your colours, you're of our party—Mr Snodgrass must go over to Emily—they're not our side of the house!

SNOD.    Willingly—willingly—for though in the opposition, I trust I shall not be out 80 of place. (WINKLE *joins* ISABELLA, *and* SNODGRASS EMILY)

WAR.    Good—good!—but where the devil is Pickwick?

WIN.    Heading the Honourable Mr Slumkey's Committee, my dear sir!—but here comes his squire, Mr Weller—now we shall know all the news.

*Enter* SAM, *ornamented with large blue favour.*

WAR.    Your servant, Mr Weller—how are you getting on? All alive, eh! 85

SAM.    Yes, sir, and kicking! Quite a reg'lar game!—there's a whole mob o' woters round the Town Arms, bawling like mad, already.

WAR.    Do they seem devoted to the popular candidate?

SAM.    Never seed sich dewotion in my life, sir!—I never seed men eat and drink so much afore—I vonder they aint afeared of burstin. 90

WAR.    Fine, fresh hearty fellows, no doubt!

SAM.    Wery fresh sir,—me and the two vaiters has been pumping on all of 'em!

WAR.    Pumping on them!

SAM.    Yes, sir!—they supp'd there last night, and every man slept vhere he fell down—so ve dragg'd 'em out von by von, and put 'em under the pump—and they're 95 all in reg'lar fine wotin order, now.

WAR.    Is it possible?

SAM.    Lord, sir!—that's nothing!—the night afore the last day of the last election, here—I've heard, the hopposition party bribed the barmaid of the Peacock, to hocus the brandy and vater of fourteen of the unpoll'd electors, as was stoppin' in 100 the house.

WAR.    Hocussing brandy and water!

SAM.    Yes, sir—puttin' laud'num into it—blest if she didn't send 'em all to sleep, till twelve hours arter the election vas over.

---

82 *the devil*: 'the devil' omitted in MS.

105 WAR.    Strange practices these, Mr Weller!
    SAM.    Not half so strange as a mirack'lous circumstance as happen'd to my own
            father, at an election time, in this 'ere wery place, Mr Vaddle.
    WAR.    What was that, Mr Weller?
    SAM.    Vy, he drives a coach through here, sir! Vell, election time comes on—and
110         he vas engag'd by von party to bring down woters from Lunnon—night afore he
            vas going to drive up—committee on 'tother side, sends for him—vell he vent,
            and wery ciwil they vas to him, to be sure—vine, and all that—at last, arter
            a bushel o' gammon, they slips a twenty pound note into his hand—and says, 'It's
            a wery bad road 'tvixt here and Lunnon aint it?' 'Wery,' says father—'specially
115         near the canal.' 'Vell, Mr Veller,' says the gen'lman—'you're a wery good vhip,
            and ve're all wery fond on you—and if you shou'd hav' a haccident, and tip these
            ere woters over into the canal, vithout hurtin on 'em, that ere twventy pounds is
            for yourself.' 'You're wery kind,' says my father.'—So he goes—and vhat's wery
            remarkable—the wery next day—on the wery spot they'd mention'd—blow'd if
120         he didn't spill 'em all into the wery 'dentical vater—and von old gen'lman newer
            vas found agin—I only mention this, as a hextraordinary vonderful coincidence—
            as the two brothers said, vhen they vas going to be hang'd together. (*Hurrahing
            heard without*)
            But look out, sir! look out—here comes our party—here comes the gowernor.—
            'Slumkey for ever.' (MOB *outside*, Hurrah!)

*Enter, Slumkey's Party in Procession, with* MR PICKWICK, *the* HONOURABLE
MR SLUMKEY, *of Slumkey Hall,* MR TUPMAN, DRUNKEN LIBERAL, *and Slumkey's*
*party, male and female, with favours, etc.*

CHORUS.—SAM *and* SLUMKEY'S PARTY.
AIR 'Hurrah! for the bonnets of blue!'

125         Here's a health to the Friends of Reform,
            Electors who're honest and true;
            And may those who will not vote for Eatanswill's good,
            Like our colours, be made to look blue!
            'Tis good to be Liberal Whigs,
130         'Tis good to be honest and true;
            'Tis good to support noble Slumkey's cause,
            And vote for the Triumph of Blue!
            Hurrah, etc.

(PICKWICK *and* SLUMKEY *ascend Hustings*)

    SAM.    Ulloa! Here come t'other party. No Fizkin, no Fizkin!

---

124.5  *AIR 'Hurrah! for the bonnets of blue!':* A Robert Burns setting by Alexander Lee, popular with singers of theatrical ballads in the 1830s.

*Enter, in Procession, the other side,* HORATIO FIZKIN, *esquire,* MAYOR, CRYER, JINGLE, TROTTER, *and their party.*

CHORUS, TROTTER, *and* FIZKIN'S PARTY.
AIR 'March, march, Ettrick and Teviotdale.'

March, march, Destructives and Radicals.                                135
Break their heads, lads, you who're friends to good order;
March, march, Democrats, Jacobins,
Make their Blue Colours yield to the Recorder!
Many a Freeholder,
Many a be-holder,                                                       140
We have addressed, with the old Tory story;
Shout, and in Eatanswill,
You shall all have your fill,
Let the Blue Party be thrown in disorder!
March, march, etc.                                                      145

(MAYOR *and* CRYER *take centre place*—FIZKIN *and* JINGLE *ascend Hustings, P.S.* JOB TROTTER *and* SAM *head their respective parties, on each side, who shout vigorously, pushing each other about,* 'Slumkey for ever,' 'Fizkin for ever,' 'No Slumkey,' 'No Fizkin,' *etc., etc.* CRYER *rings bell*)

MAY.   Silence!—Order!—Hear—hear!
D. LIB.   Success to the Mayor—and may he never forgit the nail and saucepan busi-
ness, as he got his money by—that's my sentiments.
CRY.   (*ringing bell*) Silence!
MAY.   Gentlemen!                                                       150
M. SEL.   Vell, ve hears you—go on.
MAY.   Worthy and Independent Electors of Eatanswill—we are met here, to-day, to
choose a fit and proper representative, to represent this ancient and loyal Borough!
SAM., TROT., *and their two parties,* (*tumultuously*)   'Slumkey for ever,' 'Fizkin
for ever,' etc., etc.                                                   155
CRY.   (*ringing bell*) Silence!—silence!
B. SIN.   Does your mother know you're out, old feller?
M. SEL.   (*throwing dead cat at* CRYER) There's a plumper for you!
MAY.   Order!—order!—or I'll commit the whole of you!
B. SIN.   I thinks you said commit!—                                    160
PICK.   (*on Hustings*) Gentlemen!
SAM.   Hear!—Hear!—Hear!—Silence for the gowernor.

---

134.4 *AIR 'March, march, Ettrick and Teviotdale.'*: That is, the chorus of the Jacobite song 'Blue Bonnets over the Border,' included by Sir Walter Scott in *The Monastery* published in 1820 and adopted as a theatrical and concert piece by Braham and other singers.

PICK.     Gentlemen—allow me to propose, as your representative, the Honourable Simon Slumkey, of Slumkey Hall!

165 SAM. *and* BLUES.     Hurrah!—'Slumkey for ever!'

JIN.     (*also on Hustings*) Allow me, gentlemen!

TROT.     Hurrah! Silence for Captain Fitztory.

PICK.     Captain Fitztory!—Why, hang me if it isn't that scoundrel, Jingle, disguised in a new coat; here's some villainy going on—I must keep an eye on him!—(*aside*)

170 JIN.     Gentlemen!—Electors!—Eatanswill—propose—Friend—Horatio Fizkin, Esq.—Fizkin Lodge—Representative—Loyal Borough—Fit and proper—very!

SAM.     Over the left!

TROT. *and* PARTY.     Hurrah!—'Fizkin for ever!'

SAM. *and* PARTY.     'No Fizkin!'—'Slumkey for ever!'

175 CRY.     (*ringing bell*) Silence!—Silence!

MAY.     Show of hands—Honourable Slumkey.

SAM.     I'll hold up both hands.

(SAM *and* BLUES *hold up hands for Slumkey*)

MAY.     Horatio Fizkin, Esq.

SAM.     And a rum von to look at, he is!

180 TROT.     Hurrah! now boys.

(BUFFS *hold up hands for Fizkin*)

MAY.     Show of hands in favour of Slumkey.

SAM. *and* PARTY.     Hurrah! Slumkey for ever.

JIN.     Quite a mistake—demand poll—show favour—not hands—all Fiskinites!—Mayor partial—stupid—clear case—very—very!

185 MAY.     Gentlemen, the poll is opened.

SAM.     How can that be, ven nobody's head aint broke, and ve aint any split wotes. (ELECTORS *commence polling*—MAYOR, CRYER, etc. *taking votes*—WARDLE *votes*; DRUNKEN LIBERAL *votes on both sides*)

PICK.     Friends—as a fellow-countryman—

M. SEL.     How can you be a countryman, vhen you're a Lunnoner?

190 SAM.     Hear!—Hear!—for Mr Pickvick.

B. SIN.     Aye—hear Mr Picnic.

PICK.     If you'd have meat for asking for—bread for nothing—and beer for less—vote for Slumkey!

SAM. *and* BLUES.     Hurrah!—'Slumkey for ever!'

195 JIN.     All humbug—Radicals! Destructives!—vote for Fizkin—Noble Fellow!—Glorious Constitution!—Magna Charter!—Bill of Rights!—Trial by Jury!—Wooden Walls!—Englishman's Birthright!—Make no Pledges!—

SAM.     No!—no!—they're all up the spout.

198 *up the spout*: Sam converts the tag into a joke by punning on the meanings of 'pledge' as a political promise but also an object put into pawn, 'up the spout'.

JIN.    Fizkin!—Britain's boast—take care of all your property!—

SAM.    Don't you vish you may get it?                                          200

TROT.    Order!—Order!—Hear Captain Fitztory!

JIN.    Vote for Fizkin—lots of Mock Turtle—Champagne, by pailsful—give 'em you for nothing, and pay you for taking them away.

TROT. *and* BUFFS.    Hurrah!—Fizkin for ever!

SAM.    (*twigs* JINGLE *bribing* VOTERS) Ulloa! there's that ere chap being guilty of    205
corruption—bribery!—bribery!

PICK.    The scoundrel!—I object to those votes being received—Mr Fizkin is deceived—that fellow's an impostor.

SAM.    Yes, place 'em all to our side—they belong to our side.—

CRY.    (*ringing bell*) Silence!—Silence!—Silence!                            210

MAY.    Gentlemen, the poll is closed—the numbers are—Slumkey Ninety-eight!

SAM. *and* BLUES.    Hurrah!—'Slumkey for ever!'

MAY.    Fizkin, Forty-five!—majority for Slumkey, Fifty-three!—The Honourable Simon Slumkey is, therefore, duly elected.

SAM.    Hurrah!—Chair him!—Cheer him!—Chair him!                              215

WAR.    (*to* ISABELLA, *etc.*) Let us get out of the way, while we can.

(*Exeunt* WARDLE, ISABELLA, EMILY, SNODGRASS, *and* WINKLE)

(FIZKIN *and party sneak down to front, to the air of 'Oh, dear, what can the matter be,' amidst groans of* SAM, *etc., and exeunt. Chair is brought on,* SLUMKEY, PICKWICK, MAYOR, TUPMAN, *and party, come down to the air, 'See the Conquering Hero comes.'* SAM, *shouting and capering about, runs against* TROTTER—*a concussion takes place— which leads to general combat between Blues and Buffs, in which* MR PICKWICK *and* SLUMKEY *get upset—and scene closes on general confusion*)


## SCENE 3

*Hall leading to Bar and Coffee-Room of the Town Arms Inn.*

*Enter* FAT BOY, *carrying a large goose.*

F. BOY.    (*yawning*) Master might have waited till I waked—but I suppose he didn't    1
know where I was—postillion let me ride one of the horses, and when they chang'd them, I was asleep, and didn't know anything about it, till I was thrown into the hay-loft—half-an-hour after I'd been in the stable! horse got tir'd of my making a feather-bed of his back, I suppose. (*yawns*) Well, I shan't go to the election now,    5

216.7 FIZKIN *and party…general confusion*: MS abbreviates this stage direction into 'the Two Parties come down from Hustings when a general row ensures and scene closes'.

2 *Master…where I was*: MS, which generally has many fewer lines for Fat Boy, cuts this speech down to 'I suppose'.

'cause it's all over—I shall wait for him, here—I can take a nap till he comes. (FAT BOY *retires one side, makes a pillow of goose, and sleeps*)

*Enter* WARDLE, ISABELLA *and* WINKLE, EMILY *and* SNODGRASS.

WAR.    Thank Heaven! we've got through the bustle—ah! it's lucky Joe wasn't with us—he'd have been asleep as usual, and might have been favoured with a nightcap, in the shape of an oaken cudgel—that might have prevented his ever waking
10    again.

ISA.    I told you, sir! the people would win—another victory in the cause of the population!

WAR.    You girls are devilish anxious to uphold the population, methinks!

EM.    We shall demand a scrutiny.

15  SNOD.    Yes, 'never let the noble mind despair,—though nursed in ills, and exercised in care!'—as the immortal Bard says.

WIN.    Our dear friend, Pickwick, is, no doubt, enjoying the triumphant reward of his disinterested patriotism!—Eh! what the deuce is this?

*Enter* PICKWICK *and* TUPMAN, *covered with mud and dust—and* SAM, *with a black eye, and his nose damaged.*

PICK.    Confound the villains—Exclusives do they call themselves—I wish they'd
20    been a little more exclusive, with their kicks and cuffs—a queer way of polling, theirs—cracked heads have been as plenty as blackberries. But, however, we're not so bad off as the Honourable Slumkey—for they've soused him in the horse-pond.

SAM.    *Ray*ther a rough scramble, sir, certainly—but I paid a few on 'em—and gave the t'others a receipt—I'll jist rub you down a bit, vith this ere jack towel, vhat I
25    borrow'd from the cook—and then go and see if I can't cork up my claret, here, a little. (SAM *rubs down* PICKWICK *and* TUPMAN)

WAR.    Are these the lofty principles of your high-minded, elevated party, Emily?— knocking everybody down.

PICK.    What, my dear friend Wardle, Emily, and Isabella, too!—I rejoice to meet
30    you—don't stare—Tupman and I have only been rolled in the kennel, for the good of the country.

WAR.    One half our patriots should be served in the same way.

---

9 *cudgel*: MS cuts from this point in Winkle's speech to the entry of Pickwick, removing the slight innuendo in Wardle's response to Isabella.

16 *as the immortal Bard says*: Winkle implies that his quotation is Shakespearean, but in fact it is from the last lines of Ambrose Philips's tragedy *The Distrest Mother* (1712), where the couplet is 'Though plunged in ills, and exercised in care | Yet never let the noble mind despair.'

23 *SAM*: MS cuts Sam's speech and Wardle's response.

25 *cork up my claret*: 'cork up the claret' is contemporary boxing parlance for 'staunch the blood'. Moncrieff was well acquainted with the 'fast' language of the prize ring from his work on Pierce Egan's story to produce his hit play *Tom and Jerry* (Adelphi, 1823).

32 *One half…same way*: A political claptrap which the MS omits.

TUP. I haven't a whole bone left in my body—if this is your march of intellect—to be run over, and trod down by every blackguard in the country—I've done.

SAM. (*finishing rubbing them down*) There, sir!—there you are. Now I'll go and per- 35
form my toilet. (*Exit* SAM)

WAR. Well—well—well!—I rejoice that your man has come in, however. He is a Liberal—and while we return such members as he is, the cause of Liberty and Old England must flourish!

*Re-enter* SAM, *with card.*

SAM. (*to* PICKWICK) Card for you, sir!—gen'lman a vaiting! 40

PICK. Eh! a card for me! (*reads*) 'Mrs Leo Hunter, the Den, Eatanswill.' I thought you said a gentleman?

SAM. A wery good imitation of von, if it aint, sir! He vants you partick'ler—as the devil's private secretary said, vhen he fetch'd avay Doctor Faustus!

PICK. Well, in that case, I will see him. 45

SAM. Wery vell, sir!—I'll give him the intimation. This vay, sir!

*Enter* MR LEO HUNTER.

L. HUN. Mr Pickwick, I presume. Your fame has reach'd the ears of Mrs Leo Hunter, my wife, sir!—I am Mr Leo Hunter—we are proud to number among our acquaint-ances, all those who have rendered themselves celebrated, by their works and tal-ents—more especially so distinguished a person as yourself, and the members of 50
the far-famed Club, that from you derives its name.

PICK. I shall be extremely happy to make the acquaintance of your lady, sir!

L. HUN. You shall make it, sir! To-morrow morning, we give a public breakfast—a fete champetre—to a great number of public characters.

ISA. *and* EM. Delightful!—delightful! 55

L. HUN. Permit Mrs Leo Hunter to have the gratification of seeing you at the Den.

PICK. With great pleasure.

L. HUN. You have a gentleman in your train, who has produced some beautiful little poems, I think, sir! 60

EM. (*eagerly*) Oh, yes, sir!—Mr Snodgrass—no one but must have heard of his abilities!

SNOD. Praise from beauty's lips, is the bard's sweetest nurture.

L. HUN. And another whose sporting abilities Nimrod has delighted to record—one celebrated for a thousand steeple chases. 65

ISA. And not a few wild-goose chases, I believe. (*aside*) He stands before you, sir!

---

33 *body*: MS has 'skin' for 'body'.     34 *I've done*: MS omits 'I've done'.
44 *Doctor Faustus*: MS omits this Wellerism.     46 *This vay, sir*: MS has 'walk in' for 'This vay'.
53 L. HUN: MS cuts this speech down to Pickwick's 'With great pleasure'.
63 SNOD: MS cuts Snodgrass's line.

WIN.    (*aside*) Is she sporting with me, or not?

L. HUN.    You must all come. My lady is a Hunter, you know—Mrs Leo Hunter!—
He!—he!—Writes poetry too—everybody must have heard of her 'Ode to an expir-
70    ing Frog!'—sweet composition—but she will recite it to-morrow—in the character
of Minerva!

PICK.    Minerva!

L. HUN.    Yes, sir!—I forgot to mention, it is a fancy dress dejeune—Jacob Nathan,
in the High Street, has thousands of fancy dresses—here are tickets for all your
75    friends.

TUP.    I shall go as Massaroni, the Bandit—and make prey on all mankind—it will
suit with my despairing condition.

PICK.    As a bandit—you don't mean to say, that you design to dress yourself in a
green velvet jacket, with a two inch tail—nonsense—you're too old and too fat.

80  TUP.    (*angrily*) Mr Pickwick!

ISA. *and* EM.    Oh! delightful!—charming!—It will be the very thing!—you must
consent—Mr Pickwick.

PICK.    But, a jacket with a two-inch tail. However, let it be so.

SNOD.    I shall go as Apollo—striking my lyre—in blue satin trunks and a cloak, with
85    white silk tights.

WIN.    I shall go as Actæon—with a large pair of deer horns, to mark my character.

ISA.    Dear me!—Methinks that's being somewhat premature. (*aside*)

SAM.    And I shall go as Old Nick—and play the devil with them all. (*aside*)

PICK.    You may all go as you like—but no fancy dress for me. I fancy no dress but
90    my own.

L. HUN.    My dear sir! we will make an exception in your favour. Mrs Leo Hunter will
be delighted to see you in any way—and, perhaps, it will be most gratifying to her,
and her guests, to behold so great a man as you are, in his natural state. But I am
trespassing on your valuable time—farewell, my dear sir,—farewell! Mrs Leo Hunter
95    will confidently expect and rely on the presence of yourself and your distinguished
friends, to-morrow morning. (*Exit* MR LEO HUNTER)

PICK.    We must not lose so favourable an opportunity of noting down character, and
meeting adventure, as this promises to afford us.

---

67 *Is she… not?*: MS cuts Winkle's aside.

70 *sweet composition*: MS cuts 'sweet composition'.

73 *Jacob Nathan*: MS substitutes 'Solomon Lucas' for 'Jacob Nathan'. Dickens named him as 'Solomon
Lucas, the Jew in the High Street'. The intrusion of the name of Nathan, the leading court, military and stage
costumier established in London since 1790, is perhaps another instance of Moncrieff's theatricality shaping his adaptation, like the theatre jokes between Job and Jingle.

79 *too fat*: MS cuts next three speeches.

84 *Apollo*: MS has not 'Apollo' but 'a troubadour', which is the word Dickens uses.

87 ISA: MS omits Isabella's response, with its suggestion that she will make Winkle a cuckold after he
marries her. Dickens does not specify Winkle's choice of fancy dress.

89 *You may*: MS inserts 'as well' here, making Pickwick less imperious.

93 *her guests*: MS cuts from here, ending 'farewell until tomorrow morning'.

WAR.   Well, well—I'll e'en go with you, though I can't say I much relish appearing as a man without a character! for once, I'll sport a domino. But come, I feel like drink- 100 ing—let's go in and toss off a glass of black strap, to the successful candidate, in the good old cause. Where the devil can Joe be?

(JOE *snores*)

Ulloa! Damn that boy, if he isn't here, and asleep again. But, eh! what's this I see? sleeping on the goose! Oh! you villain—but he's not the only one that has slept on goose—if it had been a saddle of mutton, it would have been just the same—he'd have made a 105 pillow of it—and thought he was sleeping on flock. But, come, friends!—come, girls!

ISA.   We will follow you directly, papa!—You must excuse us a moment; Emily and I have got a few arrangements to make.

WAR.   Very well, girls!—don't be long, or we shall think you're plotting mischief. Now, Pickwick, old boy! this way! 110

*Exeunt* WARDLE, PICKWICK, TUPMAN, SNODGRASS, *and* WINKLE; *followed by* SAM *and* FAT BOY

ISA.   I have staid behind, my dear Emily, to communicate to you a project, for which this Fancy Dress Breakfast affords us a favourable opportunity. I know your predilection for consulting Fortune Tellers, though they've never told you true. Now, as we are neither of us quite certain of our swains—mine's going as Actæon, you see, in search of some Diana—and no doubt means to rifle all the game he starts, though 115 he must handle his piece better than he did with the rooks. Mr Snodgrass is to go as Apollo, it appears, and you know what sort of a gentleman he was—he won't always harp on one theme, depend on't; suppose, therefore, we turn the tables, and instead of discovering our lovers, by having our fortunes told—tell our lovers their fortunes, and so learn ours that way. 120

EM.   What a madcap you are—but anything to satisfy myself that my Augustus truly loves me!—Oh! Snodgrass—if he would but say as much to me in plain prose, as he has in poetry, I should desire no more. Agreed!—agreed!

ISA.   You shall go to this Fete Champetre—where our lions are to be shown, as Margaret Finch, the Queen of the Gipsies, you know—I, as a simple country girl, a 125 sure bait for a sportsman—we can procure tickets, unknown to them, and thus fairly entrap them.

100 *without a character*: MS cuts to his demand for Joe, omitting also his jokes about the boy sleeping. A domino is a plain, normally black, kaftan-like garment with a hood that conceals the face, worn over ordinary clothes by guests at a masquerade who do not choose to adopt fancy dress. Black strap is a mixture of rum and molasses.

112 *opportunity*: MS abbreviates, and perhaps bowdlerizes, cutting from here to 'and instead of' and substituting 'Suppose we go as fortune tellers'.

120 *tell...fortunes*: MS substitutes 'we do so by telling them theirs' for 'tell our lovers their fortunes'.

123 *Agreed!—agreed!*: MS moves 'Agreed!—agreed!' to beginning of Isabella's speech.

126 *a sure...sportsman*: MS leaves out 'a sure bait for a sportsman' and some superfluous words in this speech.

EM.    Have it all your own way—but my life on Snodgrass's truth. Ah! Bella—I wish I
had your spirits—always buoyant—always gay.

130  ISA.    And why shouldn't I be so?—'Toujours gai,' is my motto—and through life will
I stick to it.

SONG, ISABELLA.

AIR 'Toujours Gai.'

Always gay—always gay!
If we would be always gay,
Sport at ease, and cheerful play,
135                     And on Sorrow trample!
We must not let anger stay,
But chase moody care away,
'Twill make every month, a May!
                     'Tis nature's own example!

140  We'll not nourish discontent,
Nor, as many do, resent
Injuries, that ne'er were meant,
                     Poisoning life's leisure;
We'll not grumble, pine, nor fret;
145  All that's sadd'ning we'll forget!
Part as blythe as first we met,—
                     Votaries of pleasure!

(*Exeunt* ISABELLA *and* EMILY)

*Re-enter* SAM.

SAM.    I can't get out of my canister that 'ere chap, as run avay vith the old maid, being
transmogrified into a captain, and taking the side of sich a hole-and-corner candi-
150  date as that Fizkin—he's got summat willainous on foot—or he vouldn't be mixed
up vith that 'ere party—I vish I could get hold on that mulberry man of his'n—I'd
pump it all out of him, with a high-draw-lic pressure, in no time. Vell, the devil
certainly does take care of his own children—for blow me if he isn't here, in the
wery nick—I'll pretend not to see him. (*aside*)

*Enter* JOB TROTTER.

155  TROT.    (*aside*) There he is—now to bamboozle him—and send old Pickwick a wool-
gathering, for thwarting Jingle, at the election; and prevent his interfering with him

---

130  ISA: MS omits this speech, attributes the song to Emily, and does not include its text. 'Toujours gai' is
the title of a rondo by composer Joseph Gale, published in London *c*.1805, which may be the air specified here.
154  *maid…wery nick*: MS has 'woman' for 'maid' and abbreviates this speech cutting from 'and taking'
to 'that 'ere party' and from 'in no time' to 'wery nick,' substituting 'why I'm sure that's him a'coming'.
156  *thwarting*: MS substitutes 'sporting with' for 'thwarting' and cuts from 'and prevent' to the end of the
speech.

again—morality shall be my cue—must keep up my character of Dismal Jemmy!—
never fails—got my handkerchief—and 'Collection, No. 4,'—all ready.

(*Pulls out book and appears absorbed in reading*)

SAM.    He doesn't see me—seems close wrapp'd up in his own invard meditations—
they must be as good as a flannel veskit to him—vell, if he don't speak, I must.  160
(*aside*) Ulloa! Gowernor—how are you, old feller? (*to* TROTTER)

TROT.    Eh! oh! now for it. (*aside*) Pretty well, I thank you—how are you? (*gravely*)

SAM.    Vy, I shou'd be a good deal better, if I vasn't quite so much like a walking
brandy bottle—but I've bin drinking a good deal, for the benefit of the nation—and
hav bin oblig'd to hav a ha'penny shower bath, for the good of myself—that is, I've  165
bin putting my head in the horse trough, and gettin a little boy to pump on me—so
now I'm become quvite cool and comfortable agin. Now then, I'll try the pump on
him. (*aside*) Aint your master's name Captain Fitztory?

TROT.    (*with a deep sigh*) I am sorry to say it is.

SAM.    Giv us your hand, my Patriarch—I quite likes the looks on you—what's your  170
name?

TROT.    (*casting down his eyes*) Job Trotter!

SAM.    Job!—and a wery good name it is—the only one I knows, that aint got a nickname to it—what sort of a place have you got?

TROT.    (*mournfully*) Bad—very bad!—my master's quite a dragon—he's going to  175
run away with an immense rich heiress, from a boarding school.

SAM.    Indeed!—who?

TROT.    That's not to be told to everybody.

SAM.    Oh! it's a secret, is it, old feller? I suppose your master is rich?

TROT.    Rich!—poor as a church mouse.                                            180

SAM.    Oh! that's the game, is it?—don't you think, then, you're a precious rascal—to
let your master run away vith this young heiress?

TROT.    I know that—and that is what preys upon my mind—but what can I do?
(*crying*)

SAM.    Do—dewulge to the missus, and giv up your master.

TROT.    Who would believe me?—the young lady is reckoned the very model of  185
innocence and discretion. If I knew any respectable gentleman now, who would
take the matter up.

SAM.    Say no more, my pebble—here comes the wery gentleman you vants.

*Enter* PICKWICK.

---

158 '*Collection, No. 4*': 'Collection, No. 4' is a hymn book that Job carries.

160 *they must...to him*: MS omits the remark about the waistcoat.

164 *bottle*: MS cuts the rest of the speech, substituting 'But I say, aren't you Captain Fitztory's man?' and
having Trotter reply 'I am sorry to say I am'.

170 *on you*: MS has 'of ye' for 'on you'.

176 *immense*: MS cuts 'immense' and omits the ensuing dialogue from Sam's speech to 'innocence and
discretion'.

186 *If I knew any*: MS has 'I wish I knew some' for 'If I knew any'.

Captain Fitztory's sarwant, sir! as is troubl'd vith some punctuation of conscience—
190    vat are makin a hole in his heart—his master's agoing to run avay with a young
heiress, from a boarding school.

PICK.    Another elopement! the scoundrel!

TROT.    Sorry to betray my master, sir. (*taking out pocket handkerchief, and applying it to his eyes*)

PICK.    Your feelings do you honour, my good fellow—but it is your duty,
195    nevertheless.

TROT.    I know it is my duty, sir—but still it's a hard trial to betray a master, whose clothes one wears, and whose bread one eats. (*weeps*)

SAM.    Come—come—blow this vater-cart bus'ness—it von't do no good, this von't—since your feelins is so wery fine—it's a pity you don't keep 'em in your own busum—
200    and not let 'em ewaporate in hot vater—'specially as they does no good—the next time you go out to a smokin' party, put that ere reflection in your pipe, and smoke it—and for the present, jist put up that bit o' pink gingham into your pocket—t'ant so handsome, that you need keep vawin' it about, as if you vas a tight-rope dancer.

205    PICK.    Right—Sam—right—but, come young man, in a few words—

TROT.    Well then, sir, though it cuts me to the heart—the boarding school stands a little way out of the town, the first house on the right hand—the elopement takes place to-night, this very night, at twelve o'clock!—you can catch 'em in the very act—I shall be concealed in the house—you'll be waiting in the garden, alone, and
210    at half-past eleven, I'll let you in, through the back door! and he'll soon find himself in the cage.

SAM.    Vithout his dicky bird—a wery capital plan—I'll give you a leg over the garden vall, sir.

TROT.    It's not right, sir, of me, to betray my master, bad as he is—I know it is
215    not. (*pulls out his handkerchief, and pretends to weep again*)

SAM.    Crying again—I never seed sich a feller—blow me if I don't think he's got a main in his head, as is alvays turned on.

PICK.    I don't half like the plan, but however, as the happiness of this young lady is at stake—I must e'en adopt it—I shall be sure to be there—take care to be waiting at
220    the door.

---

203 *vawin*: 'vawin' is presumably meant for 'waving' and is an instance of the unpronounceable lengths to which the v/w transposition is carried in the printed text, which cannot be corrected from the MS since that leaves this speech out *as is troubl'd...tight-rope dancer*: MS cuts from 'as is troubl'd' to 'heart' and then from Pickwick's response to 'tight-rope dancer' leaving only Job's answer as 'It's a hard trial, to betray a master, whose clothes one wears, and whose bread one eats, but it is my duty.'

205 *Sam*: MS leaves out 'Sam' and thus redirects Pickwick's speech.

206 *though...heart*: 'though...heart' omitted in MS.

207 *the...hand*: 'the...hand' omitted in MS.

208 *this...o'clock*: 'this...o'clock' omitted in MS.

212 SAM: This speech of Sam's and his next omitted in MS.

TROT.  I'll take care, sir, never fear.

PICK.  You are a fine fellow, and there's a sovereign for you—I admire your goodness of heart—no thanks—remember, eleven o'clock—let me go and prepare immediately—I'm burning with impatience to expose the scoundrel. (*Exit* PICKWICK)

SAM.  Hem!—not a bad notion, that ere crying—I'd cry like a rain-vater spout, in a shower, on sich terms as these—how do you do it? 225

TROT.  It comes from the heart, Mr Walker—but I must trot; good evening—the cunning Isaac—but I have caught him for once—now to get up the 'Agreeable Surprise' for his master. (*Exit* JOB TROTTER)

SAM.  You're a soft customer, you are—ve've got it all out of you, any how.—But let me go and get the gowernor ready for this nocturniwal expedition—as the old owl said to the young un, when he vent out a mouse-huntin'. (*Exit* SAM) 230

## SCENE 4

*Gardens, and back of Miss Tabby's Boarding School—Wall on one side—Twilight.*

*Enter, from house,* MISS TABBY, ISABELLA, *and* EMILY.

MISS T.  While your father and his friends are refreshing themselves, previous to their departure, we will breathe the cool pure air in quiet here. 1

ISA.  We could not be in your neighbourhood, my dear governess, and not visit the cherish'd scenes of our childhood—of our happiest days.

MISS T.  You must pass the night here! you know I have plenty of beds—it will be better than your sleeping at an inn—be once more joyous, thoughtless school girls. 5

EM.  Would that we could, dear governess, but that can never be! No charm can win us back that sweet springtime of life.

ISA.  But we may live it o'er again, dear sister, in talking of old times.

MISS T.  You will meet many of your old companions—many fast blooming, like yourselves, to youth's sweet may. 10

*Enter* LUCRETIA KITCHENER, *Miss Tabby's Cook.*

LUCRE.  (*to* MISS TABBY) A letter for you, ma'am, left by a most mysterious man, who wouldn't wait for any answer.

224 *I admire...immediately*: 'I admire...immediately' omitted in MS.

225 SAM: Sam's speech, and Trotter's from 'the cunning Isaac' omitted in MS.

229 *the cunning Isaac...'Agreeable Surprise'*: Trotter continues his theatrical references: *The Agreeable Surprize* is a comic opera by O'Keeffe and Arnold (Haymarket, 1784); 'cunning Isaac' refers to a character in Sheridan's *The Duenna* (Covent Garden, 1775) who mistakenly thinks himself clever.

230 *all out of you*: MS cuts from here, substituting 'clear enough—but it's getting late—I must go and prepare the governor for the expedition'.

2 *previous to their departure*: MS omits 'previous to their departure' and then Isabella's speech and in Miss Tabby's next 'it will be better than your sleeping at an inn'.

7 *but that can never be!*: MS omits 'but that can never be!' and Miss Tabby's next speech.

MISS T.    A letter for me, cook? bless me, who can this be from! (*opens letter*) Mercy
15  on me, anonymous.

LUCRE.    A nouny mouse letter to Miss Tabby—how partick'larly shocking, I must
tell all the young ladies. (*aside*)

MISS T.    Let me peruse its contents. (*reads*)

'Respected madam, as a friend to female innocence, it is my duty to inform you, that
20  a plan is laid to carry off one of your young ladies to-night, by a notorious libertine,
who will scale your garden wall, for that purpose! You will, therefore, take such
steps as you may think advisable, to foil his base intentions—Anti-Tarquin,' I am
paralyzed.

LUCRE.    How monstratiously horrid—let me go and tell all the young ladies,
25  directly. (*Exit* LUCRETIA)

EM.    What a romantic adventure!

ISA.    Very kind of Anti-Tarquin, I'm sure, to let you know, my dear governess—
though, perhaps, the young lady mayn't think so. What's to be done?

MISS T.    Ah! what, indeed, my dear girls—and not a man in the house to protect us!
30  EM.    Oh! yes!—there is my father—and my dear Mr Snodgrass!

ISA.    And pray don't forget Mr Winkle—the most renowned shot in Berkshire—and
our boy, Joe—who fortunately has got the gentlemen's fire-arms with him—ready
for to-morrow's sporting.

MISS T.    I breathe again—run, my dear girl, summon them to my aid, in this terrible
35  emergency.

ISA.    I will, I will! (*Exit* ISABELLA)

MISS T.    I wonder which of the young ladies it can be—is it Miss Biggs? or perhaps,
it's Miss Sims, she's rather forward; or more likely it's Miss Shufflebottom!—only let
me find out who it is, and she shall have black marks and double lessons for a
40  month to come—she shall, the hussey; disgracing Dilworth House establishment in
this manner.

EM.    Calm yourself, dear madam, you have luckily made the discovery of this atro-
cious plot just in time—oh, here comes my father and the interesting Augustus.

*Enter* ISABELLA, *with* WARDLE, SNODGRASS, *and* WINKLE—FAT BOY *and*
LUCRETIA *with poker.*

16  *letter to...shocking*: MS omits 'letter to...shocking'.

19  *Let me peruse...female innocence*: MS omits 'Let me peruse its contents,' the sd, and 'as a friend to
female innocence'.

22  *Anti-Tarquin*: The reference is to the story of Sextus Tarquinius, son of the last king of Rome, and his
rape of Lucretia, the wife of his cousin, which supposedly precipitated the rebellion that brought about the
Roman Republic.

24  *monstratiously*: MS omits 'monstratiously'.

28  *What a romantic... What's to be done?*: MS omits both girls' speeches.

33  *the most renowned...sporting*: MS omits 'the most renowned shot in Berkshire' and 'sporting'.

36  *I breathe...I will, I will!*: MS omits 'I breathe again' and 'in this terrible emergency' and Isabella's reply.

43  *I wonder which...interesting Augustus*: MS omits the speculations, reading only 'I wonder which of
the young ladies is disgracing Dilworth House in this manner,' and also omits Emily's response.

WAR.   The mousing scoundrel, but we'll tickle him—leave me to arrange it all—
   Snodgrass and Winkle, as Cookey, here, has been kind enough to provide you with   45
   those two oaken towels—you must lie in wait amongst the shrubs, that you may be
   ready to rush out and secure him when he comes.
EM.   This laurel bush, dear Augustus, will do capitally, and nothing can be more
   appropriate—you know it will divert the lightning from your brow, and guard a life
   so dear to all the Muses.   50
SNOD.   Life would be well resigned in woman's service.
EM.   Yes, but still I'd rather you'd keep yours for my service, for all that.
ISA.   Mr Winkle can hide himself behind this cluster of bachelors' buttons; mind
   you don't run down the parsley bed, Mr Winkle.
WIN.   Never fear, miss—I love a little night sport—been out bat-shooting many a   55
   time; no bad hand, I can tell you.
MISS T.   I'm sure I don't know how I shall make you amends, Mr Wardle, you are
   indeed the preserver of innocence—the guardian of virtue in danger.
WAR.   Don't mention it, madam, I've girls of my own, you know—Joe—Joe—damn
   that boy, he's asleep again—you must keep watch behind those tulip beds—no, con-   60
   found it, we mustn't put you near any beds, or you'll go to sleep directly—behind
   that tree will do—take care of that gun, don't you know it's on half cock?
LUCRE.   Mercy on me! a gun on half cock, in Dilworth House, how partik'larly
   shocking.
WAR.   Mind, neither of you go off now; to be sure it's only loaded with sparrow shot,   65
   merely give you a slight peppering.
F. BOY.   I'll take care, master.
MISS T.   Cook, you must be prepared to rush out on the first alarm.
LUCRE.   Oh dear! ma'am, I darn't—I can't face a strange man, after what Handy
   Tarbin has said.   70
MISS T.   Cook, I'm surprised at your impudence! I insist upon it, or a month's warn-
   ing—go and get the boarders all ready, and be prepared to rush out at their head, on
   the first alarm, to strike him with terror.
WAR.   Yes, if the presence of so many petticoats at one time don't frighten him, I
   don't know what will—Tupman would be just in his element.   75
EM.   Dear papa, you must remain indoors with us, to take care of us.
ISA.   I don't see the danger myself.

47 *as Cookey... when he comes*: MS omits 'as Cookey... towels' and 'when he comes'.

52 *brow... for all that*: MS inserts 'sacred' before 'brow' but cuts the final clause, Snodgrass's speech, and Emily's reply.

56 *cluster... I can tell you*: MS has 'clump' for 'cluster' and omits the warning about the parsley bed, and Winkle's boast in reply.

58 *I'm sure... virtue in danger*: MS substitutes 'to thank you' for 'I shall make you amends' and ends the speech after 'Mr Wardle'.

62 *Joe—damn that boy... half cock?*: MS omits 'Joe—damn that boy, he's asleep again', 'confound it', 'directly' and 'don't you know it's on half cock?' and therefore also the cook's speech.

67 *master*: MS has a long cut here, from this point to Wardle's speech beginning 'Now, then'.

WAR.    Aye—aye—but come, time's getting on, take your places; no doubt this terrible Giovanni will soon be here—how dark it is—give him a warm reception,
80  boys—don't spare your cudgels—we'll all rush out with lights, on the first alarm.

EM.    Well, it certainly is very romantic and interesting—my dear Snodgrass must
write a poem on it.

WAR.    Now, then, lie close, boys—this way, girls.

LUCRE.    What a dreadful, awful moment—I declare I'm all in a twitteration—mercy
85  on me!

(SNODGRASS *and* WINKLE *conceal themselves behind shrubs*—FAT BOY *behind tree,
where he falls asleep*—WARDLE, ISABELLA, EMILY, *and* LUCRETIA *enter house—It
has now become quite dark—Storm begins to rise*)

WIN.    (*softly to* SNODGRASS) Is that the Fat Boy, or is it the thunder, Snoddy?

SNOD.    Don't know—this is a very poetical situation—but I wish we had some gin
and water, Byron's immortal beverage! We may get the rheumatism.

WIN.    Hush! I hear footsteps—our game's breaking cover.

90  PICK.    (*to* SAM, *without, softly*) Just assist me up, and then return to the inn, and wait
for me till my return.

SAM.    (*without, cautiously*) Certainly, sir.

PICK.    Now, then, lay hold of my leg, and when I say, 'over,' raise me gently.

SAM.    (*without, softly*) All right, sir, there you are.

(PICKWICK *appears, jerked over wall into garden*)

95  SAM.    (*without, softly*) You haven't hurt yourself, I hope, sir.

PICK.    I haven't hurt *myself*, but I rather think that you have hurt me—I've fallen into
a flower-bed.

SAM.    (*without, softly*) 'Love among the roses,' sir.

PICK.    For a bed of roses, it has plenty of thorns; but never mind, you be off back to
100   the inn.

SAM.    (*without*) Wery vell; vish you safe through the business, sir. (SAM *heard
departing, whistling*)

SNOD.    (*aside*) The villain's gained admission—I must get my stick ready.

---

79  *Giovanni*: Another theatrical reference, to the myth of the rake Don Juan, current in London at the
time in versions of and spin-offs from Mozart's *Don Giovanni* (Prague, 1787).

85  *What a dreadful…mercy on me*: MS simplifies to 'I declare sir I'm all in a twitter'.

85.3  *Storm*: MS omits the sd reference to 'Storm' and therefore the exchange following, down to
Pickwick's speech without.

92  *Certainly*: MS substitutes 'I will' for 'Certainly'.

98  *without…sir*: MS omits this speech. The reference is to the favourite air 'Love Among the Roses'
which was of early eighteenth-century origin but popular in the 1820s at all levels from the repertoire of the
famous tenor Braham to garlands and chapbooks and the circus ring, where it accompanied acrobatic and
equestrian performances. In 1822 Samuel Beazley used the phrase for the title of a successful operetta premiered at the English Opera House.

101.1  *Wery vell…whistling*: MS omits this speech but not the sd, and then cuts to Pickwick's 'But it's
getting'.

WIN.    (*aside*) Let me exercise my arm a little beforehand, that I may be prepared.

PICK.    I have strange misgivings—this letter that I've received from my landlady, calling upon me to fulfil my promise of marrying her—(what can the foolish 105 woman mean?) and hinting at an action for breach of promise—troubles me—I must get off of it somehow.

SNOD.    (*listening*) Perjured seducer!

WIN.    (*aside, listening*) Oh! he's an old hand at it—got twenty wives, if the truth's known, I'll be bound. 110

PICK.    But it's getting rather blusterous—I shall catch my death, if I stay here long— let me give the signal at once—it must be time!—

TRIO, PICKWICK, SNODGRASS, *and* WINKLE.

AIR 'Haydn's Surprize.'

PICK.    (*piano*)

Let me, while the coast is clear,
To the back door softly creep;
He'll the signal surely hear,                                115
If he is not fast asleep!

SNOD. *and* WIN.    (*aside*) Softly steal, the scoundrel seize!

PICK.    All's secure

SNOD. *and* WIN.    He'll find, he lies!

PICK.    Now friend Trotter, if you please! 120

SNOD. *and* WIN.    Yield dog!

PICK.    Mercy on me!

OMNES.    A surprise!

(SNODGRASS *and* WINKLE *rush out, and commence thrashing* PICKWICK, *crying,* 'Villain, robber, ravisher, seducer,' *etc.* PICKWICK *roars out,* 'Oh, Lord! murder, thieves,'—*and falls flat on his face.* WARDLE, MISS TABBY, ISABELLA, EMILY, LUCRETIA (*with a warming pan*), *and* BOARDERS, *rush out with lights, etc. The women all set up a loud scream.* FAT BOY *wakes—starts up—fires gun, and shoots* LUCRETIA *in the bustle*)

LUCRE.    Oh, Lord! Oh, Lord! that Fat Boy has shot me behind, here—I'm assassinated. 125

WAR.    Damn that boy—he's asleep again.

F. BOY.    No I ain't—the gun's waked me—I hope I've not spoilt your bum-beseen, ma'am?

---

112.2 *AIR 'Haydn's Surprize.'*: Joseph Haydn, Surprise Symphony, No. 94 in G major, second of the London Symphonies, premiered in 1791. The lines for the Pickwickians to sing fit quite well with the opening of the second movement, up to 'the surprise' itself, the sudden fortissimo chord.

MISS T.    But where is the seducer?

130  BOARDERS.    (*eagerly*) Ah! where is he!

SNOD.    He's yielded to the prowess of our arms.

WIN.    I've brought him down.

MISS T.    Dear me! I hope you havn't kill'd him—ring the alarm bell, Cook.

PICK.    (*groaning*) Don't—don't—I'm a respectable man!

135  MISS T.    How did you come in this garden?

PICK.    (*still on his face*) I am no robber—I want the lady of the house!

LUCRE.    Oh! the ferocious monster! wants Miss Tabby!

L. GIRL.    He'll be wanting us, by-and-by!—I suppose.

WAR.    Hoist the fellow up—and let's see what he's made of.—Come, friend, show

140  your face—bring the lights this way, girls!

(SNODGRASS *and* WINKLE *raise up* MR PICKWICK—EMILY *and* ISABELLA *hold lights*)

WAR., ISA., EM., SNOD., *and* WIN.    Mr Pickwick!!

*Tableau of Astonishment*

F. BOY.    What a very odd dream. (*snores*)

SNOD.    Our illustrious leader—eloping with young ladies from a boarding school—'wonderful—wonderful!—And again wonderful, out of all whooping!'

145  WIN.    The sly old fox—who'd have thought he'd been so fond of sport?

ISA.    Oh! Mr Pickwick!

EM.    Fie! Mr Pickwick!

WAR.    Who could have supposed the solid, sedate Mr Pickwick would have come poaching on the manor grounds of a Young Ladies' Boarding School—I should

150  scarcely have suspected that, even from our friend, Mr Tupman!

WIN.    I may start any game, now!

PICK.    What a trap have I fallen into. That scoundrel, Mr Trotter. You are all wrong, indeed you are—I am no seducer—no ravisher—I didn't come to run away with any young lady.

155  L. GIRL.    (*aside*) What a disappointment!

PICK.    I came to warn the lady of the house, that one of her young ladies was going to elope to-night!

MISS T.    The hussey! who with?

PICK.    Your friend, Captain Fitztory, madam!

160  MISS T.    My friend! I don't know any such person!

PICK.    Mr Jingle, then!

MISS T.    I never heard of the man!

---

132 *brought him down*: MS has a simplified form of the sd, and then cuts the dialogue to this point.

138 *He'll be wanting . . . I suppose*: MS omits this line, and all subsequent speeches for the 'L(ittle) Girl.'

141.1 *Tableau of Astonishment*: MS omits sd and next three speeches, then has 'all' cry 'Mr Pickwick' and cuts again to his response 'What a trap' etc.

158 *MISS T*: MS omits her speech, running Pickwick's explanation on.

WAR.    I see how it is—you've been hoaxed, friend Pickwick. I will answer for my
friend, madam—he is incapable of doing any of you any harm.

L. GIRL.    Then there'll be no eloping, after all—we've been hoaxed—la! how 165
provoking! (*aside*)

WAR.    But come, the night air's cool—let's in doors, and laugh at this affair, over a
glass of your ginger wine ma'am—we've got to get ready for the Fancy Breakfast, in
the morning, you know, friends.

F. BOY.    (*yawns*) I hopes it won't be a fancy breakfast—'cos I'm very hungry—it quite 170
keeps me awake.

WAR.    Come, this way!—this way!

PICK.    Oh! my poor bones. I shan't get over it for a month—that villain,
Jingle! (*Exeunt* OMNES, *into house*)


## SCENE 5

*Tap Room of the Town Arms Inn.*

*Enter* SAM, R., *smoking a pipe, with a pot in his hand.*

SAM.    I vonder how the gowernor 'as got on by this ere time—with his assigna- 1
tion—I dare say he's in rare clover, now—all the young ladies makin much on
him, for presarwing their honour—shouldn't mind if I vas in his sitevation. I can't
find that ere young Chelsea vater vorks, Mr Job Trotter, any vere; he's given us the
slip quvite, all in a hurry, as they says at the Old Bailey. The ancient, too, hasn't 5
attended his appintment neither, he vas to come arter he'd put up his horses, and
have a little bit of tattle over old family affairs;—I don't like to puff my yard of clay
in my own company, as it vere, Pewter don't relish half so vell, ven von ain't got a
pal to bite his name in it as vell as vonself—but stop, I am magging too fast, for
here he is.                                                                          10

*Enter* OLD WELLER, L.

OLD W.    Vell, Samivel, here I am agin—got to the end of my stage—put up my prads,
and come back here to have a little comfortable talk vith you; it is quvite a hoint-
ment for the eyes to see you—vy I aint seed you for two years and better.

163 *you've...Pickwick*: MS omits 'you've...Pickwick'.
168 *ma'am*: MS omits the rest of this speech and Fat Boy's interjection.

  3 *I dare say...sitevation*: MS omits 'I dare say...sitevation'.
  5 *Trotter...quvite*: MS omits 'Trotter' and 'quvite' and ends the speech at 'Bailey'.
  9 *yard of clay...magging*: A 'yard of clay' is a long clay pipe; Pewter here means an alcoholic drink,
from the mugs used in public houses, named after the soft metal they were made of, which could presumably be soft enough to mark with the teeth; 'magging' means talking idly, a fast slang usage in 1830, now
chiefly Australian.
  13 *vy I aint...better*: MS simplifies this speech from 'stage': 'I wants to have some talk; I haven't seen you
for two years, and better.'

SAM.    No more you have, old feller; but come, you must have a bit of veed, and mois-
15    ten your thorax out of this ere tankard—it vill make your throat vork all the easier—
nothin' like vaterin the roads,—here, Tom Pots,—(*calling*)—bring a Broseley here.

*Enter* POT BOY, *with pipe*, R.

SAM.    That'll do, Tommy; I'll owe you for it. (*Exit* POT BOY) Now, then, Mr Veller,
senior, ve're on equal terms, so ve can fire away; but stay, first take a pull at this 'ere
home brewed.
20    OLD W.    Here's tovards your good health, Samivel.
SAM.    Thank'ye, let me illuminate you. (OLD WELLER *lights his pipe by* SAM'S, *and
begins smoking*)
SAM.    I quvite forgot, in our little miscellaneous conwersation, this morning, old
codger, to ax you about mother-in-law; how is she?
OLD W.    Vy, I tell you vhat, Sammy, there never vas a nicer ooman, as a vidder, than
25    that 'ere second wenture o' mine! a sveet creater she vas, Sammy, and all I can say on
her now, is, that as she vas sich an unkimmon pleasant vidder, it's a great pity she
ever changed her position! she don't act as a vife, Sammy.
SAM.    Don't she, though.
OLD W.    No, she's too much in the angel line—she's too good a creeter for me,
30    Sammy, I feel I don't desarve her.
SAM.    That's wery self-denying of you.
OLD W.    Wery! she's got hold o' some new inwention for grown up people being born
agin, Sammy, the new birth, I thinks they call it—I should wery much like to see
your mother-in-law born agin—vouldn't I put her out to nurse—vhat d'ye think
35    she did t'other day?
SAM.    Don't know—vhat?
OLD W.    Vy, blow me if she didn't go and get up a tea-drinking party for a feller they
calls the Shepherd; to raise subscriptions! and vhat d'ye think they vere for?
SAM.    Can't guess.
40    OLD W.    To pay his vater-rate—three quvarters; the Shepherd hadn't paid a farden,
so they cut it off; perhaps he didn't drink out of that 'ere tap, but more t'other.
SAM.    No doubt on't.
OLD W.    This Shepherd is von of those fellers that prowides the infant negroes in the
Vest Inges with flannel veskits and moral pocket ankerchiefs. I vas a standin' starin'

16 *but come…roads*: MS omits 'but come…veed' and 'it vill…roads.' A Broseley, named after the
Shropshire town where they were made from the seventeenth century to 1960, was a disposable item, a clay
pipe sold in pubs ready filled with tobacco.

17 *Exit* POT BOY: MS cuts from here to Sam saying 'I quite forgot to ax you about mother-in-law'. At this
date mother-in-law meant stepmother.

24 *Sammy*: MS cuts from here to 'she don't act as a vife, Sammy', omits the next three speeches, and
picks up at Old Weller's 'she's got hold,' cuts after 'agin' to 'nurse'.

38 *subscriptions*: MS cuts from here and Sam's response, includes Old Weller's 'To pay his vater-rate' but
then cuts again to his next speech, beginning 'He's one of those fellers'.

44 *Vest Inges with flannel veskits*: MS has 'Iondies' for 'Inges' and 'shirts' for 'veskits'.

in at the picture shop down at our place vhen I sees a little bill about it—'Tickets 45
half-a-crown—all applications to be made to the committee—secretary, Mrs
Veller!'—and vhen I got home there vas the committee sittin' in our back parlour;
all a passin' resolutions, and woting supplies—vhen expectin' to see all sorts of
games I vas gammoned to put my name down for a ticket, and at six o'clock on
Friday evening I goes vith the old ooman, and valks up into a first floor, vhere there 50
vas tea things for thirty—presently in comes a fat chap in black, with a great vhite
face and red nose, smiling away like clock vork, and cries, 'Here's the Shepherd,
come a wisiting his faithful flock!' and then round vent the kiss of peace.

SAM.    That is to say, a kiss a-piece! I s'pose, vell, that vosn't so much a miss.

OLD W.    So I thought—vell, arter that comes the tea; I vish you could ha' seed the 55
Shepherd walking into the ham and muffins, Sammy—then he began to preach, and
looking wery hard at me, hollows out—'Vhere's the sinner—vhere's the miserable
sinner?'—vhereupon, my blood being up, as he vouldn't make any apology, but
calls me a wessel of wrath, I lends him two or three for himself, with a little-un in,
for his deputy, and valks quvietly off.                                              60

SAM.    And wery proper; mend your draught.

OLD W.    Confound him—morning, noon, and night, is he drinking pineapple rum-
and-vater, vith your mother-in-law, in the Markis o' Granby. Capital hand at
accounts, he is—borrows eighteen pence on Monday, and comes on Tuesday for a
shilling, to make it half-a-crown—calls agin on Vednesday for another half- 65
a-crown, to make it five shillings, and goes on doubling, till he gets it up to a five
pound note in no time.

SAM.    And you lets him. (*knocking the ashes out of his pipe*) I am ashamed on you,
old two for his heels.

OLD W.    Vy, vhat can I do—I am a married man, Samivel—yes, a married man!— 70
and ven you are married, Samivel, you'll understand a good many things as you
don't understand now; but vether it's vorth vhile going through so much to larn so
little, is a matter of taste—I don't think it is.

SAM.    I can't say, for I ain't tried; but come, the pot's out, and so is my pipe.

OLD W.    Vell, then, I'll bid you good bye, Samivel: ve shall meet again in Lunnon— 75
Belle Savage tap—you must come and see us at the Markiss o' Granby, Samivel.

---

46 *I vas…applications*: MS omits 'I vas…half-a-crown' and inserts 'for tickets' after 'all applications.' It
then cuts 'and vhen I got home…games' and 'presently' to the end of the speech, substituting 'and the
Shepherd came a wisiting his faithful flock and then the kiss of peace vent round.' Sam's response is cut, and
Old Weller's next speech reduced to 'I vish you could ha' seen the Shepherd walking into the ham and muffins, Sammy.'

61 *mend your draught*: 'mend your draught' because his pipe is going out.

64 *Capital hand at accounts*: MS omits 'Capital hand at accounts'.

67 *a five pound note*: MS has 'five pounds' for 'a five pound note'.

69 *two for his heels*: The reference is to scoring in the card game cribbage, where the dealer records 'two
for his heels' if the first card turned up is a jack.

70 *vhat can I do*: MS omits the rest of the speech.

74 *for I ain't tried*: MS omits 'for I ain't tried'.

SAM.    Aye—aye! ta ta, old boy, till ve meets again—all I've got to say, is this here; if I
vas the properiator of the Markiss o' Granby, and that ere Shepherd came looking arter
my lamb, or mutton, vhatever you call it, I'd poison his rum and vater, that's all.

80 OLD W.    No, vould you, really—vould you, though?

SAM.    I vould! but I vouldn't be too hard upon him at first—I'd jist drop him in the
vater-butt, and put the lid on, and then if I found he vas insensible to kindness, I'd
try t'other persvasion.

OLD W.    You're your father's own boy, Samivel, and I'll contemplate the motion all
85   the vay, as I goes up to Lunnon, so ta ta!  (*Exit L.*)

SAM.    He's a good old cock, he is; though he shouldn't let the hen crow over him as
she does. Vell, I'll go and git everything ready for this ere fancy breakfast—ve shall
have the gowernor coming back soon—I shall go as Teddy O'Carroll, the Donnybrook
Braham—vot I met on the race-course, ven I vas helper to Charley Sveatemvell, the
90   trainer; and give the gentlefolks a specimen of my crochets and quavers; and by vay
of a vind up, I shall clap my devil's horns and tail and pitchfork into my pocket, for
I daresay I sha'n't vant an opportunity of using 'em.  (*Exit L.*)

## SCENE 6

MRS LEO HUNTER's *Grounds, The Den, Eatanswill, fitted up for Fete Champetre.*
VISITORS *discovered, in various fancy dresses.*

### SONG AND CHORUS, OMNES
AIR 'Now by the waving greenwood tree.'

1                Under the waving greenwood tree,
                    We merry, merry mortals haste;
                    Hungry and thirsty, who but we,
                    The ham and tea to taste.
5              Then away to the breakfast, away, away,
                    Hang those of care who think;
                Let all be Fancy, here to-day,
                    Except what we eat and drink!
                    Under the waving greenwood tree, etc.

*Enter* MR *and* MRS LEO HUNTER, *the latter as Minerva.*

---

80  OLD W: MS omits this speech and the next.
90  *though he…trainer*: MS omits 'though he…as she does' and 've shall…the trainer'.
91  *devil's horns*: MS inserts 'on' here, and 'put my' before 'pitchfork'.

0.4  AIR *'Now by the waving greenwood tree.'*: MS omits the song. It seems to be a parodic version of a
current street song, whose model appears on a Catnach broadside dated [1830] by the British Library.
A copy is available at <http://clio.lib.olemiss.edu/u?/kgbroadsides,1087>.

MRS L. H.    Delightful—delightful! one foreign lion, Count Smorltauk, who's come    10
expressly, from Germany, to write visiting notes on England—two London lions—
the celebrated Tobacco Pipe Player, and the great Kentuckian Tragedian—all our
country lions—two or three lionesses, one a lady that has been up in a balloon, and
another, a lady that has fall'n down in one, and then the King of all the Lions, the
president of the Pickwickians and his associates!—why we shall be the envy and    15
admiration of the whole world—only want Boz to complete it—pity he wouldn't
suffer himself to be caught.

MR L. H.    It was indeed, my dear Mrs H. I tried hard enough.

MRS L. H.    You must be on the qui vive, Mr Hunter; I have issued tickets for a hundred, but you know we have only provided breakfast for fifty, so while I cater for the    20
most distinguished of our guests, in the Zoology of Fashion and Ton, you must take
care of the attendant Jackalls, in the best manner you can—but stand out of the way,
Mr Hunter—stand out of the way—here come the Pickwickians, and their president!—oh, the dear delightful man!

*Enter* PICKWICK, *arm in arm with* SNODGRASS *as Apollo, in blue and white silk,
and a Grecian helmet; holding a lyre—on one side, and* TUPMAN *as Massaroni, the
Brigand, in green velvet jacket, sugar loaf hat, and ribbons, and Alpine leggings and
rifle—on the other—followed by* WINKLE *as Actæon, with a bow and arrow, and large
pair of horns.*

MRS L. H.    My dear Mr Pickwick, for I know it is you, by your gaiters—this is kind,    25
I rejoice to see you—you must promise not to stir from my side all the morning—I
have got a hundred people to present you to.

PICK.    You are very kind, ma'am, allow me to introduce my associates;—Mr Apollo
Snodgrass—Minerva should know Apollo. (*introduces*)

MRS L. H.    A poet, delighted to make the acquaintance—you must hear my 'Ode to    30
an expiring frog.'

---

14 *one foreign lion...of all the Lions*: MS cuts 'one foreign lion...of all the Lions'.

17 *suffer himself to be caught*: MS has 'come' for 'suffer himself to be caught'. Boz is of course Moncrieff's
addition to the satire of lionization, as are the other celebrities she lists, apart from Count Smorltauk. The
tobacco pipe player is obscure, and possibly just a joke, but the Kentuckian Tragedian may be a hit at Edwin
Forrest—American but not from Kentucky—who had made a great theatrical and social hit in London over
the winter of 1836–7, and was married in London the month before this play premiered. T.D. Rice, who was
from Kentucky, had made a great stir in London theatrical circles during 1837 by his 'Jim Crow' performances in grotesque blackface.

18 *It was...hard enough*: MS omits this speech.

20 *provided breakfast*: MS has 'prepared' for 'provided breakfast' and trims the rest of the speech in
several places, cutting 'in the Zoology of Fashion and Ton', 'Jackalls', and her injunction to her husband to
'stand out of the way'. MS also replaces her exclamation about Pickwick as 'the dear delightful man' with 'I
know him by his gaiters' (transferred from her speech in greeting to him), which indicates that the recog-
nizable image of Pickwick as a little round man in gaiters was already current.

21 *in the Zoology...Ton*: MS omits 'in the Zoology of Fashion and Ton'.

27 *I have...you to*: MS omits 'I have...you to.'

30 *acquaintance*: MS cuts here and omits his response.

SNOD.    Shall be much gratified.

PICK.    This is Mr Massaroni Tupman. (*introducing*)

MRS L. H.    I doat upon bandits—I shall enlist him to dress the lobster salad for me.

35  TUP.    With pleasure—this scene of enchantment might almost make one forget even the perfidious Rachel—heigho!

PICK.    (*introducing* WINKLE) This is Mr Actæon Winkle, the celebrated sportsman, madam; he would have worn a red hunting coat to be more in character, but he thought it made him look too much like a general postman.

40  MRS L. H.    He is fit to belong to the most noble order of the Bucks—I must know him better.

WIN.    You are very good ma'am—I wish that Jacob Nathan had given me a little more hunting room in these satin tights—confound me if I can hardly move in them—too tight by a great deal. (*aside*)

45  MRS L. H.    But come, friends, you must want some refreshments, and then I have to show you over the grounds—I've just had a new pile of old ruins erected, and a beautiful imitation cataract painted in water colours—I must trouble the bandit, here, to take care of my ridicule! Apollo, will you carry my sal volatile, as your prototype used to do for Daphne, formerly.

50  SNOD.    I shall be delighted.

MRS L. H.    Now, then, this way—this way!

(*Exit* MRS LEO HUNTER, *with* MR PICKWICK *and* TUPMAN, SNODGRASS *and* WINKLE)

*Enter* ISABELLA *and* EMILY—*the former as Cicely Homespun—the latter as Margaret Finch, the Queen of the Gypsies.*

ISA.    There they are. We have only now to watch our opportunity.

EM.    Augustus cannot detect me, now I have stained my cheeks.

ISA.    And this flaxen wig will effectually conceal me. Father will be too much taken
55  up with the novelty of the scene, to observe us, and Joe will either be eating or asleep.

EM.    Hush! away, my dear Bella—here my Apollo comes! Now, then, in telling his fortune, to learn my own.

ISA.    I'll not interfere with you. I must go and hunt up my sportsman. The stars
60  befriend you, Emmy! (*Exit* ISABELLA)

EM.    'Tis a bold step—but love dares all! Oh, Snodgrass! Snodgrass! (*retires a little on one side*)

*Re-enter* SNODGRASS.

---

36  *With pleasure...heigho*: MS omits this speech and Pickwick's remarks on Winkle's coat.
40  *Bucks*: MS ends the speech here, and omits Winkle's response and aside.
45  *refreshments*: MS ends the speech here, and omits the response.
59  *ISA*: MS begins the girls' lines here, and substitutes 'Emily' for 'Emmy'.

SNOD.  I'm glad I've got out of that refreshment room—couldn't fancy it Olympus, at all. A very anti-poetical person, that Mrs Hunter. While I was talking of the Heliconian Fountain—hang me if she didn't ask me to put some water in the pot— and instead of the Muses, wanted to stuff me with muffins.                    65

EM.  Now for it!—(*comes forward and curtsies*) Noble Apollo, spare the poor gipsey a halfpenny—have your fortune told, Celetial sir?

SNOD.  Eh! Apollo have his fortune told—No, 'tis too wild a fiction. But poetry delights in fiction.

EM.  Cross the poor gipsey's hand with a bit of silver—heavenly gentleman—it is a  70
Queen that asks you!—

SNOD.  A Queen! dark ministress of fate?

EM.  Yes, Margaret Finch, Mr Apollo.

SNOD.  But I don't think I've got any money—neither Apollo, nor his sons ever have, I believe. Let me feel in the pockets of my under waistcoat—there, Mrs Finch—  75
there's a fourpenny piece for you.—Now then, invoke the stars, and mind, as I've proved myself a goldfinch, that you don't turn out a *chaff*-finch.

EM.  La! your Godship!—do you think I could do so?—Ha!—by the lines in your palm, I perceive that you do not love true!

SNOD.  And by the line you're getting me in, I can perceive that you do not tell true,  80
brown Sybil.—I am as true as the great Bear is to the Pole.

EM.  And he's very true—anybody that's seen him in the Regent's Park, can tell that—but are you not playing one of Apollo's attributes, the lyre!

SNOD.  No, by great Jove—Oh! Emily! Emily! there is no joy without thee!

EM.  He loves me, and I am happy!—(*aside*)—I did this but to try you!—The lines of  85
life run smooth, Apollo—yours will be a happy destiny. She you love will well requite your truth—you will have riches—honours—

SNOD.  And children!

EM.  Oh, fie! My art does not extend so far as that.

SNOD.  Nay, gipsey, I must know!                                                    90

EM.  Then I must fly—his questions grow embarrassing, (*aside*) good morning, son of Jove—Jupiter wants you. (*Exit* EMILY, *hastily*)

SNOD.  Gone—confusion!—I've not learnt half I wanted—I havn't had twopennorth of prediction for my money. Mrs Finch! Mrs Finch!

---

62  *refreshment room*: MS ends the speech here.

67  *spare…halfpenny*: MS omits 'spare…halfpenny' and cuts Snodgrass's line.

70  *heavenly gentleman*: MS omits from here to Snodgrass's 'But I don't think'.

75  *neither Apollo…I believe*: MS substitutes 'in pockets, I suppose these troubadours didn't want any' for 'neither Apollo…I believe' and leaves out his handing over the fourpenny piece.

78  *La! your Godship!*: MS omits this exclamation, and the palm reading, amending 'Do you think I could do such a thing? I perceive that you do not love truly—' His response begins at 'I am as true…'

82  *can tell*: MS ends the speech here with 'you so' instead of 'that'.

84  *Jove*: MS omits the invocation of Jove.

86  *I did this but…Apollo*: MS omits 'I did this but…Apollo'.

89  *so far as that*: MS cuts to her exit.

94  *I havn't…money*: MS omits 'I havn't…money'.

(*Exit* SNODGRASS, *after* EMILY)
Enter SAM, *as Teddy O'Carrol, the Donnybrook Braham, a race-course ballad singer.*

95    SAM.    A pretty trick that onion-headed feller, Mr Job Trotter, has play'd my gowernor—I've bin reg'larly done by that ere chap—I must return him his shuttlecock
somehow—it strikes me wery sing'lar, that he and his precious master vill be comin
here—as they seems to admit all sorts of quveer cattle—and p'raps I may have an
opportunity of repayin 'em in Irish money, thirteen pence for their shilling—who
100    knows—they von't have any suspicion of me, in this ere dress. Vell, if I aint as good
as Nixon, the Cheshire conjuror! Here they are!

Enter JINGLE, *as Don Giovanni, and* JOB TROTTER, *as Doctor Cantwell.*

JIN.    Ha! ha! ha!—Capital trick—very!—wonder how old Fire-works likes it.
SAM.    (*aside*) Old Fire-works—the warmints—but I'll pay 'em off.
TROT.    And that Johnny Raw of a servant of his, who wanted to make a handle of
105    me—but the pump was dry—and all the water is in my eye. I wonder where he
is now?
SAM.    (*aside*) Johnny Raw!—I'm not raw, now. No! no! I've bin done rayther too
much—vhants to know vhere I am—they'll find that out, soon enough. (*comes
forward as Ballad Singer, singing*)

Oh, dear! vhat can the matter be,
110        Dear, dear, vhat can the matter be,
Oh, dear! vhat can the matter be,
Johnny's so long at the fair!
He promised, etc.

(*Dances grotesquely, then offers ballads to* JINGLE *and* TROTTER)

Buy a ballad, your honours, of Teddy O'Carrol! Here's 'Ve met,'—'Over the
115    Mountains,'—'The Old Maid,'—'Nothing like Money,'—'Oh, Cruel,'—'He Loves,

---

94.2 *Donnybrook Braham*: Donnybrook Fair was the great meeting for marketing and latterly pleasure—drinking, gambling, singing, and especially dancing—outside Dublin from the thirteenth century
onwards, abolished as riotous in the 1850s. John Braham, 1774–1856, was the leading tenor in England in the
1820s, and in 1835 built the St James's Theatre.

98 *p'raps*: MS begins the speech here, cutting 'money' and changing 'pence for their shilling' to 'to the
dozen for the trick he played on Mr Pickwick at the Boarding School.' The next sentence is omitted, and
'like' substituted for 'as good as' and 'prophet' for 'conjurer.' 'Here they are' is omitted.

101 *Nixon, the Cheshire conjuror!*: Dickens mentions Nixon, the author of a chapbook of prophecies
first published in 1714, in chapter 43, when Sam is getting his father to commit him to the debtor's prison.

101.1 *Don Giovanni…Doctor Cantwell*: For Don Giovanni see n.79 p.60. Dr Cantwell is the leading character from Bickerstaffe's *The Hypocrite*, a translation of Molière's *Tartuffe*, first staged at Drury Lane in 1769.

105 *handle of me*: MS omits the rest of the speech.

107 *I'm not raw, now*: MS omits the rest of the speech and the sd description of him 'as Ballad
Singer'.

and Rides avay,'—'The Conwict's Return,'—'Strike the Liar,'—and 'The Rogues March.'

JIN.    March!—hop, skip, jump—vagrant act—stocks, whipping post—interruption—busy—very!—hate singing—out of tune—no time—penny—by-and bye—come again—generous—very!    120

SAM. (*singing*)

> Oh, come to me when day-light sets,
> Sweet, oh, come to me!
> Vhile sveetly go our gondolets,
> Over the moonlight sea! etc.
>                 Tol lol de lol, etc. (*dances as before*)    125

JIN.    Off, Vagabond—now for Mrs Hunter—fresh gull—Don Giovanni—new victim—good chance—Doctor Cantwell—deep plan—very!

SAM.    I'll not lose sight on 'em. (*aside*)

(*sings*)        They brought him back, and then they found
            The spoons on this Nice Young Man, etc.    130

(*Exit* JINGLE *and* TROTTER, *annoyed, followed by* SAM, *singing*)
*Enter* ISABELLA, *followed by* WINKLE.

WIN.    All's game with a sportsman, you know, my love—that is, that's fair—Devils of fellows—can't help it—I may bounce a bit, here, with this rustic. (*aside*) Must have a kiss—all prim'd!

ISA.    Oh fie, sir!—but what will your sweetheart, at home, say?

WIN.    Like me all the better for it—fond of spirit—but won't know it—poor thing—  135 glad to have me—come, one kiss—give it at once, my pretty partridge, or I shall take a brace—licensed to kill!

ISA.    (*aside*) The impudent rogue—but I'm glad to find he can be gallant sometimes—wouldn't give a pin for a man that wasn't a little bit of a rake. But people will see us, here!—Look, they're all coming to begin the dancing.    140

---

117 *Buy a ballad… 'The Rogues March'.*: MS omits the list of wares and the dance, and abbreviates Jingle's following speech to 'penny—by and bye—come again'.

124 *Over the moonlight sea! etc.*: The list of songs Sam has to sell is miscellaneous, not all broadside ballads, and this example is by Thomas Moore, published in *National Airs* in 1818. The following couplet, however, is a snatch from a broadside, probably of the 1820s, which was reprinted by John Ashton in his *Modern Street Ballads* in 1888 and is now available online: <http://www.staggernation.com/msb/he_was_such_a_nice_young_man.php>. MS omits the sd to dance.

127 *Doctor Cantwell*: MS substitutes 'never suspect' for 'Doctor Cantwell'.

130.2 *Enter* ISABELLA, *followed by* WINKLE: MS omits this episode between Isabella and Winkle, resuming with the entrance of Mrs Leo Hunter etc.

WIN.    Little Innocent! we must be partners, never leave a pretty girl—too good a
sportsman for that.

ISA.    If you could meet me, now, at my father's.

WIN.    With all my heart, my rosebud—I'll beat the bushes in no time—but you must
145    give me your name, and where you live.

ISA.    I've got it all written down, in large hand, on a card, if you please, sir!

WIN.    Cream of the valley—Homespun Cottage, I suppose—Claybottom,
Muddington—Eh! what's this? (*reads*) 'Isabella Wardle, Dingley Dell,'—Trapp'd—
Caught—I'd give the world to be under a haycock! Miss Isabella Wardle. I—that is,
150    you—Oh Lord! I can't stand it any longer. (*runs off*)

ISA.    Ha! ha! ha! a pretty sportsman, but I've brought him down—though I havn't
done with him yet—Mr Winkle—Mr Winkle. (*Exit following him, and calling*)

*Enter* MRS LEO HUNTER *with* MR PICKWICK, WARDLE, SNODGRASS, EMILY, *in
Domino,* FAT BOY, *as the living skeleton, and Fancy Characters.*

MRS L. H.    Now then, friends, the dance—the dance.

EM.    Aye, the dance! I have eluded Augustus—this domino will enable me still to
155    enjoy the dance—(*aside*)—aye, the dance.

SONG, EMILY.

AIR 'The Cachuca'

Now to the castanet, merrily sounding,
        Dance the Cachuca, in smiling array;
Not even Duvernay, lightest when bounding,
        Shall, than ourselves, be more buoyant and gay;
160    Then join the Cachuca—la ra, la la!
        Dance, ere the sun seeks his home in the west,
        For hearts now are lightest,
        And eyes now are brightest,
        And pleasure and love, in each bosom, are guest!

165    Now while the breeze is with melody laden,
        And sighing with transport, each love-stricken youth,
Breathes a sweet tale in the ear of his maiden,
        Painting his passion, his hopes, and his truth
Dance the Cachuca—la ra, la la!
170        Each with the partner he worships the best.
        Hearts now are lightest,
        Eyes now are brightest!
Dancing in daylight robs no one of rest.

152.2 *SNODGRASS...living skeleton*: MS omits the Fat Boy.

155.2 *AIR 'The Cachuca'*: The Spanish dance, as Moncrieff's words suggest, was the basis of a set piece
introduced in the 1830s into many performances by the ballet dancer Pauline Duvernay. MS omits the song.

(*All the characters join in Pas Generale,* MRS LEO HUNTER *with* MR PICKWICK—
SNODGRASS *with* EMILY—WINKLE *who has re-entered, with* ISABELLA—
MR TUPMAN *with a* NUN, FAT BOY *with* COLUMBINE, *etc.*)
*Re-enter* JINGLE *and* JOB TROTTER.

JIN.     Ah! dear Minerva—charming Hunter, glad to see you—glorious scene—
         Eastern splendour—crowds of people—full grounds—regular Mangle—Walker's    175
         patent—hard work—very!
MRS L. H.    Well, this is apropos—we were just wishing for you, my dear Captain
         Fitztory, allow me to introduce you to my friends.
ISA.     (*screams*) Ha! the villain that carried off my aunt.
EM.      Horrible monster!                                                          180
PICK.    Jingle, here—he is an impostor!
JIN.     Allow me an explanation, Miss Emily—Miss Isabella—you're all deceived—very.
EM.      Stand off, sir.
PICK.    Secure him—duck him—the pump—the horsepond!

FINALE, OMNES.

AIR 'The quick part of the Finale to the first act of Cinderella.'

PICK.          Villain utter not a single syllable,                                 185
               But from this chosen spot directly fly.
EM.            Oh, sirs, protect us, do not forsake us,
               On your protection we do rely.
SNOD.          Dear ladies, fear not, harm you, he dare not;
               On our protection you may rely.                                      190
WAR.           Shall my authority be disregarded?
               Off rogue and vagabond—oh fie, oh fie!
GUESTS.        Off to the watchhouse, for time quick flies!
               If he resists us, the horsepond is nigh.
SERVANTS.      No more disputing, if he denies,                                     195
               Call the police in—don't let the rogue fly.

(*Towards the end of this finale,* SAM *comes in as the Devil, with pitchfork etc., and squibs
off* TROTTER *and* JINGLE. *Drop falls in confusion*)

END OF ACT II

---

176 *Walker's patent*: Dickens mentions Baker's patent mangle, which was a well-known brand, but
Moncrieff has substituted, perhaps accidentally, the name 'Walker', which was attached to many patents
for modern appliances in the period.
    180 *Charming Hunter...Horrible Monster!*: MS omits 'charming Hunter...Horrible Monster!'
    183 *Stand off, sir*: MS omits Emily's line.
    184.2 *AIR '...Cinderella.'*: Rossini's *La Cenerentola* (Rome, 1817) was popular in England from 1820.

# ACT III

## SCENE 1

*Common Room in the Great White Horse Inn, Ipswich.*

PICKWICK, SNODGRASS, WINKLE, *and* TUPMAN *discovered.*

GLEE, PICKWICKIANS
AIR 'Glorious Apollo'

1        Jove born Minerva, from on high survey'd us,
        Yearned to found a CLUB, to wisdom's praise,
        Sent noble PICKWICK, hither to aid us,
        Crowning our temples with unfading bays,
5        Thus when combining—heart and hand joining,
        Sing we in harmony, Mister Pickwick's praise!

PICK.    Well, here we are, in the Great White Horse at Ipswich—wish we were coursing to run down some better game than this vagabond, Jingle, though.

SNOD.    Right! right! but cui boni?—to what good will be our pursuit, chief?

10 PICK.    Why, how do we know whom he may deceive next, has he not already deceived a worthy man?—and we the innocent cause—he shall not do so again if I can help it—we've got a clue to him, and I'll expose him everywhere—I'll teach him to call me Old Fireworks!

TUP.    I will go with you to the end of the world, and further!—Oh, Rachel, Rachel!

15 SNOD.    We will all follow our illustrious leader—assured of Emily's affections, I can dare all. But hadn't we better see after dinner? it's half-past eight o'clock. I'll step in and order it.

WIN.    Not a poetical one, I hope, I've a sporting appetite.

SNOD.    Don't be afraid: poets are generally pretty sharp set. Shall order something light,

20    though—turtle—salmon—saddle of mutton—broiled fowl and mushrooms—five of champagne—cranberry tart—parmesan—port—pippins—that's all.

TUP.    My soul's too much to let me eat, but think I can manage the saddle of mutton.

---

0.3 *GLEE, PICKWICKIANS*: MS omits the song. Moncrieff modelled the lyric closely upon Samuel Webbe's original, written in 1787, and the anthem of the gentlemen's glee club—as Dickens knew when he named Dick Swiveller's little company after it, in *The Old Curiosity Shop*.

11 *and we…cause*: MS omits 'and we…cause'.

14 *I will go…Rachel, Rachel*: MS omits this speech and curtails the next, then cuts from Winkle's 'Not a poetical one…' to his '…this way!'

WIN.   Come along and have a glass of sherry and bitters, to tone our stomachs. I must stick up to Bella Wardle, now, or own my gallantry—all brag! She's fairly 25 bagg'd me, the baggage—this way.

PICK.   I'll follow you directly—mind, we sleep here to-night. I'll merely give my servant, Sam, a few directions—I see him coming. (*Exit*)

SNOD.   Great man! President of all—we'll wait for you. This way, associates of my toil and fame. 30

(*Exeunt* SNODGRASS, TUPMAN, *and* WINKLE)
*Enter* SAM *and* OLD WELLER.

PICK.   Well, now, Sam?

SAM.   Beg your pardon, sir, but the old un here vants to know if he's to book you for town tomorrow?

PICK.   Not till I have discovered this abandoned Jingle, Sam, if I stay here for a century. 35

SAM.   Vell, you knows best, sir, 'cause you lived longest, as the girl said to Old Parr, vhen he axed her if she thought, living single vas good for the health.

WELL.   I could have answered him at once, Samivel, for I've been married—yes, I've done it vonce too often, Sammy—take example from your father and be wery careful o' vidders all your life—'specially if they've kept a public house, Sammy. Beg 40 your pardon, sir, I hope nothing personal—I hope you ain't got a vidder.

PICK.   Don't mention it, my good friend, though you are not so very wide of the mark—but your trouble, it seems, is because you've got a widow, mine is because I won't have one. That cursed Mrs Bardell!—she has got a couple of Qui-tam fellows, Dodson and Fogg, they call themselves 'jobbing attorneys', to bring an action for 45 breach of promise of marriage—I never promised the creature marriage—and what's worse, they have subpoenaed my very friends to appear against me!

WELL.   Widders vill do anything, sir; but I beg your pardon, sir, I forgot to speak to you about my son. I hope you've no fault to find vith Sammy.

PICK.   None, whatever. 50

WELL.   Wery glad to hear it, sir. I took a good deal o' pains with his eddication, sir— let him run in the streets vhen he was wery young and shift for hisself—it's the only way to make a boy sharp, sir.

PICK.   Won't you take anything, Mr Weller.

---

29 *SNOD*: MS omits this speech.

32 *sir, but . . . here*: MS omits 'sir, but' and then 'here'.

36 *SAM*: MS omits this speech and starts the next, Old Weller's, at 'Beg your pardon'. Old (Thomas) Parr was buried in Westminster Abbey in 1635, reputedly at the age of 152, after fathering a child out of wedlock when he was 100—which may be what Sam is hinting at in his remark about living single.

47 *she has got . . . to appear*: MS omits 'she has got . . . attorneys' and again 'I never . . . worse, they' and cuts 'very' and 'to appear'.

48 *but I . . . sir*: MS omits 'but I . . . sir'.

51 *WELL*: MS omits this speech.

55 WELL.   You're very good. Perhaps a small glass of brandy, just to drink success to
Sammy, vouldn't be amiss.

PICK.   A small glass of brandy here, waiter! (*calling*)

(WAITER *brings brandy, and exits*)

SAM.   Take care, old feller, or you'll have a touch of your old complaint, the gout,
again.

60 WELL.   I've found a sovereign cure for that, Sammy. (*bolting the brandy*)

PICK.   A sovereign cure for the gout, eh! I must note that down for the club. (*takes
out a note book*) What is it?

WELL.   Vy, this, sir—the gout is a complaint that arises from too much ease and
comfort; if ever you're attacked vith the gout, sir, jist marry a widder, as has got a
65   loud woice, vith a decent notion o' usin' it, and you'll never have the gout again; it's
a capital prescription, sir, I takes it reg'lar, and can varrant it to drive away any illness as is caused by too much jollity.

SAM.   You're a perfect wictim of connubiality, father—as Blue Beard's domestic
chaplain said, vith a tear of pity, vhen he buried him.

70 PICK.   Ha! ha! ha! (*laughs*) It's rather a novel receipt, certainly; but I must go and
join my friends—I am somewhat fatigued, and shall retire to bed early—you'll be
waiting, Sam.

SAM.   As sure as death and quarter day, sir.

PICK.   I wish you good-bye, Mr Weller; hope you'll have a speedy alleviation of your
75   domestic grievances. (*Exit*)

WELL.   That's past hopin' for, Sammy, that only rests vith the undertaker; but vhat's
that letter you're twiddling about in your hand, Sammy? 'Pursuit of knowledge
under difficulties,' eh?

SAM.   Vy, to tell you the truth, it's a letter I've been writing!

80 WELL.   Not to any young ooman I hopes, Sammy?

SAM.   Vell, it ain't no use a sayin' it ain't—it's a walentine.

WELL.   A walentine? Vhat arter the varnin' you've had o' your father's wicious per-
pensities—arter all I said to you on this 'ere wery subject—arter actually seein' and
bein' in the company of your mother-in-law, vich I should ha' thought vas a moral
85   lesson as no man cou'd ever ha' forgotten, to his dying day. I didn't think you cou'd
ha' done it, Sammy! (*puts handkerchief to his eyes*)

SAM.   Vhat's the matter now?

WELL.   Never mind, Sammy, it vill be a wery agonisin' trial to me at my time o' life—
but I'm pretty tough, that's von consolation—as the wery old turkey remarked vhen
90   the farmer said he vas afear'd he shou'd be obliged to kill him for the Lunnon
Market.

---

58 *SAM*: MS cuts from here to Pickwick's 'but I must go'.

72 *you'll be waiting, Sam*: MS omits Sam's response and Pickwick's goodbye, leaving Old Weller's speech
without reference.

82 *Vhat arter the*: MS inserts 'werry good' but then omits 'arter…seein' and 'vich I…dying day' and the sd.

87 *SAM*: MS omits this and the next speech.

SAM.    Vot'll be a trial, old double wicket?

WELL.    To see you married— to see you a deluded wictim, and thinkin' in your innocence, that's all wery capital. It's a dreadful trial to a father's feelings, that 'ere, Sammy.                                                                                         95

SAM.    Nonsense, but I know you're a judge o' these things—so I'll read you the letter.

WELL.    Vell fire away, my boy; but first ve'll have a glass of the inwairiable. Waiter!

*Enter* WAITER.

A double go of the inwairiable.

WAITER.    Yes, sir!—yes, sir!  (*Exit*)                                                        100

WELL.    They know my ways here.

*Enter* WAITER *with liquor, which he gives to* OLD WELLER, *and exits.*

Now, go on, Sammy!

SAM.    (*reads*) 'Lovely creetur, I feel myself a damned—'

WELL.    Eh, that can't be damned.

SAM.    No, it ain't damned, it's shamed, there's a blot on it. 'I feel myself ashamed—'       105

WELL.    Wery good—go on.

SAM.    'Feel myself ashamed and completely cir—' I forget vhat this 'ere vord is. (*scratching his head*) Here's another blot, let me see, here's a c and i and a d.

WELL.    Circumwented, p'raps.

SAM.    No it ain't, it's circumscribed.                                                        110

WELL.    Vell, that may be a tenderer vord. Drive on.

SAM.    'Completely circumscribed in a dressing of you, for you are a nice young girl, and nothin' but it.'

WELL.    Drive on, Sammy.

SAM.    'Afore I see you, I thought all oomen vas alike, but now I find vhat a reg'lar soft     115
headed, ink red-louse turnip I must ha' bin, for there ain't nobody like you, and I like you better than nothin' at all.' I thought it best to make that rayther strong.

WELL.    Wery good, drive on.

SAM.    'I take the priviledge of the day, Mary, my dear—as the gen'lman in difficulties did vhen he walked out on a Sunday—to tell you that the first and only time I seed     120
you, your likeness vas took on my—turn over!'

WELL.    Vhat, Sammy, took on your turn over?

---

93 *To see you married*: MS omits the rest of this speech.

103 *I feel myself a*: MS avoidance of censorable words means Sam stops here, Old W replies 'what can that be' and Sam responds 'it's ashamed' and continues an abbreviated version without all OW's interjections: 'and completely cir—I forget vhat this ere word is | OW: Circumscribed, p'rhaps | Sam: Completely circumscribed in a dressing of you, for you are a nice young gal, so I take the priviledge of the day, Mary, my dear, as the gen'lman in difficulties did, ven he valked out of a Sunday, therefore except of me, Mary, my dear, as your walentine, and think over what I've said, my dear Mary! I will now conclude.'—That's all.

120 *walked out on a Sunday*: London debtors living in the sanctuary of 'the Rules' could go out on a Sunday, when they could not be arrested.

SAM.　Yes, you alvays puts 'turn over' vhen you goes t'other side. 'Your likeness took on my—turn over—heart. Except of me, Mary, my dear, as your walentine, and
125　think over vhat I've said, my dear Mary. I vill now conclude.' That's all.

WELL.　That's rather a sudden pull up, ain't it?

SAM.　Not a bit on't, she'll vish there vas more, and that's the great art o' letter writin'.

WELL.　Vell, there's somethin' in that—and I vish your mother-in-law 'ud only con-
130　duct her conwersation on the same genteel principle. Ain't you goin' to sign it?

SAM.　That's the difficulty, I don't know vhat to sign it!

WELL.　Sign it Veller.

SAM.　Von't do. Never sign a walentine vith your own name!

WELL.　Sign it Pickvick, then—it's a wery good name, and wery easy to spell.
135　P-i-k-v-i-k.

SAM.　The wery thing, I could end with a werse, couldn't I? Vhat do you think?

WELL.　I don't like it, Sammy. I never know'd a respectable coachman as wrote poetry, 'cept von as wrote an affectin' copy of werses the night afore he vas hung for a highvay robbery; but he vas only a Camberwell man, so even that's no rule.

140　SAM.　No matter, I must end with a werse, so here goes. (*writes*)

'Your lovesick Pick-vick.' Now then, to direct it. (*writes*)

'To Mary, 'Ousemaid at Mr Waddles, Manor Farm, Dingley Dell.' There, that'll do.

WELL.　Vell, now then, vy, as you consulted me—now, to vhat I vanted to consult you about, Samivel; it's a pint of domestic policy—this 'ere Stiggins, the Shepherd.

145　SAM.　The red-nosed man that I seed when I wisited mother-in-law at Dorking?

WELL.　The wery same; this 'ere red-nosed man, Sammy, wisits your mother-in-law, vith a kindness and constancy, as I never seed eqvalled! he's sitch a friend o' the family, Sammy, that vhen he's avay from us, he can't be comfortable, unless he has something to remember us by.

150　SAM.　I'd give him something as ud turpentine and beesvax his memory for the next ten years or so, if I vas you.

WELL.　Stop a minute, I vas going to say—he alvays brings a flat bottle as holds about a pint and a half vith him, and fills it vith pineapple-rum afore he goes avay—

SAM.　And empties it afore he comes back, I supposes—

155　WELL.　Clean! Never leaves nothin' in it but the cork and the smell—trust him for that, Sammy. Now these 'ere fellows, my boy, are a goin' to get up the monthly mee-tin' o' the United Grand Junction Ebenezer Temperance Society! your mother-in-law vas to be there, Sammy, but she's got the rheumatics and can't—and I, Sammy, I've got the two tickets as vas sent her.

160　SAM.　Vot are you vinking your right eye for, have you got the ticdoloreux in it?

WELL.　No, no! this is it. You and I vill go punctuval to the time; the Shepherd von't (*laughs*) Ha, ha, ha!

126　*That's rather … ain't it?*: MS cuts to 'you goin' to sign it?'
135　*P-i-k-v-i-k*: MS omits the spelling and cuts to Sam's 'No matter' for which is substituted 'Vell'.
143　WELL: MS omits all the rest of the exchange, resuming at OW's 'vell, now then I'll finish the glass'.

SAM.   Vhat are you laughin' at, old corpilence? I never seed sitch an old ghost in all
my born days.

WELL.   Hush, Sammy; two friends of mine as vorks on the Oxford Road, and is up   165
to all kinds o' games, vill get the Shepherd safe in tow, and vhen he does go to the
Ebenezer Junction, vich he's sure to do, for they'll see him to the door, and shove
him in if necessary, he'll be as far gone in rum and vater as ever he vas at the Markiss
o' Granby, at Dorkin, and that's not sayin' a little either.

SAM.   I'll go with you, father, I'll go with you, you may depend upon me.   170

WELL.   Spoke like my own boy, vell, now then I'll finish the glass and say good
bye. (*drinks*) Good night, my boy, and may this love match never cause you to
know your father's sorrows.

SAM.   I'll see you to the door, Mr Veller, senior, the governor won't want me just
yet. (*Exeunt* SAM *and* OLD WELLER)   175

*Re-enter* MR PICKWICK.

PICK.   There, I've had a mouthful, and now I'll be off to bed. Late dinners don't suit
me—they may stay as long as they like, they'll not leave their wine just yet; besides,
I've got a great deal to think about, though I declare the glass or two of wine that I've
taken seems to have got into my head as it is—that plaguy Mrs Martha Bardell and
that cursed Dodson and Fogg. But they won't bear reflecting on—they'll drive me   180
mad—let me go to bed—I only hope I may sleep. Waiter! (*calls*)

*Enter* WAITER.

WAITER.   Sir!

PICK.   I can have a bed?

WAITER.   We've none but double-bedded rooms.

PICK.   I can have one of them to myself, can't I?   185

WAITER.   Oh yes, sir—there's No. 22, will suit you capitally, sir—nice fire—all ready
in it—sheets just air'd, and everything—I'll show you up to it, sir.

PICK.   That will be the very thing; tell my servant to bring me up some hot water at
eight o'clock, and I sha'n't want him any more to-night.

WAITER.   I will, sir—this way, sir. (*Exeunt* PICKWICK *and* WAITER)   190

*Re-enter* SAM.

SAM.   I've slipped that 'ere walentine in the post, so now it is off my mind—making
love for the fust time is like going a swimmin, it's very awkvard, the fust plunge, but
it's nothing when your used to it. Now, I've only got to dewote my faculties to give

---

181 *Late…go to bed*: MS omits 'Late…as it is' and 'Martha', changing the second 'go to bed' to 'go to rest'.
183 *bed*: MS substitutes 'room'.
184 *rooms*: MS adds 'empty here at present'.
186 *22*: MS has 23.
187 *sir—nice…in it*: MS omits 'sir—nice' and 'in it', Pickwick's speech following, and Waiter's 'I will, sir'.

that ere mulberry-painted portable engine, Mr Job Trotter, some compensation for
195   the trouble he took, to let me know, I didn't know so much as I thought I did. I met
with him quvite casually, as it vere, as I vas a valking down the town—wery glad to
see me he vas—I can't say—I squeezed out of him that he was a courting of a cook,
vhat had saved some money, as he met at chapel, vere he vas singing 'No. 4
Collection!' who was going to set up in the chandlery line—and that he had every
200   reason to expect that he was to be the chandler—Hulloa! the guvenor!—what can
he vant?

*Enter* PICKWICK.

PICK.    One might as well be at the maze, at Hampton Court—quite a labyrinth—as
many ways down stairs, as there's streets in Seven Dials—glad I've found my way
here at last—odd enough—left my gold watch behind me—family concern—
205   couldn't sleep if it wasn't ticking over my head—apropos, Sam, here!—step in the
next room, Sam, and get me my watch, it's lying down on the table.
SAM.    Directly, sir! (*Exit* SAM)
PICK.    Droll—very droll—I should lose my way—it's quite certain these old inns
were built in the way they are, on purpose to make people stay in them—guests
210   must be a month in them before they get used to them—I must make a note of them
for the club.

*Re-enter* SAM.

SAM.    There's the ticker, sir!
PICK.    Thank'ye, Sam; now, then, I'll take my way back again. Hope I sha'n't make
any more mistakes. Good night, SAM. (*Exit*)
215   SAM.    And I'll take my way to the tap, and then off to the attic, as Milton said when
he was writin' 'Paradise Lost,' and drinkin' small beer! (*Exit* SAM)

*Enter* AUNT RACHEL, FAT BOY, *and* WAITER.

RACH.    Very well, waiter—you will send the chambermaid to me, and provide a bed
for my attendant here.
F. BOY.    I can sleep anywhere. (*snores*)
220   WAITER.    Find him a bed in the cock-loft directly, ma'am. (*Exit* WAITER)
RACH.    I am glad my brother has thought proper to send for me again—sorry the
coach only came part of the way and stopped here. Mine has only been a juvenile
indiscretion—susceptible hearts will sympathize.—Oh, Lothario! cruel, false,
Lothario!—much-injured Tupman, too! How my heart yearns to make you repara-
225   tion and become your wife. I was deluded, but my love is yours—heigho!

---

200   *the fust plunge … chandler*: MS omits 'the fust plunge' and 'Now … to be the chandler'.
203   *Seven Dials*: A notorious slum district of London, close to the theatres.
211   *Droll … for the club*: MS omits this speech.
222   *stopped here*: MS omits the rest of the speech.

*Enter* CHAMBERMAID.

CHAM.    No. 22, ma'm—shall I show you to your room?

RACH.    Do, my good girl. Oh, Lothario!—oh, much-injured Tupman! Get you to
bed, Joe. (*Exeunt* RACHEL *and* CHAMBERMAID)

F. BOY.    She's crack'd—that love has turned her wits! Tell me to go to bed!—as if
there was any occasion to tell me that! They says I am always asleep—they doesn't    230
know how I lays awake at nights, and everybody 'as their day-dreams sometimes,
and ain't always awake, as well as me—but what's more, are very often caught nap-
ping. How drowsy talking does make me!

SONG. FAT BOY

AIR 'We're a Noddin'.'

I'm always noddin', nid, nid, noddin',
I'm always noddin', abroad and at home.                                              235
The butler loves ale and little to do,
The cook loves a sip, and loves a drain, too,
The footman loves Mary—she loves him, he thinks,
While Mary loves the groom, but I love forty winks.
But I'm always noddin', nid, nid, noddin',                                          240
I'm always noddin', abroad and at home.

(*Falls asleep at the end of song in chair*)

WAITER *enters to show him to his room, finds him asleep—can't wake him, so carries
him off on chair.*

## SCENE 2

*Bedroom Gallery in Great White Horse Inn—Range of Bedrooms, numbered 21, 22, 23,
and 24.*

*Enter* PICKWICK.

PICK.    Well, there certainly never was such a puzzling place, as this—I've been up    1
a dozen flights of stairs, and came to the Lord knows how many landings, without
arriving at port; but I think I'm right now. This is certainly the identical gallery—two

---

233.1 *SONG. FAT BOY*: MS omits the Fat Boy's speech and song. The song is derived from a Scots traditional song 'corrected' by Burns and published in the *Scots Musical Museum*, no. 523, with the first line
'Gudeen to you kimmer'. It was printed in the cheap songbook *The Universal Songster* in 1828, in a version
'as altered for London', and was probably being sung, therefore, in the London tavern song rooms. Moncrieff
wrote many songs as well as plays, and in the late 1820s was selling sheet music in a Regent Street shop,
hence his familiarity and dexterity with the body of popular song.

numbers very much alike! 21—that can't be it! they ain't at all alike; 24—nor this;
5    22—that must be it. I'll just peep in to make sure I'm correct. (*opens door*)
Yes, a blazing fire—the candle, I suppose, has gone out. I can undress myself without it, so here goes! (*Exit* PICKWICK *into room*)

(*A short pause*)
Enter AUNT RACHEL *and* CHAMBERMAID, *with light.*

CHAM.    That is your room, ma'am, No. 22. Shall I take the light and turn down the
bed clothes?
10   RACH.    No—no—chambermaid—I will do that myself—give me the candle. You
will call me at seven—but let one of your ostlers call the stout youth, you saw with
me, at five—he always takes a couple of hours to open his eyes.
CHAM.    I'll take care, ma'am. Good night, ma'am.
RACH.    Good night! Dear me, it's very odd—but I never can help thinking of my
15   unprotected condition, just as I am going to bed. It's very hard, having two chances,
as I had, after having waited so long, that I should miss them both—I certainly cannot
afford to lose more time now! though everybody must allow I'm in the height of my
bloom; quite in my prime—not like those green, unripe, inexperienced pinafore
chits, that all the fellows run after so, now o' days, in preference to maturer beauty; but
20   I'll take care how I let slip another chance—heigho! oh, Lothario! oh, Mr Tupman!
But let me go and put my hair in curl, I've some fancy yellow paper—one likes to look
tasty, even within the arms of Morpheus. (*Exit* AUNT RACHEL *into No. 22*)

Enter SAM, *rather fresh.*

SAM.    Vell, certainly this here Ipsvich ale is werry strong, and my governor—Mr
Pickwick—is a werry good fellow—my place is a werry nice place—Mary is a werry
25   pretty girl, and that Job Trotter is a werry great willin, and everything is werry comfortable—mine's a werry cheering prospect, as the man said, as he look'd out o' the
Pillory, and saw the rotten eggs a coming—vell, it is but fit it should be, for the road
I've travelled through ain't been werry much macadamised as yet—and turn, and
turn about, is fair play, as the showman said, vhen he vhopped the boys, vho turned
30   the round-about. Talking of round-abouts, I certainly have had some quveer ups
and downs; one of these ere times, I shall make a song of my life and adwentures,
'The youthful days of Mr Samevel Veller,' a werry good idea—

(*Loud screams heard in bedroom No. 22, and cries of* 'Oh, Lord! oh, Lord!')

Ulloa! vhat's in the vind now?—as the devil said vhen he vent to collect his tithes.

5 *but I...correct*: MS omits 'but I...but, stay,' and 'that must...correct', substituting 'must be my room'.
11 *chambermaid...You will*: MS omits 'chambermaid', 'give me the candle. You will' and the chambermaid's response, and substitutes 'two' for 'a couple of'.
15 *bed*: MS omits 'Good night!' and the rest of the speech from this point, except for 'heigho!'
31 *my place...ups and downs*: MS omits 'my place...comfortable', 'as the man...should be, for', and 'and
turn,...ups and downs;'.
33 *to collect his tithes*: MS has 'out' for 'to collect his tythes'.

(*No. 22 door is burst open and* AUNT RACHEL *in white bed-gown and yellow curl papers, and* MR PICKWICK, *in flannel robe and nightcap, rush out, but in their haste stick together in the doorway—both screaming* 'Murder, thieves, fire!' *etc.—* SNODGRASS, WINKLE, *and* TUPMAN, *with* LANDLADY, SERVANTS *of inn, and* GUESTS, *half-dressed, enter from all sides in great alarm*)

SNOD.    What, in high heaven's name, is the matter?

RACH.    Preserve me from this ravisher. 35

PICK.    Oh, my dear friends! here's a woman got into my room.

TUP.    Palpitating sensation!

WIN.    Poaching again.

LAND.    Terrible old Turk!

RACH.    Joseph—why Joseph, I say. D— that boy, he's asleep again. What will become 40 of me—I'm ruined. (*faints in* TUPMAN's *arms, hiding her face*)

LAND.    The character of my house will be gone for ever—call in the mayor's officers, they're down below.—Mr Dubberly, Mr Grummer! (*calling*)

PICK.    My dear madam, on the honour of a gentleman!—

*Enter* DUBBERLY *and* GRUMMER, *with Constable's Staff and Poker.*

GRUM.    Eh! breaking the peace—where are the malefactors?—In the King's name I 45 charge you.—

SAM.    Ulloa! squalls aboard!—

WIN.    This is worse than the boarding-school.

LAND.    There stands the culprit—take him up, knock him down!

SAM.    Well, you are a-going it, old Blazes—but you must knock down afore you can 50 take him up—and that aint exactly feasible, vhile I'm here!—

GRUM.    Ah! a rescue! fire on the willains—Mr Dubberly, you've got the red hot poker—secure them—bring in the parish chair.

SNOD.    I'll protect him at the hazard of my life.

SAM.    Stand off, old Blazes! 55

GRUM.    Down with him!

OCTETTO AND CHORUS, OMNES (*severally*)

AIR 'Tow, row, row!'

PICK.    Zounds! What now—what a row,

DUB.    Keep the peace, sir! Or I'll floor you.

SAM.    Show me how—come on now—

34 SNOD: MS omits this speech.

38 WIN: MS omits this speech and transfers Rachel's speech from above to this place.

40 D— *that boy*: MS omits 'D— that boy' and the landlord's following speech.

54 *protect*: MS has 'defend' for protect' and then a speech for Tupman: 'I can't 'cause I've got my arms full'.

56.2 AIR 'Tow, row, row!': The song does not fit to the tune of 'The British Grenadiers', of which this is the burden, but nor does it clearly correspond to the Irish tune of the same name. Presumably the 1830s had another song named with the current phrase for a fight or 'general row'.

| 60 | RACH. | In the King's name, I implore you. |
| | LAND. | Lay them low—make them bow, |
| | PICK. | Rascals, soon we'll triumph o'er you. |
| | SAM. | Well, I vow—smooth your brow, |
| | | Here's your mother coming for you! |
| 65 | GRUM. | Crack his crown—knock him down, |
| | | Was there ever such a villain; |
| | SNOD. | Stupid clown—do him brown, |
| | | Give the vagabond a milling! |
| | SAM. | You may frown—all your town, |
| 70 | | I would leather for a shilling! |
| | DUB. | Self you'll drown—in his gown, |
| | | When the Mayor gives you a drilling! |
| | OMNES. | What a row, etc. |

(*During the singing this,* SAM *floors* GRUMMER—SNODGRASS *and* WINKLE *attack* DUBBERLY, MR PICKWICK *is secured by* CHAMBERMAID *and* LANDLADY. *Old sedan is brought in—*SAM *is overpowered—*PICKWICK *is placed in the chair. Exeunt* OMNES. FAT BOY *enters, half dressed, and half asleep—as they are going—yawns, stares vacantly about, and walks quietly after them, singeing his nose with the candle as he goes off*)

## SCENE 3

*Justice Hall in the Mansion of* MR NUPKINS, *the Mayor.*

*Enter* NUPKINS, *and* JINGLE *as Captain Fitztory.*

1 NUP.   Duty is my motto, in every station of life, my dear friend, Captain Fitztory. My daughter's happiness is before everything. I had certainly intended that a union should take place between her and Sydney Porkenham, but as it appears your fortune is somewhat superior, and you are a Captain, why, of course, that alters the

5 case. As an affectionate father, I shall give my free consent to your nuptials.

JIN.   Matchless man—distinguished magistrate—worlds of gratitude—happiest day of my life—Henrietta—mother's beauty, father's virtue—lovely—rich!—very.

NUP.   Why, yes! but I don't want to brag, from the days of Magna Charta, for that is my Epocha, the Nupkins' have always cut a conspicuous figure.

10 JIN.   Don't doubt it—whipping posts, stocks. (*aside*) (*bell rings, and noise heard outside*) Eh! Business, Nuppy—poaching—pheasants—peasants—joskins—whip

---

5 *my dear…father*: MS omits 'my dear…everything' and 'certainly' and substitutes 'my daughter' for 'her' below; and omits 'of course…father' at the end of the speech.

7 *rich!*: MS omits 'rich!'      9 *for that…Epocha*: MS omits 'for that…Epocha'.

11 *joskins*: Joskin as a cant term for countryman, bumpkin, is first cited by *OED* in 1811.

'em—fine 'em—sacred duty—justice—I'll vanish—Mrs Nupkins—pay respects—
see lovely bride—whisper how I'm transported—blush—sigh—dear Alfred!—tender—very—very! Come back directly—trounce the villains—trounce 'em—good
for the nation—necessary, very! (*Exit* JINGLE)                              15

NUP.     A noble fellow!—he'll do honor to me. But what is this? A charge—let me call
my clerk, Mr Jinks, and get ready to receive it.—Mr Jinks! Mr Jinks! (*calling*)

*Enter* JINKS, *with table, two chairs and writing apparatus.*

JINKS.     Yes, sir!
NUP.     Now then. To business—we must uphold the great principles of Magna
Charta, Mr Jinks—stick to this—punish everybody!                             20
JINKS.     Yes, sir.
GRUMMER.     (*without*) Bring them along, this way!
NUP.     Be firm, Mr Jinks—this looks like a serious riot—we must have the great
Bulwark to support us.

*Enter* GRUMMER, DUBBERLY, *and* CONSTABLES, *with* SAM, PICKWICK, SNODGRASS,
*and* WINKLE, *prisoners, followed by* LANDLADY, *etc.*

Hey day!—hey day!—what is the meaning of all this?                           25
PICK.     Is it thus, that the liberty of the subject—
SNOD.     I demand an ample retribution.
WIN.     I have been sported with.
SAM.     Pickvick and Principle, I says! this ere old gen'leman vill soon put everything
to rights.                                                                   30
NUP.     Silence! silence! Order, I say, or I'll commit you all, on the authority of Magna
Charta.
SAM.     And whose Carter is he?
NUP.     Silence, that ruffian. Now then, what is the charge?
LAND.     Please your worship, this man, No. 23, has been violently assaulting No. 22,  35
a most respectable lady, who will be here presently to swear to it.
GRUM.     Yes, your washup, this ere Pickvick and these ere t'other rhinosceruses—
SAM.     I say, come—come—none of that ere, old Strike-a-light. Beg your pardon, sir,
but this ere hofficer of your'n, in the gambooge tops, 'ull never earn a decent
livin', as a master of the ceremonies, any vhere; this ere's S. Pickvick, Esq.,—this ere's  40

---

15 *whipping...necessary*: MS abbreviates, omitting 'Whipping...cage', 'sacred duty...tender—very'
and 'trounce 'em' and 'necessary'.
20 *Magna Charta*: MS omits rest of speech.
22 GRUMMER: MS omits this speech and Nupkin's next.
25 *what is...this?*: MS substitutes 'what is the matter?'
26 PICK: MS omits this and next three speeches.
34 NUP: MS omits this speech.
36 *who will...swear to it*: MS substitutes 'and here comes the lady to swear it.' Then the whole of the
ensuing scene, to the entry of Aunt Rachel, is omitted.
39 *gambooge tops*: High boots with a yellow band at the top.

Mr Snodgrass, and this ere's Mr Vinkle; three wery respectable gen'l'men, as you'll
be proud to make the acquaintance on, vhen you knows 'em.

NUP.    Ulloa! ulloa! who is this man, Grummer?

GRUM.    A wery desperate character your washup, he attempted to rescue the other
45    prisoners, and assaulted the hofficers in a double capacity—so ve took him into
custody.

NUP.    You did quite right—put all the depositions down, Jinks; the fellow is evidently an outrageous ruffian!

PICK.    He is my servant, sir!

50 NUP.    Oh! oh!—another of the gang—put it all down, Mr Jinks!

SAM.    And score under it, old Bush-vig.

NUP.    What is your name, scoundrel?

SAM.    No, that ain't my name—I *ray*ther supposes as you vants to give it me—it must
be your own property.

55 PICK.    Sam! Sam! be quiet!

SAM.    I am as dumb as a drum, vith a hole in it!

NUP.    Mr Jinks, he hasn't told his name, you see, so put it down. Will you tell your
name, sir!

SAM.    Sam Veller.

60 NUP.    A very good name for the Newgate Calendar—put it down, Mr Jinks!

SAM.    Two l's, old feller.

NUP.    Do you spell it with a V or a W.

SAM.    That depends on the taste and fancy of the speller—I never had occasion to
spell it more than once or twice, in my life, and then I spell'd it vith a We!

65 NUP.    Put that down, Mr Jinks—put that down—spells W with a V—where do you
live, sir?

SAM.    Vherever I can!

NUP.    Put that down, Mr Jinks—put that down—he is a vagabond by his own confession, so I can commit him, according to Magna Charta.

70 SAM.    A wery impartial justice, this ere!—Doesn't show any preference—commits
hisself, as vell as everybody else.

NUP.    Silence, sir! I shall hold the three prisoners to bail—and fine this man, five
pounds for every assault—and keep him in custody till it's paid.

PICK.    But hadn't you better hear the evidence first, and let us know what we've
75    done?

NUP.    Not at all necessary, sir.

(JINKS *whispers* NUPKINS)

NUP.    Ah! true!—I shall in my clemency give you the privilege of our glorious Magna
Charta—call in the complainant.

SAM.    Ah! let's have somethin' to complain on.

80 NUP.    Silence, sir!

GRUM.    This ere Pickwick is a well-known, abandoned character, your washup—a
very great dilly quent—he was cotch'd trying to run away with a whole boardin

school o' young wirgins—and he's being indicted for a breach of promise of marriage and bigamy, this ere wery moment.

NUP.   Horrible profligacy! none of our wives or daughters are safe, with such a 85
hoary-headed sinner—but here comes the lady!

*Enter* AUNT RACHEL, *supported by* TUPMAN, *followed by* FAT BOY.

NUP.   Now, madam, assert your wrongs—there stands the desperado.

SAM.   (*seeing* RACHEL WARDLE) Vell, vas there ever such a start, as this ere!

PICK.   What's this? Miss Rachel Wardle.

RACH.   Good heavens! how have I been mistaken! Mr Pickwick—I beg a thousand 90
pardons!

NUP.   Eh, what—acquaintances! But that mustn't impede the course of justice. It's
contrary to the Magna Charta. Friendship mustn't suborn the evidence—can you
throw any light on this bedroom affair, youth?

(F. BOY *snores*)

Put that down, Mr Jinks. I confirm the conviction—it's a clear case—I confirm the 95
conviction.

PICK.   But, Mr Magistrate, this is entirely a mistake. I have long been intimate with
that lady. I entered her room entirely in error.

NUP.   Yes, yes! I know you did.

RACH.   I withdraw all charge. I would trust my life in the hands of that gentleman, sir.   100

NUP.   I must bind you over to prosecute, madam—in two sureties in forty pounds—
nothing but vigorous measures will do in these times; already has there been a
rebellion in the town of day-scholars, at one of the principal seminaries—a respectable apple woman's window has been broken, contrary to Magna Charta—the civil
power must be supported. I have faced greater danger than this. You recollect the 105
Suffolk Bantam and Norfolk Dumpling, Mr Jinks?

SAM.   Ve must get out of this somehow. I'll try vat Mr Trotter's influence will do.

*Enter* JINGLE.

JIN.   Now, Nuppy, lunch waiting—cold tongue—chicken—sherry—commit them
all—empty stomach bad for health—wind too—awkward—vulgar—very—
very—very.   110

SAM.   Caught at last. Vell, this beats Stilton!

PICK.   What do I see? The villain Jingle!

89   *What's this?*: MS has 'Why what is …'

99   *this is entirely…I know you did*: MS omits 'this is…mistake' and has 'this' for 'that' lady, and omits
Nupkins's speech.

100   *sir*: MS omits 'sir'.

101   *prosecute*: MS has 'appear' for 'prosecute' and omits the rest of the speech from 'these times'.

109   *cold tongue…them all*: MS omits 'cold tongue…them all'.

112   *Jingle*: MS omits next two speeches and picks up at Pickwick's 'he's an impostor—a swindling
stroller', inserts 'as my friends can prove' but omits 'ran away…expose him'.

NUP.   Jingle, no, sir, my son-in-law that is to be, Captain Fitztory.

JIN.   Angels and ministers of grace—all up—mine sprung—must bolt.

115 PICK.   Another victim. 'Captain!'—he's an impostor—a swindling stroller—ran
away with this lady to obtain her fortune—extracted money from her friends—my
associates here can prove it—but I'll expose him—I was in search of him.

NUP.   His looks convict him, and going to marry my daughter—what will the
Porkenhams, and the Griggs, and the Slummingtons say? Shall I convict him—
120 what's to prevent me?

JIN.   Pride—pride—old fellow!—wouldn't do—no go—caught a Captain, eh! ha!
ha! very good husband for daughter—biter bit—make it public—not for worlds—
look sheepish—very.

NUP.   Villain!

125 JIN.   Ha, ha! Captain for ever nothing like it—catch the girls—scarlet coat—scarlet
fever—no matter—tall young man, old lover—Sidney Porkenham rich—fine fellow—not so rich as Captain, though, eh!—turn him away—off with him—anything
for Captain—nothing like Captain anywhere—eh, Nup, eh?

NUP.   Remove the villain. Leave the house, sir.

130 PICK.   Stay sir. (*to* JINGLE) You are exposed, disgraced—I might have taken a
revenge much greater—this leniency, I hope, you will remember—but ere you go,
let me inform you, I consider you are a rascal and a ruffian, and worse than any man
I ever met with.

JIN.   Ha! ha! Good fellow, Pickwick—fine heart—stout old boy—must not be pas-
135 sionate—bad thing, very—might do you a service—thing you little dream of—but
sha'n't—bye-bye—see you again some day—keep up your spirits. Where is my servant? Job—where are you, Job?

SAM.   Ulloa! here he is—vhy ve vere, this wery moment, speaking of you—how are
you?—vere have you bin? Come in, and then I'll show you out! How does the chan-
140 dlery business go on? How happy you look—have you got the cook? You'll have a
bastin' presently! let me hand you to the door—come, come, don't baptize your wil-
lany here, you hypocrite, in that manner—now, ain't you a wery nice young man?

NUP.   Out with them—out with them—out with them!

SAM.   Vith pleasure—this vay, gen'lmen—take care how you go. (*trips up their
heels, and kicks them out*)

145 NUP.   A worthy riddance! You have nobly furthered the purpose of Magna Charta.
Gentlemen, you are at liberty!

PICK.   I'm pleased to have a second time preserved a lovely female from a scoundrel.
Miss Wardle, I have occasioned you some inconvenience—let me repair it. My
good friend, Tupman, here—relieve his anguish—soothe his despairing heart—he
150 loves you still!

114 *Angels and ministers of grace*: Jingle quotes from *Hamlet*—a very theatrical habit.
118 *but I'll expose... convict him, and*: MS omits 'but I'll expose... convict him, and'.
125 *very good... Ha, ha!*: MS omits 'very good... public', Nupkins's interjection, and Jingle's laugh.
128 *nothing like it... nothing like Captain*: MS omits 'nothing like it... eh!' and 'off with... Captain'.
133 *I ever met with*: MS omits the rest of the scene, to the general exit.

RACH.  Tracy! (*tenderly*)

TUP.  Rachel! (*they embrace—*FAT BOY *snores*)

SAM.  (*who has returned*) He's vinking at their reconciliation—vot a young bore constrictur it is. Vell, I've polished off that Mr Job—left him sprawling in an ingun bed—he can cry as long as he likes there.                                          155

PICK.  We'll now depart, with thanks, sir, for your courtesy,—come, friends, for town—the heaviest of my trials is at hand—we must be prepared.

SAM.  Aye, aye—all's now as it should be, as the oyster said to the tub, vhen the knife slipped and cut the girl's thumb off—it's all right now.

(*Exeunt* PICKWICK, SNODGRASS, *and* WINKLE, *shown off by* NUPKIN, GRUMMER, DUBBERLY, *and* JINKS, *followed by* LANDLADY, CONSTABLES, SAM, *and* FAT BOY, *snoring*)

## SCENE 4

*Old Palace Yard, outside of Westminster Hall.*

*Enter* OLD WELLER.

WELL.  Ha! Ha! ha! Vell vas there ever such a game! As my Sammy didn't come of  1
course, I didn't vait for him—so I goes to this ere Temperance Society, all alone, by myself! and there they vas, a reg'lar mixtur o' vater drinkers of every description.— Tea and vater drinkers—Gin and vater drinkers—Rum and vater drinkers, and Brandy and vater drinkers, all but salt and vater drinkers, but there varn't none o'  5
them—no thank ye—vell, arter they swallowed a draught of a report—who should come in, but the Shepherd his wery self! and the first thing he did, being wery drunk, vas, as in duty bound, to say everybody else was drunk—and it wasn't till I'd manifested the truth to him with half-a-dozen knock down arguments—that I con-
winced the reverend gen'lman—that he wasn't quite compos, and hadn't a leg to  10
stand on. Ha, ha! didn't I bonnet him, neither? (*laughs immoderately*)

*Enter* SAM.

SAM.  Ulloa old wenerable—vhat are you putting yourself into such a paroxysm for?—making yourself so precious hot, that you looks like a aggrawated glass-blower. Vhat fancy is it that is ticklin up your funny bone, in this ere vay?

WELL.  He's in for it, Sam. He's in for it!                                          15

SAM.  Who's in for it?

WELL.  Vy the Shepherd—twelve glasses deep of rum and vater—with a good hidin'—and a night's lodging in the Station House, into the bargin—all performed by me!—Your dutiful father Toney Veller—as vitness my hand!

0.1 *Old Palace Yard*: MS omits the scene between Sam and Old Weller, beginning with the entry of Wardle etc. below.

20  SAM.    Vhat, have you bin a reginerating him?—Vell, I'm glad of it—von half of these
fellows as belongs to these Temperance Societies—don't desarve nothing less, than
to die, of the Hydrofobia, under a feather bed, and not in it. Sorry I var'nt there to
have seed the lark, and ha' lent a helping hand.—But come—are you prepared to go
into the Court vith me? because the Gowernor's suit is acomin on, and I'm a
25  vitness.

WELL.    Quvite ready, Samivel,—but apropoz, as they says: if your Gowerner vants
any vitnesses as to character, or to prove a alleybi,—all I can say is, I've been turning
over the business in my mind, and he may make his-self perfectly easy, Sammy,—
I've got some friends as vill do either for him—but my adwice vill be this ere,—
30  never mind the character,—but stick to the alleybi.

SAM.    Vy, he arn't a goin to be tried at the Old Bailey!

WELL.    That ere forms no part of the present consideration, Sammy. Vherever he is
going to be tried, my boy—a alleybi is the thing to get him off—Ve got Jim Vildspark
off, that ere manslaughter of his'n, with a alleybi, vhen all the big-vigs to a man said
35  as nothing could save him, and my 'pinion is, Sammy—that if your governor don't
prove a alleybi, he'll be vot the Italians call—regularly flummuxed—and that's all
about it.

SAM.    Vell, vell, I von't argefy with you, old Prussian-blue—have it all your own vay!
But let's be off there at vonce—so come along.

40  WELL.    Aye, aye, my boy—alleybi vill do the trick. Ha! ha! ha! (*Exit* OLD WELLER
*and* SAM)

*Enter* WARDLE, ISABELLA, *and* EMILY.

WAR.    No! no! girls—I couldn't remain in Dingley Dell, and know there was so
important an affair as my friend Pickwick's trial, about to be decided! the 14th of
February—it is to come off to-day—from this spot, we gain the earliest intelligence.
Rachel must wait 'till we return.

45  ISA.    Winkle is a witness, is he not, papa?

WAR.    Yes, yes; make your mind easy, girl, you will be sure to see him.

EM.    And Mr Snodgrass, pa?

WAR.    Yes, Mr Snodgrass too.

EM.    Then there's no doubt, sir, who will win the day—noble Augustus.

50  WAR.    They're both good fellows, and when the trial is over, if you will still hold in
the same mind—

EM.    My love's unalterable as fate!

WAR.    Aye! Aye—well, if you're willing, and they're ready, I don't know that I shall
oppose your passion.

55  ISA.    That's a good dear pa! I'll take care Mr Winkle don't offend the laws! No game
without a certificate—he shan't sport, unless he has a license!

43  *14th of February*: MS omits the date.
46  *Yes, yes...him*: MS omits Wardle's response and Emily's next two speeches.
54  *Aye!...passion*: MS omits 'Aye...ready' and substitutes 'happiness' for 'passion'.
56  *he shan't...license!*: MS omits 'he shan't...license!' possibly to avoid innuendo.

EM.　I need no surety but Augustus's love—Snodgrass and truth are one!

ISA.　Winkle must quit his club—I'll have no clubs—selfish unsociable things!—I
only wish all the women had my spirit; we'd soon put down all the clubs, or else we'd
set up a Ladies' Club, of our own.　　60

EM.　Yes, sister, and admit all the gentlemen into it, the very first thing—No! no!—
that would never do!

ISA.　Why, we might leave the door open, a leetle to be sure—only just a-jar, at all
events, we shouldn't lock it. But no clubs, for me, I say!

EM.　Bless me, how imperative you've grown.　　65

ISA.　Yes, yes—we don't mean to take things as we used to do—Petticoat Government,
is the order of the day, so Petticoat Government for ever!

SONG

To woman's diplomacy all must now yield
Her ministry none shall withstand
'Gainst her, opposition, will vain take the field　　70
She'll Premier still rule in each hand [*sic*]
E'er first in Debate her pre-eminence lies
She'll make war and peace at her will
O'er the Treasury Lords it et raise up supplies
And the whole Home Department best fill　　75
Yet still every Cabinet, woman will sway
And Petticoat Government—all must obey.

Yes, first in each Cabinet, will she bear sway
And Petticoat Government all must obey.

EM.　Well, well, you may turn white-sergeant, if you please; I would but reign within　80
a living heart—my views are not so lofty!

WAR.　Dear me, I wish I could gain some intelligence—I'm all anxiety—my poor
friend Pickwick!

EM.　Hope all, sir! Snodgrass upholds him—his noble eloquence is certain to convince the judge of Mr Pickwick's innocence—he will at once get his acquittal.　　85

WAR.　Would it may prove so—but I've my doubts, my poor enthusiastic simple
Emily.

57　EM: MS omits this speech and the exchange down to and including Isabella's 'Yes, yes'.

67.1　SONG: The Song is not in 1837. Charles Dance's farce *Petticoat Government* (Drury Lane, 1832) was
often on the bills at the major theatres during the summer of 1837. MS includes the song but omits Emily's
next speech.

85　*upholds … get his*: MS omits 'upholds … his' and substitutes 'and procure him an' for 'he will at once
get his'.

86　*simple*: MS omits 'simple', Emily's song, and Isabella's following speech. 'The Bridal Ring' is by
George Rodwell, from his music for Fitzball's *Lord of the Isles* (Surrey, 1834), which was playing at the Surrey
in the spring of 1837.

EM.    Well, you will see, sir! Oh Augustus, soon may we meet once more, within that mystic circle, love's own bridal ring, never to part again.

SONG, EMILY

AIR 'The Bridal Ring.'

90      The wishes and hopes of my early years,
       Once seal'd, Love shall guard for ever;
       While other times the doubts and fears,
       Dispell'd, shall visit me never;
       Sacred and sweet, the nuptial kiss
95      From the heart to the lip will spring
       When he'll place, on my finger the pledge of bliss—
       Love's Bridal Ring—Love's Bridal Ring.

ISA.    Hey! here comes some one, father!—Ah, Mr Winkle! Now we shall know.

*Enter* WINKLE, *in great agitation.*

WAR.    Welcome, welcome, Mr Winkle. Well, the trial?
100  ISA.    Yes, it is over—is it favourable? You will excuse, sir, our anxiety.
WIN.    My dear friends—Miss Isabella—I—that is—ask Snodgrass! Oh! (*covers his face with his hands in an agony of grief, and rushes off*)
ISA.    But, Mr Winkle! Sir—bless me—very odd!
WAR.    The man's gone off as if he was shot.
EM.    No matter—here is Snodgrass, he'll soon tell us—dear me, how wild he looks!

*Enter* SNODGRASS, *wildly.*

105  Now, dear Augustus.
WAR.    Aye, aye, Snodgrass, tell us the verdict, is it over? She's nonsuited! Aye! aye! aye!
SNOD.    Adorable Emily! I—I—(*makes several ineffectual attempts to speak, then rushes out, covering his face with his handkerchief*)
WAR.    Confound it—Snodgrass—Snodgrass—Snodgrass! (*calling*)
110  Why, he is worse than t'other—he's struck dumb—the other wouldn't tell us, and he seems as if he couldn't.
EM.    Exquisite sensibility, worthy his poet's soul—tis lost—the trial's lost.
WAR.    Gad, I begin to think so—but stay, we must not judge too hastily—here's Mr Weller—we shall get a rational answer from him at all events.

---

98.1 *agitation*: MS has 'haste' for 'agitation'.      100 *ISA*: MS omits this speech.
102 *ISA*: MS omits this speech, also Wardle's, and Emily's 'No matter' and 'Now, dear Augustus!'
107 *Aye, aye…Aye! aye! aye!*: MS omits all the 'Aye's.
110 *dumb*: MS omits the rest of the speech, Emily's speech, and resumes with Wardle's 'here's Mr Weller'.

*Enter* SAM, *sorrowfully.*

Now Mr Weller—now, your news!                                                    115
ISA. *and* EM.    Ah! do, dear Mr Weller. Your master is triumphant, surely?
SAM.    Wery triumphant, indeed—that is, the reverse way; but I'll tell you about it,
and to cheer up my spirits I'll give it to you in a bit of a song.

SONG, SAM.

AIR 'Marlbrook.'

There can be no sort of denial,
That an anxious thing is a trial,                                                120
Vhen you have got to rely all
On L A W, law!
No matter what it's for—
Debt, contract, or faux-pas

(*spoken*) 'Bardell versus Pickwick'—Breach of Promise of Marriage—Mr Sergt.  125
Buzzfuzz—and Mr Simpkin for the plaintiff—Mr Sergt Snubbin, and Mr Plumky for
the Defendant—Justice Stareleigh on the Bench—are the jury all sworn—All my
Lord—then let the cause proceed—Silence! Silence! Mr Sergt. Buzzfuzz rose to state
the case—My Lord and Gentlemen of the Jury—the plaintiff in this case is a widow—
the Relict of the late Mr Bardell—my Lord is retiring for a few moments to take some  130
refreshment—

117 *that is, the reverse way*: MS substitutes 'but I'm sorry to say the reverse' for 'that is, the reverse way'.

118 *song*: The following solo section appears to be a detachable unit, with a very variable text, probably performed separately on other occasions by William Hammond: see Introduction, 'The Plays He Did Not Write'. The text here is the version submitted to the Lord Chamberlain, as being the author's version of the text. A different version, presumably inflected by Hammond's performance, appears in the 1837 printing of the play, marked out and separated in a smaller font. That version is given here in the notes.

118.2 *AIR 'Marlbrook.'*: i.e. 'Marlbrough s'en va-t-en guerre', a French traditional popular melody which has various sets of words, the best known of which today is probably 'For he's a jolly good fellow'. Early in his career Hammond had a success singing Hudson's comic song 'LAW', from which this may be derived (see Introduction, 'The Plays He Did Not Write').

124 *faux-pas*: 1837 has a further stanza: I don't want the law to disparage, | But I'll tell of a shocking miscarriage, | 'Bout a breach of promise of marriage, | In which justice showed a flaw. | I'll show the chance of Law: | Its quirks and its vexation, | Expense and ruination, | Its tricks and its evasion, | Glorious, uncertain Law.

131 *Mr Sergt. Buzzfuzz... refreshment*: 1837 has a different version of these lines: 'Mr Sergeant Buzfuz addressed the jury for the plaintiff. He pumped into 'em, how, that his client, Mrs Bardell vas a vidder as let lodgings, and how Mr Pickwick vas a gen'lman as took 'em; and then he produced two scraps of paper, about some chops and some sarce, and a slow coach and a varming pan, vich he said everybody knew, vas clearly a promise of marriage—and how that Mrs Bardell had taken Mr Pickvick in, and vanted to do it agin—and how she had contracted to lodge and do for him, and he trusted an enlightened jury would help her to accomplish her vishes, and about twelve more sacks of chaff all to the same purpose; then he call'd a whole lot o' vitnesses, and what he said they all swore to; arter vhich, the judge popp'd out of a back door to get some mutton chops and sherry, and so ended the first part of the chapter.'

For quirk and for wexation,
Expense and ruination;
For tricks and for evasion,
135                 There's nothing like the Law.

With many a fine oration,
And cross-examination,
They prove to demonstration,
                What they are contending for.
140       Each other they clapper-claw,
Till their wigs are ready to thaw;
You'd think them really at var,
But bless you it's all jaw,
For quirks and for wexation,
145       Expense and ruination;
For tricks and ewasion,
                There's nothing like the Law.

(*spoken*) Mr Sergeant Snubbins rose to address the court for the defence:—'My Lud
and gentlemen of the jury,' said he, 'this may more truly be called a cause for costs than
150    a cause for damages; it is vhat is technically call'd an attorney's cause—a cause for
which there is no cause at all. Mutton chops and matrimonial chops have been ingen-
iously mixed up together; to mislead you; my learned friend has not only served them
up to you vith Tomata sauce, but he has given you plenty of his own sauce, in addition.
He has talked to you, gentlemen, of a varming pan—he must have had his face suf-
155    ficiently rubbed vith it, to have acquired brass enough to come into this Court, with a
cause so utterly groundless and contemptible. I am much mistaken, if my learned
friend will not discover before he has done, that there are some hot coals, in this varming pan of his, that he has been unvise to stir up, as he is wery likely to *burn his fingers*
in so doing; the notes merely referred to lunches, not to love, as to the slow coach, it
160    will be found to be von, in vhich the only *fare* vill be Mrs Bardell herself, and vhich vill
require my learned friend, and his employers, Dodson and Fogg, to vork like horses,
I vill not say *asses* to drag, with any satisfaction, through the uphill undertaking in
vhich they vere engaged.' Mr Justice Stareleigh summed up and said if the plaintiff vas

---

141 *thaw*: 1837 has another quatrain here: 'Like Richard the Third at Drury, | The counsel, all sound and
fury, | Addressed the judge and jury, | And thus attention draw.'
148 *spoken*: MS omits this 'spoken' section in favour of: 'Call Samuel Weller!—Here I am sir! As the
Trigger said on whole cock—what is your name! Sam Weller, my Lord—Well now Mr Weller, I believe you
are in the service of Mr Pickwick the defendant—Speak up Mr Weller. I mean to speak up sir—I am in the
service o' that 'ere Genl'man and a wery good service it is—Little to do and plenty to get Eh—Oh! quite
enough to get sir—it's not Evidence—werry good my Lord! Gentlemen of the jury do you find for the
Plaintiff or Defendant—For the Plaintiff—Damages seven Hundred and fifty Pounds—Take your money
Jurymen!—Now break up the court—'.

right, it vas quite clear the defendant must be wrong: and if the defendant vas wrong,
it was equally evident that the plaintiff must be right. They could consult all their sagac-  165
ity, and decide accordingly. The jury returned a verdict for the plaintiff—damages
seven hundred and fifty pounds.

> For quirks and for wexation,
> Expense and ruination,
> For tricks and for ewasion  170
> There's nothing like the Law.

WAR.    What! seven hundred and fifty pounds damages. Well it may be Law, but
damn me if it's justice.

SAM.    So the eel said, sir! vhen the Lord Chancellor' cook, vas a skinning 'em for his
Lordship's dinner,—but here's the gowernor.  175

*Enter* MR PICKWICK.

PICK.    Ah! my dear friends—well, you know the result—but not a halfpenny, either
of damages or costs, do Dodson and Fogg get, if I stay in a debtors' prison all my life
for it.

WAR.    I scarce can blame you; but may not a new trial—

PICK.    No, no! I've had enough of law, my friends.  180

WAR.    Well, but they may compromise.

PICK.    I cannot hope it!

WAR.    If you want money—

PICK.    Nay, my means are ample—my mind is made up. I will not yield to such
injustice—where are you staying?  185

WAR.    At Gould's Hotel.

PICK.    I'll meet you there, perhaps, this evening. I am somewhat ruffled now.

WAR.    We shall expect you—we'll not disturb you now.—Good-bye old friend—
keep up your spirits—rely on this, should ought occur—you understand—it may,
to prevent your promised visit to my girls and me, come what will come you'll find  190
we'll visit you. Come Bella, Emily—good-bye—good-bye, God bless you.

PICK.    Thank ye—thank ye—bless ye!

(WARDLE, ISABELLA, *and* EMILY *grasp* MR PICKWICK'S *hands with expressions of
the deepest commiseration and sympathy, and silently exit.—*MR PICKWICK *is much
moved*)

---

172  *damages*: Copy text returns to 1837 here. MS omits 'Well…justice' and Sam's reply.

177  *stay*: MS has 'lay' for 'stay'.

180  *No, no!*: MS omits 'No, no!' and next two speeches, picking up at Pickwick's 'I will not'.

187  *evening*: MS ends the speech here.

191  *we'll not…God bless you*: MS omits 'we'll not…now', 'keep up…girls and me' and 'God bless you,'
and Pickwick's responses.

I must not yield to this. I wish the worst were come.

SAM.   (*looking off*) I don't know vhether this is the worst—but there seems some-
195     thing bad enough coming: who are these?

*Enter* NAMBY *and* SMOUGH, *two Bailiffs*—NAMBY *walks up to* MR PICKWICK, *and taps him on shoulder.*

PICK.   Do you want me, sir?

NAM.   Not at all, sir! we don't want you, 'cos vy, ve've got you! I've got a little bit of an execution against you; 'Bardell and Pickwick,'—you may look at the Varrant; likes to make everything agreeable.

200 SAM.   (*knocking* NAMBY's *hat off*) Vy don't you take off your hat vhen you speak to a gen'lman.

NAM.   (*to* PICKWICK) That's an assault. I call you to bear vitness.

SAM.   Don't bear no vitness at all, sir! but only give me leave—and, in five minutes, I'll so polish off these ere laughing hyenas that even their own mothers sha'n't know
205     'em agin.

PICK.   Sam, I desire you—I command you—not to molest them again—they do but do their duty—take up that hat!

SAM.   Beg your pardon, sir; but I'll be damn'd if I do—and if he wenturs to put it on agin until you're done speakin, I'll knock him into the middle of next veek.

210 NAM.   This is my card, sir! 'Namby, Bell Alley.' I suppose you'll go to my house— every accommodation, and on the most reasonable terms.

SAM.   Board, a shilling a mouthful, and lodgings five shillings a day per square yard.

PICK.   No, sir! I will at once into my destination—the prison. I've no desire to tarry on my road, especially where's there's such sorry accommodation.

215 NAM.   Hum! He's not half a good'un—not a gemman by no means. (*aside*) Oh, if you're goin' to prison, ve can't waste no time on you; ve've got to attend to a *gemman*, so come along.

SAM.   Paws off, old carcase monger. I'll wait on my master, if it's agreeable to you. You can follow.

220 PICK.   Stay, Sam. Listen to what I am going to say.

SAM.   Certainly, sir! Fire away.

PICK.   A prison is not the place to take a young man to!

SAM.   Nor an old one, either, sir.

PICK.   You are quite right, Sam! But old men may go there through their own heed-
225     lessness and inexperience, whilst young men may be brought there by the heart-

---

195 *who are these?*: MS substitutes 'as the man's leg said to the mortification' for 'who are these?'
198 *Varrant*: MS ends the speech here, and omits next three speeches and Sam's assault.
207 *I desire…hat!*: MS omits 'I desire you' and 'take up that hat!' and Sam's reply.
210 *I suppose…house*: MS omits 'I suppose…house'.
213 *prison*: MS ends speech here and omits next two, running on Pickwick's 'Stay, Sam. Listen…'
221 SAM: MS omits this response.
224 PICK: MS omits this speech and three more, picking up with Pickwick's 'you, for a time'.

lessness of those they serve—it is better for young men, in every point of view, that
they should never go—do you understand?

SAM.    (*doggedly*) No, sir, I don't think I do.

PICK.    Try, Sam!

SAM.    Vell, sir, I *ray*ther see your drift now, and if I do, it's my opinion you're comin'   230
it a great deal too strong—as the mail coach said to the snow storm vhen it overtook
him.

PICK.    I see you comprehend me—you for a time must leave me, Sam.

SAM.    (*sarcastically*) Oh, for a time—eh, sir.

PICK.    Yes, while I remain in prison—your wages I shall continue to pay you. Any   235
one of my friends would be happy to take you, were it only out of respect to me —
and if I ever do leave the prison, Sam, if I do—I pledge you my word you shall
return to my service instantly.

SAM.    Now, I tell you vot it is, sir! this here sort o' thing don't do at all; so don't let's
hear any more about it!   240

PICK.    I am sincere and resolved, Sam!

SAM.    You are, sir?

PICK.    Yes—so good-bye, my good fellow! Now, gentlemen, I am at your service.

NAM.    Oh! ve'll trundle you along in no time.

(*Exeunt* MR PICKWICK, *with* NAMBY *and* SMOUGH, R., *leaving* SAM *apparently
paralysed*)
*Enter* OLD WELLER, L.

WELL.    Oh, Samivel!—Samivel! I told you what would come, my boy, if your gower-   245
nor didn't prove a alleybi.

SAM.    (*recovering himself*) And so he's resolved, Eh!—wery good—then so am I.
You've just come in time, so don't be troubling your nob any more about alleybi's,
but jist you listen to me till I've done—the gowernor's gone to prison, and vot's
more, von't let me go with him.   250

WELL.    Vhat, stop there by his-self, poor creetur—that can't be done!

SAM.    In course it can't, I knows that.

WELL.    Vy they'll eat him up alive—do him as brown as a roasted pigeon—it oughtn't
to be.

SAM.    And what's more it shan't—certainly not!—but how to prewent it—don't you   255
see any way of taking care on him?

---

234  SAM: MS omits this speech.

236  *pay you. Any…respect to me*: MS omits 'pay you. Any…respect to me'.

237  *if I do*: MS omits 'if I do'.

242  SAM: MS omits this speech and Pickwick's 'Yes'.

244  NAM: MS omits this speech.

246  *I told you…alleybi*: MS has 'I told you it would come to this, my boy!'

250  *so don't be…more*: MS omits 'so don't be…till I've done' and has 'vorse' for 'more', then cuts five
speeches, picking up at Sam's 'I'll jist trouble you…' but omitting 'jist'.

WELL. No, I don't—no vay—unless it's gettin' him into a turn-up bedstead, unbeknown to the turnkeys; or dressin' him up like an old ooman with a green weil.

SAM. Oh! you don't, don't you?—Vell then, I'll tell you what it is—I'll jist trouble
260 you for the loan of five and twenty pounds.

WELL. What good will that do?

SAM. Never mind—p'raps you may ask me for it five minutes arterwards—and p'raps I may say I von't pay, and cut up rough—you von't think of arresting your own son for the money, and sending him to the Fleet, you unnat'ral wagabond?

265 WELL. I sees it all—capital, capital—ha! ha! ha! (*laughs immoderately*)

SAM. Vhat an old image it is, what are you standin' there for, conwertin' your face into a street door knocker, vhen there's so much to be done—vhere's the money?

WELL. In the boot here—hold my hat—now for it—(*takes out large dirty pocketbook, and gives* SAM *notes*)—and now, then, I knows a gen'leman limb of the law,
270 that'll do the rest of the business for us in no time—von that has brains like a frog—all over his body, and reaching to the very tips of his fingers—so come along Sammy, come along, and like a 'fectionate father, I'll lock you up in no time.

SAM. Vot a cruel-hearted varmint it is. Von't you take my bill at sixpence a month—ha! ha! ha! Vell, if you von't, you must have my body, as the dragon fly said, ven he
275 flew avay and left his hinder half behind him.

(*Exeunt* SAM *and* OLD WELLER)


## SCENE 5

*Interior of the Fleet*—PRISONERS *discovered.*

CHORUS, PRISONERS

AIR 'Oh! Poor Luddy, Heighho!'

1 I wish we were walking down the Strand,
 Luddites, Luddites! Oh! Poor Luddites, I—Owe!
 The Traps shouldn't nab us, when out of land,
 Luddites! Luddites! Oh ! poor Luddites, I—Owe!
5 Terms and returns, they pass away,
 Luddites, Luddites! Oh! Poor Luddites, I—Owe!

---

263 *p'raps I may*: MS has 'I mayn't pay it you' and continues 'and you may be hard-hearted enough to arrest me for it and put me into prison you old image' then omits all to '—vere's the money?'

275 *hold my hat... half behind him*: MS omits 'hold my hat—now for it', 'and now, then', 'gen'leman', 'von that has... his fingers', 'Sammy, come along', ''fectionate father', and Sam's final speech, finishing Old Weller's speech and the scene with 'like a dutiful son, I'll put you in jail and lock you up in no time'.

0.3 *AIR 'Oh! Poor Luddy, Heighho!'*: The original appears in *The Universal Songster*, vol. III (London: John Fairburn, 1826), 127, attributed to 'T. Dibdin'.

No matter, we all shall be free one day,
Luddites! Luddites! Oh ! poor Luddites, I—Owe!

TRUN.    (*without*) This way, 'squire!
1ST PRI.    Ha! another bird cag'd!—worthy subjects of King Lud! to the gate! the race   10
is not always to the Fleet, but we'll have a run for it this time, at all events! (*Exit*
PRISONERS)

*Enter* TURNKEY *with* PICKWICK, L.

TRUN.    Here you are, sir, and wery comfortable you'll find yourself in no time—
those ere gen'l'man, residents here, vill soon find out you're a new von—and you'll
have lots of acquaintances to prevent your feeling lonely—so good-bye for the present, and make yourself at home.                                                        15
PICK.    Thankye, friend.

(*Exit* TURNKEY)

So here I am, the inmate of a prison—this is the school to learn the world in; severe,
but salutary lessons. Well, I may now consider myself regularly settled here—I have
had my portrait taken; the turnkeys have been staring at me for the last hour, to
make sure they shall know me—and to-morrow I am to have a chummage ticket—a   20
lodging provided gratis—with more advantages than I am aware of, or anybody
else—strange inconsistency—as I came in, a Dutch clock ticked upon the wall—a
bird sang in a cage—wheels within wheels—a prison in a prison. (*muses*)

*Enter* JINGLE *and* JOB TROTTER (*not perceiving Pickwick*), *the latter with a little bit of
scrag of mutton in his hand.*

JIN.    Eh! scrag of mutton—half a pound—all our allowance—sorry fare—quite—
quick—hungry—very—very!                                                                 25
JOB.    I could cry without trying now, but that I've got no gingham—we have made a
mess of it—all on the poor side of things now—aye, e'en the poorest of the poor. The
Fleet, poor side!
PICK.    (*arousing*) Well, it's no use musing—I may as well perambulate this world of
mine—make the small circuit of the town, that I must henceforth live in—I've no   30
other now.
JOB.    (*seeing him*) Eh! what, but no, sure it can't be! what, Mr Pickwick!

16  *Thankye, friend*: MS begins the scene here, with Pickwick's thanks, which are repeated.
22  *this is the school . . . a Dutch clock ticked*: MS omits 'this is the school . . . lessons' and 'I have had . . . inconsistency', and changes 'a Dutch clock ticked' to 'I saw a Dutch clock upon'.
25  *all our allowance . . . very*: MS omits 'all our allowance . . . quite' and the final 'very'.
28  *I could . . . The Fleet, poor side!*: MS omits 'I could . . . gingham', changes 'mess of' to 'mess on', inserts 'of
the Fleet prison' after 'aye, e'en', and omits 'The Fleet, poor side!'
30  *make the . . . live in*: MS omits 'make the . . . live in', Job's speech, and the beginning of Jingle's, picking
up at 'A queer place.'

JIN.    Ah! Mr Pickwick! A queer place this, sir, to meet in—parted so long, sir—ain't
it? very—very! (*affecting gaiety*)

35  PICK.    Jingle, retributive powers—villain as he is, I cannot see his present misery,
without compassion—can I speak a word with you?

JIN.    Certainly, always at home—can't wander far—no danger of overwalking yourself here—Spike Park—grounds pretty, romantic, but not extensive—open for public inspection—family always in town—housekeeper desperately careful—very!

40  but what has brought you here?

PICK.    I have lost a trial, and have come here for the damages.

JIN.    Martha Bardell?

PICK.    The same—with costs, they will make near a thousand pounds.

JIN.    Ah! What—oh villain!—villain!—but mum—no matter—cannot help it

45  now. (*aside*)

PICK.    You've forgot your coat!

JIN.    Eh! Spout—dear relation—Uncle Tom! couldn't help it—must eat you know—
wants of nature—and all that.

PICK.    What do you mean?

50  JIN.    Gone, my dear sir! last coat—can't help it—lived on a pair of boots—whole
fortnight!—ill—hungry—deserved it all—but suffered much—very! (*covers his
eyes with his hands and weeps*)

PICK.    Come, come, we'll see what can be done when I know all about the matter.
Here, Job,—where is that fellow Job?

JOB.    (*coming forward*) Here, sir!

55  PICK.    Come here, sir! (*sternly*) Take that! (*gives money*) Go—get you wherewithal
to comfort you—this for the present—hereafter I may assist you with more lasting
service!

JIN.    God bless you—this I've not deserved! Let me seek means some way to recompense my villainy, and prove my gratitude—I'm not all vice! Come, Job—quick—

60  quick—food—food! (*Exit with* JOB)

34  *parted so long... very*: MS omits 'parted so long' and one 'very'.

36  *powers... without compassion*: MS had 'justice' for 'powers' and omits 'without compassion'.

40  *yourself... very! but*: MS omits 'yourself... very! but'.

43  *with costs, they*: MS omits 'with costs, they' and substitutes 'it'.

44  *but mum*: MS omits 'but mum'.

47  *Uncle Tom:* Harriet Beecher Stowe's *Uncle Tom's Cabin* was not published until 1851; here the slang
meaning is 'pawnbroker'. The term was later shortened to 'uncle'.

48  *Eh!... and all that*: MS omits 'Eh!', 'dear relation... help it', and 'and all that', and omits the next two
speeches.

51  *fortnight*: MS adds 'silk umbrella ivory handle a week—ask Job. Knows it. | PICK. Oh, I understand
you you've pawned it. | JIN. Every thing. Job's shirts too—nothing soon lie in bed. Starve—die—coroners
Inquest poor prisoner—workhouse funeral—serve him right—all over—drop curtain.'

53  *Job*: MS omits second 'Job'.

57  *you... lasting service*: MS omits 'you... lasting service', substituting 'ye'.

59  *Let me seek... all vice!*: MS omits 'Let me seek... all vice!' and Pickwick's soliloquy, to the entry of Sam.

PICK.    Poor human nature, guilt is its own avenger! We should judge gently and deal
mercifully! What can that dingy fly be creeping up that wall for, when he might rove
in freedom where he lists—the insect is decidedly insane.

*Enter* SAM, L.

Ah, Sam! my good fellow, I am glad to see you—I thank you for this visit—let me
explain to you my meaning more at large.                                            65
SAM.    Won't presently do, sir?
PICK.    Certainly—but why not now? Speak out, Sam!
SAM.    'Cos I've got a little business as I vants to do, sir! I think I'd better see after it at
once—the fact is—(*hesitates*)
PICK.    Speak out!                                                                 70
SAM.    Vell, the fact is—p'r'aps I'd better see arter my bed, afore I do anything else!
PICK.    (*with astonishment*) Your bed!
SAM.    Yes, my bed—I'm a prisoner—I vas arrested this ere wery arternoon, for debt.
PICK.    You arrested for debt!
SAM.    Yes, for debt—and the man as put me in vill never let me out till you go out    75
yourself!
PICK.    Bless my heart and soul—what do you mean?
SAM.    Vhat I say! If it's forty years to come, I shall be a prisoner, and I'm wery glad
on it, and if it had bin in Newgate, it vould ha' bin jist the same! Now the murder's
out—and damme there's an end on it!                                                 80
PICK.    Faithful, noble fellow! If anything could tempt one to pay the sum, for which
I have come here, it would be gratitude—that, through its means, I have experienced that which I never could have done but in a prison's walls—devotion without
interest—faith under every difficulty—and what true worth may still be found,
enshrined sometimes within an humble heart! I am not proof to such attachment.  85
We'll never part again—good fellow! your fortunes henceforth must be mine!
SAM.    No, none of that, sir! I arn't us'd to hear such vords as these—they somehow
comes quveer to me—it's no sich great things to brag on—to wish to keep with a
good master—and as to its being here or there—the heart, sir! the heart is the thing
vhat I looks at!                                                                    90
PICK.    Well, well, Sam! we'll say no more of this just now—I must go and look after
our accommodations, for the night—I've got a direction to a Chancery prisoner,

64  *I am glad to see you*: MS omits 'I am glad to see you'.
67  *Speak out, Sam!*: MS omits 'Speak out, Sam!'
68  SAM: MS amalgamates, making this speech, "Cos I've a little business to do, I think I'd better see arter
my bed', and cutting Sam's next and giving Pickwick both exclamations at once.
75  *for debt ... vill never*: MS omits 'for debt', has 'vont' for 'vill never', and omits Pickwick's response.
80  *Vaht I say! ... end on it!*: MS omits 'Vaht I say!', 'I shall be ... jist the same', and 'and damme there's an
end on it!'
86  *Faithful ... good fellow!*: MS has 'Generous' for 'Faithful' and omits 'If anything ... good fellow!'
88  *brag on—*: MS inserts 'vot is good' and omits 'the heart, sir! ... I looks at!'

who has been here these five-and-twenty years. I am told he can provide for me—wait for me here—I will soon return. (*Exit* PICKWICK, L.)

95    SAM.    So, I've got a footin' in here, at last—I've had some trouble in doing it—but it is done—this is a quveer start, lockin' people up, that ain't so vell off as their neighbours—them as has alvays bin sottin in public houses, don't mind it—but them as has alvays bin bustlin about, and trying to get their living, it goes hard vith—in this respect, the Law is unequval; and the sooner it's done avay vith, the better—I never

100    heard but of von man as liked being shut up, in my life; and he vas a little quveer feller, as they us'd to let go outside to smoke his pipe, every evenin; but bein threatened to be lock'd out altogether, for having staid rather late, two or three times—blow me if he'd ever go out agin, for fear they shou'd keep their vords, in good earnest.

*Enter* JINGLE.

105    JIN.    Eh! Mr Weller—you here! Eh!—snug place, this—very!—ain't it—all one's friends—see how it is—Marine—Fleet—voyage—outward bound—three months—the Straits of Portugal—clear bill—reach harbour—pleasant—aint it—very!

SAM.    Why, if this ere aint that mortal rattlesnake Jingle!—Vell, I'm damn'd!—(*stands a moment or two, stupefied, then recovers himself*)
Now I should wery much like jist to beat him into an anatomy, only sickness and

110    starvation seem to have done it afore me.

JIN.    Know what you're pondering on—can't do it—heart won't let you—true Englishman—won't strike when down—faithful fellow!—master a Christian—I, damn'd rascal—feel it—pinch'd within, here—(*placing his hand on his bosom*)—very!

115    SAM.    Vy, yes, you seem to have bin rayther close pinch'd in your pantry, lately—as the valnut said to the nut-crackers—havn't put your head in the manger so reg'larly as you us'd to do—but vhat are you driwin at, young corkscrew?

JIN.    This—don't laugh—Pickwick, fine heart—very!—not always callous—feel gratitude—sav'd me from starving—gave me money—should have given—what?—

120    blows—cuffs—deceiv'd—wrong'd—laugh'd at—no matter—didn't!—He is in prison—Dodson and Fogg—damn'd scoundrels—Martha Bardell—old hag!—my wife!

SAM.    Your wife!—wheugh—(*whistles*)—but aint you gammoning, Mister—this can't be real—it is too good!

125    JIN.    Pos—honour!—No, not honour—havn't got it—here's certificate—much better—thought she had money—found mistake, too late—left her day after mar-

93 *I must go…provide for me*: MS omits 'I must go…provide for me' and all of Sam's speech from 'I've had some' to 'in good earnest', having instead 'but who is this coming'.

106 *very!…friends*: MS omits 'very!…friends'.

108.1 *mortal…recovers himself*: MS omits 'mortal' and 'Vell, I'm damn'd!' and the sd.

114 *placing…very!*: MS omits sd and 'very!', and Sam's speech.

120 *This—don't laugh…didn't!*: MS omits 'This—don't laugh', adds 'sometimes' after 'gratitude', and omits 'gave me…didn't!'

riage—plan to fleece Pickwick—threaten'd to blab—Dodson and Fogg gave money—were to give more—knew of it all—plot between the three—thought I was dead—deceived though—very—very!—lived to repent—make reparation— and hope—live honest.                                                                              130

SAM.    Vell, vonders vill never cease—as the old lady said, vhen she'd twins—but how's this ere to sarve the governor—how's he to get out?

JIN.    Indict the parties—Conspiracy!—Old Bailey—true bill—grand jury—bail, eight hundred pounds—Judges' warrant—forty-eight hours notice—search house—Police—Newgate—Dodson and Fogg—get in—let Pickwick out—and glad  135 to get out!—very!

SAM.    Well, this is all wery fine—but how to do it?

JIN.    Leave that to me—know Jew Lawyer—Noisy Nosey!—lives in the rules—fine hand at an indictment—best in the world—take the job too, on spec.—talk to your- self—make conspiracy of it—prove it—give him ten pounds—do it in ten min-  140 utes—first rate rogue—bold!—keen—knowing—very!

SAM.    Ten pounds! I'd give him ten hundred, if I had it—if he'd only get the governor out o' this 'ere pennytentiary!

JIN.    Say no more—come along—down in the Fair—this way—all right—load off heart—better! Calmer—gayer—very!                                                     145

SAM.    Bring this to bear, and spifflicate me if that ere Job Trotter turns parson, if I von't become von o' the congregation. Now, then, follow my leader, Mr Jingle! for I don't mean to lose sight o' you, not till this ere is done—not by no means. (*Exeunt* SAM *and* JINGLE)

*Enter* TURNKEY, *with* SNODGRASS, TUPMAN, *and* WINKLE, R.

TRUN.    This way, gentlemen—you'll find Mr Pickwick in his hotel, here. (*shows them in and exits*)

SNOD.    Pickwick in exile!—Napoleon, at St. Helena!—to nought else can I liken our  150 illustrious leader—great man—much persecuted sage!

WIN.    I see him coming—he has a mackerel hanging from his finger—he gives it to an old woman!

TUP.    He is here—my dear, dear friend!

*Enter* PICKWICK, L.

---

127  *marriage*: MS adds 'no one knew of it—heard of trial'.

129  *thought I was…lived to*: MS omits 'thought I was…lived to'.

131  *as the old…twins*: MS omits 'as the old…twins', and shortens the rest of the speech to 'how's he to get out?'

135  *in*: MS confuses this too-condensed speech further by substituting 'out' for 'in' here, and omitting 'to get out!' below.

144  *know Jew Lawyer…Say no more*: MS omits 'know Jew Lawyer…Say no more'.

144  MS changes the rest of the speech to 'all—right—load off heart—feel better—don't laugh—mind easier—calmer—gayer—very—now come' and then omits Sam's response.

148.2  *TURNKEY*: MS omits the turnkey and has Pickwick and his friends enter to be met immediately by Sam, Jingle, and Job, starting the scene with Sam's cheering.

155 PICK.    Welcome, my boys! rejoiced to see you!

SNOD.    What we could do, we did for you!

PICK.    Yes—yes—you certainly did for me—preserve me from my friends, I say! No matter—this is a sorry place to come to—but we'll be merry yet—I've taken a very beautiful room, five feet by four, at a pound a week, and hir'd a most capital pair of

160    bellows, and other furniture, at thirty shillings a week—so life will wear away, as swiftly here, as it would do in any other place.

SNOD.    Sublime philosophy!

TUP.    But have you then no hope!

PICK.    None—none!

*Enter* SAM, JINGLE, *and* JOB TROTTER, L.

165 SAM.    Hurrah! Hurrah! Hurrah! Pack up your things, sir!

PICK.    Sam—Sam—compose yourself—I have provided beds, a pair of bellows, and—

SAM.    Beds!—bellows!—burn the beds—and blow the bellows.—Hurrah!—Hurrah!

PICK.    Sam, you are mad!—restrain this excitation—my friends, here, wish to walk

170    with me awhile—get my stick.

SAM.    Stick—you must cut your stick!—and prepare to take a wery long valk. Hurrah!—Hurrah!

PICK.    Why, Sam! What has come to him! how can I walk without my stick?

SAM.    Beg pardon—my heart's too full to speak!—Mr Jingle, here—is the wery best

175    scoundrel as ever vas—and the long and short of it is—you're a free man agin—Mother Bardell is married!—Dodson and Fogg's in Newgate!—all a conspiracy—Jingle, here, proved it—Mother Bardell's husband!—here's your discharge! (*gives paper*)

PICK.    Amazement!

SAM.    And wot's more—three hundred pounds, to compromise the felony—and all

180    this clever scoundrel, Jingle's, doing!

JIN.    Friend Pickwick—can't say much—feelings won't let me—fact simply this—account—your debtor—ow'd you much—yes, much—this per contra—let us strike balance—if in my favour—give your note of hand! (*takes hand*)

PICK.    This repays all—still all is not repaid—take this three hundred pounds—'tis

185    fairly yours—it will release you—live honest, and live happy!

JIN.    Study new character—play new part—eh—give up the villains—bad line of business—unprofitable—very—I will—I will—bless you, old fellow!—eternal

---

168 *bellows!...Hurrah!*: MS omits 'bellows!—burn', substitutes 'oh, hang' for 'blow', and deletes the final cheers, then omits next three speeches, running on Sam's speech with 'Beg pardon...'

178 *and the long...Amazement!*: MS omits 'and the long...in Newgate!', the handing over of the paper, and Pickwick's line.

180 *clever scoundrel*: MS substitutes 'is' for 'clever scoundrel'.

181 JIN: MS omits this speech.

185 *it will...honest*: MS omits 'it will...honest'.

186 JIN: MS omits 'Study new...I will', reverses 'repentance—gratitude', omits 'Damme', and omits Trotter's and Sam's speeches.

blessings—repentance—gratitude! (*repressing his feelings*) Damme, I want the word—Job—Job—good bye—God bless you all! (*Exit* JINGLE, L.)

TROT.    (*advancing to* PICKWICK, *and appearing deeply affected*) Everlasting grati-   190
tude! heartfelt tears!—acknowledgments!—oh! oh! (*bursting into a roar*)

SAM.    Come, I say—none o' that ere, young cullender—this is too much of a good thing! (*forces* JOB TROTTER *off*)

*Enter* WARDLE, ISABELLA, EMILY, *and* AUNT RACHEL, *followed by* MARY, *the* HOUSEMAID, *and the* FAT BOY, R.

WAR.    Where is he? Ah! my boy! (*shaking hands with* PICKWICK) What all our friends here?—There, girls, each take your partner. (ISABELLA, EMILY, *and* AUNT   195
RACHEL, *severally join* WINKLE, SNODGRASS, *and* TUPMAN. SAM *sidles round to* MARY. FAT BOY *leans against wall, and falls asleep*) We've come to stay a long while with you.

PICK.    Very sorry, my dear friends! but I'm just going out—don't look incredulous! All is discovered—the action's given up, and you've just come in time to accompany me home!   200

WAR.    And never could we do it in a more glorious moment, than the accession of Beauty, Virtue, and Grace, to reign o'er Britain, and bless every heart! We must not lose a moment—come.

SAM.    But how am I to get out?—oh, I must stay here, with Mary, I 'spose—any von might find comfort vhere she is.   205

MARY.    La! Mr Weller.

*Enter* OLD WELLER, L.

WELL.    Now Samivel.

SAM.    Eh! the old 'un—this is jist the wery ticket. Oh, you unnat'ral, hard-hearted, old warmint—vot I've got you—give me my discharge or I'll have you put under the pump.   210

WELL.    Vot's the gowernor a goin out?—Vell, then, promise to be a more dutiful lit-tle boy, for the future, and mend your prodigy vays—and you shall go out vith him. Beg pardon, gen'lfolks!

SAM.    Hurrah! Come, Mary—now, sir—and may every poor feller, vhat's in prison for debt, and can't pay, speedily follow our example—and that's the vorst vish of   215
Sam Veller! Come, father! come, Mary!

WELL.    Vhat, the walentine—oh, Samivel—Samivel!—But these ere cheeks!—vy, they're like a basket o' Love Apples—and then, she ain't a vidder, that's von thing—so

---

195 *There*: MS has 'come' for 'There' and omits all sds in the speech.

199 *discovered*: MS has 'discharged' for 'discovered', omits 'home', and begins Wardle's speech at 'We must not', thus not including the clap-trap about Victoria coming to the throne.

204 SAM: MS omits this speech and the next.

208 *Eh! the old ... ticket*: MS omits 'Eh! the old ... ticket'.

213 *then, promise ... gen'lfolks!*: MS omits 'then, promise ... little' and substitutes 'if you'll be a good' and omits 'and mend your prodigy vays', 'out', and 'Beg pardon, gen'lfolks!' The rest of the scene is omitted.

there mayn't be quvite so much wiciousness in her—so as the old coachman always
loves a smack o' the vhip, and never refuses a fare—vy, clap yourself alongside o'
your father, girl—ya hip!

WAR.    I won't have another word, till we are outside these infernal walls—so this
way—this way!

(*Exeunt* WARDLE *and* PICKWICK, AUNT RACHEL *and* TUPMAN, ISABELLA *and*
WINKLE, EMILY *and* SNODGRASS, SAM, MARY, *and* OLD WELLER *bringing up the
rear. Just as they go off,* FAT BOY *wakes himself with his own snoring, finds he's alone,
looks vacantly about, sees the spikes, is frightened, and runs off.*)


# SCENE 6

*London, on the Accession of the Queen.*

*Enter* POPULACE, *in holiday clothes.*

CHORUS, OMNES.
AIR 'Victoria' Chorus, 'Der Freischutz.'

Victoria! Victoria! Victoria!
To her be all honour and glory!
Her name shall for ever adorn Britain's story!
Victoria! Victoria! Victoria!

*Enter* WARDLE, PICKWICK, AUNT RACHEL *and* TUPMAN, ISABELLA *and* WINKLE,
EMILY *and* SNODGRASS, SAM, MARY, *and* OLD WELLER, *followed by the* FAT BOY.

PICK.    This is, indeed, a proud day for Old England!—and adds a zest e'en to the joy
we feel.—Wardle, you've acted nobly! My friends, you're each bless'd with the girls
of your hearts! and under so bright a sway, as that which now dawns o'er us—you've
but in common with all around us, to live, love, and be happy! Sam, you too, have
your Mary—We owe you all—there's something to provide your wedding dinner. (*gives pocket-book*)

SAM.    A hundred pounds! I shall only wish—as the gen'lman did, when he von but
a tenth part as much in the lottery, that we may have a wery long acquaintance. If
I've done my duty, I'm satisfied—at all ewents, I've done my best—and though there
may be a few leetle trifling errors—if my kind friends vill but generously overlook

---

0.1 *on the Accession of the Queen*: William IV died on 20 June and the procession to proclaim Victoria's
accession round London took place on 21 June. The play was licensed on 6 July, to open on or about 10 July.
MS omits 'on the Accession of the Queen' in favour of simply 'illuminations'.

0.4 *AIR 'Victoria' Chorus, 'Der Freischutz.'*: Presumably the chorus 'Victoria! Der Meister soll leben' from
Act One of Weber's opera, which was an international success from the time of its premiere in Berlin in 1821.

them—vy, all I can say is, that I'll endeavour to amend 'em—and vishing ewery 15
true Englishman vill join vith me, in heart and woice, in shouting 'God save the
Queen,' I shall take my leave, and vith their permission, appear again another
opportunity.

FINALE, OMNES

AIR 'Auber's God Save the King! Gustavus.'

Hail! All hail! Our much-lov'd Queen!
With shouts we'll waken plain and green;                          20
Ne'er was one so cherish'd, seen,
Long live the Queen!
Fenc'd round by patriot hearts,
No danger can she dread;
Fell faction backward starts,                                    25
And hides, abash'd, its head!
All hail! Our lov'd Victoria!
Old England's pride and glory!
Her name shall shine for ever,
Renown'd in regal story!                                         30
All hail! Our lov'd Victoria!
Long live the Queen!
Long live the Queen!
With shout we'll waken plain and green,
Long live the Queen!                                             35
Blessing light upon Victoria!
Peace and joy be hers for ever;
Blessing light on Queen Victoria!
Peace and joy be hers for ever!
God Save the Queen!                                              40

(*While this chorus is singing, Procession of* HERALDS, BEEFEATERS, GUARDS, *etc.,
are seen passing through Temple Bar, to proclaim the Accession of her Majesty, Queen
Victoria, and the piece concludes, amidst general shouts of joy and congratulation,
with tableau!*)

THE END

15 *when he…amend 'em*: MS omits 'when he…acquaintance' and has 'when he got the tenth in the
lottery, that it may last'. It also omits 'and though…amend 'em'.
18.2 *AIR 'Auber's God Save the King! Gustavus.'*: Auber's opera *Gustave III* premiered in Paris in 1833 and
was successfully imported to London.
28 *glory*: MS omits the rest of the song, giving only 'etc etc etc'.

# TWO

Edward Stirling, *Nicholas Nickleby*, Adelphi, 19 November 1838

## INTRODUCTION

NICHOLAS NICKLEBY was one of the most popular of Dickens's early works on the stage. Edward Stirling's *Nicholas Nickleby*, created when only eight (that is, one-third) of the parts had been published, and staged at the Adelphi, struck Dickens as 'excellent' in many respects: see the Introduction ('I Feel Sure About Her') for his opinions and a discussion of his intervention in its staging.

Edward Stirling was a very persistent and often an effective dramatizer of Dickens's works. Born Edward Lambert in Oxfordshire in 1807 or 1809, he was schooled in London and started at the age of fourteen on the bottom rungs of the theatrical ladder, by his own account[1] buying parts in disreputable private theatres and graduating to Richardson's show at Bartholomew Fair and then the East End Pavilion theatre. His marriage in 1832 to Fanny Clifton (Mary Anne Kehl) did not carry him to the theatrical heights the remarkable 'Mrs Stirling' herself attained, and she soon left him, but he did make the move with her to the West End. He was the Adelphi stage director when he wrote this play, probably his longest-running piece, from the early parts of *Nicholas Nickleby*. He wrote many more Dickensian adaptations, two of which are also included in this volume (*Barnaby Rudge* and *Martin Chuzzlewit*), as well as hundreds of other plays, and an archetypal book of rambling, detailed, deeply inaccurate but colourfully entertaining theatrical reminiscences, *Old Drury Lane*. Stirling is a rather despised jobbing dramatist, but he numbers some interesting plays amongst the many potboilers. The production of much run-of-the-mill stage matter was inevitable when yearly contracts as a stage director, like the one he had with the Adelphi at this point, could specify that the duties included the writing of six plays in the course of the season; but facility did not entirely swamp his undeniable abilities as a writer.

The Adelphi was a thriving, modern theatre in the nascent West End, newly renovated, enlarged, and decorated and with a competent, even star-studded company who worked together well in this short season as they had before.[2] In the 1838–9 season they also staged a successful *Oliver Twist*, possibly also written by Stirling. The Adelphi stage was not large, but it was technically adequate to the creation of the important tableaux in this play; Dickens praised the pictures Stirling created as well representing the Hablot Browne plates. *Nicholas Nickleby* was the hit of the season.

---

[1] Edward Stirling, *Old Drury Lane: Fifty Years' Recollections of Author, Actor, and Manager* (London: Chatto and Windus, 1881), 2 vols, vol. 1, 6–44.

[2] See Bratton, *West End*, 190; and *Adelphi Calendar*.

## THE TEXT

The copy text here is the Lord Chamberlain's MS, Add. MS 42949 ff. 636–72v; it is annotated on the front (f. 636r) 'Adelphi: recd Novr 15th 1838 / Licd Novr 16th 1838,' and its first night was 19 November. The title page calls it 'a burletta in two acts.' According to the indexes to the LC collection, it is in Stirling's own hand. He has signed the back of folio 640v, at the end of the first scene. His making of his own copy for the licenser would be consistent with his role as stage director at the theatre and gives the MS authority as to both the script and the stage directions, which, unusually for a licenser's text, include detailed placing of entrances and exits, which have accordingly been included here. The code employed is 'L.' or 'L.H.' for left and 'R.' or 'R.H.' for right, and 'U.E.' for 'upper entrance,' meaning from behind the final upstage flat.

Deletions and insertions in the MS are quite frequent, and are silently accepted except where they seem to indicate changes of mind or perhaps modifications made specifically for the licensing text, such as the removal of the word 'devil'.

The MS has been collated to repair errors and omissions with the text published by Chapman and Hall, the last play in vol. V of their series Webster's National Acting Drama (1838) as digitized by Chadwyck-Healey, English Prose Drama Full-Text Database, Cambridge, 1996. These two texts are referred to in the notes as 'MS' and '1838.'

The texts differ in a few possibly significant ways: the section discussed in the Introduction ('I Feel Sure About Her') that includes the speech about the robins is not in MS and is here taken from 1838; the tag line commending the future of the novel to the audience is transferred from Nicholas to Smike in 1838, which might reflect a change made in performance, underlining the importance of Mrs Keeley's success in this role; and, less easily explained, the role of John Browdie, played by the undistinguished company actor Henry Beverley, is noticeably enlarged in 1838. One might conjecture that the intention was to replace broad physical comedy between female characters, which is cut in 1838, with more genteel mockery of the provincial bumpkin. These and all other significant variations are noted in the present text.

## Characters and cast of the first production

| | |
|---|---|
| Ralph Nickleby | Mr William Cullenford |
| Nicholas Nickleby | Mr John Webster |
| Newman Noggs | Mr O. Smith |
| Mantilini | Mr Frederick Yates |
| Squeers | Mr James Wilkinson |
| Scaley | Mr Sanders |
| Tix | |
| Smike | Mrs Robert Keeley |
| John Browdie | Mr Henry Beverly |
| Servant | Mr Updell |
| Servant | Mr George |
| Lord Verisopht | Mr Lansdowne |
| Col. Chowser | Mr Robinson |
| Pluck | Mr Shaw |
| Pike | Mr Wellington |
| Sir Mulberry Hawke | Mr Wilson |

Servants

| | |
|---|---|
| Mrs Nickleby | Miss O'Neil |
| Kate Nickleby | Miss Cotterill |
| Madame Mantilini | Miss Shaw |
| Miss Knag | Miss Enscoe |
| Miss Squeers | Miss Gower |
| Miss Price | Miss Grove |
| Mrs Squeers | Mrs Fosbroke |

Work Ladies[3]

---

[3] Cast corrected and augmented from *Adelphi Calendar*.

**2.** Mary Ann Keeley as Smike in Stirling's *Nicholas Nickleby*.

Woodcut © Victoria and Albert Museum

# ACT I

## SCENE 1

*The Inn Yard of the Saracen's Head Snow Hill—profile Coach—L.H.—on the R.H. a large window—supposed to be that of a Coffee-Room—through which a fire is seen burning cheerfully—and a table laid for breakfast, smoking, coffee, etc.—opposite is another table, at which is seated 4 little boys, a fifth boy on a small box, eagerly watching Squeers, who is eating voraciously, cutting large slices from a round of Beef and occasionally pocketing the same—an ostler or chambermaid crosses the yard—it is snowing lightly during scene—lights half down.*

SQUEERS.    (*speaking to children while eating*) Conquer your passions boys—and    1
don't be eager after victuals! (*swallows a large piece*)

*Enter* WAITER *with large jug—and a kettle, with hot water.*

WAITER.    The milk, sir.
SQUEERS.    (*speaking with his mouth full*) Very well. (*looks into jug*) Is this two
penn'orth, William?    5
WAITER.    Two penn'orth, sir.
SQUEERS.    What a rare article milk is in London! Fill the jug up to the top with
water.
WAITER.    To the top, sir? why the milk will be drownded.
SQUEERS.    Serve it right for being so dear. Now have you brought the bread-and-    10
butter for *three*, for the *five* little boys?
WAITER.    Yes, sir. (*places a small plate of thick bread and butter a the table*)
SQUEERS.    Very good. I expect a young gentleman of the name of Nickleby, when he
arrives send him to me.
WAITER.    Yes, sir. (*going*)    15
SQUEERS.    Stop! you may leave the kettle.

WAITER    *exits*

SQUEERS.    (*tasting the milk and pouring water in*) Here's richness!—think of the
many beggars and orphans in the street that would be glad of this little boys. (*pours
more water*) Now boys—for breakfast. When I say Number one—the boy on the left
hand nearest the window may take a drink; and when I say number two, the boy    20
next him will go in; and so till number five, which is the last boy. Are you all ready—
BOYS.    Yes, if you please, sir.

---

0.7 *lights half down*: The initial picture derives from the second illustration in the first part, March 1838. Dickens was impressed by the staging at the Adelphi, and the reproduction of the illustrations. 'The tableaux from Browne's Sketches exceedingly good', he told Forster (letter of 23 November, *Letters* vol. 1, 460).

SQUEERS.    That's right—keep so till I tell you to begin. No. 1. (*boy drinks*) No.
2 (*drinks*) 3—4—and 5. (*all drink*) And now for the bread-and-butter. (*breaking it*
25    *into 5 portions*) Look sharp, for when the horn blows every boy leaves off. (*they eat*
*quickly. Squeers standing before fire*) Capital chance—this Nickleby for me—the
very man I want—it is not the first time Old Ralph has thrown me a bone to pick.

(*A horn sounds, and people cross yard with luggage*)

That's the horn! leave off, boys. No. 1 pull that crust out of your mouth; 4 & 5, I'll
knock your heads together. (*taking bread and butter from them, and placing it in*
30    *a small basket*) There, you'll want it on the road.

WAITER *re-enters.*

WAITER.    Mr Nickleby, sir.
SQUEERS.    Very well—William, get these boys on the coach—will you—

(WAITER *exits with boys*)

RALPH *and* NICHOLAS *enter*—SQUEERS *bows.*

SQUEERS.    (*to* RALPH) Servant, sir—those dear children are 5 pupils of mine, all
booked outside for the delightful village of Dotheboys Hall, near Greta Bridge, in
35    Yorkshire—where youths are boarded, clothed, booked, washed—furnished with
pocket-money, and—
RALPH.    As advertised—we know all about it, sir.
SQUEERS.    You do, sir, you do—no man better. That boy—you sent to us—Dorker—
he that died—how kind Mrs Squeers behaved to him—the attention that was
40    bestowed upon him in his illness—dry toast and warm tea offered him every night
and morning when he couldn't swallow it—a candle in his bed room on the very
night he died—and the best Walker's Dictionary to lay his head upon, yet he died.
RALPH.    (*groans*) Hem!
SQUEERS.    (*whispers to Ralph*) That half-witted fool—still lives, although we tried
45    every thing—
RALPH.    Silence! my nephew, Mr Nicholas Nickleby.
SQUEERS.    (*aside*) All mum. (*to* NICHOLAS) How do you do, sir? you'd be delighted
with Mrs Squeers—she'll be a mother to you.

(*Retire up stage with* RALPH *and* NICHOLAS *talking, and Exit*)
*Enter* NEWMAN NOGGS (*see description for dress*) U.E.L.H.—

NOGGS.    (*looking cautiously round*) Governor—not here—all right. (*producing a*
50    *dirty soiled letter*) This may be a slight assistance to his nephew—poor 'devil—he's

---

27 *a bone to pick*: MS trimmed, cutting off 'a bone to pick', supplied from 1838.
42 *yet he died*: 1838 inserts 'ungrateful'.
48.2 *see description for dress*: The description in the novel, which reads 'a suit of clothes (if the term be
allowable when they suited him not at all) much the worse for wear, very much too small, and placed upon
such a short allowance of buttons that it was marvellous how he contrived to keep them on.' (no. 1, 7).

hooked ha! ha!' widowed mother—innocent pretty sister—unprovided—not a friend to look to but Ralph Nickleby—he a *friend*—ha! ha! ha! to any thing but himself—no, no, I've heard of hard hearts—but rock marble's a feather bed to his—

(*A noise of passengers arriving. Horn sounds, and* 'Coach, coach ready')

I must not be seen—no, no, secrecy, secrecy's the word—ha! ha! (*goes up behind coach*)

*Enter* R.H.E. MRS NICKLEBY, KATE, RALPH, SQUEERS, *and* NICHOLAS.

RALPH.    (*to* MRS NICKLEBY) Don't tell me, madam—I never paid for a hackney 55
coach in my life.
MRS NICKLEBY.    I can't help it; if the dear boy had gone without seeing us I should
never have forgiven myself—without his breakfast too.
RALPH.    Breakfast! Stuff—when I first started in the world, I took a penny loaf and
a drink at the pump for my breakfast.                                        60
SQUEERS.    (*who has been placing boys on coach*) Now Nickleby, I think you'd better
get up behind. I'm afraid of one of them boys falling off and that would be a clear
loss of twenty pounds a year.
KATE.    (*to* NICHOLAS) Dear Nicholas! who is that vulgar man—
SQUEERS.    Mr Whackford Squeers, ma'am, and I'm far from being ashamed of it. 65
Them's some of my boys—all gentlemen's sons—each boy is required to bring—two
suits of clothes—six shirts, six pair of stockings—two nightcaps, two pocket-hand-
kerchiefs, two pair of shoes, two hats, and one razor.
NICHOLAS.    A razor! what's that for, sir?
SQUEERS.    To shave with.                                                    70
RALPH.    (*advancing*) My niece—Nicholas's sister—Mr Squeers.
SQUEERS.    (*bowing*) Indeed—I wish Mrs Squeers took gals, and we had you for a
teacher—I don't know tho', she might grow jealous. Eh! ha! ha! (SQUEERS *and*
RALPH *talk apart*)
KATE.    (*aside to* NICHOLAS) I don't half like the appearance of this person, Nicholas.
What kind of a place are you going to—                                       75
NICHOLAS.    I hardly know, Kate, but I suppose the Yorkshire folks are rather rough—
and uncultivated. Mr Squeers is my employer—you mustn't take his coarseness
ill—They are looking this way—I must take my place. Bless you love—and good
bye—mother, look forward to our meeting again some day—good bye. (*kisses sister
and mother and mounts coach*)
KATE *and* MRS NICKLEBY.    Good bye. (*crying*)                              80
SQUEERS.    (*aside to* RALPH) I understand—I'll hold him with a tight hand—and
for S—
RALPH.    (*aside, interrupting* SQUEERS) As you value my friendship, never let me
hear any news of the brat again—but—his—
SQUEERS.    Death—ha! ha! (*nodding his head and placing finger to his nose—they* 85
*whisper—*RALPH *gives money*)

51 *'devil...ha!'*: MS has 'devil—he's hooked ha! Ha!' deleted and 'lad' inserted.

NEWMAN NOGGS, *who has stolen on during the latter part of the scene, approaches coach cautiously.*

NOGGS.    Here!—(*holding up the letter to* NICHOLAS).
NICHOLAS.    What's this?
NOGGS.    Hush! (*points to* RALPH) Take it—read it—nobody knows—that's all—
NICHOLAS.    (*taking letter*) Stop—
90  NOGGS.    I can't. (*going*)
NICHOLAS.    Why?
NOGGS.    Because I won't.

*Tableau*

GUARD.    Now gentlemen—coach ready.


SONG
Four in hand from Piccadilly
95      Now seated in the dickey
Stop at the White Horse Cellar
Etc etc


*Horn Sounds.* SQUEERS *jumps up—*KATE *and* MRS NICKELBY *wave their hands— Coach moves slowly—snow descends heavily. Scene closed in.*


# SCENE 2

*A Chamber in* MADAME MANTILINI's *house.*

*A single knock and a bell heard as the scene opens. Enter a* LIVERY SERVANT *L.H.*

1  SERVANT.    (*yawning*) I never saw such a bore of a house as this is—knocker and bell going from morning till night—I most positively must give my master his discharge. (*Exits R. H.—re-enter—followed by* NEWMAN NOGGS *carrying a letter*)

---

92.1 *Tableau:* The print 'Nicholas Starts for Yorkshire', from the second number, realized on stage. 1838 has 'Tableau—see work' and a previous sd indicating 'all the characters for the tableau' entered with Ralph, who had briefly left the stage after his conversation with Squeers and returned as Noggs told Nicholas to 'Hush!'

97.2 *Horn . . . in:* The MS has two versions of this conclusion, from the song, on ff. 640r and 641r, which are, however, on the same paper and in the same hand, probably Stirling's, given that he had endorsed the back of 640r 'Nicholas Nickleby/2 Act/ E. Stirling'. They differ in that only f. 640 has the song, and its version of the sd is slightly briefer. It would be a reasonable deduction to say that Stirling added—possibly even sent in to the Lord Chamberlain separately—f. 640r, to include the song. The brevity of the song text suggests that it was already a published or at least known lyric, but it has not so far been traced. The White Horse Cellar in Piccadilly was a busy stop and booking office for several stagecoach lines.

NOGGS.    Give this to your master—Mr Ralph Nickleby will be here immediately—
be quick—no time to lose. (*gives letter*)                                                    5
SERVANT.    No time to lose. (*mimicking*) What a wild boar! (*Exit slowly*)
NOGGS.    Nice place the benevolent old gentleman has selected—for the pretty delicate creature—his niece—a dressmaker—a milliner—and open to all the insults
and degradations—that the wasps and butterflies of fashion may choose to heap
upon her—and for what!—why the splendid recompense of 6 shillings per week—    10
14 hours per day—and find herself in food and all the necessaries of life—The boy—
pack'd off to the worst of slavery—the drudgery of a Yorkshire school—the girl
condemned to perpetual misery—and squalid poverty. So much for the widow's
friend—kind uncle and loving brother—bah! I'm ashamed to own myself of the
same species—but a day will come—will come.                                          15

*Enter* RALPH NICKLEBY *conducting* KATE, R.H.

RALPH.    Why are you loitering here—idling your time away—go home—
NOGGS.    Yes, sir—but allow me to—
RALPH.    Go. (*loud*)
NOGGS.    Oh! (*Hobbles off R.H.*)
KATE.    Is this Madame Mantilini's, sir?                                              20
RALPH.    It is Madame Mantilini's—and what of that, pray?
KATE.    Nothing. (*timidly*)
RALPH.    Oh! I thought you might have some objections to offer—to the situation
I have been at the trouble of providing for you—
KATE.    Uncle—I must ask one question—am I to live at home—                          25
RALPH.    At home! where's that? didn't know you had one.
KATE.    I mean with my mother—*the widow*—I cannot leave her.
RALPH.    Humbug—do as you like, tho' you will live here to all intents and purposes,
for here you will take your meals—here you will be from morning till night—and
occasionally till morning again.                                                       30
KATE.    But at night—I mean—I must be with my mother—at home—although that
home may be humble—
RALPH.    *May* be humble—must be, you mean—
KATE.    Your pardon—uncle—the word slipped from my tongue.
RALPH.    I hope it did—we must have no false notions of pride.                       35
MANTALINI.    (*speaking without*) Make haste my devinity—can't exist without
you—pon my honor.

*Enter* MANTILINI.

---

4 *immediately*: MS has 'wait for an answer' deleted and 'Mr Ralph Nickleby will be here immediately'
inserted, which agrees with 1838.
27 *I cannot leave her*: MS has 'at night' deleted here.
30 *Humbug…again*: The MS has this speech, and the next four speeches to Mantalini heard off stage,
inserted as a correction on a slip, f. 642r, replacing 'yes you may go home at night /*aside*/ that's when they let you.'

MANTALINI.    Nickleby—how are you? demmit! you don't mean to say you want me
yet do you—

40  RALPH.    Not yet—my niece—

MANTALINI.    I remember—demmit—I remember now what you come for—ha!
ha! forgot the note—and thought you wanted money—you are such a rum fellow,
Nickleby—the demdest, long-headed, queerest-tempered old coiner of gold and
silver ever was—demmit.

*Enter* MADAME MANTILINI *L.H.*

45  MANTALINI.    My life! what a demn'd devil of a time you have been—

MADAME.    I didn't even know Mr Nickleby was here—love.

MANTALINI.    Then what a double d-d infernal rascal that footman must be—
my love—

MADAME.    That is entirely your fault my dear.

50  MANTALINI.    My fault, my heart's joy—

MADAME.    Certainly—you will not correct the man.

MANTALINI.    Correct the man, my soul's delight?

MADAME.    Yes—I am sure he wants speaking to—badly enough.

MANTALINI.    Then do not vex yourself—he shall be horsewhipped till he cries out
55  demnibly. (*kisses her—she pulls him playfully by the ear*)

RALPH.    Now ma'am, this is my niece. (*brings* KATE *forward*)

MADAME.    Just so—Mr Nickleby—can you speak French, child?

KATE.    Yes, ma'am. (*modestly*)

MANTALINI.    Like a demn'd native. (*eyeing* KATE *with a glass*)

60  MADAME.    We keep twenty young women constantly employed in the establishment.

MANTALINI.    Yes, and some of 'em demn'd handsome to!

MADAME.    Mantalini!

MANTALINI.    My senses' idol!

MADAME.    Do you wish to break my heart?

65  MANTALINI.    Not for twenty thousand hemispheres populated with—with—little
ballet-dancers.

MADAME.    You will pay no attention if you please to what Mr Mantalini says—he
knows nothing whatever about any of my young women—he was never even in the
work room—I do not allow it—pray what hours of work have you been accustomed to?

70  KATE.    I have never been accustomed to work at all ma'am.

RALPH.    For which reason she'll work the better.

MADAME.    I hope so—our hours are from nine to nine, with extra work when we're
very full of business, for which I allow payment—dinner and tea you will take
here—your wages will average from 5 to 7 shillings a week.

---

43  MS has the next two pages transposed and therefore mispaginated. The correct order is restored here,
and what follows (onwards from f. 641v) is f. 645r.
62  MADAME: f. 644v.

MANTALINI.    (*aside*) What she'll do with so much demn'd money I can't guess.    75

MADAME.    If you are ready to come—you had better begin to-morrow morning at nine precisely. Miss Knagg my forewoman—shall be prepared to receive you—is there any more, Mr Nickleby?

RALPH.    Nothing more, ma'am.

MADAME.    Then I believe that's all—come my love.    80

MANATALINI.    Yes, my soul—adieu—Nickleby—Au revoir—you little bonnet sylph—(*bowing to* KATE)—mind the demn'd nine—in the morning.

MADAME.    Mantilini! (*angrily*)

MANTALINI.    (*putting his arm round her waist and hurrying her off*) Silence, charment—you know I'm too demn'd fond of you. (*Exit*)    85

RALPH.    There, now you're provided for—I had some idea of providing for your mother in a pleasant part of the country—but as you want to be together I must try to do something else for her—she has a little money, hasn't she?

KATE.    A very little.

RALPH.    A little will go a great way if it's used sparingly. There's a house empty that    90 belongs to me—I can put you into it till it's let—But no time to spare now—come, I'll see you into the street—then you must find your way home—turn to the right hand—straight on—if you forget then ask—or stand still till you remember again.

(*Exit—hurriedly—dragging* KATE *after him on his arm after song*)

SONG

Money is your friend is it not?
Money is your friend is it not?    95
Is it not—is it not—
Yes, Money, money, money
Is your friend.

## SCENE 3

*A dilapidated room—supposed to be a kitchen at Dotheboys Hall—window in F. through which the snow is seen on the ground—moonlight—the reflection falls strongly*

---

75 *What…guess*: This aside would seem to be an afterthought on Stirling's part, since he began to run on the rest of Madame Mantalini's speech, as it appears in the novel, and then deleted 'If you are re' to change speaker. He offers more matter for Yates's performance as Mantalini, which was much praised.

83 MADAME: f. 643r.

93.1 *after song*: 'after song' and the song itself are inserted into the MS in a different pen, and are not in 1838. This would seem a clear instance of the addition of songs to a text to comply with the conditions of the burletta licence, which forbade drama without music in the minor houses like the Adelphi. The snatch of lyric given has not been traced.

SCENE 3: f. 645r.        0.1 *in F*: in flat.

*on Smike—who is sitting by a wretched fire—with his head leaning upon his hands—a solitary rush light illuminates the scene—table chairs—all shabby—for Smike's appearance—see book—slow music to open scene.*

1 SMIKE. (*mournfully*) (*sighs*) Oh, dear! oh, dear! he died—my heart will break—it will—it will—there is no hope for me—how many years have passed since I was a little child—younger than any that are here now. (*wildly*) Where, where are they all gone—I wish I was—with—poor Dorker—the boy that died here—I remember—
5 when I sat up with him at night—he cried no more for friends he wished to come and sit with him—but began to see faces round his bed that came from home—all smiling—ah! what faces will smile on me when I die—(*shivering*) who will talk to me in those long—long nights? they cannot come from home—I—I don't know what *home is*—nothing—nothing but pain and fear—pain and fear for me alive or
10 dead—no hope—no hope. (*buries his face in his hands*)

(*A loud knocking at the door in flat—*SMIKE *rises hastily, wipes his eyes*)

SQUEERS. (*without*) Are you coming to-night—the wind blows fit to knock a man off his legs—
SMIKE. (*sighs*) He's come again. Oh! (*opens door in flat*)

*Enter* SQUEERS *and* NICHOLAS.

SQUEERS. Is that you, Smike—
15 SMIKE. Yes, sir!
SQUEERS. Then why the devil didn't you come to the door before?
SMIKE. Please, sir, I was almost asleep over the fire.
SQUEERS. Fire—what fire?
SMIKE. The kitchen fire, sir. Missus said as I was sitting up, I might come in for a
20 warm.
SQUEERS. Your missus is a fool! you'd have been more awake in the cold I reckon—away with you, and tell Mrs Squeers *I'm* arrived—jump.
(SMIKE *steals out*)
NICHOLAS. Is this Dotheboys Hall, sir?
SQUEERS. Yes! but you needn't call it a hall down here; the fact is it isn't a hall.

0.5 *for… book*: The description of Smike is in chapter 7, 61 in the second number, and reads 'Although he could not have been less than eighteen or nineteen years old, and was tall for that age, he wore a skeleton suit, such as is usually put upon very little boys, and which, though most absurdly short in the arms and legs, was quite wide enough for his attenuated frame. In order that the lower part of his legs might be in perfect keeping with this singular dress, he had a very large pair of boots, originally made for tops, which might have been once worn by some stout farmer, but were now too patched and tattered for a beggar. Heaven knows how long he had been there, but he still wore the same linen which he had first taken down; for, round his neck, was a tattered child's frill, only half concealed by a coarse, man's neckerchief. He was lame'. Mary Ann Keeley who played the role was not as tall as an average male eighteen-year-old, but was famous for her boy roles, which until this point had been comic parts in burlesque; she recalled her difficulty, at this first appearance in the play, in getting the audience to take her seriously.

NICHOLAS.   Oh, indeed.                                                                              25
SQUEERS.   No—we call it a hall up in London—because it sounds better—a man may
   call his house an island if he likes—there's no Act of Parliament against that I believe?
Mrs SQUEERS.   Where is he? where's my deary?

*Enter* MRS SQUEERS.
*For dress see book. Rushes into* SQUEERS's *arms and kissing him.*

MRS SQUEERS.   How is my Squeery—
SQUEERS.   Quite well, love. How are the cows?                                                      30
MRS SQUEERS.   All right
SQUEERS.   And the pigs?
MRS SQUEERS.   As well as can be expected.
SQUEERS.   Come, that's a blessing. The boys are all as they were, I suppose.
MRS SQUEERS.   They're well enough—that young Pitcher's had a fever.                                35
SQUEERS.   Damn that boy—he's always at something of that sort.
MRS SQUEERS.   I say it's obstinacy—I'd beat it out of him and I told you six months
   ago.
SQUEERS.   You did, darling, you did—we'll try what can be done in that way. This is
   the new young man—my dear.                                                                       40
MRS SQUEERS.   Oh!
SQUEERS.   You must give him a shake down in the parlour to-night.
MRS SQUEERS.   We'll manage somehow—you don't much mind how you sleep I
   suppose sir?
NICHOLAS.   No—I am not particular.                                                                 45
MRS SQUEERS.   That's lucky! eh Squeery! (*laughs ha!*)

*Re-enter* SMIKE *slowly.*

SQUEERS.   Well, what do you want—eh?
SMIKE.   (*trembling*) Is there—did any body—has nothing been heard—about me?
SQUEERS.   Devil a bit—and never will be—pretty sort of thing, isn't it, that you
   should have been left here all these years and no money paid after the first six—nor   50
   no clue left who you belong to—and I've had to feed and clothe you—that's the best
   of the joke.

SMIKE *pressing his hands to his head—steals out wringing his hands.*

MRS SQUEERS.   It's my firm belief, Squeers—that young chap's turning silly.
SQUEERS.   I hope he won't make such a fool of himself—for he's a handy fellow, and
   worth his meat and drink any day; besides we should lose!—hem I'll tell you by and   55

---

28.2 *for dress see book*: This description is also in chapter 7: 'The lady, who was of a large raw-boned
figure, was about half a head taller than Mr Squeers, and was dressed in a dimity night-jacket; with her
hair in papers; she had also a dirty nightcap on, relieved by a yellow cotton handkerchief which tied it
under the chin.'

bye—let's have supper—I'm hungry—Nickleby will pick a bit with us tonight, to-
morrow we'll settle matters—and put him into his regular bed room—who sleeps
in Brookes's bed—let me see—Jennings 1—Bolder 2—Graymarsh 3—Primrose 4—
and whats' name—5—yes, Brookes is full.

60 NICHOLAS.     (*aside*) I should think he was—poor devil.

SQUEERS.     There's a place somewhere—but I can't call to mind where—7 in the
morning—7 winter 6 in the summer.

NICHOLAS.     I shall be ready, sir.

SQUEERS.     I'll come myself and show you where the well is—you'll always find a
65     little bit of soap in the kitchen-window; that belongs to you—I don't know what
boy's towel I can put you on—but if you'll make shift to-morrow morning Mrs S.
will arrange it—my dear, don't forget—

MRS SQUEERS.     I'll take care—and mind *you* take care young man—and always
get first wash—the teacher ought to have it, but the boys get the better of him if
70     they can—

SQUEERS.     (*aside*) Now for supper. We'll eat first—he can polish the bones—

MRS SQUEERS.     (*aside*) Hush! I've got a nice juicy steak for you—I bought a large
piece on purpose for—

SQUEERS.     For what—not for the—Boys—

75 MRS SQUEERS.     No—no—do you think I should make myself such a noddy
Squeers—eh—(*Exits with* SQUEERS—*arm round his waist*)

NICHOLAS.     (*walking up and down stage*) Extraordinary person!—wild, uncouth
place—can my uncle have been deceived—or has he willingly condemned me to
such a life as this—no no—I wrong him for the supposition—perhaps I am judging
80     too hastily—matters may turn out here—much better than they promise—I must
be patient—and endeavour to accommodate myself to circumstances—for my
mother and dear sister's sake (*takes out* NEWMAN NOGGS'S *letter*) what an
extraordinary hand—why did Noggs give this to me—there was an earnestness in
his manner—that has struck me forcibly—(*reads*)
85     'My dear young man, I know the world—your father did not or he would not
have done me a kindness when there was no hope of return—you do not, or you
would not be bound on such a journey. If ever you want a shelter in London—
they know where I live at the sign of the Crown in Silver-street Golden-square—
it is at the corner of Silver and James St—bar door both ways. You can come at
90     night—once nobody was ashamed—never mind that—It's all over now—
Newman Noggs
P.S.—If you should go near Barnard Castle, there is good ale at the King's Head—
Say you know me, and I am sure they will not charge you for it—You may say *Mr*
*Noggs*—there—for I was a gentleman then—I was indeed—'

*Re-enter* SMIKE *slowly.*

95 SMIKE.     You're to go in to supper, sir. (*shivering*)

NICHOLAS.     Thank you—you are shivering—are you cold—

SMIKE.     N-n-no—I am not cold—I'm used to it.

NICHOLAS.    Poor fellow. (*patting his head*) (*Exit, R.H. 1 E.*)

SMIKE.    He spoke kindly to me. I—I—can't bear it. (*sighs*) When—when shall I
hear from home—from some one that loves me? To remain longer in this dreadful 100
place will drive me mad. If I was a little bird, then I could fly far, far away, to live
happily all the summer days among the green fields and wild flowers. Yes, yes, I'll
go at once. (*runs to window*) But there are no flowers now. The cold glistening
snow is on the ground, and the green fields are buried under a large white shroud.
If I left the house now I might be starved, and drop helpless and frozen, like the 105
poor birds! (*pauses*) I've heard that good people that live away from this place feed
the pretty harmless robins when the cold days and dark nights are on—perhaps they
would feed me too, for I am very harmless—very. I'll run to them at once, and ask
them. (*going*)

SQUEERS.    (*heard without, R.H.*) Smike! you lazy rascal, where are you?          110

SMIKE.    (*creeping from window*) I dare not go—that voice renders me helpless! I'll—
I'll wait till the moon goes to sleep and the gloomy clouds come down; then—then
I'll fly away, to be my own master, to walk about all day, and sleep soundly at
night. (*laughs*) Ha! ha! that will be what some of the boys call liberty. (*clasps his
hands with joy*) Oh! I love it—I love it—I love liberty! Yes, yes; this night I will be 115
free—ha! ha! (*Exit through window carefully—the reflection of the moon is thrown
upon* SMIKE *as he gets out of window—he then closes the window-shutters, and the
scene changes*)


# SCENE 4

MANTALINI's—*the work-room—a number of girls discovered variously employed—
sewing—making bonnets etc.*—MISS KNAG—KATE—*and* MADAME MANTILINI—
*Tableau see Plate.*

MADAME.    Miss Knag this is the young person I spoke to you about—Miss 1
Nickleby—

GIRLS.    (*aside to each other*) The new country young lady—

MADAME.    I think for the present she will not be of much use—but her appearance
will—                                                                             5

---

98 *Exit, R.H. 1 E.*: The MS has Smike exit with him, and an anomalous instruction 'end scene' at this
point, which is at the foot of f. 467v, before moving on to scene 4 on the next leaf, f. 468r. This leaves out the
whole of Mrs Keeley's soliloquy and action, her big chance to impress her acting of a pathetic child role
upon the surprised audience. There is a mark in the MS, a circle diagonally crossed through, which is a
stock symbol used in various ways by copyists and prompters but most often at this date indicating the place
where additional material is to be inserted (I am indebted to Tracy Catell for this precise information).
There is no sign of the matter to be introduced, but 1838, which is followed here, shows that it was the scene
to whose sentimentality Dickens objected when he saw the play: see Introduction.

0.3 *see Plate*: 'Madame Mantalini introduces Kate to Miss Knag', the second plate in No. V, before chapter 15.

MISS KNAG.    Suit very well with mine—Miss Nickleby and I are quite a pair—he! he!—

*Door in flat opens slowly.* MANTALINI *peeps in.*

MANTALINI.    Is my life and soul there?

MADAME.    No—

(GIRLS *laugh aside*)

MANTALINI.    How can it say so, when it is blooming there like a little rose in a dem-
10    nition flower-pot—may its poppet come in and talk?

MADAME.    Certainly not. You know I never allow you in the work-room—go along—

MANTALINI.    (*walks towards her on tiptoe—blowing kisses to her*) Why will it vex—
itself—and twist its little face into bewitching nutcrackers. (*embracing*)

MADAME.    Oh I can't bear you.

15    MANTALINI.    Not bear *me*—fibs—fibs—it could not be—there's not a woman alive,
that would tell me such a thing to my face—to my own face—

(GIRLS *laugh*)

MADAME.    Ladies leave the room—(*girls rise*) Miss Knag retire a few minutes with
Miss Nickleby.

(*one of the* GIRLS—*laughs loud*)

Miss Jones—your services will not be required after to-morrow evening.

20    GIRL.    I'm sure I don't care. I can get a shilling a-day and my victuals any where, and
here I get none. (GIRLS *exit talking aside*)

MANTALINI *is seated in chair* L.H., *coquetting with* KATE NICKLEBY.

MISS K.    Isn't he a beautiful man creature?

MISS K. *and* KATE *exit* R.H. 2 E.

MADAME.    Alfred I am surprised at your conduct—why do you show yourself to the
girls—my young ladies—

25    MANTALINI.    (*tapping her chin*) If you will be odiously, demnibly outrageously jealous my soul—you will be very miserable—horrid miserable—demnition miserable.

MADAME.    I am miserable. (*pettishly*)

MANTALINI.    Do not put itself out of humour. It is a pretty bewitching little demn'd
countenance, and it should not be put out of humour, for it spoils its loveliness, and

30    makes it cross and gloomy like a frightful, naughty, demn'd hobgoblin—

MADAME.    I am not to be brought round in that way always sir—

MANTALINI.    It shall be brought round in any way it likes best—and not be brought
round at all if it likes it better.

21 *I'm . . . none*: MS omits this speech.
21.1 *MANTALINI . . . NICKLEBY*: MS omits this sd and has Miss Knag exit alone after her line.

MADAME.    You are always flirting with some new person—last night at the Ball—
your attentions to Miss—La—Spinnini was remarked by every one—                    35
MANTALINI.    No—no—pon my soul, my life—
MADAME.    They were—I had my eye upon you all the time.
MANTALINI.    Bless—the little winking twinkling eye, was it on me all the time—
Oh, demmit.
MADAME.    You ought not to waltz with any body but your own wife—and I will not    40
bear it, Mantilini, if I take poison first—(*throws herself into a chair*)
MANTALINI.    She will not take poison and have horrid pains will she—(*drawing a
chair towards her and seating himself*) She will not take poison because she had a
demd fine husband who might have married two countesses and a dowager—
MADAME.    Two countesses—you told me one before.                    45
MANTALINI.    Two—two—demd fine women, real countesses and splendid
fortunes—demmit.
MADAME.    (*playfully*) And why didn't you?—
MANTALINI.    Why didn't I! had I not seen the demd'st little fascinator in all the
world—and while that little fascinator is my wife—may not all the countesses and    50
dowagers in England be—

(MADAME M. *kisses him in time to interrupt the sentence*)

MADAME.    Dear Alfred.
MANTALINI.    Adorable—Evelina—let me worship you—can't it spare its Alfey a lit-
tle more cash—my existence's jewel—
MADAME.    Don't ask, my love, we've so little in hand.                    55
MANTALINI.    Then we must have some more—Pigeon—we must have some dis-
count out of old Nickleby to carry on the war with—demmit—
MADAME.    But you can't want any more—just now—dear—
MANTALINI.    My life and soul—there is a horse for sale at Scrubbs's—which it
would be a sin and a crime to lose—magnificent—quadruped—going my senses'    60
joy for nothing—
MADAME.    For nothing—I am glad of that.
MANTALINI.    For actually nothing—a 100 guineas down will buy him—mane—
and crest and legs and tail and all of the demdest beauty—I will ride him in the
Park, before the very chariots of the rejected countesses—the demd old dowager    65
will faint with grief and rage—and the other two will say, he is—married—he has
made away with himself, it is a demd thing, it is all up—They will hate each other
demnibly, and wish you dead and buried—ha! ha! he! He—
MADAME.    Ha! ha! you naughty flatterer—I suppose I must see what money I have
in the desk—(*going*)                    70
MANTALINI.    Make haste, angel of bounty—get me the 100—or I shall devour you
with kisses—absolutely swallow its little body, clothes and all, demmit!

*Exits coquetting with* MADAME MANTALINI *after song*

SONG, MANTALINI
Oh love is a Fairy power
That weaves our chain of bliss
75    Tis another land's stolen hour
To sweeten whole years in this
Etc etc etc

*Exit coquetting with Madam*


# SCENE 5

*—a parlour meanly furnished in Dotheboys Hall—Enter* MISS SQUEERS *and* MISS PRICE—*followed by a little* SERVANT-GIRL *who places table and 4 chairs, tea things etc—*

1  MISS PRICE.    So Fanny—you've really—got a right-down sweet heart at last, eh—
MISS SQUEERS.    Yes Tilda—and I flatter myself such a *one* as folks don't meet with every day—he's a perfect gentleman bred and born—
MISS PRICE.    Lor, how nice.
5  MISS SQUEERS.    Ain't it—we fell in love with one another at first sight—he's only been here—a fortnight—now can't you guess who it is Tilly dear?
MISS PRICE.    Is it the new tutor—Mr Nickleby?
MISS SQUEERS.    (*simpers*) Y—e—s—although he's only Pa's assistant he's a young gentleman of high birth—and immense connections—I mustn't tell you all I know
10    just yet—but he will have heaps of money—and perhaps a title or two. Ain't I a fortunate girl at last?
MISS PRICE.    (*slyly*) Uncommon!—what has he said to you?
MISS SQUEERS.    Oh! don't ask me—when I begged him to make a soft pen for me this morning he looked so *soft* at me—oh dear—I'm a lost girl Tilly. (*sighs*)
15  MISS PRICE.    Did he look this way, Fanny—(*leering*)
MISS SQUEERS.    Yes, only much more genteel.—Pa and Ma being out I've invited him to meet you and your intended Mr Browdie and to drink tea and play cards in the parlour—this evening.

72.2 *SONG, MANTALINI*: Song not in 1838; it is on a new sheet in the MS (650r) which is left partially blank before the next scene begins on the lower half of 650v, suggesting that the scrap of the song given is an insertion; it is probably here to satisfy the terms of the burletta licence. The lyric may be from 'Sing to Love a Roundelay' by Joseph Augustine Wade.

9 *mustn't*: 1838; MS has 'must'.
10 *and . . . two*: MS begins the scene anew at this point, repeating the entrance but having the characters carry the tea equipage, and then deletes the sd and a line for Miss Squeers: 'Now isn't it an extraordinary thing Tilda!'
13 *don't ask me*: 1838; MS inserts and then deletes 'he a real gentleman born—of high birth—although he's only my Pa's teacher'.

MISS PRICE.    How delicious—John will soon be here—he's only gone home to clean himself. (*fetches chairs, they sit*) Between ourselves, Mr John's grown rather jeal-   20
ous—I must take him down a bit—I'll give myself a few airs.

MISS SQUEERS.    I do so palpitate! (*placing her hand on her heart*)

MISS PRICE.    Ah poor thing! I know what it is—you'll soon get the better of it dear. (*A slight knock,* R.H.)

MISS SQUEERS.    Oh Tilda!—there he is—is my hair in order?    25

MISS PRICE.    Yes—hush! (*whispers*) Say come in.

MISS SQUEERS.    Oh! come in. (*whispering*)

*Enter* NICHOLAS.

NICHOLAS.    Good evening. (*bowing*) I understood from Mr Squeers that—

MISS SQUEERS.    O yes it's all right—Father—Pa don't tea with us—but you won't mind that I dare say—we are only waiting for one more gentleman.    30

MISS PRICE.    Don't mind me a bit; for I'm quite as bad. Go on just as you would if you were alone.

MISS SQUEERS.    La! 'Tilda! I'm ashamed—of you. (*both giggle*)

NICHOLAS.    (*aside*) What are they about—oh—well, as I am here—and seem expected (for some reason unknown to myself)—to be amiable, why it's no use   35
looking like a goose—ladies, allow me—the honour. (*places chairs—girls giggle*)

MISS SQUEERS.    Ain't he a duck, 'Tilly! (*a heavy footstep heard without*)

MISS PRICE.    That's John Browdie's step! (*runs to wing*) Well, John!

*Enter* JOHN BROWDIE (*see work*).

BROWDIE.    Weel, *Mat*-ilda! (*grinning*) I be here at last. I had to clean the horses, and milk 'tould cow, before mother would gi I my Sunday coat, to come out a   40
sweethearting.

MISS SQUEERS.    I beg your pardon Mr Nickleby—Mr John Browdie, sir, a perfect gentleman.

(NICHOLAS *bows*)

BROWDIE.    'Ees! and a miller, grazier, and cow doctor. For eating bacon, drinking yale, and killing a pig, I won't turn my hand upon any chap in Yorkshire—gi' us thy   45
fist, lad! (*grinning*)

MISS SQUEERS.    Now—sit down the tea's drawn—Mr Nickleby, will you sit here. (*placing chair next her*)

MISS PRICE.    To be *sure* he will—here should he sit—

*They all seat themselves at table.* NICHOLAS *eats very heartily.*

---

20 *fetches chairs, they sit*: 1838; MS omits the sd and the ensuing explanation.

38.1 *see work*: i.e. see Dickens's description of Browdie. It is in chapter 9, 81 of No. III: 'his hair very damp from recent washing, and a clean shirt, whereof the collar might have belonged to some giant ancestor, forming, together with a white waistcoat of similar dimensions, the chief ornament of his person' and he was 'something over six feet high, with a face and body rather above the due proportion than below it.'

39 *Weel…last*: The rest of this speech and his next are from 1838, not occurring in MS (nor in Dickens).

50  BROWDIE.     (*speaks with his mouth full*) Old wooman out, beant she (MISS S.
     *nods*)—glad of it—ye weant get bread and butther ev'ry night I expect, mun—
     (*aside*) Ecod, how he does put it away! ha! ha! (*laughs, and appears to choke with a
     mouthful of bread*)
     NICHOLAS.     (*sharply*) Sir—
     BROWDIE.     (*laughing*) Ecod If you stop here at school long eneaf—ye'll be nout but
55   skeen and boans ha! ha!—t'other teacher wur a lean un, ecod he weir—a mopstick
     was a Daniel Lambert to un—ha! ha!
     NICHOLAS.     Your remarks are ungentlemanly and offensive sir, and—I—

(*All rise*)

     BROWDIE.     Dang it—does want to fight? Come on. (*squaring up to* NICHOLAS)
     MISS PRICE.     (*stopping* BROWDIE's *mouth*) If you say another word, John, I'll never
60   forgive you—
     BROWDIE.     Weel, weel—I won't. Kiss I, lass, and we'll say no more about school-
     master chap. (*kisses* MISS P. *heartily*)
     MISS SQUEERS.     Oh! (*sighing*)
     MISS PRICE.     What's the matter, Fanny?
65   MISS SQUEERS.     Nothing, 'Tilda, dear.
     MISS PRICE.     I'm sure there is. (*to* NICHOLAS) Say something to her—shall I and
     John go into the little kitchen, and come back presently—
     NICHOLAS.     What on earth should you do that for?
     MISS PRICE.     What for—well you *are* a one to keep company. (*a* LITTLE SERVANT
     GIRL *clears off tea things*)
70   MISS SQUEERS.     We're going to have a game at cards if it's agreeable and as there are
     only four of us Tilda—we had better go partners two against two.
     MISS PRICE.     With all my heart—what do you say, Mr Nickleby?
     BROWDIE.     (*aside*) She doant ask I.
     NICHOLAS.     I shall feel a pleasure—allow me to be your partner.
75   BROWDIE.     (*aside*) That Lunnon chap wants to court her. I'll—
     MISS SQUEERS.     Well, I never! Mr Browdie—shall we join partners against
     'em? (*reseat themselves*)
     NICHOLAS.     (*dealing cards*) We intend to win every thing.
     MISS SQUEERS.     Tilda has won something she didn't expect.
80   MISS PRICE.     La, dear! your hair's coming out of curl.
     MISS SQUEERS.     Never mind me.
     MISS PRICE.     I never had such luck—I should always like to have you for a partner,
     Mr Nickleby—

---

51 *Old…mun*: MS ends the speech here; 1838 apparently seeks to build up the broad comedy in the role
of Browdie.
     56 *a…ha!*: MS omits 'a mopstick…ha! ha!'
     58 *Dang…* NICHOLAS: MS omits this speech and sd.
     62 *Kiss…heartily*: MS omits 'Kiss…chap' and sd.          73 *She doant ask I*: MS omits this speech.
     75 *That…I'll*: MS omits this speech.

NICHOLAS.    I wish you had.

MISS SQUEERS.    (*aside*) Did ever any body hear—                                    85

MISS PRICE.    John why don't you say something—and not sit there so silent and glum.

BROWDIE.    Weel then—what I say is this—Dang me if I stan' this ony longer—Do ye gang whoame wi me, and do yon bright an' tight young whipster, look sharp out for a broken head next time he cums under my hond. (*strikes table violently*)

MISS PRICE.    Mercy on us what's all this John?                                         90

BROWDIE.    Cum whoam I tell ye, cum whoam. (*pulling her*)

MISS SQUEERS.    (*sobbing violently*) oh!—oh!—I had 5 trumps in my hand too oh!

MISS PRICE.    Why here's Fanny in tears now—what can the matter be—

MISS SQUEERS.    Oh you don't know Miss of course—pray don't trouble yourself to enquire—                                                                          95

MISS PRICE.    Well I'm sure Miss Pert—

MISS SQUEERS.    and who cares whether you are sure or not ma'am.

MISS PRICE.    You are monstrous polite—Ma'am—

MISS SQUEERS.    I shall not come to you to take lessons in the art ma'am—

NICHOLAS.    Ladies allow me to—                                                          100

MISS SQUEERS.    I shan't—

MISS PRICE.    That's pretty treatment to a real gentleman oh! Miss Fanny Squeers— wheres your manners?

MISS SQUEERS.    Low person—I despise you—

MISS PRICE.    Ha! ha! despise me poor thing—a petty school master's daughter talk  105 to me indeed—ha! its too funny—

MISS SQUEERS.    Petty schoolmaster's daughter—(*screams*) Tilda I hate you.

MISS PRICE.    There's no love lost between us—young woman.

MISS SQUEERS.    Young woman—I scorn your words Minx.

MISS PRICE.    If you call names I slap your face madam. (*advancing towards her*)    110

MISS SQUEERS.    I'll box your ears if you dare to threaten me—hussy—(*advancing*)

BROWDIE.    (*pulling MISS PRICE away*) Dang it cum whoam will ee?

---

87 *Weel...longer*: 1838 ends the scene very differently, from this point on:

> Do you think I'm going to let that cockney chap, make luve to you, after all I've done and spent? haven't I treated ye to all the races, fairs, and bull-baitings in t'country? didn't I last Tadcaster fair pay for two pound of gingerbread-nuts, two combs as good as tortoise-shell, and a chap that dances when they pulls a string?—besides spending a matther o' nine pence in the lucky bag, tea totums, cherrybounce, and sweet stuff? after all this, dost think I'm going to stand ony Lunnon nonsense? No! I be dom'd if I do. (*going up to Nicholas*) Stand up like a mon, and let me knock you down. (*Pulls off coat, and squares up to Nicholas*)
>
> MISS PRICE.    Well, I'm sure, sir! what's all this about? ha! ha! (*laughs*)
>
> BROWDIE.    Don't laugh. I beant a bit jealous; oh no—oh no—no—ha! ha! ha! it be capital fun beant it? Eh! ha! (*stamping with rage*) Oh you two-faced Jezebel! where be all my money—the lucky bag—I'll be revenged—I'll be revenged—(*kicks over table*) I wool—I wool.
>
> (*Exit, R.H. 1 E. dragging off MISS PRICE*)
>
> MISS SQUEERS (*sobbing violently*) Oh! Oh! I had five trumps in my hand. (*falls into Nicholas's arms*)
>
> (*Exit, L.H. 1 E. with NICKLEBY*)

MISS PRICE.   I won't—let me—scratch her face—

MISS SQUEERS.   I'll tear her eyes out—(*slaps* MISS PRICE's *face*)

(THE GIRLS *struggle for a moment*—BROWDIE *carries* MISS PRICE *off*—*screaming violently* R.H. MISS SQUEERS. *falls violently into* NICHOLAS *arms squalling*)

115 NICHOLAS.   (*dragging her off* L.H.) What the devil am I to do with her?

(MISS SQUEERS *drag out*)

END SCENE

## SCENE 6

*The school-room at Do-the-boys Hall. Desks, forms, etc.*

MR *and* MRS SQUEERS *discovered*—MRS SQUEERS *looking in a cupboard.*

1 BOYS.   Bab—bab—by—Bab—by—l—o—b—on Babbylon. (*this is done with a confused noise*)

MRS SQUEERS.   Drat the things—I can't find the school spoon any where.

SQUEERS.   Never mind it, dear—it's of no consequence—

MRS SQUEERS.   No consequence—why how you talk—isn't it brimstone morning?

5 SQUEERS.   I forgot my dear—yes—we must not neglect purifying the boys' blood.

MRS SQUEERS.   Besides if they hadn't something or other in the way of medicine they'd be always ailing and giving a world of trouble, and it spoils their appetites and comes cheaper than breakfast and dinner.

MRS SQUEERS.   That Smike must have hid it somewhere or other. (*calls*) Smike,

10 where are you—

SQUEERS.   I haven't seen the young gentleman this morning—since Nickleby's been here—he's grown dull and lazy—a good thrashing will bring him to his senses—I'm thinking.

MRS SQUEERS.   You're always thinking Squeery—why don't you act? That *Nuckleboy*

15 will set all the boys against you—with his proud stuck-up ways. I hate the very look of him—

SQUEERS.   My love, you are indiscreet—

MRS SQUEERS.   Stuff don't tell me—I know what's what. Smike! where the devil are you? *Exit* R.H.

115.1 *MISS SQUEERS drag out*: This final sd is in the MS, but deleted.

1.1 *this... noise*: Sd not in MS.

6 *MRS SQUEERS*: Deleted in MS: 'Purify fiddlesticks, and you know they have to partly because...' 1838 gives this speech to Squeers.

7 *and*: MS has 'partly because' deleted.

19 *Exit* R.H.: MS and 1838 are contradictory about the entrances and exits at this point. MS has Squeers and Mrs S exit disputing before Nicholas enters, but deletes that instruction, and inserts an exit for Squeers but not his wife, before Nicholas enters, but does not indicate his re-entry. 1838 has the configuration here.

SQUEERS.   He shall have a double allowance of brimstone for this, and a sound 20
caning—(*retires up to his desk,* R.H.)

*Enter* NICHOLAS 1 E.L.H.

NICHOLAS.   When will the day arrive that enables me to turn my back upon this
accursed place—never to set foot in it again or to think of it—even think of it—but
with loathing and disgust—added to my other sufferings, as if they were inefficient,
is the pretended affection towards me advanced by Miss Squeers, the disgusting 25
prototype of her more disgusting father—By rejecting her attentions I have set
these people by the ears—and made more enemies—when heaven knows I needed
none—The unfeeling, dastardly conduct pursued by Squeers towards the poor
helpless boy Smike, is beyond all forbearance. I am determined to oppose such
barbarity the next time—let the consequence be what it may. (*seats himself at* 30
*desk—a low murmur heard without* R.H.)

SQUEERS.   Boys, boys, silence, or I'll—

*Enter groups of boys of all ages dressed shabbily—surrounding* MRS SQUEERS.—*she car-*
*ries a large brown pan—filled with treacle—which she places on a desk—and stands*
*behind it—Boys make faces—*SQUEERS *strikes form with cane, they are instantly silent.*

SQUEERS.   Have you seen Smike this morning Mr Nickleby?

NICHOLAS.   I have seen nothing of him since last night.

SQUEERS.   Come sir you won't save him this way where is he? he is missing.

1ST BOY.   Please—sir—I think Smike's run away. 35

SQUEERS.   Ha! who said that?

BOYS.   Tomkins—sir—

SQUEERS.   (*seizing boy*) And what reason have you to suppose any boy would run
away from *this* establishment, eh, sir—take that—(*boxes his ears*) I give you all
notice if I catch Master Smike, I'll only stop short of flaying him. 40

MRS SQUEERS.   If you catch him—you can't help it, stupid—he hadn't any money,
had he?

SQUEERS.   Never had a penny in all his life.

MRS SQUEERS.   And he didn't take any thing to eat with him—I'll answer for, ha!
ha!—then of course he must beg his way, and he could do that nowhere but on the 45
public road.

SQUEERS.   That's true—

MRS SQUEERS.   I have sent one chaise one way—and Swallow's man another, so we
are sure to catch the rascal before night.

NICHOLAS.   (*aside*) Wretches! 50

SQUEERS.   (*rapping desk with cane*) Now, 1st class treacle—

---

30 *the next time*: 'the next time' 1838, not in MS.

(*The boys all advance slowly and reluctantly and* MRS SQUEERS *gives each a spoonful of treacle, some a rap of the head with spoon*)

*see plate*

*Music*

SQUEERS.    Now is that physicking nearly over—

MRS SQUEERS.    Just over. (*giving a little boy a very large spoonful*)—There that's the last—(*takes pan away—boys make wry faces*).

55 SQUEERS.    Now Mr Nickleby—we'll begin bus. for the day—1st class—English Spelling and Philosophy come forward—

(*6 ragged boys advance with tattered books—*NICHOLAS *places himself near* SQUEERS)

We'll get up a Latin class by and by which I shall turn over to you Nickleby—now then where's the first boy?

BOY.    Please sir, he's cleaning the back-parlour windows.

60 SQUEERS.    So he is to be sure—we always go upon the practical mode of teaching, the regular educational system, C-L-E-A-N, clean, verb active, to make bright, to scour. W-I-N—win—D-E-R—der—winder, a casement—when the boy knows this out of book, he goes and does it. It's just the same principle as the use of the globes—now—where's the second boy?

65 BOY.    Please sir, he's weeding the garden.

SQUEERS.    To be sure he is—B-O-T—bot—, T-I-N—tin—N-E-Y—ney, bottinney noun substantive, a knowledge of plants—when he has learned that bottinney means a knowledge of plants, he goes and knows 'em—that's our system, what do you think of it?

70 NICHOLAS.    It's a *useful* one at any rate.

SQUEERS.    I believe you—third boy, what's a horse?

BOY.    A beast, sir.

SQUEERS.    So it is, ain't it Nickleby?

NICHOLAS.    I believe there is no doubt of that, sir.

75 SQUEERS.    Of course there isn't—a horse is a quadruped, and quadruped's Latin for beast, as every body that's gone through the grammar knows—or else where's the use of having grammars at all?—so as you're in that, go and look after *my* horse, and rub him down well—the rest of the class Philosophy go and draw water up, till somebody tells you to leave off—for it's washing-day to-morrow.

*Enter* MRS SQUEERS *hastily 3 E.R.H.*

80 MRS SQUEERS.    We've got the gentleman at last—Swallow's man caught him on the road to York—and they've tied him hand and foot to prevent him giving them the slip again.

SQUEERS.    Bring him in—bring him.

51.3 *see plate*: The plate is the first in No. III.

MRS SQUEERS *exits, and returns immediately dragging in* SMIKE—*trembling and dejected 3 E.R.H.*

NICHOLAS.    Poor fellow! (*aside*) my heart bleeds for him.

SQUEERS.    Let every boy keep his place. (*striking the desk*) Nickleby attend sir— 85
   Now, sir, (*to* SMIKE) have you any thing to say for yourself? (*flourishing his cane*)
   Stand a little out of the way Mrs Squeers, my dear, I've hardly got room enough—

SMIKE.    Spare me, sir I was driven to do it—

SQUEERS.    Driven to do it, were you—Oh! it wasn't your fault, it was mine I suppose, eh?    90

MRS SQUEERS.    What does he mean by that?

SQUEERS.    We'll try and find out. (*seizes* SMIKE, *and is in the act of striking him
   when* NICHOLAS *stands before them*)—

NICHOLAS.    Stop!

SQUEERS.    Who cried stop?

NICHOLAS.    I—this must not go on.    95

SQUEERS.    Must not go on.

NICHOLAS.    No—I say must not—I will prevent it, you have disregarded all my
   quiet entreaties on this poor miserable boy's behalf—therefore don't blame me for
   this public interference—you have brought it on yourself.

SQUEERS.    (*violently enraged*) Sit down, beggar. (*endeavouring to strike* SMIKE) 100
   Stand back.

NICHOLAS.    Wretch I will not stand by and see it done—I have a long series of
   insults to avenge, and my indignation is aggravated by the dastardly cruelties practised on helpless infancy in this foul den—have a care, for if you do raise the devil
   within me, the consequences shall fall heavily on your own head—    105

SQUEERS.    Dog—rascal!—take that (*strikes* NICHOLAS *a blow with the cane—
   NICHOLAS *wrests cane from him and beats him without mercy—Boys shout—*MISS
   SQUEERS *rushes in—and belabours* NICHOLAS—MASTER SQUEERS *and* MRS
   SQUEERS *join in—universal confusion and Picture see Plate*).

*Music*

## END OF ACT

106.3 *see Plate*: The second plate in No. IV.

# ACT II

## SCENE 1

*A desolate wild heath—with a barn or outhouse painted on one of the flats—small practicable door in same—day break—music piano—*SMIKE *discovered crouching on the stage and peeping through barn door.*

1 SMIKE.    Yes—he's there—I'll watch beside him till he wakes then hide behind the
tall bushes lest he should see and send me back. Oh—no—no he would not be so
cruel—they'd kill me now he's gone—I am cold and hungry—yet very happy—for I
am near the only being that ever spoke kindly to me since I was a little child,
5 eh! (*wildly*) What am I now? a man ha! ha! a brave man? No—I'm nothing—a
fool!—those cruel people always told me so.

(*Barn door slowly opens* NICHOLAS *enters from it.* SMIKE *partially conceals himself
behind door*)

NICHOLAS.    I have slept well spite of the fatigue and vexation that overwhelmed me
tho' I cannot banish entirely from my mind the certain painful misgivings as to the
probable fate of the poor boy—Smike—it makes me shudder, to even think of his
10 unhappy situation.

(SMIKE *advances*)

What is this?—can it be some lingering creation of the visions that have disturbed
me—it cannot be real—and yet I—I—am awake—Smike!
SMIKE.    (*kneeling*) Y—e—s don't beat me—
NICHOLAS.    (*raising*) Wretched boy—why do you kneel to me?
15 SMIKE.    To go with you, anywhere—everywhere—to the world's end—to the
churchyard grave—let me—do let me go with you—you are my home—my kind
friend—take me with you, pray!
NICHOLAS.    I am a friend who can do little for you—how came you here?
SMIKE.    I—I have followed your footsteps—a long—long way—from *there* (*shud-*
20 *ders*) watched when you slept—and crouched like a hare in the grass—when you
stopped to eat—I—I—am very—hungry—but I dare not ask for bread, or you
might have discovered and sent me back.
NICHOLAS.    Poor fellow—your hard fate denies you any friend but one, and he is
nearly as helpless as yourself—
25 SMIKE.    May I—may I—go with you?—I will be your faithful hard-working servant, I will indeed—I want no clothes—these will do very well; I only want to be near
you. (*taking* NICHOLAS's *hand*)
NICHOLAS.    And you shall—we'll walk to London together—and the world shall
deal by you as it does by me, till one or both of us shall quit it for a better—(*shaking*
30 SMIKE's *hand*) come.

SMIKE.    (*laughing wildly*) Ha! ha! I'm so happy—I—I don't feel a bit hungry now—
Come, come, let us run all the way.

JOHN BROWDIE *whistles without, R. H.*

SMIKE.    Hush—they are coming to carry me back don't let 'em, don't let 'em. (*clings
to* NICHOLAS)

NICHOLAS.    Silence—boy—you've nothing to dread. (*looks off R. H.*) Unfortunate!—
tis my late rival, Mr John Browdie—I'm in no mood for noise and riot and yet do    35
what I will—I shall not escape altercation with this honest blockhead and perhaps
a blow or two with his staff.

SMIKE.    No, no, he shall beat me, not you.

*Enter* JOHN BROWDIE *carrying a huge stick.*

BROWDIE.    Barn-door open, eh! what the devils in't wind now? (*seeing* NICHOLAS)
Gadzooks—thee be'st out betimes this morning, sur. Servant young gentleman—    40
(*bows*)

NICHOLAS.    Yours. (*bows*)

BROWDIE.    Weel—we—ha' met at last—eh? (*whistling, striking his stick on the
ground—*SMIKE *shrinks away*)

NICHOLAS.    Yes—Come, we parted on no very good terms—the last time we met—
it was my fault, I believe but—I had no intention of offending you, and no idea that
I was doing so—I was very sorry for it afterwards—will you shake hands? (*offers*    45
*his hand*)

BROWDIE.    Shake hands—ah that I will—(*shakes hands*)

SMIKE.    (*running forward*) Mine—mine, too. (*offers his*)

BROWDIE.    Dong it, mun—what does this scarecrow do wi' thee?—why, thy feace be
all broken loike—wa-at be the matter?

NICHOLAS.    It is a cut—a blow but I returned it to the giver and with good interest too.    50

BROWDIE.    Noa, did'ee though? I loike un for that—

NICHOLAS.    The fact is—I have been ill-treated—

SMIKE.    For me. (*mournfully*)

BROWDIE.    Noa—don't say that.

NICHOLAS.    Yes—I have been—by that man Squeers; and I have beaten him    55
soundly—and have left the place in consequence—

BROWDIE.    What—beaten the school measther? ho! ho! ho! Who ever heard o' the
loike o' that noo!—Gi' us thee hond again youngster. Beaten a schoolmeaster—
Dang it—I loove thee for't ho! ho! (*shakes* NICHOLAS's *hand violently*)

SMIKE.    (*laughs*) ha! ha! ha!    60

BROWDIE.    Capital! Capital!—Mun, and what does mean to do lad—now?

NICHOLAS.    Go immediately to London—we are now on our way.

BROWDIE.    (*shaking his head*) Dost know how much coaches charge?

NICHOLAS.    No—I do not—but that is of no consequence, for we intend walking.

BROWDIE.    Gang awa to Lunnun afoot, a matter of 190 mile?    65

NICHOLAS.    Every step of the way.

SMIKE.    We'll be there by night.

NICHOLAS.   Silly lad—good bye, Browdie—We must walk 40 miles before night—(*going*)

70  BROWDIE.   Stan' still noo—Hoo much cash hast thee gotten—mun—

NICHOLAS.   Not much—perhaps five shillings—but I can make it enough—where there's a will there's a way.

BROWDIE.   Five shillings for two lads to walk up to Lunnun wi', 190 wearisome miles—No I'm dang'd if they shall while John Browdie's gotten a golden guinea in

75  his t'ould leather purse—(*pulling out a shabby purse and offering it to* NICHOLAS) There he be, lad—tak as much as likes mun.

NICHOLAS.   You are too kind—

BROWDIE.   Too koind—pack a stuff—bean't it duty of one mon to assist another? If every body—would stick to that—there wouldn't be quite so much mischief done

80  in't world—tak' eneaf to carry thee whoam—thee'lt pay me yan day a' warrant—

NICHOLAS.   I will not refuse your generous-hearted kindness (*taking money*) a sovereign will be quite enough.

BROWDIE.   One—dong it lad tak' one a piece—

NICHOLAS.   No—thank you, one will be sufficient for both—

85  BROWDIE.   If thee won't ha it, t'other chap shall—here—Smike here be one for thee—

SMIKE.   (*taking money and giving it to* NICHOLAS) Both for you!—ha! ha!

NICHOLAS.   Heaven will reward you for this kindness.

BROWDIE.   It be all right. Something be a *thumping* up and down under my waistcoat that tells me so. (*shakes hands with both*) Good bye, bless ee—stop—tak' this

90  bit o' timber to help thee on wi' mun, keep a good heart, and bless thee—Beaten schoolmaster! 'cod it's the best thing a've heard this twenty year—ho! ho! ha! (*Exits* R. H.—NICHOLAS *and* SMIKE L.H, NICHOLAS *carrying his bundle on the stick over his shoulder and waving his hand to* BROWDIE, SMIKE *looking back and nodding his head, holding* NICHOLAS's *coat-tail in one hand; Music*)

*Re-enter* BROWDIE.

BROWDIE.   Well—I do feel so happy—I could dance—sing or do any thing now—so I'll try a stave—

SONG

In Yorkshire I was born and bred

95

And learn'd a thing or two sir,<br>
And what be more my mother said<br>
My wit would bring me through sir<br>
Etc etc.

(*Exit laughing*)

98 *In Yorkshire...Etc etc*: 1838 ends scene with the exit of Nicholas and Smike. The MS has Browdie's re-entry and song in fainter ink, apparently an addition; songs were necessary to satisfy the terms of the Adelphi's licence. This one has not been traced, but appears perhaps to be based on the tune and verse of 'The Vicar of Bray.'

## SCENE 2

*The Show Room at* MADAME MANTALINI's—KATE *discovered arranging various articles of dress and bijouterie—large cheval glass—dresses, bonnets, etc. scattered about scene.*

KATE.   I am almost tired of this wretched state of existence—no relief—no relaxa-  1
tion—perpetually associating with these odious people—not one being in the
world—that can understand or sympathize with my situation but my mother—and
that kind—good creature—Newman Noggs! innumerable are the little acts of delicate attention shown by him towards us—I quite love him—Amidst all our trou-  5
bles—it is a comfort to learn from Nicholas—that he is likely to do well—it's a
bright star in our dark horizon—(*approaches glass, at the same moment* MR SCALEY—
*pops his head up behind it*—KATE *screams*)
SCALEY.   Don't be alarmed Miss—this here's the manti-making con-sarn 'an't
it? (*advancing towards door in flat*)
KATE.   Yes—what did you want—                                                    10
SCALEY.   (*opening door*—Enter MR TIX—*see book*) Wait a minnit, young ooman—
vere's your Governor?
KATE.   My what—did you say?
SCALEY.   Mr Muntlehiney—wot's come of him?—is he at home?
KATE.   He is above stairs, I believe—do you want him?                           15
SCALEY.   No—I don't ezactly want him, if it's made a favour on—you can jist gi' him
that 'ere card and tell him if he wants to speak to *me* and save trouble, here I am,
that's all—(*gives card to* KATE)
KATE.   I'll take the card to him immediately. (*Exits*)
SCALEY.   As you likes, Miss—(*touching glass with stick*) Good plate, this here, Tix—  20
and this here article warn't made for nothing, mind you. (*pointing to silk*)

*Enter* MADAME MANTALINI *and* KATE—SCALEY *is arranging his neckcloth at glass.*

MADAME.   Gracious heaven!—the wretch!
SCALEY.   Oh! is this the Missus?
KATE.   It is Madame Mantalini—sir. (MADAME *sits in a chair*)
SCALEY.   Then—this is a writ of execution—and if it's not convenient to settle we'll  25
go over the house at wunst—and take the inwentory. (*Enter* MANTILINI *hastily
with a razor in his hand.*)
MANTALINI.   Stop—stop! what's the dem'd total.

---

11 *Enter... book*: The description is in chapter 21, No. VII, 95: 'a little man in brown, very much the worse
for wear, who brought with him a mingled fumigation of stale tobacco and fresh onions. The clothes of this
gentleman were much bespeckled with flue; and his shoes, stockings, and nether garments, from his heels
to the waist buttons of his coat inclusive, were profusely embroidered with splashes of mud, caught a fortnight previously—before the setting-in of the fine weather.'

SCALEY.　Fifteen hundred and twenty-seven pound, four and ninepence ha'penny—

MANTALINI.　The half-penny be dem'd.

30 SCALEY.　By all means if you vish it, and the ninepence too—but whats this rig to be,
only a small crack, or a out-and-out smash?

MANTALINI.　(*hurriedly*) A dem'd smash!

SCALEY.　Wery good—then Mr Tom Tix, esk-vire, you must inform your angel wife
and lovely family as you won't sleep at home for three nights to come—along of

35 being in possession here—Now let's walk our precious legs—up stairs—and begin
bus—Wot's the good of fretting yourself Ma'am a good half of wots here isn't paid
for I des-say, and wot a consolation oughtn't that to be to her feelings. (*Exit with*
TIX, MADAME MANTALINI *sobs*)

MANTALINI.　(*approaches her*) My cup of happiness's sweetener will you listen to
me for two minutes?

40 MADAME.　Oh! don't speak to me (*sobbing*) you have ruined me, that's enough—
oh! oh!—

MANTALINI.　Have I—the infernal rascal—to ruin such a poppet—let me cut its—
villain's dem'd throat. (*raises razor to his throat*)

MADAME.　Oh! Alfred—if you love me, don't. Miss Nickleby—arrest his arm for

45 heaven's sake, he will destroy himself!—I spoke unkindly to him, and he cannot
bear it from me—Alfred, my darling Alfred, d—o—n—t (*embracing him*)

MANTALINI.　I'm not fit to live—to breathe the same air with my angel wife—I am
too dem'd bad, let me die—fall a dem'd bleeding object at your pretty little feet.

MADAME.　Alfred—I didn't mean to say it—I didn't mean to say it. (*clinging to him*)

50 MANTALINI.　Ruined! (*starting*) haven't I brought ruin on the best and purest creature that ever blest a demnation vagabond! (*flourishing razor*) let me go—let me
make myself—a horrid object—

MADAME.　Pray—compose yourself my own angel—it was nobody's fault.

MANTALINI.　(*groans*) Oh! this is too beautiful!—

55 MADAME.　Never mind—dear—we shall do very well yet.

MANTALINI.　(*starting and feeling the razor with his finger*) Yes, in the prison—it's
dem'd sharp!

MADAME.　If you talk so, Alfred, you'll drive me mad.

MANTALINI.　Who talks of madness? I'm dem'd mad—is there no dem'd mineral

60 poison in the world—will no kind, invaluable, dem'd friend, blow my brains out?
Fly far from me—I cannot dare not—gaze upon your heavenly beauties, dare not
reflect on the wreck my dem'd conduct has made—let me go—I can't live, let me
hide in some solitary corner and cut my dem'd throat quietly. (*rushes out*)

---

56 *Yes, in the prison*: MS has 'yes, in the prison' deleted, and 'It's dem'd sharp' substituted; 1838 has 'Oh!
Dem it, the razor's too dem'd sharp'.

63 *Who…quietly*: MS has changes to this speech, deleting 'Who talks of madness? I'm demd' and 'Fly far
from me…conduct has made' and inserting 'dem'd' before 'mineral' and 'friend'; 1838 has the abbreviated
version, including the inserted words.

SONG, KATE

When thy bosom heaves a sigh
When a tear o'erflows thine eye 65
Thy fond heart with passion sighs
To cheer mine heart and glad mine eyes
Etc etc

*Rushes out following* MADAME

MADAME. Help—help—for heaven's sake—Alfred—Alfred—cut mine first. (*Exits*)

MANTALINI. (*without*) I will—I will—with the same dem'd razor. 70

## SCENE 3

*Lodgings of* NEWMAN NOGGS—*a meanly furnished garret—scene half dark.*

NOGGS. (*speaking without*) This way, come this way, my dear boy— 1

*Enter* NEWMAN NOGGS *carrying a glass of rum-and-water—a candlestick* (*very old and shabby*) *with a small candle in it alight—and pushing in* NICHOLAS *and* SMIKE— *the two latter appear much fatigued and* SMIKE *is splashed with mud.*

NOGGS. Taste this. (*pouring rum-and-water down both their mouths*) You are wet through—and I—haven't even a change—to offer you.

NICHOLAS. I have dry clothes in my bundle—if you look so distressed to see me you will add to the pain I feel already, at being compelled to cast myself upon your 5 slender means for shelter—

NOGGS. (*grasping him*) Good lad—good lad—you won't refuse to eat, will you— (*runs off and brings—two old chairs on—*SMIKE *eats heartily*)

NOGGS. It is the best I have—eat heartily—bless you—

NICHOLAS. Thankye—thankye, now tell me—of my mother and sister—are they well? 10

63.1 *SONG, KATE*: This seems a particularly unlikely place for a song, and it does not occur in 1838; the exits are also confused in MS, which has Kate 'rushes out following Madame' after her song and, at the top of the next sheet (663v), 'Madame and Kate following hastily'. We might conjecture that it was inserted as a legal fiction, and not performed.

0.1 *scene half dark*: 'scene half dark' 1838.

1.3 *carrying...mud*: sd augmented from 1838: 'a candlestick...alight'; 1838 also adds that Smike 'carries bundle and stick'.

7.1 *SMIKE eats heartily*: 1838 has instead of this sd '*taking some bread and cheese from his pocket, wrapped in a piece of paper*'.

NOGGS.   Well, both well.

NICHOLAS.   Now listen to me—before I would make an effort to see them, I deemed it expedient to come to you, lest by gratifying my own selfish desires—I should injure them—What has my uncle heard from Yorkshire?

(SMIKE *picks up the crumbs which he has dropped on the stage and eats them*)

NOGGS.   (*smiles and shakes his head*)

15 NICHOLAS.   What has he heard—I am prepared to hear the very worst that malice has suggested—tell me at once pray—

NOGGS.   To-morrow—hear it to-morrow.

NICHOLAS.   What purpose would that answer?

NOGGS.   You would sleep the better—that's all.

20 NICHOLAS.   I should sleep the worse—I cannot hope to close my eyes—unless you tell me every thing—don't fear—you may rouse my indignation—or wound my pride—but you will not break my rest, for if the scene were acted over again, I could take no other part than I have taken—never—if I starve or beg in conse-quence. If I had stood by tamely and passively, I should have hated myself and

25 merited the contempt of every man in existence—the black-hearted scoundrel Squeers!

SMIKE.   Oh! (*shudders*)

NOGGS.   My dear young man—you must not give way to—this sort of thing will never do, you know—as to getting on in the world, if you take every body's part

30 that's ill-treated—why—why—(*seizing* NICHOLAS's *hand and shaking it violently*) Damn it—I am proud to hear of it—and would have done it myself—the day before yesterday, your uncle received this letter—I took a hasty copy of it while he was out—(*produces dirty letter*) Shall I read it?

NICHOLAS.   If you please.

35 NOGGS.   (*reading*) 'Sir—My Pa requests me to write to you—the doctors consider-ing it doubtful whether he will ever recuvver the use of his *legs* which prevents his holding a pen—he is one mask of brooses both blue and green—likewise two forms which is steepled in his goar—when your nevew—that you recommended for a teacher, had done this to my Pa—and jumped upon his body with his feet—he

40 assaulted my Ma—dashed her to the earth—and drove her back comb several inches into her head—a very little more and it must have entered her skull—me and my brother were then the victims of his fury—I am screaming out loud all the time I write with pain—the monster having satiated his thirst for blood run away taking with him a boy of desperate character—called Smike—and a Garnet Ring belong-

45 ing to Ma—my Pa begs that if he comes to you the ring may be returned and that you will let the thief and assassin go, as if we prosecuted him he would only be

---

12 *NICHOLAS*: MS has a different speech for Nicholas before this, deleted: 'and is my sister still engaged in the trade which she wrote to tell me she thought she would like so much?'

transported and if he is let go, he is sure to be hung before long—hoping to hear from you when convenient

> I remain

> > yours and                                                                    50

> > > cetrer

> > > > Fanny Squeers

P.S.    I pity his ignorance and despise him.'

NOGGS.    (*aside and looking at* SMIKE) Is that the boy of desperate character? Poor fellow—poor fellow.                                                                    55

NICHOLAS.    Mr Noggs, I must go out at once—(*putting on his hat*)

NOGGS.    Go out?

NICHOLAS.    Yes, to Golden Square—nobody who knows me would believe this story of the ring—but it is due to myself that I should state the truth—besides, I have a word or two to exchange with Mr Ralph Nickleby—which will not keep cool.  60

NOGGS.    They must.

NICHOLAS.    They must not, indeed. (*going*)

NOGGS.    You have nothing to fear at present—your uncle is too much employed to think of you—he had hardly read this letter when he was called away—its contents are known to nobody but himself and us—                                          65

NICHOLAS.    Not even to my mother and sister? If I thought that they—I will go there—I will see him immediately—I am determined—

NOGGS.    Then I'll go with you—Let me see your uncle first—to pave the way for you—he may be at the counting-house—we'll try that first—he gives a grand party and dinner tonight at home to his friends—ha! ha! his friends—poor devils—that  70 he plunges into ruin by his kindness, he once was *kind* to me—*very*—ha!—You can wait the corner of Silver Street—while I go in—I'll give you the signal to enter—don't be impetuous—meet him calmly—he's a dangerous man—I know it too well—too well—follow me. (*Exit*)

NICHOLAS.    (*thoughtfully gazing on the ground and sighs*) What a miserable,  75 wretched fate is mine—

SMIKE.    (*creeping towards him, and placing his hand on his arms*) Don't—pray don't—look so sad—I know you have got into great trouble by bringing me away—I ought to have known that and stopped behind—you—you are not rich, you have not enough for yourself and I should not be here—you grow thinner every day,  80 your cheek is paler, and your eye more sunk—I—cannot bear to look at you—to-day I tried to leave you—but I could not without a word—I—I love you too much—

NICHOLAS.    The word which separates us—shall never be said by me—I would not lose you now for all the world could give—Give me your hand—my heart is linked to yours—what if I am steeped in poverty? you lighten it, and we will be poor or  85 rich together—

(*Exits grasping* SMIKE's *hand*)

## SCENE 4

*The counting-house of* RALPH NICKLEBY—*two desks—stools: window practicable in flat and door—the window opens to Golden Square.*

RALPH NICKLEBY *discovered seated at his desk looking over a pile of papers—*

1 RALPH.   Curses on them both! to think that all my plans should be overthrown, rendered abortive by the headstrong rashness of this boy, Nicholas—he shall never have one penny of my money, or one crust of my bread, or one grasp of my hand—no— not to save him from the loftiest gallows in all Europe, (*rises*) at every risk Smike—

5        must be separated from him—or some unforeseen events might—reveal all. (*pauses*) Yes—yes—they will surely make for London—I'll be upon the watch—for them— my dutiful nephew—shall see the inside of a prison—the garnet ring will fix him there—and the poor fool that accompanies him—shall back to Yorkshire—ha! ha! (*chuckles*) he'll be safe *this* time with his kind master—Squeers—I'll warrant—

10      (*collecting papers—and putting them in desk*) These deeds shall go with me—I am at last resolved to destroy them—present circumstances demand it for my own secu- rity—(*puts them in pocket book*)

NOGGS *enters, L. with a very shabby umbrella under his arm, which he opens and places on stage near his desk, he then takes his hat off and hangs it up and hobbles to his desk (which is a high one) and commences mending a pen.*

        RALPH.   So sir—you are here at last?—pray why didn't you come before—when you knew I wanted to leave the office earlier?
15 NOGGS.   Humph! (*affecting to write at desk*)
        RALPH.   Fool!
        NOGGS.   (*aside*) Brute!
        RALPH.   Why I keep such an idle dog about me I can't tell.
        NOGGS.   *Keep—starve* you mean—
20 RALPH.   What's that you're mumbling, sir, eh?
        NOGGS.   A thing you don't understand—the truth—
        RALPH.   Bah! I wish I had never seen you.
        NOGGS.   So do I—with all my soul—
        RALPH.   Is this your gratitude—to me—Rascal—
25 NOGGS.   What have I to be grateful for? Is it—the knowledge—that your cruel con- duct—brought me to ruin—or is it for the miserable Pittance that you begrudgingly bestow upon me weekly—in the shape of wages—
        RALPH.   Do you know me Sir? (*passionately*)
        NOGGS.   I *do* worse luck.
30 RALPH.   Scoundrel!—did I not release you from *prison*—and take you into my employment—
        NOGGS.   You did! but you first sent me there—as long as I had houses and land to mortgage—Mr Ralph Nickleby was my good friend—when they ceased—his

friendship ceased—and his very dear friend, Newman Noggs—became—a fool—
an idle vagabond and a prison was much too good for him in the opinion of the  35
honest—warm-hearted, conscientious Ralph Nickleby.

RALPH.    Very good, sir—very good—now be kind enough to listen to me for one minute—We part—sir—and if after to morrow you dare to place your foot in my house—
I'll send you back to prison—to starve—sir—to starve!—don't let me be disturbed
to-night—I have friends at home—to-morrow, remember my promise—beggar!          40

(*During this speech he has taken the pocket book from the desk—and placed it apparently in his breast pocket, but wearing a spencer coat over his other, the book slips between
them and falls on the stage unnoticed.* RALPH *exits shaking his finger at* NOGGS)

NOGGS.    (*walking up and down stage*) Perhaps I have acted wrong—quarrelling
with the oppressor is not the best way of serving the oppressed—Nicholas must not
see his uncle while this angry fit lasts—he called me beggar—he that made me
one—Oh! if I could but repay the villain. (*kicks pocket book*) What's this? (*picking
it up*) his pocket book—it will be safe here till morning. (*he is in the act of placing it*  45
*on desk—when the papers—which are much longer than the book—catch his eye—
turning them over and reading*) 'The copy of a will'—perhaps his own—I should like
to see what he has done for poor Nicholas—for once in his life he may have acted
with a little generosity—towards his fellow-creatures—at all events there's no great
harm in peeping (*opens will—reads*) Eh! am I awake—(*speaking and reading rapidly*) 'I—give and bequeath—all my—personal estates, land—houses—funded  50
property—to my executor, Mr Ralph Nickleby—in the event of the death of my
only child—Thomas Smike—Oh!—I shall choke!—20,000—three and ½—per
cents—landed estate in Surrey—House in Portland Place—Oh! oh! I see it all
now—Ralph Nickleby you old rascal. (*laughs*) ha! ha! (*rubbing his hands violently*)
Now—now—the beggar may have a chance of sending you to prison—to starve—  55
to starve—ha! (*runs to window throws it up and calls*—Nickleby! Nickleby!
(NICHOLAS *and* SMIKE *appear at window*—)

NOGGS.    Come in—come in—(*opens door in flat*)

(*they enter*) Don't speak a word, my dear boy, let me talk—

NICHOLAS.    But my uncle—

NOGGS.    Damn your uncle!—listen to me—I'll be a mother and father to you—(*tak-*  60
*ing* SMIKE's *hand*) I want to ask—this boy a question or two—has he a good
memory?

NICHOLAS.    I don't know.

SMIKE.    I had once—but it's all gone now—all gone. (*sighs*)

NICHOLAS.    Why do you think, you had once?                                     65

SMIKE.    Because I could remember when I was a child—before I went to that
place. (*shuddering*)

---

41 *Perhaps … wrong*: 1838 inserts 'but that's nothing new—I'm never right—'.
54 *old*: MS has 'damned' replaced by 'old'.

NOGGS.  Think no more of that place—can you remember the first day you went to Yorkshire? Did you find your way there alone?

70  SMIKE.  No—oh—no.

NOGGS.  Who was with you?

SMIKE.  A man—a dark withered man—I was glad to leave him, I was so afraid of him.

NOGGS.  Do you recollect any thing about the house you lived in—before that

75  man—took you into Yorkshire?

SMIKE.  No. (*suddenly remembers*) Yes—a room I remember I slept in a room, a large lonesome room at the top of the house, where there was a trap door in the ceiling—I have covered my head with clothes often, not to see it, for it frightened me, a young child with no one near at night, and I used to wonder what was on the other side—

80  NOGGS.  Do you recollect—the man's name?—

SMIKE.  Name—no!—(*shakes his head*) No!—

NOGGS.  That's a pity—Nickleby—(*to* NICHOLAS)

SMIKE.  (*starting*) Nickleby—Nickleby (*clapping his hands*) that's it—that's the name—they called him it at the school!—

85  NOGGS.  (*laughing and singing*) Ha! ha! Tol-lol, diddle-lol. (*hugging* SMIKE) It's all right—you shall have your own. Tol—lol—my dear boy—

NICHOLAS.  Are you mad—Mr Noggs?

NOGGS.  Yes—yes with joy—don't ask me any questions now—you shall learn all presently—jump into a coach with me—we'll fetch your mother—then drive to

90  your uncle's—your sister is there already—he gives a grand party to-night—and I'm sure he'll be delighted to see us all—very—ha! ha—come along, boys I'm proud of you—I wish I'd been mother and father—to you both—

(*Exits hastily—dragging* NICHOLAS *and* SMIKE)


# SCENE 5

*A handsome suite of rooms—at* RALPH NICKLEBY'S—*richly furnished, carpeted— etc—chandeliers sofas etc—*

RALPH—KATE—MANTALINI—LORD VERISOPHT—SIR MULBERRY HAWKE— HONOURABLE MR SNOBB—COLONEL CHOWSER—MESSRS. PLUCK AND PYKE *etc—discovered—See Tableau, No. 6th Music.*

---

69  *Think... Yorkshire*: MS deletes and 1838 omits 'Think no more... Yorkshire'.

72  *withered man*: 1838 inserts sd '*imitates the look of Ralph Nickleby*'.

80  *Do... name*: 1838 omits this and next three speeches, cutting out the recollection of the name.

92.1  *Exits... SMIKE*: MS has a blank half page here, f. 668v, suggesting perhaps a space for another interpolated song.

0.5  *See Tableau, No. 6th*: i.e. the first plate in part No. VI, 'Miss Nickleby introduced to her uncle's friends.'

RALPH.   Lord Verisopht—my niece Miss Nickleby—   1
LORD VERISOPHT   (*lispingly*) de—light—ed to know her—(*bows*)
RALPH.   Colonel Chowser—Honourable Mr Snobb—Mr Pike—and Mr Pluck—my dear—Gentlemen my niece—(*gentlemen bow*—KATE *curtseys*)
MANTALINI.   (*advancing*) Dem it Nickleby—don't leave me out—   5
RALPH.   You have met my niece—before—I believe—at—
MANTALINI.   (*interrupting him*) Yes, I believe so too. (*aside to* LORD VERISOPHT) The old boy's jealous—the fact is, niece—is most outrageously—demnibly in love with me—poor little pet—how can she help it—I'm so dem'd beautiful—(*retires up, talking to* LORD VERISOPHT—*and followed by the gentlemen laughing*)
OMNES.   Oh! Oh! Manti—   10
MANTALINI.   Truth—the dem'd truth—pon honour—(*saunters off, shaking his hand to* KATE *unobserved by* RALPH—)
RALPH.   Now—let me lead you down—dinner will soon be served—
KATE.   Pray uncle—are there any ladies here?—
RALPH.   No—I don't know any—come—
KATE.   Must I go immediately—I should like to arrange my dress—   15
RALPH.   Oh! Very—well—you can do that here—there's a glass—I'll come for you in a few minutes—(*aside and exits*) Humph! these women always want something!—
KATE.   (*arranging her hair at the glass*) I wish my dear mother—was here with me; the rude gaze—of uncle's guests annoy me—beyond measure—

*Re-enter* MANTILINI *on tiptoe U.E.*

MANTALINI.   There she is—the charming—Rosy—Posy—I'll make her dem'd   20
happy—by whispering demd soft pretty nonsense into her delicate little ear. (*advancing*)
KATE.   I'm astonished at meeting Mr Mantilini here, after the scene at his house.
MANTALINI.   My name! She dotes upon me. Mantilini you—dem'd—wicked—lucky—lady's pet—
KATE.   (*aside*) Poor Nicholas! I wonder what he is doing now—I wish I could see   25
him.
MANTALINI.   (*aside*) She wants to see me—I am a dem'd happy woman's tormentor!—(*kneeling at* KATE's *feet*) adorable—enchantress—behold me at your delicious little ten toes.
KATE.   (*starting back*) You here—sir!   30
MANTALINI.   Yes—ain't it dem'd kind?—jump into its adorer's arms at once—and let it stop its pretty—mouth—with demnibly sweet kisses.
KATE.   (*aside*) What does he mean?
MANTALINI.   (*aside*) Poor thing—she's—overwhelmed by my dem'd kind declaration—so she ought to be—for pon my soul—if I had not—been so dem'd fond of   35
her—I should have let her make the first move—I'm so dem'd particular—ain't you—delighted with me love—eh!
KATE.   Sir! dare you address this language to me under my uncle's roof—Shame upon you sir—if you have no respect for yourself—remember your wife.

40 MANTALINI.   Never mind its ugly wife moppet poppet—we'll fly—far enough from her reach—love me—and it shall have every thing it wishes for—a new cab—a dem'd little tiger—and a box at the opera—you'll dote upon me—when you know me better—'pon my soul—you will dear—This—dem'd beautiful hair—and these outrageously beautiful whiskers are real—no dem'd macassar. (*aside*) If she resists
45     the dem'd whiskers—she's not worth having—
KATE.   Your behaviour sir—offends and disgusts me beyond measure—if you have one spark of gentlemanly feeling you will leave me instantly.
MANTALINI.   (*laughs*) ha! ha!—now its making fun of its devoted darling—cruel—dem'd—cruel—Kitty—(*taking her hand and kissing it*)
50 KATE.   Unhand me, sir this instant—Uncle—help! help!—(*They struggle—a second or two—*NICHOLAS *rushes in followed by* RALPH *who enters on the opposite side—and* MRS NICKLEBY)
NICHOLAS.   (*knocking* MANTILINI *down*) Scoundrel!

KATE *runs to her mother,* RALPH—*stands—astonished at seeing* NICHOLAS—Picture—music*

MANTALINI.   (*rising*) Dem that fellow! he's ruffled my whiskers—the next time—it speaks first to a woman—may its whiskers entirely drop off—and no dem'd bear's grease be able to bring them back again—demit. (*Exit*)
55 NICHOLAS.   (*to* RALPH) Is it thus—sir—you expose beneath your own roof—a helpless girl—your dead brother's child—to insult and degradation?—You shrink—to look at me—you well may—shame—shame upon you.
RALPH.   (*recovering from his surprise*) How dare you sir—enter my house unbidden after your disgraceful conduct in Yorkshire—if I did my duty I should immediately
60     deliver you up to justice.
KATE.   Justice—what does he mean Nicholas? I'm sure you're innocent. (*embracing him*)
RALPH.   Innocent, indeed! (*sneeringly*) pray do innocent men inveigle nameless vagabonds and prowl about the country—assault riot, theft—what do you call these?
65 NICHOLAS.   A lie!—and well you know it—you who under the pretence of serv-ing—heaped every insult, wrong, and indignity, upon my head—you, who sent me to a den, where, indeed, cruelty, worthy of yourself, runs wanton and youthful mis-ery stalks precocious; where the lightness of childhood shrinks into the heaviness of age, and its every promise blights, and withers as it grows—
70 KATE.   Of what does he accuse you, brother?
RALPH.   First of attacking his master—and being within an ace of qualifying him-self for a trial for murder—and robbing his mistress of a valuable ring.
NICHOLAS.   Tis false—the woman—the wife of the fellow from whom these charges come—dropped—as I suppose—a worthless ring among some clothes of mine—
75     early on the morning on which I left the house—I found it when I opened my bundle on the road—and returned it at once by coach—and they have it now.

KATE.  I knew it.—I was sure you would scorn so mean an act—but about this boy—
in whose company they say you left?

NICHOLAS.  That boy! a silly, helpless creature that I rescued from brutality and
hard usage, is with me now.                                                            80

RALPH.  Do you choose to restore that boy sir?

NICHOLAS.  No—I do not.

RALPH.  You do not?

NICHOLAS.  No—

NOGGS *enters followed by* ALL THE VISITORS *U.E. Advances down centre.*

NOGGS.  No, I'm d-d if he does—                                                         85

RALPH.  Dog!—what brings you here—?

NOGGS.  Buss!—I know you are fond of that—(*producing pocket book*)
This pocket book belongs to you—you lost it—I found it.

RALPH.  (*aside*) Confusion! give it to me—give it me.

NOGGS.  To be sure I will!—there's the book—its contents—I keep for the right        90
owner—(*offering book*)

RALPH.  (*enraged*) Give me the papers—would you *rob* me?

NOGGS.  Rob!—no, I leave the robbing for you to do—these papers belong to a poor
persecuted orphan—named Smike. (*bringing* SMIKE *in from U.E.*) Do you know
him—                                                                                   95

*Chord. Picture.* RALPH *appears overwhelmed with confusion.*

SMIKE.  (*running to* NICHOLAS) Tis he—tis he—the cruel man that left me at the
school!

NOGGS.  (*rubbing his hands joyfully*) Ha! I knew it—I knew it, (*giving papers to*
NICHOLAS) look over these—chance gave them to my hands—Deeds which your
uncle unlawfully withheld—seeking to deprive this lad of his property—                100

NICHOLAS.  (*looking hastily over the papers*) Villain!

KATE  (*to* SMIKE) Poor boy! (*patting his head*—SMIKE *kisses her hand*)

NOGGS.  (*walking up to* RALPH *rubbing his hands*) And now, Mr Ralph Nickleby—I
think—the dog!—the beggar!—the fool!—that you kept from starving and rescued
from prison—is more than a match for you now—Eh? (*chuckles*) ha! ha!               105

RALPH.  Wretch, you show your teeth do you—Beware—I'll be revenged—
The law—the law will protect me—against your plots—I'll indite you all—
(*rushes out*)

NOGGS.  (*laughs 'ha' and rubs his hands*)

NICHOLAS.  (*giving paper to* SMIKE) These papers place you for ever—far beyond
the reach of poverty—riches are yours.                                                 110

SMIKE.  (*returning papers to* NICHOLAS) For you—not for me—I only want to live
and die—with you, my kind, my only friend—

NICHOLAS.  (*advances*) Boy! Not your *only* friend—I hope that we have been fortunate enough to secure the good wishes and approbation of a numerous circle of

115   kind friends (*pointing to the audience*) who by their generous sympathy and
      support—will ensure the future career of NICHOLAS NICKLEBY.

*Picture*

CHORUS, OMNES

Thus all our Sorrows ended
And all our griefs are past
By your applause befriended
120   We hope that this may last.

CURTAIN

116 *NICHOLAS NICKLEBY*: 1838 gives the tag to Smike, not Nicholas, running his speech on: 'my only friend—no, not my only friend' and ending '...the future career of Smike and Nicholas Nickleby.' It also offers a diagrammatic 'disposition of characters' for the final tableau.

# THREE

Edward Stirling, *Barnaby Rudge*, New Strand Theatre, August 1841

## INTRODUCTION

STIRLING's *Barnaby Rudge* appeared at the little New Strand Theatre in August 1841; it was written, therefore, when the serialization of the novel in the weekly *Master Humphrey's Clock* had reached chapter 48, the scene on Westminster Bridge when Barnaby and his mother arrive in London, and he joins the mob. This incident forms the penultimate scene of the dramatization, followed only by Stirling's invented ending in which, in the midst of the riots, Dolly Varden is molested by Hugh and rescued by Joe Willet, as a dragoon, and the Stranger is revealed as Barnaby's father and the murderer of Reuben Haredale.

Edward Stirling was by this stage already an experienced dramatizer of Dickens, as well as a sometimes remarkably innovative maker and remaker of plays from all sources, with a strong interest in experiments in staging derived from the French stage.[1] Hence his facility in completing Dickensian plots when he needed to, and, in the case of *The Old Curiosity Shop*, for example, making a shrewd guess at Dickens's intentions from the story so far.[2] Here he has wound up the melodramatic murder story in an obvious way, and the play gleaned condescending praise from one reviewer as providing a 'fair transcription' of the original dialogue and an effective deployment of 'stage-trick'.[3] More strikingly, Stirling's vigorous, economic version has also anticipated the book's climactic plunge into the Gordon Riots, and presents a stage picture of mob violence which seems to have alarmed another critic. *The Examiner* on 14 August (probably John Forster) calls the act of transferring the book to the stage 'detestable', the inclusion of the riots 'not an improvement' on the earlier version at the English Opera House, and pronounces that 'the whole thing was distasteful'. His squeamishness extends to his criticism of Mary Ann Keeley's Barnaby: 'there is great art and experience about Mrs Keeley, but the artlessness of the other [Julia Fortesque at the English Opera House] carries it hollow'. The long-running creative interaction between Mary Ann Keeley and Dickens is discussed in the Introduction ('I Feel Sure About Her'). It is clearly marked in this play, where it seems to have been uppermost in Stirling's mind, guiding his choices and elaborations: the dramaturg could be said to have created the text to showcase the art of Mary Ann Keeley in another widely varying boy role.

---

[1] See Bratton, *West End*, 178–9.   [2] Bolton, 47.   [3] *The Oddfellow*, 3 August 1841.

## THE TEXT

The play was not printed, and the licensing copy, BL Add. MS 42959 ff. 452–482, is the sole text. It was apparently submitted for scrutiny on 6 July, according to the index to the volume in which it appears, but the usual annotation on the front of the MS itself showing date submitted and date licence sent is lacking. From internal evidence, especially the habit throughout of omitting the letters 'in' in words ending 'ing' and the use of other abbreviations such as 'wod' and 'shd' for 'would' and 'should', especially but not solely in stage directions, this appears to be the work of a professional copyist. Spelling and punctuation have been regularized, except for the retention of dashes which might indicate the intended rhythms of delivery.

The tableaux in the play are derived from the woodcut illustrations in the novel as it appeared in *Master Humphrey's Clock*, published weekly and then as a three-volume whole by Chapman and Hall in 1841. The notes specify the probable originals.

## Characters and cast of the first production[4]

John Willet
Joe Willet
Edward Chester
Mr/Sir John Chester
Gabriel Varden
Geoffrey Haredale
Barnaby Rudge                            Mrs Robert Keeley
Stranger (Rudge)
Simon Tappertit                          Mr Attwood
Hugh                                     Mr H. Hall
Dennis the hangman
Solomon Daisy
Tom Cobb
Parkes
Servants, Mob
Emma Haredale
Mrs Rudge
Mrs Varden
Dolly Varden
Miggs

---

[4] This list is created from the MS itself, which, as is usually the case, does not actually include a cast list. Few of the actors' names are known; those included are supplied from advertisements and reviews.

**3.** Interior of the New Strand Theatre in 1832, by Robert Blemmel Schnebbelie. When *Barnaby Rudge* was staged there in 1841 the stage and auditorium had not been much changed.

# ACT I

## SCENE 1

*The Maypole.*
*Music—Tableau—No.1.*

JOHN WILLET, SOLOMON DAISY, TOM COBB, PARKES, JOE WILLET, YOUNG
CHESTER, *and* STRANGER *discovered.*

DAISY.   (*aside to* JNO. WILLET) He must be a highwayman.                                    1

WILLET.   Stuff man—do you suppose highwaymen don't dress handsomer than
that—it's a better business than you think for—leave him to me I'll soon tackle
him (*looks at* STRANGER *and coughs*) hem! (*smoking*)

STRANGER.   (*turning round*) Well?                                                                              5

WILLET.   (*confused*) Well—I thought you gave an order master—

STRANGER.   I had forgotten—bring me a can of ale—what house is that stands a
mile or so from here, Landlord?

WILLET.   Public House?

JOE.   Public House—no, father—he means the great house—the Warren—the red   10
brick house, Sir—that stands in its own grounds?

STRANGER.   Ay lad—and the owner's name is?

JOE.   Haredale—Mr Geoffrey Hardale—a worthy gentleman too.

STRANGER.   Indeed! I turned out of my way coming here—to look at the grounds—
who was the young lady that I saw entering a carriage—his daughter?                           15

JOE.   Why how should I know, honest man—I did not see the lady.

STRANGER.   Has Mr Haredale a daughter?

JOE.   No—no—he's a single gentleman.

STRANGER.   Single men have had daughters before now.

JOE.   (*shaking his head violently and plucking him by the sleeve*) You'll come in for it   20
presently, I know you will, from him. (*aside pointing to* CHESTER)

STRANGER.   I mean no harm, or treason to King George. I am a stranger to these
parts—I merely asked a few questions about a remarkable house in your neighbourhood. (*to* CHESTER *rising*) Perhaps you can tell me, sir.

CHESTER.   (*rising*) Really my good friend I can give you no information relating   25
to the Warren House or its inhabitants—(*beckoning* JOE *to door*) Good night,
sir. (*Exits whispering to* JOE)

STRANGER.   A shy cock that—(*aside*) I'll ruffle his feathers.

---

0.2 *Music—Tableau—No.1*: The second illustration in the story, the woodcut showing the interior of the
inn on p. 233 of *Master Humphrey's Clock*, which first appeared in chapter 1, part 11, is probably intended.

JOE.    (*closing door*) What a thing love is—he has set off to walk to London—and
30    gives up a good hot supper and our best bed—because Miss Haredale has gone to a
masquerade up in town, and he has set his heart upon seeing her.

STRANGER.    He is in love then?

JOE.    Rather.

WILLET.    Silence sir—what do you mean by talking when you see people, that are
35    more than two or three times your age—sitting still and saying nothing?

JOE.    Then that's the proper time for me to talk—isn't it?

WILLET.    No sir—the proper time's no time, sir—when I was your age I never talked,
I listened.

JOE.    It's all very fine talking—but if you mean to tell me I'm never to open my lips—

40    WILLET.    Silence—sir—you never are—when you're spoke to speak—I'll answer
your questions master.

STRANGER.    Thank you—is her father alive?

WILLET.    No—he is not alive—and he isn't dead.

STRANGER.    Not dead?

45    WILLET.    No—not in the common sort of a way.

STRANGER.    What the deuce do you mean—not dead in the common sort of a
way—what do you mean?

WILLET.    Well—as it's a Maypole story—and belongs to the house, I'll tell it—
hem!—Twenty years ago Mr Reuben Haredale—was owner of the Warren—his
50    lady was dead and he was left with one child that young lady you've been enquiring
about—he left the Warren House when his wife died—feeling it lonely—and went
up to London—he suddenly came back bringing with him his little girl—two
women servants—his steward, Mr Rudge—and a gardener.

COBB.    That was on the 19th of March 1753—two and twenty years ago.

55    WILLET.    Very good Cobb—and the 20th of March—the very morning after his
arrival—poor Mr Haredale was found murdered in his bed—his bureau open and
a cash box supposed to contain a large sum of money gone—

STRANGER.    Was there no clue to this mystery?

WILLET.    No—the steward and gardener were both missing and both suspected for
60    a long time—but some months afterwards the body of poor Mr Rudge was found
with a deep gash in his breast, at the bottom of a piece of water in the grounds—
Everybody now knew that the gardener must be the murderer—he has never been
heard of from that time to this—the murder will be discovered on the 19th of March,
in some way or other—mark my words sir.

65    STRANGER.    Strange story. (*rising*) My horse young man. Landlord take the reckoning—I must be in London tonight—

JOE.    Tonight—

STRANGER.    Tonight—what do you stare at—you'll know me again I see!

JOE.    The man's worth knowing, master, who travels a road he don't know—mounted
70    on a jaded horse—on such a night as this.

STRANGER.    You have sharp eyes and a sharp tongue I find.

JOE.    Yes, but they grows rusty sometimes for want of using.

STRANGER.    (*striking* JOE *with whip*) Use your tongue less, Boy—and keep your
eyes for your sweethearts. (*Exits hastily*)

WILLET.    Serve you right—hold your tongue Joe.                                        75

JOE.    I won't father—it's all along with you that he dared to do what he did—seeing
me treated like a child and put down like a fool he plucks up a heart and has a fling
at me—but he's mistaken—I'll show him—I'll show all of you before long (*tucking
up his sleeves*) I will.

WILLET.    Joe—Joe Willet—are you mad, sir?                                             80

JOE.    Father—I know what I say—and what I mean. I can't bear the contempt that
you treat me with—I won't—I can't bear it.

WILLET.    (*dropping his pipe*) The world's turn'd upside down—here's a pretty state of
things—my boy Joe wants to be master and make me, his lawful father,—nothing
and nobody—it's too monstrous! I shall die under it. (*weeps and drinks*)            85

OMNES.    Master Willet. (*all rise surround him*)

JOE.    I shall—there an't any boys left now—they're all gone—there's nothing left now
between a male baby and a man—all the boys went out with the blessed Majesty
King George the 2$^{nd}$.

COBB.    Joe you're a bad 'un—a very bad one.                                           90

JOE.    Don't you talk to me!

WILLET.    Hold your tongue sir—

JOE.    I won't father—it's hard enough to bear it from you—and I won't from any
body else.

COBB.    Why who are you that you're not to be talked to—ha! ha!—what a nice boy    95
to be sure.

JOE.    (*upsets the table—they all fall down over each other*)

JOE.    I have done it now—I knew it would come to this—the Maypole and I must
part company—it's all over—I'll hang myself—or go for a soldier—(*bursts out*)

*The scene ends in confusion—all endeavouring to get up.*


# SCENE 2

*An old-fashioned street in the outskirts of London—1775—Wind and rain.*

BARNABY RUDGE    *enters—apparently buried in thought.*

BARNA.    (*looking up*) Yes—yes we have stars here—bonny bright stars—which      1
shine blythely on the graves; and I love to watch them as they wink their eyes in
mockery of the dull earth they look on—and we have our Lady Moon too shining
among the clouds like a silver ball—and throwing her slender threads over the trees
and the streams—I'll home now and back to the Warren again, I and Grip—before    5
the light gets up—it is a brave spot. I go there to hear the wind whistle among the
trees—when they bow their heads, as I do mine to the gentry when they cross my

path—Mother chides me for going there—and I never let her find me among the bushes—no, no, I can hide like a hare among the fern and tall grass—ha! ha!—
10    mother! I know where it grows rank and rich—(*he pauses and is suddenly roused by a noise of footsteps* R.H. *He looks off*)—ah—the lover has light steps—for his mistress' heart—I know the fine gentleman does not go to the old Warren to gaze on bright eyes—and steals back by the moon—he comes this way; (*listens*) heavier steps follow his—(*retires cautiously behind wing*)

CHESTER *enters closely followed by the* STRANGER.

15    STRANGER.    Good night.
CHESTER.    Good night sir—why do you dog my steps?
STRANGER.    Powerful reasons—young man—you are rich—I am poor—you have money—I want it—(*draws sword*) Deliver up your purse!
CHESTER.    Never, ruffian!

(*Buss—*BARNABY *rushes out and seizes the* STRANGER)

20    BARNA.    No—no—he's good—I'll tear you to pieces I'm strong at heart—help—ho—mother—Hugh—Grip!
STRANGER.    Off and unloose me—or I'll dash your brains out—off I say—(*tries to fling off* BARNABY *who clings to him calling for help.* GABRIEL VARDEN'S *voice is heard* L.H.)
GAB.    Yo—ho—this way.
STRANGER.    (*dashing* BARNABY *off and striking at him with his sword*) Curses on
25    you—I'm beat after all—I must to horse again without all my prize. (*Exits hastily*)
GAB.    (*nearer*) Who's in danger—where are you?
BARNA.    (*recognizes the voice*) Yes—yes—I know—I know him!

(RUNS *off and re-enters immediately with* GABRIEL VARDEN *closely muffled up*)

GAB.    Why—what's here to do—how's this—what, Barnaby?
BARNA.    (*pointing to* EDWARD) There's blood upon him (*shudders*) it makes me sick.
30    GAB.    How came it there?
BARNA.    Steel—steel—steel. (*imitates a sword thrust*)
GAB.    Is he robbed?
BARNA.    Yes—(*points to where the* STRANGER *exits*)
GAB.    Oh—I see—the robber made off that way—did he—well well, never mind that
35    just now—hold your torch this way—now stand quiet while I try to see what harm is done. (*tableau*) This man is not dead—he has a wound in his side and is in a fainting fit.
BARNA.    I know him—I know him.
GAB.    Know him?
40    BARNA.    Hush! (*lays finger on lip*) He went out today a wooing—I wouldn't for a light guinea that he should never go a wooing again, for if he did, some eyes would

---

36 *tableau*: Probably indicates reproduction of the woodcut on 252 of *Master Humphrey's Clock*, at the end of the third chapter, in part 11.

grow dim that are now as bright—see when I talk of eyes the stars come out—
whose eyes are they—if they are angels' eyes why do they look down here and see
good men hurt—and only wink and sparkle all the night?

GAB.   Heaven help the silly fellow—can he know this gentleman—his mother's 45
house is not far off. I'd better see if she can tell me who he is—Barnaby my man—
help me to put him in the chaise and we'll ride home together.

BARNA.   I can't touch him—he's bloody.

GAB.   It's in his nature I know—it's cruel to ask him—but I must have help—Barnaby
if you know this gentleman—for the sake of his life—and the lives of every body 50
who loves him help me raise him—

BARNA.   Cover him then, wrap him close don't let me see it—smell it—don't speak
the word—don't—

GAB.   (*covers* EDWARD *with coat*) There—you see he's covered now—(*they raise the
body*) well done—well done—now for the chaise lad— 55

*Music. They carry* EDWARD *off.*

## SCENE 3

*A Chamber in the House of* GABRIEL VARDEN *the Locksmith.*

*Enter* MIGGS *cautiously with a light.*

MIGGS.   Here's mysteries—oh gracious! Why I wish I may have only a walking 1
funeral and never be buried decent with a mourning coach, if Simon Tappertit an't
been out all night—he's made a key for himself the little villain but I'll do for him—
(*stops up keyhole of door with paper*) There now—let's see whether you won't be glad
to take some notice of me, mister—he! he!—you'll have eyes for somebody besides 5
Miss Dolly now I think. (*sits at window*) I don't go to bed this night till you come
home my lad—no—not for five and forty pounds. (*noise at door*) That's him—(*buss*)

MIGGS.   Who's there?

TAP.   Hush!

MIGGS.   Is it thieves? 10

TAP.   No—no—don't you know me Miggs—it's Sim.

MIGGS.   Oh—what of him—is he in danger? Is he in the midst of flames and blazes—

TAP.   No—I'm here ain't I—what a fool you are Miggs—

MIGGS.   Lor—so it is—(*loud*) If you please Mum—here's—

TAP.   No—don't—I've been out without leave—and something's the matter with the 15
lock—undo the door.

MIGGS.   I dursn't Simon—I dursn't do it!

TAP.   Do—for my sake do—you know I'm in love with you—hang the keyhole!

MIGGS.   But if I do—you'll try to kiss me—

TAP.   No—that I won't—but do undo the door there's a dear. 20

MIGGS.   Well I suppose I must—

*She opens the door.* TAPPERTIT *enters.*

MIGGS.  Lor our Simmy—what a figure—(*aside*) he don't kiss me—

TAP.  (*kisses her*) I knew I could quench her—Go to bed charming—creep up softly—I'll climb up to my room without my shoes—adieu.

25  MIGGS.  Oh Simmie—what a Turk you are—(*aside*) he may be as cool as he likes now—but I'm in his confidence and he can't help himself—no—not if he was twenty Simminses. (*Exit R.H.*)

TAP.  Oh! I had been born a pirate. (*looks at lock*) I wonder who has been stuffing paper in here—Miggs or some secret foe—perhaps Joe Willet my rival—no he's at
30  Chigwell—who then—I'd give him up to vengeance and the Prentice Knights if I only knew—why warn't I eddicated as a—corsair or genteel highwayman or a patriot—it's all one—and not left to drag out a miserable existence unbeknown to mankind in general—it's too much—but I shall burst out one of these days then— what power can keep me down—I feel my soul getting into my head. (*takes off his*
35  *shoes*) I want something to drink all spirit like myself, gunpowder soaked in blazing oil—(*a knock heard*) my hateful master—baseborn tyrant—now I must change these sainted things for rubbish—lead on, we follow thee—(*struts off and nearly oversets* MIGGS *who enters*) Hush—if you love me—He's there at the door Miggs— He that stops our beer and makes us eat fat meat—but he dies for it some day.

(*Exit* TAPPERTIT—MIGGS *opens door*)

40  MIGGS.  Who's there?

GAB.  Me, Girl.

*Enter* GABRIEL.

MIGGS.  Lor Sir—Missus has been *so* bad—(*calling*) Master's come home Mum—

*Enter* MRS VARDEN *in nightcap reading.*

GAB.  You had better go to bed, Miggs.

MIGGS.  Thank you sir—not before my Missus—by rights—she ought to have been
45  there three hours ago.

MRS V.  Miggs, be silent.

MIGGS.  Yes Mem—I will—

GAB.  How do you find yourself my dear?

MRS V.  You're very anxious to know an't you. You've not been near me all day and
50  wouldn't if I was dying.

GAB.  My dear Martha how can you say such things—if there was anything the mat- ter with you shouldn't I be in constant attendance upon you?

MRS V.  Yes (*in tears*) yes you would I don't doubt it Varden—that is as much as to tell me you would be hovering round me like a vulture—waiting till the breath was
55  out of my body that you might marry somebody else.

MIGGS.  It's no use mem—I can't bear to see angels suffering.

MRS V.  But you'll break my heart you will one of these days—I only want to see Dolly settled then you may settle me as soon as you please.

GAB.    Martha—what is it you complain of?

MRS V.    Is it a chilling thing to have one's husband sulking and falling asleep directly   60
he comes home—Is it natural when he goes out that I should want to know anything that happens—and that he should tell me without my begging and praying
him to do it—is that natural—or is it not?

GAB.    I was really afraid you were not disposed to talk—I'll tell you everything my
dear—something dreadful had happened—young Barnaby Rudge met me—          65

MRS V.    No Varden—I dare say—thank you, sir, not a child to be corrected one minute and petted the next—I'm a little too old for that—Miggs carry the light—*you*
can be cheerful, Miggs, at least.

(*Exits reading,* MIGGS *lighting her*)

GAB.    Now who would think that woman could ever be pleasant and agreeable—
well—well—all of us have our faults—I'll not be hard upon hers—we have been   70
man and wife too long for that—all I wish is—that somebody would drown or
marry Miggs—(*sighs*)


# SCENE 4

*A parlor in* VARDEN'S *House.*

TAPPERTIT *discovered.*

TAP.    Joe—yes Joe Willet– is here in this house at this time in the morning unbeknown   1
to all save me and Dolly—but never mind—something will come of this—something
dreadful—(*flourishes hammer*) I only hope it mayn't be human gore. (*retires*)

DOLLY VARDEN *and* JOE. *Enter* R.H.

JOE.    I have come this early to say—goodbye, for I don't know how many years—
perhaps for ever—I am going abroad (*TAP enters*) or about to turn soldier.          5

DOLLY.    Indeed! I hope you'll have a pleasant voyage—but I am extremely sorry that
you should have taken so much trouble on my account—it is such a long way to
Chigwell—and how is Mr Willet your father, that dear old gentleman?

JOE.    And this is all you have to say, Dolly?

DOLLY.    All—why good gracious what do you expect Mr Joseph?          10

JOE.    Not one 'Goodbye'—not one—'Don't go'—(*shaking her hand*) Goodbye—bless
you.

DOLLY.    (*smiling*) Goodbye.

JOE.    Come Dolly—dear Dolly—don't let us part like this—I love you dearly with all
my heart and soul as ever man loved woman in this world—I am a poor fellow as   15

---

5 *TAP enters*: Sic; but he has 'retired' rather than left the stage, and would perhaps come down to over-
hear the action at this point.

you know—poorer now than ever—for I have fled from home—not being able to bear it any longer—but give me a word of comfort, say something kind to me—I have no right to ask it of you, but I love you and shall treasure the slightest word from you all through my life—Dolly dearest have you nothing to say?—

*Tableau*

20 DOLLY.    I have said—Goodbye, twice. (*he puts his arm around her waist*) Take your arm away directly Mr Joseph or I'll call Miggs to you.

JOE.    Very well—I'll not reproach you—it's my fault no doubt—I have thought sometimes that you didn't quite despise me—but I was a fool to think so—Goodbye—God bless you. (*Exits hastily*)

25 DOLLY.    He's not actually gone—I don't care if he is—I'm sure the coachmaker is much better and I don't like Joe—a bit tha-a-at I don't. (*bursts into tears and exits* R.H.)

TAP.    (*advances*) Have my ears deceived me—or—do I dream—am I to thank thee fortune—he's gone—my rival—she's left—Tremble, Willet, and despair—She's mine! (*dances and sings*)

30
> 'Tis a folly to talk of life's troubles
> There's always two sides of the way
> If one's in the shade the chance doubles
> The other is pleasant and gay
> etc. etc. etc.

35    (*looks off*) The Governor and Dolly—(*runs to his work*) I know I shall poison him before his time.

*Enter* GABRIEL *and* DOLLY.

GAB.    What have you been crying about my dear? you'll spoil your good looks if you fret, child.

DOLLY.    Father—what is it you say about last night—young Mr Chester robbed
40    lying wounded in the road—La! If the news should reach poor Miss Emma at the Manor!

GAB.    That's what I was coming to Dolly—it must reach her—and through you—Mr Edward has written a letter and begged I would give it her—now you shall go with me to the Manor House—you'll see your old friend Joe too—I am going to see Mr
45    Edward tonight—he's at Mrs Rudge's—and tomorrow we'll start to the Maypole.

(MRS V. *and* MIGGS *enter* R.H.)

---

19.1 *Tableau*: The tableau seems to be independently conceived, not based on a woodcut from the book: the scene is from chapter 13, which has no illustration.

33 *'Tis…gay*: The first stanza of a comic song billed as 'new' when John Reeve sang it in the Adelphi Lenten entertainment *Trifles Light as Air* in April 1823.

MRS V.   I hear you Varden—but no you won't go to that depraved Maypole and wicked John Willet.

GAB.   I am sorry my dear you have such an objection to the old inn—and old John—for otherwise, as tomorrow is not a busy day—we might have all three gone in the chaise—and a happy day we'd have of it.                                    50

MRS V.   Oh—Miggs—come here.

MIGGS.   —Yes mem—

GAB.   What is the matter now?

MRS V.   Ask Miggs—she's a comfort to me—whatever she may be to others.

GAB.   She's a misery of my life—she's all the plagues of Egypt in one—what is the   55 matter?

MIGGS.   You talk'd about happy days and my blessed missus is too good to be happy—run Miss Dolly for a little drop of brandy and water—not over weak, poor thing—that'll bring her sufferings round.

(DOLLY *is going*)

MRS V.   Stay child—I'll mix for myself—(*Exits*)                                    60

GAB.   Doll—Doll—if ever you have a husband of your own—never faint my darling—remember that my dear—and a word in your ear—never have a Miggs about you.

(MIGGS *re-enters*)

MIGGS.   Missus is come round, Sir—and I think if you was to persuade a bit she might see you—she has such a forgiving spirit, she'll forget all that's pass'd—

GAB.   Come Dolly—I suppose we must humour your mother or no peace shall we   65 get tomorrow—come, my dear. (*Exit with* DOLLY)

MIGGS.   (*going*) Oh! What happiness it is when man and wife come round together. (*Exit following them*)


# SCENE 5

*The House of* MRS RUDGE.

*Enter* MRS RUDGE *followed by the* STRANGER.

STRANGER.   Stay—I have been looking for you many nights—is this house   1 empty? (*she nods her head*) is this your house?

MRS R.   It is—why in heaven's name do you darken it?

STRANGER.   Give me meat and drink—or I dare do more than that.

MRS R.   You were the robber on the Chigwell road.                                    5

STRANGER.   I was.

MRS R.   And nearly a murderer.

62.1 *MIGGS re-enters*: No exit is marked for Miggs; she perhaps followed her mistress.

STRANGER.   The will was not wanting—there was one came upon me and rais'd the hue and cry—but I made a thrust at him.

10  MRS R.   Wretch!—you thrust at *him*—do not touch me with a finger or you are lost—

STRANGER.   Hear me—Give the alarm—refuse to shelter me—I will not hurt you—But I will not be taken alive—give me to eat and drink.

MRS R.   Will you leave me if I do this much? And return no more?

STRANGER.   I will promise nothing—nothing but this—I will execute my threat if

15  you betray me.

(*Sits at table—*MRS R. *places food—he eats*)

STRANGER.   (*eating*) Do you live alone?

MRS R.   No.

STRANGER.   Who dwells here beside?

MRS R.   One—it is no matter who—you had best begone, or he may find you here.

20  STRANGER.   You are rich.

MRS R.   Very—very rich.

STRANGER.   You have some money—give me your purse—you had it in your hand at the door—Give it me. (*she gives it—he counts a few pieces out*)

MRS R.   Take all—but go before it is too late—begone—I hear wayward steps—fly

25  from this place.

STRANGER.   If there are spies without I am safer here—

(*A slight knock at door*)

MRS R.   It is too late—it is my son, my idiot son.

STRANGER.   Let him come in.

MRS R.   The dread of this hour has been upon me all my life—and I will not.

(*Shutters shake*)

30  BARNA.   (*without*) Mother, Mother dear—Grip and I are cold.

STRANGER.   He calls you—that voice—it was he who grappled with me in the road!—was it he?

BARNABY *opens window—*MRS R. *pushes* STRANGER *in closet*

BARNA.   Are you there mother—how long you keep us from the fire and light—

MRS R. (*opens door—*BARNABY *enters carrying Grip the raven in basket*)

MRS R.   My boy—(*embraces and kisses him*)

35  BARNA.   We have been near a field, mother, leaping ditches—the wind has been blowing and the rushes and young plants bowing to it lest it should do them harm—cowards—and Grip—ha! ha! brave Grip—when the wind rolls him over in the dust—he turns and manfully tries to bite it—he has quarrell'd with every little twig—thinking, he told me—that it mocked him—ha! ha! ha!—He takes such care

40  of me besides—such care mother—he watches all the time I sleep.

(*Closes window and is about seating himself before closet when* MRS R. *takes the chair and points to another*)

How pale you are tonight—we have been cruel Grip and made her anxious.

*Tableau (The* STRANGER *hastily withdraws—*BARNABY *turns round hastily)*

MRS R.  (*agitated*) What is it, my son?

BARNA.  He flaps his wings as if there was somebody here—but Grip is wiser than to fancy that—jump then! (*buss*) Mother I'll tell you where we have been today—and what we have been doing—shall I?                                    45

MRS R.  Yes, dear.

BARNA.  You mustn't tell—for it's a secret mind only known to me and Grip and Hugh—you seem frightened, Mother—you don't see—(*starting up*)

MRS R.  See what?

BARNA.  There's—none of that about—blood—is there? (*showing the mark on his*  50 *breast*) I am afraid there is somewhere—you make my hair stand on end and my flesh creep—is it in this room, tell me, is it? (*covers his face with his hands*) is it gone?

MRS R.  There has been nothing here dear Barnaby, look—you see there are but you and me.                                                              55

BARNA.  (*looks round*) No—no—but let's see—were we talking—was it you and me?—where have we been?

MRS R.  Nowhere but here.

BARNA.  Aye—Hugh and I—That's it—Maypole Hugh and I you know and Grip— we have been lying in the forest and among the trees by the road side with a dog in  60 a noose ready to slip him when the man came by.

MRS R.  What man?

BARNA.  The robber—him that the stars winked at—we have waited for him after dark—and we shall have him. (*buss*) Ha! ha! we shall have him—you shall see him Mother bound hand and foot and you shall hear him at Tyburn Tree if we have  65 luck—so Hugh says—you're pale again and trembling and why *do* you look behind me so?

MRS R.  It is nothing—I am not quite well—Go you to bed and leave me here.

BARNA.  To bed—I don't like bed—I like to lie before the fire—I am hungry too— and Grip has eaten nothing since broad noon—Let us have supper—Grip!—to sup-  70 per lad. (*sits at table with Grip and feeds him*) That's all—Mother won't you taste? (*she shakes her head*) I want more bread from the closet—(*he is going to closet* MRS R. *prevents him*)

MRS R.  Sit still—I'll fetch it for you.

BARNA.  Mother—is today my birthday?

MRS R.  Don't you recall, it was a week ago?                                75

BARNA.  I remember that—but I think today must be my birthday too for all that— and I'll tell you why—I have always seen you on the evening of that day grow very

---

41.1 *Tableau*: Another picture which does not seem to be directly drawn from the plates in the book, but is probably based upon the woodcut in vol. 3, 28 of *Master Humphrey's Clock*, chapter 17, part 13.

44 *buss*: The business indicated is Barnaby putting Grip through his tricks.

sad—I have seen you cry, when Grip and I were most glad—as it is now you have looked as you have done ever since, Mother, towards night on my birthday—you

80      see I have found that out—tho' I am silly—this must be my birthday—Grip—(*he appears sleepy*)

MRS R.      Go to bed my child.

BARNA.      No—I'll lie here. (*lies on the floor*) I shall soon dream Mother—to sleep Grip—lad—to sleep.

MRS R.      Wretched boy. (*she watches him*)

85   BARNA.      (*in his sleep*) Now Lad—lie—Hugh—we shall have him yet—bold Grip— whoop—and away.

(STRANGER *cautiously comes from closet and extinguishes the candle*—MRS R. *and the* STRANGER *stand looking at each other. She motions the* STRANGER *to the door*)

STRANGER.      Stay—you teach your son well.

MRS R.      I have taught him nothing that you heard tonight—Depart instantly—or—I will rouse him.

90   STRANGER.      Shall *I* rouse him?

MRS R.      You dare not do that.

STRANGER.      I dare do anything—he knows me well it seems—I will know him— (*advances to him*)

MRS R.      Would you kill him in his sleep?

STRANGER.      Woman—I would see him nearer—and I will (*looks at Barnaby's face*)

95      observe in him of whose existence I was ignorant till to night—be careful how you use me—I may take a slow and sure revenge—(*going*)

MRS R.      There is a dreadful meaning in your words—I do not fathom it.

STRANGER.      There is a meaning in them and I see you do fathom it to the very depth— I leave you to digest it—do not forget my memory. (*Exits pointing at* BARNABY)

100   MRS R.      (*on her knees*) Oh thou who has taught me such deep love for this one remnant of the promise of a happy life—help him in his sad walk through this darken'd world, or my poor heart is broken—

*Closed in*


# SCENE 6

*Room in the Maypole.*

*Enter* WILLET, VARDEN, MRS VARDEN, *and* DOLLY.

1   GAB.      There, my love, we are safe arrived at last—this is the Maypole and this is my worthy friend John Willet– the best landlord in England.

---

102.1 *Closed in*: Flats close in slowly, probably to solemn music, changing the scene to the Maypole and a livelier tune.

WILLET.    That'll do—I hope you're well Ma'am and young Miss—may I have the
honor to lead you to our bar?

GAB.    And it *is* a bar, Martha.                                                          5

MRS V.    Gabriel Varden, I dare say you know it—you're a wicked man, Mr Willet, to
keep my husband here so long at all times.

GAB.    Never mind, John, let's have something nice and easy for dinner—(*aside to*
DOLLY) you can run over to Miss Haredale's with the letter, while the dinner is getting ready. (DOLLY *nods*)                                                                 10

WILLET.    This way ma'am if you please.

MRS V.    (*taking his arm*) I'm very troublesome, Mr Willet; come Varden—Dolly
child—you can amuse yourself—don't lose yourself—oh! Mr Willet—never have
any girls—they are such plagues.

WILLET.    (*going with her*) So are the boys—but there an't none of them left here   15
now—mine was the last—and he's run away.

*Exits with* GABRIEL *following*

GAB.    (*going*) Now Dolly, run to the Manor House child—(*Exits*)

DOLLY.    Yes Father—I will—Oh! poor Joe—I wish he was here.

SONG

Oh love is a fairy power
That weaves our chain of bliss                                                            20
'Tis another land's stolen hour
To sweeten whole years in this
etc etc etc                                                              *Exits*

*Enter* WILLET *and* MR CHESTER.

MR C.    You can give my horse a good feed and stabling can you, and me an early
dinner—I want this note conveyed to Mr Haredale's—have you a messenger at       25
hand?

WILLET.    Yes Sir. (*calls*) Halloa there, Hugh!

MR C.    And who is this Hugh my good friend?

WILLET.    A dreadful idle fellow—always sleeping in the sun in the summer and in
the straw in the winter—(*calls*) Hugh!—                                                   30

MR C.    Is there no other person?

WILLET.    Why yes—there is a sort of half natural as one may say—quick of foot—
and may be trusted.

MR C.    You don't mean—Barnaby!

WILLET.    Yes I do—shall I send him sir?                                                   35

MR C.    Yes, Mr Willet, if you please.

18.1 *Song*: The stanza is from 'Sing to love a roundelay' by Joseph Augustine Wade, 1796–1845, composer
of many songs; this was published *c*.1821.

WILLET.    Yes sir—(*exits calling*) Barnaby, come here lad.

BARNA.    (*without*) Coming—this way Grip—jump lad—jump. (*enters hastily with basket etc*)

MR C.    My good lad—you know Mr Haredale's?

BARNA.    (*nods and laughs*)

40  MR C.    Give this note into his own hands—wait for an answer—and here is money for thy pains—(*gives money*)

BARNA.    For Grip and me and Hugh to share—well, we shall spend it pretty soon.

MR C.    Away and use speed, my good boy.

BARNA.    Speed—speed—if you want to see hurry and speed—come here. (*leads*

45     MR CHESTER *to window*) Do you see there—how they whirl and plunge—and now they stop again and whisper together—I say what is it that they plot and hatch?—Do you know?

MR C.    They are only clothes—such as we wear—drying on those lines and fluttering in the wind.

50  BARNA.    Clothes—ha! ha!—why how much better to be silly, than as wise as you—you don't see shadowy people there—not you—I lead a merrier life than you with all your cleverness—ha! ha! I'll not change with you, no not I—(*Exits*)

MR C.    A strange creature, upon my word—it was a fortunate circumstance that I gleaned from Mrs Rudge—that my hopeful son—seriously paid his attentions to

55     Miss Emma Haredale—I must put a stop to it—he must marry well and rich—my debts must be paid out of his wife's fortune—there is a sort of holy bond between father and son—he must run away with an heiress. (*Exits taking snuff*)


SCENE 7


*A wood near the Warren.*

DOLLY *enters hurrying.*

1  DOLLY.    (*agitated*) I—I am sure someone is following me—stopping when I stop—moving when I move—I—I am not frightened—no—no—(*attempts to sing and walks on*—MAYPOLE HUGH *jumps through the bushes and stands before her—she screams—Tableau*)

DOLLY.    Was it you then after all—how glad I am to see you. (*aside*) I'm almost afraid of him.

5  HUGH.    Why do you spend so much breath in trying to avoid me—you're always proud to *me*, mistress.

DOLLY.    I am proud to no one—fall back if you please—or go on.

---

2.2 *Tableau*: The picture probably derives from the woodcut in vol. 3, 49, chapter 21, part 13 in *Master Humphrey's Clock.*

HUGH.　Nay, Mistress—I'll walk with you. (*buss*) Ha! ha! well done—strike again do—I like it.

DOLLY.　Let me go—Let me go this moment—Hugh—good—if you will leave me I 10 will give you anything—everything I have and never tell one word of this to any living creature.

HUGH.　You best had not—hark'ye little dove—you had best not—all about here know me and what I dare do—if I have a mind—if ever you are going to tell— stop—when the word's on your lip and think on the mischief you'll bring if you 15 do—upon some innocent heads—bring trouble on me and I'll bring trouble and something more on them—I care no more for them than for so many dogs—why should I—I'd sooner kill a man than a dog any day—

(*She attempts to run—he catches her arm*)

DOLLY.　Have pity—

HUGH.　To some I will—softly—softly darling—would you fly from rough Hugh, 20 that loves you as well as any drawing room gallant, bless you—I have the tenderest heart alive—I love all the ladies—you wouldn't run from me—look at me!

DOLLY.　I would—I will—Help! (*struggling*)

HUGH.　A fine for crying out—ha!—ha!—ha! a fine pretty one from your lips—I pay myself. 25

DOLLY.　Help! Help!

(*He attempts to kiss her—she screams.* BARNABY *runs on—and strikes* HUGH *on the head, who falls, then places himself before* DOLLY—*she has dropped the letter during the struggle*)

DOLLY.　Thank heaven—I am saved!

BARNA.　Run Mistress—run—be swift of foot. Brave Hugh is thick of skull and will soon wake up from his hurt—I and Grip will hold him down—(HUGH *half raises himself*) run—run—swift as the wind— 30

(HUGH *rises and is advancing towards* DOLLY *when* BARNABY *stands between them with his pole and keeps him at bay with it—*DOLLY *receding*)

BARNA.　Ha! ha! ha! which is best now Hugh—brave Hugh—the strong man or the fool—eh?

HUGH *appears much enraged and makes several attempts to seize* DOLLY, BARNABY *always preventing him as the Act Drop descends on the Picture.*

### END OF ACT ONE

---

8 *buss*: The business is that Hugh walks beside her, 'endeavouring to draw her arm through his', and she punches him 'with right good will' (chapter 21).

32.2 *Picture*: The end-of-act tableau is not drawn from the novel, since Dolly's rescuer there is Joe, not Barnaby.

# ACT II

## SCENE 1

*A Library in the Warren House.*

MR HAREDALE, MISS HAREDALE, MRS RUDGE, *and* BARNABY *discovered.*

1 MR H.   At length you have mustered heart to visit the old place, Mary—I am glad you have.

MRS R.   For the first time and the last, sir.

MR H.   The first for many years—but I hope not the last—I have often wished to see

5 you should you return here—as to Barnaby, it is quite his home.

BARNA.   And Grip.

MR H.   Yes—call him down, Barnaby.

BARNA.   Call him—but who can make him come—he calls me and makes me go where he will—he goes on before and I follow—he's the master and I'm the man—is

10 that the truth, Grip?—I make *him* come—him who never goes to sleep or so much as winks—why, any time of night you may see his eyes open in any dark room, shining like two sparks—I make him come—ha! ha!

MR H.   Hear me Mary—it's enough to know that you were cruelly involved in the calamity which deprived me of my only brother—and Emma of her father—with-

15 out being obliged to suppose  (as I something am) that you associate me with the author of our joint misfortune.

MRS R.   Associate *you* with them Sir?

MR H.   Indeed I think you do—your husband died in my brother's service and defence—it is natural you should—do so—we are a fallen house.

20 EMMA.   Pray ring dear Uncle—or stay, Barnaby will run himself and ask for wine.

BARNA.   Yes—and some for Grip—bold fellow.

MRS R.   Not for the world—I could not touch it—Sir—I scarcely know how to begin—you will think my mind disordered—

MR H.   Not so—any advice or assistance I can give you—you know is yours of

25 right—truly yours—

MRS R.   I must leave—your kind protection—as I am deeply thankful for the kindness of those alive and dead, who have occupied this house—and as I would not have its roof fall down and crush me, or its very walls drip blood, my name being spoken in their hearing—I never will again subsist upon its bounty—or let them

30 help me to subsistence.

MR H.   These are strange riddles.

MRS R.   You do not know to what uses they may be applied—into what hands it may pass.

MR H.   Surely its uses rest with you?

MRS R.   They did—they rest with me no longer—it may be—it *is*—devoted to pur- 35
poses that mock the dead in their graves—it never can prosper with me.

MR H.   What words are these?—you give up house and home—the annuity we settled on you twenty years ago—to wander forth and begin the world anew—and this
for some secret—or monstrous fancy—among what associates are you fallen—into
what guilt have you ever been betrayed? 40

MRS R.   I am guilty—and yet innocent—wrong yet right—good in intention though
constrained to shield and aid the bad—ask me no more questions sir—I must leave
my house tomorrow. My future dwelling, if I am to live in peace, must be a secret—
if we are hunted, we must fly again—and now this load is off my mind I beseech
you—and you dear Miss Haredale—to think well of me as you have been used to 45
do. Even if I die and cannot tell my secret—come child—I will pray for—and thank
you both—and trouble you no more. (*going*)

MR H.   I will accompany you to the park gates. Mary—your resolve almost makes
me doubtful of my senses.

MRS R.   Farewell Miss—perhaps for ever. 50

*Kisses* MISS HAREDALE *and exits with* MR HAREDALE.

BARNA.   (*takes* MISS HAREDALE's *hand*) I love you—I love your low voice and your
soft eyes—and it does me good to see that there are tears in them, for I thought that
no one cried but Mother—when she gives me all that she has, to stay my hunger and
while she fasts herself, weeps when I ask for more.

EMMA.   Poor boy—this will buy some comforts for you. (*gives money*) 55

BARNA.   —and Grip—come with me Grip—Mother shall work for you—and I will
walk with you in the green fields, among the leaves and the birds—and the wild
flowers where the brook dances in the light where I dip for pebbles shining beside
our path—and making a looking glass for the blue sky—will you come?

MRS R.   (*without*) Barnaby, I am waiting for you dear— 60

BARNA.   Hush! We must go Grip—don't tell Mother—(*places his finger on lip*) don't
tell. (*Exits*)

EMMA.   Helpless child—what a love of nature, despite his sad infirmity, is mixed up
in his wandering fancies.

EDWARD CHESTER *enters—he embraces* EMMA.

EDWD.   Dearest Girl—I have been long waiting anxiously in the park for this oppor- 65
tunity and have just watched your uncle leave the house—look up—speak—say one
word I entreat.

EMMA.   I dread to think of this rash visit—he will return on the instant—then—

EDWD.   Then what sweet—one moment with you—is worth every risk—say—that
you do not mind the cruel obstacles—constantly thrown in our path—say that— 70

MR HAREDALE *enters and thrusts* EDWARD *from her.*

MR H.   Say that, this is well done of you Sir—to corrupt my servants and enter my
house—in secret like a thief.

EDWD.    Miss Haredale's presence Sir and your relationship—gives you a licence
which if you are a brave man you will not abuse—you have compelled me to this
75    course and the fault is yours—not mine.

MR H.    It is not the act of a true man to tamper with the affections of a weak girl—
begone—I forbid you my house—your presence here is offensive to me—and dis-
tressing to my niece. (*places his arm round* EMMA's *waist*)

EDWD.    Mr Haredale your arm encircles her on whom I have set my every hope and
80    thought—she has plighted her faith to me—you shall not cancel the bond between
us—I will not abandon the pursuit—I leave her with a confidence in her pure faith,
which you will never weaken—and with no concern—but that I do not leave her in
some gentler care—your froward sullen temper chills and freezes all around you,
cold, unfeeling man! (*Exits kissing* EMMA's *hand*)

*The Scene is closed in.*

## SCENE 2

VARDEN's *House and workshop.*

*Enter* TAPPERTIT *and* MR CHESTER.

1    MR C.    Pray my good sir—is this the house of G. Varden—Locksmith of Clerkenwell,
London?

TAP.    It is—and I am the Prentice Simon Tappertit.

MR C.    Indeed! was it from your kindness Mr Tappertit that I am endebted for
5    this? (*shews card and reads*) 'A Friend—desiring of a Conference Immediate—
Private—Burn it when you've read it—S.T.'

TAP.    I am the individual that writ it and left it at your chambers—you was out—or
I would have explained the point then.

MR C.    Really I am exceedingly sorry that it so happened, my good friend.

10    TAP.    Don't apologize Sir—we'll to Buss.

MR C.    If you please.

TAP.    From what passes in our house I am aware that your son keeps company still
against your inclinations—now Sir—I am on your side—what I tell you is this—
that as long as our people go backwards and forwards to that jolly old Maypole
15    fetching and carrying you can't help your son keeping company with that young
lady—now I'll tell you how it is to be prevented—if an honest civil gentleman like
you, was only to talk to our old woman—that's Mrs Varden—and flatter her up a
bit—you'd gain her over for ever—then there's the point got—she wouldn't let her
daughter Dolly play the go-between and carry letters for your son any longer.

20    MR C.    What a profound knowledge of human nature you possess—is Mrs Varden in?

TAP.    She is—did you wish to see her? (MR C. *nods*) (TAP. *exits, calling*) Mr Chester
Ma'am—and not Mr Edward, it's his father.

*Enter* MRS VARDEN, DOLLY, *and* MIGGS.

MR C.   (*bowing*) But do not let his father be any check or restraint on your domestic
occupation, Miss Varden.

MIGGS.   Oh—now—there—an't I always a saying it—(*claps her hands*) If he an't   25
been and took Missus for her own daughter—well she do look like it—that she do.

MR C.   Is it possible that this is Mrs Varden? I am amazed—that is not your daughter
Ma'am—no—no; your sister.

MRS V.   (*simperingly*) My daughter indeed, Sir.

MR C.   My friend Gabriel, whose acquaintance I only made this evening—should be   30
a happy man.

MRS V.   (*sighs and shakes her head*) Ah!

MR C.   Is that the case—dear me—you're a mother, Mrs Varden—you may guess the
object of my visit—I love my son—and would save him from marriage—certain
misery. He has had—I am told—your lovely daughter's aid in conveying letters etc.   35
to Miss Haredale—and your open-hearted husband's—

MRS V.   Much more than mine Sir—It's a—

MR C.   Bad example—it is. No doubt you will prevent it—I am sure.

MRS V.   Prevent it, Sir—I'll put a stop to it. Varden had better mind his home—and
for you miss—I'll shut you up night and day.                                              40

MR C.   Dear Madam—I shall ever live your grateful debtor—I expect my dear boy
will be waiting for me at my chambers; adieu—convey my deep regards to amiable
Gabriel—farewell love (*to* DOLLY) Madam I am ever your devoted slave (*to* MRS
VARDEN—*salutes her pompously*) will this young lady condescend to light me to the
door? (*to* MIGGS)                                                                       45

(*Exiting*—MIGGS *lights him to wing*)

MIGGS.   (*returning*) Oh mim—oh gracious mim, there's a gentleman—to think of his
taking you for Miss Dolly and me for a young lady—if I was Master wouldn't I be
jealous of him!

DOLLY.   For my part I half believe Mr Chester, with all his politeness, was making
game of us more than once.                                                               50

MRS V.   How dare you—I'm astonished—but it's just like you. (*weeps*) Did ever any
body ever hear of a daughter telling her own mother—she has been made game
of. (*strikes* DOLLY *with her fan and rushes off—followed by* MIGGS)

DOLLY.   Well what will this world come to—it is turning quite round—all thro' love,
as the song says.                                                                        55

SONG

Oh, 'tis love—'tis love—<br>
That makes the world go round<br>
etc etc

*Exit*

---

57 *Oh…round*: A popular song since the early 1820s, appearing anonymously by 1831 in *The Universal
Songster*.

## SCENE 3

*The Chambers of* CHESTER.

MR CHESTER *and* EDWARD *discovered.*

1 MR C.    So you have had a cool dismissal have you—I told you last night what would
    happen—Poor Ned—may I ask you for the nut crackers?
  EDWD.    She has been tampered with and most vilely deceived—my heart will break.
  MR C.    There again (*sipping wine*) you are wrong—hearts—we know they are—of
5 animals—of bullocks and sheep and so forth—are cooked and devoured I am told
    by the lower classes with a great deal of relish—Men are sometimes stabbed to the
    heart—but as to hearts being broken—is all nonsense, Ned—
  EDWD.    Hear me—I love Emma fervently, truly—and cannot give her up—
  MR C.    Indeed Sir—if you will do me the favor to ring the bell—the servant will shew
10 you the door—Go to the deuce at my express desire—Good day. (EDWARD *exits*)
    Very awkward this—his marriage with this wealthy heiress I had selected for him
    would have paid my debts and provided handsomely for me—(*takes snuff*) If time
    were money I would compound with my creditors and give them three hours a
    day—they might pay themselves in calls then (*a knock at door*) who's there—come in.

*Enter* HUGH.

15 MR C.    Ah—my Maypole centaur, are you here?
  HUGH.    (*sulkily*) Here I am—and trouble enough I've had to get here—what do you
    ask me to come for and keep me out when I *do* come?
  MR C.    My good fellow—your being here is the very best proof that you are not kept
    out—how are you?
20 HUGH.    I'm well enough.
  MR C.    Sit down.
  HUGH.    I'd rather stand.
  MR C.    Please yourself by all means.

(*A pause*)

  HUGH.    are you going to speak to me, Master?
25 MR C.    My worthy creature—you are a little ruffled and out of humour—I'll wait till
    you're quite yourself again—I am in no hurry.
  HUGH.    Why—lookye sir—am I the man that you privately left your whip with
    before you rode away from the Maypole and told to bring it back whenever he
    might want to see you on a certain subject?
30 MR C.    No doubt the same—or you have a twin brother.
  HUGH.    Then I have come, sir—and I have brought it back, and something else along
    with it—a letter sir—that I took from the person that had charge of it. (*places* DOLLY'S
    *letter in* 1ˢᵗ *Act and whip on the table*)
  MR C.    Did you obtain this by force?

HUGH.   Not quite—partly.

MR C.   Who was the messenger from whom you took it? (*opens letter and reads it*)   35

HUGH.   A woman—One Varden's daughter.

MR C.   Oh indeed—what else did you take from her?

HUGH.   What else?

MR C.   Yes.

HUGH.   Nothing.   40

MR C.   I think—there was one thing else.

HUGH.   Well—a kiss—nothing else.

MR C.   I have heard a trifle of jewellery spoken of, such as a bracelet now, for instance.

HUGH.   Curse him—(*draws from his bosom bracelet wrapped in hay, lays it on table*) there.   45

MR C.   Pray put it up again—my excellent friend you took it for yourself and may keep it—I am neither a thief nor a receiver—you had better hide it—

HUGH.   You're not a receiver—what do you call *that* Master? (*striking letter with his hand*)

MR C.   I call that quite another thing—I shall prove it presently—as you will see— you are thirsty I suppose?   50

HUGH.   Yes.

MR C.   Step into that closet, and bring me a bottle you will see there, and a glass (HUGH *fetches it*) now fill and drink—(*he fills several glasses—all of which* HUGH *rapidly drinks*)

MR C.   How many can you bear?

HUGH.   As many as you like—go on—fill high—give me a bumper of this and I'll do   55 murder if you ask me.

MR C.   As I don't mean to ask you, and as you might possibly do it without—we will stop at the next glass—you were drinking before you came here.

HUGH.   I always do when I can get it (*waving the glass over his head*) why not? Ha! ha! what's so good to me as this? What else has ever given me the strength and cour-   60 age of a man—I should have died in a ditch. Where's he who, when I was a weak and sickly wretch, with trembling legs and fading sight, bade me cheer up, as this did?— I never knew him—not I—I drink to the drink Master—and this arm (*raises it*) it once was mere skin and bone—and would have been dust in some church yard by this time—but for the drink I should never have been spirited up to take a kiss from   65 the proud little beauty, Master, but for the drink—I thank the drink for it—I'll drink again, Master—fill me one more, come, one more.

MR C.   You are such a promising fellow—what's your age?

HUGH.   I don't know.

MR C.   At any rate—you must have confidence to trust me with your life—Robbery   70 on the King's highway, my young friend, is a very dangerous and ticklish occupation.

HUGH.   How's this—who was it set me on?

MR C.   Who—I didn't hear you—who was it? Your neck is as safe in my hands—my good fellow—as though a baby's fingers clasped your throat I assure you—take   75 another glass—you are quieter now—by the bye—what is your name—my good soul—you are called Hugh—I know—of course—your other name.

HUGH.    I have no other name.

MR C.    Do you mean that you never knew one or that you don't choose to tell
80    it—which?

HUGH.    I'd tell if I could—I have been always called Hugh—nothing more I never knew, nor saw, nor thought about a father, and I was a boy of six—that's not very old—when they hung my mother upon Tyburn—they might have let her live, she was poor enough—you see that dog of mine, such a dog as that and one of the same
85    breed was the only living thing except me that howled that day—If he'd have been a man, he'd have been glad to be quit of her—for she had been forced to keep him lean and half starved, but being a dog, and not having a man's sense—he was sorry.

MR C.    It was dull of the brute—but good night—remember you are safe with me—so long as you deserve it—and I hope you always will—be careful—pray do—
90    good night—bless you.

(*Bows* HUGH *out*)

MR C.    They shouldn't have hanged his mother—I'm sure she was handsome—red nosed perhaps—aye—it was all for the best—Peak, my chair. (*calls*) Foh! Buy some scent and sprinkle the floor—the very atmosphere is tainted by the Centaur.

PEAK *and 2 chairmen bring in a sedan chair.*

*Tableau—scene closes*

# SCENE 4

MRS RUDGE's *House as in 1ˢᵗ Act.*

*Enter* HAREDALE *and* VARDEN.

1    GAB.    The sight of you is good for sore eyes, sir. Why have you brought me to this house?

HARE.    Varden, you will be amazed to hear what errand I am on.

GAB.    I have no doubt it's a reasonable one.

5    HARE.    But half an hour ago—

GAB.    Bringing you news of Barnaby and his mother—ah—you needn't shake your head sir—it was a wild goose chase—quite hopeless—quite hopeless. The world is a wild place.

HARE.    My good fellow—I have a deeper meaning in my present anxiety to find
10    them than you can fathom—It is not a mere whim—but an earnest solemn purpose—

93.2 *Tableau—scene closes*: From the woodcut in vol. 3, 68, end of chapter 23, in part 14 of *Master Humphrey's Clock.*

my thoughts and dreams all tend to it—I have no rest by night or day—I cannot lie
quiet in any sleep—since the night of the storm—in short since the 19th of March.

GAB.   The anniversary of your poor brother's murder.

HARE.   You know the furniture still remains here—belonging to Mrs Rudge; the
house has been shut up, by my orders, since she left it—I now intend to occupy   15
it—and am now here to pass the night—and not tonight alone—but many nights.
This is a secret I trust you with only—you will not come to me unless in case of
strong necessity—from dusk to broad daylight—I shall be here.

GAB.   For what purpose?

HARE.   No morbid purpose—but there is a mysterious connection with this house   20
and the sad event that I am certain will be brought to light here—(*lights a taper*) will
you like to walk through the house—speak low.

GAB.   No—I'm obliged to you—I might frighten the rats—this is a dull place—may
no-one share your watch?

HARE.   Thank you—my good friend if you remained with me—you would think me   25
the victim of some hideous fancy—do you think Mrs Rudge can have married
again?

GAB.   Not without our knowledge, sir.

HARE.   She may have done so—suppose she has married incautiously—and the
man turned out a ruffian—is it not possible that such a connection may have been   30
formed in her husband's lifetime, and led to his and my brother's death?

GAB.   Gracious providence—don't entertain such dark thoughts for a moment—five
and twenty years ago, ne'er was a girl like her—a gay, handsome, laughing, bright
eyed damsel—think what she was then and what she is now. We all change—but
that's time—time does his work honestly—but care and suffering and these devils   35
have changed her. They are devils—secret—stealthy—undermining devils that do
more havoc in a month—than time does in a year—picture to yourself what Mary
Rudge was before they went to work with her fresh heart and face—do her that
justice and say whether such a thing is possible.

HARE.   You are a good fellow Varden—and are quite right—any suspicions are unjust.   40

GAB.   It isn't, sir, because I courted her before Rudge and failed, that I say she was
too good for him—she would have been as much too good for me. But she *was* too
good for him—he wasn't free and frank enough with her—for myself I'll always
keep her old picture in my mind—stand by her—and try to win her back to peace—
and sir—I'd do the same if she had married fifty highwaymen—poor thing.   45

HARE.   (*takes his hand*) Good night friend—good night—remember my injunction—don't let me be disturbed—I feel—this mystery will soon be revealed—darkness—gives way to light. Farewell. (*Exits L.H.*)

GAB.   Good night Sir. (*bows*) What a very odd notion to shut himself up here with
the cobwebs and dust—well—well—for my part—I'd rather be snugly seated at   50
home—with Toby in one hand and a pipe in the other—yes—tho' Miggs was in the
background—at it tooth and nail. (*Exits*)

## SCENE 5

*The Wanderer's Home* (*sunset*).

BARNABY *and* MRS RUDGE *discovered.*

1 BARNA.    A brave evening, Mother—if we had clinking in our pockets, but a few specks of that gold which is piled up yonder in the sky—we should be rich for life— we'd dress fine—you and I, I mean—not Grip—Keep horses, dogs—wear bright fine colours and feathers, do no more work—live delicately and at our ease—oh!

5 We'd find uses for it—I would I knew where gold was buried—how hard I'd work to dig it up!

MRS R.    My boy—it always glitters brightest at a distance—Do you not see how red it is? Nothing bears so many stains of blood as gold—avoid it my son—I'd rather we were dead—and laid in our graves—than you should ever come to love it.

10 BARNA.    (*looks at sky—then on the mark on his wrist*) Why should you fear it Mother—no good man fears it—and will not—I'll watch over you—nothing shall harm you—or touch one hair of your head if it did—is not the curse read—the curse!

*The* STRANGER *disguised as a blind beggar enters.*

STRANGER.    A blessing on those voices—they are like eyes to me—will they speak

15 again and cheer the poor traveller—I struck my stick just now upon the bucket of your well—Be pleased to let me have a draught of water lady—

BARNA.    Come round this way. (*crossing to him*) Put your hand in mine—you're blind—and always in the dark, eh?—are you frightened in the dark? Do you see great crowds of faces now? Do they grin and chatter? (*places chair for him*)

20 MRS R.    You have wandered from the road—

STRANGER.    May be—may be—that's likely. (BARNABY *brings a jug of water to him and he drinks*) Thank you for this rest and drink—(*takes pence from wallet*) might I make bold to ask that one who has the gift of sight would lay this out for me in bread to keep me on my way?

25 BARNA.    Yes—(*takes money*) yes—I'll go—then I'll hunt for glow worms to light up his dark way—seek the smooth grass and the holly bush to make his bed—Grip shall watch over him while he sleeps—(*Exits*)

STRANGER.    (*rises and removes patch from eye—*MRS R. *starts*) You know me.

MRS R.    Too well—too well—what do you want?

30 STRANGER.    I am poor. (*holds out hand*) To eat and drink I must have money— I say no more—I've been long searching for you.

MRS R.    Do you know how pinched and destitute I am—Let your heart be soft-ened—have mercy—

---

0.1 *The Wanderer's Home*: i.e. the cottage in which Mrs Rudge and Barnaby took refuge, five years before, according to Dickens's chapter 45. The play takes little account of time passing.

STRANGER. (*snaps his fingers*) You have a roof over your head—always have had—a son to comfort and assist you—he is a likely lad—now in a word—I want twenty 35 pounds—you can get it—give up an annuity or borrow it—consider of it—I'll enjoy the air the while.

MRS R. (*appears overpowered by grief*)

STRANGER (*draws patch over his eye*)

BARNABY (*re-enters with bread*)

BARNA. Here's bread—good man.

STRANGER. Thanks—taste this lad for your pains.

BARNA. (*drinks from a flask bottle*)

STRANGER. Is it good (BARNABY *coughs*) drink more—you don't taste anything like 40 that often.

BARNA. Often—never!

STRANGER. Too poor—your mother, poor soul, would be happier if she was richer.

BARNA. Why so I tell her—this very thing I told her just now—Tell me, is there any way of being rich I could find out? 45

STRANGER. Any way—a hundred ways.

BARNA. Ay—ay—do you say so—what are they—nay Mother it's for your sake I ask—not mine—what are they?

STRANGER. Why—they are not to be found out by stay-at-homes my friend.

BARNA. Stay-at-homes—But I am not one—I am often out before the sun and 50 travel home when he has gone to rest—I dream of digging gold up in heaps—but I never find it—tell me where it is—I'd go there—if the journey were a whole year long—because I know she would be happier—Speak again—

STRANGER. It's in the world—bold Barnaby, the merry world—not in solitary places like those you pass your time in—but in crowds—and where there's noise 55 and rattle.

MRS R. (*hastily approaching the* STRANGER, *whispering*) Let me speak to you— (STRANGER *rises*) Take these—they are the savings of years—if you *can* take them do—on condition that you leave this place instantly—that you do not tempt my child.

STRANGER. Six guineas fall short of twenty pounds. 60

MRS R. For such a sum I must write to a distant part of the country—return on this day week—at the same hour—but not to the house—wait at the corner of the lane.

STRANGER. Of course I shall find you there—I'll trust you—on this day week at sunset—and think of him within doors—good night—bless you Ma'am (*assuming another voice*) farewell bold Barnaby, farewell—(*Exits*) 65

BARNA. Mother what is the matter—why does he go?

MRS R. I don't know—You must not follow him—besides we must leave this place to night—this instant.

BARNA. This place—this cottage and the little garden, Mother?

MRS R. Yes—we must travel to London—and find some new abode. 70

MRS R. (*puts on bonnet and cloak*—BARNABY *places basket at his back*—MRS R. *takes his hand, shuts cottage door and locks it*)

MRS R.   Now. (*looks round eagerly*)

BARNA.   Yes—yes—oh I'm glad, laugh Grip—laugh—(*going, suddenly stops*) But the poor dog that licks me and jumps for joy when I see him—how mournful he will be Mother, when he scratches at the door and finds it always shut—and I am
75   gone. (*Exits, his mother leading him away*)


# SCENE 6

*The 'Boot,' a low public house.*

*A number of persons shabbily dressed and led on by* DENNIS *enter shouting.* TAPPERTIT *enters bowing lowly to the mob.*

1   TAP.   Gentlemen—well met—my Lord Gordon—does me and you the honour of sending his compliments per self.

DEN.   You've seen my Lord too, have you—I see this afternoon.

TAP.   My duty called me to the lobby when I shut up our shop—and I saw him
5   there—how do you do?

DEN.   Lively—Master, lively—here's a new brother regularly put down in black and white—sent by Master Gashford, a credit to our cause, one of the stick-at-nothing sort—one arter my own heart—come in Muster Maypole. (HUGH *enters*) D'ye see him? (*slapping him on the back*) An't he got the right sort of looks?

10   HUGH.   Looks—or no looks—I'm the man you want.

TAP.   Do you know me feller?

HUGH.   Not I? ha! ha! ha! but I should like to.

TAP.   You are the hostler of the Maypole.

HUGH.   (*staring*) Why it—aren't—

15   TAP.   Arnt it? You remember G. Varden—Bells made and mended in Town and Country—you remember coming down here—to ask after a vagabond Joe Willet, don't you?—you was sent by his father—and you said hated him wuss than pisin.

HUGH.   To be sure.

TAP.   And are you in the same mind now?

20   HUGH.   Yes.

TAP.   Give's your hand (*looks at* HUGH's *hand*) is your other one at all cleaner?

HUGH.   Much the same.

TAP.   Well then—I'll owe you a shake.

DEN.   Huzza—my lovely infant—we shall make something of you by and by.

25   HUGH.   You may make anything you like of me. Put me on what duty you please— I'm your man—I'll fight all London—Single-handed (*he strikes* TAPPERTIT *on head—and knocks his hat over his eyes* ) Noble Captain.

(*All Shout*)

TAP.    Now to dress—United Bulldogs—Lord George will soon—call upon us to be doing—the eyes of all the world are upon us—how much money have we collected this week?    30

DEN.    Here's the list—Muster Gashford sent it—

*Gives list to* TAPPERTIT—*a tub is rolled on.* TAPPERTIT *mounts—Tableau.*

TAP.    (*reads*) Boys—we are 60 thousand strong.

MOB.    Hoorah!

TAP.    Our funds *not* very improving—40 Scavengers—3 and 4 pence—the united Link Boys—3 shillings—a Friend in Bedlam—½ a crown—The Jolly Bull Dogs 2    35 pence and the United Bull Dogs ½ a guinea—(*shouts*) the last brave hearts comes much welcome—(*descends*)

HUGH.    I like you brave Captain—you're a Bull Dog—to the heart's core—lead on anywhere—I'll follow you.

TAP.    Aye—That man will prove a credit to my *corps*—and let me see—(*pauses*)    40 things is coming to a *crisis*—Lord George leads us on tomorrow then for the row— then in an altered state of society—which must follow—he, the Maypole brother might marry Miggs—if he was drunk enough—yes—it shall be done—I'll make a note of it—March!

(*Exits slowly—writing in a small dirty book—the rest following*)

## SCENE 7

*Westminster Bridge, the end leading to the Hall.*

MR CHESTER, *now Sir John, enters from the Hall—at the same time* MR HAREDALE *wrapped in a large cloak passes from the opposite side.*

MR C.    (*stopping him*) Haredale!—God bless me—this is strange indeed.    1

HARE.    Yes—It is—yes—a—(*endeavouring to pass*)

MR C.    My dear friend—why such speed—one minute—for the sake of old acquaintance.

HARE.    I am in haste—neither of us has sought this meeting—Let it be a brief one—    5 Good night.

MR C.    Fie!—fie! How very churlish—your name was on my lips—this is really a most remarkable meeting.

MOB.    (*without*) Huzza! Lord George for ever!—on to St George's Fields—down with everybody!    10

31.1 *Tableau*: Woodcut in *Master Humphrey's Clock* vol. 3, 161, chapter 39, part 16.

MR C.   You hear the people, Haredale—Lord George is leading them to St George's
Fields to commence our great undertaking—but I believe you're not one of us—we
have nothing in common.
HARE.   We have much in common—many things—all that *he* gave us—and com-
15    mon charity, not to say common sense and common decency—should teach you to
refrain from these proceedings—shame upon you to mislead these ignorant men.
MR C.   Really, you are wrong—my friend.
MOB.   *Shouting without*
HARE.   You hear your dupes—sir—I hope there is but one gentleman in England
mixed up with this sad affair.
MOB.   *Enter shouting*
20  MR C.   I don't hear you sir—Brothers (*to* MOB) on to St George's Fields.
HUGH.   (*aside to* DENNIS) I know that proud squire and owe him an old grudge—
Let's down with him.
DEN.   With all my heart—Boys—here's one against us—this black-looking cove—
MOB.   Down with him!
25  TAP.   Duck him!
DEN.   Hang him!

HUGH.   (*hurls a stone and strikes Haredale on the head*)

HARE.   (*turning round*) Who is that? Show me the man who did it—Dog! was it
you? (*seizing one of the* MOB *throws him down and draws sword*)

*Tableau*

MR C.   My dear friend—are you mad?—you are blinded by passion—you don't
30    know your friends from your foes.
HARE.   I know them all sir—I can distinguish well—Sir John, you are answerable for
this—draw if you are a gentleman. (*pause*) Coward! (*strikes* CHESTER—MOB *groan
and* VARDEN *rushes through crowd*)
VARDEN.   Sir—for heavens sake—don't mind—what can you do against this number? Away—sir—Dolly shall bring all you want to night—make haste, sir—as quick
35    as you can. (*forces* HAREDALE *off reluctantly*)
HARE.   Sir John Chester—we shall meet again; look to it.

MOB *yell*

CHESTER.   I hope so my dear friend (*aside*) that blow shall be answered in the
churl's blood (*beckons* HUGH *and* DENNIS) mind, my worthy friends—to your care
I consign Mr Haredale and his house in the coming struggle—you may do as you
40    please with him or his—provided you show no mercy—and no quarter—sack—
burn or do as you like with his house—but it must come down and he must die—
you understand. (*all in a loud whisper*)
DEN.   Oh my eye—I believe you!

28.1 *Tableau*: From the woodcut in *Master Humphrey's Clock* vol. 3, 188, chapter 43, part 16.

HUGH.    Understand—yes—you speak plain enough Master—why this is hearty.

CHESTER.    I knew you would like it—poor lambs, be cautious—watch his steps for 45
a few minutes then return here—I'll rejoin you after receiving orders from Lord
George. (*Exits followed by* MOB)

MRS RUDGE *and* BARNABY *enter—they pause on the bridge.*

BARNA.    Mother—now we've reached London shall we see the blind man again?

MRS R.    No (*aside*) I pray heaven. Why do you ask—why do you desire to see him,
love?                                                                                             50

BARNA.    Because he talked to me about gold—and because he came and went away
so strangely—just as the whiteheaded man comes sometimes to my bed-foot in
the night—and says what I can't remember when the bright day returns—he told
me he'd come back—(*laughs*) ay—ay—he will—oh yes—(MOB *shout without*)
see—look Mother—do you hear that—(*looks off*) that's the brave crowd he talked 55
of—come—come—

MRS R.    Not to join it!

BARNA.    Yes—yes—why not? (*endeavours to drag her with him*—MOB *shout*)

MRS R.    No—no—dear Barnaby—for my sake!

BARNA.    For your sake—well—it's for your sake Mother—remember what the blind 60
man said about gold—Here's the brave crowd—come—or—wait until I come
back—yes wait. (*he stoops to buckle his shoe*)

CHESTER. (*re-enters—passes and sees* BARNABY)

CHESTER. Young man.

BARNA.    Who's that? (*looks up*)

CHESTER.    Do you wear this ornament? (*produces a blue cockade*)                65

MRS R.    No—pray not—Do not give it to him.

CHESTER.    Speak for yourself, my dear Madam—will you wear the sign of a loyal
Englishman?

BARNA.    Yes—I will—I will. (*pins it in his hat*)

CHESTER.    Hasten to St George's Fields—the hour of assembling is ten.           70

MRS R.    Oh mercy Sir—do not tempt him into danger—we are but just come from
the country and know nothing of these matters.

CHESTER.    My good woman—what do you mean by tempting—dear me (*to*
BARNABY) you desire to make one of our great body, do you my man?

BARNA.    Yes—to be sure I do—I told her so—myself.                                75

CHESTER.    What a very unnatural mother you must be—follow me my lad—and
you shall have your wish. (*he is going when the* MOB *all enter—wearing blue cock-
ades etc.*)

HUGH.    (*to* CHESTER) All right master—we've kennelled the old fox—and I'll soon
burn him out. (*sees* BARNABY) What, Barnaby Rudge—how now lad, where have
you been hiding for these hundred years—ha! ha! ha! (*strikes him on shoulder*)     80

BARNA.    What, Hugh!

HUGH.     Ay—Maypole Hugh—you remember my dog—he's alive now and will know
you I warrant—what, you wear the colour do you—well done ha! ha! (*shakes his
hand*)

CHESTER.     You know this young man, I see.

85   HUGH.     Know him as well as I know my right hand—My Captain knows him—we
all know him.

DEN.     —Yes, Master Sir John, we all know him.

TAP.     I only slightly, Sir John—he's a shallow idiot.

CHESTER.     Take him into your division—I'll leave him to your care—(*Exits*)

90   HUGH.     Yes—and it hasn't a better nor a nimbler nor a more active man, than
Barnaby—show me the man who says it has—fall in Barnaby—fall in lad—he shall
march between me and Dennis—and he shall carry the gayest silken streamer in
this valiant army. (*gives* BARNABY *a Blue Flag*)

MRS R.     (*clinging to* BARNABY) No—in the name of Heaven, Barnaby—come
95   with me.

HUGH.     Halloa! Women in the field. (*holding her back*) My Captain there—

TAP.     What's the matter now—do you call this order?

HUGH.     Nothing like it—It's against all orders—Ladies are carrying off our gallant
soldiers from their duty—the word of command, Captain—quick.

100   TAP.     Close Form—March—

*The* MOB *march off with* BARNABY *who proudly carries the flag—*HUGH *keeping* MRS
RUDGE *back—shots are heard in the distance and military music—*MRS RUDGE *continues to follow them, vainly endeavouring to reach* BARNABY; *the scene changes.*

## THE LAST SCENE

*A chamber in the House of* MRS RUDGE *overlooking the City.*

DOLLY *seen entering with a small basket.*

1   DOLLY.     I'm sure I shall never get back again—I'm so frightened—and the streets are
so crowded by ill-looking men—I scarcely know how I reached Mrs Rudge's in
safety—I shouldn't though, if it hadn't been for the soldiers—oh—how I do love a
soldier—poor Joe—I almost wish they'd make me one—so that I could see you once

---

100.3   *the scene changes*: This is the end of the portion of the novel published by the time Stirling wrote
his play; he had the ending, therefore, to invent, in the final scene that follows. The MS has from here a different appearance, in the same handwriting but in much paler ink with wider spacing, suggesting it was not
written out at the same time.

0.2   *A chamber... basket*: It is unclear how the staging is to work here. Dolly is 'seen entering' but might
be indoors or still out in the street when she avoids the mob and 'staggers to the steps'. If the heading did not
specify 'a chamber in the house of Mrs Rudge' the scene could more easily be imagined as taking place in
the street, with steps up to the door at the centre.

more—Father desired me to carry this basket of nice little things for poor Mr 5
Haredale—the mob are setting fire to the houses and coming this way what shall I
do—I'm so frightened  (*shouts heard without*) the mob beat back the soldiers—they
are coming here with horrid looks—how—how—shall I escape—(*the* MOB *are seen
hurrying through the street—she endeavours to avoid them. She staggers to the steps
and falls exhausted*)

DOLLY.    Father, Joe—don't leave me!

(MOB *shouting—Guns firing and soldiers pursuing*)

DENNIS.    This is the old Haredales' house—go to work my boys—down with it!    10

HUGH.    Stop my masters—before we burn the kennel—let's look after the fox—he
may escape us else—and I want life! Lead the men, brave Captain—round the
house—and leave me to deal with those within—I'll do the work well, never fear ha!
ha! (*shews large knife*) I've had it ground up—give the word, Captain!

TAPP.    Go back all of you—then go forward and march over again.    15

MOB *exit shouting*

HUGH.    I never was so happy in my life—I'm no longer a dog, a brute—among my
fellow men—but a master of men—all London's ours—it's all in our hands now—
I've only waited for such a day as this—I'll burn and kill for what's past—kill as they
killed her, without mercy—without hope—knife for rope. (*sees* DOLLY) My beauty
of the wood—Hugh lad, you're in luck tonight—here's a dainty damsel ready to your 20
hands—(*he raises her up*) Look up—it's an old friend—one that must please you.

DOLLY.    (*recovering*) who is it—where am I—why am I here?

HUGH.    I can't tell my beauty unless you came to meet me here—I've long liked you.
I've kept it to myself many a year but I needn't do so any longer—times are altered
now—I'm a man as good as the next—mine you shall be sweet. (*attempts to kiss her*) 25

DOLLY.    Help!

HUGH.    Ay ay—call away, mistress, there's no bold Barnaby to crack my crown and
save your life.

*She calls for help—Drums heard without. He is just forcing her off when the* MOB
*repass—pursued by* SOLDIERS—JOE WILLET *dressed as a* DRAGOON *rushes in, sees*
DOLLY—*fires a pistol.* HUGH *falls—*JOE *catches* DOLLY *in his arms—*

*Tableau*

JOE.    My own love—look up—it is I—I ever yours faithfully—Dolly, dear girl, do
speak to me—I'll place you in safety then again to duty—the streets are filled with 30
lawless misguided men—all seeking ill—now love, fear nothing—leave that dog to
his fate—he is well served. (*points to* HUGH, *and leads* DOLLY *off*)

HUGH.    (*rising slowly*) He's hit me in the right place—curse on his aim—if we'd have
come to a fair struggle my knife would have spoilt him. (*appears faint*) I want some

28.4 *Tableau*: A new tableau, since the incident is not in Dickens's storyline.

35  drink courage in me—courage Hugh—bold Hugh—I should have liked to have
died in the green woods—not in this dark place and with this blood and red glare
about me  (*wildly*) but I helped do it ha! ha! Huzza boys—burn away—kill—(*falls
dead*)

MRS RUDGE *enters dragging in* BARNABY *who still carries the flag*—MOB *shouting.*

BARNA.    Let me go Mother—this is brave work—I like it, they call me Captain—
general—noble Barnaby—and shout and follow his silken thing when I wave it over
40  their heads—Let me go back to them!

MRS R.    Barnaby—stay here with me—we shall be safe now in the old house—would
you break my heart?

BARNA.    No, no Mother dear, I only go to make you rich and happy—they're calling
for me.

45  MRS R.    (*seeing* HUGH) See, see my boy—if you go—they will kill you as they have
killed this bad man.

BARNA.    Kill—another—what do you mean? He will rise up again when he wakes
won't he? He sleeps soundly—I'll wait by him. (*sits*)

MRS R.    Come with me to your old bed place—come.

50  BARNA.    I like that place—I always had pleasant dreams there—let's go—hush!
Mother don't wake poor Hugh—

(*Exit up stairs, followed by* MRS RUDGE)

MR HAREDALE *rushes in fighting with* STRANGER *and* MOB.

HAREDALE.    Dogs, would you murder me? Is this fair or manly?

STRANGER.    Die, proud Tyrant! (*he is about stabbing him when* BARNABY *rushes
forward and seizes him by the throat*)

BARNA.    It is he mother—the robber—we've caught him now—ha! ha! Hugh, he's
55  trapped lad—I'll hold him—till you wake!

STRANGER.    (*struggling*) Loose your hold fool or I'll brain you—let go, I say.

*He is about to strike* BARNABY *with sword when he tears off the handkerchief round his
head*—HAREDALE *starts.*

HARE.    Does the grave give up the dead?

*Buss.*

MRS R.    (*tearing* BARNABY *away*) Yes—Rudge—the false steward—my husband—
and the murderer of your brother—felon like—he robbed and slew him in the
60  night.

SOLDIERS *enter headed by* JOE WILLET; *they seize the felon.*

*A grand Tableau by all the characters as the Act Drop descends*

END OF PIECE

# FOUR

Charles Webb, *Old Scrooge*, Sadler's Wells and New Strand
Theatre, February 1844

## INTRODUCTION

'I F Mr Charles Dickens be enamored of the fame accorded by the play-goers of the minor theatres, he has every reason to be satisfied, for managers, in all directions, have taken French leave with his "Christmas Carol," determined to make the world better, if not wiser, by depicting impossibilities', opined the theatre columnist of the *Era*, on 18 February 1844. Dickens tried but failed to contain this explosion, and to profit from it himself, by authorizing Stirling to make a version for the Adelphi, which is discussed in the Introduction ('Like the Brilliant Ballet-Pantomime'). The most widely used dramatization in the minors was a flexible script created by Charles Webb which was first staged at Sadler's Wells as 'Boz's Christmas Carol, entitled Old Scrooge, or, The Miser's Dream, and The Past!—The Present!!—and—The Future!!!' It was then refocused into less of an allegorically costumed romp and more a vehicle for a grand central performance at the Strand, a smaller stage with less room for such spectacles and a more intimate auditorium. Webb's version was then variously mounted at the Queen's, the Britannia in Hoxton, and the transpontine Victoria.

Charles Webb is now an entirely forgotten man of the mid-century whose main distinction was that he had an identical twin, Harry. They were both in the theatre business, and made a good thing of reviving *A Comedy of Errors*, previously little known to the nineteenth-century stage, to take advantage of their similarity to play the two Dromios. They had to make do with their wives (who were also sisters, if not twins) as the Antipholus brothers, but toured successfully over several seasons. They were even picked up for a London season, at the Princess's in 1864. Apart from this, Harry was relatively successful, and went into management in Ireland, but Charles lived, apparently, the hidden life of a Bohemian hack in London; Nicoll credits him with seventeen plays, his count including a *Martin Chuzzlewit* but missing *Old Scrooge*, and no doubt there were many more. He and his brother sprang from a City family, who might—or might not—have been the same Webbs who advertised their 'International, Musical, and Equestrian Star Agency' at Messrs George Webb and Company's, Designers, Lithographers, and Printers' at Snow Hill near Newgate and provided 'Whole Companies' of professional entertainers to all and sundry. The brothers' 'life of honourable professional labour' lies largely beneath the radar of modern theatre history.[1]

---

[1] *Era*, 9 August 1863; Harry Webb died leaving five young children in 1868, one of whom was provided with a place at Christ's Hospital school by the Lord Mayor of London because Harry's family had 'long been respected residents of the Bread Street ward of the City of London' (*Era*, 5 July 1868).

## THE TEXT

No printed copies of this text survive, but, anomalously, two were submitted for licensing: Add. MS 42972 ff. 976–1008, dated by the office 1/29/44 and also 2/3/44, which has a heading 'for representation on Monday July 5th 44 at Sadler's Wells' and Add. MS 42973 ff. 78–144, which was submitted for the New Strand and dated by the office 2/7/44. The July date is almost certainly a slip of the pen—by July the house was in the hands of Warner and Phelps. *Old Scrooge* opened at the Wells on 5 February and then at the Strand on 12 February. The two texts vary considerably. Internal evidence suggests strongly that the Strand MS is a revision of the Sadler's Wells, the latter containing, for example, several instances of deletions and emendations which have been accepted in the making of the second copy. The Sadler's Wells version, of which only the first act is present in the licenser's copy, is of interest for its marked divergence from the story. The present text therefore has Add. MS 42973 ff. 78–144, licensed for the Strand, as its copy text, collated with the earlier MS as far as f. 992, where they part company radically. This is the point at which the Shade of Jacob Marley begins to show Scrooge visions: in the Sadler's Wells version these are largely un-Dickensian. The rest of the act is therefore appended to the present text separately. It is of interest to show what Sadler's Wells was doing just before Warner and Phelps arrived to gentrify its programmes.

### Characters and cast lists of first performances

At Sadler's Wells

| | |
|---|---|
| Old Scrooge | H. Marston |
| Fred Pleasant | Mr Bird |
| Bob Cratchit | Mr Coreno |
| Marley's Ghost | Mr Williams |
| Old Fezziwig | Mr Richardson |
| Goodfellow | Mr Franks |
| Topper | Mr Lamb |
| Ghost of Christmas past | Master G. Newman |
| Ghost of Christmas present | Mr C.J. Smith |
| Ghost of Christmas future | Mr Dry |
| Tiny Tim | Master Newman |
| Master Peter Cratchit | Mr Richardson |
| The two smaller Cratchits | Messrs Grammani & Andrews |
| | |
| Joe Badger | Mr Williamson |
| Dick the Waggoner | Mr Franks |
| Dick Wilkins | Mr Smithson |
| Mr Berry | Mr C. Fenton |
| Mrs Cratchit | Mrs R. Barnett |
| Martha Cratchit | Miss Backhouse |

| | |
|---|---|
| Mrs Pleasant | Miss Stephens |
| Ellen Williams | Miss Caroline Rankley |
| Mrs Fezziwig | Miss Cooke |
| Mrs Dilber | Mrs Wilton |
| Mrs Mangle | Mrs Andrews |
| The Three Misses Fezziwig | Misses Morrelli, Melville, Andrews |
| | |
| The Six young followers, whose hearts they break | Mr Grammani, Mr James, Mr Wilson, Mr Thompson |
| The Housemaid | Miss Collins |
| Her Cousin (the baker) | Mr Hill |
| Neighbour | Mrs Smart |
| The Milkman | Mr Wells |
| Slabs | Mr Austin |
| Christmas Customers | Messrs Gray, James, Willis, West. Mesdames Smart, Mason, Watkins |
| | |
| Scrooge's niece's sisters | Miss Williams & Miss Anderson |
| | |
| Merchants at Royal Exchange | Messrs Smithson, Morris & Burton |

At the New Strand

| | |
|---|---|
| Ebenezer Scrooge | Mr G. Bennett |
| Bob Cratchit | Mr Attwood |
| Fred Pleasant | Mr Roberts |
| Mr Goodfellow | Mr R. Romer |
| Mr Topper | Mr Rance[2] |

---

[2] Since the texts are derived from MSS, and were performed at minor theatres, these lists have been created from a single playbill for a performance at Sadler's Wells (for 5 February 1844, in the Bodleian Library) and from a review (*Morning Post*, 13 February 1844) of the New Strand production. The Sadler's Wells bill is puzzling in that it does not describe the masque-like visions in this text, though it apparently details all the scenes of the play, and so it does not bill the actors in that episode.

**4.** Harry and Charles Webb (kneeling) with John Nelson and George Vining in *The Comedy of Errors* at The Princess's Theatre, taken 1864. Charles Webb wrote *Old Scrooge*.

# ACT I

## SCENE 1

*The Counting House of Ebenezer* SCROOGE, *in Tokenhouse Yard.*

*It is dark and heavy in appearance. Window in F and do[or]—Shelves with Boxes, Parchments &c &c. Desk at which* SCROOGE *is seated in an old leathern arm chair— poring ove[r] his banker's book. near him is a small stove with a very small fire burning—by its side a coal box—in the R near 1.E. is a capacious japan deed box, with this inscription* 'Deeds' '1814–1843'. *In a recess, very dirty and dingy—divided from the room by a glazed partition with practicable door—*BOB CRATCHIT *is seen copying letters before a very much smaller fire than his master's—lighted candle on his desk and one on* SCROOGE'S.

*Clock strikes four.*

BOB.    *(looking up)* Four o'clock, and quite dark!                                               1

SCROOGE.    *(telling up his book)* 27 . 28 . 29 . 30 .—£30,000 balance in the hands of Messrs Jones the Bankers.

BOB.    *(leaving his seat, blowing his fingers, and stamping his feet)* Oh! ain't it precious cold, rather—the fog's pouring in at every chink and keyhole.                   5

SCROOGE.    *(to himself)* Warm—very warm, all my own earning, all my own saving!

BOB.    *(standing at door with a very small shovel in ha[nd])* If you please sir, may I put another coal on?

SCROOGE.    Hark ye, sir—if you attempt to put another coal on, I'll put a period to   10 your service—that's all. Put coal on such a fire as that! have you no blood in your veins?—no warmth?

BOB.    I've very little money sir—perhaps that accounts for it.

SCROOGE.    Scoundrel! say that again and you shall have less! Every Saturday of my life I pay you fifteen good shillings—and that's meat, drink, board, lodging, wash-   15 ing, firing—*(goes on with his book)*

BOB.    *(returning to his own room)* But not sufficient coal to keep the pot a boiling for a wife and five young 'uns—never mind, cold as I am, my heart's not half so frozen as

---

0.2 *Window in F and do[or]*: The sd is taken from Add. MS 42972 ff. 976-1008 (hereinafter referred to as the Sadler's Wells text, SWT) which has a longer version. This folio, f. 997, however, is shaved on the outer edge, hence the several conjectural restorations.

0.10 *Clock strikes four*: SWT inserts 'with the last bar of the overture & just before the curtain rises' before the striking of the clock, the whole sd marked out with crosses, indicating a music cue.

5 *and keyhole*: SWT omits 'and keyhole'.

10 SCROOGE: SWT has deletion: 'Prodigal! Would you ruin me? Loading coal on that fire!'

yours, old master—I'll warm myself. (*mounts stool—reaches down a white comforter,*
20 *puts his fingers to his mouth—then hold his hands to the candle, to warm them*) It's
Christmas eve—I don't think it's been really light, all day—I'll put on my comforter—
and this is not the only comforter I've got—(*smiles to himself*) I've a much better
comforter than this at home—my wife—rather—she is a comfort!

*Enter* PLEASANT *door in flat.*

PLEASANT.    Master at home, Cratchit—where is he?
25 BOB.    There sir. (*pointing*)
PLEASANT.    How is he, on Christmas Eve? Merry—pleasant, eh?
BOB.    Much as usual sir—as 'per last,' rather.
PLEASANT.    (*to* SCROOGE) A merry Christmas, uncle—God save you!
SCROOGE.    Oh, it's you—humbug!
30 PLEASANT.    Come, come Uncle, don't say that—humbug indeed! Which do you
mean, Christmas, or me?
SCROOGE.    Christmas!—humbug!
PLEASANT.    Christmas—humbug uncle? You don't mean it, I'm sure!
SCROOGE.    I do—Merry Christmas! What right have you to be merry? What rea-
35 son? You're *poor* enough!
PLEASANT.    And you are rich enough—so what right have you to be dismal, morose,
and savage, when you ought to be pleasant? Answer me that, uncle of mine!
BOB.    (*having listened, starts up, and flourishes ruler*) Ay, answer him that! (*half
aside*) if you can!
40 SCROOGE.    Bah! humbug!
PLEASANT.    Don't be cross, uncle!
SCROOGE.    What else can I be, when I live in such a world of fools as this? Merry
Christmas! Out upon Merry Christmas! What's Christmas time for you, but a time
for paying your bills, without money—a time for finding yourself a year older, and
45 not an hour richer—a time for balancing your books, and having every item in
them, through a round dozen of months, presented dead against you? If I could
work my will, every idiot who goes about with 'Merry Christmas' on his lips, should
be boiled with his own pudding, and buried with a stake of holly through his heart.
He should!
50 PLEASANT.    That wouldn't be pleasant, uncle!
SCROOGE.    Pleasant! I have no pleasure, except in this! (*holds up banker's book*)
BOB.    Hurrah! Master can speak truth, when he's not driving a bargain.
PLEASANT.    And that's all your pleasure at Christmas uncle? Your banker's book,
with its thousands is the only pleasant reflection you have—God help you, then!
55 SCROOGE.    (*sternly*) Nephew, keep Christmas in your own way, and let me keep it in
mine!

21 *It's Christmas eve*: SWT has deletion: 'cold, bleak, biting, bitter weather'.
23 *comforter than this*: MS omits 'comforter than this'.
37 *Answer . . . mine*: SWT adds another 'answer me that?'

PLEASANT.   But you don't keep it.

BOB.   Bray-vo!

SCROOGE.   Let me leave it alone then—much good may it do you! Much good it has done you!   60

PLEASANT.   There are many things from which I might have derived good, by which I haven't profited, I daresay—Christmas among the rest,—I am sure I have always thought on Christmas time, as a good time—the only time I know of, when people seem, by one consent, to open their shut up hearts freely, and to think of people below them, as if they really were fellow passengers to the grave, and not   65   another race of creatures bound on other journeys—and therefore Uncle, though it has never put a scrap of gold or silver in my pocket, I believe that it has done me good—that it will do one good—and therefore I say again, God bless it!

BOB.   (*involuntarily waving ruler*) Hurrah!

SCROOGE.   (*stands for a moment amazed—seizes the ruler from his own desk—and flings it at the head of the excited clerk—he ducks, and avoids it*) Let me hear another   70   word from you, and you'll keep your Christmas, by losing your situation! (*to* PLEASANT) You're quite a powerful speaker, sir, I wonder you don't go into parliament.

PLEASANT.   There are quite nonentities enough there Uncle, without my adding to the number!—Come, don't be angry, dine with us tomorrow.   75

SCROOGE.   I'll see you hanged first!

PLEASANT.   That's pleasant—but why, uncle?

SCROOGE.   Why did you get married?

PLEASANT.   For pleasure, Uncle—I fell in love.

SCROOGE.   Fell in love!—Good afternoon! (*writes*)   80

PLEASANT.   But you never came to see me before that happened—why give it as a reason now?

SCROOGE.   Good afternoon!

PLEASANT.   I want nothing from you—why can't we be friends? I'm sorry to find you so resolute—we never had any quarrel, to which I have been a party—but I   85   have made the trial in homage to Christmas, and I'll keep my Christmas humour to the last—so a Merry Christmas, Uncle!

SCROOGE.   Good afternoon!

PLEASANT.   And a happy New Year!

SCROOGE.   Good afternoon. (*writes*)   90

PLEASANT.   (*leaving* SCROOGE) Bob Cratchit!

BOB.   (*quitting his stool*) Sir !—I'm glad you've spoke to me, sir—I am indeed, rather!

---

58 *Bray-vo*: The spelling, only thus in SWT, suggests the intention to give Bob the expressions and accent of the London clerk.

63 *Christmas time*: SWT has a deletion: 'when it has come round'.

64 *people*: SWT has 'men and women' for 'people'.   77 *but why, uncle*: SWT repeats 'why?'

84 *friends*: SWT repeats Scrooge's 'Good afternoon' here.

PLEASANT.   (*shaking his hand*) A Merry Christmas and a Happy New Year to you, with all my heart!

95  BOB.   The same to you, Sir—with all my soul!

PLEASANT.   And to Mrs Cratchit—and all the little Cratchits, not forgetting poor Tiny Tim!

BOB.   God Bless you Sir—you've touched a father's heart, Sir—I am a father!

SCROOGE.   (*looking up*) Have done with that foolery, or I discharge you!

100  BOB.   (*goes to desk*) Yes, Sir—yes, it's all over—Sir! (*to* PLEASANT) Good bye!

PLEASANT.   Meet me at 7 o'clock, by the Exchange, before you go home—I must have a word with you, Bob—I must have a glass with you, Bob, on Christmas eve, so don't fail!—Uncle Scrooge.

SCROOGE.   Well, Sir?

105  PLEASANT.   A Merry Christmas, Uncle! Good bye, good bye—(*Exit*)

SCROOGE.   You're a pretty fellow, to talk about a merry Christmas! My clerk, too, with 15 shillings a week and a wife and family—he talk about a merry Christmas. Bah! I'll retire to Bedlam, for here you're all lunatics together!

MESSRS GOODFELLOW *and* TOPPER *appear at door in flat.*

GOODFELLOW.   Scrooge and Marley's Counting House, I believe?

110  SCROOGE.   (*leaving his seat*) It is Sir—what then?

(GOODFELLOW *takes off his hat—bows—*TOPPER *does the same*)

GOODFELLOW.   Have I the pleasure of addressing Mr Scrooge or Mr Marley?

SCROOGE.   Mr Marley has been dead this seven years,—he died seven years go, this very night!

GOODFELLOW.   (*looking over book and papers in his hand & giving him a list*) We

115  have no doubt his liberality will be well represented by his surviving partner, have we, Topper?

TOPPER.   None in the least!

SCROOGE.   (*coldly*) Liberality—a word I don't understand, Sir.

BOB.   (*aside*) The truth again—wonderful!

120  GOODFELLOW.   Well then, Mr Scrooge—Topper will have no objection to enlighten you, I dare say.

TOPPER.   None in the least! You are no doubt aware, Mr Scrooge, that at this festive season, it is more than usually desirable that we should make some provision for the poor and destitute, who suffer greatly at the present time—Many thousands are

125  in want of common necessaries—there is no chance, sir, unless the really wealthy do something for them, of these of their regaling on roast beef and plum pudding this year—

---

96  *and all the little Cratchits*: only in SWT.      103  *so don't fail*: SWT has 'so don't fail' inserted.

107  *talk about a*: SWT has 'talk about a' inserted.

113  *he died... very night*: SWT has 'he died... very night' doubly underlined.

SCROOGE.    Are there no prisons?

GOODFELLOW.    Plenty of prisons.

SCROOGE.    And the Union workhouses?                                                        130

GOODFELLOW.    Are in full operation—I would I could say they are not!

SCROOGE.    The treadmill, and the Poor Law are in full vigour, then?

TOPPER.    Both very busy, Sir.

SCROOGE.    No obstacles to stop or impede them in their useful course?

TOPPER.    None in the least!                                                                135

SCROOGE.    I'm glad to hear it!—I was afraid, from what you said at first, that something had occurred!

GOODFELLOW.    Under the impression that they scarcely furnish Christmas cheer of
mind and body to the multitude, a few of us are endeavouring to raise a fund, to buy
the poor some meat and drink, and means of warmth—we chuse this time, because   140
it is one, of all others, when want is keenly felt, and abundance rejoices. What shall
I put you down for?

SCROOGE.    Nothing!

TOPPER.    You wish to be anonymous.

SCROOGE.    Not in the least, I wish to be alone—I don't make myself merry at   145
Christmas.

BOB.    (*aside*) True, again!

SCROOGE.    And I can't afford to make idle people merry. I help to support the estab-
lishments I have mentioned—they cost enough—and those who are badly off, must
go there!                                                                                     150

GOODFELLOW.    Many can't go there, and many would rather die!

SCROOGE.    Then they had better do it, and decrease the surplus population. It's not
my business, it's enough for a man to understand his own affairs, and not interfere
with other people's. Mine occupies me constantly. Good afternoon, gentlemen!

GOODFELLOW.    And this is your answer to a mission of charity and mercy?   155

SCROOGE.    It is!

TOPPER.    Then Sir allow me to say a few words.—I've no ill feeling against you—not
half so much as you have exhibited against your poorer fellow creatures—but, when
you are balancing your long and last account—there, Sir there, up there—(*points to
Heaven*) the debit side will, must, be dreadfully heavy against you!   160

SCROOGE.    Why do you say this?

TOPPER.    Because you'll not find a single action of your life that will redound to
your *Credit*—Good afternoon, Sir!

(*Exit with* GOODFELLOW)

SCROOGE.    All humbug!

BOB.    (*approaching*) It's time to shut up the counting house.   165

137 *I'm glad…occurred*: SWT repeats 'I'm very glad to hear it'.
161 SCROOGE: SWT begins the speech 'And why sir?—Why?'
164 SCROOGE: SWT begins the speech 'Bah! Humbug!'

SCROOGE.    Oh! yes, you're always in a hurry to leave your business—you're not in
        such a hurry to come to it! You'll want all day tomorrow, I suppose?

BOB.    If quite convenient, sir.

SCROOGE.    It is not! If I was to stop half a crown for it, you'd think yourself ill used,
170        I'll be bound!

BOB.    (*with a faint smile, and scratching his head*) Rather, sir!

SCROOGE.    And yet you don't think me ill used, when I pay a day's wages, for no
        work.

BOB.    It's only once a year, sir!

175 SCROOGE.    A poor excuse for picking a man's pocket, every 25ᵗʰ of December. (*but-
        tons his coat up to the chin*) But I suppose you must have the whole day. Be here all
        the earlier next morning.

BOB.    (*gladly*) Yes, sir, I will!—is there anything else I can do for you, before I go?

SCROOGE.    (*seizing his ear*) Would you ruin me by your waste and extravagence?

180 BOB.    Land sir, what's the matter?

SCROOGE.    (*points to desk*) The candle—put it out! Extinguish it! Is it not enough
        that you rob me of your time, but you must also dissipate my substance. (*flings him
        from him towards desk*)

BOB.    (*puts out candle*) It's done, sir!

SCROOGE.    Close the shutters!

185 BOB.    (*going*) It's done, Sir!
        (*without*) Hurrah! It's Christmas Eve!

SCROOGE.    Go, fellow!

BOB.    I wouldn't stand that—only—

SCROOGE.    What are you muttering?

190 BOB.    Only I've got a wife and family, and poor little tiny Tim, to cherish.—But I
        won't wish him good night, for it—nor a merry Christmas; nor a happy new year—I
        won't!

SCROOGE.    Are you gone?

BOB.    Rather! (*Exit*)

195 SCROOGE.    A good riddance!—I'm now alone, with all my leases, and mortgages
        to look over, and my deeds to think on! (*he has just reached the door, when it is
        pushed—he starts back*) Who the devil's that?

168 *If quite convenient, sir*: SWT has deletion 'It being Christmas day'.

169 *It is not*: SWT adds 'convenient, and not fair'.

179 *seizing his ear*: SWT has him seize Bob by the arm, rather than the ear, and begins the speech 'Yes,
prodigal,—yes!'

182.1 *The candle...desk*: MS ends the speech at 'put it out!' and omits sd.

183 *It's done, sir*: SWT has a sd here: 'Stage light ½ down' deleted, replaced with 'border lights down'
marked with the six crosses that indicate a lighting cue in this text.

187 *SCROOGE*: SWT parts company from the Strand version of the play here, having Bob re-enter and
wait upon Scrooge as he gets out his gruel pan, changes into his dressing gown, and moves into the next
scene, which corresponds to scene 3 below, without a change of location and omitting the door knocker
incident.

BOB. (*reappears at the door*) I can't do it sir!

SCROOGE. Can't do what, sir?

BOB. I can't go without wishing you a merry—  200

SCROOGE. (*shutting door*) Bah! Humbug! (*locks door*) let me see that all's safe (*he takes up light & examines the room*)

BOB. (*sings, at keyhole*) God bless you, merry gentleman! Let nothing you dismay!—

SCROOGE. (*rushes to door*) It's well you've gone, or you should have been *merry* to some tune! I'm bilious at the word—I'll go home, and sleep, while these idle fools  205 pass their hours in useless mummery—Christmas! Bah! *Exit*

## SCENE 2

*Exterior of* SCROOGE's *House.*

SCROOGE *enters, feeling his way.*

SCROOGE. Pretty night this, to be out in—fog like a dark wall hanging round you!—  1 I'm obliged to grope my way to the door! It's well for me, that I know every stone in the yard, for not a ray of light from the gas lamp penetrates the black old gateway— Ha! I'm at home at last! Where's the key? (*feeling his pockets*) I'm so cold, my fingers are quite numbed! what is there to make a man merry in that, I should like to know.  5

(*Inserts the key—the door resists his efforts—he looks up—recoils, at seeing the knocker become illuminated, shewing the face of Jacob Marley*)

Marley's face!—'tis not a shadow, for it gleams like a bad lobster, in a dark cellar. It is not angry, or ferocious, but looks at me as Marley used to look, with ghostly spectacles turned up upon its ghostly forehead—the eyes are wide open, and perfectly motionless—the dismal light about it—its livid colour—'tis horrible—Jacob— Jacob Marley! (*knocker resumes its shape*) Pooh! It's only the knocker!  10

(*Opens door—walks in—lights rushlight—with the door half open, he is seen to look behind it, at the fastening of the knocker*)

Pooh! It's only the knocker!

(*Bangs the door, which closes with a loud noise*)

---

SCENE 2: SW does not make a break here, and omits this small scene, continuing in the office—see below.

# SCENE 3

*Apartment in* SCROOGE'*s House.*

SCROOGE *appears at door—he pauses, to look behind—enters, closes door, and searches the room.*

1   SCROOGE.    Nobody under the table—Nobody in the closet—Nobody stirring but
    myself, and the house as still as death—Death—ha!—It's exactly seven years ago,
    and as near about this very hour as may be, since old Jacob Marley died! (*bell
    heard—he looks towards the wall, amazed*) What can make that bell ring—it's a
5   disused bell and communicates with the highest story of the building! (*different
    bells heard*) why there's every bell in the house going! What can it mean? Am I
    awake?

(*Bells cease—Noise of a heavy chain—Crash, as if a door was burst open, at a distance—
footsteps heard*)

    It's humbug still!—I won't believe it!

(*Door flies open—as he is warming his hands, the* SHADE OF JACOB MARLEY *stands
before him*)

---

0.3  SCROOGE...*room*: SWT, which follows from the exit of Cratchit and continues scene 1, begins:

'SCROOGE. *banging the door in his face* Bah! Humbug! (*locks the door*) [deleted: the next visitor that calls on me to night must get through the walls] let me see that's all safe [deleted: before I sit down] (*music piano—he takes up light & examines every part of the room closely*)—Nobody under the table—nobody under the desk—(*looking into Cratchit's room*) Nobody here—(*opening closet*)—Nobody in the closet—Nobody [del:here ins: stirring] but myself—and the house as still as death. Death! I wonder why—(*the closet door swings to and the candle is extinguished by the current of air*)—My candle out, well the fire gives light enough for me, and I shall save its burning away. (*comes towards front*)—I wonder *why*, I thought of old Jacob Marley's *death* [del:today], exactly 7 years ago and about this very hour as near as many be? (*a bell is heard to ring very softly & increases; he looks towards the wall in amazement*) [del:why] what can make that bell ring?—it's a disused bell and communicates with the highest story of the building (*a peal of different bells—very loud—as if every bell in the house was ringing*)—why there's every bell in the [ins:old] house going! What is it? What can it mean? Am I asleep or awake? (*rubs his eyes*) I cannot be awake, I must be dreaming (*half in terror he looks round—a part of the window—becomes transparent—and the face of Jacob Marley is seen*) No, it's not a dream for there is Jacob Marley's face looking at me, as it used to look! (*The Face disappears*)—Pooh—Pooh—I'm a fool, a child, this is all imagination, the bells did not ring—there was no face—it was all an illusion a—a—humbug—humbug—humbug—(*hastens to his chair, throws himself in it. The Shade of Marley stands before him; he seems riveted to his seat in horror: 'Tableau' 'Marley's Ghost'*)—Its humbug still! (*starts up from his seat gazing intently*)—I won't believe it! And yet it's the same face: the very same: Marley in his pigtail, usual waistcoat, tights, and boots;—a chain too clasped about his middle! And made up of cash-boxes, keys, padlocks, ledgers, deeds, and heavy quires wrought in steel—and yet I can see through old Jacob—he's transparent—I often heard he had no bowels but never till this moment did I believe it. Can you sit down?'

From this point it rejoins the MS text, though with differences as noted.

It is him! Marley, in his usual waistcoat, tights, and boots, and pigtail—a chain,
too, clasped about his middle, and made of cash-boxes, keys, padlocks, ledgers,  10
deeds, and heavy purses, wrought in steel—yet I can see through old Jacob—he's
transparent—Why, Jacob Marley, I often heard he had no bowels, but never, till
this moment, did I believe it.—Can you sit down?

SHADE.    I can! (*sits—they stare at each other*)

SCROOGE.    What do you want with me?                                              15

SHADE.    Much!

SCROOGE.    Marley's voice! He can't be really dead!

SHADE.    You don't believe in me?

SCROOGE.    I—I don't!

SHADE.    Why do you doubt your senses?                                            20

SCROOGE.    Because a little thing affects them—a slight disorder of the stomach,
makes them cheats—you may be an undigested bit of beef—a crumb of cheese—
there's more of gravy than of grave about you. Who are you?

SHADE.    Ask me who I *was*.

SCROOGE.    Who *were* you then?                                                   25

SHADE.    In life, I was your partner, Jacob Marley.

SCROOGE.    In life!—then—you're really dead—there's no—humbug?

SHADE.    None.

SCROOGE.    His voice disturbs the very marrow in my bones! If I sit staring at those
fixed, glazed eyes, in silence for a moment—they will drive me mad! Something, to  30
divert the vision's stony gaze from me!

(SHADE *starts up—so does* SCROOGE—SHADE *undoes wrapper—the jaw falls—then
makes a step towards him—*SCROOGE *falls on his knees and clasps his hands before his
face*)

Mercy, dreadful apparition! why do you trouble me?

SHADE.    Man of the worldly mind! Do you believe in me?

SCROOGE.    I do—I must—But why do spirits walk the earth—and why do they
come to me?                                                                        35

SHADE.    It is required of every man, that the spirit within him should walk abroad
among his fellow men—if that spirit goes not forth in life, it is doomed to do so after
death—to wander through the world, and witness what it cannot share—but might
have shared on earth, and turned to happiness.

SCROOGE.    Jacob, tell me more—speak comfort to me!                               40

---

25 *Who were you then*: SWT adds 'for you're rather particular—for a shade'.

27 SCROOGE: SWT omits this speech and the reply.

31 *me*: SWT has a deletion: '(*pulls out boot jack*) You see this boot jack? / SHADE. I do. / SCROOGE. You
are not looking at it. / SHADE. But I see it notwithstanding. / SCROOGE. Well—I have but to swallow this'
with the MS text inserted instead.

33 *Do you believe in me*: SWT adds 'or not?'

38 *it is doomed…death*: SWT repeats 'doomed'.          40 *Jacob*: SWT adds 'old Jacob Marley'.

SHADE.   I have none to give—I cannot rest—I cannot stay any where. In life my
spirit never roved beyond the narrow limits of this, our money changing hole—and
weary journeys lie before me still.

SCROOGE.   But you have been dead seven years, have you been travelling all the
45   time?

SHADE.   The whole time—no rest—incessant torture of remorse.

SCROOGE.   You travel fast—what a *rail*-er you must be!

SHADE.   On the wings of the wind—on we flit—never stop!

SCROOGE.   You beat the railway then! What a quantity of ground you must have
50   gone over.

SHADE.   Oh! captive bound, and double ironed—

SCROOGE.   (*looking round*) Double ironed!

SHADE.   Not to know that ages of incessant labour by immortal creatures from this
earth must pass into eternity before the good of which it is susceptible is all developed—
55   not to know that any Christian spirit, working kindly in its little sphere, will find its
mortal life too short for its vast means of usefulness—not to know that no space of
regret can make amends for one life's opportunities misused! Yet such was I!

SCROOGE.   But you were always a good man of business, Jacob!

SHADE.   Mankind was my business—the common welfare was my business—char-
60   ity, mercy, forbearance, were all my business—and I looked to none—not one of
these! Why did I walk through crowds of fellow beings, with my eyes turned
inwards, caring only for myself.

SCROOGE.   (*trembling*) You make me quake, good Jacob!

SHADE.   Arise! Awake!

65   SCROOGE.   I've been awake all my life—wide awake! But don't be hard upon me
Jacob!

SHADE.   Pray, then, that a change in spirit may be wrought—seek your old arm
chair! (SCROOGE *totters towards it and seats himself, his eyes still fixed on the*
SHADE) dream not of your gold—your leases—mortgages—your sordid gains—
70   but look into our streets and face the squalid misery that stares at you, with fam-
ine's hollow eyes—and if you remain in heart as you now are, you cannot escape
my fate!

SCROOGE.   (*in chair*) Cannot!

---

46  *torture of remorse*: SWT omits 'torture of remorse'.

47  *rail-er*: A neologism in 1844, meaning one who travels by train; *OED*'s first recorded instance
is in 1834.

50  *over*: SWT adds 'in seven years!'        57  *Yet such was I*: SWT repeats 'Such was I'.

63  *You make me quake*: SWT has 'exceedingly' and 'kind Jacob!' at the end of the line.

65  SCROOGE: SWT begins 'I am awake good Jacob'.

69  *gold*: SWT includes 'your money bags' here and 'your funded property, your estates' before 'your
sordid gains'.

70  *misery*: SWT adds 'and haggard want and wretchedness and ignorance'.

71  *eyes*: SWT has 'look well and closely'.

SHADE.    This chain I wear, I made, in life, link by link—I girded it on, of my own free will, and of my own free will, I wore it! Is its pattern strange to you? Or would you 75 know the weight and length of the strong coil you bear yourself? It was full as heavy, and as long as this, seven Christmases ago—you have laboured on it since—it is a ponderous chain! Hear me—my time is nearly gone!

SCROOGE.    And mine's to come, I suppose?

SHADE.    How it is that I appear before you in a shape that you can see, I may not 80 tell—I have sat invisible beside you, many a day—I am here tonight to warn you, that you have yet a chance, and hope of escape—a chance and hope of my procuring, Ebenezer.

SCROOGE.    Thank'ee!

SHADE.    You will be haunted by three Spirits. 85

SCROOGE.    Is that the chance and hope, you mentioned?

SHADE.    It is! Without their visits, you cannot hope to shun the path I tread. Expect the first, when the bell tolls one!

SCROOGE.    Couldn't I take 'em all at once, and have it over?

SHADE.    Expect the second, on the next night, at the same hour. The third, upon the 90 next night, when the last toll of 12 has ceased. Look to see me no more—and look for your own sake—you remember what has passed between us!

(*Puts wrapper round his face, and confronts* SCROOGE, *with the chain wound round his arm—steps backwards towards window—at each step, window rises.* SHADE *beckons* SCROOGE—*he totters towards it—It extends its arm, forbidding further approach. Discordant music—It glides through window*)

SCROOGE.    He floats away upon bleak dark clouds—Jacob Marley, come what will, mine eyes shall follow you!

(*Rushes to window—*SPIRITS *appear—he staggers back—they disperse—and* SCROOGE *is discovered, with the* SPIRIT OF CHRISTMAS PAST. *Bell strikes One*)

Are you the Spirit, Sir, whose coming was foretold to me? 95

SPIRIT.    I am!

SCROOGE.    Who, and what are you?

SPIRIT.    The Ghost of Christmas Past!

SCROOGE.    Long past?

SPIRIT.    No—your past! 100

SCROOGE.    Be covered, sir—you may catch cold!

SPIRIT.    What! Would you so soon with worldly hands, put out the light I give? Is it not enough that you are one of those, whose passions made this cap, and force me thro' whole trains of years, to wear it low upon my brow?

SCROOGE.    What business brings you here? 105

SPIRIT.    Your welfare.

---

74 *SHADE*: SWT parts from the MS here, bridging into a different interpretation of the apparition of the Spirits of Christmas; see appendix.

SCROOGE.    Much obliged!—but a good night's rest would have been more condu-
cive to the end.

SPIRIT.    Your reclamation, then—take heed! (*clasps his arm*) Rise, and walk forth
110    with me!

SCROOGE.    (*rises, reluctantly*) How odd!—I'm obliged to rise at one o'clock in the
morning! Spirit, I'm a mortal, and liable to fall.

SPIRIT.    (*laying his hand on Scrooge's breast*) Bear but a touch of my hand *there*, and
you shall be upheld in more than this.

115    SCROOGE.    This is very strange!

(*Scene vanishes, a snow landscape appears*)

Good Heaven! I was bred in this place—I was a boy here—a thousand odours float
in the air, each one connected with a thousand hopes, and delights, and joys, and
cares, long forgotten!

SPIRIT.    Your lip is trembling—what is that, upon your cheek?

120    SCROOGE.    That—that is—

SPIRIT.    A tear?

SCROOGE.    No—only a pimple! (*brushes it away*)

SPIRIT.    You recollect the way?

SCROOGE.    Recollect it?—I could walk it, blindfold!

125    SPIRIT.    Strange! to have forgotten it, so many years! Let us on!

(*Scene disappears—Diorama passes*)

SCROOGE.    Is it possible?—there, Haydon's meadows! Do you see that gate? Many
times I've sat on it! and that tree—I climbed it often, for a bird's nest—happy recollections—and there's the market town—dear old Hollythorn, with its bridges, and
river, the church, too, whose chimes, on Sabbath morn, would call us, and bid us
130    not forget whose day it was. Those were joyous times!

SPIRIT.    That was a long while ago!

SCROOGE.    Very, indeed! (*two or three figures pass*) Heaven save me! Farmer
Williams, and Reuben Thornley, and Martin Jones—(*calls*) Reuben! Martin!
Farmer!—look! Do you not know me?

135    SPIRIT.    (*restraining him*) These are but shadows of things that might have been—
they have no consciousness of us!

SCROOGE.    No consciousness? Why is it, then, that I was rejoiced beyond all
bounds to see them? Why was it that my eyes glistened and my heart leaped up as
they went past?—why was it that my whole soul felt filled with gladness at these
140    endearing recollections of home and boyhood! Why was all this?—Answer me
Spirit—Answer?

SPIRIT.    Look!

137 *beyond*: There is a change of copyist in MS here, and the next section uses 'Cs Past' as the speech
ascription, but it is here regularized.

*(Music—In place of Diorama—The School Room is apparent, in which is a window in F.)*

SCROOGE.   The very place where I went to school—the form, the desk—
SPIRIT.   *(points to boy seated reading)* The school is not quite deserted.
SCROOGE.   No, I see—                                                           145
SPIRIT.   A solitary child, neglected by his friends, is left there.
SCROOGE.   I know it—I know it.
SPIRIT.   The image of your former self.
SCROOGE.   Yes—I was a little child then, quite friendless and deserted—no one to
   speak a kind word for me—ill-treated, half starved—beaten *(sobs)*—poor boy—   150
   poor boy!
SPIRIT.   *(pointing to window)* Look again.

*(Characteristic music—the window becomes transparent & the figure of Ali Baba leading the ass laden with wood appears)*

SCROOGE.   *(in ecstasy)* Why it's Ali Baba!—it's dear old honest Ali Baba!—Yes—
   yes—I know one Christmas time when yonder solitary child was left here all alone,
   he *did* come for the first time just like that—he did, he did, upon my soul he did   155
   *(earnestly)* poor boy! *(half crying)*

*(Music changes, Ali Baba disappears—succeeded by Valentine & Orson in transparency)*

   *(in rapture)* Ah look—look—Valentine and now his wild brother Orson—look
   how they threaten each other—Ah spare him! Valentine—he's but a brute—no
   sense—no reason—but still he is your brother. *(they disappear)*

*(Music changes again to 'Oh poor Robinson Crusoe' etc, Robinson Crusoe & his Man Friday in transparency)*

   *(in delight)* Robinson Crusoe—poor Robinson Crusoe—where have you been   160
   Robin Crusoe—and there's his man Friday running for his life—Holloa!—stop!
   Holloo! *(calls—the vision disappears)*—I wish, poor boy—*(putting his hand into his
   pocket—and drying his eyes with his cuff)* but no—it's too late now.

SPIRIT.   What's the matter?
SCROOGE.   Nothing—nothing—There was a boy singing a Christmas carol at my   165
   door last night—I should have liked to give him something, that's all.
SPIRIT.   Indeed? *(smiling doubtfully)*
SCROOGE.   *(the figure of the boy is pacing up and down despairingly)*
   Oh—yes—old as I am—I feel what it is to be a boy again. There—I used to do that—
   walk up and down and pace the dreary school room when I was left quite by

159.1 *'Oh poor Robinson Crusoe'*: This popular song appears in chapbooks from the previous century, and early nineteenth-century printings of Samuel Foote's *The Mayor of Garratt*, first staged in 1763 soon after the publication of Defoe's novel, print it as a song often introduced into the performance of the character of Jerry Sneak in that play. In 1844 the play was still in the repertoire, and in 1841 it was included in the farewell benefit of the actor Russell, nicknamed for his famous Jerry Sneak.

170    myself—and all he other boys had gone home for the jolly holidays. O—I know what it is to be alone—I do—I do—

(*Music—'Home—sweet home'—played con spirito*)

(*A little girl runs in and clasps her arms about the neck of the boy*)

SCROOGE.   (*carried beyond himself*)—Jessie—dear Jessie! My sister Jessie!

SPIRIT.   A Shadow.

SCROOGE.   (*despondingly*)—I forgot—I forgot—I forgot!

175  SPIRIT.   See, she clasps her tiny hands around him, she leads him with her—she is about to take him home.

SCROOGE.   To be sure she is—I recollect—Home for good and all—Home for ever and ever—kind Jessie—gentle Jessie! (*she is leading the boy away, they disappear*) dear—dear Jessie—

180  SPIRIT.   Always a delicate creature whom a breath might have withered—but she had a large heart.

SCROOGE.   So she did, you're right—I'll not gainsay it, Spirit, Heaven forbid.

SPIRIT.   She died a woman—and had as I think children.

SCROOGE.   One child.

185  SPIRIT.   True, your nephew.

SCROOGE.   (*fidgety*) My nephew!—yes—his mother fetched me from dreary dull school—and I have repaid her by driving her son away from me.

CHRISTMAS PAST *waves his hand—Music—The Scene changes to Fezziwig's ball (see plate)* SCROOGE *aroused by the cheerful scene looks up amazed*

SCROOGE.   Why it's old Fezziwig—Bless his heart; it's Fezziwig alive again and there I am just as I was thirty-seven years back. (*the dancing is kept up to the greatest*

190   *pitch of hilarity*) Go it Fezziwig!—Well done Dick!—Yo—ho—yoho!—(*commences dancing & snapping his fingers*) that's it—Shuffle—cut—cut, shuffle—thread the needle—hand half round and back again—down the middle—go it—hurrah! Oh here's a merry dance! (*shouting & dancing*) Go it (*keeps capering and frisking about— the image of his former self turns out the lights—Stage dark—gauze rises—he stops*)— Where am I again?—Mr Fezziwig—Dick! Mrs Fezziwig—where are you all?

195  SPIRIT.   You saw how delighted—how grateful they all were—a small matter to make silly folks so full of gratitude.

SCROOGE.   Small?

SPIRIT.   Why, is it not?—he has spent but a few pounds of your mortal money— three or four perhaps—is that much?

200  SCROOGE.   It isn't that, Spirit, it isn't that—He had the power to render us happy or unhappy—to make our service light or burdensome, a pleasure or a toil—Say that his power lies in words and looks alone—in things so slight and insignificant that it

---

171.1 '*Home—sweet home*': The famous air from Bishop's *The Maid of Milan* (1823).

187.2 *see plate*: One of the four hand-coloured illustrations by John Leech.

is impossible to add and count them up; what then—the happiness he gives is quite as great as if it cost a fortune.

SPIRIT.    (*glancing at him*) Oh, you think so—what's the matter?                     205

SCROOGE.    (*turning away*) Nothing particular.

SPIRIT.    Something, I think.

SCROOGE.    No—no—I should like to be able—to say a word or two to my clerk just now—That's all.—

SPIRIT.    (*waving his hand and speaking to some one invisible*)—My time grows     210 short—quick!

(*Music. Gauze sinks—open country discovered—*FIGURE OF SCROOGE—(*older than at Fezziwigs*) *discovered with* ELLEN WILLIAMS *in mourning dress. She is seated on bank, [he beside] her with his eyes cast to the ground, fidgety and restless—*SCROOGE *becomes violently agitated and is fixed with emotion & amazement*)

FIGURE OF SCROOGE.    It matters little, I tell you.

ELLEN.    It matters little to you, very little—Another idol has displaced me; and, if it can cheer and comfort you in time to come as I would have tried to do, I have no just cause to grieve.                                                       215

FIGURE OF SCROOGE.    What idol has displaced you?

ELLEN.    A golden one! The lust of wealth.

SCROOGE.    It did—It did.

FIGURE OF SCROOGE.    This is the even handed dealing of the world! There is nothing on which it is so hard as poverty—and there is nothing it professes to condemn   220 with so much severity as the pursuit of wealth.

ELLEN.    You fear the world to much, all your other hopes have merged into the hope of being beyond the chance of its sordid reproach—I have seen your nobler aspirations fall off one by one until the master passion—gain—has quite engrossed you.

FIGURE OF SCROOGE.    What then? I am not changed towards you, am I?            225

ELLEN.    Our contract is an old one.—It was made when we were both poor and content to be so, until in good season we could improve our worldly fortune by patient industry—you *are* changed. When it was made you were another man.

SCROOGE.    Oh—true—true!

FIGURE OF SCROOGE.    I was a boy—                                           230

ELLEN.    A boy! (*rises*) enough—I see your own feeling tells you that you *were* not what you *are*—I am—That which promised happiness when we were one in heart is fraught with misery now that we are two. How often and how keenly I have thought of this—I will not say—It is enough that I *have* thought of it and can release you.

FIGURE OF SCROOGE.    Have I ever sought release?                             235

ELLEN.    In words?—No—never!

SCROOGE.    Ellen!

FIGURE OF SCROOGE.    In what then?

211.3  *he beside*: MS has a blank here, as if the copyist could not make out the words.
216  *FIGURE OF SCROOGE*: MS mistakenly ascribes this response to SCROOGE.

ELLEN.    In a changed nature—an altered spirit—in another atmosphere of life—in
240      another hope as its great end—in every thing that made my love of any worth or
         value in your sight. If this had never been between us—tell me—would you seek me
         out and try to win me now that you are rich? Ah—no!

FIGURE OF SCROOGE.    You think not—

ELLEN.    I would gladly think otherwise if I could—

245  SCROOGE.    (*to himself*) She cannot!—I did—I did desert her.

ELLEN.    But it is against my reason to believe you would choose a dowerless girl—
         you—who in your every confidence with her, weigh every thing by gain—do I not
         know—if for a moment—you were false enough to your own guiding principle—
         do I not know that your repentance and regret would surely follow? I do—and I
250      release you—release you with a full heart—for the love of him you once were.

FIGURE OF SCROOGE.    Hear me!

ELLEN.    Hear me—you may—the memory of what is past half makes me hope you
         will—have pain in this—A very brief time, and you will dismiss the recollection of
         it as an unprofitable dream—from which it happened well that you awoke—
255      Farewell—may you be happy in the life you have chosen. (*she disappears—leaving
         the figure musing*)—

SCROOGE.    Spirit!—shew me no more—

(*Music—*SPIRIT *waves his hand—Gauze rises*)

SCROOGE.    Conduct me home—why do you delight to torture me?

SPIRIT.    One shadow more—one!

SCROOGE.    No—never—no more—I don't wish to see it—Shew me no more. (*in a
260      broken voice*)—Remove me—remove me from this place.

SPIRIT.    I told you these were shadows of things that have been—That they *are*—
         what they are blame not me.

SCROOGE.    You have worked me to madness—desperation (*seizes* SPIRIT) I tell
         you I cannot bear it longer. (*struggle*)

(*Music commenced—piano—then crescendo*)

265      Leave me—take me back—haunt me no longer—(*seizes the extinguisher shaped
         cap—presses it forcibly on the head of the* SPIRIT—*he commences sinking through
         gauze at the same time full flood of light poured up through trap*) Down—down—
         busy—meddling—torturing Spirit of the Past—Down—down! (SPIRIT *disap-
         pears—*SCROOGE *is in his own Chamber again—See etching page 73*)

*Drop curtain quickly*

267.1 *See etching page 73:* The Leech illustration cited shows the flood of light streaming out at ground
level, as Scrooge presses the extinguisher, as Dickens describes; exactly how the gauze was used to achieve
the Spirit's disappearance is not clear. A large gauze is present at the back of the stage, with the scene
between Ellen and the Figure of Scrooge seen through it, and then made to disappear, in favour of Scrooge's
house, by the lighting change. It is worth recalling that the Strand, at which this version premiered, had a
small stage, only fourteen feet deep.

# ACT II

## SCENE 1

SCROOGE's *house as before.*

SCROOGE *in his chair.*

SCROOGE.   (*in his dream*) Spirit! I cannot extinguish the light—you—your light, in   1
one unbroken stream, still pours upon my bewildered mind—remove me from
these scenes of former days—remove me! (*rises frantically, and rushes to* L)

(*Tableau*)

(*seeing Spirit*) who art thou?

SPIRIT.   The Ghost of Christmas Present—look upon me!   5
SCROOGE.   I do!
SPIRIT.   You have never seen the like of me before.
SCROOGE.   Never!
SPIRIT.   Have never walked forth with the younger branches of my family, mean-
ing—for I am very young—my elder brothers, born in these later years?   10
SCROOGE.   I don't think I have—I am afraid I have not. Have you had many broth-
ers, Spirit?
SPIRIT.   More than eighteen hundred!
SCROOGE.   A tremendous family to provide for.
SPIRIT.   What you have seen, are shadows of the things that have been—that they   15
are what they are, blame not us.
SCROOGE.   Let me not see them again—let me not think of them—they drive me
mad—remove me, I cannot bear it!
SPIRIT.   Walk forth, then.
SCROOGE.   Whither?   20
SPIRIT.   Among your kith and kind—your fellow men—your brethren—don thy
gear—arise—and look on that, which is! Go! Mingle with the busy scenes of life—
take active parts—yet be invisible, among the jostling crowd—invisible!
SCROOGE.   Is the whole world blind then?
SPIRIT.   Blind! Ho! Ho! Ho!—blind! Fool, it is your soul that wanders—your   25
thoughts—your body's sleeping, there! (*points to chair*)
SCROOGE.   (*looking through glass*) Is it?—I can't say that I see it!

---

3.1 *Tableau*: Presumably based upon Leech's plate 'Scrooge's third visitor', showing the huge figure of
Christmas Present holding up a smoking torch and extending a hand to a small shivering Scrooge in his
nightshirt.

SPIRIT.    See it? Ho! Ho! Ho! Gold dazzles your sight—avarice steals the light insidi-
ously away, that ought to guide you to the poor man's home—I shall be at your side,
30    depend on't!

SCROOGE.    Shall you? You are a very good fellow—I should like your acquaintance.

SPIRIT.    You never liked my family—but we may be friends yet.

SCROOGE.    How?

SPIRIT.    Learn to know me better—learn to be jolly, merry, blithe! Learn to be chari-
35    table—kind, forgiving, generous, benevolent—and you and I will shake hands
warmly.

SCROOGE.    Spirit, conduct me where you will—I went forth last night on compul-
sion, and I learnt a lesson, which is working now. Tonight, if you have ought to
teach me, let me profit by it.

40  SPIRIT.    Touch my robe!

*Scene sinks*


## SCENE 2

*Part of Cornhill and new Exchange by gaslight.*
*Men and boys sliding,* BOB CRATCHIT *among them.*


### CHORUS

1                  Hurrah! hurrah! Away we go!
                   What do we care for falling snow?
                   Now up, now down, now to and fro!
                   Over the frozen earth we go!


5  BOYS etc.    (*as* CRATCHIT *slides*) Go it, Bob—keep it up, Bob—go it, Bob!

BOB.    Hooray! Won't I, rather! Ain't I warm now!

HABS.    Go it, ye cripples, go it!

BOB.    Who said that?

HABS.    Why I did, to be sure, Mr Cratchit!

10  BOB.    Don't say it again, that's a good lad, don't say it again!

HABS.    Lor, why not, Mr Cratchit—it ain't swearing.

BOB.    No, no, but I don't like it!

HABS.    Why, Mr Cratchit?

BOB.    (*patting his head kindly*) Because I've got a little boy at home, that's a cripple,
15    and it puts me in mind of him—it does indeed, rather—poor Tiny Tim!

*Enter* PLEASANT (*a goose in his hand*).


7 *HABS*: This appears to be the speech ascription in the MS, but its reference is obscure. There is no
minor character listed by anything resembling the name on the extant bills.

PLEASANT.    Well, Cratchit, here you are—not kept you waiting, have I? that would
    not be pleasant!

BOB.    Yes it would, Sir, rather.

PLEASANT.    Why?

BOB.    Anything would be pleasant, for the pleasure of seeing your pleasant face!    20
    And, Sir, there's not the least family resemblance 'twixt you and master—not a bit!

PLEASANT.    Yet I've tried hard to make him like me—very hard!

BOB.    He's too hard to be softened, Sir, you can't mollify him—I've tried to mollify
    him myself, but it's no go!

PLEASANT.    Mollify him, Cratchit?    25

BOB.    Yes, Sir, to make him tender, like—but you can't—he'd take more boiling to do
    it, than the oldest dunghill cock that ever lived—it's my opinion, you might boil
    him for fifty years, and then he wouldn't be tender!

PLEASANT.    Ha! ha! I wish he had been with me just now, round Leadenhall market,
    to have seen the glorious piles of turkeys, capons, geese—to have seen the fruiter-    30
    ers, all radiant in their glory—pears and apples—bunches of grapes—piles of fil-
    berts, mossy brown—recalling, in their fragrance, ancient walks among the wood,
    and pleasant shufflings, ankle deep, through withered leaves—and there were
    Norfolk Biffens, squat and swarthy—piles of oranges and lemons—

BOB.    Oh, don't, Sir, don't—you do make my mouth water, rather!    35

PLEASANT.    And there were cherry cheeked girls—and mothers, and their hopeful
    sons—carrying huge baskets—and there were fathers there, with a huge sirloin—
    there, with a turkey dangling from his horny hands—and there to hear the laughs
    and jokes—to see the bright eyes, and brighter smiles—the happy faces—all push-
    ing, shuffling, jostling, laughing—oh, Bob, if my old Uncle had only been there, he    40
    must have said, as I said—that it was glorious, Bob! And that there was nothing half
    so pleasant in this world, as witnessing the happiness of our fellow creatures!

BOB.    He wouldn't have done it, Sir.

PLEASANT.    Why?

BOB.    Because, coming from him, the lie would have choked him, 'ere it reached his lips.    45

PLEASANT.    Bob, what have you for dinner tomorrow?

BOB.    A beautiful cushion of bacon, and some potatoes, Sir—that's what we mean to
    have rather—I've got my salary in my pocket—15/- you know—so as soon as I get
    home, I mean Mrs Cratchit, and my son Peter, and myself, to go out and buy it—I
    do, rather—and won't we have a jovial dinner, thank Heaven!    50

(CHRISTMAS PRESENT *and* SCROOGE *enter pausing at the back*)

PLEASANT.    Here's a goose!

BOB.    A goose, sir!

PLEASANT.    Take it!

BOB.    A goose, sir! (*taking it*)

PLEASANT.    Have your family round, enjoy yourselves—be happy—and to me, it    55
    will be the greatest satisfaction—damme, it will be one of the most pleasant
    moments of my life! (*Exit*)

SPIRIT.   You see! (*to* SCROOGE)

BOB.    A fat goose!

60  SCROOGE.    That was a good action of Fred's—but—

BOB.    I—I—God bless him! I've got a goose! A goose!

(*Music—Air—'Run! Run!' (from Giovanni)*)

*People appear, carrying dinners to bakehouse.*

SCROOGE *observes the busy scene.* TWO PERSONS, *each carrying a dinner, run against each other, in doorway.*

1ST PERSON.    Why didn't you mind where you're coming—you've upset half my pudding!

2ND PERSON.    Serves you right—you ran against me!

65  1ST PERSON.   No I didn't!

2ND PERSON.    Yes, you did!

1ST PERSON.    For two pins, I'd serve you out!

2ND PERSON.    You can't! (*they prepare to fight*)

SCROOGE.    Spirit! Spirit of Christmas!

70  SPIRIT.    I am here!

SCROOGE.    Look!—they're going to fight!

SPIRIT.    Not at all—there's not a dinner of the poor today, but I have sprinkled it with incense from my torch—they'll not fight!

SCROOGE.    But can't you put them in a good humour with each other? Everybody

75    seems so full of glee—so cosy—I can't bear to see clenched fists, and angry brows—put them in a good humour, Spirit—a good humour!

SPIRIT.    You begin to take some interest in what is passing round you?

SCROOGE.    I confess I do!

SPIRIT.    There! (*flashes torch*)

80  SCROOGE.    Why, they smile kindly on each other!

SPIRIT.    They do!

SCROOGE.    They clasp each other's hands!

SPIRIT.    They do—so easy is it to reconcile mankind, by deeds of good will!

1ST PERSON.    It's a shame to quarrel on Christmas day!

85  2ND PERSON.    God love it, so it is! Come along!

(*Exeunt, arm in arm*)

SPIRIT.    You see!

SCROOGE.    Spirit! Is there a peculiar flavour in what you sprinkled from your torch?

SPIRIT.    There is—my own!

SCROOGE.    Would it apply to any kind of dinner, on this day?

90  SPIRIT.    To any; kindly given to a poor one, most.

SCROOGE.    Why to a poor one, most?

SPIRIT.    Because it needs it most.

SCROOGE.    But, I've observed a remarkable quality in you—when my eyes were first
    opened to your spiritual presence, you were a giant in form and stature—now,
    you're only the size of an ordinary man—and that's very extraordinary!                95
SPIRIT.    Not at all—I can accommodate myself to any place, with ease—and stand
    beneath a lowly roof, as gracefully, and like a supernatural creature, as I could in the
    loftiest hall, that monarch ever graced.
SCROOGE.    You're a wonderful Spirit, for your size—generous, hearty Spirit!
SPIRIT.    We'll walk on, if you please.                                                  100
SCROOGE.    Where?
SPIRIT.    To the dwelling of your poor clerk, Bob Cratchit—I'll bless his dwelling
    with the sprinklings of my torch—and so, come on!

(*Leads him off*)


# SCENE 3

*Cratchit's family party—House of* BOB CRATCHIT.
*Music lively and characteristic.*

MRS CRATCHIT *and* MISS BELINDA CRATCHIT—*both decked in ribbons—laying the
cloth.* MASTER PETER CRATCHIT *with a very large shirt collar sticking up is plunging
a fork in a saucepan of potatoes on the fire—*TWO YOUNG CRATCHITS—(*a boy and a
girl*) *rush through door in flat.*

BOY & GIRL.    Oh mother!—hurray, mother!—mother—                                          1
MRS C.    (*pausing in her work*) Well my dears?

(MARTHA CRATCHIT *appears at door the two young ones following and stopping just
on the threshold*)

BOY & GIRL.    Here's Martha, mother!—Hurrah—there's such a goose Martha!
    (*Exeunt*)
MRS C.    Why bless your heart alive my dear, how late you are! Come let me take off
    your shawl and bonnet—and sit down my dear—do! And are you quite well my    5
    darling Martha? (*kissing her*) And here—Belinda, put away your sister's bonnet
    and shawl, and now tell me my dear what has kept you so?

(BELINDA *hangs up bonnet and shawl*)

MARTHA.    We'd a deal of work to finish up last night—and had to clear away this
    morning all our litter, mother.
MRS C.    —Well, never mind, so long as you are come! Peter put your sister a chair,   10
    by the fire.
PETER.    Yes, mother.

MRS C.   (*pointing to chair*) Sit down there my dear—and have a good warm—Lord
   bless ye!
15 BOY & GIRL.   (*appearing at door*) No—no mother—father's coming—hide
   Martha—hide!

*Music—'Nora Creina'—*MARTHA *hides—*BOB CRATCHIT *appears at door with a little
humpbacked boy on his shoulder—*TINY TIM—*he has a short crutch in his hand—*BOB
*advances dancing down to the music, as if to keep him warm.*

BOB.   (*to his wife*) Well mother, here I am! And Tim's been so pleased! Ain't you Tim
   rather?
TIM.   Yes father!
20 BOB.   (*looking round*) But where's Martha?
MRS C.   Not coming—
BOB.   (*his face changing*) Not coming! (*lifts* TIM *down*) not coming upon Christmas
   day—well now that is a disappointment to me—it is indeed.
MARTHA.   Yes father, yes—I am coming (*rushes out*) am coming father, I am
25 here. (*rushes into his arms he embraces her*)
ALL THE YOUNG CRATCHITS.   Hooray! Hooray! Hooray! Won't we be happy!

(*Picture—*PETER *flourishing a fork—*JACK *throwing his cap up—*TINY TIM *waving his
little crutch*)

PETER.   (*catching up* TIM *in his arms*) Come along Tim and hear the pudding singing in the copper—
BOB.   Go for the goose, Peter.
30 PETER.   Yes father.
BOY & GIRL.   (*catching hold of* PETER *on each side*) Come along Peter hooray—hooray—for the goose.

(*Exit* PETER, BOY, & GIRL)

BOB.   And Tim, go and sit down on the stool before the fire, and Martha reach the
   jug (*she does so*)—and Belinda bring me the lemons (*she does so*)—And mother—
35 pour me out some boiling water—and here's the cream, rather! (*producing bottle
   from pocket*) And now won't we mix the gin punch Tim—Tiny Tim—Eh, my
   boy?—(*begins mixing—turning up cuffs of his coat*) here, you mount your stool—
   now stir it round and round. Mother—girls—the very steam of it's grateful ain't it?
   And now put it on the hob to simmer. (TIM *does so*)

(*Re-enter* PETER *with the goose—followed by the* TWO YOUNG CRATCHITS—*he places
it on table*)

40 OMNES.   Hooray!—here it is—

16.1 *'Nora Creina'*: A traditional Irish air, arranged for piano and published in 1818 by Augustus Meves,
current as a song in concerts and lectures in the early 1840s.
   26.2 *Picture…crutch*: Not a Leech illustration.

BOB. (*lifting the dish cover*) Look at it—there never was such a goose. Heaven bless the generous heart who gave it.

MRS C. And so say I—amen—

OMNES. And I—and I—and I—and I—

BOB. Peter—mash the potatoes (PETER *seizes the saucepan*) and mother—take up 45 the pudding—

(*Exeunt* MRS CRATCHIT *and the two elder girls*)

BOY & GIRL. Hooray!—Pudding—Pudding ! (*dancing about in glee*) Hooray for the pudding!

BOY. Suppose it should not be done enough.

TIM. Suppose it should break in turning out. 50

BOB. Suppose somebody should have got over the back wall and stolen it!

BOY. (*running to side*) It can't be father, look there's a lot of steam—it's a coming— it's a coming—Hooray! It's out of the copper—

BOB. (*sniffing*) A smell like washing day.

PETER. (*sniffing*) A smell like an eating house and a pastry cook's next door to each 55 other.

BOB. With a laundresses next door to that, rather!

(MRS CRATCHIT—*re-enters with pudding followed by* MARTHA & BELINDA—*It is placed on table*)

MRS C. And here's the pudding.

BOB. A wonderful pudding!

CHILDREN. A beautiful pudding! 60

BOB. A glorious pudding. (*seizing his wife's hand*) My dear it's the greatest success you have achieved since our wedding day.

MRS C. Well—now that the weight is off my mind—I do confess I had my doubts about the quality of the flour.

BOB. Form a circle, children, give me the gin punch, Peter, and all the family glass 65 you can collect—that's two tumblers and a custard cup without a handle—

(*He pours out the punch—while he is doing this* CHRISTMAS PRESENT *and* SCROOGE— *enter noiselessly and take their stand* L.H. *corner*)

Well my dears—here is a merry Christmas to us all—God bless us!

OMNES. A merry Christmas to us!

TINY TIM. And God bless us every one.

BOB. (*taking him in his arms*) And God bless my poor little fellow and preserve you 70 to me. (*he takes the child's hand in his, kisses him & sits him by his side, they then sit down to dinner very quietly—the foreground of the stage being occupied by* SCROOGE *and the* SPIRIT)

SCROOGE. (*closely observing them*) Spirit—I feel an interest in this I never felt before—a working in my heart I never felt till now. Tell me if Tiny Tim will live?

C. PRESENT. What would you give to save his life?

75  SCROOGE.    Give! I give? I see a vacant seat and a crutch without an owner carefully
      preserved.

C. PRESENT.    If those shadows remain unaltered by the future the child will die.

SCROOGE.    (*struggling with his miserly spirit*) I could almost part with my own life—
      but my wealth—my money—

80  C. PRESENT.    Nonsense man—he'd better die.

SCROOGE.    (*in agony*) Better die!

C. PRESENT.    (*with energy*) Yes—and so decrease the surplus population.

(*Momentary Picture—*SCROOGE *abashed and overcome with penitence & grief—drops
his head without replying*)

Man, if man you be in heart, not adamant, forebear that wicked cant until you
have discovered what the surplus is and where it is—will you decide what men
85      shall live and what men shall die? It may be in sight of heaven you are more worthless and less fit to live than millions like this poor man's child—Oh heaven!—to
hear the insect on the leaf pronouncing on the too much life among his hungry
brothers in the dust!—But—listen.

BOB.    (*raising glass in his hand*) Mr Scrooge!—(SCROOGE *whose eyes have been cast
      on the ground at the* SPIRIT'S *rebuke raises them quickly and looks towards the table*)
90      yes—he's my master—he pays me and I'll do it—I'll give you Mr Scrooge, the
      founder of the feast—

MRS C.    (*rises rather angrily*) The founder of the feast indeed! I wish I had him
      here—I'd give him a piece of my mind and a drumstick to swallow—and I hope he'd
      have a good appetite for the sauce I'd give him for seasoning.

95  BOB.    (*disparagingly*) My dear!—the children—Christmas Day—

MRS C.    It should be Christmas Day, I'm sure, on which one drinks the health of
      such an odious stingy hard unfeeling man as Mr Scrooge—you know he is, Robert—
      nobody knows it better than you do, poor fellow.

BOB.    (*as before*) My dear, Christmas Day!—

100  MRS C.    I'll drink his health for your sake and the day's—not for his—Long life to
      him—a merry Christmas & a happy new year, he'll be very merry and very happy
      in his old counting house—I've no doubt—

TINY TIM.    (*rising*) Now I'll give you a toast father & mother dear—I've been think-
      ing of it ever so long.

105  BOB.    What is't, my boy, what is't?

TINY TIM.    Mr Pleasant—Mr Scrooge's nephew—the gentleman who gave us the
      goose.

OMNES.    Hurrah! Hurrah! Hip! Hip! Hip! Hurrah! Hip! Hip! Hip! Hurrah!

*All the* CRATCHITS *rise and amidst the prolonged voices of the family—jingling of
glasses—clattering of knives & forks—*

*The scene closes.*

## SCENE 4

*A bleak and deserted moor whose monstrous masses of rude stone are cast about as though it were the burial place of giants (for description see work p. 102).*

*Music agitated & hurried—after a slight pause the earth opens and* CHRISTMAS PRESENT *and* SCROOGE *ascend.* SCROOGE *pale, trembling & exhausted.*

SCROOGE.    Spirit, pause—I pray you pause, I am exhausted bewildered with my  1
     rapid flight, tarry but a moment if only to recruit my exhausted frame.
C. PRESENT.    Ha! ha!—what matters that? 'tis better you should see all that I can
     show you while I have the power. I have not long to live.
SCROOGE.    (*trembling*) Not long to live?                                      5
C. PRESENT.    On the Twelfth Night I expire.
SCROOGE.    So soon!
C. PRESENT.    Beware of my brother, I mean my younger brother, my next of kin, he
     who follows close upon me—I have shewn you all I can—my race is nearly run.
SCROOGE.    You may say *race, race* indeed, for no race was ever done half so quickly,  10
     not even the Derby—I touched your robe and there we were in a Palace, now in a
     hovel, then on the peak of some lofty mountain—anon soaring across a plain and
     then like a seabird skimming the wide and fathomless track of waters—listening to
     their wild and angry roar as they beat relentless against the rocks as though they
     would soften their cold, flinty surface by incessant singing.                15
C. PRESENT.    (*in a marked manner*) So have I beat against your heart—with what
     effect, time alone can shew.
SCROOGE.    Against my heart!
C. PRESENT.    Yes; you have now seen Christmas in all its various forms and phases—
     Built upon a dismal reef of sunken rocks o'er which the water chafed and foamed  20
     the wild year through, we saw a solitary lighthouse, but even there those two men
     who watched the light had made a fire that through the thick stone would shed a ray
     of lightness o'er the awful sea—yes—even there they joined their horny hands over
     the rough table at which they sat and wished each other a merry Christmas in their
     can of grog.                                                                 25
SCROOGE.    And so they did—and so they did!
C. PRESENT.    (*with meaning*) They said not, as I have heard it said, out upon
     Christmas!—Christmas humbug!
SCROOGE.    No! no!—
C. PRESENT.    And when we flitted on above the black and heaving sea until we  30
     lighted on a ship—What heard we there as we stood beside the helmsman at the
     wheel?—the lookout in the bow and the officers who had the watch? I say, what
     heard we then?
SCROOGE.    Why, every man among them hummed a Christmas tune or had a
     Christmas thought, or spoke below his breath to his companion of some bygone  35
     Christmas day with homeward hopes belonging to it.

C. PRESENT.    True and more than that,—every man on board, waking or sleeping, good or bad, had a kinder word for another on that day than on any day of the year and had shared to some extent in its festivities and had remembered those he cared
40    for at a distance and had known that they delighted to remember him—Now, in all your long life for fifty-seven years have you ever done as much?

SCROOGE.    I cannot say I have, but tell me, Spirit—what dark abyss is it through which I have just come, what dismal place is it we have just left?

C. PRESENT.    A place where miners live and labour in the bowels of the earth and
45    among them and within a circle of mud and stone you saw around a glowing fire an old man and woman with their children and their children's children and another generation beyond that all decked and gaily in their holiday attire—yes, even they gave a blithe and loud welcome to Christmas—but my race is nearly run—One more scene we pass together—it is the last—Behold!

(*Lively Music—waves his torch, the moon disappears and in its place is seen a bright, gay, gleaming cheerful room at* PLEASANT's *on twelfth night—*PLEASANT, MRS PLEASANT, GOODFELLOW, TOPPER, MISS EASY—LADY & GENTLEMEN *in a hearty laugh*)

50    PLEASANT.    Ha! ha! ha!—would you believe it ladies—ha! ha! ha!

OMNES.    Ha! ha! ha!—

PLEASANT.    Would you believe it gentlemen—Ha! ha! ha!—he said, he said that Christmas was a humbug—as I live—ha! ha! ha! Aye, and he believed it too.

MRS P.    More shame for him Fred, but I'm not surprised at any thing he says, are you
55    Mr Topper?

TOPPER.    Not in the least.

PLEASANT.    To say truth he's a comical old fellow and not so pleasant as he might be, however his offences carry their own punishment and I have nothing to say against him.

60    SCROOGE.    Well done Fred, I'll remember you.

C. PRESENT.    Do—in your will.

MRS P.    I'm sure he's very rich, at least you always tell me so.

PLEASANT.    What of that my dear, his wealth is of no use to him—he don't do any good with it, he hasn't the satisfaction of thinking ha! ha! that he's going to benefit
65    *us* with it!

SCROOGE.    Certainly not—I'm not going to die yet.

MRS P.    I've no patience with him.

LADIES.    No more have I—no more have I—have you Mr Topper?

TOPPER.    None in the least.

70    PLEASANT.    Oh I have—I'm sorry for him, I couldn't be angry with him if I tried— who suffers by his ill whims? Himself always—Here he takes into his head to dislike us and he won't come to dine with us—what's the consequence? He don't lose much of a dinner.

MRS P.    Indeed—I think he loses a very good dinner!

75    LADIES.    And so do I—and so do I—and so do we all.

PLEASANT.    I'm glad to hear it, because I haven't any great faith in these young housekeepers, have you Topper?

TOPPER.    None in the least.

MRS P.    Mr Topper!

TOPPER.    —(*disconcerted*) My dear lady—I—hem, upon my word I didn't know— 80
habit—apologize—you're not offended my dear lady I hope?

MRS P.    Not in the least—ha! ha! ha! Come Pleasant—finish what you have to say about Uncle Scrooge and bury him for the rest of the evening.

SCROOGE.    (*aside*) Bury me!

PLEASANT.    Well, I was only going to say that in consequence of his not making 85
merry with us he loses a great many pleasant moments which could do him no harm;
I'm sure he loves pleasanter companions than he can find in his own thoughts in his
mouldy counting house or his dusty chambers—I mean to give him the same chance
every year whether he likes it or not for I pity him—he may rail at Christmas till he
dies—but I can't help thinking better of it I defy him—if he finds me going there in 90
good temper year after year and saying Uncle Scrooge how are you?—If it only puts
him in the vein to leave his poor clerk £50 at his death—that's something ain't it?

SCROOGE.    My death!

C. PRESENT.    (*to him*) You must die and you cannot take your money with you.

PLEASANT.    But as my wife says let's put Uncle Scrooge under ground and have a 95
pleasant quadrille or a rattling Galop Diable—I've seen some excellent music for it
and Topper will have no objection to lead the orchestra by whistling—will you
Topper my boy?

TOPPER.    None in the least.

PLEASANT.    Then clear away for the Galoppade—                                               100

(*They begin clearing away the furniture—Gents choose partners etc*)

C. PRESENT.    (*to* SCROOGE) We must depart.

SCROOGE.    No—no Spirit, let me stay one half hour, only one—see, they are choosing partners—they are taking places—I had none of these enjoyments in my youth, let me stay a few minutes longer—if only to gaze upon yon fair girl, the image of poor Ellen Williams.                                                                                               105

C. PRESENT.    You remember her with regret then?

SCROOGE.    I do.

C. PRESENT.    Stay.

(*Clash from the orchestra—Galop de Diable—*SPIRIT *seizes* SCROOGE *and forces him into circle—he stands amazed bewildered looking on. When the other characters are at the height of this exciting whirl—the stage darkens—they dance right off—Scene disappears to a Street during a very heavy snow storm—Clock begins to slowly toll Twelve— the robe & hair of the* SPIRIT *are quite white—*SCROOGE *looks petrified.*)

C. PRESENT.    (*with the first stroke of* 12) Hark—my life is ending!

SCROOGE.    Spirit, Spirit—where am I?—forgive me if I am not justified in what I 110
ask, but I see something strange protruding from your robe—Is it a hoof or a claw?

C. PRESENT.    (*with the 3rd stroke of the bell*) A claw! For all the flesh there is upon it. (*opening his robe and ushering the gaunt forms of the 2 Children seen in [the illustration]*)

C. PRESENT.    Oh man look here—look—look—look down here—yellow—meagre—ragged—scowling, wolfish, yet prostrate too in their humility—they are forms
115     of those to whom you refused a *penny* when you had thousands at your command. (SCROOGE *starts back appalled*) Here where graceful youth should have filled their features and here where angels might sit enthroned, devils lurk. No change, no degradation, no perversion of humanity in any grade through all the mysteries of wonderful creation has monsters half so horrible and dread—

120  SCROOGE.    Spirit, are they yours?

C. PRESENT.    (*with 8th stroke of bell*) They are man's and they cling to me appealing from their fathers—this boy is *Ignorance*, this girl is *Want!*—Beware them both and all of their degree—but most of all beware this boy—for on his brow I see that written which is *Doom* unless the writing be erased  (*sinks slowly*)—deny it—deny it if
125     you can—

(SCROOGE *looking round appalled and trembling*—A FIGURE *in a black mantle approaches slowly from the back*—*with one finger extended*—*beckons* SCROOGE)

C. PRESENT.    (*disappearing with last stroke of 12*) The Future!
PHANTOM OF THE FUTURE.    I await you!

SCROOGE *shudderingly falls on his knees—averts his gaze from the* PHANTOM—*clasps the ragged children and Drop falls.*

*End of Act Two*

---

112.2  *the illustration*: The MS is defective here, at a change in the sheets, from f. 126 to f. 127. For f. 127 a different paper is used, suggesting perhaps a change of the time of copying, or of the copyist. The sense seems to indicate that what is missing is a reference to Leech's unnamed illustration at the end of Stave III.

# ACT III

## SCENE 1

*The new Royal Exchange, 'Even there where merchants most do congregate'.*

*Discovered*—GRIBBLE, WOLF, THOMPSON, SMITH, GOODFELLOW, *and* TOPPER.

GRIBBLE.    Ha! ha! ha! so, the old hunks has cut us at last.                                    1
PARTY.    (*all laugh*)
GOODFELLOW.    There's no doubt about his death, Topper?
TOPPER.    Oh! No, not an atom—none in the least!

(*During this, the* PHANTOM OF THE FUTURE *and* SCROOGE *glide silently on— and as each party speaks,* SCROOGE *walks round, peeping anxiously in their different faces*)

SCROOGE.    I know this place—these men—I have met them daily! (*his thoughts wander*) Poor Ellen Williams! Spirit, or whatsoe'er thou art, you say you will shew 5 me visions of the things that have not happened, but will happen in the time before us—if so, how comes it, I see no shadow of myself among my former companions? It cannot be, that I shall be taken hence!
PHANTOM.    Listen!
GRIBBLE.    When did he die?                                                                        .    10
SMITH.    Last night! (*all laugh*)
SCROOGE.    They jest, they laugh at death! Oh, that they had witnessed the scene, that I have just passed through! Let me leave this place—I am heart sick!
PHANTOM.    Listen!
GOODFELLOW.    Has he left his nephew anything—any legacy?                                         15
TOPPER.    Cut him off, without a shilling!
SCROOGE.    They do mean me—they must mean me! Am I to die then?—so soon?
PHANTOM.    Speak not—but watch, and learn!

(*Clock strikes 4—a bell ringing*)

GRIBBLE.    Four o'clock!
WOLF.    Change over!                                                                               20
SMITH AND THOMPSON.    Let's go and see what the Funds have closed at!

*Exeunt*

---

0.1 *'Even...congregate'*: From *Merchant of Venice* Act 1 scene 3, presumably suggested by the book, but not quoted therein.

PHANTOM.   Men walk on, you see, about their occupations, their pursuits, their pleasures—and you, a drop, an atom, a speck in the vast tide of human life—your withdrawal from the current, is not felt by a single heart!

25 SCROOGE.   Too true! But lead me further, Spirit—whatever may be my end, I feel, I know your purpose is to do me good. I hope to live—to be another man from what I was—to make amends for all that's past—I am prepared to bear you company, and do it with a thankful heart! You will not take my life—will you, dread Phantom? You will let me live, to repent, will you not? (PHANTOM *beckons him along*) No,

30 no—speak, in answer!

PHANTOM.   Obey thy destiny, and murmur not—on! on!

SCROOGE.   No hope—not one word of comfort! Lead on!—the night is waning fast, and each fleeting moment is precious time to me! Ellen! wronged girl, I shall rejoin you! Lead on!

*Exeunt*


# SCENE 2

*Interior of* OLD JOE BADGER'S *Marine store shop—Saffron Hill.*

OLD JOE *seated in the midst of the articles of his trade, before a charcoal fire, a brazier, smoking—he shrugs, as if with cold—draws an old curtain before the window—trims his lamp, with end of pipe.* PHANTOM *appears at door, beckons* SCROOGE, *who follows him behind curtain.*

1 PHANTOM.   (*to* SCROOGE) Listen!

JOE.   Come! The old curtain will keep the cold air from my poor old bones!—I've not lived seventy odd years and upwards, without knowing how to make myself *warm*, I warrant! No, no—leave old Joe alone for that! (*a knock*) who's there?

5 MRS DIBBLER.   (*without*) It's me, Mr Badger! I've got some little articles for you!

JOE.   Come in, my dear! (*goes towards door, as she enters, with a bundle*) What have you brought me? Anything I can give a price for, eh?

MRS MANGLES.   (*entering, with a bundle*) If she hasn't I have Joe, I can assure you!

BERRY.   (*entering*) And I've brought a trifle or two, merely for old acquaintance sake!

10 MRS D.   Mother Mangles, as I'm a sinner! And Mr Berry!

MRS M.   Mary Dibbler! As I'm alive! why, what has brought you here?

MRS D.   The same as has brought you, I guess—legs!

JOE.   I reckon you guess right ha! ha!—Well, Mr Berry, you don't seem lively?

MRS D.   Uncommon mute for an undertaker's man, I must say! (*they all laugh, at find-*

15 *ing themselves together*) Well, I'll say this—let the charwoman alone, to be the first.

MRS M.   Let the laundress alone, to be the second.

BERRY.   And let the death hunter alone, to be the third! Look here, Joe—here's a chance! If we haven't all met here, without a meaning.

MRS M.   Every one has a right to take care of themselves, Mr Berry—the old cur-
mudgeon always did!                                                                    20
MRS D.   True!—no man more so!
MRS M.   We're not going to pick holes in each other's coats, I suppose.
JOE.   Certainly not—none of you blow the gaff—I'll swear you're all honest, ha! ha!
for that!
THE THREE.   We should hope so—ha! ha!                                                 25
MRS D.   Then who's the worse, for the loss of a few rags? Not the dead man, I suppose.
MRS M.   If he wanted to keep his musty things after he was dead, the wicked old
screw, why wasn't he natural, in his life time?
MRS D.   Our helping ourselves to a few things, is a judgement on him—it is!
MRS M.   Open that bundle, Joe, and let me know the value on't—don't be afraid to   30
speak out—I'm not afraid to be the first!
BERRY.   No, Mother Mangles—if you are, I'm hanged!—my gallantry will ne'er
stand that neither—if there is to be any risk, I'll be the first to mount the breach—
providing old Joe promises to come nothing of the screwing-down system.
JOE.   Well, I'll give you a fair price.                                               35
BERRY.   Here's two seals—a silver pencil case—a pair of sleeve buttons—and a
brooch—mind ye, no tick for 'em—We never give tick, at our shop—but always sends
in our bills for funerals, while the tears are in the people's eyes—so no tick for me!
JOE.   (*after examining them chalks on table*) That's your account—and I wouldn't
give another sixpence, if I was to be boiled for not doing so!                         40
BERRY.   Hand over the tin—tho' you're worse than any other Jew that ever lived!
Five shillings for a lot like that! You're the deadest nail at a bargain, and the downiest
hammer at driving it, I ever knew!—I thought you would have shelled out a little
more handsome! (*Exit*)
JOE.   (*calls after him, then sinks his voice*) Not another farthing, to save the thief from   45
hanging, would I give! Who's next?
MRS D.   I'm next—look here!
JOE.   Two sheets—two towels—an old waistcoat—two old fashioned silver tea
spoons—a air of sugar tongs—and a few boots—(*marks, with chalk*)
MRS D.   Fifteen shillings—the man's mad!                                              50
JOE.   It's a weakness of mine, to give too much to ladies—that's the only madness I
have—and that's the way I ruin myself.
MRS D.   Give me the money! It'll cost me an extra sixpence, to get a drop of some-
thing comfortable, to solace my disappointment! Mangles, dear, you'll find me at
the bar, at the corner! (*Exit*)                                                       55
JOE.   (*to himself*) If you'd been brought to the bar 30 years ago, t'wouldn't have been
much matter!
MRS M.   Now, my bundle, Joe!
JOE.   (*drags out a large dark roll of heavy stuff*) What do you call this—bed curtains?
MRS M.   I should think so—bed curtains!                                               60
SCROOGE.   (*peeping*) They are mine!
JOE.   You don't mean to say you took them down, rings and all!

MRS M.   Yes, I do!

JOE.   You were born to make your fortune, and you'll certainly do it! (*examines the things*)

65 SCROOGE.   The vile harpies!

MRS M.   I shan't hold my hand, when I can get anything in it, for the sake of such a man as *he* was! Don't drop the oil on that blanket now!

JOE.   (*drops them*) His blankets!

SCROOGE.   Let me pass—I cannot endure this!

70 PHANTOM.   You must; in vain you wrestle with the future!

(SCROOGE *struggles—his back is towards* JOE *and* MRS MANGLES—*while he is doing so, they sink through the stage, with table etc*)

*Scene changes to a dark gloomy room—in which is a bed, supporting a recumbent* FIGURE, *covered with a sheet.*

SCROOGE.   Spirit, I see—the case of this unhappy man, I feel to be my own—my life tends that way now—but they shall not rob me, before my face—the property they are bartering for, is mine—it cost me money and that cost me every friend on earth! Now let me go!

75 PHANTOM.   (*releases him*) Fool, can you grasp shadows? If so, there is one, touch it!

SCROOGE.   (*perceiving changes*) Merciful Heaven—what is this? A bare, uncurtain'd bed!—and on it—passive, still, and motionless, lying beneath a ragged sheet—a form, that speaketh in awful language, dumb though it be!

PHANTOM.   (*points to bed*) Unwatched, unwept, uncared for!

80 SCROOGE.   If I dared remove that covering, my future fate would be revealed, at once! Oh! Cold, cold, rigid, dreadful death, set up thine altar here, and dress it with such terrors as thou hast at thy command, for this is thy dominion! (*kneels*) But the loved, revered, and honored head, thou can'st not turn one hair to thy dread purposes, or make one feature odious! It is not that the heart and pulse are still—but

85 that the hand was open, generous, and true—the heart, brave, warm, and tender, and the pulse a man's! tell me, if this prostrate figure could be raised up now, what would be its foremost thought?

PHANTOM.   Avarice, hard dealing—griping cares!

SCROOGE.   Then they have brought him to a rich end! Truly, Spirit, this is a fearful

90 place—in leaving it, I shall not leave its lesson, trust me! Let us go! (PHANTOM *points to bed*) I understand you; and would do it, if I could—but have not the power! Let us go—let us go!

*Exeunt*

## SCENE 3

*Room in* FRED PLEASANT'S *House.*

*Double knock heard—*MRS PLEASANT *hastens in, to meet* PLEASANT *who enters.*

MRS P.   Well, Fred, my dear, you're home at last! What news?   1
PLEASANT.   Pleasant my dear—tho' upon a sad subject!
MRS P.   Do not jest, Fred, with our misfortunes—is it good, or bad?
PLEASANT.   Bad!
MRS P.   We are quite ruined, then!   5
PLEASANT.   Smile again—there is hope yet!
MRS P.   If he relents, there is—nothing is past hope, if such a miracle has happened to your uncle.
PLEASANT.   He is past relenting—he is dead!
MRS P.   To whom will our debt for the rent, be transferred?   10
PLEASANT.   I don't know yet; but it must be a bad fortune indeed, to find so merciless a creditor in his executor, as he was.
MRS P.   We may sleep, tonight, with light hearts then, Fred!
PLEASANT.   We may! Yes, disguise it as we will, we may sleep with lighter hearts than we have slept with, for this many a month!   15

*Exeunt*

PHANTOM *appears, followed by* SCROOGE.

PHANTOM.   You have heard!
SCROOGE.   To my grief, my sorrow, my shame! Every house seems happier—the only emotion you have ever shown me, caused by my death, has been one of pleasure—let me see some tenderness—regret—connected with the close of life, or that dark chamber, which we left just now, will be for ever present with me.   20
PHANTOM.   Behold! (*motions with his hand*)

*Scene changes to Interior of* BOB CRATCHIT'S.

MRS CRATCHIT *and* CHILDREN *seated round the fire.*

PETER.   (*reading*) 'and in the midst of their comfort, the little child was taken from them.'

(MRS CRATCHIT *lays down her work, and puts her hand to her face*)

SCROOGE.   Where have I heard those words? I surely have not dreamed them? Why does not the boy read on?   25
PHANTOM.   Listen!
CHILDREN.   What's the matter, mother?
MRS C.   Nothing—the colour hurts my eyes—they're better now.
MARTHA.   It must be near my father's time, mother—
PETER.   (*shuts book*) Past it, rather—but I think he walked a little slower than he   30
used, these last four evenings, mother.

MRS C.    I have known him walk—with—tiny Tim upon his shoulders, very fast, indeed!

PETER.    And so have I!

35 MRS C.    But he was very light to carry—and his father loved him so, that it was no trouble—(*a single knock—she hastens up*) and there's your father—be quiet, there's good children—don't disturb him!

(*Goes to meet* BOB—MARTHA *places a chair*—PETER *pours out tea*—BOB *enters, dejectedly, yet striving to assume cheerfulness*)

Well, Robert, I'm glad you're come! How do you feel? Are you better?

BOB.    (*sits*) Yes, mother, yes—rather.

PETER.    (*handing tea*) Here, father!

40 BOB.    No! I can't eat—I can't!

CHILDREN.    Don't mind it, father—don't be grieved!

BOB.    My dears, I'm not grieved—I'm rather tired—that's all! (*forces a smile*) Look, mother, I'm cheerful!—resigned!—Poor things, how well you've got on with your work! They'll be done, long before Sunday—rather—rather!

45 MRS C.    Sunday—you've been then, today, Robert?

BOB.    Yes, my dear—I wish you could have gone—it would have done you good, to see how green a place it is—but you'll see it often—I promised him I would—work there, on Sunday—(*unable to bear up*) My little, little child—Don't heed me—I can't help it—I shall be more a man presently, and less like him!

50 MRS C.    Robert!

BOB.    I shall be better in a moment! (*firmly*) No! I do not murmur—I am quite happy in all our trouble, we are not destitute of friends—and kind ones, too! I met Mr Scrooge's nephew this morning—I'm sure it's a happy name, to call him Pleasant—for he is the kindest, and pleasantest spoken gentleman, you ever

55 heard!—And kindly he behaved—he pulled out half a sovereign, pressed it into my hand, and walked out, crying 'remember me to your good wife.' Now who could have told him you were a good wife? How could he have come to know that?

PETER.    Everybody knows that, to be sure, father.

BOB.    Very well observed—rather—I hope they do.

60 MRS C.    I'm sure Mr Pleasant's a good young man!

BOB.    You would be surer of it, if you saw, and spoke to him! I shouldn't be at all surprised—mark what I say—if he got Peter a better situation.

MRS C.    Only hear that, Peter!

MARTHA.    And then Peter will be keeping company with some one, and setting up

65 for himself!

PETER.    Get along with you, do, Martha!

BOB.    Just as likely as not, rather, one of these odd days—though there's plenty of time for that. But however, and where ever we part from one another, I am sure we shall none of us forget poor tiny Tim, shall we? Or this first parting, there was amongst us—

70 ALL.    Never!

BOB.    And I know, my dears, that when we recollect how patient he was, altho' he was a little, little child—we shall not quarrel among ourselves—and forget poor tiny Tim, in doing so—

ALL.   Never, father!

BOB.   I am vey happy, though—poor little tiny Tim!   75

(*Picture—During this,* SCROOGE *has seated himself and with his hand resting on his head, been a silent listener—the* PHANTOM *with its face towards* SCROOGE*—he touches him—*SCROOGE *looks up, imploringly*)

## SCENE 4

*Front Scene, with iron gates.*

PHANTOM *appears—*SCROOGE *tottering after.*

SCROOGE.   Pause, Spirit, pray! I can scarcely crawl—something informs me that our   1
parting moment is at hand—I know it—but I know not how! Torture me not, but
answer—let me know the worst—is it so?   (PHANTOM *points through gate*) No, not
that way—'tis gloomy, fearful—'tis like the entrance of a charnel house—the very
air is rife with odours exhaling from the remains of poor humanity!—Not there! I   5
pray you not!

(*Bell tolls, at intervals*)

PHANTOM.   Come!   (*Exit through gate*)

SCROOGE.   Cold, cold, deadly cold!   (*as he reaches gate, bell tolls—he shudders, as he
passes through gate*)

## SCENE 5

*Churchyard. A flat grave stone.* PHANTOM *stands near it, pointing.* SCROOGE *pale, and
almost prostrate with his fears, at back.*

SCROOGE.   A churchyard!   1

PHANTOM.   The wretched being, whose name you dread, yet wish to unfold, lies
underneath this ground. I speak not further. Approach!

SCROOGE.   Before I draw nearer to that stone to which you point—at least answer
me this—are these the shadows of things that will be, or shadows of things that may   5
be, only   (PHANTOM *points*) men's evil courses will foreshadow certain events—to
which, if persevered in, they must head—but if the courses are departed from, the
ends will change. Say, it is thus, with what you show me.

PHANTOM.   Approach!

SCROOGE.   I will!   (*creeps towards the stone*) I cannot read—my sight fails me—I see   10
letters—they are dark, indistinct—No! they flash before my eyes, in characters of
flame!   (*falls on his knees—catches* PHANTOM's *robe*) Spirit, am I that man, who lay
upon the bed?

PHANTOM.   You are!

15 SCROOGE.   No, Spirit—oh, no! no! (PHANTOM *still points*) Spirit, hear me! I am not the man I was—I will not be the man I must have been, but for this inter-course—why shew me this? Why shew me, if I'm past all hope?

PHANTOM.   It is the end!

SCROOGE.   Good Spirit! I will live in the past, the present, and the future—the spir-
20 its of all three, shall strive within me—I will not shut out the lesson that they teach—Oh! Tell me—may I purge away the writing on this stone?

PHANTOM.   It is recorded there! (*points down*)

SCROOGE.   No, no—I am not fit to die—I have been a sinner all my life—wicked, hard of heart, selfish, cruel—have had no time for repentance—I cannot die—I will
25 not—let me live—another year,—only a month—a day, even! Ha! you're forcing me down, deep into the earth! Give me an hour, only—let me live!

PHANTOM.   No!

SCROOGE.   You're strangling me—you stop my respiration—my breath—I will not die!

*The whole scene disappears—with it, the* PHANTOM—*and* SCROOGE *is standing in the counting house.* FRED, *holding him by the wrists—bells ringing a merry peal.*

30 PLEASANT.   And who, in heaven's name, wishes you to die? (*shakes him*) why, Uncle Scrooge, what's the matter with you?

SCROOGE.   The churchyard—the horrible black Phantom—the deep tolling of the hideous bell!

PLEASANT.   What hideous bell? The bells are ringing out the blithest peal you've
35 heard for many a day—convince yourself—listen!

SCROOGE.   I do—I do hear them! (*looks round*) And this place—no—it cannot be—Yes, it is! It is my own house!

PLEASANT.   To be sure it is! Where else should it be? You have properly frightened us all, I can tell you—you've not been in bed, all night!

40 SCROOGE.   Not in bed!

PLEASANT.   I came to dress you, and found you fast asleep!

SCROOGE.   Are you sure of all this?

PLEASANT.   Am I alive?

SCROOGE.   (*seizes his hand*) Yes, yes, you are! (*shakes hands warmly*) I feel you are!
45 my dear Fred, I'm so happy—so very happy—ha! ha!

PLEASANT.   Why, Uncle Scrooge! He's mad! I never heard him laugh before!

SCROOGE.   Ha! ha! Huzza!—it's a dream, then, after all—hurrah!—only a dream!—the room's my own—the chair's my own—Fred's my own nephew—and best, and happiest of all, the time before me is my own, to make amends in! everything's here,
50 as I left it, overnight—I am here—the Shadows of the things that would have been, may be dispelled—they will be—I know they will—and I shall live! Fred! Open the

---

46 *PLEASANT*: MS attributes this speech to Bob, but he has not yet entered, and the form of address makes clear that it is Pleasant's speech.

window (PLEASANT *does so*) that I mayn't lose a tinkle of those merry sounds! It's Christmas day, ain't it?

PLEASANT.   To be sure it is!

SCROOGE.   (*dancing*) I'm happy as an angel—as merry as a schoolboy—as giddy as 55 a drunken man! A merry Christmas to everybody—a happy new year to all the world! (*pops his head out of window*) Come along, Bob! Hurrah, Bob! (BOB *appears at door*) Tol de rol lol! (*shakes his hand*) Dance, Bob! Bob, you're a good fellow—tol de rol lol! (*frisks about*)

BOB.   (*to* PLEASANT) I thought something had happened! 60

PLEASANT.   Only a pleasant change, that's all!

BOB.   A change! Old master's mad, surely, or I'm in a dream, rather!

SCROOGE.   No! all dreams are past, Bob! One remembrance only haunts me still— tiny Tim—tell me, Bob—is little tiny Tim alive?

BOB.   Lord bless me, Sir, alive, and kicking, and screaming out for bread and butter, 65 like anything, this morning!

SCROOGE.   I'll butter his bread on both sides for him! Go and fetch him—fetch all your family—every one!—go, Bob!

BOB.   I don't believe it! (*shakes himself*) Am I awake? Pinch, kick me, somebody, and let me be convinced! 70

SCROOGE.   I'm going to give a dance, Pleasant—a dance, Bob—I'll turn the old counting house into a ballroom, and open the ball myself! Don't stand there, Bob, staring—and winking and blinking, but go along—fetch them all!

BOB.   Is that old master, or is it not?

SCROOGE.   Your old master, Bob, but a new man! (*takes his hand*) I'm not drunk— 75 nor mad—Mammon has fettered me all my life—but Providence has thought fit to alter me—so don't pause, Bob—do as I bid you! Take a cab—ride home—take twenty cabs, and ride back—I'll pay for it all!

BOB.   (*going*) Yes, Sir.

SCROOGE.   And Bob— 80

BOB.   Yes, sir?

SCROOGE.   Call at the fruiterers—tell them to send a cart load of holly and mistletoe—oranges—apples—grapes—everything! And run to Birch's, at Cornhill— order a dinner for twenty, Bob! Go, Bob, run all the way!

BOB.   Rather—rather! (*Exits*) 85

SCROOGE.   As for you, Pleasant—I never felt so happy in all my life as I do, in finding you here, flourishing, alive, & well! Why, there's a lady coming here, Fred, I declare!

PLEASANT.   My wife, I dare say, come to look after me!

SCROOGE.   Your wife! Let me escort her in. (*hastens to door*) Gad! I feel quite young 90 again! I feel like a boy of thirty—boy of thirty?—I feel like a child, of ten! (*meets* MRS PLEASANT *at door*) Welcome, my dear girl, welcome! (*handing her in*) I'm all safe, you see—quite safe—pleasant—you dog, Fred!

PLEASANT.   Yes, sir!

SCROOGE.   She's a beauty, you dog! She has good taste—good taste! 95

MRS P.    A merry Christmas, sir, and a happy new year!

SCROOGE.    The same to you, my dear, and  (*kisses her hand*) Oh! Delicious!

PLEASANT.    Ha! ha! Pleasant!

SCROOGE.    Remarkably pleasant—never had such a treat, for forty years!

*Enter* ELLEN WILLIAMS.

100  ELLEN.    I hope there has nothing happened to Mr Scrooge!

SCROOGE.    Nothing in the world, my good creature, but the best of fortune! Who are you, that make the inquiry? I know your face—your features—tho' I can't say where—for till this day, I've not been much in the habit of looking beyond myself; but I'm an altered man!

105  ELLEN.    And I'm an altered woman—fifteen, when we first parted—

SCROOGE.    God! Ellen Williams!

ELLEN.    The same, in heart and affection! Eight and thirty years have dimmed, but not extinguished it—I released you from your vows, but never forgot mine—'tis I, who have been the humble attendant at your chambers, though unseen, unknown,

110  by you.

BOB.    (*without*) Come along, my dear—come along—come along—Peter, come along—Martha—come along—Jack—come along, all—and here we are, the whole family, rather! (*enters, carrying* TINY TIM—*followed by* MRS CRATCHIT, CHILDREN *etc*)

SCROOGE.    Welcome to you all! A merry Christmas, Bob—aye, and you shall have a

115  merrier one than you've had, for many a year! I'll raise your salary, Bob, to £200 a year!

ALL.    (*except* BOB) Hurrah!

BOB.    No, no—I can't stand all this!

SCROOGE.    I'll assist all your family—and tiny Tim—give me tiny Tim—(*they do*

120  *so*) Heaven bless you, poor boy—may you sit in your father's chimney corner, and gladden his heart, for many a day to come! But clear away, and let's have a dance! (*they take their places, he advances*) Stay! I must have another word or two—kind friends, be assured I shall never forget the lesson a peep into the future has taught me. While the past will be always present to my imagination—may it

125  enable me to fill my part in a 'Christmas Carol' on many, many merry nights to come! And so, to use the words of little tiny Tim here (*pats children's heads*) Heaven bless us every one!

END

# APPENDIX TO WEBB'S *OLD SCROOGE*

A week before the production of this play at the New Strand, Sadler's Wells stole a march on the many London theatres getting up versions of *A Christmas Carol* and produced theirs first. It was also written by Charles Webb. For some reason both Webb plays were submitted for licensing: perhaps the management at the Strand felt theirs differed too much from that at Sadler's Wells to be admissible for licensing purposes as the same play, or perhaps Webb failed to mention that the Strand had already bought it from him. None of the other theatres who produced the work subsequently felt it necessary to reapply for a licence, so we may deduce that they all used either the Strand version on which this edition is based, or something closer to that produced at Sadler's Wells. This appendix therefore includes all that survives of the Wells MS, Add. MS 42972 ff. 976–1008, from the point in Act I scene 3 where the two decisively part company. The transcription begins on f. 992 of the Wells MS, as the Shade of Jacob Marley puts Scrooge to sleep and begins to show him visions. It is incomplete, the surviving MS extending no further than the end of Act I.

SHADE.      No! But I am here tonight to warn you, that you have yet a chance and hope    1
of escape, a chance and hope of my procuring Ebenezer:—*ponder* on what I have
said; *think well:—think deeply—*
SCROOGE.      (*drowsily rubbing his eyes*) I will Jacob—I will.
SHADE.      *Sleep on it! Sleep! Sleep!*                                                       5
SCROOGE.      (*tossing restlessly in his chair*) Jacob you're trying to mesmerize me!—its
all—all humbug! (*struggling faintly*) and yet *sleep*—deep *sleep*—presses on me in
spite of myself—closes my eye lids—steals away the light—the bright sense of life—
my brain is in chaos—the *past*, the *present*, and the *future*, all undefined are struggling there—struggling—this is not death, Jacob? This is not death?                        10
SHADE.      (*again outstretching its arm*) Sleep!

SCROOGE *remains passive and sleeping in the chair.*

*Music. 'I remember—I remember—how my childhood fleeted by' played very piano. The Lid of the Japan Deed Box flies open—light & vapour ascend and from it the Spirit of the Past arises. It was a strange figure—like a child. Tableau 1st.*

___

2 *of escape*: 'of escape' deleted.          8 *in spite of myself*: 'in spite of myself' deleted.

8 *bright*: 'bright' deleted.          10 *struggling*: 'struggling' deleted.

11.2 *'I remember...fleeted by'*: Mrs Edward Fitzgerald's setting of this ballad by W.M. Praed was heard in London soirées in 1833, and published in 1834.

11.4 *It was...child*: 'it was a strange figure—like a child' is inserted, written on the opposite leaf (992v) with the instruction in the text on f. 993r to see the 'description' opposite.

11.4 *Tableau 1st*: The tableau does not derive from one of Leech's illustrations.

SCROOGE.    (*in sleep*) What is this, what rises up before me?

SHADE.    Turn thine eyes around, man. Ask thy soul.

SCROOGE.    (*sleeping*) It is the Spirit of the Past, and now 'tis dark—now light—'tis
15    now a pair of legs without a head—and now a head without a Body; now a thing
with one leg—now with one arm—now with 2 arms! Now it sparkles brilliantly—
now grows indistinct—and now 'tis gone!

*Spirit of the Past vanishes.*

SHADE.    I will visit thee once more, and in the scenes of boyhood and of youth walk
by thy side—but look again, for though externally thy sense of vision's shut—yet
20    can it conjure up an image of the present.

*Music 'The Roast Beef of Old England'—music marked & forte. The scene at back divides
and discovers Tableau 2nd 'THE GHOST OF CHRISTMAS PRESENT'—SCROOGE starts
up momentarily.*

SHADE.    You have never seen the like of him before!

SCROOGE.    Never.

SHADE.    Never walked forth with the younger members of his family or his elder
brothers, born in later years?

25    SCROOGE.    I am afraid I have not;—has he many brothers?

SHADE.    More than 1800.

SCROOGE.    A tremendous family to provide for.

SHADE.    He will be with thee again—but look, he is receding fast away—fading
from you—(THE GHOST OF CHRISTMAS PRESENT *disappears*) and in his place
30    dim vapours rise—look through the dark'ning veil (*Music—of a peculiar and solemn character*) and tell me what you see.

*Stage quite dark.*

SCROOGE.    (*sinking in his chair*) Nothing—in vain I try to pierce this hideous
obscurity—all is darkness—all gloom—

SHADE.    Wake not, till the Future stands clearly and terribly defined before thee! But
35    let thy slumbering spirit soar far away to scenes long past—long forgotten.

---

20.1 *'The Roast Beef of Old England'*: The popular tune was composed by Richard Leveridge twenty years
after Henry Fielding included the original lyric in his *Grub Street Opera* in 1731.

20.2 *'THE GHOST OF CHRISTMAS PRESENT'*: This tableau is derived from the Leech illustration called
'Scrooge's third visitor'.

31.1 *Stage quite dark*: The sd is surrounded with triple xs, the mark for a cue which is to be transmitted
to the stage crew. At this point the MS sets off into a scene in which the Spirit of the Future appears to
Scrooge in a churchyard, but it halts and is deleted after a dozen lines.

35 *long forgotten*: Another false start is deleted here, which was to begin a scene on Cornhill, outside
the new Stock Exchange.

*The* SHADE OF JACOB MARLEY *sinks*—SCROOGE *snores loudly. The stage becomes filled with clouds.* MIRTH—JOLLITY—MOMUS—APOLLO—PUCK—BACCHANAL *&c all rush on the stage*—PAN *with his pipe,* PUNCH *&c*

[OMNES] Jolly Father Christmas with eyes laughing bright
Whose Sceptre of holly's a weapon of might,
Whose torch flashes kindly its genial ray
And lightens dull hearts on his Natal day.
To the poor in their homes—give plenty & pleasure 40
Content & good company—ne'er stint them I measure
In mirth or in merriment; but bid 'em like good'uns
Eat their Roast Beef, and swallow their puddings

PAN. (*solus*) Hot! Hot! All *piping* hot. (*they dance a movement*)

CHRISTMAS PRESENT *ascends through stage into the midst of Circle.*

CHRISTMAS PRESENT. Yo, ho, my friends! Welcome, ye merry bands 45
Pan I see has *piped* all hands.
Or called a *Court*; then I shan't shilly shally
But when I've *said* my *say*, I'll bid you *'Allez'*
The facts are these: an old curmudgeon elf
Who never thought on any but himself 50
Now doubts our power, and with his withered rum mug
Has dared to say that I'm a humbug—

(*great sensation*)

PUNCH. Roo-too-it! May he ne'er taste breakfast, lunch
MOMUS. Or banquet on thy *spirit*, glorious Punch.
PUCK. Philanthropy's wide march he'll but retard 55
PUNCH. (*shaking his cudgel*) As I'm a *head-hitter*, I'll *hit* him hard.
Unless he alters—
APOLLO. Will music charm him?
PUNCH. No, bold Pol, a *Lyre's* sure to harm him.
MIRTH. I'll make him laugh— 60
MOMUS. I'll make him jolly
PUNCH. And lessons teach, from *life,* of folly.
CHRISTMAS PRESENT. Silence uproarious knaves! I have a plan

35.2 *clouds*: A new leaf, f. 995r, begins here, with the entry of pantomime/allegorical characters who are not in the original, but would be a familiar part of Sadler's Wells entertainments.
35.3 *PUNCH*: The figure of Punch here is intended directly to invoke the magazine of that name, then in its early years; hence the ensuing puns.
45 *CHRISTMAS PRESENT*: Deleted: 'Well done my children—I come to join your jovial'.
56 *head-hitter*: *Punch* pun: head-hitter = editor.

To work a reformation in our man.
65  Old Christmas past—my peaked and dwindled sire
Shall shew him *that*, will light a fire
In his cold heart! Shall shew him truth!
And call him back to days of youth
Spirit of ages, long since fled
70  Whose sons are mingled with the mighty dead,
Whose glorious truth a light hath shed
That burns in halo round thy head

*Music*

SPIRIT OF CHRISTMAS PAST.    (*rises*) What need ye *Son*—
CHRISTMAS PRESENT.    (*seizes his hand*) Welcome, Father.
75  PUNCH.    He is *well-come*, I own that, rather.
OMNES.    Welcome! Welcome!
CHRISTMAS PAST.    Zounds, what a clatter—
On Earth there's something sure the matter.
CHRISTMAS PRESENT.    A soul that scorns me, that homage will not pay
80  Whose life in selfishness hath past away
Whose hand should scatter comfort on the earth
Raise drooping want, and rescue starving worth
A man that ought to taste good Christmas cheer
Nor when 'tis paid for deem it dear,
85  A man that ought to join my Christmas band
Nor grasp at all with greedy hand
CHRISTMAS PAST.    I'll walk abroad, I'll shew him what he's lost
What *happiness* his gold hath cost.
CHRISTMAS PRESENT.    I'll shew him mirth and laughter, faces pleasant
90  And from the past drop to the present.
But for the future—
CHRISTMAS PAST.    Let time unveil it
I'm off—
PUNCH.    Pray are you going to rail it—
95  No, call a cab—we're at a stand.
CHRISTMAS PAST.    Where?
PUNCH.    —One, Nine, Four, Strand
MIRTH—JOLLITY—MOMUS—APOLLO—PAN.    You'll need me, and me, and me,
and me—
100  CHRISTMAS PRESENT.    We need ye all, Choice spirits free!

---

97 *One, Nine, Four, Strand*: This is the address of the *Punch* offices from May 1843 to January 1845; see
M.H. Spielmann, *The History of Punch* (London: Cassell and Co., 1895), 258. Presumably there was a cab
stand outside.

Yet 'ere on wind we're born along
We'll revel in a jovial song
Strike up Pol, Pan your pipes play
And when in a Christmas day—

*Song & Chorus*

Revel—laugh and shout—'tis Christmas time                    105
See the holly and the mistletoe and hear the merry chime
Lovers kind are meeting—Friends are blithely greeting
Welcome—then—O welcome to merry Christmas time.

*Repeat, and dance off in groups—the Clouds disperse and open to*

## SCENE 3

*The village of Holly-Thorn by sunlight on Christmas Day of 1805*—EBENEZER SCROOGE
*aged 18 seated on a stile, the chimes are ringing merrily.*

SCROOGE.    I wish those noisy bells would hold their clatter—from my part I hate  1
Christmas day—I always did hate it—it's only a day's work lost to me and I'd any
time sooner have the money than the holiday—well, I shalln't pass another here,
that's one comfort—No, I've saved up 20 guineas and come what will on't, I'll seek
my fortune in London, that's the place to make money—if I could save up 20 guin-  5
eas by dint of pinching, scraping, and self denial out of 5/- a week—why mayn't I by
the same process make 20,000 guineas in a larger place—yes, yes—London's the
place for me! London! London's a much wider *field* to till than any 'bout these
parts—I'll go, come what will on't.
ELLEN.    (*heard singing without*)

'Tis a merry, merry morn—And there hangs on the thorn                    10
        Hoar frost sparkling bright
    A sparkling gem—ne'er found in diadem
        A jewel, a jewel of light.

*Enters.*

SCROOGE.    What are you making that noise for?
ELLEN.    Ebenezer!—It's Christmas Day—Mayn't one carol a song on such a blythe  15
morning? I came purposely after you to wish you a merry—
SCROOGE.    Nonsense—I'd rather you'd wish me *plenty* of *money*.
ELLEN.    (*seriously*) Well then I came after you for another purpose, to ask—to ask if
it is really true that you are going to London? That you are going to leave the
village?                    20
SCROOGE.    Yes it is—what then?

ELLEN.    What then! Have you forgotten all your vows, all your promises made to me? Have you forgotten five years since—just at this season—when you were left alone, friendless, solitary at school, with no one to bid you welcome to a home—
25  have you forgotten the morning when I dashed into the room—kissed your cheek—and bore you with me to my father's farm? Have you forgotten the kindly welcome you received under the poor man's roof? Have you indeed forgotten all this?

SCROOGE.    No I've not, or if I had it matters little. I've been industrious—faithful, hard working—saving—and now I see a way to better my fortune.

30  ELLEN.    It matters little, to you very little, for I see another idol has displaced me and if it can cheer up and comfort you in time to come, as I would have tried to do, I have no just cause to grieve.

SCROOGE.    What idol has displaced you, tell me that?

ELLEN.    A golden one—the lust of wealth, little by little I have seen the frank and
35  generous spirit of your youth pine and die away, even now your face begins to wear the signs of care and avarice. There is an eager, greedy & restless motion in your eye which shews the passion that has taken root, and where the shadow of the growing tree will fall.

SCROOGE.    This is the even handed dealing of the world! There is nothing on which
40  it is so hard as poverty; and there is nothing it professes to condemn with such severity as the pursuit of wealth.

ELLEN.    Can you wonder, have I not watched the nobler aspirations of your soul fall one by one until the master passion, Gain, has quite engrossed you? Have I not?

SCROOGE.    What then? Even if I have grown so much the wiser, what then? I am not
45  changed towards you.

ELLEN.    You are changed. When our contract was made you were a different being and that which promised happiness when we were one in heart, is fraught with misery now that we are two.

SCROOGE.    Have I sought release?

50  ELLEN.    In words, no, never.

SCROOGE.    In what then?

ELLEN.    In an altered spirit; in another atmosphere of life; another hope as to its great end. In every thing that made my love of any worth and value in your sight.

SCROOGE.    I shall come back from London—rich, very rich, I shall claim you then—

55  ELLEN.    You will not even attempt to.

SCROOGE.    Why?

ELLEN.    I shall be *poor* and I am certain you will never wed a dowerless girl—you who in your very confidence with her weigh every thing by gain, but be assured—if you are bent on leaving us—

60  SCROOGE.    I am determined.

ELLEN.    Well then I release you—release you from all promises—release you with a full heart for the love of him—you once were.

SCROOGE.    Ellen!

ELLEN.    You may—the memory of what is past—half makes me hope you will
65  have pain in this. A very, very brief time, and you will dismiss the recollection

of it, gladly, as an unprofitable dream from which it happened well that you awoke. (*Exit*)

SCROOGE. (*calling after her*) Why Ellen! What, gone! Gone! Given me up, left me thus! (*goes to wing*) Why Ellen I say!—she hastens on, as though she would thrust me from heart and sight at once—she does not even turn to give me a parting 70 look—why should I follow her then? Why care for her? I've got my money—my money—(*pulling out a leather bag and jingling it*)—aye and enough to take me far away from here—that's a comfort she can't deprive me of, no, no. (*mounts the stile*) Well, I'll have a look at the old village Church and the Bridge and the mill stream before I leave them (*Music very piano 'My Boyhood's Home'*) I—Aye, there they are, 75 all at my feet, and so is fortune—I'll kick the ball merrily along and make it gather, gather, as it rolls—and there go little George and James riding our ponies down the town—(*listens*) now I hear them call to Farmer Giles's sons and hallo and shout to each other till the broad fields seem to ring with merry music, and the crisp air laughs at their jovial Christmas greetings. (*descends from stile*) Christmas! What 80 care I for Christmas? Out upon Christmas, I'll go to London!

*Music changes to Gee-Ho-Dobbin & jingling of waggon bells.*

And in the very nick of time here comes the waggon!

WAGGONER. (*heard without*) Woa there Smiler—woa Dobbin—gently—gently!

SCROOGE. Ho there! Waggoner!

WAGGONER. (*looking over stile*) Well. (*stares*) What Master Ebenezer Scrooge, be 85 that you? What do you want, mun?

SCROOGE. To go to London with you. What will you take me for?

WAGGONER. Oh, for three shilling—and that won't hurt you.

SCROOGE. Three shillings—no *two*, not a fraction more, I'll sooner walk every step of the way first. 90

WAGGONER. Hoa—well,—you and I mun wonan't quarrel about *straws*.

SCROOGE. Call money, *straws*?

WAGGONER. Jump up!—Jump up mun!

SCROOGE. You're off at once then?

WAGGONER. This very minute, (*disappears cracking his whip—Bells heard again*) 95

SCROOGE. (*jumping over stile*) Farewell Hollythorn—farewell; and now for dingy, smoky London, the heart of wealth and commerce. (*disappears*)

*Music: 'Over the Hills and far away' close in by*

75 'My Boyhood's Home': From William Michael Rooke's opera *Amilie* (Covent Garden, 1837). It is marked with triple crosses as a music cue, in the MS.

81.1 *Gee-Ho-Dobbin*: 'Gee ho Dobbin' is a traditional air which reached the public stage in Arne's *Love in a Village*, with new words by Bickerstaffe (Covent Garden, 1762).

97.1 'Over the Hills and far away': Another traditional tune that appeared early in plays and ballad operas, including *The Recruiting Officer* (1706) and Gay's *The Beggar's Opera* (1728).

## SCENE 4

*Room in Mr Fezziwig's House, Christmas eve 1806, 1st Grooves*
*Music 'The Fine Old English Gentleman'.*

*Enter* MR *and* MRS FEZZIWIG.

1    FEZZIWIG.    (*in a great bustle*) Hilli-ho Mrs Fezziwig! Chirrup Mrs Fezziwig!
    MRS F.    But I can't chirrup Mr Fezziwig!
    FEZZIWIG.    Yes you can, bless your heart you can my dear—as blithely as a bird—
      here we are Christmas Eve 1806; let's be merry, let's be jolly—have you made the
5    cake, and have you made the negus? And have you the great piece of cold roast
      ready and have you the great piece of cold boiled? And are there plenty of mince
      pies, and plenty of beer? Hilli-ho! Chirrup chirrup!
    MRS F.    My dear Mr Fezziwig, you are so boisterous.
    FEZZIWIG.    Boisterous! I'm happy—come to my arms! (*embraces her*) Chirrup!
10    Chirrup!
    MRS F.    (*smoothing her dress*) Mr F., I do declare you're quite rambunctious.
    FEZZIWIG.    Never mind my dear—only once a year you know, kiss me!
    MRS F.    Bless your good tempered, round, jolly jovial, oily, comfortable looking
      face—there!—(*kisses him a hearty smack*)
15 FEZZIWIG.    Ah, that's hearty, I like it!
    MRS F.    You like to make everybody around you comfortable.
    FEZZIWIG.    To be sure I do—we'll have in the Fiddler—we'll have in all our own
      little band of Fezziwigs—we'll have in all the young men and women employed in
      the business—we'll have in the housemaid and her cousin the baker, we'll have in
20    the cook and her brother's particular friend the milkman—we'll have in the boy
      from over the way who don't get half board enough from his master—
    MRS F.    and we'll have in the girl who lives next door whose mistress I know has
      pulled her ears—
    FEZZIWIG.    Hilli-ho! Ho!—We'll have 'em all in! We'll have a happy jovial night! Yo
25    ho, there my boys. (*calling off*) No more work tonight! Christmas Eve, Dick!

*Enter* DICK *an apprentice.*

    DICK.    Yes sir!
    FEZZIWIG.    (*calling loudly*) Christmas Mr Ebenezer Scrooge, my chief shopman!

*Enter* SCROOGE (*in Shopman's apron and sleeves*)

    SCROOGE.    Yes sir.
    FEZZIWIG.    Christmas Ebenezer! Let's have the shutters up (*clapping his hands*
30    *sharply together*) before man or boy can say, Jack Robinson!

---

0.2 *'The Fine Old English Gentleman'*: The air of 'A Fine Old English Gentleman' was one of the many tunes
from the popular melting pot to which ownership was asserted during the nineteenth century, when they were
published and became valuable; there was a court case disputing the rights. See *Morning Chronicle*, 17 June 1834.

SCROOGE *and* DICK.  (*together*) Yes—sir. (*Exeunt hastily*)

FEZZIWIG.   Hark, how the two fellows go at it!

MRS F.   How the shutters are going up surely! An *industrious* young man that Ebenezer—a *nice* young man, and a *prudent* young man.

FEZZIWIG.   Hark how they go—one—two—three—Four—five—six—bar 'em, pin 35 'em—seven—eight—nine—all right and here they are again panting like race horses.

SCROOGE.   (*out of breath*) What shall we do next, sir?

FEZZIWIG.   Hilli-ho! Clean away my lads—the next warehouse—let's have lots of room! Hilli-ho Dick! Chirrup Ebenezer!

SCROOGE.   Clean away! With you looking on sir it shall be done in a minute! Every 40 moveable shall be packed off as if dismissed from public life evermore—the floors shall be swept and watered; the lamps trimmed; fresh fuel heaped upon the fire; and the warehouse shall become as snug and dry, and warm and bright a ball room, as you could wish to see upon a winter's night! Come along Dick! Come along!

FEZZIWIG.   (*taking* MRS F's *hand*) Come along Mrs Fezziwig—to the ball room! 45 You and I will open the ball;—Sir Roger de Coverly for ever! Hilli-ho I feel quite young again—Chirrup! Chirrup! (*Exeunt hand in hand*)


## SCENE 5

FEZZIWIG *Ball. Fiddler in the Desk. Fire blazing—Mistletoe suspended from Ceiling, the room full of various Characters as described; as they are discovered they strike off into the following Chorus*

CHORUS

The Christmas log with its bright red glow 1
Give light and warmth to the heart we know
Crack nuts—and jokes—sip toast and ale,
And list to the song and merry tale.
Shout for the log! The Christmas log! 5
As from year to year we onward jog
Shout for the log! The old Yule log!
Where is the hearth on which ye gaze
That would not miss its cheerful blaze
When the ground is covered with frost and snow 10
And the winter's winds, they chilly blow
Shout for the log! The Christmas log!

*Enter* MR *and* MRS FEZZIWIG *followed by* SCROOGE & DICK.

FEZZIWIG.   Chirrup away Neighbours—Chirrup! A merry Christmas to you all— and we'll have a dance any how and every how; take your places—fifteen couple at once; the figure—hand half round and back again the other way; down the middle 15 and up again—shuffle—cut—cut and shuffle—all top couples and none at the bottom—advance and retire—hold hands with your partner; bow and curtsey; corkscrew; thread-the-needle—and back again to places—I'll shew you how to cut too—bless you I can cut till the very calves of my legs wink again.

20    MRS F.     Are you ready fiddler?

FEZZIWIG.     Chirrup! Scrape! Fiddle away! Hilli-ho, off we go!

*General dance—kept up to the greatest pitch of hilarity—*SCROOGE *in his youth is nowhere to be seen but when a close circle that has been dancing round divide—he is discovered, dressed as in scene 1ˢᵗ, dancing away as if for life—one by one the couples dance off, Mr & Mrs Fezziwig last couple—then the Fiddler dances off—the music ceases—Stage becomes quite dark.*

SCROOGE.     Hollo! Where am I? Where are you all? This moment I saw old Fezziwig— my companion Dick—my heart and soul were in the scene, and with my former self! I remembered every thing,—enjoyed every thing! (*calls*) where are you all?

25    Where are you?

CHRISTMAS PAST.     (*glides in*) Gone! Past!—The Spirit of the Present now awaits you.

SCROOGE.     (*pressing his hand on the* SPIRIT'S *cap*) At least I'll drive you from me! Down busy meddler—down! down! Haunt me no more!

*As* SCROOGE *presses—the ground opens—the* SPIRIT OF THE PAST *sinks through—a flood of light pours upwards in the face & figure of* SCROOGE *& the act drop descends quickly.*

# FIVE

Edward Stirling, *Martin Chuzzlewit*, Lyceum, July 1844

## INTRODUCTION

THIS highly successful melodrama was the outstanding hit of Mary Ann Keeley's first season as manager at the Lyceum. Having waited until publication was complete, the dramatist had no need this time to invent the working-out of the plot, nor to worry too much about making the story clear: he could expect his audience to recognize the characters and their doings, which the review in the *Age and Argus* asserted 'everyone knows, or ought to know.' This reviewer was satisfied that Stirling had 'admirably' got in all that was possible of 'the original particulars', and his fellow critics tended to agree, unworried by what to a modern reader might seem a somewhat brusque and unexplained progress through the story, omitting the American section. To the original audience one of the important successes of the piece was the staging: 'the wood, where the deed of death was done' was 'most invitingly true to nature', and of especial note was Act II Scene 7, the climax of the second act, the 'grand stage effect of...the view of London Bridge Wharf with a built steamer, and a lighter that glides along the water, and receives goods from a crane. This scene, with all the attendant bustle, is very cleverly managed.'[1] Visually, also, the costuming and make-up were highly successful, evoking the novel's plates at every turn.

These high production values backed up the other, more important strength of the piece, the acting, which all agreed was admirable. The *Era* critic noted the many acting opportunities of the play. 'Mr Stirling has very skilfully mixed his materials together, of broad farce, sprightly comedy, deep pathos, and stirring melodrame.' The weight of the melodrama fell upon Emery, playing Jonas with very little plot build-up but some big scenes in which to render his 'thorough-bred villain' 'an excellent and faithfully disgusting' reading, 'accompanied with thrilling melo-dramatic "effect"' which, after the first few nights, he brought down to a human level, and delivered 'without rant'.[2] He played against Miss Woolgar as Mercy, who made the transition 'to the drooping wife absolutely painful to contemplate. Who can survey such pictures', the *Era* continued, 'and say that there is no moral in the stage?' Wigan as Tigg, Frank Matthews as Pecksniff, and Meadows as Tom Pinch were generally admired as having walked out of the plates on to the stage, and achieved a spectrum of comic successes. Vining was understood to have done his best with Martin, who could not really be much more than a walking

---

[1] *Age and Argus*, 13 July 1844; *Family Companion*, Manchester, 13 July 1844; *Era*, 14 July 1844.
[2] *Age and Argus*, 13 July 1844.

gentleman in the plot as it came to the stage. The outstanding performances, however, were in the 'broad farce' scenes, especially those involving Bob and Mary Ann Keeley. 'Mrs Keeley's Bailey was the delight of the house. Shrewd, sly, intelligent little cockney—witty, and fully aware of the fact—knowing and assuming the innocence of a babe—the *beau ideal* of the "tiger"—the essence of premature assurance, slang, and precocious boyhood.'[3] 'Whilst his wife was flourishing away in either lodging-house livery or leathers and top-boots, her funny little helpmate had transmogrified himself into Mrs Sairey Gamp...the way in which the muzzy nurse maunders over violated friendship, and the impropriety of indulgence in strong liquors...receives a commentary of the most racy description in her mode of steadying herself by the table, and lurching against the side scene as she makes her exit, in a most delicious state of inebriation.'[4] Separately, as in Act I Scene 6, the climax of the first act, when Bailey orchestrates and comments upon the banquet at Todgers's and its culminating brawl, across a two-level set, and Act III Scene 2, Mrs Gamp's falling-out with Collier as Betsy Prig to which the reviewer refers, and also together, in a series of brief, intertheatrical vignettes, 'the two dear delightful Keeleys would have saved the piece in themselves if it had ever been in jeopardy, which it was not for a moment.'[5]

For discussion of the play as the first triumph of the Keeley management at the Lyceum see Introduction ('1843 and the Keeley Management') and for Stirling himself see the headnote to *Nicholas Nickleby* in this volume.

### THE TEXT

The text derives initially from Lord Chamberlain's Collection Add. MS 42976 ff. 516–35, which still has the letter requesting a licence from Mary Ann Keeley attached, but now only contains the first of the play's three acts. Acts II and III are therefore derived from the printed text published by Lacy, undated, with which Act I is collated to repair errors and omissions; they are designated 'MS' and 'Lacy' in the notes.

---

[3] *Age and Argus*, 13 July 1844.     [4] *Era*, 14 July 1844.     [5] *Era*, 14 July 1844.

Characters and cast of the first production

| | |
|---|---|
| Martin Chuzzlewit snr | Mr Richard Younge |
| Martin Chuzzlewit jnr | Mr Frederick Vining |
| Jonas Chuzzlewit | Mr Emery |
| Seth Pecksniff | Mr Frank Matthews |
| Tom Pinch | Mr Drinkwater Meadows |
| Tigg Montague | Mr Alfred Wigan |
| Bailey | Mrs Mary Ann Keeley |
| Nadgett | Mr Turner |
| John Westlock | |
| Mark Tapley | |
| Charity Pecksniff | Mrs Leonora Wigan |
| Mercy Pecksniff | Miss Sarah Jane Woolgar |
| Ruth Pinch | Miss Grove |
| Mary Graham | Miss Fortesque |
| Mrs Sarah Gamp | Mr Robert Keeley |
| Mrs Betsy Prig | Mr J.W. Collier |
| Mrs Todger | Mrs Woolidge |
| Mrs Lupin | Mrs Usher |
| Newsmen, Watermen, Porters | |

**5.** 'Mrs Gamp Propoges a Toast.' Etching by Phiz (Hablot K. Browne) June 1844, plate 35 in No. XVIII of *Martin Chuzzlewit*, which is indicated in the stage direction to Act III Scene 2 of the play as the setting for that scene.

# THE PROLOGUE

No ghostly legend from some mouldering page,          1
And 'carefully adapted for the stage,'
No grand romantic drama, deep and dire,
Full of 'tyerrific combat' and red fire
Boast we tonight. No flimsy plot shall trench        5
Upon our scene 'translated from the French'
But one in deep emotions far more rife
The powerful romance of common life.

We owe this story of the present hour
To that great master-hand—whose graphic power    10
Can call up laughter—bid the tear to start,
And find an echoing chord in every heart.
Whom we have learn'd to deem an household friend,
Who, 'midst his varied writings never penned
One line that might his guileless pages spot,    15
'One word that, dying, he would wish to blot.'

We know there is, around his simple name,
A prestige thrown your sympathies to claim,
But still our playwright, feeling well his task,
Has sent me forth, your clemency to ask.    20
And some old friends, selected from the rest
Of humankind, the sweetest and the best,
Crowd forth, your patient hearing to implore
Presuming on the fellowship of yore.

Good 'Mr Pickwick' first, with smiling face    25
And kindly heart, entreats your courteous grace;
Then, arm in arm, led onwards by one will,
The 'Brothers Cheeryble' endorse our bill,
And warm by kindness—ever both alike—
The timid hopes of poor neglected 'Smike';    30
Whilst not unmindful of your past kind deeds,
'Oliver Twist' next for a hearing pleads.
'Dick Swiveller,' who has crept here quite by stealth,

---

*THE PROLOGUE*: By Albert Smith, spoken on the first night by Mary Ann Keeley, and taken here from the newspaper report in the *Age and Argus*, 13 July 1844.

'Passes the Rosy' 'ere he drinks your health;
35    With all those kindred friends we know so well,
Watched over by the shade of 'Little Nell.'
Next, laughing at 'Joe Willett' in her train,
Dear 'Dolly Varden' flirts, and laughs again,
And hopes your pleasure will not be alloyed
40    Because she knows that 'Miggs' will be annoyed.
And, lastly, whilst around both cot and hall
The echoes of the 'Christmas Carol' fall,
'Bob Cratchit' on raised wages, spruce and trim,
Leads forward, with his crutch, poor 'Tiny Tim.'

45    The others are to come. In anxious state
Behind the scenes your fiat they await.
Be certain, both for your and their behoof,
They'll do the best they can. Now to the proof.

# ACT I

## SCENE 1

*A neatly furnished Parlour in* MR PECKSNIFF's *house. Fire—pictures—table—chairs— candles—work, books—*

MERCY *and* CHARITY *Discovered.* MERCY *on a stool dressing a large doll.* CHARITY *making night caps. Tea things on table—*

*Music. Wind very loud.*

CHARITY.    What in the name of Providence can detain pa so long, Mercy?    1
MERCY.    Can't guess, Cherry. Perhaps the weather—only listen to the wind—there's
a gust! whew! how it blows! what will become of our poor chimney pots!

(*The noise of a door opening and very loud knocking*)

PECKSNIFF.    (*without*) I see you!—a runaway knock. You'll catch it Sir. (*a loud slam
of the door shutting*) Murder!    5
MERCY.    That voice? My parent! (*rushes out door in flat*)
CHARITY.    (*taking a light*) Is he gone? Is he extinct? Oh, speak!

(*Exit. They re-enter supporting* PECKSNIFF *covered with mud his hat off and
manner wild*)

BOTH.    Speak Pa, even if you are dead. don't look so wild dearest Pa! (*they place him
on a chair and embrace him*)
PECKSNIFF.    (*looking round*) That'll do. I'm better.
MERCY.    (*wildly*) He speaks!    10
CHARITY.    He lives!

(*Both kissing him.* CHARITY *pours out some brandy for him*)

PECKSNIFF.    Mercy! Charity! My bright eyed pair, fetch the ham and eggs.

(MERCY *exits* R. H. CHARITY *places a large piece of brown paper and vinegar over his
forehead*)

CHARITY.    How could you fall, pa?
PECKSNIFF.    Ask Providence, how it could knock me off my legs—The wind, child,
did it, the unruly wind. (*sighs*) What's virtue to wind? Nothing. (*re-enter* MERCY 15
*with ham and eggs. They seat themselves at Table. Charity helps the tea*)
MERCY.    Ain't tea delicious Pa, such evenings as this?
PECKSNIFF.    (*eating*) Truly so!
CHARITY.    And eggs?

PECKSNIFF.    Eggs are transitory, for they come and go. Every pleasure is. We can't
20    even eat long. If we indulge in harmless fluids, we get the dropsy. If in exciting
liquids, we get drunk.

MERCY.    Not *we*, Pa.

PECKSNIFF.    I mean mankind in general. There's nothing personal in morality,
Love, we're all worms! (*sighs*) My sweet pets, you will rejoice to hear that I have
25    again been fortunate. A new inmate will soon come among us, to settle in our ark.

CHARITY.    A youth?

PECKSNIFF.    Yes. He will avail himself of the eligible opportunity which now offers,
for uniting advantages of the best practical architectural education with the comforts of a home. Together with—

30    MERCY.    Oh, pa! (*shaking her finger*) See advertisement. (*laughing*)

PECKSNIFF.    Playful, playful warbler.

MERCY.    Is he handsome?

CHARITY.    Is he rich?

MERCY.    Oh, good gracious Cherry! what a mercenary girl you are, you prudent
35    thing, you. (*they slap each other playfully*)

PECKSNIFF.    Silly house pigeons! Our pupil is well looking. As to his *worldly* gear,
I do not positively expect any immediate premium, with him. But what of that?
There is disinterestedness in the world I hope. The youth I allude to is your cousin
Martin Chuzzlewit. He will take up his residence to-morrow in this abode of inno
40    cence. Mr Pinch must meet him at Salisbury. Now tell me the domestic news since
I left.

CHARITY.    Nothing Pa, except Mrs Lupin of the Dragon called to ask your advice.
An elderly gentleman has been taken ill at her inn, he is a perfect stranger. No one
with him but a young girl, about whom there seems a mystery.

45    PECKSNIFF.    Indeed!

CHARITY.    Mrs Lupin wishes you to speak to him, for he won't let anybody approach
him. She says he appears rich.

PECKSNIFF.    Rich Eh? Poor Pilgrim. I'll watch his progress. Is John Westlock
gone? (*to* CHARITY)

50    CHARITY.    No, Pa.

PECKSNIFF.    And why not? His time expired yesterday.

CHARITY.    He slept at Mrs Lupin's last night. Mr Pinch spent the evening with him
and was not home till late.

MERCY.    And when I met him on the stairs this morning he looked such a monster—
55    his eyes as dull as if they'd been boiled and his clothes smelt so strong of smoke and
punch. (*shuddering*)

PECKSNIFF.    I think Mr Pinch might have done better, than choose for his companion
one who wounded me so deeply.

38 *I hope*: 'The Youth...I hope' omitted from Lacy.
52 CHARITY: This and the next three speeches, to Pinch's knock, omitted in Lacy.
54 MERCY: Mercy's speech deleted in MS.

CHARITY.   What can we expect from Mr Pinch?

PECKSNIFF.   Mr Pinch is a fellow creature my dear, an item in the vast sum total of   60
humanity, and we have a right to expect…

(PINCH *timidly opens the door in flat and peeps in*)

PINCH.   Only me, sir. (*very humbly*)

PECKSNIFF.   Come in! (*blandly.* PINCH *enters slowly, keeping his hand on the lock*)

PINCH.   I beg your pardon for intruding sir but… (*bowing*)

PECKSNIFF.   No intrusion—pray be seated Mr Pinch. Shut the door, if you please,   65
Mr Pinch.

PINCH.   Certainly Sir. (*he throws it open and beckons*) Mr Westlock hearing that
you were come home wishes to say good bye before he leaves for good and all, he—he
hopes to leave none but friends behind him although you have had some little
differences.   70

CHARITY *and* MERCY.   Little differences!

PECKSNIFF.   My domestic turtles! Proceed Mr Pinch.

PINCH.   Well Sir Mr Westlock wants to—to—

(*Hesitates and beckons at the door.* JOHN WESTLOCK *entering*)

WESTLOCK.   Say good bye and shake your hand. Come Mr Pecksniff don't let there
be any ill blood between us. I'm sorry I've ever given you an offence. Bear me no ill   75
will at parting.

PECKSNIFF.   I bear no ill will to any man.

PINCH.   (*joyfully*) I told you he didn't, I knew he didn't—he always says he don't.

WESTLOCK.   Then you will shake hands, Sir.

PECKSNIFF.   No, John. I have forgiven you my wrongs, but I won't shake hands.   80

WESTLOCK.   Pinch, didn't I tell you so. Here's a pretty fellow. Wrongs! Wrong I have
done him—after the five hundred pounds he had with me under false pretences
and the seventy pounds a year for board and lodging, that would have been dear at
seventeen.

PECKSNIFF.   Money, John, is the root of all evil. I grieve to see it is already bearing   85
evil fruit in you—but I forgive you in spirit—I forgive you. Go, go   (*waves his hand*)
in peace.

WESTLOCK.   Bah!

PECKSNIFF.   Savage!

MERCY.   Beast!   90

PECKSNIFF.   Come, my injured ones. our domestic hearth is rudely ploughed up.
We must suffer, but I still forgive. Oh, Thomas Pinch, oh! (*wipes his eyes*) I didn't
expect this no, no. (*Exit with his daughters*)

---

82   *under false pretences*: 'under false pretences' omitted in Lacy.

90   *Money, John… Beast*: 'Money, John' to 'Beast!' deleted in MS and omitted in Lacy.

91   *Come, my*: MS has 'ethereal' deleted before 'injured'.

WESTLOCK.    Bah! Pinch, I was right, you were wrong. (*slapping his shoulder*)
95    You haven't half devil enough in you for this Pecksniff—you haven't half—you
haven't any.

PINCH.    I must have a good deal of what you call devil, to make him so uncomfortable—how grieved he was.

WESTLOCK.    He grieved?

100    PINCH.    Yes didn't you see his tears? It's all my fault. I did it—I am an ungrateful
fellow!

WESTLOCK.    What have you to be grateful for?

PINCH.    Everything. Didn't he take me as his pupil for much less than he asked? My
poor old grandmother died happy in seeing me with such a man. I have grown up
105    in his house. I am in his confidence. I am his assistant. He allows me no salary, but
when his business improves, my prospects are to improve too.

WESTLOCK.    I believe you are one of the best fellows in the world Tom Pinch.

PINCH.    Not at all. If you only knew Pecksniff, as well as I do, you'd love him as I do.

WESTLOCK.    Poor Tom, he never scraped and clawed into his pouch your poor
110    grandmother's hard savings, dazzling her with prospects of your happiness; he
never speculated and traded on her pride in you that you should live to be a gentleman, not he.

PINCH.    No, of course not.

WESTLOCK.    Nonsense, man—you know he's a deceptive humbug.

115    (*a coach horn*) There's the coach. Good bye; give me your hand, Tom.

PINCH.    Both hands, John. (*shakes his hands*)

WESTLOCK.    I shall write to you from London. Heaven bless you, Tom—you're too
good for PECKSNIFF. (*Exit rapidly*)

PINCH.    Good bye. Mind you write my dear fellow. Stop, stop, you're going without
120    the knife I bought you for a remembrance. (*coach heard*) He's gone (*sighs*) it seems
but yesterday that he came. He's a fine fellow—a good fellow—no faults, none—
Yes—*one* only *one*—he won't love Pecksniff! (*Exits R.H.*)


# SCENE 2

*A Chamber at* MRS LUPIN's, *'The Blue Dragon.'*

*Door in flat opening inside; keyhole. Enter* MRS LUPIN *conducting* PECKSNIFF R.H.

---

96 *you haven't half—you haven't any*: MS omits 'you haven't half—you haven't any'.

105 *He allows me no salary*: Lacy substitutes 'he allows a little salary', which is nearer to the novel, which
has 'he allows me a salary' (chapter 2).

109 *WESTLOCK*: MS has this speech and the next deleted; Lacy omits them. In this case the first version
of the MS is closer to the novel.

116 *John*: MS deletes 'John' and Lacy omits it.

119 *Good bye...fellow*: MS deletes 'Good bye...fellow' and 'seems but...came' and Lacy has only 'Stop
stop!' before 'He's a fine fellow'.

MRS L.    Oh, dear me Sir! I'm so glad you've come. The poor gentleman's so bad and  1
so fractious.

PECKSNIFF.    Fractious is he, Mrs Lupin?

MRS L.    Uncommon. There must be weighty matters on his conscience, for he groans
and grumbles, makes wills, then makes a bonfire of them over the candle. I know  5
he wants proper advice, and that's why I called on you, sir. (*curtseys*)

PECKSNIFF.    (*sighs*) Mrs Lupin—

MRS L.    The young thing with him can't be able to advise, she's too much
overcome.

PECKSNIFF.    Is she very young? (MRS L. *nods*) Oh, dear me, dear me.    10

MRS L.    I'm afraid they ain't married, either, Sir.

PECKSNIFF.    Your fears are natural. I'll wait on the travellers.

MRS L.    This is the door. Shall I knock?

PECKSNIFF.    No I'll enter. (*peeps through keyhole*) The old gentleman is in bed, the
young person reading—this looks artful.    15

MRS L.    She reads nothing—but good books, poor thing.

PECKSNIFF.    Good books. Yes, yes, it's very artful—deep thing, very.

MRS L.    Since he's been ill several parties have come to the Dragon wishing to see
him, but he won't hear of anybody of the name of Chuzzlewit.

PECKSNIFF.    Chuzzlewit!    20

MRS L.    Yes, sir—that's the rich gentleman's name—Martin Chuzzlewit.

PECKSNIFF.    My venerable cousin. Let me see him—let me fold him to this sensitive
breast. I know he hates me—but he shall see me—he shall behold my affectionate
tears. He may scoff at them, and attribute them to snuff, onions, or smelling salts.
Still I will bless him for hating me. (*Exits door in flat*)    25

MRS L.    What a martyr to goodness! he's the pride of the whole village. Such a gentleman, too! he is willing to do anything for anybody when it costs him nothing, so
Mark says. (*a bell rings*) Coming! That's no. 2 again. The shabby coat and mostachios: I'm sure he'll never pay for the brandy. (*bell again*) Cuss that no. 2.
Coming! (*Exits rapidly* R.H.)    30

*Enter* MR MONTAGUE TIGG, L.H. *singing piano. For dress see work. He steps lightly,
looks round cautiously.*

TIGG.    This must be the tiger's den. Strike me ferocious! (*approaches the door*)
Yes this is the wild beast's apartment. (*noise of voices within*) What a delicious
growl!

OLD MARTIN.    (*within*) Go sir—I won't hear you—go!

TIGG.    Won't hear him? Who is the buffalo? (*peeps at keyhole*)    35

---

5 *There must be…candle*: Lacy omits 'There must be…candle'.

11 *I'm afraid…Sir*: Lacy omits this speech and Pecksniff's 'Your fears are natural', having him say instead
'Oh dear me—dear me.' Both versions derive from the novel (chapter 3).

14 *peeps through keyhole*: Lacy omits the rest of this speech, and the next two.

28 *That's no. 2 again*: Lacy omits 'The shabby coat and mostachios' and 'Cuss that no. 2'.

A sleek oily looking customer, eh! Another invader of the old boy's purse strings. (*the door opens as he is peeping, he falls.* PECKSNIFF *appears dejected, with his white handkerchief, wiping his eyes. The door is shut*)

PECKSNIFF.    You were eaves-dropping at the door, you vagabond. Where is Mrs Lupin? who are you?

40  TIGG.    The accredited agent of Chevy Slyme, esquire. Ambassador from the Court of Chiv. Ha! ha!

PECKSNIFF.    Do you know, sir, that I am the friend and relative of the sick gentleman within? his Protector, his guardian?

TIGG.    What, the cousin that lives in this place? *the* Pecksniff?

45  PECKSNIFF.    I am the Pecksniff.

TIGG.    Are you, though? Proud to know you, Sir. I'm interested, deeply interested, in the old boy's affairs. (*pointing to the door*) Read that.

(*Gives a soiled letter which he takes from his hat*)

PECKSNIFF.    This is addressed to my cousin Chevy Slyme, Esq. You are not the person.

50  TIGG.    You know Chevy! Wait a bit—I understand—you mistake—and I'm not offended Sir—if there is a man on earth whom a gentleman would feel honoured and proud to be mistaken for, that is my friend Slyme, for he is the most original, spiritual, classical, talented, disgustingly unappreciated dog. I don't know another man in the wide world I'm not equal to, but Chiv is a great many cuts above me.

55  PECKSNIFF.    I judged from this—(*holding out letter*)

TIGG.    No doubt you did. No Sir, my friend Slyme is round the corner. He is perpetually round the corner. (*placing finger on nose*) He is my adopted brother. My name is Tigg, Sir, Montague Tigg. Perhaps the name will be familiar to you in connexion with all the remarkable events of the Peninsular war. (PECKSNIFF *shakes

60  his head*) No? No matter. You are Slyme's relation—relations never did agree. He expects, or hopes for something from the venerable miser, there, for whose demise he's waiting round the corner. This brought *us* here; being here, I act upon my own responsibility. When I ask a man of your undoubted talent for the loan of a crown piece, don't look surprised—it's the queer state of existence one finds oneself forced

65  into. Well never mind, moralize as we will the world goes on. As Hamlet says. Hercules may lay about him with his club, but he can't prevent the cats from making a most intolerable row on the roofs of the houses, or the dogs from being shot in the hot weather, if they run about the streets unmuzzled. Life's a riddle, a most infernal hard riddle to guess Mr Pecksnuff, sniff I mean! I beg pardon—

70  PECK.    Sir!

46 *deeply interested*: Lacy omits 'deeply interested'.

55 *I judged from this*: Lacy substitutes 'Sir, I…' and starts the next speech at 'My name is Tigg'.

62 *for whose…corner*: MS deletes 'for whose…corner', Lacy omits it and also omits a large section, down to 'Nothing can be done.'

69 *guess*: MS deletes the rest of the speech, Pecksniff's response and 'I can't stand…nephew'.

TIGG.    I can't stand by and see you and Chiv cutting each other's throats when there's
nothing to be got by it, you're the cousin and my friend's the nephew. Nothing can
be done with the old tiger I give you my brightest honour, I've been ever since nine
o'clock this morning looking through that keyhole, waiting for an answer to a most
gentlemanly application for the loan of £15, on my personal security—*mine*, sir—  75
and no reply.

PECKSNIFF.    Mr Chuzzlewit has an undoubted right to regulate his own proceedings Sir. Good evening.

TIGG.    All the Chuzzlewits are here. The sour crout Anthony and his very nice son
Jonas, and half a dozen women—all on the scent for the old boy's money.          80

PECKSNIFF.    Oh, Mammon! Mammon!

TIGG.    Everybody feels interested about his health. The whole family's pouring into
the place. The time is come for Union against the common enemy. The common
enemy is the whole family; unite with Chiv and drive them from their game, then
bag it yourself, bowl away on your own accounts at the testator's wicket—think of  85
it—you'll find us in the Seven Stars, in the village. Have you five shillings, Eh?
(*a pause*) five shillings. To be punctually paid next week. You're not in want of
change, are you, Sir?

PECKSNIFF.    No, thank you. (*going*)

TIGG.    (*following*) If you had been I'd have got it for you. (*whistles and walks after*  90
PECKSNIFF) Perhaps you'd rather not lend Chiv five shillings?

PECKSNIFF.    Much rather not.

TIGG.    Perhaps you're right—will you lend *me* five shillings?

PECKSNIFF.    I couldn't do it!

TIGG.    Not even half a crown perhaps?                                            95

PECKSNIFF.    Not even half a crown.

TIGG.    (*laughing*) Why, then we are come to the ridiculously small amount of eighteen pence. Ha, ha!

PECKSNIFF.    And that would be equally objectionable. (*Exits*)

TIGG.    Pon my life that ain't so bad! Not lend eighteen pence? Pon my soul it's the  100
queerest thing—just like the celebrated conundrum, Why's a man in jail like a man
out of jail? There's no answer to it—none (*Exits laughing*)—none—dem it!


# SCENE 3

*A Cross Country Lane leading to the high road. A finger post in the centre of Stage.* TOM
PINCH *discovered seated on a wheelbarrow full of boxes, bags, hat boxes, &c.*

PINCH.    (*wiping his face*) It is rather warm—but what of it—the barrow's here in  1
time for the coach, who'd ever have guessed that Mr Pecksniff and the two young

86 *Everybody...in the village*: Lacy omits 'Everybody...in the village.'

1 *it*: Lacy has 'that?' for 'it'.

ladies—were going to London—for a whole week too—(*taking letter from his pocket*) Mr Pecksniff promised to deliver this to my sister Ruth—bless her—ah,
5  he's a good man! I'm sure I must have been born with a silver spoon in my mouth to come across him—and what a clever dashing youth his cousin is, our new pupil—so clever that he could cut his way through the world as it were cheese— how affable he is to me—he's coming down the lane—walking just as if the lane belonged to him—

*Enter* MARTIN—*down the lane—he appears dull—without noticing* PINCH *he leans against the fingerpost.*

10  PINCH.    What's the matter?
MARTIN.    I'm out of spirits—vexed—annoyed. I'll talk openly to you—for you're a good fellow Pinch, and I like you—
PINCH.    Thank you.
MARTIN.    To be brief—I've been bred up with great expectations of riches by an old
15  grandfather—a selfish, self willed man, whom I had an affection for, and bore a great deal—we often quarrelled, once fatally—the reason you see me here a disin- herited man, is because I presumed to fall in love without his consent—that's the cream of the story.
PINCH.    The cream—why love's the *milk* of human kindness.
20  MARTIN.    I say I'm in love—with the best—the loveliest girl the sun ever shone upon. But she is entirely dependant on the pleasure of my grandfather—when he first discovered our affection for each other he accused me of endeavouring to cor- rupt her—my Mary! I was enraged and told him I would not be knocked down by him in marriage to the highest bidder—for he wished to dispose of my hand like an
25  auctioneer—he stormed—I resisted—and he turned me out of doors—left penni- less I wrote to Pecksniff, offered my services—and here I am.

(*Sits on boxes—one of them, a bandbox, breaks*)

PINCH.    Oh, gracious me—it's Miss Charity's best bonnet. (*takes bonnet out crushed*) Here's a horrid ship-wreck—what's to be done with it—(*tries to put it into shape— places it on his head.* MARTIN *laughs*)
PINCH.    Don't laugh—think of the beautiful silk. (*replaces it in box*)

(MARK TAPLEY *is heard singing without 'When we're young, etc.'*)

30  PINCH.    Good bye, Mark. Pleasant walk to you. I'm sorry you will leave the Dragon, though you do say it's too jolly for you—goodbye—(MARTIN *is sitting very thought- ful on the boxes*) Poor fellow—he's melancholy—(*touching his shoulder*) Cheer up a bit—laugh, if it's only a smile—can I help you?
MARTIN.    You might as well be a toasting fork or a frying pan, for any help you can
35  render me. (*sits by him*)

---

29.1 'When we're young, etc.': Mark's song might be 'Oh the merry days when we were young', words by Miss F. Byron and music by the popular composer Edward Loder, which was being advertised as 'new' in 1837.

(MR TIGG *enters singing down the lane—swinging his cane jauntily. They don't observe him*)

TIGG.    (*seeing them—aside*) Two precious babes in the wood! How do you do—(*bowing*) 'Pon my soul, I'm grateful to my friend Pecksniff for helping me to the contemplation of such a delicious picture—(*eyeing them with his glass*) you remind me of Whittington, thrice lord mayor of London—You are in fact a pair of Whittingtons without the cat—my name is Tigg—the Tigg—you are Pinch—and I    40 respect you—if I don't grind me. (*takes* TOM's *hand*)

PINCH.    I'm obliged to you, sir.

TIGG.    Not at all—I'm come for the letter Pecksniff left for Chevy Slyme Esq.

PINCH.    He didn't leave one with me sir—he's not gone yet.

TIGG.    (*aside*) I'm sorry for it. (*whispers to* TOM) It's the money he gave you for me—    45

PINCH.    What money?

TIGG.    For a bill, a paltry bill. Chevy is positively detained at the Blue Dragon, a low-minded, clod-hopping ale house in the village, for his bill. You have heard of Fox's Book of Martyrs, but you never heard of such cruelty as this. Locked up for his Bill!    50

PINCH.    I'm very sorry, I'm sure.

TIGG.    To be sure you are. Locked up for a low performance on a slate, or chalked on the back of a door. There's a screw of such magnitude loose somewhere, that the whole framework of society is shaken.

MARTIN.    What is the amount, sir?    55

TIGG.    Three pund five. Extraordinary low, ain't it?

MARTIN.    (*to* PINCH) This Slyme is a relation of mine—I don't want him here just now. Have you money enough to pay the bill?

PINCH.    No, bless you!

MARTIN.    If we told Mrs Lupin, we'd see it paid, it would answer the same    60 purpose?

TIGG.    (*taking his hand*) Sir you're a trump—you're both trumps. A handful of trumps—it's not the temporary assistance you're going to offer—it's not the 3 pund 5, no, but it's the vindication of the high principle that Nature's Nobs feel with Nature's Nobs. (*shaking their hands*)    65

PINCH.    Mr Pecksniff, and the ladies, are coming down the lane.

TIGG.    Then I'm going *up* it.—Don't forget the 'Blue Dragon.' (*to* TOM, *aside*) Oh! if you could have seen me in Africa at the head of my regiment, charging in a hollow square, with the women, children, and plate chest, in the centre, you wouldn't think me the same man. But to all men I've a right to make an appeal on Chevy's behalf;    70 and so sir I ask the loan of 3 half crowns to be returned post paid in a week.

(PINCH *draws out a little purse in which is a sovereign.* TIGG *seeing it*)

---

49 *You have heard…as this*: Lacy omits 'You have heard…as this'.

52 *you*: Lacy ends the speech here, and MS deletes the sentence 'There's a screw…shaken.'

TIGG.   Stay perhaps for the better convenience of posting make it gold.
(*takes sovereign*) Thank you, a general direction I suppose Mr Pinch at Mr Pecksniff's
will find you. We said this week to be repaid.

75  PINCH.   Monday will do.

TIGG.   Monday will not do. Saturday is the last day stipulated. Adieu. (*writes the
date in pocket book*) Don't forget the 3 pund 5. (*Exits singing*)

MARTIN.   I see Pecksniff and my cousins coming. Don't say you saw me. I wish for
no leave taking; besides, Mary is waiting for me. Not a word. (*Exits as* PECKSNIFF,
MERCY *and* CHARITY *on his arm, enter down the lane*)

80  PECKSNIFF.   Before I quit our peaceful ark on this professional visit to London,
I wish you to understand we leave you in charge of everything. All is *free* and open.
Unlike the young man trusted by his Master in the Eastern tale, who is described as
a one-eyed almanac if I'm not mistaken Mr Pinch.

PINCH.   A one-eyed Calender, sir.

85  PECKSNIFF.   It's all the same. Be jovial but don't neglect your architectural pursuits.
Suppose you give me your idea of a monument to a Lord Mayor of London or a low
house to be erected in a Gentleman's Park. (*a distant horn*) Give this letter to
Mr Martin immediately. (*gives letter*)

PINCH.   The coach is coming sir.

90  PECKSNIFF.   Ah what are we all but coaches? Some of us are slow coaches.

CHARITY.   Goodness, Pa!

PECKSNIFF.   Some of us slow, some fast coaches, our passions are the horses, and
rampant animals, too.

MERCY.   Really, Pa, how very unpleasant!

95  PECKSNIFF.   And rampant animals too, and virtue is the drag. We start from the
Mother's Arms, and we run to the Dust Shovel. (*at this moment a coach and four or
pair, loaded with passengers stops at the end of the lane. Horn blowing. Music*)

GUARD.   Now sir. (CHARITY *and* MERCY *are handed in,* TOM, *hurrying the wheel-
barrow on, runs against* PECKSNIFF. *He falls with all the trunks over him. The
Passengers laugh.* MERCY *and* CHARITY *scream.* GUARD *helps him up,* TOM *throws
up boxes. The coach drives off, horn playing, as the Scene is closed in on Picture*)


# SCENE 4

*Tableau: A park. Enter* MARTIN *and* MARY, MARTIN's *arm round her waist.*

1  MARY.   My dear Martin.

---

83  *if... Mr Pinch*: MS deletes and Lacy omits 'if I'm not mistaken Mr Pinch'.
87  *Suppose... Park*: MS deletes and Lacy omits 'Suppose... Park'.

0.1  *Tableau... waist*: The stage picture derives from the plate in part 7, chapter 14, entitled 'Mr Tapley
succeeds in finding a "jolly" subject for contemplation', which shows Martin and Mary in the park, his arm
round her waist, he reading her the letter he has written to Tom Pinch (see Hatton & Cleaver, 196).

MARTIN.    My dear Mary, if you have changed at all, my love, since we parted, it is
only to be more beautiful than ever.

MARY.    You look more anxious and more thoughtful than you used Martin?

MARTIN.    It would be strange if I did not; my life, since I left my grandfather's, has 5
been a hard one.

MARY.    It must have been—you have paid a dear price for a poor heart, Martin; but
it is your own, and a true one.

MARTIN.    Of course.—I feel certain of that.—Now, I am about to break a design to
you, dearest, which will startle you—I am not happy with Pecksniff—he is a hypo- 10
crite, can teach me nothing; I will go abroad.

MARY.    Abroad!

MARTIN.    Only to America. See how you droop directly.

MARY.    I would not venture to dissuade you—but it is a long, long distance,—there
is a wide ocean to cross—illness and want are sad calamities in any place, but in a 15
foreign country, dreadful to endure.

MARTIN.    What am I to do? Come, come, do not hang your head down love; for
I need encouragement, that your sweet face alone can give me. Why that's well—
now you are brave again. (*kisses her*) Now I can tell you all my plans, cheerfully, as
if you were my little wife already Mary—You see grandfather will ever relent, when 20
I am gone—

MARY.    Gone!

MARTIN.    Yes—Come (*holds up his finger*) a friend of mine—a fellow clerk of
Pecksniff's, Tom Pinch—a poor, strange, simple oddity, full of zeal and honesty—
quite an infant; I shall commit you to his care during my absence—he will receive 25
all your letters and forward you all mine—he knows all about us—I have told him
our history—I call him my dear Tom Pinch because it pleases him.

MARY.    Very right, and very kind.

MARTIN.    Does my grandfather ever speak of me?

MARY.    Never—Since your separation that I was the unhappy cause of—he has 30
never once uttered your name, but he has never abated in his kindness to me.

MARTIN.    I thank him for that last act—I neither expect nor desire that he'll mention my name again—he may once, to couple it with reproach, in his will—let
him—by the time it reaches me he will be in his grave.

MARY.    Martin—if you would but sometimes, in some quiet hour, beside the winter 35
fire—in the summer air—when you hear gentle music—or think of death—or
home—or childhood—if you would at such a season, think of him—or any one
who ever wronged you, you would forgive him in your breast, I know.

MARTIN.    I was not born to be the toy, and puppet of any man, far less him to whom
my whole youth was sacrificed.                                                            40

(*Enter* TOM PINCH *with a letter*)

32 *act*: Lacy omits the rest of this speech, and the next two, going straight to Pinch's entrance.

PINCH.    Here's a letter Mr Pecksniff desired me to give you—I knew I should find you here.

MARTIN.    For me! (*taking it*) My love—my friend, Mr Pinch. Tom—this is the fair girl who used to listen to your organ playing. (MARY *offers her hand.* TOM *takes it awkwardly*)

45  PINCH.    You love music, Miss?

MARY.    Devotedly! And you were the organist?

MARTIN.    (*violently agitated*) I knew he was a villain! Scoundrel! (*reading letter*)

PINCH *and* MARY.    Who?

MARTIN.    Who! Why your Idol—Pecksniff—He has dared to order me from his

50  house calls me an impostor, and mourns over my corruption.

MARY.    What is it, dear Martin?

MARTIN.    Oh—nothing. More persecution—my grandfather has seen this oily rascal and he upon his advice turns me out of doors—absolutely out of doors! (*reads*) 'Go forth serpent from the flow'ry path of Purity and Peace go forth—like all who

55  know you, I renounce you!' (*tears the letter up*) Renounce me! Oh! If he were here! a lying fawning servile hound! *He* renounce me!

MARY.    Dear Martin—

MARTIN.    I *must* go now to America—you would not have me starve—or hold horses in the street to earn my roll of bread? Would you?—There don't fret—Pinch

60  will see you home. (*kisses her*) Heaven bless you! I will write to you from New York—I will go at once.

PINCH.    Going!—Across the sea. In this bad weather—on foot—without your clothes—without money?

MARTIN.    Yes—to America.

65  PINCH.    No—no—don't go there!

MARTIN.    My mind is made up. Good bye Tom! bless you, Mary! Tom—watch over her—(*shakes his hand, kisses* MARY *and hurries off*)

MARY.    (*faintly*) Dear—(*sobs*)

PINCH.    Stop, stop—take this. (*pulls out his little purse, throws it after* MARTIN; *sees*

70  MARY *almost fainting; runs to her*) Oh dear don't Miss pray come back Mr Martin, she's very bad, and (*she faints in his arms*) I don't know what to do with her! (*bears her off gently. Music*).

43  *taking it*: MS has 'It's Pecksniff's hand' deleted here.
56  *hound*: MS has 'Mark me, Pinch; the day will come!' deleted here.
59  *or hold…bread*: MS deletes and Lacy omits 'or hold…bread?'
69  *take this*: MS deletes and Lacy omits 'take this' and the business with the purse.
71  *arms*: MS has a deleted exclamation of 'Oh Mercy' here.

# SCENE 5

*A Chamber in the Boarding House of* MRS TODGERS.

*Enter* MRS TODGERS, MERCY, *and* CHARITY, *dressed very gay.*

MRS T.    I hope my sweet loves that you have been perfectly happy since you have   1
been in my establishment. I devotedly hope so for your dear Pa's sake. He is an old
a very old acquaintance of mine. (*sighs*) Your Pa was once a little particular in his
attentions to me loves. But to be your *Ma* was too much happiness for me. That
wretch Todgers snapped the link and ran away with me in a cab.                5
CHARITY.    Dear Mrs Todgers!
MRS T.    (*wiping her eyes*) Yes. And after we were married, only a month—he unlawfully
ran away from his happiness, and established himself as a bachelor in foreign parts.
MERCY.    Wretch!
MRS T.    And I sunk down into a boarding house for commercial gents, and it's kill-   10
ing me—the gravy kills me—the anxiety of that one item is intense—the amount of
gravy the commercials expect each day at dinner, no one would believe it. I must
run down stairs, and look to the supper—I would not have anything wrong—on
such a festive occasion—Mr Jenkins would go mad. Ah, you little Venuses—you've
turned all my poor boarders' heads—you have, just like me, before that ravaging   15
Todgers crushed my hopes. (*Exits*)
CHARITY.    Well—this *is* living in London at last! Mercy—invited to supper by all
the gents—how pleasant!
MERCY.    Delicious! We only want—I beg pardon—*you* only want Mr Jonas
Chuzzlewit—your devoted admirer to complete your happiness.                  20
CHARITY.    Well I am sure Miss—you need not sneer at Mr Jonas, though he be your
cousin—the grapes are sour!
MERCY.    Oh, the creature! Don't be offended Cherry love, you may keep him all to
yourself—I give up my share. (*laughs*)

(*Enter* MR BAILEY JUNIOR—*a dirty errand boy, in clothes too large for him—he
appears, winks, and grins at the ladies*)

BAILEY.    There you are! (*sniffs*) An't it nice? It's a-cooking—rather a spicy sort, too.   25
CHARITY.    Will the supper be long Bailey?
BAILEY.    No—When I com'd up—Missus was dodging about the dish for the tender
pieces with a fork, and eatin'—there'll be soup, she's makin' it now—ain't she puttin'
in the water—oh, not at all neither. (*laughs*)
MERCY.    What!                                                              30
BAILEY.    There's fowls, too—not skinny ones, Oh, no. (*putting his fingers to his nose*)
There's a fish just come—(*makes a wry face*) Don't eat none of him, I say. I shan't stay

---

6 *CHARITY*: MS deletes and Lacy omits this speech and the next.
12 *believe it*: MS has a deleted interjection of 'Yes' from Charity here.

here much longer—to be kept short and 'sulted—the chaps calls me Old Bailey and
Top-boots—it's too much for the wages. I'll go into the army.

35 MERCY.    Into the army! (*laughs*)

BAILEY.    Oh! Why not? There's many drummers in the Tower—don't their country
walley 'em, mind?—Oh not at all, neither.

CHARITY.    You'll be shot.

BAILEY.    What if I am? There's something gamey in it—ain't there—I'd sooner be hit

40 with a cannon-ball nor a rolling pin, and she's always a catching up something o'
that sort and chucking it at me, when the gentlemen's appetites is good—I won't
stop—no. So whatever you means to give me you'd better give it all at once—because
if ever you come back I shan't be here—and as to the other boy he won't deserve
nothing—*I* know.

(*Re-enter* MRS TODGERS *over-hearing him*)

45 MRS T.    Oh, you little villain—you bad, false boy—(*slapping his head*)

BAILEY.    No worse than yourself, come now. Do that again, will you.

MRS T.    He is a most dreadful child—the gentlemen spoil him. I'm sure nothing but
hanging will do him good.

BAILEY.    Won't it? Oh—yes—what do you go a lowerin' the table for then, and

50 destroyin' my constitution? (*going*)

MRS T.    Go down stairs, you vicious boy—(*pushing him*) Go, do you hear? Go along—

BAILEY.    Well, an't I goin' (*half crying*) you know you grudges the wittles, and steals
all the best bits yourself (*Exits sulkily*) you does.

MRS T.    Don't mind that little rascal, loves—supper will be served in a minute or

55 two. Your Pa is taking a glass of grog with the gents below—go into the drawing
room. I'll join you immediately, sweet loves. (MERCY *and* CHARITY *exiting*) Stuck
up minxes, ignorant as hay stacks, too.

(*Enter* PECKSNIFF, *rather elevated, smiling blandly*)

MRS T.    Well, Mr Pecksniff, how have my gentlemen used you down stairs?

PECKSNIFF.    (*hesitating*) Their conduct has been such my dear Madam as I can

60 never remember it without a tear. Oh Todgers. (*taking her hand. Weeps*)

MRS T.    My goodness! how low you are in spirits.

PECKSNIFF.    I am a man, Madam, also a father, also a widower. My feelings, Mrs
Podgers—

MRS T.    Todgers.

65 PECKSNIFF.    —Todgers, will not consent to be entirely smothered, like the young
children in the Tower. (*sighs*) She was beautiful—she had a small property...my
departed Sally—Oh! Todgers! (*leans on her arm*)

MRS T.    Are you ill, sir?

PECKSNIFF.    (*smiling*) Chronic. It is carrying me to my grave—

---

62 *I am...widower*: MS deletes and Lacy omits 'I am...widower.'
64 MRS T: MS omits her interjection.

MRS T.    Heaven forbid!                                                                    70
PECKSNIFF.    It is. I'm rather glad of it. You are like *her*, Mrs Codgers.
MRS T.    Don't squeeze me so tight—if any of the gentlemen should come in.
PECKSNIFF.    For *her* sake, permit me to squeeze you. For the sake of a voice from
     the tomb. Oh! heavenly Todgers. Give me your other hand.
MRS T.    La Mr Pecksniff, pray don't. I can't—I don't like—                                 75
PECKSNIFF.    Has a voice from the grave no influence? Take pity dear creature.
     (*attempts to kiss her*)
MRS T.    Really you mustn't. Hush!
PECKSNIFF.    It's not me it's the voice, *her* voice I am lonely in the world. What
     am I?
MRS T.    An excellent gentleman.                                                            80
PECKSNIFF.    Am I? The happiness of others is my chief object. My pupils. I dote on
     'em. They dote upon *me* too, *sometimes*. Do you know any parent or guardian who
     wishes to place his boy, one with three or four hundred pounds? An orphan would
     be preferred.
MRS T.    (*shaking her head*) I wish I did.                                                  85
PECKSNIFF.    So do I, oh Mrs T—let's have a drop of something to drink. Chronic!
     chronic again. Kiss me! You're so like *her*—Sally's voice from the grave cries out kiss
     her. (*he attempts to embrace her. She retreats. He catches her, and is kissing her, when*
     BAILEY *re-enters. Seeing them sets up a loud laugh. Picture*)
BAILEY.    Oh, Crikey! ain't you a going it, neither? Oh, no. (*laughs*)
MRS T.    Mr Pecksniff—sir!                                                                   90
PECKSNIFF.    Chronic again, chronic. (*sighs*)
MRS T.    What is it, you little imp?
BAILEY.    The wittles is up.
MRS T.    Come Sir. Supper waits. (*leading* PECKSNIFF *out*)
PECKSNIFF.    Oh Sally, if you could but get up and see my wretchedness and then go          95
     back again. (*Exits sighing*)
BAILEY.    (*grimacing at them*) Here's a lark! Won't I tell 'em all? Oh, no, not at all nei-
     ther. What a go this supper is—the best I ever seed here. The lodgers pays for it
     though. Ketch missus giving a treat—oh, no! Lots of everything—Dozens of
     oranges. this is one of 'em. (*sucks one*) Soup plates full of nuts. Pounds of raisins.     100
     Quarts of almonds. (*a bell rings*) That's for the smashed taters. (*sucks orange. Bell
     again*) That's for me.
MRS T.    (*without*) Are the potatoes coming up, Adolphus?
BAILEY.    How should I know? She always calls me 'Dolphus, in the Parlor and nasty
     little wiper in the kitchen. (*Exits*)                                                   105


73  *squeeze you*: MS corrects to this version, which Lacy also has, deleting 'in honour of her memory'.
79  *What am I*: Lacy omits 'What am I?' and the next two speeches, resuming at 'let's have a drop'.
88.1  *he attempts…Picture*: Dickens does not have Pecksniff attempt the kiss, so the tableau is not one
taken from the plates.

## SCENE 6

*The drawing room and landing place leading to the bed chambers in Todgers's Establishment—a divided Scene—occupying all the stage. The drawing room the lower part. Side doors R. & L. a long table prepared for supper. Fowls, fish, tarts, punch, &c. Chairs—lights. The upper part over the drawing room is a landing place extending across the stage. Three doors communicating with it. When the Scene opens* MR JENKINS *at the head of the table,* MR GANDER, MR MOBBLE, THE SPORTING GENTLEMAN, BOARDERS—PECKSNIFF, MERCY, CHARITY, *and* MRS TODGERS *discovered, all seated at supper.*

1  OMNES.    Hear, hear. Bravo, Jenks!

JENKS.    Every thing is up to the mark, and true to time. We'll show the world Todgers' can do it, when it chooses.

OMNES.    Bravo, Bravo.

5  MOBBLE.    (*faintly*) Bravo. (BAILEY *brings in dishes of potatoes in each hand. He drops one*)

MRS T.    (*screaming*) The viper has spoiled my best set.

BAILEY.    I didn't go to do it! (*aside*) That was for larriping me  (*all eat*) I say—Mrs Todgers.

JENKS.    (*to* MERCY) Pickles, miss?

10  MERCY.    Thank you, sir.

PECKSNIFF.    (*eating and talking*) Oh if defunct Sarah could see me now. (*To* MRS TODGERS *who is opposite him*)

MOBBLE.    (*in a gentle voice*) I'll take some—

JENKS.    (*helping* GANDER) Goose! Gander?

OMNES.    Capital. Ha, ha!

15  BAILEY.    Oh, lor. (*very loud laughing.* MRS T. *looks at him, he suddenly stops*)

MRS T.    Adolphus! (*sternly*)

BAILEY.    (*aside places a corkscrew to his nose playfully*)

JENKS.    A glass of wine, Miss Charity—

CHARITY.    With pleasure, sir. (*they drink*)

PECKSNIFF.    Mrs Todgers, I'll join you. (*sighs*) I wish I could for ever. (*drinks*) Oh!

20  GANDER.    May I take wine with *you* Miss? (*to* MERCY) have mercy—

OMNES.    Bravo. Gander's last. (*laughing*)

BAILEY.    Ha, ha! (*he is laughing, and coughs*)

JENKS.    Collars! (*reprovingly*) Mr Pecksniff happy to take wine with you, Sir.

PECKSNIFF.    Mr Jenkins you're a noble minded man overflowing with milk

25  (*hiccups*) of human k'd…

MERCY.    Kindness, Pa. (*whispering to him*)

MRS T.    (*to* CHARITY) Your Pa's poorly, we'd better retire. (*they rise, curtsey, and exit arm in arm.* MOBBLES *attempts to open the door but is thrust aside by* GANDER)

JENKS.    Now, gentlemen—

OMNES.    Hear, hear.

JENKS.   Let us drink 'The Ladies.'                                    30
BAILEY.   Oh, crikey—they're going to drink the ladies—ha, ha!
OMNES.   The ladies. (*loud applause*—BAILEY *helps himself to a beer bottle*)
JENKS.   Our rugged natures have been softened by the presence of lovely Woman.
The fountain of their existence is before us. Gentlemen I give you his health the
health of Mr Pecksniff.                                                35
OMNES.   (*applause.* THE LADIES *are seen with candles going into the rooms on the
Landing R & C, after kissing each other*)
MOBBLE.   I rise to—
GANDER.   Sit down.
PECKSNIFF.   (*rises with difficulty wipes his eyes*)
JENKS.   Order, hear, bravo!
BAILEY.   Bravo! Go it! Hurray!—Never say die!
PECKSNIFF.   (*hiccuping*) Gentlemen—brothers—we're all of one family. (*hear,*  40
*hear*) This auspicious moment is by many degrees the happiest of my life. Shall I,
can I, ever forget this night? Can I forget Todgers and her noble inmates? When I
look upon you beloved objects, can I ever forget Gander? (*hear, hear*) my feelings
of a, a—Mother (*hiccups*) and a father. For I'm both, gentlemen, to my doves. Since
sainted Sally flew away. (*wipes his eyes. Hear, hear.* BAILEY *grinds an imaginary*  45
*coffee mill at this. Picture*)
PECKSNIFF.   I—I—(*hiccups*) want words to express my bursting feelings I'm I'm—
(*sobs, falls on the floor*)
BAILEY.   Down! (*runs to him; all the guests surround him*)
JENKS.   Mr Pecksniff—Sir! (*shaking him.* GANDER *pulls his cravat off*)
PECKSNIFF.   Don't weep for me. (*hiccups*) It's chronic, chronic.
OMNES.   Pull off his coat.                                            50
MOBBLE.   He's dying.
BAILEY.   He's tossicated. (*laughs*) Oh no not at all.
JENKS.   Take him to bed.
PECKSNIFF.   To bed. Bed! (*hiccup, sings drawlingly*) 'Tis the voice of the Sluggard I
hear him complain, You have woke me too soon, I must slumber again'.      55
BAILEY.   (*laughs*)
JENKS.   Carry him up. Bailey, you watch him to sleep.

(TWO GENTS *carry* PECKSNIFF *off, R.H. door*)

PECKSNIFF.   Let us be moral! Hic, Oh, Sarah! Todgers! Another glass. It's all
chronic. (*talking as they carry him off*)
BAILEY.   I don't lose my supper tho' (*taking a plate full*) I know what's o'clock! (*Exits
after him*)

43 *This auspicious … Gander*: Lacy omits 'This auspicious … Gander'.
45.1 BAILEY … *Picture*: The novel has no Phiz plate for this scene, so the tableau is again of Stirling's
invention. Bailey's coffee-grinding gesture seems to mean tedious persistence, in 1840s cant.
47 *Down!*: Bailey's exclamation is drawn from the prize-ring, where it would have stopped the fight
when one man fell.

60 JENKS.    Pecksniff's a jolly dog, one of the right sort. (*they all join in chorus*)

> All hail to the vessel of Pecksniff the Sire
> And favouring breezes to fan
> While suitors flock round it and proudly admire
> The Architect, Artist and Man!

65 OMNES.    Huzza!

(PECKSNIFF *is carried by the* GENTS *across the landing to centre door preceded by* BAILEY *with a light. He sits at door eating his supper.* GENTS *having placed* PECKSNIFF *in his chamber, return. All this is done during the Chorus*)

PECKSNIFF.    (*opens the door, and shows his head in his night-cap. All are drinking below*) If you know a young orphan, with two or three hundred a year—hic—

BAILEY.    (*trying to push him in*) Go in will yer? What a guy! go in.

PECKSNIFF.    Where's Jenkins? I'm too tender, too *soft*—

BAILEY.    A precious deal. Go to sleep! (*pushing him in*)

70 PECKSNIFF.    I pine for Todgers (*reappearing*) hic. Another glass. Can you dance my pretty page? (*dances on landing*)

BAILEY.    Come, none of that 'ere—I ain't no pretty page. Ulloa! Mister Peck Snuff, Ulloa. (*clings to him. All laugh below at* MOBBLE)

MOBBLE.    (*starting up*) You're a villain Jenkins. (*throwing a plate at him. All start up.* JENKINS *throws oranges at him, and at each person who interferes. They strike each other. All talk loudly*)

75 BAILEY.    He'll tumble over the bannisters. Ullo, Missus! Murder—I can't hold him—Murder—Murder! (*screams heard in rooms R. & L. The doors open,* MERCY *and* CHARITY *appear with lights, in their night-caps.* MRS TODGERS *rushes out with a bald head and in her night gown.* PECKSNIFF *rushes to her, and embraces her. She screams violently.* BAILEY *laughs, & claps his hands—Two or three* GENTS *run on the landing with candles.* MOBBLE *is knocked down, below. General Picture. Music*)

End of Act

---

64 *All…Man*: Lacy omits the chorus.

73 *clings to him*: Lacy omits the sd 'clings to him', modifying the suggestiveness of Bailey (played by Mary Ann Keeley) wrestling with an amorous Pecksniff.

# ACT II

## SCENE 1

*A Parlour at* PECKSNIFF'S.

MR JONAS CHUZZLEWIT, *R.H. and* PECKSNIFF, L.H. *in mourning, discovered drinking wine.* JONAS *smoothing his hat band. A cane and gloves on table.*

JONAS.    Pecksniff, what do you mean to give your daughters when they marry?    1
PECKSNIFF.    What a very singular enquiry, dear Jonas!
JONAS.    Never you mind whether it's singular or plural—answer or let it alone. (*sulkily*) How much will you give 'em—come!
PECKSNIFF.    Four thousand each—but I shall sadly pinch and cramp myself.    5
JONAS.    Well, then, I'll marry the young 'un, though she has led me a nice life.
PECKSNIFF.    Jonas, Jonas—the dearest wish of my heart is now fulfilled! (*clasping both his hands, and weeping*)
JONAS.    I'm glad to hear it. That'll do. I say, you must come down with another thousand—make it five, and keep the old 'un, the treasure, to yourself. (*laughs and drinks*)
PECKSNIFF.    What a blessed hour this is! If your dear departed father, Anthony,    10 had but—
JONAS.    (*drops his glass, and starts up, wildly*) Drop that, Pecksniff, do you hear? Drop it now, and for ever—you had better. You an't going to crow over me, because I feared to look on him after death—because I didn't like dead company—
PECKSNIFF.    Forgive me—I forgot it was a tender string.    15
JONAS.    Don't talk to me about tender strings—I won't have it! I advise you not to revive the subject to me, or any one else. (*wipes his forehead*) I'll go to the gals, and tell 'em who I've fixed on. Mind—not a word of him again! (*Exit R.H.*)
PECKSNIFF.    Filial boy! such affection I never saw. A funeral that cost two hundred pounds—unlimited expense! (*drinks*) The sun shines mildly on my roof. My long    20 estranged cousin, Martin Chuzzlewit, Senior, comes with his fair companion to nestle in the bosom of my humble family. The children are retiring. I'll leave them to their innocent prattle. It's a hard thing to part with one's chickens—but Nature demands it, and I submit.

(*Exit 2 E.L.H.* JONAS *re-enters, with* MERCY *and* CHARITY, *R.H.*)

JONAS.    Sit down—(*pushes sofa to them*)—I want to talk to you.    25
MERCY.    Talk to us, griffin?
JONAS.    What, you're as lively as ever, eh? Oh, you're a wicked one! (*touches her hand*)
MERCY.    There, go along—(*going*)

JONAS.    Hollo! don't go.

30  MERCY.    Oh, I dare say you've very anxious I should stay, fright, an't you?

(JONAS *seizes her by the waist*)

CHARITY.    Upon my word, Merry, I wonder at your absurdity.

MERCY.    Thank you, my sweet—much obliged to it for its advice. Leave me alone, monster.

JONAS.    (*pulls her on sofa, and clasps both their waists*) Now, then, I've got both arms
35   full. (*to* MERCY) I don't mind pinching a bit.

MERCY.    Pinch him for me, Cherry—I do so hate him!

JONAS.    No, no—I want to have some sober talk, to prevent mistakes.
     (*to* CHARITY) She'll not believe what I am going to say, will she, cousin?

CHARITY.    Really I can't tell. What is it?

40  JONAS.    Why, you see—I know she'll make game of me—but you know what pains
     I took to get into her company in London—I always asked you about her, didn't I
     cousin—so I don't mind speaking before you. Cousin Merry, will you have me for
     a husband?

CHARITY.    (*starting up*) A what, you wretch? after all your attentions to me! (*slaps
     his face*)

45  MERCY.    Let me go, fright! (*slaps his face on the other side*) I won't have you—let
     me go—

JONAS.    Say yes—then I will.

MERCY.    If ever I did, it should only be that I might hate and tease you.

JONAS.    It's a bargain. We're a pair, if ever there was one!

50  CHARITY.    (*bursting into tears*) You—you—vile deceitful wretch, you! Pa—pa!
     (*loud. Rings bell violently*)

*Enter* PECKSNIFF, L.H.

PECKSNIFF.    Children—girls, what is this?

CHARITY.    (*runs to him*) The false, mean, odious villain, has, before my face, pro-
     posed to Mercy—(*sobs*)—not me!

PECKSNIFF.    Oh, fie—for shame! Can the triumphs of a sister move you to this ter
55   rible display? I am hurt to see it!

CHARITY.    You against me, too? I shall go mad! (*sinking into a chair*)

PECKSNIFF.    Mercy, my girl—bless you! See to her. Ah, envy! what a passion
     you are!

PINCH *appears*, L.H.D.

PINCH.    Mr Martin Chuzzlewit and Miss Mary—he told me not to knock.

(OLD MARTIN *and* MARY *enter—*PECKSNIFF *runs to him*)

60  PECKSNIFF.    (*bowing, and taking his hand*) My dear and honoured sir—how
     delighted I am to see you! Welcome—thrice welcome to my humble home. Thomas,
     why did you bring Mr Chuzzlewit into this room?

OLD MARTIN.    I desired him. I have rooms at 'The Dragon' to-night. When I have
spoken to you, we will return.
PECKSNIFF.    I will guide your steps with a lanthorn.                                    65
OLD MARTIN.    No—I won't trouble you. Mr Pinch has promised to do it.
PECKSNIFF.    I bow, my dear sir. My loves, welcome the young stranger. Let us adjourn
to the parlour—it is more cosy. (*presenting* JONAS) Our young relative, Mr Jonas—
OLD MARTIN.    Don't let me see him—I wish to see none of the name! Come—
come! (*hurrying out,* R.H. *followed by* MERCY, CHARITY, PECKSNIFF, *and* MARY,    70
PINCH *is following*—JONAS *walks round, shuts the door, and places his back against
it, with his cane behind him*)
JONAS.    The old fool! Who wants to see him, or his money either. Now, Mr Pitch, or
Witch, or Stitch, or whatever your name is—
PINCH.    My name is Pinch, sir—what have you got to say to me?
JONAS.    (*advancing*) Just this, Mr Pinch. I advise you to keep to yourself, and not to
cut in where you're not wanted. I have heard of you, and your meek ways. Don't try    75
to curry favour with my relations. Damme, who are you, that you should walk
home with them? unless it's behind 'em, like any other servant out of livery.
PINCH.    Come—let me go, if you please.
JONAS.    Not till I choose, sneak! You're afraid of my making you split upon some of
your babbling, eh?                                                                       80
PINCH.    I am not afraid of many things, I hope—and certainly not of anything you
will do. I am not a talebearer—I despise all meanness. You quite mistake. Oh, is this
manly from one in your position to one in mine? Please to make room for me to
pass—the less I say the better.
JONAS.    I should like to know what goes on between you and a vagabond member of    85
my family.
PINCH.    I know no vagabond.
JONAS.    You do!
PINCH.    I don't. Your uncle's namesake—young Master Martin, in America—if you
mean him, he's no vagabond. Any comparison between you and him is immeasur-      90
ably to your disadvantage.
JONAS.    Oh, indeed! And what do you think of his gal—his deary—his beggarly
leavings, eh? (*sneeringly*)
PINCH.    I won't stay to hear this—let me go—I won't stay!
JONAS.    You lie, sneak—you shall, and I'll make you! (*he raises the stick to strike*    95
PINCH—PINCH *runs at him, forces it from him, and belabours him heartily—he calls
loudly for mercy*—CHARITY *runs on—seeing* PINCH *beating him, she claps her
hands*)
CHARITY.    Dear Mr Pinch, don't spare him! Another for me—oh, you wretch!
(*laughs*—JONAS *falls*—PINCH *drops the stick*—PECKSNIFF *re-enters with* MERCY,
R. *They form tableau. Scene closes in*)

96.2 *They form tableau. Scene closes in*: Another stage picture not derived from Phiz, since the scene is
not derived from the novel.

## SCENE 2

*A room in the House of* JONAS CHUZZLEWIT, *London.*

*A violent knocking and bell ringing,* R.H.
*Enter* MRS SARAH GAMP, *with a candle,* L.H.

1   MRS GAMP.    Cus that bell! I know it's got the ague! Whenever I'm disposed to nap a
bit, it begins its tantarums—ring, ring, ring! there's no rest for Sarey Gamp in this
wale of tears, as Mrs Harris says. (*bell rings,* R.H.) Coming—coming! (*Exit* R.H.,
*and re-enter with* MR BAILEY, *drest in a smart livery frock coat, top boots, &c.,* R.H.)
BAILEY.    What Sa-ri-ah! my blessed virgin! this is a treat to meet you here—I needn't
5   ask you how you've been this long time, for I see you're in full bloom—all a blowin'
and a growin'!
MRS GAMP.    What a imperant young cock sparrow it is.
BAILEY.    Gently—softly, Sa-ri-ah—go with the grain! How is your constitution?
MRS GAMP.    Don't talk of constitooshuns! a person need be made of bricks to stand
10   what I endoors, Mrs Harris justly says to me, but t'other day, 'Oh, Sarey Gamp,' she
says, 'How is it done?' 'Mrs Harris, ma'am,' I says to her, 'we gives no trust ourselves,
and puts a deal of trust elsewhere—these is our religious feelings, and we finds 'em
answer.' 'Sarey,' says she, 'sich is life, which, likewise, is the hend of all things.'
BAILEY.    You're so full of zeal—boiling over with it—you worret yourself too much,
15   Sa-ri-ah!
MRS GAMP.    Worret myself—you speak the truth in that! Come, Mr Pert, what do
you want here at Mr Chuzzlewit's?
BAILEY.    Business, my beauty, business—here's a letter from my governor, for Mr
Jonas Chuzzlewit, Esq.—(*gives letter*) to be delivered immediately, postage paid.
20   I've cut Mother Todgers—don't you twig my toot ong tong? (*turns round*) Reether
spicey, eh? my governor's the right sort of man—you can't see his face for his whiskers, and can't see his whiskers for the dye upon 'em. Do you know a pair of topboots
when you see them? cos I rather think they'll take the dust out of your eyes,
Sa-ri-ah! (*touching his boots, and strutting over the stage*)
25   MRS GAMP.    Drat the braggin' boldness of that boy! Mr Chuzzlewit ain't at home—
though I expects him to-night with his newly married wife.
BAILEY.    His wife—don't I know her? not at all! I'm intimate with her when she first
kept company with him! She was a nice girl—reether! (*winks at* MRS GAMP)
MRS GAMP.    There's nothing you don't know—all the wretchedness of the world is
30   print to that 'ere boy.
BAILEY.    Softly, Sa-ri-ah! go gently!
MRS GAMP.    As you know her, perhaps you knows her crisen name.
BAILEY.    Charity!
MRS GAMP.    That it ain't!
35   BAILEY.    Cherry, that's short for it.
MRS GAMP.    It don't commenge with a C at all—it's a M!

BAILEY.   (*slapping his boots*) Then he's been and married the merry one!

MRS GAMP.   Merry is the poor thing! I feels for her a comin' to this mournful house—such a mollycholy place! (*sighs*)

BAILEY.   Never sigh, Mrs Gamp—you're too affectionate.                                    40

MRS GAMP.   There you speaks the truth—I feels the sufferins of other people more than I feels my own, though no one may suppoge it.

BAILEY.   Well, give my love to the happy bride, and the letter to the ugly bridegroom—it's a invite to master's. Bye, bye, my beauty! (*kisses his hand*) You're the remains of a fine woman, Sa-ri-ah—a very fine woman—but a trifle too fat! 45 (*Exit R.H.*)

MRS GAMP.   I wouldn't be that creeter's mother for fifty pounds! Ah, a hard hard life mine is, as many a time I says to Mrs Harris, but though I goes out work in for my bread, I maintains my independency in this pilgrim's progress of a mortal wale, and will till death! My earnins is not great, but I will not be impoged upon. Bless the babe and save the mother is my motter—but I makes so free as add to that, don't try 50 no impogition with the nuss, for she will not abear it! I wonder they ain't here afore this—considering they comes on the wings of love, they're precious slow! (*the noise of a carriage heard—a double knock and bell R.H.*) There them is! (*hurries out, re-enters, curtseying before* JONAS *and* MERCY, *in travelling dresses*, R.H.) Wishing you hall happiness and joy with hall my art, and you, too, sir! Your lady looks tired 55 with her journey, pretty dear!

JONAS.   She has bothered enough about it.

MRS GAMP.   Things has been made has comfortable has they could be. Ah, sweet thing! (*aside*) She don't look much like a merry one.

JONAS.   (*dusting his boots*) How's Chuff? still in the land of the living?          60

MRS GAMP.   Yes, sir—and Mr Chuffey may thank you for it, as many and many a time I've told him so.

JONAS.   We don't want you any more, you know.

MRS GAMP.   I'm going immegant, sir, unless there's nuffin I can do for you. (*to* MERCY)

MERCY.   (*faintly*) No, thank you—you had better leave us.                              65

MRS GAMP.   (*giving a dirty card*) Will you be so good, my darling dovey of a dear young married lady, as to keep this? it's my card—Gamp is my name, and Gamp my nater!

(*Tableau*)

I wish you good night, sir! (*curtseying out. Aside*) Well, I will say she don't look like a merry one—I'll say it, if I'm led a Martha to the stakes for it! (*Exit, curtseying*, L.H.) 70

JONAS.   What are you looking so miserable for? I suppose the place ain't good enough for you.

MERCY.   It is dull!

68.1 *Tableau*: This picture is from Phiz's plate 20, 'Mrs Gamp has her Eye on the Future', chapter 26, in part 10 (Hatton & Cleaver, 199).

JONAS.    It'll be duller before you've done with it! You're a nice article to turn sulky
75    on first coming home! Ecod, you used to have life enough when you could plague
me with it. Hark'ye, madam, you have made me bear your pretty humours once,
and now I'll make you bear mine!

MERCY.    Dear Jonas!

JONAS.    I married you that I might! I'll know who's master and who's slave!

80 MERCY.    Heaven knows I'll be obedient.

JONAS.    What, you're finding it out already, are you? Griffins have claws my girl!
there's not a pretty slight you have ever put upon me that I won't pay back a hundred
fold! what else did I marry you for? Ring the bell for supper, while I take off my
boots—the gal's down stairs. (*Exit L.H.*)

85 MERCY.    And this is my welcome home! (*Exit, sobbing violently*)


## SCENE 3

*A wood, with a set hedge terminated by a tree. There is a path behind the hedge.*
*Music.* MARY GRAHAM *is discovered, reading a letter, which she frequently kisses.*

1 MARY.    Dear Martin! how glad I am to hear from you.

(PECKSNIFF *sings without—she starts on hearing him and conceals the letter*)

PECKSNIFF.    (*entering*) Communing with nature, sweet girl? so am I.

MARY.    The morning is so beautiful, that I've prolonged my walk. I am returning now.

PECKSNIFF.    I'll return with you. Take my arm.

5 MARY.    (*trying to pass him*) No, thank you, sir. (*crosses R.H.*)

PECKSNIFF.    Why not? You would not shun me, would you? (*he takes her hand*)

MARY.    Yes, I would—you know I would. Release me, sir—your touch is disagreeable to me.

PECKSNIFF.    This is harsh. I love you, Mary! (*she starts*) Although I am a widower,
10    with two daughters, I am not encumbered, my love. Will you be mine?

MARY.    Pray release me, Mr Pecksniff. By what arts or unhappy chances you have
gained your influence over Mr Chuzzlewit I do not know, but you warp and change
his very nature, adapt his prejudices to your own bad ends, and harden a heart
naturally kind by shutting out the truth. Now you are coarse, cruel, and cowardly to
15    me. But my guardian shall know it.

PECKSNIFF.    Come, come—a word or two will set this matter right. There are two
Martin Chuzzlewits, my dear, and your carrying your anger to one, might injure the
other. You wouldn't wish to hurt him, would you?

MARY.    Wretch!

20 PECKSNIFF.    Have I influence with our venerable friend? If so, not a word of our
meeting, or Martin, Junior, suffers for it. Think of my proposal. Mr Pinch is coming.
I'll watch my pretty bride! (*Exit behind the hedge*)

MARY.   Disgusting hypocrite! And I dare not speak of his conduct, lest it should injure him!

(*Enter* TOM PINCH, *L.H.*)

PINCH.   I've been searching for you, miss—fearful you had missed your way in the  25 woods.

MARY.   No, I thank you, Thomas. You have no more letters for me, I suppose?

PINCH.   No, miss.

MARY.   Not hearing is a great weight on my mind. (PECKSNIFF *peeps over the hedge*)

PECKSNIFF.   (*aside*) Is it?  30

PINCH.   But you mustn't let it be. I would do anything—risk my life, to save you a moment's uneasiness—indeed I would.

MARY.   Dear Mr Pinch!

PECKSNIFF.   (*aside*) Dear Mr Pinch!

MARY.   (*giving her hand*) I cannot tell you how your kindness moves me. But you  35 have ever been a good angel to me—filling me with hope and courage.

PINCH.   I am little like an angel, miss.

PECKSNIFF.   (*peeping*) Very!

MARY.   Why I haven't spoken to you more of Martin is, because I feared it might be noticed, and that it would injure you with your employer.  40

PINCH.   With Pecksniff? He'd never think of us. He's the best of men. He is no spy— (PECKSNIFF *hastily pops his head down*)

MARY.   You mistake him. The person you think the best of men is the worst—the falsest, craftiest, meanest, most sordid, most shameless!

PINCH.   Lor bless us, Miss Graham! Who—what is he? (*clasping his hands*)

MARY.   What is he, who receiving me into his house his unwilling guest, knowing  45 my history and how defenceless I am, presuming before his daughters to affront me so, that if I had a brother but a child, who saw it, he would intuitively have helped me.

PINCH.   He is a scoundrel—yes, a scoundrel!

MARY.   And he now dares assail me with a proposition to become his wife—his,  50 though he knows my love for Martin, and threatens, if I refuse his hand, to plunge him into deeper ruin. He dared—here, in the broad light of day, to tell me this— holding to his lips this hand—(*extending it*)—which I would have struck off, if with it I could lose the shame and degradation of his touch! (*Exit L.H.*)

PINCH.   And he—Pecksniff, did this, did he? The villain! the double-dyed intolera-  55 ble villain! Oh, if I had him here! I wouldn't have minded anything he might have done to me, but to injure her—insult her—he's—he's—he's—he's—(*Exit rapidly, in a passion*)

PECKSNIFF.   (*peeps over, then cautiously advances from hedge*) I have a duty to dis- charge which I owe society, and it shall be performed by discharging you. Oh, Thomas Pinch! how it tries me—grates upon my feelings! I'll go and shed a few  60 tears over it in the back garden. (*Exit L.H.*)

## SCENE 4

*A very showily furnished apartment, at the Anglo Bengalee Disinterested Loan and Life
Insurance Company.*

*Enter* TIGG MONTAGUE, *dressed in the extreme of fashion, followed by* JONAS.

1  JONAS.    If I come here to ask a question or two about your Company, I don't bind
   myself to any thing, you know.
   TIGG.    My dear fellow, I applaud your frankness. Why should I disguise what you
   well know? You're in our secret. I knew my man—that's why I wrote to you. But, my
5  dear sir, if in double lining our nest you can single line yours, why not do it, and join
   us? We are not children, Mr Chuzzlewit. Take a glass of wine—
   JONAS.    No, no—no wine over business. None of that, thankee. (*winks*)
   TIGG.    What an old hand you are!
   JONAS.    You're right there, mister—
10 TIGG.    Tigg Montague. Don't you remember me?
   JONAS.    No. Though I think I have seen you before.
   TIGG.    To be sure you have—in Pecksniff's parlour.
   JONAS.    Why, you don't mean—
   TIGG.    Yes—at that little charming family party, at which yourself and father assisted.
15 JONAS.    Well, well—never mind him—he's dead!
   TIGG.    Dead, is he? (*eyeing him*) You're very like him—(*aside*)—only much uglier!
   Do you find me changed at all? Speak plainly.
   JONAS.    Rather, ecod!
   TIGG.    Was I at all seedy, then?
20 JONAS.    Precious! Ecod, you were another figure when I saw you first—ha, ha, ha! I
   see no rents and patches now.
   TIGG.    You're right. Why don't you join us? 'The Anglo Bengalee Disinterested Loan
   and Life Insurance Company.' Join us—take premiums instead of paying them. You
   shall come in cheap. We do all the world, but you're too deep to be done, you
25 dog! (*nudging him*—JONAS *laughs*) Dine with me to-morrow in Pall Mall?
   JONAS.    I will. But how do you do this? (*pointing round*)
   TIGG.    (*gives paper*) Easily—see. B. is a little tradesman—B. wants a loan—say fifty
   pounds—B. proposes self and two securities—B. is accepted—insures his life, and
   brings his friends to insure theirs, to patronize the office. B. pays the highest lawful
30 interest. (*aside*) Done brown! Take these papers with you, and look over them—
   you'll see how we do it. (*gives papers*) Here's my card—we dine at seven. Look over
   the documents. We coin money—do wonders with old ladies and gentlemen down
   in the country—wonders—money down—capital fun! I'll tell you all at dinner—
   though you're such a deep one! (*rings bell*)

*Enter* BULLAMY, *a fat Porter, in rich livery.*

35 TIGG.    (*points to him. Aside to* JONAS) Mine, too! The door, Bullamy!

(*Exit* BULLAMY)

Adieu! On my sacred word of honour, you are the deepest dog I ever met.

(JONAS *laughs and exit* L.H.)

Hooked—hooked with strong iron, the gull! Nadgett—Nadgett!

(*Enter* NADGETT. *He bows without speaking*)

Mr Nadgett, any information you can gather I shall be glad to have myself. Mr Jonas Chuzzlewit—(*gives card*)—don't mind what it is—anything you can scrape together bring to me, Mr Nadgett.                                                                                 40

(NADGETT *puts on his spectacles, reads card, nods his head, bows to* TIGG, *puts card in old pocket book, then, with another bow glides out*)

Yes, Mr Jonas Chuzzlewit—we, the Anglo Bengalee Disinterested Loan and Life Insurance Company, will have every shilling of your money, on my sacred word of honour! (*Exit* L.H.)


## SCENE 5

*A chamber in* PECKSNIFF's *House. Door in* R.F. *Window,* L.H.

MARY GRAHAM *discovered with* OLD MARTIN, *who is seated on an easy chair,* R.

MARY.    There, dear sir, it will be more cheerful for you in this room.                       1

(*A noise without—the door is thrown open, and* PECKSNIFF *is thrust in, followed by* MARTIN JUNIOR *and* TAPLEY, L. PECKSNIFF *stands before* OLD MARTIN)

MARY.    Martin!
PECKSNIFF.    (*striking his bosom*) Strike here—strike here, sir—launch your arrows at me, sir—not at him—(*pointing to* OLD MARTIN)
MARY.    Grandfather, hear me—I implore you let me speak.                                      5
PECKSNIFF.    Is it not enough, sir, that you come into my house like a thief—bringing your dissolute companions with you—but you must strike at venerable virtue? But I will be its shield! Assail me! strike here! Fire away!
OLD MARTIN.    Stand aside! Let me see what it is I used to love so dearly—
MARTIN.    Grandfather! from a painful journey, from a hard life, from a sick bed,   10
from privation and distress, I have come back to you. But for this faithful man—(*points to* TAPLEY)—I must have died abroad far from home, far from any help or consolation.
PECKSNIFF.    Let him go on, sir.
OLD MARTIN.    (*mechanically*) Go on!                                                         15
MARTIN.    I now come now to ask your forgiveness—not so much in hope for the future, as in regret for the past—all I ask you is that you will aid me to live—help me to get honest work. Try if I be self-willed, obdurate, and haughty as I was. No, no—I have disciplined in a rough school. Let the voice of nature plead between us, Grandfather, and do not for one fault quite reject me.                                          20

(OLD MARTIN *weeps*)

PECKSNIFF.     My dear sir, you must not give way thus—it is very amiable, but you must not allow the shameless conduct of one you cast away to move you so far—rouse yourself—think of me, my friend.

OLD MARTIN.     I will! you recall me to myself—I will!

25 PECKSNIFF.     That's well! Shall I give expression to your thoughts?

OLD MARTIN.     Yes, speak for me—you are true to me.

PECKSNIFF.     Young man! blush if you can—begone without a blush if you can't! (*pointing*) You shall not wrong him further—you may bestride my senseless corse, but you shan't wrong him!

30 MARTIN.     Will you give me no answer—not a word? (*to* OLD MARTIN)

OLD MARTIN.     (*rising, and leaning on* PECKSNIFF's *arm*) You have heard him—go away—it's all over—go! (*waves his hand, and exit with* PECKSNIFF. MARY, *in tears, throws herself into* MARTIN's *arms.* TAPLEY *follows* OLD MARTIN)

MARTIN.     You are not changed, Mary.

MARY.     You have restrained yourself so nobly—you have borne so much!

35 MARTIN.     Sickness, distance, were the causes of my only writing once. I have heard of Pecksniff's suit to you—does my grandfather encourage it?

MARY.     No!

MARTIN.     Thank heaven!

MARY.     His kindness to me remains unchanged. If I were his only child I could not
40     have a gentler father.

MARTIN.     I would not urge you to abandon him, dearest, but the influence this fellow exercises over him has steadily increased, I fear.

MARY.     It does—he refers to him in everything, and has no opinion upon any question but that which is forced upon him by this treacherous man.

45 MARTIN.     Mrs Lupin tells me Tom Pinch is sent away.

MARY.     Yes, because he befriended me—because he loved you—he is now in London, doing well.

MARTIN.     Poor Tom! I'll try my fortune in London—Tom Pinch has succeeded—with his advice to guide me, I may do the same. I took Tom under my protection once,
50     heaven save the mark, and promised I would make his fortune—perhaps he will take me under his now, and teach me how to earn my bread. (*Exit with her,* 2 E.L.D.)

## SCENE 6

*A handsome bedchamber at* MR TIGG MONTAGUE's. *French bedstead F. Fireplace R.F. Window. Table, two chairs, and glass brought on,* L.H.

*Enter* TIGG, *in dishabille, followed by* NADGETT, R.H.

1 TIGG.     Well, Mr Nadgett, any news of Mr Jonas Chuzzlewit's affairs?

NADGETT.    I think we have some, sir.

TIGG.    I am happy to hear it—I began to fear you were off the scent.

NADGETT.    Yes, yes—I think it is a good case. (*he carefully places his pocket book on a chair, R.H., takes a number of papers, arranges them*) Look at No. 1 if you please, 5 sir. (*gives paper to* TIGG) Now, No. 2—read two—there's more interest as you go on—three, four, and five—there, sir, read five—I think five will do it. (*rubs his hands*)

TIGG.    (*starts astounded*) You are a wonderful man, Mr Nadgett!

NADGETT.    I think it is a pretty good case now, sir, eh? (*laughs, rubs his hands*) It cost some trouble.    10

TIGG.    The trouble shall be well repaid! (NADGETT *bows*) You are a capital hand at a secret! (*aside*) Now, Mr Jonas, you are in my grasp—your purse is mine! (*double knock, R.H.*) Who is that?

NADGETT.    (*looks from window*) Mr Chuzzlewit, sir—shall I go?

TIGG.    No, remain with me, if you please—don't leave us alone together—mind you 15 don't—now follow me. (*aside*) By the Lord we don't know what may happen! (*Exit with* NADGETT, *L.H.*)

*Enter* MR BAILEY, *ushers in* JONAS, *R.H.*

JONAS.    Is Mr Montague at home?

BAILEY.    I should hope he was at home, and waiting breakfast, too. Will you take your hat up with you, or leave it here?

JONAS.    Take my name.    20

BAILEY.    The hold name, I suppose! (*laughing.* JONAS *looks at him*) What don't you remember hold Todgers? don't you remember me? when you used to come a courting there—times is changed, and they with us reether—look at my boots—I say how ugly you're grown!

JONAS.    Ugly!    25

BAILEY.    Amazing! (*aside*)

(*Re-enter* TIGG, *L.H., followed by* NADGETT. TIGG *has two brushes in his hand.* BAILEY *bows and exit*)

TIGG.    (*taking* JONAS *by the hand*) My dear sir, I am delighted to see you!

(NADGETT *affects to dry his handkerchief at the fire, R.H., but listens to the conversation*)

What an early visit this is.    Excuse me, completing my toilet. Though you go to bed with the nightingale, you rise with the lark—you're such a light sleeper.

JONAS.    I should be very glad not to get up with the lark, if I could help it. Hollo! 30 who's that? Eh? oh! old what's his name, looking as if he wanted to skulk up the chimney—he knows what a light sleeper is.

TIGG.    I've no doubt he does.

JONAS.    Of all the precious old dummies in appearance that ever I saw, he's about the worst! He's afraid of me, I think.    35

TIGG.    Quite true! he is too shy to cope with such a man as you, but does his duty well. Tell me what a light sleeper is.

JONAS.    Hang a light sleeper!

TIGG.    No, no—we'll not do that! What is it?

40 JONAS.    A light sleeper ain't a heavy one—don't sleep much, and don't sleep well, and don't sleep sound.

TIGG.    And dreams, and cries out in an ugly manner, and when the candle burns down in the socket, is in an agony, and all that sort of thing—I see!

JONAS.    Never mind that—I want to have a word with you. I'm not satisfied with the
45 state of affairs.

TIGG.    Not satisfied? the money comes in well.

JONAS.    The money may come in well enough, but it don't come out—it's all in your hands—I'm not going to stand it, you know. (*sits,* R.H.)

TIGG.    (*brushing his hair at table,* L.H.) No!

(*Tableau*)

50 JONAS.    No, I'm not, indeed—I'll play old gooseberry with the office, and make you glad to buy me out at a good high figure, if you try any of your tricks with me.

TIGG.    Play old gooseberry with us! I give you my honour!

JONAS.    Oh, confound your honour! I want a little control over the money—you may have all the honour—give me the money—I'm not going to stand it!

55 TIGG.    I am unfortunate to find you in this humour, for I was going to propose that you should induce Mr. Pecksniff to join us, and venture a little more money yourself.

JONAS.    Hear you—by—

TIGG.    Hush, my dear sir—hush! (*smiling*) You know how delighted I should be to know him.

60 JONAS.    How kind of you!

TIGG.    I give you my sacred word of honour, we should.

JONAS.    Exactly, when you catch 'em!

TIGG.    It will be to your advantage!

JONAS.    Perhaps you'll tell me how?

65 TIGG.    Shall I tell you how?

JONAS.    I think you had better—strange things have been done in the insurance way before now, and I mean to take care of myself!

TIGG.    Chuzzlewit, strange things have been done, and are done every day, not only in our way, but in a variety of other ways, and no one suspects them. Sometimes we
70 come into the knowledge of strange events.

JONAS.    What do you mean?

TIGG.    (*beckons* JONAS *to him, and whispers in his ear—he becomes violently agitated, and falls in the chair*) You'll not object to venture further with us now?

JONAS.    (*faintly*) No!

49.1 *Tableau*: This is the Phiz plate no. 28 in part 14, ''Mr Nadgett breathes, as usual, an atmosphere of mystery' (see Hatton & Cleaver, 205).

TIGG.　To be sure you won't—and your father-in-law—he has money?

JONAS.　Yes! 75

TIGG.　To be sure he has—it must be ours! Shall I leave Mr Pecksniff to you?

JONAS.　I'll do my best!

TIGG.　To be sure you will! On second thoughts, we'll see him together! I'll drive you down to his place to-morrow—he cannot be enticed too soon.

JONAS.　(*rising, wildly laughing*) Ecod, there's some fun in catching that old hypo- 80 crite—I hate him! shall we go tonight?

TIGG.　(*slapping him on the shoulder*) Come, that's like yourself—this is business— we can concert our plans on the road. I may trouble you for a trifle to-morrow before we start—say five or six thousand—nothing though—not worth mention- ing. Mr Nadgett, have the kindness to see Mr Chuzzlewit down. Adieu! respects to 85 Mrs C! By the bye, make it ten thousand!

JONAS.　(*aside*) Curse you! (*going, preceded by* NADGETT) I won't—I can't!

TIGG.　You will!

JONAS.　Ten thousand! I won't!

TIGG.　You will—you will, my sweet friend—remember! 90

(*whispers*—JONAS *rushes out*—TIGG *laughs and exits, waving his hand*) Adieu! adieu!


# SCENE 7

*London Bridge Wharf. The river and the quarter deck of a large steamer moored off the wharf. Various boats in the distance. Persons, male and female, embarking—Porters with luggage—orange boys, newspaper men, policemen, watermen. The scene occupies the whole of the stage—the front forming part of the wharf,* R.H. *Another which is reached by a broad flight of steps—the whole wharf railed from the river—the access to the steamer is by broad planks from the wharf. When the scene opens, all is hustle and movement. Music.*

NEWSMEN.　Post—Times—Morning Chronicle—Punch—Punch! 1

WATERMEN.　Gravesend—Antwerp—Margate—Greenwich!

(TOM PINCH *and his* SISTER *enter from upper wharf, descend, and leaning over the rails, look at the steamer.* MRS GAMP *is seen descending with a large umbrella and pattens. She is knocked down by a* PORTER, *who is carrying a large trunk—she screams, strikes the* PORTER *with umbrella, and descends to lower wharf—all laugh— her bonnet is squeezed double*)

MRS GAMP.　Pelise! pelise! Cus that imperent feller! There's no manner of respect paid to us women! (BAILEY *is seen strutting on—he unconsciously pushes against* MRS GAMP) You little imp, I'll— 5

BAILEY.　What, my lovely virgin! What brings you into the city? How is our friend, Sairah? How is she?

MRS GAMP.    Oh, don't ask me. I'm almost scratched to pieces. You look well enough. Smarter by day than by candlelight. I never seed such a tight young dasher!

10   BAILEY.    Gently—gently, Sairah—go a tiptoe!

MRS GAMP.    What indooces you to come down here among the packages?

BAILEY.    Pleasure. We drove down in our cab.

MRS GAMP.    Our cab!

BAILEY.    (*pointing off*) Rather so. There it is—a spicy sort. Look at the horse—he's

15   first cousin to Cauliflower, and sister to Samerhoo. That horse, ma'am's, a noble animal! He's been through the windows of two China shops, and was sold for killing his mistress. We're come into the city to look for a friend, who ought to have dined with us yesterday.

MRS GAMP.    Who's hus?

20   BAILEY.    I and the governor. There he is—(*pointing*)—I must tear myself away from you. (*sings*) 'Adieu, my only love—my honour calls me from yer!'

MRS GAMP.    I never did see sich a himp as that! (*bell rings—People crowd to edge of wharf*) Lor! I suppoge they're hoff! (*pushing among the crowd, her umbrella hooks* PINCH *by the coat collar—she pulls it, endeavouring to release herself—Persons press against her*)

PINCH.    (*mildly*) Pray mind your umbrella, ma'am.

25   MRS GAMP.    Don't speak to me, feller! I'm scrouged to a mummy! (*another person pushes her aside*) Pelise! where's the pelise? (*shaking her umbrella at* TOM) I'll give you in charge. Where's the pelise? If they greased their whiskers less, and minded their dooties a little more, no one need be druv mad by scrouging so!

PINCH.    Can I help you, ma'am? What boat do you want to go on board?

30   MRS GAMP.    I suppoge as nobody but yourself can look at a steam package, without wanting to go a boarding of it, can they booby!

PINCH.    What one do you want to look at, then? Don't be so ill-tempered.

MRS GAMP.    Ill-tempered! No blessed creetur as ever I was with in my trying times, ever brought such a charge agin me. I'm always mild and equal in spirits, but I won't

35   deny that I'm worretted and wexed this day, and with good ragion. Lord forbid! which of all them smoking monsters is the Ankwork's boat, I wonder?

RUTH.    What boat?

MRS GAMP.    The Ankworks package, my sweet.

RUTH.    That is the Antwerp packet next the wharf.

40   MRS GAMP.    And I wish it was in Jonage's belly, I do!

(NADGETT *is seen shuffling from place to place on the wharf, during this dialogue.* MRS GAMP *groans, leaning over the rails*)

RUTH.    You seem affected—perhaps your children or husband are going aboard this morning?

---

21 'Adieu...yer!': Bailey's song would seem to be derived from Dibdin's 'The soldier's adieu' which appeared in *The Universal Songster* in 1834, and begins 'Adieu, adieu, my only life! | My honour calls me from thee.'

MRS GAMP.   No, miss—my own children are all gone long ago. One fell out of a
three-pair back—another had a damp doorstep settle on her lungs, and t'other was
turned up smilin in a bedstead unbeknown. My dear, you're single, an't you?          45
RUTH.   (*smiling*) Yes.
MRS GAMP.   Keep so. Worse luck for some parties as is married. There is a dear
young creeter a coming down this morning to that very package, who's no more fit
to trust herself to sea than nothing.

(JONAS *and* MERCY *enter on the upper wharf. He is wrapped in a large cloak—she
is closely veiled—*JONAS *appears hurried in his manner—they are followed by a* PORTER,
*with luggage—*NADGETT *observes them*)

There she goes—a crossing that little bridge—that's her—ugh!          50
PINCH.   Do you mean the lady who is with that man with his face hid in his cloak?
MRS GAMP.   Yes. Well he may hide it. Do you see him a jerking of her wrist,
there? Ugh!
PINCH.   He seems to be hasty with her, indeed.

(JONAS *and* MERCY *are concealed by the passengers on board*)

NADGETT.   (*touching* PINCH's *arm, aside*) I beg your pardon, Mr Pinch—my eyes   55
are not very good—do you see a man muffled up from head to foot in a cloak? Will
you put this letter into his hands? (*gives letter*) I am nervous, and should never
hobble across the planks in time.
PINCH.   Certainly, Mr Nadgett—certainly.
NADGETT.   Thanks—thanks!          60

(*Disappears among the crowd—*PINCH *crosses the plank, and delivers the letter to*
JONAS *on board—*JONAS *starts—bell rings—a hoarse voice cries out—'Anybody for
shore?'*)

JONAS.   Yes, yes—we're for shore! I—I am coming—give me time! Where's that
woman? Come back—here! (*wildly—dragging* MERCY)
MERCY.   Where are we going?
JONAS.   Back—back!

(*Drags her over plank—as he reaches wharf,* TIGG MONTAGUE *encounters him, followed by* BAILEY)

TIGG.   I ask pardon a thousand times for interfering with your domestic trip, but   65
business must be attended to. (*aside*) You would fly, eh? but the letter prevented it.
Introduce me—(*points to* MERCY)
JONAS.   This is Mr Montague—
TIGG.   Sorry, Mrs Chuzzlewit—(*bowing*)—for having been the means of spoiling
this excursion. May I die, but I am shocked! (MRS GAMP *curtsies, and pushes*   70
*against him*) Who is this singular old female? does anybody know her?
JONAS.   You are here, too, are you?

MRS GAMP.     I hope, sir, as no bones is broke by me and Mrs Harris a walkin down a
   public wharf?

75  JONAS.     As you are here, you had better see to her, and take her home.

(MRS GAMP *crosses to* MERCY)

MERCY.     (*snatching* JONAS's *hand*) What is all this? What is it?

(*Music. The steamer bell rings, and voice through speaking trumpet cries—'Anybody for
shore?'* JONAS *throws* MERCY *over to* R.H. *She falls into* MRS GAMP's *arms. He is about
to strike her, when* BAILEY *throws himself between them in a boxing attitude—*TIGG
*looks exultingly at the group. Tableau. Act Drop descends quickly*)

76.4  *Tableau. Act Drop descends quickly:* The picture does not derive from the novel, where Bailey is not
present on the wharf.

# ACT III

## SCENE 1

*A dirty room in the house of* JONAS, *enclosed on all sides. Wall,* L.H. *A small door, and almost blocked up window, looking into a court. A very old bedstead. A portmanteau,* R.H. *A rusty fireplace. In the flat there is also a door. Both doors have locks.*

JONAS *is discovered, with* MERCY, *trembling.*

JONAS.   So, so, madam—these are your friends, when I'm away. You didn't expect   1
me back from your father's so soon, eh? You plot and tamper with these sort of
people, do you?

MERCY.   No, indeed—I have no knowledge of their secrets—I have never seen him
since I left home but once—but twice before.   5

JONAS.   Oh, but once—but twice, eh? Twice and once—perhaps three times. How
many more, you lying jade? (*raises his hand—she shrinks down*)

MERCY.   No more!

(*Clock strikes eight—the lights begin to darken*)

JONAS.   Get up—don't lie there! (*rudely jerks her up*) Listen to me, young lady, and
don't whine. If I find him in my house again—this Mr Pinch—or find that you have   10
seen him, you'll repent it, if you don't obey exactly what I order. Now, attend. What's
the time?

MERCY.   It struck eight a minute ago.

JONAS.   I shall sleep here to-night—maybe to-morrow night—and if I can sleep all
day to-morrow, so much the better. Keep the house quiet, and don't call me. Don't   15
let anybody call me—let me lie still!

MERCY.   You shall not be disturbed. Is that all?

JONAS.   What more do you want to know?

MERCY.   I want to know nothing, Jonas. All hope of confidence between us has long
deserted me.   20

JONAS.   Ecod, I should hope so!

MERCY.   But if you will tell me what you wish, I will try to please you. I make no
merit of that, for I have no friend in my father or sister, but am quite alone. You told
me you would break my spirit—you have done so—do not break my heart,
too! (*placing her hand on his shoulder*)   25

JONAS.   (*shaking her off*) Go! show your obedience by leaving me—(*opens door*)—
and if you are not deaf and dumb to everything that concerns me, you'll repent it!

(*She exits slowly, weeping—he shuts, and locks the door*)

It's no use doing things by halves. Mr Chuff's been babbling, Mrs Gamp tells me. He shall be provided for in a madhouse when I return. It's damned strange his drivell

30     ings should have taken this turn just now! (*he paces the room—appears uneasy— drags his portmanteau from under the bed—unlocks it, takes out a pair of clumsy shoes, leather leggings, and a frock of dark jean—he sits on the bed, takes off his shoes and coat, and puts on the heavy shoes, leggings, frock, and coloured handkerchief, talking to himself through the music—the moon rises, and* NADGETT's *face is seen through the window, watching*).    Old dog! He shall be gagged! No one will dare call me before to-morrow night! (*tumbles the bed clothes, puts his shoes and hat in the portmanteau—re-locks it, and places it under the bed—takes down key from the wall—looks round cautiously—listens at door—shuffling footsteps are heard without— he stoops down—they grow faint—he gently unlocks the door—it opens with diffi- culty—he peeps out*) Hush! No one's in the court. The coach'll soon take me up! (*laughs*) Ha, ha! (*aside*) And Mr Tigg and I will settle old scores! (*Exit softly, closing the door*)


# SCENE 2

MRS GAMP's *Apartment, Kingsgate Street, Holborn. A shabby room, with a tent bed, dresser, drawers, bandboxes, and cupboard, all painted on F. (see illustration). A side piece* L.H. *with a small grate, over which are the three portraits, almanack, &c. painted.*

MRS GAMP *enters, dressed in her best, carrying a small table, prepared for tea. Pickled salmon, bread, &c. &c. She then places two chairs, and her pattens and umbrella near the fire.*

1     MRS GAMP.    (*talking during her preparation*) There's a new loaf—a plate of fresh but- ter—pound best lump and some gunpowder, and two pound of Newcastle pickled salmon. A tea fit for the King of Rooshy! Now, drat you, Betty, don't be long, for I can't bear to wait. I do assure you, it is but little as I wants, but I must have that little

5     of the best and regular. That's my motter! (*taking snuff—bell rings violently,* R.) There's that Sweedlepipe's bell ringing again! Is the Thames a-fire, and cooking its own fish?

*Enter* MRS BETSY PRIG.

My precious Betsy, how late you is!
MRS PRIG.    It an't no fault of mine. (*takes off her bonnet and shawl—looks at table*)
10     I know'd she wouldn't have a cucumber! (*very cross*)
MRS GAMP.    Lor bless you, Betsy Prig—I quite forgot it!

---

0.2 *see illustration*: The Phiz plate 35, in part 18, 'Mrs Gamp propoges a toast' (see Hatton & Cleaver, 210).

MRS PRIG.   I thought it! (*takes from her pocket a large lettuce, onion, small salad, and beet root—throws it on table*) There—I brought my own garden stuff. Put plenty of vinegar, and don't drop none of your snuff into it!

MRS GAMP.   (*preparing salad*) How can you talk so?　　　　　　　　　　15

MRS PRIG.   Why an't your patients, wotever their diseases is, always a sneezing their very heads off, along of your snuff?

MRS GAMP.   And wot if they are?

MRS PRIG.   Nothing if they are—but don't deny it, Sarah.

MRS GAMP.   Who denyges of it, Betsy—who denyges it?　　　　　　　　20

MRS PRIG.   Nobody, if you don't. I want my tea! (*sits at table—*MRS GAMP *pours out—both join in the repast—*MRS PRIG *talking with her mouth full*) Have you heard about young Bailey? I read it in the 'Tizer, that he's been throwed from a gig with his master, and all but killed. He was breathin his last when the account came up.

MRS GAMP.   He was born in a wale, and he lived in a wale, and he must take the  25 consequence of such a situation.

MRS PRIG.   Your old master, Mr Jonas Chuzzlewit's, fine Assurance Company's all gone to pieces. One manager's gone off with the money, and the principal's missing. This I read, too.

MRS GAMP.   Lord keep us! (*she opens cupboard in* F. *takes out a teapot and two*  30 *glasses*) My frequent pardner, Betsy, I'll now propose a toast. I keeps the liquor in a teapot, to avoid observations. (*pours out gin*) Here's Betsy Prig! (*drinks*)

MRS PRIG.   Which, haltering to the name of Sarah Gamp, I drink with all my heart. (*drinks*) Now, jining bisness with pleasure—what is this case in which you've sent for me? Is it Mrs Harris?　　　　　　　　　　　　　　　　　35

MRS GAMP.   No, Betty, it an't!

MRS PRIG.   I am glad of it. Who is it, then? (*drinks*)

MRS GAMP.   You have heard me mention a person as I took care on, when you and I was pardners in that fever at 'The Bull'?

MRS PRIG.   Do you mean old Snuffy?　　　　　　　　　　　　　　40

MRS GAMP.   Chuffy, you mean—Mr Chuzzlewit's clerk.

MRS PRIG.   Well, it's all one.

MRS GAMP.   Mr Chuffy, Betsy, is weak in his intellects—p'rhaps not so weak as they thinks for. What I knows, I knows—and what you don't, you don't—so don't ask me. (*winks*) I was asked to take charge on him—says I, No—but I'll recommendge a  45 friend of mine, Mrs Prig—one has as passed like gold through a furnage—(MRS PRIG *helps herself again—*MRS GAMP *stops her hand*) No, Betsy—drink fair, votever you do.

MRS PRIG.   Go on.

MRS GAMP.   I'm a goin. I says, she is to be trusted—I'll answer for her—and Mrs Harris—　　　　　　　　　　　　　　　　　　　　　50

MRS PRIG.   Bother Mrs Harris! I don't believe there's sich a person!

(*Snapping her fingers in* MRS GAMP'S *face, then putting on her bonnet*)

MRS GAMP.   (*rising*) What! you base cretur! have I known Mrs Harris five-and-thirty years, to be told that there an't no sich a person livin, which her own dear

sister's child, by her first husband, a master sawyer, is marked with a mad bull in
55 Wellington boots, on account of her precious mother having been worretted by one
into a shoemaker's shop, when in a situation, which blessed is the man as has his
quiver full of such!

MRS PRIG.    Stuff!

MRS GAMP.    Stuff, Betsy! Well, you mayn't believe there's no sich creeter, for she
60 wouldn't demean herself by looking at you. Go along, you—

MRS PRIG.    I'm agoing, ma'am, an't I?

MRS GAMP.    You'd better, ma'am.

MRS PRIG.    Better! Do you know who you're talking to, ma'am?

MRS GAMP.    Aperiently to Betsy Prig—aperiently so. I know her—no one better—
65 but I won't debage myself. Go along, do!

MRS PRIG.    And you was going to take me under you, was you? Recommend me to
a lunatic, eh? How kind! Devil take your himperence! What do you mean?  (*placing
her arms a kimbo*)

MRS GAMP.    (*snatches her umbrella*) I blushes for you—go!

MRS PRIG.    You'd better blush for yourself. You and your Chuffeys! What, the poor
70 creature an't mad enough?

MRS GAMP.    He'd very soon be mad enough, if you had anything to do with him.
I know your tricks at Bartlemy's!

MRS PRIG.    My tricks, ma'am?

MRS GAMP.    Yes, lots of 'em, to stimulates the patients.
75 MRS PRIG.    I hates you, Sarah—I hates you!

MRS GAMP.    And I hates you, Betsy, ten hundred times worser!

MRS PRIG.    Insignificant wretch!

MRS GAMP.    Never darken my doors no more, you twining serpent!

MRS PRIG.    What! call me a serpent, will you ma'am? Take that!

(*Throws a tea cup at* MRS GAMP, *which she returns with the pattens, chairs, &c.*
MRS PRIG *pelts her with tea cups—*MRS GAMP *returns to* R. *puts up the umbrella to
shelter herself, and calls 'Pelise!'* MRS PRIG *runs off—*MRS GAMP *throws all the things
after her*)

80 MRS GAMP.    Oh, Betsy Prig—Betsy Prig! What I have endoored from you this
blessed night! (*drinks*) If she had abuged me being in liquor, which I thought I
smelt her when she came, but couldn't so believe, not bein uged myself. (*drinks.
Getting gradually drunk*) Never shall she have another stroke of work from
me! (*drinks*) That I should hear from that same woman's lips what I have heard her
85 speak of Mrs Harris, which dear woman is expocting me at this minnit, and is looking out of winder down the street, with little Tommy Harris in her arms. (*drinks
and weeps*) Oh, Betsy Prig what wickedness you have showed this night, but never
shall you darken Sarey's doors agin! (*staggers out*)

## SCENE 3

*A set wood with a winding path C., paths R. & L. A rude stile on which* JONAS *is discovered sitting, cutting a stick with a large knife—his hat is slouched, and handkerchief half concealing his face. Sunset. Music. Stage half dark.*

JONAS.    I'm ready for him now—so well disguised that even the coachman took me     1
for a common country fellow—so much the better! He's sure to pass through this
wood to Salisbury, for I heard Pecksniff promise to shew him through some pleasant fields at the inn where they're dining—very pleasant it'll be to him!  (*smiles*)
Rob and threaten me, will he? we'll see—we'll see!  (*a noise of voices in the distance,*    5
*and a gig.* JONAS *crosses over and listens—throwing aside his stick*) They're leaving
the gig—Pecksniff is shewing him down the path.  (*conceals himself over the stile.*
*Laughing without*)
TIGG.    (*without*) No—upon my sacred honour!
JONAS.    Ah, laugh away—do my fine fellow!

*Enter* PECKSNIFF *and* TIGG, R.H. *path, arm in arm—laughing.*

PECKSNIFF.    You tear yourself away too soon—much too soon, my dear friend.        10
TIGG.    No, no—I wish to reach Salisbury before dark.
PECKSNIFF.    This is the path—beautiful walk—go straight through the little wood
you'll come to. I'm sorry Jonas hurried away so yesterday—he had business in town,
I suppose.
TIGG.    Doubtless! You'll be in London in a few days, then?                          15
PECKSNIFF.    Certainly!
TIGG.    You are one of us.
PECKSNIFF.    Decidedly to the last farthing—you have my bond!
TIGG.    Adieu!  (*shakes his hand*) Good night!
PECKSNIFF.    Good night, dear sir—remember me to Jonas. Keep the path, and go    20
straight.  (*noise of gig,* R.H. *Pecksniff exits* R.H.)
TIGG.    (*kissing his hand to him*) Adieu! farewell! Mr Pecksniff's money's mine!  (*turns
towards C. path*) 'Pon my sacred honour, this is devilish black! a dismal looking
place! I'm not fond of your rural solitudes and flowery dells! I would rather have
missed a thousand pounds than lost the boy Bailey just now. His accident was a    25
severe one, poor lad! and to remove him from Salisbury would be madness! This is
Pecksniff's inviting rural path. I presume—very pleasant, upon my soul!  (*eyeing it*
*with his glass*) I don't like it—shall I return? no! anything is better than the company
of my amiable friend Jonas—I wouldn't have trusted my life in his hands for worlds!

(*Music. Exit slowly up C. path, humming a tune.* JONAS *emerges from his concealment,*
*follows him cautiously crouching down at intervals*)

30  TIGG.    (*without*) Mercy! mercy! spare me! (*a deep groan and pause.* JONAS *returns, dreadfully agitated—his knife stained with blood—he looks pale and terrified—he springs from the thicket, breaking down the branches, young boughs, etc. Picture*)

JONAS.    My secret's safe! he is dead, and I am free—free from his accursed persecution! (*laughs wildly*) Ha, ha! he little knew me! he lies there among the old leaves just as if he'd fallen head long down by accident! (*replaces knife*) Now for London—home—there I'm safe! (*whip and coach horn without,* R.H. *He starts*) What's

35  that? (*runs towards C. path—suddenly stops*) No, no—I dare not look on that dead man's face—the blood scents the summer night from earth to heaven—this way—through the woods—I—I—cannot look on him again.

(*Exit rapidly over the stile,* L.H. *Music*)


# SCENE 4

*Chamber in the Temple.*

*Enter* JOHN WESTLOCK, TOM PINCH, *and* MARTIN CHUZZLEWIT, JUN., L.H.

1  PINCH.    I knew you'd be glad to see Mr Martin, John—I told him so, but he'd scarce believe it. He's come to London to seek employment—I'm sure you'll help him.

MARTIN.    Yes, Tom, I am in London, no longer to make my fortune, but to try to live—my hopes do not soar above that now.

5  PINCH.    Your hopes do soar above that—yes, they do—how can you talk so? they soar up to the time when you will be happy with her—with Miss Mary—as for advice and friendly counsel, John Westlock will give it us, won't you?

WEST.    Readily, Tom. Your visit is rather opportune, for I was engaged on business connected with a member of your family, sir.

10  MARTIN.    Indeed!

WEST.    Yes, I have just heard a most extraordinary story from an old companion of mine, who has long been under my care at the Bull Inn, Holborn—the person's name is Lewsome—he made the communication to me first yesterday—it relates to a person whose name is Jonas Chuzzlewit, and affects his life.

15  MARTIN.    His life!

WEST.    You shall hear the story from my friend's own lips. (*Exit* R.H., *and re-enter, conducting* LEWSOME, *a gaunt pale young man, labouring under the effects of severe illness—he bows*) This is Mr Lewsome, sir—my friend Lewsome, Mr Chuzzlewit.

LEW.    What relation was Mr Anthony Chuzzlewit to you—who—

MARTIN.    Died! He was my grandfather's brother.

20  LEW.    I fear he was made away with—murdered!


30.2 *Picture*: Another purely stage picture, described in the novel (chapter 47) but not illustrated.

MARTIN.  By whom?

LEW.  I fear by me.

MARTIN.  By you!

LEW.  Not by my act—but I fear by my means.

MARTIN.  Speak out—speak the truth!  25

LEW.  I fear this is the truth: Jonas Chuzzlewit is the principal in this deed!

MARTIN.  What do you mean? do you know he is the son of the old man of whom you have spoken?

LEW.  I do! I have reason to know it, for I've often heard him wish his old father dead—he was in the habit of doing so at a place of meeting we had—he and I were  30 alone together—he told me his father was weak, imbecile, and in his second childhood—it would be a charity to put him out of the way! He swore he'd often thought of mixing something with the stuff he took for his cough, which should help him to die easily!

WEST.  Listen!  35

LEW.  He asked me to get him some of two sorts of drugs, one that was instantaneous in its effects, one that was slow—he said to kill rats—what did it matter to me? I was going to a distant colony, he said—this was true, but for my illness. He offered to forgive me my debt, and pay me five pounds. The next day I gave him the drugs— we have never met since.  40

MARTIN.  This disclosure has paralysed me!

WEST.  Leave us, Lewsome, but remain at hand—this matter shall be thoroughly investigated. (*Exit Lewsome, R.H., despondingly*)

MARTIN.  It shall—it shall—but how are we to set about it? who is to bring this monstrous sin to light? This man's story may be false—or even admitting it true, the  45 old man might have died a natural death.

PINCH.  I hope so.

WEST.  We'll find the nurse, Mrs Gamp, she attended Mr Chuffey, Anthony's old clerk, in his illness after his master's death. She's well known to me, having waited on Lewsome by my order at the 'Bull'. We must approach her with caution, and I've  50 little doubt, from the hints she has already dropped, some important information may be gathered. Let us seek Mrs Gamp at once.

MARTIN.  It seems cruel in me to bring this unnatural charge against a relative.

WEST.  Being in possession of the secret, and taking no measures for further inquiry would make you a partner in the guilty act. Remain here, Tom—a surprise awaits  55 you. (*Exit with* Martin, L.H.)

PINCH.  (*raising his hands*) A surprise! the whole world appears to be one huge surprise to me since I left Pecksniff's. Dear me! poison his own father! I cannot wonder at his treatment to me. What new surprise has John in waiting for me? perhaps Mr Frip's friend, my unknown employer, comes to receive the key of the offices—all's  60 prepared—every book numbered, and in place, orderly and neat. (*noise of footsteps*) The surprise coming up. (*counting the footsteps*) Forty-one, forty-two—I'm so flurried—forty-three, forty-four—forty-four takes away my breath, it's so near the door—forty—forty—(*hesitates*) I can't get the five out.

*Enter* OLD MARTIN CHUZZLEWIT *L.H., entirely changed in appearance and manner. Tableau.*

65 OLD MARTIN.    You have expected me a long time.

PINCH.    I was told my employer would soon arrive, sir—but—

OLD MARTIN.    You were ignorant who he was. It was by my desire. (*takes* PINCH'S *hand*) I have been waiting to unmask a scoundrel!—I have suffered him to treat me like a tool and instrument. You know it, Pinch—you have seen me there—you

70 know it—who better, my true heart? I've had his base soul before me day by day, and have not betrayed myself once. Follow me—come, we'll make amends for all. (*grasping* PINCH'S *arm*) The time is drawing on—I wouldn't have him die or hang himself before we meet, no, not for millions of golden pieces—come—come!

(*Exits L.H., laughing, and dragging* PINCH *with him, who looks astonished*)


# SCENE 5

*A Chamber in the House of* JONAS CHUZZLEWIT, *with a glass door, in F., leading to an inner room.*

JONAS *discovered, seated—he looks pale and haggard.*

1 JONAS.    I wish that old fool would come! I'm determined to go through with it—Mr Chuffey goes off to-night—he shall be gagged if he speaks—poisoned if he writes— he is mad enough—everything sets in against me to worry and annoy. I shall be called to account for all the swindles of that insurance office. They're all off but me,

5 and—(*shudders and starts up*) He's safe in the wood. (*a slight knock,* C.) What's that?

*Enter* MRS GAMP, C.D.

MRS GAMP.    Sairey Gamp, sir—a pleasant evening, though rather warm, which we must expect when cowcumbers is three to twopence.

JONAS.    Did you see my precious wife when you came in?

10 MRS GAMP.    No, sir, but the servant told me she'd been gone to Mrs Todgers's this three hours.

JONAS.    Of course, she's always stealing away to that woman, to hatch mischief—let her be fetched home, and get that old madman out of my house.

MRS GAMP.    I will—the blessed old chick—he shall go with his own Sairey!

15 JONAS.    Where's the other woman, I forget her name, she is to be trusted, is she?

MRS GAMP.    Betsy Prig, sir? That she an't—I've brought another instead what engages to give every satiswaction!

64.2 *Tableau*: Phiz's plate 36, 'Mr Pinch is amazed by an unexpected apparition', illustrating chapter 50 in part 18 (Hatton & Cleaver, 210).

JONAS.   What's her name?

MRS GAMP.   Harris—Mrs Harris—she's well be-known, sir—we meant to take turn and turn about with him.                                                                    20

JONAS.   We shan't quarrel about terms. Let me see the other.

MRS GAMP.   The other person, sir? It is your wish to see the other person, sir? (*confused*)

JONAS.   Yes!

MRS GAMP.   (*throwing open* C.D.) Then here him is!                                25

*Enter* OLD MARTIN *and* TAPLEY. JONAS *starts—*MRS GAMP *retreats behind* TAPLEY, *curtseys, and exits,* C.D.

OLD MARTIN.   If he attempts it, though he is my brother's son, throw up the window and call for help.

JONAS.   What right have you to give such directions in this house?

OLD MARTIN.   The right of your wrong doing. Come in there!

*Enter* LEWSOME, *supported by* JOHN WESTLOCK *and* TOM PINCH, C.

JONAS.   (*leans on the back of a chair*) I know that fellow—he is the greatest liar alive!  30 What's his tale? Ha, ha, ha!

PINCH.   This is the man, is it? (*pointing to* JONAS)

LEW.   You need do no more than look at him, to be sure of that.

*Enter* MARTIN.

PINCH.   Well, well—does he speak out—are his senses wandering?

MARTIN.   No, sir, he is perfectly sensible, and, bad as the conduct of this man  35 appears, he is not his father's actual murderer.

JONAS.   Are you satisfied now—or have you any more plots to broach? That fellow, Lewsome, will invent 'em for you by the score. Is this all? Go! Do you see that door? (*he points* C.D.)

MARTIN.   Do you see it? Look at it! (NADGETT *is standing in it, rubbing his hands,*  40 *with* POLICE OFFICERS *in attendance*)

NADGETT.   That's your man! (*points to* JONAS—*the* OFFICER *places handcuffs on his wrists*) Arrest him for murder! Let no one interfere. I have not been watching him so long for nothing.

JONAS.   (*sinks in a chair with emotion*)

MARTIN.   Where have you watched, and what have you seen?

NADGETT.   Many places without rest or relief. I accuse him of the murder of Mr  45 Montague, who was found last night killed in the wood. I saw him steal out of this house, disguised as a countryman. I kept my watch in the streets—a night, and all next day—then he came creeping home, the same countryman. I never closed my eyes—at night again he came out with a bundle—he went down the steps of London Bridge, and sunk it in the river. I gave warning to the police—it was fished up—it is  50 here! (*shews the countryman's clothes*)—stained with clay—spotted with blood! A coach is waiting to carry him to jail! Come—

(*The* OFFICERS *lead* JONAS *off,* C.D.—NADGETT *and* LEWSOME *following*)

PINCH.    Heaven pardon you! We must keep this dreadful matter from his heart-stricken wife—for a time, at least. I'll take her under my care, since I shall lose my
55    dear Mary soon. (*looks at* MARTIN) Mark, bid Mr Pecksniff and the Ladies enter.

(*Exit* MARK. *He re-enters with* MARY, RUTH, *and* MRS LUPIN—MARTIN *takes*
MARY'S *hand*—JOHN WESTLOCK *embraces* RUTH—MARK *places his arm round* MRS
LUPIN'S *waist.* PECKSNIFF *rushes in,* C.)

PECKSNIFF.    Where is my venerable friend? (*running to* OLD MARTIN *with open
arms.* OLD MARTIN *strikes him with his stick—he falls—*OLD MARTIN *belabours
him—*PECKSNIFF *rises, rubbing his shoulders*)

PINCH.    Take him out of my reach, or I can't help it! My dear Martin—(*takes*
MARTIN'S *hand*)—you speak for me, as that reptile once affected to speak in my
words to you.

60    PECKSNIFF.    I can bear much!

MARTIN.    Listen, hypocrite—listen, smooth-tongued, crawling knave! When I
was seeking reconciliation, you had already spread your shallow nets. Counting on
the restoration of the love he bore me, you designed me for one of your daughters,
did you? Why even then I knew you—scorned and despised you, hound! Didn't
65    I, Tom?

PINCH.    That you did, heartily!

PECKSNIFF.    Go on—I am not angry.

MARTIN.    Pandering to the worst of human passions was the office of your nature,
and well you did your work.

70    PECKSNIFF.    I cannot be angry with you. Mr Chuzzlewit. (*to* OLD MARTIN, *placing
his hand on his heart*) You have partaken of my hospitality—

MARTIN.    And paid you for it.

PECKSNIFF.    (*bowing*) Thank you. You have deceived me. There's hardly a person
present by whom I have not been deceived. I forgive 'em on the spot—it's my duty,
75    and I do it. I've been struck with a walking stick with knobs upon it, on that exqui-site portion of human anatomy, the brain, but harder knocks have been inflicted
without a walking stick, on a tenderer portion—my heart. (*wipes his eyes—bows to
all*) Good morning. (*Exit* L.H.)

PINCH.    Let him go, my children—he is rightly punished. The penance I have done
80    in his house is well repaid. He is a ruined bankrupt!

BAILEY *runs on* C.D. *his head bandaged, carrying an open letter—he is closely followed
by* MRS GAMP.

OMNES.    Bailey!

BAILEY.    Ra-a-ather! alive and hearty. Not killed—only a little shook and bruised.
I've just come from Todgers's—such a plummy wedding! Oh, not at all, neither—
ha, ha, ha! The bridegroom Noddle's, off—made a bolt of it—slipt his collar, after
85    keeping them all waiting three hours. He's off to Dieman's Land, by the first ship.

This letter'll tell you all about it. I picked it up as it fell from the bride's hand, when she fainted.

MRS GAMP.   You must indulge him. (*curtseying*) He's sich a boy. It's all his fun.

OLD MARTIN.   Was the person paid for the trouble we gave her?

WEST.   Yes, sir—liberally.   90

MRS GAMP.   And thank you kindly.

OLD MARTIN.   Then we'll close our acquaintance, Mrs Gamp. (*gives money to* BAILEY) Bailey, is your name, I believe?

BAILEY.   Ra-a-ather, a little sir.

OLD MARTIN.   You have been a good lad—a feeling lad, to one I regard. See that   95 woman to the door, then return.

(BAILEY *bows*)

Tell her to take less liquor, and a little more humanity, with a trifle of additional honesty into her notice, if you please. There—go—

BAILEY.   You hear, my lovely Sairey? Reether less of the tea pot—(*laughing, and leading her off*)—and the bottle on the chimbley piece—oh, not at all, never!   100

MRS GAMP.   Sarah Gamp—less liquor—out of the teapot—bottle in the chimbley piece—if I have, a rager should cut the noge off my own face! (*Exit with* BAILEY)

OLD MARTIN (*embracing* MARY *and* RUTH) My children! (*placing their hands in those of* MARTIN *and* WESTLOCK) No blushes, silly ones!

PINCH.   I can't help it!   105

OLD MARTIN.   Be happy in each other's affection. Your fortunes shall be my care. Mrs Lupin, too—Lupin is a pretty name.

MRS L.   (*curtseying*) Tapley's a betterer, sir, if you please.

OLD MARTIN.   I do please to see everybody happy. My children, may your wealth never be like mine—a source of disquietude. Mary knows how much it tor-   110 tured me.

MARY.   In spite of which, you have been so gentle—so kind to me—so even tempered, and so self-denying—never giving me a hasty look or irritable word. Thank him, dearest Martin, for such a deep fervent love as father seldom gives a child! Thank him from your heart! (*kneels*)   115

MARTIN.   I do—I do, Mary, from my soul! (*kneels*)

OLD MARTIN.   (*raising them*) Bless you—bless you—

MARY.   And Tom—dear Tom Pinch, too!

PINCH.   (*sobbing*) Do—don't—talk about me, miss—I can't hear it!

RUTH.   (*kisses him*) Brother!   120

MARY.   I must talk, and think of your simple-hearted worth and love for me, when I was almost alone. (*taking his hand*) We'll never—never part! It shall be my delight, with your sister, to anticipate thy wants, and never cease to honour thee— and our kind, dear Martin, for they well know and prize the value of an honest heart.   125

(*To the audience*)

Yes, yes—I see—joy unutterable—I see by their smiles Martin, they're all in love with Tom!

BAILEY *re-enters, C.D.*

BAILEY.    (*laughs*) Reether! Oh, no—not a little, neither.  (*picture*)

THE CURTAIN FALLS

---

128  *picture*: The final tableau is of course entirely of the stage.

# SIX

## Gilbert Abbott A'Beckett and Mark Lemon, *The Chimes*, Adelphi, December 1844

## INTRODUCTION

*T*HE *Chimes* is not much read today, and was not as well received in 1844 as the previous year's *A Christmas Carol*; but it is a remarkable Dickensian work in many ways—Forster, whose friendship the author valued particularly highly at this point, thought it his best piece so far.[1] It is arguably his most Radical piece of writing, most uncompromisingly outspoken against the inhumanity of class-based and Malthusian attitudes to the poor and of hard-line Political Economy. It was also the book which revealed to Dickens the personal rewards of performing rather than simply writing about such matters. He made a flying visit to London before it was published to read it aloud to his circle of intimate friends, and this proved to be 'a triumphant hour' for him: he was moved by the sight of his friend Maclise 'undisguisedly sobbing' to confide to his wife 'what a thing it is to have Power' and to begin planning with Forster that they would put on plays.[2] He had already made provision, by sending advance proof sheets, for an official theatrical version to be crafted by his friends Gilbert Abbott A'Beckett and Mark Lemon. For a discussion of this move in Dickens's progressive rapprochement with the stage, see the Introduction ('1843 and the Keeley Management' and 'Like the Brilliant Ballet-Pantomime').

Dickens was close to both these men, who were important Radical writers in the 1830s and 1840s. A'Beckett had founded and edited the cutting-edge satirical journal *Figaro in London* (1831–9) and contributed to *Punch* from its inception in 1841; his continuing to write for the stage, alongside prolific journalism and a career as a barrister, may have been encouraged by his marriage in 1835 to Mary Anne, daughter of Joseph Glossop, builder and manager of the Coburg. Similarly Mark Lemon, who founded *Punch* and sank his profits from several plays into keeping it going in its earliest days in 1841, was a man of middle-class mercantile origins who married into a stage family, meeting the singer Helen Romer, whom he married in 1839, when he wrote a play for the Surrey with her brother Frank, an actor and composer. The success of *Punch* owed much to A'Beckett's writing and Lemon's editorial skill in choosing contributors, and in 1844 *The Chimes* was thoroughly in accord with the paper's central humanitarian/Radical message: its circulation had tripled at Christmas 1843 when

---

[1] See Tomalin, 157.    [2] Tomalin, 159.

Lemon insisted upon publishing Hood's indictment of the oppression of seamstresses, *The Song of the Shirt*.[3]

## THE TEXT

The present edition is of the official A'Beckett/Lemon adaptation, taken from the licensing manuscript, Add. MS 42980 ff. 809r–838r, collated with the printed version published in the National Acting Drama: Mark Lemon and Gilbert Abbott À Beckett, *The Chimes: A Goblin Story, of Some Bells that Rang an Old Year Out and a New Year In; A Drama, in Four Quarters*, London, National Acting Drama Office (1887), consulted via the Chadwyck-Healey English Prose Drama Full-Text Database, Cambridge, 1996. I have not made much use of the detailed stage directions with which the printed version is adorned except where they help towards an understanding of the spectacular nature of the play, with its apparitions, visions, and jump cuts between Trotty Veck's mundane and dream-world realities. Lemon's penchant for extreme sentimentality is clear in the added directions, which strive to give a reader access to the expansive feelings of the original story. The modern reader/realizer of the piece is unlikely to be grateful for them. Indeed it is arguably an advantage for us, with our attitude to affect, that the dramatized versions often free us from the luxuriantly sentimental writing with which Dickens regaled his first readers of the Christmas books.

[3] Most of this information about A'Beckett and Lemon is derived from the *DNB*.

Characters and cast of the first production

| | |
|---|---|
| Prologue (The Spirit of the Chimes) | Miss E. Chaplin |
| Toby Veck | Mr O. Smith |
| Alderman Cute | Mr Wright |
| Filer | Mr Lambert |
| Choker | Mr Cullenford |
| Richard | Mr Selby |
| Jabez | Mr Munyard |
| John | Mr Saunders |
| Tugby | Mr Wilkinson |
| Sir Joseph Bowley | Mr Paul Bedford |
| Mr Fish | Mr C.J. Smith |
| Will Fern | Mr Hudson |
| Mr Lint | Mr Cowell |
| Goblin Of The Bell | Mr Worrell |
| Goblin | Mr Freeborn |
| Goblin | Mr Glennaire |
| Goblin | Mr Waye |
| Meggy Veck | Miss Fortescue |
| Mrs Chickenstalker | Mrs F. Matthews |
| Lady Bowley | Miss E. Harding |
| Lilian | Miss Turtle |

**6.** Playbill for the Adelphi production of the version of *The Chimes* prepared for Dickens by Gilbert Abbott A'Beckett and Mark Lemon. The design is derived from the standing card advertisement drawn by Cruickshank for use by booksellers, which was also copied on the Lyceum bill for the play.

# THE CHIMES,

## A GOBLIN STORY, OF SOME BELLS THAT RANG AN OLD YEAR OUT AND A NEW ONE IN

### PROLOGUE

Spoken (as a SPIRIT OF THE CHIMES) by Miss E. Chaplin.

| | |
|---|---:|
| High up above the city's noise and light | 1 |
| Dwelt the old Chimes of which we tell to-night, | |
| Their iron voices fell upon the ear, | |
| Not speechless were those bells, but loud and clear | |
| And none e'er listened for their measured sound, | 5 |
| Or in their booming clearer language found, | |
| Than poor old Trotty Veck. For many a year | |
| The Chimes were wont his drooping heart to cheer; | |
| They told of newer hopes and better times, | |
| And poor old Trotty dearly lov'd the chimes. | 10 |
| But Trotty oft would doubt—when want hath cried, | |
| And roused sleek Plenty's anger—as it died. | |
| When he hath heard the 'putters down' of woe | |
| Taunting Despair and mocking every throe, | |
| Then would he doubt if poverty had claim | 15 |
| To any goodness—whatsoe'r its name. | |
| He doubted if the poor man's heart could own | |
| The sympathies he deem'd were wealth's alone, | |
| Then grew repining—mourn'd the 'good old times'— | |
| Until he learned a lesson from our chimes. | 20 |

*PROLOGUE*: The prologue is not in the MS, but included here from the National Acting Drama printed edition, hereafter referred to as P[rinted] T[ext], PT.

# 1ST QUARTER

## SCENE 1

*The Tower of the Chimes.*

JABEZ *and* BAND *discovered playing some popular melody.*

*Footman opens door.*

1 FOOTMAN.   I say go away with you—*Can't* you play afore nobody's door but our'n? making a noise!

JABEZ.   Making a noise, sir—the original Tivoli professors.

FOOTMAN.   I dare say you are—but you're to go away—master says so. *Can't* you go!

5 JABEZ.   Why, this is the last day of the old year and we thought worthy Alderman Cute would give us something to drink the health of the new 'un.

FOOTMAN.   Well, then, he won't—mind that. Mr Alderman Cute hates street musicianers—he means to put 'em down—so go on—can't you go on? (*shuts door*)

JABEZ.   Well, we've got as much as I expected and that was nothing—(*enter* MRS

10 CHICKENSTALKER) Ah, good day, Mrs Chickenstalker.

MRS C.   Ah Jabez, how d'ye do?

JABEZ.   Tidyish, thank'ee. (*to the* BAND) Just go down the corner there—they're wery partial to Marble Halls if you give it 'em with inflections—I'll be down in time for the Polka. (*exit* BAND) Are you looking for old Toby Veck, or Trotty Veck as we

15 call him, Mrs Chickenstalker?

MRS C.   I was just wishing to say good day to him if he had been here.

JABEZ.   I suppose he's got a job or else it's a wonder to miss him from the old porch.

MRS C.   It is, indeed, Jabez—though a breezy, goose-skinned, blue-nosed, tooth chattering place it is in winter time.

20 JABEZ.   I believe you, Mrs C.

MRS C.   During an east wind it's bitter Jabez—bitter—It seems to come express to have a blow at Toby—or it pops on him round that corner as though it said 'why, here he is.'

JABEZ.   Ah, and whips his white apron over his head like a naughty boy's garment.

25 MRS C.   I expect some day it will whisk him up and drop him again in a distant part of the world where ticket porters are unknown—Why, that must be Meg, old Trotty's daughter.

JABEZ.   Yes, and Richard the smith—I think that'll be a match.

MRS C.   I hope so, for a worthier couple couldn't be found in a day's march,

30 Jabez. (*going*)

(*Polka heard in distance*)

JABEZ.  Hollo! they've began the Polka first—so I'm wanted to mark the beats. Good day, Mrs Chickenstalker. (*Exit*)

MRS C.  Good day, Jabez. (*looking off*) I'll not interrupt them, they seem to be very earnest—Ah me! I declare they put me in mind of my own sweethearting with poor dear Chickenstalker. (*Exit*) 35

*Enter* TOBY (*Chimes*)

TOBY.  Dinner time, eh! Ah, I'm a long way upon the frosty side of cool—Dinner time, eh! (*rising his right hand muffler and punishing his chest for being cold*) Ah-h-h! there's nothing (*stopping short, feeling his nose carefully*) I thought it was gone! I'm sure I couldn't blame it, if it was to go—it has a precious hard service of it in the bitter weather and precious little to look forward to—for I don't take snuff 40 myself—It's a good deal tried, poor creetur, at the best of times; for when it *does* get hold of a pleasant whiff or so  (which an't too often), it's generally from somebody else's dinner, a-coming home from the baker's. There's nothing more regular in its coming round than dinner-time, and nothing less regular in its coming round than dinner—That's the great difference between 'em—It's took me a long time to find it 45 out—I wonder whether it would be worth any gentleman's while, now, to buy that obserwation for the papers or the Parliament—Why, Lord! the papers is full of obserwations, as it is, and so's the Parliament—Here's last week's paper, now (*taking a very dirty one from his pocket, and holding it from him at arm's length*) full of obserwations! full of obserwations! I like to know the news, as well as any man (*fold-* 50 *ing it up smaller, and putting it in his pocket again*)—but it almost goes against the grain with me, to read a paper now—It frightens me almost—I don't know what we poor people are coming to—Lord send we may be coming to something better in the new year, nigh upon us!

MEG.  (*without*) Why, father, father! 55

TOBY.  (*not hearing, continues to trot backwards and forwards*) It seems as if we can't go right, or do right or be righted—I hadn't much schooling myself when I was young, and I can't make out whether we have any business on the face of the earth or not—Sometimes I think we must have a little, and sometimes I think we must be intruding—I get so puzzled sometimes, that I am not even able to make up my 60 mind whether there is any good at all in us, or whether we are born bad—We seem to do dreadful things, we seem to give a deal of trouble—We are always being complained of and guarded against—one way or another we fill the papers—Talk of a new year! I can bear up as well as another man, at most times, better than a good many, for I am as strong as a lion and all men an't—but supposing it should really 65 be that we have no right to a new year—supposing we really *are* intruding.

37 *rising*: Both MS and PT have 'rising', thought sense suggests 'raising', and the source text, Dickens's, has instead the phrase 'using his right-hand muffler like a boxing glove'.

44 *dinner-time...than*: MS omits 'dinner-time...than', apparently a case of eye-slip in copying.

49 *taking...arm's length*: This sd, and many following, augmented from PT, the MS not including much detail in its directions.

MEG.    (*without*) Why father, father! (*enters*)

TOBY.    (*starts, stops, and after embracing* MEG, *regards her attentively*) Yes, I think we have some business here—a little. (*kisses Meg, and squeezes her face between his hands*) Why, pet, what's to do? I didn't expect you today, Meg—

70  MEG.    Neither did I expect to come father—but here I am; and not alone—not alone.

TOBY.    Why, you don't mean to say (*looking at her covered basket*) that you—

MEG.    Smell it, father dear—only smell it (TOBY *going to lift up the cover,* MEG *interposes her hand*) No—no—no! (*with glee*) Lengthen it out a little—let me just lift up

75  the corner—just the lit-tle ti-ny cor-ner you know—There, now—what's that?

TOBY.    (*takes a sniff*) Why, it's hot!

MEG.    It's burning hot! ha! ha! it's scalding hot.

TOBY.    Ha! ha! ha! (*with a sort of kick*) It's scalding hot.

MEG.    But what is it, father? Come, you haven't guessed what it is—I can't think of

80  taking it out, 'till you guess what it is. Don't be in such a hurry—wait a minute—A little bit more of the cover—Now guess.

TOBY.    (*bends his nose to the* basket) Ah! it's very nice—It ain't—I suppose it an't polonies?

MEG.    No, no, no—Nothing like polonies.

85  TOBY.    No! (*after another sniff*) It's—it's mellower than polonies—it's very nice—it improves every moment—it's too decided for trotters, an't it? Liver? No! there's a mildness about it that don't answer to liver—Pettitoes? No! it an't faint enough for pettitoes—alas! I know it an't sausages—I'll tell you what it is—it's chitterlings.

MEG.    No, it an't! (*laughing*) no, it an't!

90  TOBY.    Why what am I a thinking of. I shall forget my own name next—it's tripe!

MEG.    Yes—yes—and in half a minute more you shall say it's the best tripe ever stewed—and so I'll lay the cloth at once father, for I have brought the tripe in a basin and tied the basin up in a pocket-handkerchief, and if I like to be proud for once, and spread that for a cloth and call it a cloth, there's no law to prevent me—is there, father?

95  TOBY.    Not that I know of, my dear—But they're always a bringing up some new law or other.

MEG.    And according to what I was reading you in the paper the other day, father, what the judge said, you know, we poor people are supposed to know 'em all—Ha! ha! what a mistake! my goodness me, how clever they think us.

100  TOBY.    Yes my dear and they'd be very fond of any one of us that did know 'em all— He'd grow fat upon the work he'd get that man, and be popular with the gentlefolks in his neighbourhood—very much so.

MEG.    He'd eat his dinner with an appetite, whoever he was, if it smelt like this— Make haste, for there's a hot potato besides and half a pint of fresh drawn beer in a

105  bottle—Where will you dine, father? On the post or on the steps? Dear dear, how grand we are—two places to choose from!

---

102 *He'd grow fat ... neighbourhood*: PT omits 'He'd grow fat ... neighbourhood'.

TOBY.    The steps today, my pet! Steps in dry weather—post in wet—There's a greater conveniency in the steps at all times because of the sitting down, but they're rheumatic in the damp.

MEG.    Then here—here it is, all ready! and beautiful it looks—come father, come.    110

TOBY.    (*aside*) Bless her! we are not all born bad—No—no—yet there may come a time, when she may find (*the Chimes strike three quarters*) Amen! (*pulling off his hat, and looking towards the belfry*)

MEG.    Amen to the bells, father!

TOBY.    They broke in like a grace, my dear. (*taking a seat*) They'd say a good one I am sure if they could—many's the kind thing they say to me.    115

MEG.    The bells do, father. (*setting the basin and a knife and fork before him*)—Well?

TOBY.    Seem to, my pet (*falling to*) and where's the difference? If I hear 'em, what does it matter whether they speak it or not? Why bless you my dear—how often have I heard them bells say, 'Toby Veck, Toby Veck, keep a good heart. Toby, Toby Veck, Toby Veck, keep a good heart, Toby'. A million times? More!    120

MEG.    Well I never—I have though.

TOBY.    When things is very bad—very bad indeed I mean almost at the worst—then its 'Toby Veck, Toby Veck, job coming soon, Toby' that way.

MEG.    And it comes at last, father.

TOBY.    Always—never fails. (*eats heartily*) Why (*dropping his knife and fork*) my    125
dove—Meg—why didn't you tell me what a beast I was?

MEG.    Father!

TOBY.    Sitting here cramming and stuffing and you before me there never so much as breaking your precious fast, nor wanting to, when—

MEG.    But I have broken it, father, all to bits—I have had my dinner.    130

TOBY.    Nonsense! two dinners in one day an't possible—you might as well tell me that two new year's days will come together or that I have had a gold head all my life, and never changed it.

MEG.    I have had my dinner father for all that (*coming nearer to him*) and if you'll go on with yours I'll tell you how, and where—and how your dinner came to be    135
brought, and—and something else besides. (*Toby eats slowly*) I had my dinner, father (*after a little hesitation*)—with—with Richard. His dinner time was early and as he brought his dinner with him when he came to see me, we—we had it together, father.

TOBY.    (*takes a little beer, and smacks his lips*) Oh!    140

MEG.    And Richard says, father—

TOBY.    What does Richard say, Meg?

MEG.    Richard, says, father—

TOBY.    Richard's a long time saying it.

MEG.    He says then father 'another year is nearly gone, and where is the use of wait-    145
ing on from year to year, when it is so unlikely we shall ever be better off, than we

---

121  *I have though*: MS omits 'I have though'.

are now?' He says we are poor now, father, and we shall be poor then; but we are young now, and years will make us old, before we know it—He says that if we wait—people in our condition—until we can see our way quite clearly, the way will
150     be a narrow one indeed—the common way—the grave, father. And how hard, father, to grow old, and die, and think we might have cheered and helped each other! How hard in all our lives to love each other, and to grieve apart, to see each other working, changing, growing old and grey. Even if I got the better of it and forgot him—which I never could—Oh father dear, how hard to have a heart so full
155     as mine is now, and live to have it slowly drained out every drop, without the recollection of one happy moment of a woman's life to stay behind and comfort me and make me better! (TOBY *ceases to eat and forces a faint laugh and then a sob*). So Richard says, father, as his work was yesterday made certain for some time to come and as I love him, and have loved him full three years—ah! longer than that if he
160     knew it! will I marry him on New Year's day, the best and happiest day, he says, in the whole year, and one that is almost sure to bring good fortune with it—It's a short notice father isn't it? but I havn't my fortune to be settled or my wedding dresses to be made, like the great ladies, father, have I?

(*Enter* RICHARD *unperceived*)

and he said so much, and said it in his way; so strong and earnest and all the time
165     so kind and gentle that I said I'd come and talk to you, father—And as they paid the money for that work of mine this morning—unexpectedly I am sure and as you have fared very poorly for a whole week, and as I couldn't help wishing there should be something to make this day a sort of holiday to you, as well as a dear and happy day to me father, I made a little treat, and brought it to surprise you!
170 RICHARD.     And see how he leaves it cooling on the step. Meg don't know what he likes not she!

*Door opens suddenly and a* FOOTMAN *nearly puts his foot in the tripe.*

FOOTMAN.     Out of the vays here will you! You must always go and be a settin' on our steps, must you. (TOBY *rises*) You can't go and give a turn to none of the neighbours never, can't you! *Will* you clear the road, or won't you?

*Enter* CUTE, FILER, *and* CHOKER *from house. Tableau.*

175 CUTE.     What's the matter? what's the matter?
FOOTMAN.     You're always a being begged and prayed upon your bended knees, you are to let our door steps be—Why don't you let 'em be? *Can't* you let them be?
CUTE.     There! that'll do, that'll do! Holloa there, Porter! Come here! What's that? Your dinner?

---

174.1 *Tableau*: MS has a gap for Choker and omits the tableau sd. The tableau probably drew upon the Leech illustration of Cute, Filer, and Choker emerging from the house, called 'dinner on the steps' on p. 34 of the volume, though that shows Filer peering into the dinner dish, rather than the gentlemen first emerging.

TOBY.　Yes, sir! (*hiding it*) 180

CUTE.　Don't leave it there! bring it here, bring it here! So this is your dinner, is it?

TOBY.　Yes, sir! (CUTE *turns it over and over on the end of the fork*)

CUTE.　Filer!

FILER.　(*examining the tripe closely*) This is a description of animal food (*making little punches in it with a pencil case*) commonly known to the labouring population 185 of this country, by the name of tripe. (CUTE *laughs, and winks*) But who eats tripe? (*looking round*) Tripe is, without an exception, the least economical, and the most wasteful article of consumption that the markets of this country can by possibility produce—the loss upon a pound of tripe has been found to be in the boiling, seven eighths of a fifth more than the loss upon a pound of any other animal sub- 190 stance—Tripe is more expensive than the hot house pine-apple. I find that the waste on that amount of tripe boiled would victual a garrison of 500 men for 5 months of 31 days each, and a February over—The waste! the waste!

TOBY.　(*aghast*) I have starved a Garrison of 500 men with my own hand!

FILER.　Who eats tripe? (*warmly*) Who eats tripe? (TOBY *makes a miserable bow*) 195 You do, do you? Then I'll tell you something. You snatch your tripe my friend out of the mouths of widows and orphans.

TOBY.　I hope not, sir—I'd sooner die of want.

FILER.　Divide the amount of tripe before-mentioned, Alderman, by the estimated number of widows and orphans, and the result will be one pennyweight of tripe to 200 each. Not a grain is left for that man. Consequently he's a robber! (CUTE *eats the tripe*)

CUTE.　And what do you say? You have heard friend Filer. What do you say?

CHOKER.　What *is* to be said? Who can take any interest in a fellow like this, in such degenerate times as these—look at him! Ah! the good old times! those were the times for a bold peasantry, and all that sort of thing—those were the times for every 205 sort of thing, in fact. There's nothing now a-days.

FILER.　No, no, the good old times; the good old times! It's of no use talking of any other times!

CHOKER.　You don't call these times do you? I don't—look into Strutt's Costumes, and see what a porter used to be in any of the good old English reigns. 210

FILER.　He hadn't in his very best circumstances a shirt to his back, or a stocking to his foot, and there was scarcely a vegetable in all England for him to put into his mouth—I can prove it by tables.

TOBY.　No, no, we can't go right or do right. (*in despair*) There is no good in us, we are born bad—and Meg, too—(*signs to* RICHARD *to take* MEG *away*) God help her, 215 she will know it soon enough. (MEG *and* RICHARD *retire up*)

CUTE.　Stop—Now you know (*addresses his two friends*) I am a plain man and a practical man, and I go to work in a plain practical way—That's my way—There is not the least mystery or difficulty in dealing with this sort of people if you understand 'em, and can talk to them in their own manner—Now you porter, don't you 220 ever tell me or anybody else my friend, that you haven't always enough to eat, and of the best, because I know better—I have tasted your tripe you know and you can't

chaff me—You understand what 'chaff' means eh? That's the right word isn't it? Ha!
ha! ha! Lord bless you it's the easiest thing on earth to deal with this sort of people
225　if you only understand 'em.

RICHARD. 　(*aside to* MEG) Easy affable joking, capital gentleman!

CUTE. 　You see, my friend, there's a great deal of nonsense talked about want—hard
up you know—that's the phrase, isn't it? ha! ha! ha! and I intend to put it down.
There's a certain amount of cant in vogue about starvation and I mean to put it
230　down. That's all—Lord bless you, you may put down anything among this sort of
people if you only know the way to set about it. (TOBY *takes* MEG's *hand, and
draws it through his arm*) Your daughter, eh? Where's her mother?

TOBY. 　Dead. Her mother got up linen and was called to Heaven when she was
born.

235　CUTE. 　And you're making love to her, are you?

RICHARD. 　Yes, and we are going to be married on New Year's day.

FILER. 　What do you mean? Married!

RICHARD. 　Why yes, we're thinking of it master. We're rather in a hurry, you see, in
case it should be put down first.

240　FILER. 　Ah! Put *that* down indeed Alderman, and you'll do something—Married!
married! The ignorance of the first principles of political economy on the part of
these people, their improvidence, their wickedness, is, by Heavens, enough to—
Now, look at that couple, will you!

TOBY. 　(*aside*) Well, they are worth looking at.

245　FILER. 　A man may live to be as old as Methusalam and may labour all his life for the
benefit of such people as these; and may heap up facts on figures, facts on figures,
mountains high and dry—and he can no more hope to persuade 'em that they have
no right or business to get married, than he can hope to persuade 'em that they have
no earthly right or business to be born. And *that* we know they haven't—it's a math
250　ematical certainty.

CUTE. 　Observe me, will you? Keep your eye on the practical man. Come here my
girl—Now, I'm going to give you a word or two of good advice, my girl—it's my
place to give advice, you know, because I'm a Justice—You know I'm a Justice, don't
you?

255　MEG. 　Yes.

CUTE. 　You are going to be married you say—very unbecoming and indelicate, in
one of your sex—But never mind that—After you are married you'll quarrel with
your husband and come to be a distressed wife—You may think not—but you will
because I tell you so—Now I give you fair warning that I have made up my mind to
260　put distressed wives down—so don't be brought before me—you'll have children—
boys. Those boys will grow up bad, of course, and run wild in the streets without
shoes and stockings—Mind my young friend I'll convict 'em, summarily, every one,
for I'm determined to put boys without shoes and stockings down.

233 *called to Heaven*: PT has 'died' for 'called to Heaven'.
247 *as these…hope to*: PT omits 'as these…hope to' inserting 'and'.

FILER.    Good, very good.

CUTE.    Perhaps your husband will die young—most likely—and leave you with a   265
baby—then you'll be turned out of doors and wander up and down the streets—Now
don't wander near me, my dear, for I am resolved to put all wandering mothers down.

FILER.    Better and better.

CUTE.    And if you attempt desperately and ungratefully and impiously to drown
yourself I'll have no pity on you, for I have made up my mind to put all suicide   270
down. So don't try it on, that's the phrase, isn't it? Ha! ha! ha! now we understand
each other—as for you, dull dog, what are you thinking of being married for? If I
was a fine young strapping chap like you I should be ashamed of being milksop
enough to pin myself to a woman's apron strings—and a pretty figure you'll cut then
with a draggle-tailed wife and a crowd of squalling children crying after you wher-   275
ever you go! There, don't make such a fool of yourself, as to get married on new
year's day—a trim young fellow like you, with all the young girls looking after you.
There—go along with you.

(MEG *goes off slowly in tears*—RICHARD *following moodily*)

TOBY.    Ah! he has put them down.

CUTE.    As you happen to be here you shall carry a letter for me. Can you be quick?—   280
you're an old man.

TOBY.    Sir—oh! yes, sir, I'm very quick and very strong.

CUTE.    How old are you?

TOBY.    I'm over sixty sir.

FILER.    Oh! this man's a great deal past the average age, you know.   285

TOBY.    I feel I'm intruding, sir—I—I misdoubted it this morning. Oh dear me!

CUTE.    There's the letter and a shilling.

FILER.    A shilling, Cute! Sixpence, for I can prove—

CUTE.    Not for a sixpence—there.

TOBY.    Thank you, sir. (*going*)   290

CUTE.    Porter!

TOBY.    Sir!

CUTE.    Take care of that daughter of yours—she's much too handsome.

TOBY.    Even her good looks are stolen from somebody or other, I suppose. (*looking
at the shilling*) She's been and robbed five hundred ladies of a bloom a piece—it's   295
very dreadful.

CUTE.    She's much too handsome, my man, the chances are that she'll come to no
good, I clearly see—Observe what I say—take care of her.

---

272 *other*: PT has an interjected speech for Richard: 'Why, Meg, never mind.'

289 *there*: PT has sd, (*he takes back the shilling and gives sixpence*), which seems necessary to the sense
of the line, but below MS has Toby look at the shilling.

293 *handsome*: PT adds 'she'll come to no good, mind that, I shall have to put her down.' And has the trio
exit, therefore cutting Cute's repetition.

*Exit* FILER, CUTE, *and* CHOKER *arm in arm.*

TOBY.   Wrong every way—wrong every way! Born bad—no business here. (*the*
300      *Chimes play very loudly*) The tune's changed—I have no business with the New Year,
nor with the old one neither—let me die! Put 'em down—Put 'em down.

*Chorus*

End of Act

---

    298.1 CHOKER: MS has 'Friend' for 'Choker'.
    300 *The tune's changed*: PT, running this speech on uninterrupted, except by the Chimes and '*music*',
from 'Even her good looks,' omits 'the tune's changed' but adds 'Dreadful' before 'Wrong every way.'
    301.1 *Chorus*: Having cued music in the course of the speech, PT gives words for this chorus, 'Good old
times—good old times! | Facts and figures—facts and figures, | Put 'em down—put 'em down.' Neither text
makes clear who is to sing the chorus, but we may assume it comes from offstage voices representing the
imps of the bells, seen later.

# 2<sup>ND</sup> QUARTER

## SCENE 1

*Hall of* SIR JOSEPH BOWLEY'S *House.*

TUGBY *discovered, dozing and waking in chair.*

*A knock and ring.*

TUG.    Another! oh lord! should I ever get sentenced to hard labour, I wonder what   1
they'll give me to do.

*Enter* TOBY.

TOBY.    A letter sir, for Sir Joseph Bowley.
TUG.    Who—who's it from?
TOBY.    Alderman Cute, sir.                                                                                5
TUG.    You're to take it in, yourself, everything goes straight in on this day of the
year.—What are you thinking on?
TOBY.    Only that the name on this letter, looked like a thousand a year.
TUG.    A thousand—ten thousand, at least. (*sits*) Ugh, I hope he's the last.
TOBY.    How different from us! Divide the lively turtles on the bills of mortality by   10
the gentlefolks able to buy 'em, and whose share does he take but his own? As to
snatching tripe from anybody's mouth, he'd scorn it!
TUG.    I dread this day, I do, the New Year, everybody's talking about the New Year as
though the old 'un was dead, and they was selling off his effects, for the benefit of
his creditors.                                                                                                        15
TOBY.    His children—his daughters—gentlemen may win their hearts and marry
them, they may be happy wives, and mothers—they may be handsome, like my
M—e—g. (*weeps*)
TUG.    What's the matter old boy?
TOBY.    Nothing, sir, nothing; I'm a poor, silly old man, sir, that's all, that's all.   20
TUG.    Poor and silly! what's that to you? You must fight up against such things! What
would become of me, if I was to give way? Why, we had as many as six runaway
carriage doubles at our door, in one night—but I fell back upon my strength of
mind, and didn't open it—
TOBY.    Dear me, sir, what a strong mind you must have!                              25

---

5 *sir*: MS omits the foregoing two speeches.

9 *Ugh…last*: MS omits the sd and 'Ugh…last' while PT omits the Dickensian but difficult sum, 'Divide
the lively turtles…but his own?' from Toby's following speech.

22 *What would become…to give way?*: MS omits 'What would become…to give way?'

25 *Dear…have*: MS omits this speech.

TUG.   But you'd better take it in, for the carriage is at the door, they've only come to
town for two hours on purpose—I'll shew you the way.

TOBY.   Thankee, sir. (*Exit,* TUGBY *follows*)

TUG.   There that way to the left—that's the door.

## SCENE 2

*A library.*

SIR JOSEPH and LADY BOWLEY, *discovered,—*MR FISH *at a table, with a cash box and
check book.* TOBY *seen at the door.*

1   SIR J.   What is this? Mr Fish, will you have the goodness to attend.

FISH.   I beg pardon, Sir Joseph. (*takes the letter from* TOBY) From Alderman Cute,
Sir Joseph.

SIR J.   Have you nothing else, porter?

5   TOBY.   No Sir—Joseph.

SIR J.   You have no bill or demand upon me—my name is Bowley, Sir Joseph
Bowley—of any kind from anybody, have you? If you have, present it. There is a
cash box by the side of Mr Fish. I allow nothing to be carried into the new year,
every description of account is settled in this house at the close of the old one, so

10   that if death was to—to—

FISH.   To cut—

SIR J.   To sever, sir, the cord of existence, my affairs would be found, I hope in a state
of preparation.

LADY B.   My dear Sir Joseph, how shocking!

15   SIR J.   My Lady Bowley, at this season of the year we should think of—of—ourselves. We should look into our—our accounts. We should feel that every return of
so eventful a period involves matters of deep moment between a man and his—and
his banker. (*to* TOBY, *who is going*) Wait a minute! You were desiring Mr Fish to
say, my lady—

20   LADY B.   Mr Fish, has said that, I believe—(*glancing at a letter*) But, upon my word,
I don't think I can let it go, after all—it is so very dear.

SIR J.   What is dear?

LADY B.   That charity, my love—they only allow two votes for a subscription of five
pounds—really monstrous!

25   SIR J.   My Lady, you surprise me. Is the luxury of feeling in proportion to the number of votes? Is there no excitement of the purest kind, in having two votes to dispose of among fifty people?

---

29 *There...door*: MS omits Tugby's speech.

14 *My...shocking*: MS omits Lady Bowley's speech and cuts Sir Joseph's to begin at 'You were desiring...'.
24 *really monstrous!*: MS omits 'really monstrous!'

LADY B.   Not to me—I acknowledge it bores one—Besides one can't oblige one's
acquaintance—but you are the poor man's friend, you know, Sir Joseph—you think
otherwise.                                                                              30

SIR J.   I am the poor man's friend. (*glancing at* TOBY) As such I may be taunted—as
such I have been taunted—but I ask no other title.

TOBY.   (*aside*) Bless him, for a noble gentleman!

SIR J.   I don't agree with Cute here—I don't agree with the Filer party—my friend,
the poor man, has no business with anything of that sort, and nothing of that sort   35
has any business with him—no man has any right to interfere between my friend
and me—I assume a paternal character towards my friend—I say, my good fellow,
I will treat you paternally.

TOBY.   (*aside*) Paternally—good gracious!

SIR J.   Your only business, my good fellow, is with me, you needn't trouble yourself  40
to think about anything, I will think for you—now the design of your creation is
not that you should swill and guzzle, and associate your enjoyments, brutally with
food, but that you should feel the dignity of labour, go forth erect into the cheerful
morning air, and stop there. Bring up your family on next to nothing—pay your
rent as regularly as the clock strikes. I set you a good example—you will find Mr   45
Fish, with a cash box before him, at all times—you may trust me to be your friend
and father.

TOBY.   (*greatly moved*) Bless him again, I say—what a father!

LADY B.   Oh you have a thankful family, Sir Joseph!

SIR J.   My lady, ingratitude is known to be the sin of that class, I expect no other  50
return.

TOBY.   (*aside*) He, too has found us bad—black-hearted ingratitude—oh dear!

SIR J.   (*opens* CUTE's *letter*) Very polite and attentive, I am sure! My lady, the
Alderman, is so obliging as to remind me that he has had 'the distinguished honor'
of meeting me at the house of our mutual friend Deedles, the banker, and inquires  55
whether it will be agreeable to me to have Will Fern, you know Will Fern, put down.

LADY B.   Most agreeable, the worst man among them! He has been committing a
robbery, I hope.

SIR J.   Why, no—not quite, very near. He came up to London, trying to better himself, that's his story, and being found at night asleep in a shed, was taken into cus-  60
tody, and carried next morning before the Alderman. The Alderman is determined
to put this sort of thing down, and that if it will be agreeable to me, to have Will
Fern, put down, he will be happy to begin with him.

---

28 *I acknowledge*: MS omits 'I acknowledge' and 'you know, Sir Joseph'.
31 *friend*: MS omits the rest of the speech.
38 *paternally*: MS begins this speech at 'I assume a...'.
41 *you needn't trouble...think for you*: MS omits 'you needn't trouble...think for you' and then probably
accidentally, the words 'and associate your enjoyments, brutally'.
44 *go forth erect...stop there*: MS omits 'go forth erect...stop there'.
46 *I set you...at all times*: PT omits 'I set you...at all times'.
56 *you know Will Fern*: MS omits 'you know Will Fern'.

LADY B.   Let him be made an example of, by all means! Last winter, when I intro
65   duced pinking and eyelet-holeing among the men and boys in the village, he
objected to the employment, Sir Joseph.
SIR J.   Hem! Mr Fish, if you'll have the goodness to attend. (FISH *seizes his pen—
dictating*) 'Private' My dear Sir, I am very much endebted to you for your courtesy,
in the matter of the man William Fern, of whom I regret to add, I can say nothing
70   favorable, he has opposed all my plans—nothing will persuade him to be happy,
when he might—Under these circumstances it appears to me, I own, that when he
comes before you again, as you informed me he promises to do tomorrow, his com-
mittal for some short term as a vagabond, would be a service to society—I am and
so forth. It appears strange, really, at the close of the year, I wind up my account, and
75   strike my balance even with William Fern. Here my friend take the letter with my
compliments, and thanks—my friend, can you say that you have also made preparation for a New Year?
TOBY.   I am afraid sir, that I am, a little, behind hand with the world.
SIR J.   Behind hand with the world! (*in a tone of terrible distinctness*)
80   TOBY.   I am afraid sir, that there's a matter of ten or twelve shillings owing to Mrs
Chickenstalker.
SIR J.   To Mrs Chickenstalker! (*in the same tone as before*)
TOBY.   A shop sir, in the general line. Also, a-a-little money, on account, of rent—a
very little, sir—it oughtn't to be owing, I know sir, but we have been hard put to it,
85   indeed!
SIR J.   (*looking at* LADY B, *then at* FISH *and at* TOBY) How a man even among this
improvident race, an old man, can look a new year in the face, with his affairs in this
condition—how he can lie down on his bed at night, and get up again in the morning, and—There! take the letter.
90   TOBY.   I heartily wish it was otherwise, sir,—we have been tried very hard!
SIR J.   Take the letter—take the letter.
FISH.   Take the letter, man, take the letter. (*points to the door*)
TOBY.   Yes, sir! Ah, bad! bad!—we must be intruding, we must! (*Exit*)

SIR JOSEPH *raises his eyes and hands*—LADY BOWLEY *yawns, and* FISH *mends
his pen.*

*Scene closes.*

66  *Last winter…Sir Joseph*: MS omits 'Last winter…Sir Joseph'.
76  *Private…compliments, and thanks*: PT omits the dictation, cutting 'Private…compliments, and
thanks' inserting instead 'Mr Fish inform the alderman, that as Fern has opposed all my plans, he may put
him down. You have heard my remarks; now'. MS omits 'also' in the final question.
82  *in the same tone as before*: The sds describing Sir Joseph's tone in PT are taken directly from Dickens.
MS has a simplified version of the exchange, cutting his first response completely and describing his second
as uttered 'with asperity'.
84  *a very little, sir*: MS omits 'a very little, sir'.
91  *Take…letter*: MS omits Sir Joseph's repetition and Fish's echo.

## SCENE 3

*A street.*

*Enter Toby.*

TOBY.    I'm glad I've got rid of that letter! We poor folks are sad plagues! I trotted fast   1
by the old church, for I feared to hear the chimes again! We seem to get no hold on
the new year, any how!

*Enter* WILL FERN *carrying little* LILIAN—TOBY *runs against him.*

I beg your pardon, I'm sure—I hope I haven't hurt you.
WILL.    No friend, you have not hurt me.                                                      5
TOBY.    Nor the child, I hope?
WILL.    Nor the child—I thank you kindly. (*glancing at a little girl he carries—asleep*)
You can tell me, perhaps, and if you can, I am sure you will, where Alderman
Cute lives?
TOBY.    Close at hand, I'll show you his house, with pleasure.                                10
WILL.    I was to have gone to him elsewhere to-morrow, but I'm uneasy under suspi-
cion, and want to clear myself, and to be free to go, and seek my bread—I don't
know where. So maybe he'll forgive my going to his house to-night.
TOBY.    It's impossible  (*with a start*) that your name's Fern?
WILL.    That's my name.                                                                       15
TOBY.    Why then—for Heaven's sake don't go to him—he'll put you down, as sure as
ever you was born—don't go to him! Sir Joseph Bowley has written to him, to put
you down, because—because you wouldn't do eyelet holeing and wouldn't be his
child. I mean wouldn't have him for a friend, and a father—and because, because—
WILL.    Truly, I have gone against his plans, to my misfortun'—I can't help it. As to     20
character, them gentlefolks will search and search, and pry and pry, and have it as
free from spot or speck in us, afore they'll help us to a dry word! Well! I hope they
don't lose good opinion as easy as we do, or their lives is strict indeed, and hardly
worth the keeping. For myself, master, I never took with that hand, (*holding it
before him*) what wasn't my own, and never held it back from work, however hard,   25
or poorly paid. Whoever can deny it, let him chop it off! But when work won't
maintain me like a human creature—when I am hungry, out of doors and in—when
I see a whole working life begin that way, go on that way, and end that way, without
a chance or change—then I say to the gentlefolks, keep away from me! let my cottage be—my doors is dark enough, without your darkening of 'em more. Don't look   30
for me to come up into the Park to help the show when there's a birthday, or a fine

---

4 *I hope I haven't hurt you*: PT repeats 'I hope I haven't hurt you?' and gives an elaborate sd from the
Dickensian description.

8 *will*: PT adds 'and I'd rather ask you than another'.

14 *Fern*: PT adds 'WILL. (*astonished*) Eh!/ TOBY. Fern! Will Fern!'

17 *don't go to him*: MS omits second 'don't go to him!' and then omits 'you wouldn't do…I mean.'

speechmaking, or what not. Act your plays and games without me, and be welcome
to 'em, and enjoy 'em—we've nought to do with one another—I'm best let alone. (*the*
CHILD *wakes*) What, I've waked you, Lil, have I? Stand down, love—bless thy pretty
35  locks!

TOBY.    Dear me, more trouble!

WILL.    I am not a cross grained man, by nature, and easy satisfied, I'm sure—I bear
no ill-will against none of 'em—I only want to live like one of the Almighty's
creeturs—I can't—I don't, so there's a pit dug, between me and them that can and
40  do,—well, I don't know as this Alderman could hurt *me* much, by sending me to
jail, but without a friend to speak a word for me, he might do it, and you see! (*pointing to* CHILD)

TOBY.    She has a beautiful face!

WILL.    Why yes! I've thought so many times,—when my hearth was very cold, and
my cupboard very bare. I thought so t'other night, when we were taken like two
45  thieves—But they—they shouldn't try the little face too often—should they, Lil?
That's hardly fair upon a man.

TOBY.    Is your wife living?

WILL.    I never had one,—she's my brother's child,—an orphan,—nine year old,
though you'd hardly think it, but she's tired, and worn out now. They'd have taken
50  care of her, the Union, eight and twenty mile away from where we live, between
four walls, as they took care of my old father when he couldn't work no more, tho'
he didn't trouble 'em long—but I took her instead, and she's lived with me ever
since. Her mother had a friend once, in London here—we are trying to find her, and
to find work too—but it's a large place—Never mind—more room for us to walk
55  about in Lilly. I don't so much as know your name, but I've opened my heart free to
you, for I'm thankful to you, with good reason. I'll take your advice, and keep clear
of this—

TOBY.    Justice!

WILL.    Ah! if that's the name they give him—this Justice—And to-morrow will try
60  whether there's better fortun' to be met with, somewheres near London. Good
night! a happy New Year.

TOBY.    Stay!—the New Year never can be happy to me if we part like this—the New
Year never can be happy to me, if I see the child and you go wandering away you
don't know where, without a shelter for your heads—Come home with me; I'm a
65  poor man, living in a poor place, but I can give you a lodging for one night, and
never miss it. Come home with me! Here! I'll take her! (*lifting* CHILD) A pretty one!

---

33  *alone*: MS has several omissions in this speech: 'Well! I hope...worth the keeping', 'Whoever can
deny it, let him chop it off!', 'when I see a whole...chance or change', 'don't look for me...I'm best let alone'.

38  *against none of 'em*: MS omits 'against none of 'em'.

38  *Almighty's*: MS substitutes 'Heaven's' for 'the Almighty's'.

40  *so there's a pit...can and do*: PT substitutes, for 'so there's a pit...can and do' 'I've got a bad name, and
I'm not likely, I'm afeard, to get a better. 'Tain't lawful to be out of sorts, and I am out of sorts—though
Heaven knows I'd sooner bear a cheerful spirit, if I could'. Both are from the scene as Dickens wrote it.

49  *nine year old...worn out now*: MS omits 'nine year old...worn out now' and then 'between four walls'.

I'd carry twenty times her weight, and never know I'd got it. Tell me, if I go to quick for you, I'm very fast, I always was. (*going*)

WILL.   She'll tire you, master.

TOBY.   Why she's as light—as light as a feather! Lighter than a peacock's feather—a 70 great deal lighter! Here we are, and there we go! Round this first turning to the right, Uncle Will, and past that pump, and sharp off up the passage to the left, right opposite the public house. Here we are, and there we go! Cross over Uncle Will, and mind the kidney pieman at the corner—Here we are, and there we go! Down the mews here, Uncle Will, and stop at the black door, with 'T. Veck, Ticket Porter,' 75 wrote upon a board—and here we are, and there we go!

(*Trots up and down the stage, and then Exeunt*)

## SCENE 4

TOBY's *lodgings.*

MEG *discovered.*

MEG.   Richard is hasty—very hasty—tho' I can scarcely blame him—for it was cruel, 1 to speak to us so hardly!

*Enter* TOBY—WILL—*and* CHILD.

TOBY.   Here we are, indeed, my precious Meg, surprising you!

MEG.   A surprise, indeed!—Well! (*holds out her arms, the* CHILD *runs to her*)

TOBY.   Here we are, and there we go! (*running round the room, and choking audibly*) 5 Here Uncle Will! here's a fire, you know!—why don't you come to the fire—Meg my precious darling, where's the kettle?—Here it is, and here it goes—and it'll bile in no time. (*puts it on the fire,* MEG *places* CHILD *by fire*)

MEG.   Why, father, you're crazy to-night, I think—I don't know what the bells would say to that—poor little feet, how cold they are.          10

LIL.   Oh, they're warmer now,—they're quite warm now.

MEG.   Why, father!

TOBY.   Here I am, and here I go, my dear.

---

68 *Come home . . . always was*: MS omits the second 'Come home with me' and 'Tell me, . . . I always was'.
71 *Why . . . lighter*: LCSM omits the repetition of 'as light' and 'lighter than a . . . great deal lighter!' PT omits 'and sharp off up the passage to the left'.

2 *hardly*: PT inserts here 'Poor dear father! I think I could not marry even Richard to part from you; what a host of kind words and kinder deeds crowd upon me now; words and deeds that have taken the sting from poverty. (*weeps. The door opens.*) Oh!'
11 *now*: PT has another speech for Meg here: 'No! no! no! we haven't rubbed 'em half enough, we're so busy, so busy; and when they're done, we'll brush out the damp hair, and when that's done we'll bring some colour to the poor pale face, with fresh water—and when that's done, we'll be so gay, and brisk, and happy.'

MEG.    Good gracious me, he's crazy! he's put the dear child's bonnet on the kettle,
15    and hung the lid behind the door.

TOBY.    I didn't go to do it, my love! (*repairing his mistake*) Meg, my dear! I see my
dear, as I was coming in half an ounce of tea lying somewhere on the stairs. (*produces it, and slice of bacon, which he re-pockets*) And I'm pretty sure there was a bit
of bacon, too—as I don't remember where it was, exactly, I'll go myself and try to
20    find 'em. (*Exit*)

WILL.    I thank you, miss, a hundred times, poor child, she has had none but these
rough hands to tend her, for many a year.

MEG.    She is a good child, I am sure, and loves you dearly, do you not? (*kisses her*)

*Enter* TOBY.

TOBY.    I have had a job to find 'em, the stairs are so dark—but here they are at last,
25    all correct—Meg, my pet, if you'll just make the tea, while your unworthy father
toasts the bacon, we shall be ready immediately.

MEG.    That I will, father.

TOBY.    It's a curious circumstance—curious—but well known to my friends, that I
never care, myself, for rashers, nor for tea—I like to see other people enjoy 'em—
30    (*speaking very loud, to impress the fact upon his guest*) but to me, as food, they're
disagreeable—There, uncle Will—now, Lilly, fall to, whilst it's hot! (*sniffs*)

WILL.    This is kind, indeed, master—though I fear I do you a wrong, by taking it.

TOBY.    Not at all—I'll just take a mere morsel, for form sake—tho' I don't care for
bacon, that I don't. (*Meg busies herself with the tea etc*)
35    Now I'll tell you what—the little one sleeps with Meg, I know.

LIL.    With good Meg! (*caressing her*) with Meg!

TOBY.    That's right! And I shouldn't wonder if she kiss Meg's father, won't she? I'm
Meg's father. (*the* CHILD *goes timidly towards him, and having kissed him, returns
to* MEG) She's as sensible as Solomon! Here we come, and here we—no, we don't—I
40    don't mean that—I—what was I saying, Meg, my precious? (MEG *looks towards*
WILL, *who has leaned upon her chair, and with his face turned from her, fondled the*
CHILD's *head, half hidden in her lap*) To be sure! to be sure! I don't know what I'm
rambling on about, tonight—my wits are wool-gathering, I think—Will Fern, you
come along with me—you're tired to death, and broken down, for want of rest—
Meg, get the child to bed! (*Exit* MEG *with* CHILD) Will, I'll shew you where you
45    lie—it's not much of a place, only a loft, but having a loft, I always say, is one of the
great conveniences of living in a mews, and till this coachhouse, and stables, gets a

---

25  *correct*: PT inserts 'I was pretty sure it was tea, and a rasher—so it is!'

31  *It's a curious…it's hot!*: MS omits this speech.

36  *LIL*: MS omits Lilian's speech, and Toby's speech and sds down to '…wool-gathering, I think'.

43  *me*: PT has an elaborate sd here, deriving directly from Dickens: *Will still plays with the Child's curls,
and still leans upon Meg's chair, turning away his face—but, in his coarse rough fingers, clenching and expand-
ing the Child's hair.*

better let, we live here cheap. There's plenty of sweet hay up there, belonging to a neighbour; and it's as clean as hands and Meg can make it. Cheer up, don't give way, A new heart for a new year, always. There's the ladder, good night, Uncle Will. (*Exit* WILL. TOBY *goes to the door*) The pretty one is praying—that is Meg's 50 name—dear, dear Meg!—Bless her, she pauses and asks for mine—she prays for me! It must be getting late. (*takes out the paper*) Full of obserwations (*reads carelessly*) more trouble by the poor—and—Eh! what's this?—Impossible! a woman, take the life of her own child—plunge with it, into the river—Unnatural! Cruel! (*lays his head on the table—soft Music and then the Chimes*)

CHORUS

Toby Veck! Toby Veck!                                           55
Waiting for you, Toby!
Toby Veck! Toby Veck!
Come and see us!
Come and see us!
Drag him to us!                                                60
Drag him to us!
Haunt and hunt him!
Haunt and hunt him!
Break his slumbers!
Break his slumbers!                                            65
Toby Veck! Toby Veck!
Door open wide, Toby!
Toby Veck! Toby Veck!
Door open wide, Toby!

(TOBY *starts and appears bewildered—listens*)

TOBY.  Meg! (*softly opening door*) Do you hear anything?                70
MEG.  (*within*) I hear the bells, father—surely, they're very strange to-night.
TOBY.  Is she asleep? (*peeps in*)
MEG.  So peacefully and happily! I can't leave her yet though father! Look how she holds my hand!
TOBY.  Meg! listen to the bells! They call me! If the tower door is really open— 75 (*hastily laying aside his apron, but never thinking of his hat*)—what's to hinder me, from going up into the steeple, and satisfying myself? If it's shut, I don't want any other satisfaction—that's enough.

*The Chimes louder.*

*End of Second Quarter.*

48 *There's plenty … can make it*: MS omits 'There's plenty … can make it.'
75 *They call me!*: MS omits 'They call me!'

# 3<sup>RD</sup> QUARTER

## SCENE 1

*The Bell Tower shewing the bells.*

*As* TOBY *enters the Chimes ring, and the bells assume spectral forms. The* GOBLIN OF
THE BELL *appears, up C. trap.*

1 GOB.   What visitor is this?
TOBY.   I thought my name was called by the Chimes—I hardly know why I am here,
or how I came—I have listened to the chimes these many years, they have cheered
me often.
5 GOB.   And you have thanked them?
TOBY.   A thousand times.
GOB.   How?
TOBY.   I am a poor man, and could only thank them in words.
GOB.   And always so? have you never done us wrong in words?
10 TOBY.   No.
GOB.   Never done us foul and false and wicked wrong, in words?
TOBY.   Nev—
GOB.   The voice of time cries to man, advance!—Time is for his advancement and
improvement. Who seeks to turn him back or stay him on his course arrests a
15 mighty engine which will strike the meddler dead; and be the fiercer and the wilder,
ever for its momentary check.
TOBY.   I never did so to my knowledge sir—It was quite by accident if I did—I
wouldn't go to do it, I'm sure.
GOB.   Who puts into the mouth of time, or of its servants, a cry of lamentation for
20 days which have had their trial and their failure, does a wrong—and you have done
that wrong to us, the chimes.
TOBY.   If you knew—or perhaps you do know—if you know how often you have
kept me company, how often you have cheered me up when I've been low—how
you were quite the plaything of my little daughter Meg, almost the only one she ever
25 had—when first her mother died, and she and me were left alone—you won't bear
malice for a hasty word.
GOB.   Who hears us make response to any creed that gauges human nature and
affections as it gauges the amount of miserable food on which humanity may pine
and dwindle does us wrong—that wrong you have done us.

---

0.3 *up C. trap*: MS omits 'up C. trap'.      25 *and she…alone*: MS omits 'and she…alone'.
29 *Who hears…done us*: PT omits this speech and Toby's response.

TOBY.    I have—please forgive me.                                                                                        30
GOB.    Who hears us echo the putters-down of crushed and broken natures formed
    to be raised up higher than such maggots of the time can crawl or can conceive?
    Who does so, does us wrong; and you have done that wrong.
TOBY.    Not meaning it—in my ignorance—not meaning it!
GOB.    Lastly, and most of all, who turns his back upon the fallen and disfigured of his   35
    kind; abandons them as vile; does wrong to Heaven and man—and you have done
    that wrong!
TOBY.    Spare me for mercy's sake!
GOB.    Listen.
SPECTRES.    Listen!                                                                                                          40
GOB.    Listen! (*the organ sounds faintly in church—A dirge heard*)
TOBY.    She is dead! Meg is dead—her Spirit calls to me—I hear it!
GOB.    The spirit of your child bewails the dead and mingles with the dead—dead
    hopes, dead fancies, dead imaginings of youth; but she is living—learn from her life
    a living truth—learn from the creature dearest to your heart, how bad the bad are   45
    born—follow her to desperation! The Spirit of the Chimes is your companion—
    go—it stands behind you.

(TOBY *turns and sees* LILIAN *still a child, but appearing as a spirit*)

TOBY.    I carried her myself to-night in these arms.
GOB.    Show him what he calls himself.

(*The Tower opens at his feet*)

TOBY.    A form crushed and motionless—no more a living man—dead!                          50
SPECTRES.    Dead!
TOBY.    Gracious Heaven! And the new year?
SPECTRES.    Past!
TOBY.    What! I missed my way, and coming on the outside of this Tower in the dark,
    fell down—a year ago?                                                                                             55
GOB.    Nine years ago.

*Chimes play. The* SPECTRES *vanish.*

TOBY.    What are these? If I am not mad, what are these?
GOB.    Spirits of the Bells—their sound upon the air—they take such shapes and
    occupations as the hopes and thoughts of mortals and the recollections they have
    stored up give them.                                                                                                 60

---

   32 *formed to be...conceive?*: PT omits 'formed to be...conceive?'
   40 *Listen*: PT omits this line for the Spectres, who are presumably the bells 'in spectral form' revealed at
the beginning of the scene.
   51 SPECTRES: PT attributes this and the following line for the Spectres to the Goblin.
   60 *What are these?...give them*: PT omits Toby's question about the Spectres and the Goblin's answer,
but then has the Goblin respond 'The Spirit of the Bell!' to his next question.

TOBY.    And you—what are you?
GOB.    Hush! hush! look here!

*Scene opens and shows a poor mean room, working at embroidery his daughter*
MEG *appears.*

TOBY.    Ah changed! changed! the light of the clear eye how dimmed—the bloom,
how faded from the cheek! Beautiful she is, as she has been—but hope—hope—
65     hope! Oh where was the fresh hope that had spoken to me like a voice!

MEG *looks up from her work at a companion—a figure dressed as the child* LILIAN, *but*
*9 years older.*

GOB.    Hark! they were speaking.
LIL.    Meg—how often you raise your head from your work to look at me.
MEG.    Are my looks so altered, Lilian, that they frighten you?
LIL.    Nay, dear—but you smile at that, yourself—why not smile when you look at
70     me, Meg?
MEG.    I do so, do I not?
LIL.    Now you do, but not usually. When you think I'm busy and don't see you, you
look so anxious and so doubtful that I hardly like to raise my eyes—There is little
cause for smiling, in this hard and toilsome life—but you were once so cheerful.
75  MEG.    Am I not now—Do I make our weary life more weary to you, Lilian?
LIL.    You have been the only thing that made it life, sometimes the only thing that
made me care to live so, Meg—such work, such work! So many hours, so many
days, so many long, long nights of hopeless, cheerless, never-ending work and not
to live upon enough, however coarse—but to earn bare bread—Oh Meg, Meg! how
80     can the cruel world go round, and bear to look upon such lives.
MEG.    Lilly! Why, Lilly, you so young and pretty!
LIL.    Oh, Meg! the worst of all, the worst of all! Make me old, Meg, wither me, and
shrivel me, and free me from the dreadful thoughts that tempt me in my youth!

*The vision closes—*TOBY *sinks upon his knees. Bells are heard and the*

*Scene changes to Bowley Hall*

*an opening at the back shews the Park.*

*Chorus of* PEASANTS

*during which Enter* FILER, CUTE, SIR JOSEPH BOWLEY, MASTER BOWLEY, *and*
*others.* TOBY *recovers.*

---

65  *hope*: PT cuts repetitions of 'hope' and has Lilian revealed at the beginning of the vision, not entering after this speech.
78  *work*: PT inserts here 'not to heap up riches, not to live grandly or gaily'.
83.4  *Chorus of* PEASANTS: Neither MS nor PT offer the words for the chorus, though MS has a space for
their insertion (f. 826r).

SIR J.  Now, friends and children the plum pudding will be ready in half an hour—barely time for the match of skittles, which, as your friend and father, I have prom- 85 ised to play with the humblest of my tenants. Fish, lead the way.

PEASANTS *shout and exeunt* SIR JOSEPH *and others.*

CUTE.  Skittles eh! It quite reminds one of the days of bluff King Hal. Ah! fine character!

FILER.  Very. (*dryly*) He married women, and murdered 'em.

CUTE.  (*to* MASTER BOWLEY) You'll marry the beautiful ladies, and not murder 90 'em, eh? Sweet boy!—we shall have this little gentleman in parliament now, before we know where we are—we shall hear of his brilliant achievements of all kinds—and we shall make orations about him in the Common Council, I'll be bound. (*Exit* MASTER B.)

TOBY.  (*aside*) Oh! the difference of shoes and stockings. Richard—where is he? I can't find Richard! Where is Richard?  95

*Enter* FISH.

FISH.  Bless my heart and soul—where's Alderman Cute? The most dreadful circumstance has occurred. I think it will be best not to acquaint Sir Joseph with it 'till the day is over—the most frightful and deplorable event.

CUTE.  Fish, Fish, my good fellow, what is the matter?

FISH.  Deedles, the banker.  100

CUTE.  Not stopped—It can't be!

FISH.  Shot himself—no motive—princely circumstances.

CUTE.  Circumstances! a man of noble fortune—Suicide, Mr Fish, by his own hand?

FISH.  This very morning.  105

CUTE.  Oh! the brain, the brain! oh! the nerves, the nerves! the mysteries of this machine, called man! oh! the little that unhinges it—poor creatures that we are! perhaps a dinner, Mr Fish—perhaps the conduct of his son, who, I have heard, ran very wild, and was in the habit of drawing bills upon him, without the least authority! A most respectable man—one of the most respectable men I ever knew—a 110 public calamity—I shall make a point of wearing the deepest mourning—a most respectable man!

TOBY.  (*aside*) What Alderman! no word of putting down?

CUTE.  Mr Fish, I will break this melancholy intelligence to Sir Joseph—Good bye, Mr Fish.  115

94 *Sweet boy!...stockings*: MS omits 'Sweet boy!...I'll be bound' and also Toby's aside 'Oh! The difference of shoes and stockings'.

104 *Suicide...own hand?*: PT substitutes 'one of the most respectable of men' for 'Suicide, Mr Fish, by his own hand?'

112 *Oh! the brain...most respectable man*: MS omits 'Oh! the brain...the nerves' and 'oh! the little... A most'

*Shouts. Enter* SIR JOSEPH *and others.*

Well, Sir Joseph, what success?

SIR J.    Capital, Cute, capital—to use your favorite phrase, I put them down famously.

SERVANT.    The dinner is served up, Sir Joseph!

SIR J.    Very well—then your friend and father invites you to plum pudding! John,
120    madeira for my friends, and XX for my children.

*A noise.* WILL FERN *forces his way in*—FERN *looks haggard and faint.*

SIR J.    What is this? Who gave this man admittance? This is a criminal from prison!
Mr Fish, sir, will you have the goodness—

WILL.    A minute—a minute—Gentlefolks, look at me. You see I'm at the worst—
beyond all hurt or harm—beyond your help. Let me say a word for these (*pointing
125    to the labouring people*) and when you're met together hear the real truth spoken
out for once.

SIR J.    There's not a man here who'd have him for a spokesman.

WILL.    Like enough, Sir Joseph—not the less true, perhaps, is what I say—perhaps
that's a proof of it. Gentlefolks—I've lived many a year in this place—you may see
130    the cottage from the sunk fence over yonder—well, I lived there—How hard, how
bitter hard I lived there I won't say—that I growed up a man and not a brute says
something for me, as I was then—As I am now there's nothing can be said for me or
done for me—I'm past it.

SIR J.    I am glad this man has entered—don't disturb him—he is an example—a liv
135    ing example I hope and trust, and confidently expect, that it will not be lost upon
my friends here.

WILL.    I dragged on somehow—neither me, nor any other man knows how—but so
heavy, that I could'nt put a cheerful face upon it, or make believe that I was anything
but what I was. Now, gentlemen, you gentlemen, that sits at sessions—when you see
140    a man with discontent writ on his face, you says to one another 'He's suspicious—I
has my doubts,' says you, 'about Will Fern—watch that fellow' I don't say gentlemen
it ayn't quite nat'ral but I say 'tis so—and from that hour, whatever Will Fern does,
or lets alone,—all one; it goes against him.

CUTE.    Of course—I told you so—common cry. Lord bless you, we are up to all this
145    sort of thing—myself and human nature.

WILL.    Now, gentlemen, see how your laws are made to trap and hunt us when we're
brought to this—I tries to live elsewhere and I'm a vagabond—to jail with him! At
last, the constable, the keeper, anybody finds me anywhere a-doing anything—to

---

120  *xx for my children*: XX means ale, so presumably the children referred to are Sir Joseph's peasantry,
not Master Bowley. MS omits the order for drinks, and has Will Fern enter at once, while PT has the peasants sit at a table on the left of the stage and the guests at another on the right.

124  *help*: PT inserts 'for the time when your kind words, or kind actions, could have done me good is
gone, with the scent of last year's beans or clover on the air.'

139  *but so heavy … what I was*: MS omits 'but so heavy … what I was.'

145  *Lord bless you … human nature*: MS omits 'Lord bless you … human nature.'

jail with him for he's a vagrant and a jail-bird known, and jail's the only home
he's got.                                                                                              150

CUTE.   A very good home, too.

WILL.   Do I say this to serve *my* cause? Who can give me back my liberty—who can
give me back my good name—who can give me back my innocent niece—who can
give me back myself? Not all the lords and ladies in wide England—But Gentlemen,
Gentlemen, dealing with other men like me, begin at the right end—give us, in  155
mercy, better homes when we're a lying in our cradles—give us better food, when
we're a working for our lives—give us kinder laws to bring us back, when we're a
going wrong—and don't set jail, jail, afore us, every where we turn.

*The whole of the persons make a movement towards* FERN, *Tableau.*

*Chimes, and Scene changes to a poor and mean garret.*

MEG *working at an embroidery frame.*

TOBY.   No Lilian—where is Lilian?

MEG.   It is almost too dark to see the threads! Poor father! I fancy he is looking down  160
upon me lovingly—Oh, how lovingly! and talking about the old times and the Bells.

TOBY.   Sweet Meg, dear, suffering Meg!

MEG.   I must light a candle, or I shall spoil the flowers.

TOBY.   But where is Richard? why is he not here to comfort her he loved? where is
Richard.                                                                                              165

(*A knock*)

MEG.   Who's there?

RICHARD.   May I come in, Meg?

MEG.   Yes—come in—come in.

*Enter* RICHARD—MEG *gives Chair—Tableau.*

RICHARD.   Still at work, Margaret? You work late.

MEG.   I generally do.                                                                                170

RICHARD.   And early?

MEG.   And early.

150 *Now, gentlemen… home he's got*: PT has a longer version of this speech: 'Now, gentlemen—(*holding out
his hands*)—I tries to live elsewhere, and I'm a vagabond—to jail with him! One of your keepers sees me in the
broad day, near my own patch of garden, with a gun—to jail with him! It's twenty mile away; and coming back,
I begs a trifle on the road—to jail with him! At last, the constable, the keeper—anybody—finds me anywhere, a
doing anything—to jail with him, for he's a vagrant, and a jail-bird known—and jail's the only home he's got.'

158.1 *Tableau*: Dickens has an inversion of a biblical quotation (Ruth 1:16) to crown this speech, but that
would not be allowed on stage; the tableau is a visual equivalent of the bitterness of Fern's rejection.

168.1 *Tableau*: PT has '(*see sketch*) he is crossing to take the chair which is turned to the wall. Meg rises
and stops him.' She then gives him the one she was sitting on, saying the other was Lilian's. The Dickensian
text (p. 125) has a sketch of Meg working and the empty chair; Richard is seen not in the room but in a
linked drawing below, approaching the door.

RICHARD.   So she said.

TOBY.   She! he means Lilian.

175 RICHARD.   She said you never tired, or never owned that you tired—not all the time you lived together—not even when you fainted, between work and fasting—But I told you that, the last time I came.

MEG.   You did; and I implored you to tell me nothing more and yet you made me a solemn promise, Richard, you never would.

180 RICHARD.   A solemn promise—a solemn promise to be sure—a solemn promise—how can I help it, Margaret? what am I to do—she has been to me again!

MEG.   Again! Oh! does she think of me so often? has she been again?

RICHARD.   Twenty times again, Margaret—she haunts me—she comes behind me in the street, and thrusts it in my hand. (*shews purse*) I hear her foot upon the ashes

185 when I'm at my work—Ha! Ha! that ain't often, and before I can turn my head her voice is in my ear saying 'Richard don't look round, for Heaven's love give her this!' She brings it where I live—she sends it in letters—she taps at the window, and lays it on the sill. What *can* I do? *look* at it!

MEG.   Hide it! hide it! When she comes again tell her, Richard, that I love her in my

190 soul—that I never lie down to sleep but I bless her and pray for her—that she is with me, night and day—that if I died tomorrow I would remember her with my last breath—but that I cannot look upon it.

RICHARD.   (*crushing purse*) I told her so—I told her so as plain as words could speak. I've taken this gift back and left it at her door a dozen times since then, but

195 when she came at last and stood before me, face to face, what could I do?

MEG.   You saw her! you saw her! Oh! Lilian, my sweet girl!

RICHARD.   I saw her there she stood trembling. 'How does she look, Richard? does she ever speak of me? Is she thinner? my old place at the table—what's in my old place? And the frame she taught me our old work on—has she burnt it, Richard?'

200 There she was—I heard her say it—'Richard I have fallen very low, and you may guess how much I have suffered in having this sent back, when I can bear to bring it in my hand to you—but you loved her once, even in my memory, dearly—Others stepped in between you—fears and jealousies and doubts, and vanities estranged you from her—but you did love her, even in my memory'—I suppose I did—I did—

205 that's neither here nor there.—Well, Lilian went on 'Oh Richard, if you ever did—if you have any memory for what is gone and lost, take it to her once more—once more! tell her how I begged and prayed—tell her how I laid my head upon your shoulder where her own might have lain, and was so humble to you, Richard—tell her that you looked into my face, and saw the beauty which she used to praise all

210 gone—all gone—and in its place a poor, wan, hollow cheek that she would weep to see—tell her everything, and take it back, and she will not refuse again—she will

---

194 *a dozen times*: MS omits 'a dozen times'.

196 *Oh! Lilian, my sweet girl!*: PT repeats 'Oh! Lilian! Lilian!'

203 *and doubts, and vanities*: MS omits 'and doubts, and vanities'.

not have the heart.' (*a pause*) You won't take it, Margaret? (*she motions him to leave her*) Good night, Margaret.

MEG.    Good night!

(*Exit* RICHARD)

Is that the Richard of my girlish love? Yet it is he, debased—degraded! (*weeps*) I must    215
to work—in any mood, in any grief, in any torture of the mind or body, work must
be done. It is very cold! (*Chimes*) Half-past twelve. (*a knock*) A knock, at this
unusual hour!

(*Door opens. Enter* LILIAN, *who rushes to* MEG *and falls upon her knees*)

Lilian! up dear! up! Lilian! my own dearest.

LIL.    Never more, Meg—never more! here! here! close to you, holding to you, feeling    220
your dear breath upon my face—

MEG.    Sweet Lilian! darling Lilian! child of my heart—no mother's love can be more
tender—lay your head upon my breast!

LIL.    Never more, Meg, never more—When I first looked into your face, you knelt
before me—on my knees before you, let me die—let it be here.    225

MEG.    You have come back, my treasure! We will live together, work together, hope
together—die together!

LIL.    Ah! kiss my lips Meg, fold your arms about me—press me to your bosom—
look kindly on me—but don't raise me. Let it be here—let me see the last of your
dear face upon my knees.    230

MEG.    Oh youth and beauty, happy as ye should be, look at this!

LIL.    Forgive me Meg—so dear, so dear! forgive me! I know you do—I see you do—
but say so, Meg!

MEG.    I do—I do, dear Lilian!

LIL.    His blessing on you dearest love! kiss me once more! He suffered her to    235
sit beside his feet and dry them with her hair—Oh Meg what mercy and
compassion. (*faints*)

*Tableau*

236  *he suffered . . . with her hair*: PT omits 'he suffered . . . with her hair.' This is unexpected: the biblical
reference would seem more likely to be cut from the censorship text rather than the printed version.

237.1  *Tableau*: The volume has no picture on which this tableau would have been based. Its next illustration does follow, p. 135, as a frontispiece to the fourth quarter, but shows the goblins, and Toby, floating
above Meg as she kneels on the river bank.

# 4<sup>TH</sup> QUARTER

## SCENE 1

*A Chandler's Shop, Back Parlour.*

TUGBY *and* MRS CHICKENSTALKER *discovered.*

1  TUG.    What sort of a night is it, Anne? Here I am if it's bad, and I don't want to go out
if it's good.

MRS C.    Blowing and sleeting hard—and threatening snow—dark and very cold.

TUG.    I'm glad to think, we had muffins. It's a sort of night that's meant for muffins—
5  likewise crumpets. Also Sally Lunns.

MRS C.    You're in spirits, Tugby, my dear.

TUG.    No, not particular—I'm a little elevated—The muffins came so pat—So it's
blowing hard, and sleeting, and threatening snow, and it's dark, and very cold, is it,
my dear? Poke the fire—it's hard weather—Aye, aye! Years are like Christians in that
10  respect—Some of 'em die hard, some of 'em easy,—This one hasn't many days to run,
and is making a fight for it—I like him all the better—

*Enter* DOCTOR.

DOCTOR.    How do ye do? this is a bad business, up stairs, Mrs Tugby, the man can't
live.

TUG.    Not the back attic can't?

15  DOCTOR.    The back attic, Mr Tugby, is coming down stairs very fast, and will be
below the basement, very soon—the back attic, Mr Tugby, is going.

TUG.    (*turning to his wife*) He must go, you know, before he's gone.

DOCTOR.    I don't think you can move him. I wouldn't take the responsibility of saying it could be done, myself. You had better leave him where he is—he can't live
20  long.

TUG.    It's the only subject, that we've ever had a word upon, she and me, and look
what it comes to—he's going to die here, after all—going to die upon the premises—
going to die in our house!

MRS C.    And where should he have died, Tugby?

25  TUG.    In the workhouse. What are workhouses for?

---

2 *Here I am … if it's good*: MS omits 'Here I am … if it's good'.

6 *Tugby, my dear*: MS omits 'Tugby, my dear'.

7 *pat*: PT extends this exchange with more material from Dickens's account of Tugby and his apoplectic
chuckling, and having them assume for a moment the doctor is a customer entering their shop.

17 *He must … he's gone*: MS omits Tugby's interjection.

22 *after all … premises*: MS cuts 'after all' and 'He's going to die on the premises'.

MRS C.    Not for that—neither did I marry you for that—don't think it, Tugby—I won't have it, I'd be separated first, and never see your face again—I told you so when Richard, Meggy Veck's husband, was in the same plight—for I knew Richard, as a handsome, steady, manly, independent youth—I knew Meg, as the sweetest looking girl, eyes ever saw—I knew her father, for the simplest, hardest working, childest-hearted man, that ever drew the breath of life; and when I turn such, out of house, and home, may angels turn me out of Heaven! As they would! And serve me right! Bless her! Bless her!

(TUG *looks indignant, and empties the contents of the till*)

DOCTOR.    There's something interesting about that woman now—how did she come to marry him?

MRS C.    Why, that is not the least cruel part of her story, sir—You see they kept company, she and Richard, many years ago. But, somehow, Richard got it into his head, through what a gentleman told him, that a young man of spirit had no business to be married—and the gentleman frightened her, and made her timid of his deserting her, and of her children coming to the gallows—And in short the thing lingered and lingered, and their trust in one another was broken, and so at last was the match.

DOCTOR.    Oh, then he went wrong, did he?

MRS C.    I think his mind was troubled by their having broke with one another. He took to drinking, idling, bad companions—he lost his looks, his character, his friends, his work—everything!

DOCTOR.    Not everything, because he gained a wife—and I want to know how he gained her?

MRS C.    I'm coming to it, sir, in a moment. This went on for five years, he sinking lower, and lower, she enduring poor thing, miseries enough to wear her life away— At last, he was so cast down, and cast out, that no one would employ or notice him—But coming, for the hundredth time, to one gentleman, who had often and often tried him, and knew his history, [who] said, 'I believe there is only one person in the world, who has a chance of reclaiming you; ask me to trust you no more until she tries to do it.'

DOCTOR.    Ah! Well!

MRS C.    Well, he went to her and kneeled to her, and said it was so—said it ever had been, and made a prayer to her to save him.

DOCTOR.    And she—don't distress yourself, Mrs Tugby!

MRS C.    She came to me that night, to ask me about living here. 'What he was once to me,' she said, 'is buried in a grave—side by side with what I was to him. I will

---

33  *childest-hearted... Bless her!*: MS omits 'childest-hearted' and 'As they would ... Bless her!'
42  *and the gentleman... was the match*: PT omits 'and the gentleman... was the match'.
45  *idling, bad companions*: PT omits 'idling, bad companions'.
49  *I'm coming to... in a moment*: MS omit s 'I'm coming to... in a moment'.
56  DOCTOR: MS omits the Doctor's interruption and his next.

make the trial, in the hope of saving him, for the love of the light hearted girl who was to have been married on a New Year's day, and for the love of her Richard.'

DOCTOR.    I suppose he used her ill, as soon as they were married?

65 MRS C.    I don't think he ever did that. I think he always felt for her until he died. He went on better for a little time, but his habits were too old, and strong to be got rid of, he soon fell back a little, and was falling fast back, when his illness came so strong upon him. There he was lying for weeks and months—between him and her baby, she was not able to do her old work—How she has lived, I know not!

70 TUG.    I know!—Like a fighting cock!

(*A loud scream behind*)

What's that?

DOCTOR.    My friend, you needn't discuss whether your lodger should be removed or not. He has spared you that trouble I believe—Let us see!

*Exeunt*

## SCENE 2

*A mean Attic.* TOBY *discovered.*

*Enter* MEG.

1 MEG.    (*opens a door and looks in*) She still sleeps, unconscious of her wretched mother's sorrows! bless you! bless you!

TOBY.    Thank heaven! she loves her child!

MEG.    I have sought for work in vain—for any sum I have offered the labour of my

5 hands, yet none will aid me—It is not for myself I care but you, my pretty one, my helpless child.—hark, she wakes.

CHILD.    Mother!

MEG.    O, the worth of that one word! (*Exit*)

TOBY.    She feels there's comfort in its voice—she loves her child!

*Re-enter* MEG *with the* CHILD.

10 MEG.    Your mother has come home again—(*kisses it*) you smile to see her.

*Enter* WILL FERN.

65 *I suppose... he died*: MS omits the Doctor's supposition and Mrs C's answer, 'I don't think... until he died', and PT omits her next remarks, 'He went on better... so strong upon him'.

73.1 *Exeunt*: PT has a speech apparently for the Goblin of the Bell saying 'Follow her—learn it from the creature dearest to your heart' which is ascribed to Toby; neither of them is given an entrance; so presumably the supposition is that they are somewhere visible, watching. Dickens ascribes this injunction to the voices Toby is hearing.

2 *bless you*: PT substitutes 'my only solace, my only happiness' for the second blessing. It also has 'God' for 'heaven' in Toby's speech following.

6 *child*: PT interjects a repetition from Toby: 'There is comfort yet, she loves it still.'

WILL.    For the last time—

MEG.    William Fern!

WILL.    For the last time. (*listens as though pursued*) Margaret, my race is nearly
run,—I couldn't finish it without a parting word with you—without one grateful
word.                                                                                    15

MEG.    What have you done?

WILL.    It's long ago, Margaret, now, but that night is as fresh here,  (*putting his hand
upon his breast*) as ever 'twas—We little thought then, that we should ever meet like
this. Your child, Margaret? Let me look at your child—Is it a girl?

MEG.    Yes.                                                                             20

WILL.    (*puts his hand upon the child's face*) See how weak I'm grown, Margaret, when
I want the courage to look at it! Let her be a moment. I won't hurt her. It's long ago,
but—what's her name?

MEG.    (*quickly*) Margaret.

WILL.    I'm glad of that, I'm glad of that, (*looks upon the child's face*) Margaret, it   25
is Lilian's face! I held the same face in my arms, when Lilian's mother died and
left her.

MEG.    (*wildly*) When Lilian's mother died and left her!

WILL.    How shrill you speak! Why do you fix your eyes, upon me so, Margaret?

TOBY.    (*wringing his hands*) Ah! follow her! learn it from the creature dearest to   30
your heart.

WILL.    Margaret, I thank thee for the last time. Good night. Good bye—put your
hand in mine and tell me you'll forget me from this hour, and try to think the end
of me was here.

MEG.    What have you done?                                                              35

WILL.    There'll be a fire to-night—When you see the distant sky red, they'll be blazing—and then think of me no more, or if you do, remember what a hell was lighted
up inside of me, and think you see its flames, reflected in the clouds. Good night.
Good bye. (*Exit*)

MEG.    Fern! Will Fern!—Like Lilian, when her mother died and left her!            40

TOBY.    But it is love! it is love! She'll never cease to love it—my poor Meg!

*Enter* TUGBY.

TUG.    (*softly*) Oh, you have come back—don't you think you have lived here long
enough without paying any rent? Don't you think that without any money, you've
been a pretty constant customer at this shop, now? Suppose you try and deal somewhere else. And suppose you provide yourself with another lodging. Come, don't  45
you think you could manage it?

---

12 *William Fern*: MS omits this speech and the preceding one.

17.1 *See how weak … It's long ago, but—*: MS omits 'See how weak … It's long ago, but—'.

26 *Lilian's face*: PT interjects 'Lilian's!' from Meg.

39 *Good night. Good bye*: MS omits 'Good night. Good bye'.

46 *Don't you think … manage it?*: MS omits 'Don't you think … somewhere else. And' and also 'Come,
don't you … manage it?'

MEG.    It is very late—tomorrow!

TUG.    Now, I know what you want, what you mean, you know there are two parties in this house, about you, and you delight in setting 'em by the ears—But you shan't
50     stay, that I'm determined—This is the last night of an old year, and I won't carry ill-blood, and quarrellings, into a new one, to please you nor nobody else.—go along with you—mind I give you half an hour—I've said it! and I'll do it! (*Exit*)

MEG.    Yes, we will go—we will find rest somewhere my precious one—I can bear no longer—yes, we will go, Meg,—like Lilian—Oh, never, like Lilian! (*Exit*)
55  VOICES.    Follow her to desperation!

TOBY.    She loves it—(*Chimes*) she loves it still. (*Exit*)


# SCENE 3

*A desolate landscape, and river.*

*Enter* MEG *and* CHILD—*she pauses and kneels.*
*Enter* TOBY; *he stands spell-bound, then enter* TWO FIGURES, *robed.*

1  MEG.    Like Lilian—to be changed like Lilian!

TOBY.    Oh, for anything to awaken her—for any gentle image of the past to rise before her. O, have mercy on her! I was her father, I was her father!—Where does she go? Turn her back, I was her father!
5  VOICES.    To desperation! Learn it from the creature dearest to your heart!

TOBY.    Now, turn her back! (*tearing his hair*) My child Meg! Turn her back! Great father, turn her back!

(MEG *moves to the river and pauses*)

MEG.    To the rolling river, swift and dim, the scatter'd lights upon the banks gleam sullen, red, and dull, as torches that are burning there, to show the way to death.
10  TOBY.    O, that I could wind my fingers in her dress—could hold it! Have mercy on her! think what her misery must have been, when such seeds bear such fruit—Oh have mercy on my child, who even at this pass means mercy to her own, and dies herself to save it!

(*Music.* MEG *sees* TOBY, *and falls into his arms*)

I see the Spirit of the Chimes, among you. (THE SPIRIT OF THE CHIMES *appears*)
15  I know that our inheritance is held in store for us, by Time!—I know that we must

---

3 *for any gentle... her father*: MS omits 'for any gentle... before her' and the first repetition of 'I was her father'.

7 *Now, turn her back!... turn her back*: MS omits this speech.

11 *think what her... bear such fruit*: PT omits 'think what her... bear such fruit'.

trust and hope, nor doubt ourselves, nor doubt the good in one another. Oh, spirits, merciful and good, I am grateful!

*Chimes—cloth—then*


# SCENE 4

*Same as in Scene IV. of the 2nd quarter—everything in the same situation.* TOBY *by fire,* MEG *leaning over him.*

MEG.　And whatever you do father, don't eat tripe again, without asking some Doctor　1
whether it's likely to agree with you, for how you *have* been going on, good gracious!

(TOBY *goes to clasp her in his arms. Enter* RICHARD)

RICHARD.　No, not even you—The first kiss of Meg, in the New Year, is mine—I
have been waiting outside the house this hour, to hear the Bells, and claim it—Meg,
my precious prize, a happy year! A life of happy years, my darling wife! (*kisses her*)　5
TOBY.　Here we are, and here we go—oh, good gracious! And tomorrow's, your
wedding-day, my pet!
RICHARD.　Today! today!—The Chimes are ringing in the New Year!
TOBY.　Richard, my boy, you was turned up trumps originally, and trumps, you
must be till you die! But you were crying by the fire tonight my Pet, when I came　10
home! Why did you cry by the fire?
MEG.　I was thinking of the years we've passed together father—only that—And
thinking you might miss me, and be lonely.

*Enter* LILIAN *and* CHILD.

TOBY.　Why here she is! Here's little Lilian! Ha, ha, ha! Here we are and here we go!
Oh, here we are and here we go again! And here we are and here we go!—and here　15
we are, and here we go, and Uncle Will, too!

*Enter* WILL FERN.

Oh, Uncle Will, the vision that I've had to-night, through lodging you! Oh, Uncle
Will, the obligations that you've laid me under, by your coming my good friend!

---

17　*Oh, Spirits…grateful!*: MS omits 'Oh, Spirits…grateful!'
17.1　*cloth*: 'cloth' indicates the dropping of a scenic backcloth, representing in this case the interior of Toby's lodgings, where he fell asleep at the end of the Second Quarter.

7　*pet*: PT adds 'Your real happy wedding-day!'
10　*Richard, my boy…die*: Instead of this sentence, PT has 'But to-day, my pet—you and Richard had some words to-day. | MEG. Because he's such a bad fellow, father. An't you, Richard? Such a headstrong, violent man! He'd have made no more of speaking his mind to that great Alderman, and putting him down I don't know where, than he would of—| RICHARD. Kissing Meg! | MEG. No, not a bit more, but I wouldn't let him, father. Where would have been the use?' before Toby's next line.

*Enter* NEIGHBOURS *and* THE DRUM.

NEIGHBOURS.    A happy New Year! Meg!—a happy wedding! many of 'em!

20  DRUM.    Trotty Veck, my boy! It's got about that your daughter is going to be married to-morrow. There an't a soul that knows you, that don't wish you both all the happiness the New Year can bring—and here we are to play it in, and dance it in, accordingly!

TOBY.    What a happiness it is, I'm sure, to be so esteemed! How kind and neigh
25  bourly you all are! It is all along of my dear daughter. She deserves it!

(*Enter* MRS CHICKENSTALKER *and a* MAN *bearing a jug*)

It's Mrs Chickenstalker!

MRS C.    Married, and not tell me, Meg! Never! I couldn't rest on the last night of the Old Year, without coming to wish you joy. I couldn't have done it, Meg—not if I had been bed-ridden.—So here I am; and as it's New Year's Eve, and the eve of your
30  wedding too, my dear, I had a little flip made, and brought it with me.

TOBY.    Mrs Tugby! (*going round and round her, in an ecstasy*) I should say Mrs Chickenstalker, bless your heart and soul, a happy New Year, and many of 'em! Mrs Tugby, (*after saluting her*) I *should* say, Mrs Chickenstalker—this is William Fern and Lilian!

35  MRS C.    Not Lilian Fern, whose mother died in Hertfordshire!

WILL.    Yes! (*they exchange words—she shakes both his hands, and embraces the child*)

TOBY.    Will Fern! Not the friend, you was hoping to find?

WILL.    Aye! And like to prove a most as good a friend if that can be, as one I found.

TOBY.    Oh! please to play up there—will you have the goodness?

40  MEG.    Stay, father—one minute. (*to audience*) Has Trotty dreamed? or are his joys and sorrows, and the actors in them, but a dream—himself a dream—If it be so, oh listener, dear to him in all his visions, try to bear in mind, the stern realities from which these shadows come, and in your sphere—none is too wide, and none too limited for such an end—endeavour to correct, improve, and soften them—So may
45  the New Year, be a happy one, to you—and happy to many more, whose happiness depends on you.

ALL.    A dance! A dance!

*A general country dance by all the characters*

*Tableau.*

END

---

26 *How kind…Chickenstalker!*: MS omits 'How kind…all are!', 'She deserves it', and 'It's Mrs Chickenstalker!'

29 *I couldn't have…been bed-ridden*: MS omits 'I couldn't have…been bed-ridden'.

46 *you*: MS terminates here.        47.2 *Tableau*: The final illustration from the book, p. 174.

# SEVEN

Albert Smith, *The Cricket on the Hearth*, Lyceum, December 1845

## INTRODUCTION

*T*HE *Cricket on the Hearth* was the high point in the series of Christmas books/ plays with which Dickens and his friendly dramaturgs and actors addressed the public at their winter firesides and in the West End. It was widely understood that, for good or ill, the author was now producing these works 'concocted chiefly with a view to...production at the Lyceum theatre'.[1] For a discussion of the contribution of the Keeleys to his inspiration and success in this, as well as the hostility of the press to Dickens's alliance with them, see the Introduction ('1843 and the Keeley Management' and 'Like the Brilliant Ballet-Pantomime').

On this occasion the writer Dickens used to take the dramatist's credit—credit for the dramatization of something barely in need of such an intervention, since it left his own hand practically ready for the stage—was his friend Albert Smith, who had also provided the prologue to the Lyceum version of *The Chimes* the previous year. Smith is an important connection in the chain that linked Dickens and the West End. He was something of a British Barnum, a showman and self-publicist who was eventually to become famously successful for his one-man shows at the Egyptian Hall, in which he talked and sang about the ascent of the Alps and his other travels and triumphs. His two popular novels had been published in 1842 and 1844, and his rooms in Percy Street were a centre of successful Bohemian London life in the 1840s and 1850s, much frequented by Sala, the young Edmund Yates, and Dickens himself. When the Keeleys entered management they were able to call on him for their most brilliant extravaganzas of 1844/5, *Open Sesame* and *Aladdin*. The effects of the company playing, on the same bill as the Christmas books, in such satirical fantasies as these should not be overlooked—Bob Keeley appeared as Ebenezer, and Mary Ann as Aladdin, on nights which had begun with their Sarah Gamp and Bailey in *Martin Chuzzlewit*, and they were playing the wild man and the civilized knight from the nursery tale of *Valentine and Orson* before they went on in *The Chimes*.[2]

Smith was content to remain a Bohemian, making scornful remarks about High Art and falling out with the aspirant *Punch* journalists. Dickens and he remained friends, and the novelist admired the business abilities Smith's brother Arthur brought to the exploitation of the one-man show, eventually choosing Arthur to run his own

---

[1] *Times*, 27 December 1845.    [2] See Bratton, *West End*, 183.

programme of touring with the Readings. Albert cemented his alliance with the stage by living with the Keeleys' daughter Mary, who made her debut as a fifteen-year-old in *The Cricket*, and eventually marrying her shortly before his unexpected death in 1860.[3]

## THE TEXT

The text is derived from the Add. MS 42990 ff. 145–204, collated with a printer's proof copy of the edition published by W.S. Johnson, London n.d. [1846], BL shelf mark Dex154. They are designated 'MS' and 'Johnson' in the notes. There is little variation between the two except in punctuation. Since the manuscript is in Albert Smith's autograph, his habit of indicating a pause by a colon [:] rather than the more usual dash has been generally preserved here, to show his sense of the rhythm of the dialogue.

---

[3] For a life of Smith, see Raymund Fitzsimons, *The Baron of Piccadilly: The Travels and Entertainments of Albert Smith, 1816–1860* (London: Geoffrey Bles, 1967).

Characters and cast of the first production

| | |
|---|---|
| John Peerybingle | Mr Emery |
| Mr Tackleton | Mr Meadows |
| Caleb Plummer | Mr Keeley |
| Old Gentleman | Mr Vining |
| Porter | Mr Yarnold |
| Dot's Father | Mr Bender |
| A Little John Peerybingle | Master Forest |

Neighbours: Mr H. Pearson, Mr T.B. Johnston, Mr J. Jefferson

| | |
|---|---|
| Dot | Mrs Keeley |
| Bertha | Miss Mary Keeley |
| Mrs Fielding | Mrs Woollidge |
| May Fielding | Miss Howard |
| Tilly Slowboy | Miss Turner |
| Dot's Mother | Miss Forster |
| Spirit of the Cricket | Miss Dawson |
| A Little Dot | Miss Frampton |

7. *The Cricket on the Hearth*: the tableau just before the end of Chirp the First, when Dot recognizes the Old Man. *Illustrated London News*, 27 December 1845.

# CHIRP THE FIRST

*The Scene represents the interior of* JOHN PEERYBINGLE'S *Cottage. A fire alight in the grate, on which is the kettle, practicable spout to steam. Table and tea-things: chairs by the fire. Cradle. Door, L. Window with curtain; furniture.*

*At the rising of the curtain, music.* TILLY SLOWBOY *is sitting down on a low stool nursing the baby.* DOT *is busy about.*

DOT.  There! there's the ham: and there's the tea: and there's the bread: now all is   1
comfortable against John comes home. Dear me! if it had been for anybody else
how tired I should have been, and cross, too: oh! very cross. I'm sure there was
enough to make me so. First, when I went to fill the kettle I lost my pattens and
splashed my legs: that's hard to bear, when one rather plumes oneself upon one's legs   5
and keeps oneself particularly neat in point of stockings. Then the lid of the kettle
first turned itself topsy-turvey and then dived sideways in—right down to the very
bottom: and was as difficult to get up as if it had been the wreck of the Royal George.
But now everything's right: and I can sit down for a minute in comfort and
cheerfulness.   10

(*Music. She sits down at the fireside. The chirp of the cricket is heard—the kettle steams*)

Ah! there's the cricket on the hearth again. I thought it wouldn't be quiet long when
the kettle began to sing. How its voice sounds through the house, and seems to
twinkle in the outer darkness like a star. Why I declare it's racing with the kettle:
trying to get before it. It can't, though; no, no,—the kettle's not to be finished like
that. How I love its fireside song of comfort, and John loves it too. He says it always   15
seems to say, 'Welcome home, old fellow; welcome home, my boy!' He's very late
to-night. Hush! I hear him. Yes, I'm sure it is. (*rises*) Give me baby, Tilly: I know it
is John coming home.

*Music. She takes the baby from* TILLY, *and going to the door opens it. Part of the cart is seen with a lantern.* JOHN *comes in stamping with cold: snow on him. He shakes his hat.*

DOT.  Oh: goodness, John! what a state you're in with the weather. (*she assists him to undress*)
JOHN.  Why you see Dot it—it ain't exactly summer weather. So no wonder. (*puts   20
down parcels*)
DOT.  I wish you wouldn't call me Dot, John. I don't like it.

---

0.3 *Door, L*: MS has an alteration in pencil here, from R. to L., which suggests that the copy was used or at least checked over during the rehearsal process or against a finalized prompt copy.

JOHN.    (*drawing her to him*) Why, little woman, what else are you? A dot, and (*looks at baby*) a Dot and carry—No: I won't make a joke. I should only spoil it. I don't know that I ever was nearer one though.

25 DOT.    You don't notice baby, John. Ain't he beautiful? Now don't he look precious in his sleep?

JOHN.    Very. He generally *is* asleep. Ain't he?

DOT.    Lor, John!—Good gracious—no!

JOHN.    Oh! I thought his eyes was generally shut. Holloa! (*shouts in baby's ear*)

30 DOT.    Goodness John, how you startle one.

JOHN.    It ain't right for him to turn 'em up, in that way—is it? See how he's winking with 'em both at once! and look at his mouth! Why, he's gasping like a gold and silver fish!

DOT.    (*with dignity*) You don't deserve to be a father—you don't. But how should you know what little complaints babies are troubled with, John?

35 JOHN.    No—it's very true, Dot. I don't know much about it, I only know the wind's been blowing north-east, straight into the cart, the whole way home.

DOT.    Poor old man! so it has. Here take the precious darling, Tilly, while I make myself of some use. Bless it, I could smother it with kissing it, I could. Now see me bustle about, John, like a busy bee—'How doth the little—' and all the rest of it you

40 know, John. Did you ever learn 'How doth the little' when you went to school, John?

JOHN.    Not quite to know it. I was very near it once. But I should only have spoilt it, I dare say.

DOT.    (*laughs*) Ha ! ha! what a dear old dunce you are, John, to be sure. Here Tilly: take baby: and don't let him fall under the grate, whatever you do. (*at the table*)

45 There there's the tea-pot ready on the hob: and the cold knuckle of ham and the crusty loaf. And there's the cricket!

JOHN.    Heyday! It's merrier than ever, tonight, I think.

DOT.    And it's sure to bring us good fortune, John!

JOHN.    It always has done so. To have a cricket on the hearth, is the luckiest thing in

50 all the world.

DOT.    (*sits by his side, and takes his hand*) The first time I heard its cheerful little note, John, was on that night, when you brought me to my new home here, as its little mistress. Nearly a year ago. You recollect, John?

JOHN.    I should think so, Dot.

55 DOT.    Its chirp was such a welcome to me! It seemed so full of promise and encouragement. It seemed to say you would be kind and gentle with me and would not expect (I had a fear of that, John, then) to find an old head on the shoulders of your foolish little wife.

JOHN.    (*patting her*) No no—I was quite content to take them as they were.

60 DOT.    It spoke the truth, John, when it seemed to say so: for you have ever been, I am sure, the best, the most considerate, the most affectionate of husbands to me. This has been a happy home, John: and I love the cricket for its sake.

JOHN.    Why, so do I then: so do I, Dot.

---

23 *it*: MS has 'I always do' deleted.

DOT.  I love it, for the many times I have heard it, and the many thoughts its harmless music has given me. Sometimes, in the twilight, when I have felt a little solitary  65
and down-hearted, John—before baby was here, to keep me company, and make
the house gay—when I have thought how lonely you would be if I should die, how
lonely I should be, if I could know that you had lost me, dear; its chirp, chirp, chirp,
upon the hearth has seemed to tell me of another little voice, so sweet, so very dear
to me before whose coming sound my trouble vanished like a dream. And when I  70
used to fear—I did fear once John—I was very young you know—that ours might
be an ill-assorted marriage: I being such a child, and you more like my guardian
than my husband; and that you might not, however hard you tried, be able to learn
to love me as you hoped and prayed you might; its chirp, chirp, chirp, has cheered
me up again, and filled me with new trust and confidence. I was thinking of these  75
things to-night, dear, when I sat expecting you; and I love the cricket, for their sake.
JOHN.  And so do I. But, Dot? *I* hope and pray that I might learn to love you? How
you talk! I had learnt that, long before I brought you here to be the cricket's little
mistress, Dot. (*kisses her, then she rises*)
DOT.  There are not many parcels to-night, John. (*she goes to those he has put down*)  80
Why, what's this round box? Heart alive, John, it's a wedding cake!
JOHN.  Leave a woman alone to find out that. Now a man would never have thought
of it, whereas it's my belief that if you was to pack a wedding cake up in a tea chest
or a turn-up bedstead, or a pickled salmon keg, or any unlikely thing, a woman
would be sure to find it out directly. Yes, I called for it at the pastry-cook's.  85
DOT.  (*reading*) Why, John! good gracious, John! you never mean to say it's Gruff
and Tackleton, the toy maker's!
TILLY.  (*dancing the baby*) Was it Gruffs and Tackletons the toy-maker's then, and
would it call at pastry cooks, for wedding cakes, and did its mothers know the boxes
when its fathers brought them homes. Ketcher! ketcher! ketcher!  90
DOT.  (*still looking at the parcel*) And so it's really come about. Why she and I were
girls at school together John—and he's as old—as unlike her. How many years older
is Gruff and Tackleton, John?
JOHN.  (*going to the table*) How many more cups of tea shall I drink tonight in one
sitting, than Gruff and Tackleton ever took in four, I wonder. (*sitting*) Ah! as to  95
eating, I eat but little but that little I enjoy, Dot. Why, Dot! (*raps with the knife on
the table*) Dot!

(DOT *has remained plunged in thought, since she last spoke. She starts at the noise*)

DOT.  Lor' bless me, John! I beg your pardon. I was thinking—I was thinking—Ah!
so, these are all the parcels, are they, John?
JOHN.  That's all, why—no—I—(*he lays down his knife and fork*) I declare—I've  100
clean forgotten the old gentleman!
DOT.  The old gentleman!

79 *Dot*: MS has a music cue here, deleted.

JOHN.      In the cart. He was asleep amongst the straw the last time I saw him. I've very
      nearly remembered him twice since I came in, but he went out of my head again.
105      Halloo! yahip there! (*goes out of the door*) Rouse up there! That's my hearty!

*Music*—TILLY *looks alarmed, as she hears the words 'the old gentleman' and crossing to*
DOT *runs against the* STRANGER *with baby's head as he enters, introduced by* JOHN.
*The* STRANGER *removes his hat and remains bare-headed in the centre of the room.*

JOHN.      You're such an undeniable good sleeper sir, that I had a mind to ask you
      where the other six are, only that would be a joke, and I know I should spoil it. Ha!
      ha! very near, though, very near.

(*Music—The* STRANGER *looks round him, and bows to* JOHN *and* DOT, *gravely. Then
striking a club he carries, on the stage, it falls asunder and forms a species of camp stool.
He sits down on it*)

JOHN.      There! that's the way I found him, sitting by the road-side. Upright as a mile-
110      stone, and almost as deaf.
DOT.      Sitting in the open air, John!
JOHN.      In the open air, just at dusk. 'Carriage paid,' he said; and gave me eighteen
      pence. Then he got in, and there he is.
STRANGER.      If you please, I was to be left till called for. Don't mind me.

*He puts on a pair of large spectacles: takes a book from his pocket, and begins to read.*
JOHN *and* DOT *look at him with astonishment.*

115      STRANGER.      (*to* JOHN, *nodding his head towards* DOT) Your daughter, my good friend?
JOHN.      Wife!
STRANGER.      Niece?
JOHN.      (*loud*). Wife!
STRANGER.      Indeed: surely—very young. (*he reads for an instant, then resumes*)
120      Baby yours?

(JOHN *and* DOT *nod eagerly*)

      Girl?
JOHN.      (*bawling*) B-o-o-oy!
STRANGER.      Also very young—eh?
DOT.      (*bawls in* STRANGER's *ear*) Two months and three days!—vaccinated just six
125      weeks ago! Took very finely. Considered by the doctor a remarkably fine child:
      equal to the general run of children at five months old. Takes notice in a way quite
      wonderful. May seem impossible to you, but feels his legs already.

(*A knocking at the door*)

---

113 *there he is*: MS has a speech for Dot here: 'he's going John, I think'.

JOHN.   Hark—he's called for sure enough. There's somebody at the door. Open it, Tilly.

*Music.* TILLY *goes to the door: opens it: and lets in* CALEB, *in his sackcloth coat.*

CALEB.   Good evening, John. Good evening, mum. Good evening, Tilly. Good 130 evening, unbeknown. How's baby, mum? Boxer's pretty well, I hope?
DOT.   All thriving, Caleb. I am sure you need only to look at the dear child, for one, to know that.
CALEB.   And I'm sure I need only look at you, for another; or at John, for another. Or at Tilly, as far as that goes. 135
JOHN.   Busy just now, Caleb?
CALEB.   Why pretty well, John: this is a good time of year for the toy business. There's rather a run upon Noah's Arks just at present. I wish I could improve Noah's family, but I don't see how it's to be done at the price. It would be a satisfaction to one's mind to make it clearer, which was Shems and Hams, and which was wives. 140 Flies ain't on that scale neither, as compared with the elephants, you know. Ah, well—have you got anything in the parcel line for me, John?

JOHN *searches his coat pocket, and brings out a little plant in a flower-pot, packed up.*

JOHN.   There it is! not so much as a leaf damaged. Full of buds! It was very dear, though, Caleb, at this season.
CALEB.   Never mind that: it would be cheap to me whatever it cost. Anything else, 145 John?
JOHN.   A small box. Here you are. (*gives the box*)
CALEB.   (*spelling*) 'For Caleb Plummer: with cash'. With cash, John: I don't think it's for me.
JOHN.   With *care*. Where do you make out 'cash'? 150
CALEB.   Oh! to be sure. It's all right—'with care'? Yes, yes, that's mine. Ah—if my dear boy in the golden South Americas had lived, John: it might have been cash indeed. You loved him like a son: didn't you? You needn't say you did. I know, of course. (*reads*) 'Caleb Plummer, with care.' Yes—yes; for my poor blind daughter's work: it's a box of dolls' eyes. I wish it was her own sight in a box, John. 155
JOHN.   I wish it was—or could be.
CALEB.   Thankee—you speak very hearty. To think she should never see the dolls: and them a staring at her bold all day long: That's where it cuts. What's the damage, John?
JOHN.   I'll damage you, if you inquire. Dot! nearly a joke: very near: wasn't it? Stop 160 Caleb: here's something for your Governor, old Gruff and Tackleton.
CALEB.   He hasn't been here, has he?
JOHN.   Not he: he's too busy courting.
CALEB.   He's coming round though: he told me so. He isn't a pleasant man, is he, John—though he does sell toys. 'Pon my honour I think he only likes to sell those 165

---

161 *old Gruff and Tackleton*: MS omits 'old Gruff and Tackleton'.

that make children uncomfortable. He makes all the grim faces to the brown paper
farmers who drive the pigs, and the moveable old ladies who carve the pies and
darn the stockings. And if you knew how he revelled in those demoniacal tumblers—dreadful things that won't lie down, but are always flinging up to stare
170    infants out of countenance; and those hideous, hairy, red-eyed jacks in boxes: Oh!
he loves them! I think I'd better go. By the bye, you couldn't have the goodness to let
me pinch Boxer's tail, mum, for half a moment, could you?

DOT.    Why, Caleb, what a question!

CALEB.    Oh—never mind, mum: he mightn't like it perhaps. There's a small order
175    just come in for barking dogs: and I should wish to go as close to nature as I could
for sixpence. That's all—never mind, mum; good-bye. (*he puts the box on his shoulder: and is going out, when he is met by* TACKLETON *on the threshold*)

TACKLETON.    (*entering*) Oh! here you are, are you? Wait a bit. I'll take you home.
John Peerybingle my service to you: more of my service to your pretty wife:
Handsomer every day: Better, too, it possible. (*aside*) and younger: there's the devil
180    of it.

DOT.    I should be astonished at your paying compliments, Mr Tackleton, but for
your condition.

TACKLETON.    Oh! you know all about it then?

DOT.    I have got myself to believe it, somehow.

185 TACKLETON.    After a very hard struggle I suppose.

DOT.   Very.

TACKLETON.    In three days' time—next Thursday. That's to be my wedding-day.

JOHN.    Why, it's our wedding-day, too.

TACKLETON.    Ha! ha! odd: you're just such another couple, just.

190 DOT.    (*half aside*) What next? He'll say just another such baby, perhaps. The man's
mad.

TACKLETON.    (*to* JOHN) I say, a word with you. You'll come to the wedding. We're
in the same boat, you know.

JOHN.    How, in the same boat?

195 TACKLETON.    (*nudging him*) A little disparity, you know. Come and spend an evening with us, beforehand.

JOHN.    Why?

TACKLETON.    Why? That's a new way of receiving an invitation. Why—for pleasure:
sociability, you know: and all that.

200 JOHN.    I thought you were never sociable.

TACKLETON.    Tchah! It's of no use to be anything but free with you, I see. Why then
the truth is you have a—what the tea drinking people call a—a sort of comfortable
appearance together, you and your wife. We know better you know, but—

JOHN.    No, we *don't* know better. What are you talking about?

---

168 *stockings*: MS has 'brown paper' as an insertion, but Johnson omits 'the moveable old ladies…darn
the stockings' and 'demoniacal tumblers…and those'.

TACKLETON.    Well, we *don't* know better, then: as you like: what does it matter? I  205
was going to say, as you have a sort of an appearance, your company will produce a
favorable effect on Mrs Tackleton that will be.

JOHN.    We've made a promise to ourselves these six months to keep our wedding-
day at home. We think you see that home—

TACKLETON.    Bah! What's home? (*cricket is heard*) Four walls and a ceiling! Why  210
don't you kill that cricket—I would. I always do. I hate their noise.

JOHN.    You kill your crickets, eh?

TACKLETON.    Scrunch 'em, sir. You'll say you'll come: because, you know, whatever
one woman says, another woman is determined to clinch, always. There's that spirit
of emulation among 'em, sir, that if your wife says to my wife 'I'm the happiest  215
woman in the world, and mine's the best husband in the world and I dote on him'
my wife will say the some to yours, or more; and *half believe it.*

JOHN.    Do you mean to say she don't, then?

TACKLETON.    Don't! Ha! ha!—don' t what?

JOHN.    Pshaw: that she don't believe it!  220

TACKLETON.    You're joking. I have the humour, Sir, to marry a young wife, and a
pretty wife. I'm able to gratify that humour and I do. It's my whim. But—now look
there! (*he points to* DOT, *who is sitting at the fire*) She honors and obeys, no doubt,
you know: and that, as I am not a man of sentiment, is quite enough for *me.* But do
you think there's anything more in it?  225

JOHN.    I think I should chuck any man out of window who said there wasn't.

TACKLETON.    Exactly so: we're exactly alike in reality I see. Good night: you won't
give us tomorrow evening. Well, next day you go visiting, I know. I'll meet you
there, and bring my wife that is to be. It'll do her good. Good night.

(*As he is going* DOT *gives a loud shriek: starts up from her seat: and remains transfixed
with terror and surprise. Picture. Music*)

JOHN.    Dot! Mary darling! what's the matter? Are you ill? (*he supports her*) What  230
is it? Tell me dear. (STRANGER *rises and stands.* DOT *falls into a fit of hysterical
laughter: claps her hands together, and sinks upon the ground*)

JOHN.    What is this, Mary?—my own little wife. Speak to me!

DOT.    (*recovering*) I'm better, John—I'm quite well—now—I—a kind of shock:
a something came suddenly before my eyes. I don't know what it was—it's quite
gone—quite gone.  235

TACKLETON.    I'm glad it's gone. I wonder where it is gone, and what it was? Humph!
Caleb, come here. Who's that, with the grey hair? (*points to* STRANGER)

---

221 *You're joking*: MS omits 'You're joking'.

229.2 *Picture. Music*: This moment is not illustrated by Leech; Smith derives the tableau from Dickens's
text, as he does several more. See illustration 7 for the *ILN* rendition of the picture.

231 STRANGER *rises and stands*: MS omits 'STRANGER *rises and stands*'.

CALEB.    I don't know, sir. Never see him before, in all my life. A beautiful figure for a nutcracker; quite a new model. With a screw jaw opening down into his waistcoat,
240    he'd be lovely.

TACKLETON.    Not ugly enough.

CALEB.    Or for a firebox, either: what a model. Unscrew his head to put the matches in: turn him heels upwards for a light: and what a firebox for a gentleman's mantel-piece, just as he stands!

245  TACKLETON.    Not half ugly enough. Come—bring that box. All right now, I hope.

DOT.    (*hurriedly*) Oh! quite gone: quite gone: Good night.

TACKLETON.    Good night. Good night, John Peerybingle.

JOHN.    Stop: this good gentleman may be glad of company. I must give him a hint to go.

250  STRANGER.    (*rises, and advances towards* JOHN) I beg your pardon friend: the more so, as I fear your wife has not been well: but the attendant whom my infirmity (*he points to his ears*) renders almost indispensable not having arrived I fear there must be some mistake. The bad night is still as bad as ever. Would you, in your kindness, suffer me to rent a bed here?

255  DOT.    (*eagerly*) Yes yes—certainly.

JOHN.    Oh! well, I don't object; but still, I'm not quite sure that—

DOT.    Hush—dear John!

TACKLETON.    Hush! why, he's stone deaf. Odd (*to* JOHN) isn't it?

DOT.    I know he is, but—yes sir: certainly. There's the spare room, and the bed ready
260    made up.

TACKLETON.    Well—now I'm off. Good night, John—good night, Mrs Peerybingle. Take care, Caleb, let that box fall, and I'll murder you.

DOT.    (*to* STRANGER) This way sir—this is your room.

(*She takes a candle, and beckons the* STRANGER *to an apartment at the side.* TACKLETON *who is going, preceded by* CALEB, *turns back and laying his hand on* JOHN'S *shoulder, points towards his wife, and the* STRANGER. *The curtain falls to the music of the commencement*)

# CHIRP THE SECOND

*The abode of* CALEB PLUMMER—*a poor half tumbling down interior. A dresser on which some common broken crockery is placed. The room is filled with toys of all descriptions, especially dolls' houses, and dolls. There are moveable sand toys and musical carts: fiddles, drums, weapons, Noah's Arks, horses etc., etc.* CALEB'S *coat hung up.*

*As the curtain rises* CALEB *is discovered making a baby-house.*

CALEB. (*sings*)     The glasses sparkle on the board,     1
                      The wine is ruby bright, etc.
Ah! me! my voice seems to get fainter and fainter every day: I'm often afraid that
my poor blind child will perceive it. And then I shall not be able to make her
believe that I am still young and lively, by my songs. Poor Bertha! yet I often think 5
her blindness may be a blessing. She never knew that the walls are blotched and
bare of plaster or that the iron is rusting, the wood rotting, and the paper peeling
off. If my poor boy had lived to come back from the golden South Americas, how
different it would have been. She knows not now that Tackleton is a cold and exact-
ing master. Poor girl, I have made her believe by a little affectionate artifice that all 10
his harsh and unfeeling reproofs are meant in joke to enliven us—and she thinks he
is our guardian angel: and she imagines her poor old father to be a man still young
and handsome. Hush! Caleb: she is here!

*Music. The door opens:* CALEB *rises and goes towards it.* BERTHA *enters, and feels her
way to the spot where he was sitting. He takes her hand.*

CALEB.   Bertha!
BERTHA.   Father! So you were out in the rain last night in your beautiful new 15
   great coat.
CALEB.   (*looking at his coat and shrugging his shoulders*) In my beautiful new
   great coat.
BERTHA.   How glad I am you bought it, father.
CALEB.   And of such a fashionable tailor too: it's too good for me.     20
BERTHA.   Too good for you, father: what can be too good for you?
CALEB.   I'm half ashamed to wear it though, upon my word. When I hear the boys
   and people behind me say, 'Holloa! here's a swell' I don't know which way to look.

---

0.3 *sand toys*: A sand toy is a mechanical figure suspended in a frame which moves its limbs when, concealed behind it, sand falls from an upper reservoir onto a wheel.

2 *The glasses...ruby bright, etc.*: Music by Thomas A. Geary, words by W.D. Diggs, published around
1800.

5 *believe that*: MS has a deletion: 'we are well'.

11 *Poor girl...enliven us—and*: MS omits 'Poor girl...enliven us—and'.

And when the beggar wouldn't go away last night: and when I said I was a very
common man said 'No, your Honour! bless your honour, don't say that,' I was quite
ashamed—I really felt as if I hadn't a right to wear it.

BERTHA.     (*clapping her hands with delight*) I see you, father, as plainly as if I had the
eyes I never want, when you are with me. A blue coat—

CALEB.     Bright blue.

BERTHA.     Yes, yes! bright blue! the colour I can just remember in the blessed sky.
A bright blue coat.

CALEB.     Made loose to the figure.

BERTHA.     Yes, loose to the figure—(*laughing*) and in it you, dear father, with your
merry eye, your smiling face, your free step, and your dark hair—looking so young
and handsome.

CALEB.     Halloa! halloa! I shall be vain, presently.

BERTHA.     Not at all, dear father: not at all. But I am idling; I can talk just as well whilst
I am at work.  (*she feels about for her basket: finds it: and begins to dress some dolls*)

CALEB.     (*taking up the dolls' house*) There we are, as near the real thing as sixpenn'orth
of half-pence is to sixpence. What a pity that the whole front of the house opens at
once. If there was only a staircase in it now, and regular doors to the rooms to go in
at, but that's the worst of my calling. I'm always deluding myself and swindling
myself. (*in a low tone*)

BERTHA.     You are speaking quite softly. You are not tired, father?

CALEB.     Tired! What could tire me, Bertha? I was never tired. What does it
mean? (*sings with forced energy*)
We'll drown it in a bowl,
We'll drown a bowl, etc., etc.

*As he is singing* TACKLETON *enters.*

TACKLETON.     What! you're singing, are you? Go it—*I* can't sing. I can't afford it. I'm
glad you can. I hope you can afford to work too. Hardly time for both, I should
think.

CALEB.     (*to* BERTHA) If you could only see him, Bertha, how he's winking at me.
Such a man to joke: you'd think, if you didn't know him, he was in earnest: wouldn't
you now?

(BERTHA *nods assent*)

TACKLETON.     The bird that can sing, and won't sing, must be made to sing, they say.
What about the owl that can't sing, and oughtn't to sing, and will sing—is there
anything that *he* should be made to do?

CALEB.     (*aside to* BERTHA) The extent to which he's winking at this moment! Oh!
my gracious!

BERTHA.     Always merry and lighthearted with us, Mr Tackleton.

TACKLETON.     Oh—there you are—are you? Poor idiot! Umph! well—and being
there, how are you?

BERTHA.    Oh—well—quite well: as happy as even you can wish me to be. As happy as you would make the whole world if you could.

TACKLETON.    Poor idiot. No gleam of reason: not a gleam.    65

(BERTHA, *who does not hear him, takes* TACKLETON's *hand, and presses it to her lips*)

What's the matter now?

BERTHA.    I stood the little plant you sent me close beside my pillow when I went to sleep last night, and remembered it in my dreams. And when the day broke, and the glorious red sun, father—the *red* sun—

CALEB.    Red in the mornings and evenings Bertha. (*aside*) Poor thing! How I   70 deceive her, to make her believe he was less harsh and cold!

BERTHA.    When the sun rose, and the bright light I almost fear to strike myself against it in walking, came into the room, I turned the little plant towards it and blessed heaven for making things so precious, and blessed you for sending them to cheer me.    75

TACKLETON.    (*aside*) Bedlam broke loose. We shall arrive at the straight waistcoat and mufflers soon. We're getting on. Ugh! Bertha—come here. Shall I tell you a secret?

BERTHA.    If you will.

TACKLETON.    This is the day on which little what's her name: the spoiled child,   80 Peerybingle's wife: pays her regular visit to you—makes her fantastic pic-nic here: isn't it?

BERTHA.    Yes—this is the day.

TACKLETON.    I thought so! I should like to join the party.

BERTHA.    (*gladly*) Do you hear that, father?    85

CALEB.    Yes—yes: I hear it: but I don't believe it. It's one of my lies, no doubt.

TACKLETON.    You see. I want to bring the Peerybingles a little more into company with May Fielding. I am going to be married to May.

BERTHA.    Married!

TACKLETON.    (*muttering*) She's such a con-founded idiot, that I was afraid she'd   90 never comprehend me. (*aloud*) Yes—married! Church, parson, clerk, beadle, glass coach, bells, breakfast, bride-cake, favours, marrowbones, cleavers, and all the rest of the tom-foolery. A wedding, you know: a wedding. Don't you know what a wedding is?

BERTHA.    I know; I understand.    95

TACKLETON.    Do you? It's more than I expected. Well—I want to join the party and to bring May and her mother—I'll send in a little something or other before the afternoon. A cold leg of mutton, or some comfortable trifle of that sort. You'll expect me.

BERTHA.    Yes. (*she turns away, and her head droops*)    100

TACKLETON.    I don't think you will, for you seem to have forgotten all about it already. Caleb!

---

71 *How I deceive her*: Johnson has not 'How I deceive her' but 'I must deceive her still'.

CALEB.    (*to himself*) I may venture to say I'm here I suppose. (*aloud*) Sir!

TACKLETON.    Take care she don't forget what I've been saying to her.

105 CALEB.    *She* never forgets. It's one of the few things she an't clever in.

TACKLETON.    Every man thinks his own geese swans. Well—good bye. Umph! poor devil! (*Exit*)

CALEB.    (*To himself, taking up a toy waggon and horses, which he proceeds to put harness on*) Phew! I'm glad he's gone. (*sings*) The glasses sparkle etc.

BERTHA    (*puts her hand on his shoulder*) Father—I am lonely, in the dark—I want

110 my eyes: my patient, willing eyes.

CALEB.    Here they are: always ready. They are more yours than mine Bertha. What shall your eyes do for you, dear?

BERTHA.    Look round the room, father.

CALEB.    All right—no sooner said than done, Bertha.

115 BERTHA.    Tell me about it.

CALEB.    It's much the same as usual: homely, but very snug. The gay colours on the walls: the bright flowers on the plates and dishes: the shining wood where there are beams and panels: the general cheerfulness and neatness of the building make it very pretty.

120 BERTHA.    You have your working dress on, and are not so gallant as when you wear the handsome coat? (*touches him*)

CALEB.    Not quite so gallant. Pretty brisk, though.

BERTHA.    (*putting her hand around his neck*) Father, tell me something about May— she is very beautiful?

125 CALEB.    She is indeed.

BERTHA.    Her hair is dark, darker than mine. Her voice is sweet and musical, I know. I have often loved to hear it—Her shape—

CALEB.    There's not a doll's in all the room to equal it; and her eyes—

BERTHA.    (*sadly*). Her *eyes*—father—(*hides her face, and her head sinks on his arm*)

130 CALEB.    (*aside*) Fool that I was! (*sings*) 'We'll drown it in a bowl.'

BERTHA.    But Mr Tackleton—our kind noble friend, father—he is older than May.

CALEB.    (*hesitating*) Ye-e-es—he's a little older. But that don't signify.

BERTHA.    Oh father, yes. To be his patient companion in infirmity and age: to be his gentle nurse in sickness, and his constant friend in suffering and sorrow: to sit beside his

135 bed, and talk to him, awake, and pray for him, asleep! Would she do all this dear father?

CALEB.    No doubt of it.

BERTHA.    I love her, father: I can love her from my soul. (*clings to her father: and is affected*)

CALEB.    Come, Bertha: cheerly! cheerly! I declare all the dolls are staring at us, as if they were mad with hunger, to remind us that our company will be here soon.

140 Come, Bertha: let us go and see about the potatoes in that handsome wooden bowl that is so beautiful to look at. Come, come.

*Music. They exit. The tune changes to 'Gee ho dobbin' and the door opens. Enter* MRS PEERYBINGLE, *carrying all sorts of parcels: followed by* JOHN, *doing the same: and lastly,* TILLY, *carrying the baby.*

DOT.   (*putting the parcels down*) Oh! My goodness! How heavy they are! Nobody here to receive us and nobody come yet. Never mind; we're not proud, John, are we?

JOHN.   Well—I don't know, Dot: I'm proud of you when you're admired: knowing that you don't mind it.   145

DOT.   Now, John—

JOHN.   In fact, that you rather like it, perhaps.

DOT.   Now hush, John! I'm sure I'm only proud of our cart, and who wouldn't be—and Boxer.

JOHN.   And just getting into the cart—the legs, Dot, eh?   150

DOT.   Now, John: how can you! Think of Tilly. And are you sure you've got the basket with the veal and ham pie and things, and the bottles of beer? Because if you haven't, we must go back.

JOHN.   You're a nice little article to talk about going back, when you kept me a quarter of an hour after time. They're all right.   155

DOT.   I declare I wouldn't come without the veal and ham pie, and things, and the bottles of beer, for any money. Regularly once a fortnight since we have been married John, we've made our little pic-nic here. If anything were to go wrong with it, I should almost think we were never going to be lucky again.

JOHN.   It was a kind thought, in the first instance, and I honour you for it, little   160 woman.

DOT.   My dear John! don't talk of honouring me—my gracious!

JOHN.   By the bye—that old gentleman—he's an odd fish. I can't make him out. I don't believe there's any harm in him.

DOT.   Not at all—I'm sure there's none at all.   165

JOHN.   (*with meaning*) I'm glad you feel so certain: because it's a confirmation to me. It's curious he should have taken it into his head to ask leave to go on lodging with us: an't it. Things come about so strangely.

DOT.   (*almost aside*) So very strangely.

JOHN.   However—he's a good-natured old gentleman: and pays as a gentleman—   170 doesn't he. Why, Dot! what are you thinking about.

DOT.   (*starting*). Thinking of John? I—I was listening to you.

JOHN.   Oh! that's all right, I was afraid from the look of your face I had set you thinking about something else.

DOT.   Oh no, John, no! But here comes Caleb and Bertha. Now they shall help us put   175 the veal and ham pie and things and bottles of beer, all in order.

*Enter* CALEB *and* BERTHA.

CALEB.   Halloa, John: here you are then: and Missus, too. How d'ye do, mum?

BERTHA.   (*going to* DOT) Dear Mary!

CALEB.   The rest of the company will be here directly. The potatoes is all right: you never see such pictures—I don't think I could make any half so natural, not if dolls   180

---

142 *Oh! My goodness ... they are!*: MS has sd and 'Oh! My goodness ... they are!' deleted, and it is omitted in Johnson.

wouldn't have nothing else in their kitchens. Ah! (*a knock*) There's May, and her mother, and Gruff and Tackleton. Come in—come in!

*Enter* TACKLETON *with* MAY FIELDING *on one arm and* MRS FIELDING *on the other, wearing a calash over her cap, which is very fine.* TACKLETON *is carrying a parcel.* CALEB *receives them awkwardly.*

TACKLETON.   Well—we're come. I don't suppose you wanted me much though.
DOT.   (*going to* MAY) May! my dear old friend! what a happiness to see you.

(*They embrace*)

185  TACKLETON.   Ah—that's it: women always are so deuced affectionate before people. It's all trick: only to make us envious: don't you think so Peerybingle?
JOHN.   No I don't. I call that as pleasant a sight as a man might see in a long day. Their faces quite set one another's off. They ought to have been born sisters.
MAY.   (*to* BERTHA) And are you quite well and happy, Bertha?
190  BERTHA.   Quite, dear May. How can I be otherwise, when you are here?
CALEB.   Bless me: I'm quite nervous. I feel as if somebody was pulling a string, and making me jump all ways at once. I'll go and get the potatoes. (*Exit*)
TACKLETON.   There—there's a leg of mutton. (*puts it on the table*) And there's a tart. Ah—you may stare: but we don't mind a little dissipation when our brides are
195  in the case. I hav'nt been married a year, you know, John.
DOT.   (*aside*) Spiteful creature!
JOHN.   Come—let us begin dinner—You have not driven along the road three or four miles. I'm hungry.
CALEB.   (*enters with a bowl of smoking potatoes*) You shan't be long John: you shan't
200  be long. There they are, look at 'em: it's almost a shame to eat 'em. Now sit down: sit down. You there, mum, if you please (*to* MRS FIELDING) and you there. (*to* TACKLETON) Perhaps too, sir, you'd like May next you: it's natural you should: and Mrs Peerybingle: you'll go to the side of your old friend, John here: and Bertha next to me. There we are—beautiful!
205  DOT.   Oh—how comfortable this is. It seems but yesterday May, that we were at school: and now to think you are quite a woman grown.
MAY.   And you, Dot—married!
JOHN.   Yes—and got a baby!
DOT.   Now, John!
210  JOHN.   Well—is it anything to be ashamed of. I always thought—
DOT.   (*interrupts him*) You dear, good, awkward John. There take some pie—and there's a nice bit of egg—and now don't talk with your mouth full.
CALEB.   But you, May: you don't eat anything.

---

182.2  *calash*: A calash is a hood supported on hoops over the head.
  204  *beautiful*: MS has a diagram of the table here with Mrs Fielding at the top, an oblong going down from her with, reading across, written to the sides of it 'Caleb...Tackelton' | 'Bertha...May Fielding' | 'John...Dot', and a separate square down R. from it labelled 'TILLY and Baby'.

DOT.    Oh May's in love, you know Caleb: and people in love are never hungry. Bless
   you, it wouldn't be proper. I never was, was I John?                                    215
TACKLETON.    Perhaps you were never in love. Ha! ha!
DOT.    (*imitating his hollow laugh*) Ha! ha! what a funny man you are. (*aside*) He
   looks about as much in his own element as a fresh young salmon on the top of the
   pyramid.
MRS FIELDING.    (*gravely*) Ah! girls are girls, and byegones byegones, and as long as  220
   young people are young and thoughtless, they'll behave as young and thoughtless
   people do.
DOT.    Dear May—To talk of those merry school days makes one young again.
TACKLETON.    Why you ain't particularly old at any time, are you?
DOT.    Look at my sober plodding husband there. He adds twenty years to my age at  225
   least, don't you, John?
JOHN.    Forty.
DOT.    How many you'll add to May's I'm sure I don't know. But she can't be less than
   a hundred years of age, on her next birthday.
TACKLETON.    Ha! ha! (*aside*) I could twist her neck like a sparrow's.                   230
DOT.    Dear! dear! Only to remember how we used to talk, at school, about the husbands we should choose. I don't know how handsome, and young, and how gay and
   how lively, mine was to be! And as to May's! Ah dear! I don't know whether to laugh
   or cry, when I think what silly girls we were.
TACKLETON.    Ah! you couldn't help yourselves; for all that you couldn't resist us,     235
   you see. Here we are! here we are! Where are your gay young bridegrooms now?
DOT.    Some of them are dead: and some of them forgotten. Some of them, if they
   could stand among us at this moment, would not believe we were the same creatures,
   or that we could forget them so. No no: they would not believe one word of it.
JOHN.    Why, Dot—little woman? what are you thinking of? Come, come: I think       240
   we're slighting the bottled beer. I'll give a toast. Here's to-morrow, (*they pass the
   beer round*) the wedding day: and we'll drink a bumper to it.
CALEB.    Yes—the wedding day.
ALL.    The wedding day—the wedding day.

(BERTHA *gets up and leaves the table*)

JOHN.    And now a song—a song!                                                           245
ALL.    Yes a song.
CALEB.    (*rising*) Here's a harp—a rude thing—I made for Bertha. But Mrs
   Peerybingle knows how to play it.
DOT.    I'll do my best, John.

*Song Dot*

215 *was I John?*: MS has 'was I John?' deleted, and Johnson omits it.
249.1 *Song Dot*: MS has the direction for a song and the text from 'JOHN And now a song' deleted, and
Johnson omits it; MS also deletes the preparation for another entry here, '*at the conclusion of the song, a
knocking at the doors.* | CALEB. More visitors! I suppose we must say we're all of us…'

250  JOHN.     Well: this is all very well, but I must be stirring. I have got several parcels to
deliver now.

CALEB.     But you won't be long, John?

JOHN.     Oh no! the old horse has had a bait as well as myself, and we shall soon get
over the ground.

255  CALEB.     Well—good bye, John.

JOHN.     Good bye: good bye, all! (*To baby*) Good bye: young shaver. Time will come
I suppose when you'll turn out into the cold, my little friend, and leave your old
father to enjoy his pipe and his rheumatics in the chimney-corner. Eh! where's Dot?

DOT.     (*starting*) I'm here, John.

260  JOHN.     (*claps his hands*) Come, come: where's the pipe?

DOT.     I forgot the pipe, John. I'll fill it directly. (*she takes pipe from his coat*)

JOHN.     Forgot the pipe! Was such a wonder ever heard of. Why, what a clumsy Dot
you are this afternoon. I could have done it better myself, I verily believe.

TACKLETON.     I'll go with you, John Peerybingle, a little way if you'll take me. I've

265  got to go down the town.

JOHN.     Oh—willingly—willingly: Good bye, Caleb: good bye, all. I shall be back
very soon.

ALL.     Good bye, John. (*Exeunt* JOHN *and* TACKLETON)

DOT.     And now, Tilly: bring me the precious baby: and whilst you help May put the

270  things to rights, and do everything she tells you, I shall sit with Mrs Fielding at the fire.

MRS FIELDING.     I should have sat by fireplaces of a very different kind, if people had
done by other people as the first people ought to do, especially in the Indigo trade.

DOT.     (*shaking her head*) Ah, I'm sure you would.

MRS FIELDING.     But when a friend asks any one to befriend that friend's friend, and

275  the friend's friend does not act as such, we must put up with what other friends have
to offer us.

DOT.     Yes—it's very true, ma'am. But now, (*putting a chair*) sit down here: and while
baby is in my lap, perhaps you will tell me how to manage it, and put me right upon
twenty points, where I am as wrong as can be. Won't you, Mrs Fielding?

280  MRS FIELDING.     I see no objection; although, before that occurrence with the
Indigo, which I always thought would happen, and told Mr F. so often, but he
wouldn't believe me, I never managed my babies at all, but had proper persons
whom we paid. My husband was quite enough for me to manage.

DOT.     Ah—I should think so.

(DOT *seats herself upon a stool, with baby, near the fire, and close to* MRS FIELDING.
MAY *and* TILLY *are putting the room to rights.* CALEB *and* BERTHA *come forward*)

285  CALEB.     Bertha, what has happened? How changed you are, my darling, and in so
short a time. What is it? Tell me.

BERTHA.     (*bursts into tears*) Oh, father—father: my hard, hard fate!

CALEB.     But think how cheerful and how happy you have been, Bertha! How good
and how much loved by many people, although I know, to be—to be blind, is a great

290  affliction: but—

BERTHA.    I have never felt it, in its fullness. Oh my good gentle father, bear with me if I am wicked. This is not the sorrow that so weighs me down.

CALEB.    (*aside*) I cannot understand her: what does this mean?

BERTHA.    Bring her to me. I cannot hold it closed and shut within myself. May. Bring May.    295

(MAY *hearing it comes towards her, and touches her arm.* BERTHA *seizes her by the hands*)

BERTHA.    Look into my face, dear heart, sweet heart! Read it with your beautiful eyes, and tell me if truth is written on it?

MAY.    Dear Bertha—yes.

BERTHA.    There is not in my soul, a wish, or thought, that is not for your good, bright May. There is not in my soul a grateful recollection, stronger than the deep    300 remembrance which is stored there of the many, many times, when in the full pride of sight and beauty, you have had consideration for Blind Bertha, even when we two were children, or when Bertha was as much a child, as ever blindness can be! Every blessing on your head light upon your happy course! Not the less, my dear May— not the less, my bird—because to-day, the knowledge that you are to be *his* wife, has    305 wrung my heart almost to breaking.

CALEB.    Is it possible—she loves him, then—Tackleton!

BERTHA.    Father—May—Mary! oh! forgive me that it is so, for the sake of all he has done to relieve the weariness of my dark life; and for the sake of the belief you have in me, when I call Heaven to witness that I could not wish him married to a wife    310 more worthy of his goodness.

CALEB.    Gracious Heaven, is it possible! Have I deceived her then to break her heart at last!

DOT.    (*who has been listening, advances*) Come, come, dear Bertha! come away with me: give her your arm, May. So! How composed she is, you see, already, and how    315 good it is of her to mind us. (*kisses her*) There dear: come and sit by us. Stop—I hear some footsteps I know.

BERTHA.    (*starts*) Whose—step is that?

CALEB.    Whose! why it's John's.

(JOHN PEERYBINGLE *enters*)

DOT.    Why John: how soon you have returned.    320

JOHN.    Well—ain't you glad of it, Dot? I met young Hobbins in the street, and he is going to take the cart on: and call for us on his way back.

BERTHA.    But whose is the other's step—that of a man's—behind you?

CALEB.    She's not to be deceived.

---

294 *I cannot… within myself:* Johnson omits 'I cannot… within myself'.

303 *There is not in my soul… blindness can be:* Johnson omits 'There is not in my soul… blindness can be!'

325 JOHN.    Why—who should I overtake, but our old deaf gentleman, who'd been up town to buy some things, so I brought him along with me. Come along sir, you'll be welcome—never fear!—

(*The* STRANGER *enters*)

He's not so much a stranger that you haven't seen him once, Caleb. You'll give him house-room till we go?

330 CALEB.    Oh surely, John; and take it as an honour.

JOHN.    He's the best company on earth to talk secrets in. I have reasonable good lungs but he tries 'em, I can tell you. Sit down, sir. All friends here, and glad to see you.

CALEB.    What can we do to entertain him, John.

335 JOHN.    Oh—nothing. A chair in the corner, and leave to sit quite silent, and look pleasantly about him, is all he cares for. He's easily pleased.

(JOHN *leads* STRANGER *to a chair.* BERTHA *and* MAY *are talking. So also* DOT *and* MRS FIELDING)

JOHN    (*to* DOT) A clumsy Dot she was, this afternoon; and yet I like her, somehow, See yonder, Dot. (*he points to* STRANGER)

DOT.    Well—John. (*confused*) What is there, there? (*aside*) Can he suspect 340 anything?

JOHN.    He's—ha! ha! ha!—he's full of admiration for you. Talks of nobody else.

DOT.    I wish he had a better subject, John.

JOHN.    A better subject: there's no such thing. Come, off with the heavy wrappers, and a cosy half hour by the fire. (*to* MRS FIELDING) My humble service, mistress. 345 A game at cribbage, you and I? That's hearty: the cards and board, Dot. And a glass of beer here, if there's any left, small wife.

DOT.    Yes John—plenty.

(MAY *arranges the table and cards, whilst* DOT *gets the beer.* TACKLETON *enters at the door*)

MRS FIELDING.    That's quite right, my dear. Thank heaven I have always found May a dutiful child, though I say it, that ought not: and an excellent wife she will make.

350 TACKLETON.    Well, I don't doubt that.

MRS FIELDING.    And with regard to our family, though we are reduced in purse—I don't say this, sir, out of regard to what we are to play for—but though we are reduced in purse, we have always had some pretensions to gentility.

JOHN.    Which nobody doubts who knows you, mum, or May either. There's a good 355 Dot. (DOT *brings beer*) And now we will cut for deal. (*cuts*) Seven.

MRS FIELDING.    Nine.

JOHN.    Ah—you are fortunate, mistress.

(*The* STRANGER *who has been exchanging looks with* DOT, *gets up, unperceived, and goes towards door P.S.* DOT *appears anxious to follow him, as he beckons to her. This is through the dialogue*)

MRS FIELDING.    Well—I will go to say that if the Indigo trade had turned out different, which, however, is not a pleasant subject to allude to, we *might* have
been lucky.                                                                360
JOHN.    Well—here goes. (*he deals*) Now I wonder what my fortune will be to-night.
Hum! (*takes his cards*) What ought I to throw out? Here, Dot—Dot.

(DOT *is about to follow the* STRANGER, *who is gone out. She starts at* JOHN's *voice, and
turns back*)

What would you do, Dot?
DOT.    (*alarmed*) I, John? nothing.
JOHN.    Pshaw! You—no, the cards. Which shall I throw out? (DOT *takes out the* 365
*cards and throws them down*) There, little woman, that will do. I won't call you away
from May again.

(DOT *retires.The others except* TACKLETON, *who watches her, gather round*)

MRS FIELDING.    I play, I think.

(*Music. During the game,* DOT *has taken a candle from the table timidly, and followed
the* STRANGER. *The light is seen directly afterwards behind the blind of the large window. When it becomes stationary,* TACKLETON *advances, and lays his hand upon*
JOHN's *shoulder*)

TACKLETON.    I'm sorry to disturb you: but, a word, immediately.
JOHN.    I'm going to deal—it's a crisis.                                  370
TACKLETON.    It is—come here man: come.
JOHN.    (*rising and alarmed*) What do you mean?
TACKLETON.    (*leading him from the cards*) Hush, John Peerybingle; I'm sorry for
this: I am indeed. I have been afraid of it. I have suspected it from the first.
JOHN.    What is it?                                                        375
TACKLETON.    Hush! I'll show you. Can you bear to look through that window, do
you think?
JOHN.    Why not? (*advancing*)
TACKLETON.    A moment more. Don't commit any violence; it's of no use. It's dan-
gerous too. You're a strong made man; and you might do murder before you 380
know it.
JOHN.    What do you mean, I say? Stand on one side.

(JOHN *puts* TACKLETON *back, and advancing to the window, draws back the blind. The
window looks into a warehouse, now lighted; in which are seen* DOT *and
the* STRANGER, *as a young man, with his arm around her waist. She takes his white wig,
and laughs as she puts it on his head*)

---

368 *I play, I think*: MS has a gap here to the foot of page, with, in pencil, 'Cribbage dialogue to be written
in here according to the time required for the action. Mrs Fielding pegs too many.'

JOHN.     What do I see! Dot! May? Faithless. Yes, she adjusts the lie upon his head,
   and laughs at me, as she does it!  (*wildly*) May this hand have power enough to dash
385   them to the earth. But no—I cannot—she was my wife—gone! lost forever.

*He falls down upon the ground. As the others gather round him,* TACKLETON *draws the
curtain.*

*Tableau.*

*End of Chirp the Second.*

---

385.3 *Tableau*: Not derived from the Leech illustrations.

# CHIRP THE THIRD

*The Scene is the same as for Chirp the First—the interior of* JOHN PEERYBINGLE'S *cottage. As the curtain rises slowly, to plaintive music,* JOHN *is discovered sitting by the fire place, with his head upon his hands.*

JOHN.    I have sat here through the long, long night, until the stars grew pale, and the  1
cold day broke—and the more I have thought about her, the more I feel how desolate I am become—how totally the great bond of my life is rent asunder.

*Music.* DOT *enters mournfully, and sits down on the little stool at his feet. He is about to kiss her, but recollecting what has occurred, he reclines his head upon the table, hiding his face with his hands.* DOT *goes out, expressing great anxiety.*

And *he* is still beneath my roof! the lover of her early choice; of whom she has thought and dreamed: for whom she has pined and pined, when I fancied her so  5
happy by my side. Oh agony, to think of it! (*he sees the gun hanging on the wall*)
What monstrous demon has taken possession of my thoughts, and now whispers to me that it is just, to shoot this man as I would a wild beast. A step will bring me to his side. I can kill him—kill him in his bed! (*takes down the gun*) It is loaded—
I know that; and again the demon has changed my thoughts to scourges, to urge me  10
on. I will kill him—here in his bed!

(*As he speaks, the fire, which was before nearly extinguished, burns up, and the cricket is heard. Music. He stops and listens for an instant: then speaks through the music*)

The cricket on the hearth! (*puts down gun*) That she so loved and told me so, with her pleasant voice: oh! what a voice it was for making household music at the fireside of an honest man—and she is nothing now to me. Her love is another's—another's!

(*He bursts into tears and sits down again by the fireside. Music continued. The hearth opens—and the* FAIRY CRICKET *is seen, covered with a filmy grey veil. The* CRICKET *keeps chirping but faintly, so as not to interfere with the dialogue*)

CRICKET.    'I love it John: for the many times I have heard it, and the many thoughts  15
its harmless music has given me.'
JOHN.    Her very words! she said so! True.
CRICKET.    'This has been a happy home, John, and I love the cricket for its sake.'

---

3.3 DOT *enters...great anxiety*: MS omits this entry and silent business. We may conjecture that it developed as Mary Ann Keeley worked on the role of Dot; it is singled out for praise in the reviews. The MS sd is simply 'he starts up'.

6 *on the wall*: MS has the melodramatic interjection 'Ha!' deleted.

14 *honest man*: MS deletes 'I feel as if weakened from a fright'.

JOHN.     It has been, Heaven knows. She made it happy always until now.

20  CRICKET.     So gracefully sweet tempered: so domestic, joyful, busy, and lighthearted.

JOHN.     Otherwise, I never could have loved her as I did.

CRICKET.     As you *do*.

JOHN.     (*faltering*) As I did.

CRICKET.     Upon your own hearth—

25  JOHN.     The hearth she has blighted!

CRICKET.     The hearth she has, how often, blessed and brightened: the hearth, which but for her, were only a few stones, and bricks, and rusty bars, but which has been, through her, the altar of your home on which you have nightly sacrificed some petty passion, selfishness or care, and offered up the homage of a tranquil mind, a
30      trusting nature, and an overflowing heart: so that the smoke from this poor chimney has gone upward with a better fragrance than the incense that is burnt before the richest shrines in all the gaudy temples of this world. Upon your own hearth: in its quiet sanctuary: surrounded by its gentle influence and associations. Hear her! hear me! hear everything that speaks the language of your hearth and home!

35  JOHN.     And pleads for her?

CRICKET.     All things that speak of the language of your hearth and home must plead for her: for they speak the truth. Behold!

*As the* FAIRY CRICKET *finishes speaking, the chimney, above the mantel piece, opens slowly and discovers a tableau vivant—a facsimile view of the interior of the cottage, with a miniature figure of* DOT, *sitting by the fireside, as in Act 1.* TILLY SLOWBOY, BABY, *etc. At the same time troops of* SMALL FAIRIES *appear from every available position— some forming a sort of border to the tableau: others run to* JOHN, *and pull him by the skirts, to call his attention to the picture.*

CRICKET.     Is this the light wife you are mourning for?

*The figure of* DOT *rises, and an equally miniature resemblance of* JOHN PEERYBINGLE *comes in at the door. She rises to meet him: helps him off with his things etc. repeating the business of the first scene.*

CRICKET.     Is this the wife who has forsaken you?

*The Music becomes louder and hurried—a film descends in front of the tableau; the scene becomes darker; and a shadow of the* STRANGER *appears to obscure it. The* FAIRIES *express consternation and strive to rub it out, or put it on one side. When it goes away, it discovers* DOT, *sitting by the side of the cradle, with her hands clasped on her forehead and her hair hanging down. The* FAIRIES *get round her—kiss her, and try to fondle her.*

---

37  *Behold!*: Johnson omits 'Behold!'

37.2  *tableau*: These pictures are only indirectly derived from the book, where the first woodcut on p. 114 shows John sitting at a table, head in hand, with his visions around his head, and the second on p. 120 has him alone, hunched before the fireplace.

39.1  *film descends*: MS has the instruction that the film should rise, corrected to 'descends'.

CRICKET.   Is this the wife who has betrayed your confidence? Do you think that 40
these household spirits to whom falsehood is annihilation, would thus comfort her
if they did not believe her to be true—Reflect on this; for in all truth and kindness
has it been presented to you.

*The* FAIRY CRICKET *disappears, and the tableau closes. The Music also ceases.* JOHN
*starts, as if from sleep.*

JOHN.   Can it be a dream that I have seen these things? I hear the question still: 'Is
that the wife that has betrayed my confidence?' But no—no: again the terrible 45
shadow rises on my hearth. (*a knocking.* JOHN *starts*) Who is that? (*knocking
repeated*) Come in.

TACKLETON *enters.*

TACKLETON.   John Peerybingle, my good fellow: how do you find yourself this
morning?
JOHN.   I have had a poor night, master Tackleton, for I have been a good deal dis- 50
turbed in my mind. But it's over now. I wish to speak a word or two with you. You
are not married before noon.
TACKLETON.   No—plenty of time: plenty of time.

TILLY *enters.*

TILLY.   If you please I can't make nobody hear. I hope nobody ain't gone and died, if
you please. (*she knocks at the* STRANGER'S *door, and then exits*) 55
TACKLETON.   John Peerybingle, I hope there has been nothing—nothing rash in
the night.
JOHN.   What do you mean?
TACKLETON.   Because as I came here I looked into the window of his room. It was
empty and he was gone. There has been—no scuffle—eh? 60
JOHN.   Make yourself easy. He went into that room last night without word or harm
from me, and nobody has entered it since.
TACKLETON.   Oh! Well: I think he has got off pretty easily.
JOHN.   Look'ye Master Tackleton, you showed me last night my wife: my wife, that I
love: secretly— 65
TACKLETON.   And tenderly.
JOHN.   Conniving at that man's disguise, and giving him opportunities of meeting
her alone. I think there's no sight I wouldn't rather have seen than that. I think
there's no man in the world I wouldn't have rather had to show it me.
TACKLETON.   I confess to having had my suspicions always. And that has made me 70
objectionable here, I know.

---

41 *annihilation*: Johnson has 'annihilated', which would mean something different—that they always
saw the truth, not that they were destroyed by falsehood. Dickens has 'annihilation'.
44 *Can it be . . . these things?*: Johnson omits the first sentence.
46 *my hearth*: MS deletes 'She is—she must be guilty'.

JOHN.    But as you did shew it me: and as you saw her: my wife: *my wife that I love*, at this disadvantage, it is right and just that you should also see with my eyes, and look into my breast and know what my mind is upon the subject. For it's settled: and
75    nothing can shake it now.

TACKLETON.    Go on, John Peerybingle, I'll listen to you.

JOHN.    I am a plain rough man, with very little to recommend me. I am not a clever man, as you very well know. I am not a young man. I loved my little Dot, because I had seen her grow up from a child in her father's house: because I knew how pre-
80    cious she was: because she had been my life, for years and years. There's many men I can't compare with, who never could have loved my little Dot like me, I think. But I did not—I feel it now—sufficiently consider her.

TACKLETON.    To be sure. Giddiness, frivolity, fickleness, love of admiration! Not considered; all left out of sight. Hah!

85    JOHN.    You had best not interrupt me, till you understand me: and you're wide of doing so. If yesterday, I'd have struck down that man with a blow, who dared to breathe a word against her: today I'd set my foot upon his face, if he was my brother.

TACKLETON.    I did not mean anything, John Peerybingle: go on.

JOHN.    Did I consider that I took her: at her age and with her beauty: from her young
90    companions, and the many scenes of which she was the ornament: in which she was the brightest little star that ever shone: to shut her up from day to day in my dull house, and keep my tedious company? Did I consider how little suited I was to her sprightly humour, and how wearisome a plodding man like me must be to one of her quick spirit? Did I consider that it was no merit in me, or claim in me, that I
95    loved her, when everybody must who knew her? Never. I took advantage of her hopeful nature, and her cheerful disposition, and I married her. I wish I never had. For her sake, not for mine.

TACKLETON.    For your own as well, John.

JOHN.    I say *no*. Heaven bless her for the constancy with which she has tried to keep
100    the knowledge of this from me. Poor girl: that I could ever hope she would be fond of me. That I could ever believe she was.

TACKLETON.    She made a show of it: she made such a show of it, that, to tell you the truth, it was the origin of my misgivings. Look at May Fielding: *she* never pretends to be so fond of me.

105    JOHN.    I only now begin to know how hard she has tried to be my dutiful and zeal-ous wife. That will be some comfort to me when I am here alone.

TACKLETON.    Here alone? Oh, then you do mean to take some notice of this?

JOHN.    I mean to do her the greatest kindness, and make her the best reparation in my power.

110    TACKLETON.    Make *her* reparation? There must be something wrong here. You didn't mean that of course?

JOHN.    (*seizing* TACKLETON *by the collar*) Listen to me, and take care you hear me right. Listen to me. Do I speak plainly?

TACKLETON.    Very plainly indeed.

115    JOHN.    As if I meant it?

TACKLETON.   Very much as if you meant it.

JOHN.   I sat upon that hearth, last night, all night: on the spot where she has often sat beside me with her sweet face looking into mine. I called up her whole life—its every passage, in review before me. And upon my soul she is innocent, if there is one to judge the innocent and the guilty.                                                                          120

TACKLETON.   Very likely, John Peerybingle, very likely.

JOHN.   Passion and distrust have left me: nothing but my grief remains. In an unhappy moment some old lover—forsaken perhaps for me, against her will—returned. In an unhappy moment, wanting time to think of what she did, she made herself a party to his treachery by concealing it. Last night she saw him, in the   125
interview we witnessed. It was wrong. But otherwise than this she is innocent, if there is truth on earth.

TACKLETON.   If that is your opinion—

JOHN.   So let her go. Go, with my blessing for the many happy hours she has given me and my forgiveness for any pang she has caused me. She'll never hate me. She'll   130
learn to like me better, when I am not a drag upon her.

(DOT *appears at the back, pale and anxious*)

This is the day on which I took her, with so little thought for her enjoyment, from her home. To-day she shall return to it, and I will trouble her no more. Her father and mother will be here today—we had made a little plan for keeping it together—and they shall take her home. I can trust her there, or anywhere. She leaves me without   135
blame—and she will live so, I am sure. If I should die—I may perhaps while she is still young—I have lost some courage in a few hours—she'll find that I remembered her, and loved her to the last! This is the end of what you showed me. Now it's over.

DOT.   (*coming forward*) Oh no John—not over. Do not say it's over, yet; I have heard your noble words, I will not steal away pretending to be ignorant of what has affected   140
me with such deep gratitude. Do not say it's over, till the clock has struck again.

JOHN.   No hand can make the clock which will strike again for me the hours that are gone. But let it be so, if you will, my dear. It will strike soon. It's of little matter what we say. I'd try to please you in a harder case than that.

TACKLETON.   Well—I must be off: for when the clock strikes again, it'll be neces-   145
sary for me to be on my way to church. Good morning John Peerybingle. I'm sorry to be deprived of the pleasure of your company, for the loss, and the occasion of it, too.

JOHN.   I have spoken plainly?

TACKLETON.   Oh quite.                                                                          150

JOHN.   And you'll remember what I've said?

TACKLETON.   Well, if you compel me to make the observation, I'm not likely to forget it.

JOHN.   I'll see you into your chaise. I shall not come back until the clock strikes.

TACKLETON *makes a rude obeisance to* DOT: *As he is going out with* JOHN, TILLY
*enters with the* BABY. JOHN *pauses: kisses it: and rushes out.* DOT *bursts into tears.*

155 TILLY.   (*howling*) Oh if you please, don't. It's enough to dead and bury the baby, so it
is if you please.

DOT.   Will you bring him sometimes to see his father Tilly, when I can't live here,
and have gone to my old home?

TILLY.   Ow-w if you please don't! Ow, what has everybody gone and been and done
160   with everybody, making everybody else so wretched. Ow—w—w.

*As she is going off, she meets* CALEB *and* BERTHA *entering.*

CALEB.   Hey day—what's the matter here?

BERTHA.   What! Mary—not at the marriage!

CALEB.   (*aside to* DOT) I told her you would not be there mum. I heard as much last
night, but bless you, I don't care for what they say. *I* don't believe 'em. There an't
165   much of me, but that little should be torn to pieces rather than I'd trust a word
against you. (*he takes her hand*)

DOT.   You are very kind, Caleb: very.

BERTHA.   Mary—where is your hand. Ah! Here it is, here it is. (*she kisses it*) I heard
them speaking softly among themselves last night, of some blame against you. They
170   are wrong.

CALEB.   They are wrong.

BERTHA.   I know it. I told them so, I scorned to hear a word. There is nothing half
so real or so true about me as she is. My sister!

CALEB.   Bertha my dear. I have something on my mind I want to tell you while we
175   three are alone. Hear me kindly. I have a confession to make to you, my darling.

BERTHA.   A confession, father?

CALEB.   I have wandered from the truth, and lost myself, intending to be kind to
you. My dear blind daughter—hear me and forgive me.

BERTHA.   Forgive *you* father—so good, so kind!

180 CALEB.   Your road in life was rough, my poor one, and I meant to smooth it for you.
I have altered objects, changed the characters of people, invented many things that
never have been, to make you happier—Heaven forgive me—and surrounded you
with fancies.

BERTHA.   But living people are not fancies, father, you can't change them.

185 CALEB.   I have done so, Bertha. There is one person that you know, my dove—

BERTHA.   Oh father! Why do you say I know? what and whom do I know—I who
have no leader. I am miserably blind.

CALEB.   The marriage that takes place today, May's marriage, is with a sordid, stern,
grinding man. A harsh master to you and me, my dear, for many years. Ugly in his
190   looks and in his nature. Cold and callous always. Unlike what I have painted him
for you in every thing, my child: in every thing.

BERTHA.   Oh! why did you ever fill my heart so full, and then—come in like death
and tear away the object of my love! Oh Heaven, how blind I am: how helpless and
alone! *Mary*—tell me what my home is—what it really is.

---

188 *May's marriage*: MS omits 'May's marriage'.

DOT. It is a poor place, Bertha: very poor and bare indeed. The house will scarcely 195
keep out wind and rain another winter. It is as roughly shielded from the weather,
Bertha, as your father in his sackcloth coat.

BERTHA. (*leading* DOT *aside*) And the presents, Mary, that came at my wish. Who
sent them: did you?

DOT. No. 200

BERTHA. (*shaking her head, presses her hands to her eyes*) Dear Mary, a moment
more—look across the room to where my father is and tell me what you see.

DOT. I see an old man worn with care and work, but striving hard, in many ways,
for one great sacred object; and I honour his grey head, and bless it.

(BERTHA *leaves* DOT, *goes towards her father, and falls at his knees*)

BERTHA. I feel as if my sight was restored. There is not a gallant figure on the earth 205
that I would cherish so devotedly as this. The greyer and more worn the dearer,
father.

CALEB. Bertha!

BERTHA. And, in my blindness, I believed him to be so different!

CALEB. The fresh smart father in the blue coat Bertha—he's gone. 210

BERTHA. Nothing is gone, dearest father—no—everything is there in you.
Father—Mary.

CALEB. Yes, my dear—here she is.

BERTHA. There is no change in *her*? You never told me anything of *her* that was not
true? 215

CALEB. I should have done it, my dear, I fear, if I could have made her better than
she was. But I must have changed her for the worse, if I had changed her at all.
Nothing could improve her, Bertha.

DOT. More changes than you think for may happen, though. You mustn't let them
startle you to much if they do. Bertha! hark! are those wheels upon the road? 220

BERTHA. (*listens*) Yes—coming very fast.

DOT. (*flurried*) I—I—I know you have a quick ear. Though, as I said just now (*listens*) there are great changes in the world, great changes and we can't do better—we
can't do better, I say, than prepare ourselves to be surprised at hardly anything. They
are wheels indeed—coming nearer—nearer! *Very* close, and now you hear them 225
stopping at the garden gate. And now you hear a step outside the door—and now—
ah! he is here.

*Music. She utters a cry of delight. The* STRANGER, *now a young man, comes in, throwing his hat upon the ground.* DOT *puts both her hands before* CALEB's *eyes.*

DOT. Is it over?

EDWARD. Yes.

DOT. Happily yes? 230

EDWARD. Yes.

DOT. Do you recollect the voice, dear Caleb? Did you ever hear the like of it before?

CALEB. If my boy in the golden South Americas was alive—

DOT.    He is alive! (*takes her hands away from* CALEB's *eyes*) Look at him! See where
235    he stands before you, healthy and strong! Your own son: your own dear living loving brother, Bertha.

(*They embrace.* JOHN PEERYBINGLE *enters and starts back*)

JOHN.    Why—how's this? What does this mean?

CALEB.    It means, John, that my own boy is come back from the golden South
Americas. Him you fitted out, and sent away yourself. Him that you were always
240    such a friend to.

JOHN.    (*advances to shake hands & then recoils*) Edward! Was it you?

DOT.    Now tell him all, Edward: tell him all. And don't spare me: for nothing shall
make me spare myself in his eyes, ever again.

EDWARD.    I was the man.

245    JOHN.    And could you steal disguised into the house of your old friend? There was a
frank boy, once—how many years is it, Caleb, since we heard he was dead, and had
it proved as we thought—who never would have done that.

EDWARD.    There was a generous friend of mine, once more than a father to me than
a friend, who never would have judged me, or any other man, unheard. You were
250    he. So I am certain you will hear me now.

JOHN.    Well—that's but fair. I will.

EDWARD.    You must know that when I left here: a boy: I was in love: and my love was
returned. She was a very young girl—who, perhaps, (you may tell me) did't know
her own mind. But I knew mine: and I had a passion for her.

255    JOHN.    You had—*you*.

EDWARD.    Indeed I had: and she returned it, I have ever since believed she did, and
now I am sure she did.

JOHN.    Heaven help me, this is worse than all.

EDWARD.    Constant to her and returning full of hope, after many hardships and
260    perils, to redeem my part of our old contract, I heard, twenty miles away, that she
was false to me: that she had forgotten me, and had bestowed herself upon another
and a richer man. I had no mind to reproach her, but I wished to see her, and to
prove beyond dispute that this were true. That I might have the truth—the real
truth—observing freely for myself, without obstruction on the one hand, or pre-
265    senting my own influence, if I had any, before her, on the other, I dressed myself
unlike myself—you know how—and waited on the road, you know where. You had
no suspicion of me: neither had—had she (*points to* DOT) until I whispered into
her ear at the fireside, and she so nearly betrayed me.

DOT.    (*eagerly*) But when she knew that Edward was alive and well and had come
270    back, and when she knew his purpose, she advised him by all means to keep his
secret close: for his old friend John Peerybingle was much too open in his nature,
and too clumsy in all artifice—being a clumsy man in general—to keep it for him.
And so she—that's me John, told him all, and how his sweetheart had believed him
to be dead; and how she had at last been over-persuaded by her mother into mar-
275    riage, which the silly dear old thing called advantageous: and when she—that's me

again, John—told him they were not yet married (though close upon it) and that it
would be nothing but a sacrifice if it went on, for that there was no love on her side,
and when he went nearly mad with joy to hear it, then she—that's me again—said
she would go between them, as she had often done before in old times, John, and
they were brought together John; and were married John, an hour ago and here, 280
here, (*she runs to the door and brings in* MAY) and here's the bride, and Gruff and
Tackleton may die a bachelor, and I'm a happy little woman, may God bless you.

JOHN.    (*advancing*) My own, my darling Dot!

DOT.    (*retreats*) No, John, no! Hear all. Don't love me any more John, till you've
heard every word I have to say. It was wrong to have a secret from you John: I'm 285
very sorry, I didn't think it any harm, till I came and sat down by you on the little stool,
last night: but when I knew, by what was written in your face, that you had seen me
walking in the gallery with Edward, and knew what you thought: I felt how giddy
and how wrong it was. But oh, dear John, how could you, how could you think so?

JOHN.    Little woman! Dot! How could I indeed!                          290

DOT.    Don't love me yet, please John. Not for a long time yet. When I was sad about
this intended marriage, dear, it was because I remembered May and Edward such
young lovers: and knew that her heart was far away from Gruff & Tackleton. You
believe that now, don't you, John?

JOHN.    I do, I do. (*advances*)                                        295

DOT.    No—keep your place, John. When I laugh at you, as I sometimes do John, and
call you clumsy and a dear old goose, and names of that sort, it's because I love you
John, so well, and take such pleasure in your ways, and wouldn't see you altered in
the least respect to have you made a king tomorrow.

CALEB.    Hoorar! hoorar! My opinion!                                    300

DOT.    When I first came home here, I was half afraid I mightn't learn to love you every
bit as well as I hoped and prayed I might, being so very young. But, dear John, every
day and hour I loved you more and more. And if I could have loved you better than I
do, the noble words I heard you say this morning would have made me. But I can't; all
the affection I had—it was a great deal, John—I gave you, as you well deserve, long 305
long ago, and I have no more left to give. Now my dear husband, take me to your heart
again! That's my home, John and never, never, think of sending me to any other.

*She rushes into his arms. At this moment* TACKLETON *enters.*

TACKLETON.    Ah—what the devil's this John Peerybingle? There's some mistake.
I beg your pardon sir (*to* EDWARD) I haven't the pleasure of knowing you: but if
you can do me the favour to spare that young lady, she has rather a particular 310
engagement with me this morning.

EDWARD.    But I can't spare her. I couldn't think of it.

TACKLETON.    What do you mean—you vagabond—

EDWARD.    I mean that, as I can make allowance for your being vexed, I am as deaf
to harsh discourse this morning, as I was to all discourse last night.             315

---

302 *being so very young*: Johnson omits 'being so very young'.

TACKLETON.    I don't understand you.

EDWARD.    I am sorry, Sir (*holding out* MAY's *ring finger*) that the young lady can't accompany you to church: but as she has been there once this morning perhaps you'll excuse her.

TACKLETON *looks at* MAY: *scratches his ear and takes a little parcel, containing a ring from his pocket.*

320   TACKLETON.    Miss Slowboy will you have the kindness to throw that in the fire. (*she does so*) Thankee.

EDWARD.    It was a previous engagement—quite an old engagement, that prevented my wife from keeping her appointment with you, I assure you.

MAY.    Mr Tackleton, will do me justice to acknowledge that I revealed it to him
325   faithfully: and that I told him many times I never could forget it.

TACKLETON.    Ah! Certainly: oh! To be sure: oh! It's all right. It's quite correct. Mrs Edward Plummer, I infer?

EDWARD.    That's the name.

TACKLETON.    Ah! I shouldn't have known you, sir, I give you joy, sir.

330   EDWARD.    Thankee.

TACKLETON.    Mrs Peerybingle I am sorry. You haven't done me a very great kindness, but upon my life I'm sorry. You are better than I thought you. John Peerybingle I am sorry. You understand me: that's enough. It's quite correct, ladies and gentlemen all, and perfectly satisfactory. Good morning. (*Exit*)

335   JOHN.    Now we'll make a day of it, if ever there was one.

DOT.    And we'll have such a feast: and such a merrymaking! Dear dear John! I hardly know whether to laugh or cry. My goodness John. There's old Mrs Fielding at the door all the time, and nobody has asked her out of the chaise. Go and fetch her in. (*Exit* JOHN) And Caleb—run round to father's, and bring him in, and mother
340   too: and anything they have got to eat and drink that's ready. (CALEB *goes*) And May—spare her for a few minutes, Edward—there's the tub of ale in the cellar and there's the key: and Bertha shall look after these vegetables, and we've a nice ham. What a happy, happy little woman I mean to be.

*She bustles about, with the others, moving tables, plates etc.* JOHN *enters with* MRS FIELDING.

JOHN.    There, mum: there's your son-in-law, and a fine fellow he is.

345   MRS F.    That ever I should have lived to see the day! When that unfortunate affair happened in the Indigo trade I knew throughout my life I should meet only insults, and here they are. Carry me to my grave.

JOHN.    Not at all, mum: you're not dead, nor anything like it, nor won't be, we hope, for many a year to come. There, let them tell their own story, and get out of their
350   scrape as they can, and as I am sure they will.

---

347 *When that unfortunate...here they are*: Johnson omits 'When that unfortunate...here they are.'

*He brings* EDWARD, MAY, *and* MRS F. *together, and pushes them towards the fire place.* CALEB *returns with* DOT'S FATHER *and* MOTHER *and one or two* NEIGHBOURS. *They embrace* DOT.

CALEB.   How d'ye do, everybody. Here they are, and here we are: and won't we be jolly. Hallo, who are you?

*A* MAN *enters with two parcels.*

MAN.   Mr Tackleton's compliments, and as he hasn't got no use for the cake himself perhaps you'll eat it: there it is.

CALEB.   Law!                                                                                355

MAN.   And Mr Tackleton's compliments, and he's sent a few toys for the baby. They an't ugly.

DOT.   Why—what can he mean?

TACKLETON *enters.*

TACKLETON.   Mrs Peerybingle, it means this. I'm sorry, more sorry than I was this morning. John Peerybingle, I'm sour by disposition, but I can't help being sweet- 360 ened more or less by coming face to face with such a man as you. Caleb! The unconscious little nurse gave me a broken hint last night of which I have found the thread. I blush to think how easily I might have bound you and your daughter to me: and what a miserable idiot I was when I took her for one! Friends, one and all—my house is very lonely today. I have not so much as a cricket on my hearth—I have 365 scared them all away. Be gracious to me. Let me join this happy party.

JOHN.   Of course—and heartily glad we are to see you. We'll make you so jolly that you shalln't believe you're yourself.

DOT.   John! You won't send me home this evening—will you?

(JOHN *embraces her*)

EDWARD.   A dance—a dance! Bertha, here's your harp: now play us your liveliest 370 tune. Won't you dance, Mary? (DOT *shakes her head*) Nor you John? No? then here goes.

(BERTHA *plays the harp. Music.* MAY *and* EDWARD *get up and dance, for a little time, alone. Then* JOHN *throws his pipe away, takes* DOT *round the waist, and joins them. Presently* TACKLETON *goes off with* MRS FIELDING. *Then* DOT'S FATHER *and* MOTHER *join in. Lastly* CALEB *and* TILLY SLOWBOY, *and* NEIGHBOURS)

*General Dance and*

*The Curtain Falls*

# EIGHT

Albert Smith, *The Battle of Life*, Lyceum, December 1846

## INTRODUCTION

AFTER the resounding success of *The Cricket on the Hearth*, this next Christmas book was eagerly awaited by audiences, and was perhaps bound to be some kind of departure. The Keeleys bought it in advance, Albert Smith was sent the proof sheets, and the Lyceum lavished a visually spectacular production upon the result. The little theatres were more eager than ever to mount their versions too, but the play did not achieve an afterlife of new British adaptations, as its immediate predecessor had done. The press, by this time thoroughly hostile to this apparently back-door theatrical activity, and perhaps also hostile to the possibility that Dickens was making his fortune by taking over the whole artistic scene in London, and so seeking ways to diminish him, attributed what success *The Battle of Life* had entirely to Mary Ann Keeley and Smith. For deductions about the implications of this odd failure, see the Introduction ('Like the Brilliant Ballet-Pantomime').

### THE TEXT

Dickens followed his established practice of sending his proof sheets to Smith, who then acted as dramaturg. The basis of this edition is the Lord Chamberlain's MS, Add. MS 42998 ff. 512–87, which was submitted by Mrs Keeley on 14 December 1846. It is in Smith's hand, with his characteristic punctuation that uses colons where his contemporary dramatists use a dash. This has been collated with a copy of the printed text of 1847 published by W.S. Johnson with a title page declaring Smith's official status as Dickens's chosen dramatizer, which has many small emendations that occur in the MS incorporated into the text. The copy I have used is in the British Library, BL Dex211, from the Dexter collection of Dickens rare books, and is annotated 'Charles Dickens had a hand in this play, both as regards the writing and the production on the stage.'

Characters and cast of the first production

| | |
|---|---|
| Dr Jeddler | Mr Frank Matthews |
| Alfred Heathfield | Mr Leigh Murray |
| Michael Warden | Mr F. Vining |
| Mr Snitchey | Mr Meadows |
| Mr Craggs | Mr Turner |
| Benjamin Britain | Mr Robert Keeley |
| Grace Jeddler | Miss Ellen Daly |
| Marion Jeddler | Miss May |
| Mrs Snitchey | Mrs Woollidge |
| Mrs Craggs | Miss Grove |
| Aunt Martha | Miss Foster |
| Clemency Newcome | Mrs Mary Ann Keeley |

Musicians, guests, coachman, and passengers.

**8.** *The Battle of Life*: Bob and Mary Ann Keeley as Clemency and Britain. *Illustrated London News*, 26 December 1846.

# ACT I

## SCENE 1

*The stage represents an orchard attached to an old stone house, with a honeysuckle porch, and terminating in a view of a picturesque open country with church, water-mill, cornfields etc. The porch and the trees are practicable; the back ground is made by a series of sets. The first set must be contrived for the coach to drive along behind. On the rising of the curtain several persons are in the scene.*

MEN *and* WOMEN *are up the trees on ladders, and* CLEMENCY *is sitting on a branch.* GRACE *and* MARION *are dancing together on the grass before the house, to the music of a harp and fiddle. As they conclude* DR JEDDLER *appears in the porch.*

DR J.  Music and dancing *today*! (*aside*) I thought they dreaded today, but it's a world of contradictions. (*aloud*) Why Grace—why Marion, is the world more mad than usual this morning?

MARION.  Make some allowance for it, father, if it be: for it's somebody's birth-day.

DR J.  Somebody's birth-day, Puss! Don't you know it's always somebody's birthday? Did you never hear how many new performers enter on this—ha! ha! ha!—it's impossible to speak gravely of it—on this preposterous and ridiculous business called life, every minute?

MARION.  No, father.

DR J.  No—not you, of course: you're a woman—almost. By the bye: I suppose it's *your* birthday?

MARION.  No! do you really father?

DR J.  (*kisses her*) There! Take my love with it, and many happy returns of—the idea!—the day. The notion of wishing happy returns, in such a great practical joke as the world, is good. Ha! ha! ha! But how did you get this music? Poultry stealers of course. Where did the minstrels come from?

GRACE.  (*twisting flowers in her sister's hair*) Alfred sent it, father.

DR J.  Oh! Alfred sent it, did he?

GRACE.  Yes: he met it coming out of the town as he was entering, early—the men are travelling on foot, and rested there last night; and as it was Marion's birth-day,

1

5

10

15

20

---

0.8 MEN *and* WOMEN...*porch*: The opening picture is not derived from the book in all its details: the illustration (p. 3) has a top line of the aftermath of the old battle, and the three figures of Grace, Marion, and Dr Jeddler against the apple trees, with no one else present.

15 *The notion...returns*: MS has a deleted version of this line, 'on such a farce as this is good for ha! ha! ha! look upon the world as,' worth noting for its retention of Dickens's theatrical image in Jeddler's philosophizing.

and he thought it would please her, he sent them on, with a pencilled note to me, saying that if I thought so too, they had come to serenade her.

DR J.     Aye, aye: he always takes your opinion.

25 GRACE.     And my opinion (*admiring her sister*) being favourable, and Marion being in high spirits and beginning to dance, I joined her: and so we danced to Alfred's music till we were out of breath and we thought the music all the gayer for being sent by Alfred. Didn't we, dear Marion?

MARION.     Oh—I don't know, Grace. How you teaze me about Alfred.

30 GRACE.     Teaze you, by mentioning your lover!

MARION.     (*picking a flower to pieces*) I am sure I don't much care to have him mentioned. I am almost tired of hearing of him: and as to his being my lover—

GRACE.     Hush. Don't speak lightly of a true heart which is all your own, Marion, even in jest. There is not a truer heart than Alfred's in the world.

35 MARION.     No—no. Perhaps not. But I don't know that there's any great merit in that. I—I don't want him to be so very true—I never asked him. If he expects that I—but, dear Grace, why need we talk of him at all, just now? (*they put their arms round each other's waist and go up the stage*)

DR J.     Ah! they are two dear girls. Grace is but four years older that Marion, and yet she has been a mother to her. I am sorry for her sake—sorry for them both—that 40 life should be such a very ridiculous business as it is. Pshaw! All love is folly—an idle imposition which young people practice on themselves. Nothing in it—a bubble. Ha! ha! (*looks at his watch*) Hey day. Here Britain! Benjamin Britain! Holloa!

(BRITAIN *comes from the house*)

BRITAIN.     Now then. Here I am. What is it?

DR J.     Where's the breakfast table?

45 BRITAIN.     In the house.

DR J.     Are you going to spread it out here, as you were told last night? Don't you know there are gentlemen coming? That there's business to be done this morning before the coach comes by? That this is a very particular occasion?

BRITAIN.     (*gradually raising his voice*) Yes—I know all about it, but I couldn't do 50 anything, Doctor Jeddler, till the women had done getting in the apples, could I?

DR J.     Well—they have done now! (*claps his hands*) Come—make haste! Where's Clemency?

CLEM.     (*from the tree*) Here am I, Mister: here am I. It's all done now. (*coming down the ladder*) Clear away, gals. Everything shall be ready for you in half a minute, 55 Mister. (*comes to front and pulls her dress into shape*) It's all very well to be in a hurry when you haven't got to put yourself to rights: but I like to be tidy, though they do say I've got two left legs and somebody else's arms, and that all four of 'em are out of joint: and that my shoes never will go where my feet want them to. Well— never mind—I'm sure they're good shoes; and my legs and arms are no business of 60 mine: I'm quite content to take them as they come—everything—all except my

---

41 *young*: MS omits 'young'.

elbows: and they do get grazed dreadful, and always where I can't see 'em. (*begins to lay the table, which* BRITAIN *and one of the women have brought out*) I wonder how many's a-coming. One—two—three—four: more than that. Two more cups Britain: and saucers: and spoons. Mr Alfred's going away today, to learn how to make doctor's stuff, in foreign parts. Well—I hope it will do him good, I'm sure. I wonder 65 how Miss Marion likes it. (SNITCHEY *and* CRAGGS *appear at the orchard gate*) Oh—this is the other company. (*aloud*) here are them two lawyers a-coming, Mister.

DR J. (*advancing to meet them*) Aha! Good morning, good morning! Grace my dear! Marion! Here are Messrs Snitchey and Craggs: where's Alfred?

GRACE. He'll be back directly father, no doubt. He had so much to do this morning 70 in his preparations for departure, that he was up and out by day-break. Good morning, gentlemen.

SNITCH. Ladies—for self and Craggs—(*they both bow*) good morning. Miss (*to* MARION) I kiss your hand. (*he kisses it*)

CLEM. (*looks at him with no very good will*) Humph! So long as he don't kiss mine, 75 I don't care. He might kiss my elbows if it would make 'em well.

SNITCH. And I wish you (*still to* MARION) a hundred happy returns of this auspicious day.

CLEM. I dare say. He don't look much like a gentleman who *could* wish anybody much good, if he would. 80

DR J. A hundred happy returns: Ha! ha! think of that. The great farce, in a hundred acts.

SNITCH. (*standing his blue bag against the leg of the table*) You wouldn't—I am sure—cut the great farce short for this actress, at all events, Dr Jeddler.

DR J. No—Heaven forbid! May she live to laugh at it, as long as she can laugh, and 85 then say, with the French wit, 'The farce is ended—draw the curtain.'

SNITCH. (*looking into his blue bag*) The French wit was wrong, Dr Jeddler, and your philosophy is altogether wrong, depend upon it, as I have often told you. Nothing serious in life? What do you call law?

DR J. A joke. 90

SNITCH. Did you ever go to law?

DR J. Never.

SNITCH. If you ever do, perhaps you'll alter your opinion.

CRAGGS. It's made a great deal too easy.

DR J. Law is? 95

CRAGGS. Yes: everything is, now-a-days: it's the vice of the times. If the world is a joke—and I'm not prepared to say it isn't—it ought to be made a very difficult joke to crack. But it's being made far too easy. We're oiling the gates of life, when they ought to be rusty. We shall have them beginning to turn soon, with a smooth sound. Whereas, they ought to grate upon their hinges, sir. 100

BRIT. (*to* CLEM) He seems to grate upon his own hinges rather: eh, Clemency?

CLEM. Nasty cold hard, dry man: in his grey and white, he looks just like a flint. I should like to make him strike some sparks, by hitting him hard against a bit of steel.

105  BRIT.    T'other's like a raven, or a magpie: and the doctor's like a winter pippin, with
here and there a dimple to express the peckings of the birds, and his pigtail behind
stands for a stalk. There's the three nat'ral kingdoms there. Animal, wegetable, and
mineral—all ready. Hulloa! Here's Mr Alfred!

ALFRED *comes through the orchard gate followed by a porter carrying baskets and*
*packages.*

DR J.    Happy returns, Alf.
110  SNITCH.    A hundred happy returns of this auspicious day, Mr Heathfield. (*bows*)
CRAGGS.    Returns. (*bows*)
ALF.    Why—what a battery! And one—two—three: all foreboders of no good in the
great sea before me.
BRIT.    They look like the Graces, them three, Clemency; don't they?
115  CLEM.    Uncommon disguised, if they are.
ALF.    I am glad you are not the first I have met this morning. I should have taken it
as a bad omen: but Grace was the first—sweet, pleasant Grace—so I defy you all!
CLEM.    If you please, mister, *I* was the first you know. He was a walking, out here,
before sunrise, you remember. *I* was in the house.
120  ALF.    That's true: Clemency was the first. So I defy you with Clemency.
SNITCH.    Ha! ha! ha! for self and Craggs. What a defiance.
ALF.    (*shakes hands with the* DOCTOR, *and* SNITCHEY, *and* CRAGGS) Not so bad a
one as it appears, may be. But where are the—my goodness! (*he recognizes* MARION
*and* GRACE, *and going to them, salutes them*)
SNITCH.    I say (*to* CRAGGS) did you see that?
125  CRAGGS.    Yes: and all too easy: like everything else. A good deal too easy.
DR J.    Now come—to breakfast—to breakfast. Grace, you take your usual place.
Marion—Alfred—next to her. Messrs Snitchey and Craggs, will you be seated?

*They place themselves at the table.* CLEMENCY *in waiting.* BRITAIN *at a side table on*
*which some cold meat has been placed.*

BRIT.    (*to* SNITCHEY, *holding up carving knife and fork at him*) Meat?
SNITCH.    Certainly.
130  BRIT.    (*to* CRAGGS) Do *you* want any?
CRAGGS.    Lean and well done.
BRIT.    There (*helps him*) I know nobody else won't have any.
CLEM.    (*pouring out water in teapot*) Say *when*, Miss.
GRACE.    That will do, Clemency.
135  CLEM.    That's it, miss. (*coming to* BRITAIN *and looking at* CRAGGS) I say, Britain; he
don't complain of the beef being too easy—does he?

---

107  *with here and…for a stalk*: MS omits 'with here and…for a stalk'.
125  *A good deal too easy*: The printed text (referred to hereinafter as 1847) omits the speeches of Snitchey
and Craggs here.
136  *does he?*: MS initially gives the remark about Craggs to Britain, as he serves, above.

CRAGGS *is seized with a fit of coughing.* CLEMENCY *runs and thumps his back. He recovers.*

BRIT.  (*chuckling*) Ha! ha! I thought he was gone—that I did. What a pity! (*slaps the cold meat with the blade of his knife*)

DR J.  Now Alfred: for a word or two of business whilst we are yet at breakfast.

SNITCH.  Whilst we are *yet* at breakfast. (*they eat*)

ALF.  If you please, sir.                                                                     140

DR J.  If anything could be serious in such a—

ALF.  Farce as this—(*smiling*)

DR J.  In such a farce as this, it might be the recurrence on the eve of separation of a double birthday which is connected with many associations pleasant to us four, and with the recollection of a long and amicable intercourse. That's not to the purpose.  145

ALF.  Ah—yes, yes, Dr Jeddler: it is much to the purpose, as my heart bears witness this morning, and as yours does too, if you would let it speak. Today I leave your house, and cease to be your ward. We part with tender relations stretching far behind us, that can never be exactly renewed, and with others (*looks at* MARION) with others dawning yet before us, fraught with such considerations as I must not  150 trust myself to speak of now. Come, come! There's a serious grain in this large foolish dust-heap, doctor. Let us allow to day, that there is *one*.

DR J.  Today! Hear him! ha! ha! ha! of all days in the foolish year. Why, on this day there was once a great battle fought on this very ground, and so many lives were lost, that within my recollection, generations afterwards, a church yard full of  155 bones, and dust of bones, and chips of cloven skulls has been dug up from underneath our feet here—yet not a hundred people in that battle knew for what they fought, or why: and not half a hundred were the better for the gain or the loss. Not half a dozen agree, to this hour, on the cause or merits: and nobody in short can ever know anything distinct about it, but the mourners of the slain. Serious too!  160 Such a system!

ALF.  But all this seems to me to be very serious.

DR J.  Serious! If you allowed such things to be serious, you must go mad, or die, or climb up to the top of a mountain and turn hermit.

ALF.  Besides—so long ago.                                                                     165

DR J.  Long ago: do you know what the world has been doing since? *I* don't.

SNITCH.  (*stirring his tea*) It has been going to law a little.

CRAGGS.  Although the way out has always been made too easy.

CLEMENCY *tumbles against the table.*

DR J.  Hey day: what's that?

CLEM.  It's this evil-inclined blue-bag: always a tripping up somebody.                        170

SNITCH.  (*looks cross, and moves it away*) I was going to say, doctor, that war *is* foolish. There we agree. The idea of any man exposing himself voluntarily to fire and

---

150 *dawning*: 1847 substitutes 'opening' for 'dawning'.

155 *generations*: MS has 'a generation' but 1847 agrees with Dickens and his timescale by using the plural.

sword! Stupid, wasteful, positively ridiculous. But look upon this battle-field as real property. Think of the laws belonging to it: to the bequest and devise of real prop-
175   erty: to the mortgage and redemption of real property: ah! (*smacks his lips*) of the complicated laws relating to title, and the contradictory acts of parliament connected with them, and the ingenious and interminable chancery suits. There's a green spot in life you like. I believe I speak for self and Craggs.

(CRAGGS *bows*)

SNITCH.    Then I'll have another cup of tea, and a little more beef, thankee. I don't
180   stand up for life in general: it's full of folly, or something worse. But you mustn't laugh at life: you've got a game to play; everybody's playing against you, you know; and you're playing against them. There are deep moves on the board. You must only laugh, Dr Jeddler, when you win: and then not much. He! he!

(CLEMENCY *imitates his laugh and finishes with an expression of scorn*)

DR J.    Well, Alfred, what do you say now?
185   ALF.    Really sir, I wish you would forget this battle in the broader battle-field of life, on which the sun looks every day.
SNITCH.    I'm afraid that won't soften his opinions, Mr Alfred. The combatants are very eager, and very bitter, in that same Battle of Life. There's a great deal of cutting and slashing, and firing into people's heads from behind: terrible treading down
190   and trampling on; it's rather a bad business.
ALF.    (*with emphasis, clearly and distinctly*) I believe, Mr Snitchey, there are quiet victories and struggles; great sacrifices of self, and noble acts of heroism in it—even in many of its apparent contradictions and lightness—not the less difficult to achieve, because they have no earthly chronicle or audience: done every day in
195   nooks and corners, and in little households, and in men's and women's hearts—any one of which might reconcile the sternest man to such a world, and fill him with belief and hope in it, though two-fourths of the people are at war and another fourth at law—and that's a bold war.
DR J.    Well—well: I'm too old to be converted. Sixty years have gone over my head,
200   and—I have never seen the Christian world—including Heaven knows how many loving mothers and good enough girls, like mine here, *anything* but mad for a battle-field. The same contradictions prevail in everything. One must either laugh or cry at such stupendous inconsistencies: and I prefer to laugh.
BRIT.    (*who has been listening attentively*) Ha! ha! ha! so do I.
205   CLEM.    (*knocks him with her elbow*) I say: what are you laughing at?
BRIT.    Not you.
CLEM.    Who then?

---

198 *bold war*: 1847 ends the speech at 'hope in it'. MS is not entirely clear at the end of its version, which reads either 'and that's a cold war' or '…a bold war'. Dickens, however, had 'a bold word', which was presumably what Smith had before him, even if he altered it to describe a 'war' referring to 'the law'. He apparently decided to eliminate uncertainty by omission in the text for printing.

BRIT.    Humanity. That's the joke.

CLEM.    (*to herself, speaking of* BRITAIN) What between master and them lawyers,
he's getting more and more addle-headed every day. (*she nudges him with her*   210
*elbow*) Do you know where you are? Do you want to get warning?

BRIT.    I don't know anything. I don't care for anything. I don't make out anything. I
don't believe anything. And I don't want anything.

CLEM.    Ah—you're getting quite muddled in the depths of your ignorance. Truth at
the bottom of her well is quite up high compared to you.                        215

DR J.    But this is not to our purpose, Alfred. Ceasing to be my ward (as you have
said) today, and leaving us full to the brim of such learning as the Grammar School
down here was able to give you, and your studies in London could add to that, and
such practical knowledge as a dull old doctor like myself, could graft upon both,
you are away, now, into the world. The first term of probation appointed by your   220
poor father being over, away you go now, your own master, to fulfil his second
desire: and long before your three years tour among the foreign schools of medicine
is finished you'll have forgotten us. Lord, you'll forget us easily, in six months.

ALF.    If I do—But, you know better: why should I speak to you! (*laughing*)

DR J.    I don't know anything of the sort. What do you say, Marion? Eh? Nothing?   225

(MARION *plays with her teacup*)

I haven't been a very unjust steward, I hope, in the execution of my trust: but I am
to be, at any rate, formally discharged and released, and what not, this morning, and
here are our good friends Snitchey and Craggs with a bagful of papers, accounts and
documents for the transfer of the balance of the trust fund to you,  (I wish it was a
more difficult one to dispose of, Alfred, but you must get to be a great man and make   230
it so) and other drolleries of that sort, which are to be signed, sealed, and delivered.

SNITCH.    (*pushing away his plate and taking out the papers*) And duly witnessed, as
by the law required; and self and Craggs having been co-trustees with you, doctor,
in so far as the fund was concerned, we shall want your two servants to attest the
signatures. Can you read, Mrs Newcome?                                          235

CLEM.    I a'n't married, Mister.

SNITCH.    Oh: I beg your pardon. (*looking at her*) He! He! I should think not. You
*can* read?

CLEM.    A little.

SNATCH.    The marriage service, night and morning, eh?                         240

CLEM.    No, too hard. I only reads a thimble.

SNITCH.    Read a thimble! What are you talking about, young woman?

CLEM.    (*nods*) And a nutmeg-grater.

SNITCH.    Why, this is a lunatic: a subject for the Lord High Chancellor!

CRAGGS.    If possessed of any property.                                        245

---

212 *I don't care for anything*: 1847 omits 'I don't care for anything'.

GRACE.   You do not quite understand her. She has got a thimble and a nutmeg-grater, and each has a motto on them, which she can read.

BRIT.   They form her pocket library: that's all. She is not much given to study great books.

250 SNITCH.   Oh, that's it, is it? Ha! ha! ha! I thought our friend was an idiot. She looks uncommonly like it. And what does the thimble say, Mrs Newcome?

CLEM.   I ain't married, Mister.

SNITCH.   Well, Newcome: will that do? What does the thimble say, Newcome?

CLEMENCY *looks down into her pocket and takes therefrom all sorts of articles, scissors, apple, orange, penny, balls of cotton, curl papers etc which she gives* BRITAIN *to hold, detailing them as she pulls them out. At last she produces the thimble: puts it on her finger, and rattles the nutmeg grater against it.*

SNITCH.   That's the thimble, is it young woman? And what does the thimble say?

255 CLEM.   (*reading round it*) It says 'For-get and for-give.'

(SNITCHEY *and* CRAGGS *laugh*)

SNITCH.   So new!

CRAGGS.   So easy.

SNITCH.   Such a knowledge of human nature in it.

CRAGGS.   So applicable to the affairs of life.

260 SNITCH.   And the nutmeg grater?

CLEM.   The grater says 'do-as-you-would-be-done-by.'

SNITCH.   'Do, or you'll be done brown' you mean.

CLEM.   (*shakes her head*) I don't understand. I a'n't no lawyer.

SNITCH.   I am afraid that if she was, doctor, she'd find it to be the golden rule of half
265 her clients. If Mr Britain will oblige us with a mouthful of ink, we'll sign, seal, and deliver as soon as possible; or the coach will be coming past before we know where we are.

BRIT.   (*vacantly*) It'll come by before I know where *I* am. I'm quite bewildered.

CLEM.   Here, Britain; here's the ink  (*jogs him*) now do be a little brisk and fresh.

270 SNITCH.   (*to* BRITAIN) You'll be good enough, Mr Britain, to sign your name—there.

BRIT.   Well, I'd rather not, you know: I don't want anything, and I don't want to sign away what little I've got. I'd rather not commit myself, if it's all the same.

DR J.   But this is not committing yourself, Britain. We only want your name as a witness—you understand. Come, sign it man: you're only a witness.

275 BRIT.   Stop a minute: let me see what it is I'm going to put my name to. Um! Ah! (*reading it*) If it was so much Chinese—and I rather think it is—it couldn't be worse. Stop a minute I tell you. Perhaps there's something on the other side. No, I don't think I like it much, though.

SNITCH.   Now, Mr Britain: if you have finished. Here, if you please.

280 BRIT.   (*signing*) Oh yes: it's easy to say, 'here'—very easy. There—I've been and done it. Now, I'll be bound, I ain't worth a farthing in the world. Oh dear.

SNITCH.   Now, Newcome: we will trouble you for your name.

CLEM.    (*laughing*) Lor! To think they want my name—mine! Give us the pen, mister and don't hurry me, else—now there's a blot to begin with (*takes up ink with her finger and wipes it on her head: then sucks her pen*) C. L.—E.—oh! There's a long hair in the pen. Cle—M—there—can you read that? 285

DR J.    Britain—run to the gate and watch for the coach. Time flies, Alfred.

ALF.    Yes, sir, yes. Dear Grace! A moment Marion: so young and beautiful: so winning and so much admired: dear to my heart as nothing else in life is: remember! I leave Marion to you. 290

GRACE.    She always has been a sacred charge to me Alfred. She is doubly so now. I will be faithful to my trust, believe me.

ALF.    I do believe it Grace. I know it well. Who could look upon your face, and hear your earnest voice, and not know it! Ah, good Grace! If I had your well-governed heart and tranquil mind, how bravely I would leave this place to day. 295

GRACE.    Would you?

ALF.    And yet Grace—sister seems the natural word—

GRACE.    (*quickly*) Use it. I am glad to hear it. Call me nothing else.

ALF.    And yet, sister then, Marion and I had better have your true and steadfast qualities serving us here and making us both happier and better; I wouldn't carry them away to sustain myself, if I could. 300

BRIT.    (*on the wall*) Coach is on the hill-top. (*horn music*)

DR J.    Time flies, Alfred.

ALF.    (*to* MARION, *who has been standing apart*) I have been telling Grace, dear Marion, that you are her charge: my precious trust at parting. And when I come back, and reclaim you dearest, and the bright prospect of our married life lies stretched before us, it shall be one of our chief pleasures to consult how we can make Grace happy: how we can shew our gratitude and love to her, to return her something of the debt she will have heaped upon us. 305

MARION.    (*puts her hand on her sister's neck*) Dear Grace! 310

ALF.    And when the time comes, as it must one day,—I wonder it has never come yet, but Grace knows best, for Grace is always right, when *she* will want a friend to open her whole heart to—then Marion, how faithful we will prove, and what delight to us to know that she, our dear good sister, loves, and is loved again as we would have her.

BRIT.    Coach coming through the wood! (*music*) 315

ALF.    And when all is passed, and we are old, and living (as we must) together—close together—talking of the old times, there shall be favourite times among them—this day most of all—and telling each other what we thought and felt; and hoped and feared at parting, and how we couldn't bear to say good bye—

CLEM.    Coach out of the wood! 320

GRACE.    Alfred! Don't linger: there's no time. Say good bye to Marion, and heaven be with you!

(ALFRED *embraces* MARION)

302 *horn music*: MS omits this and the next music cue.

DR J.  Farewell my boy! To talk about anything serious is such a—ha! ha! ha!—you
know what I mean. But all I can say is that if you and Marion should continue in the
325 same foolish minds, I shall not object to have you for a son-in-law one of these days.

BRIT.  Coach on the bridge!

ALF.  Let it come! (*to* DR JEDDLER) Think of me sometimes, my old friend and
guardian, as seriously as you can. Adieu Mr Snitchey! Farewell Mr Craggs.

CLEM.  Coach coming down the road.

330 ALF.  A kiss of Clemency Newcome for long acquaintance sake. (*kisses her*)

CLEM.  Oh: my goodness! I never did. And now he's rumpled me.

*(The horn sounds without)*

ALF.  Shake hands, Britain. Marion, dearest heart: good bye! Sister Grace!
remember.

*Music. The coach comes up to the back. Bustle.* ALFRED *mounts. The people come on.*

BRIT.  Hallow there! Some of you, let's give him a good one at going.

335 GRACE.  See, he waves his hat to you, my love. Your chosen husband, darling. Look.

MARION.  Heaven bless you, Grace. But I cannot bear to see it. It breaks my
heart. (*falls on her sister's neck, sobbing*)

BRIT.  Now then a good one. Here's jolly luck to him. Hurray!

*The people huzzah.* ALFRED *continues to wave his hat in reply to the farewells of* DR
JEDDLER *and the others. The horn sounds: and as the coach moves away the curtain
falls.*

End of Act I

# ACT II

## SCENE 1

*The office of* SNITCHEY *and* CRAGGS. *A dark wainscot room, furnished with high-backed leathern chairs. A framed print of a judge's head. Bales of papers on the shelves, and tiers of deed boxes, labelled 'Snaggles', 'Hall and Clifford', 'Saunders, Maurice, and Co', 'Douglas', 'Brandram', 'Marmy'. An office table and three chairs in the centre: the table covered with documents, and on it a deed-box labelled 'Michael Warden, Esquire.' A candle burning on the table.*

SNITCHEY *and* CRAGGS *are seated opposite to each other at desk,* MICHAEL WARDEN *in a larger chair, in an attitude of thought.*

SNITCH.  (*laying down a deed*) That's all. Really there's no other resource. No other  1
  resource.
WARD.  All lost, spent, wasted, pawned, borrowed, and sold, eh?
SNITCH.  All.
WARD.  Nothing else to be done you say?  5
SNITCH.  Nothing at all.
WARD.  And I am not personally safe in England. You hold to that; do you?
SNITCH.  In no part of the United Kingdom of Great Britain and Ireland.
WARD.  A mere prodigal son with no father to go back to, no swine to keep, and no
  husks to share with them. Eh?  10

SNITCHEY *and* CRAGGS *cough, one after the other.*

WARD.  Ruined at thirty. Humph!
SNITCH.  Not ruined Mr Warden. Not so bad as that. You have done a good deal
  towards it I must say: but you are not ruined. A little nursing—
WARD.  A little devil!
SNITCH.  Mr Craggs: will you oblige me with a pinch of snuff. Thank you sir.  15
WARD.  Humph! You talk of nursing. How long nursing?
SNITCH.  (*dusting snuff from his fingers*) How long nursing? For your involved
  estate, Sir? In good hands? S and C's, say? Six or seven years.
WARD.  (*with a sneering laugh*) To starve for six or seven years.
SNITCH.  To starve for six or seven years, would be very uncommon indeed. You  20
  might get another estate in that time by shewing yourself as a wonder. But we don't
  think you could do it—speaking for Self and Craggs—and consequently don't
  advise it.
WARD.  What *do* you advise?
SNITCH.  Nursing, I say. Some years of nursing by Self and Craggs would bring it  25
  round. But to enable us to make terms, and hold terms, and you to keep terms, you

must go away: you must live abroad. As to starvation, we would insure you some
hundreds a year to starve upon, even in the beginning, I dare say, Mr Warden.

WARD.     Hundreds! And I have spent thousands.

30 SNITCH.     That there is no doubt about. (*he puts back papers in box*) No doubt
about.

WARD.     After all, my iron-headed friend—

SNITCH.     Self and—excuse me—Craggs.

WARD.     I beg Mr Craggs' pardon. After all my iron-headed friends: you don't know
35 half my ruin yet.

(*The lawyers stare eagerly at him*)

I'm not only deep in debt, I am deep in—

SNITCH.     Not in love!

WARD.     Yes, deep in love.

SNITCH.     And not with an heiress, sir?

40 WARD.     Not with an heiress.

CRAGGS.     Nor a rich lady?

WARD.     Nor a rich lady, that I know of—except in beauty and merit.

SNITCH.     A *single* lady I trust?

WARD.     Certainly.

45 SNITCH.     It's not one of Dr Jeddler's daughters?

WARD.     Yes.

SNITCH.     Not his youngest daughter?

WARD.     Yes.

SNITCH.     Mr Craggs, will you oblige me with another pinch of snuff? Thank you.
50 I'm happy to say it don't signify, Mr Warden: she's engaged, sir: she's bespoke. My
partner can corroborate me. We know the fact.

CRAGGS.     We know the fact.

WARD.     Why, so do I perhaps. What of that? Are you men of the world, and did you
never hear of a woman changing her mind?

55 SNITCH.     There certainly have been actions for breach, brought against both spin-
sters, and widows: but in the majority of cases—

WARD.     Cases! Don't talk to me of cases. The general precedent is a much larger
volume than any of your law books. Besides, do you think I have lived six weeks in
the doctor's house for nothing?

60 SNITCH.     (*to* CRAGGS) I think, Mr Craggs, that of all the scrapes Mr Warden's horses
have brought him into at one time or another, the worst scrape may turn out to be,
if he talks in this way, his having been ever left by one of them at the Doctor's garden
wall, with three broken ribs, a snapped collar bone, and the Lord knows how many
bruises. We didn't think as much of it at the time when we knew he was going on

---

50 *to say*: MS omits 'to say'.

61 *one time or another*: MS deletes an elaboration: 'and they have been pretty numerous and pretty
expensive, as none know better than himself and you and I'.

well under the Doctor's hands, and roof, but it looks bad now Sir. Bad! It looks *very* 65
bad. Dr Jeddler too—our client, Mr Craggs.

CRAGGS.    Mr Alfred Heathfield, too, a sort of client, Mr Snitchey.

WARD.    Mr Michael Warden too, a sort of client: and no bad one either: having
played the fool for ten or twelve years. However, Mr Michael Warden has sown his
wild oats now—there's their crop in that box—and means to repent and be wise. 70
And in proof of it Mr Michael Warden means, if he can, to marry Marion, the doctor's lovely daughter: and to carry her away with him.

SNITCH.    Really, Mr Craggs—

WARD.    Really, Mr Snitchey, and Mr Craggs, partners both, you have little to do with
this. There's nothing illegal in it. I never was Mr Heathfield's bosom friend. I violate 75
no confidence of his. I love where he loves, and I mean to win where he would win
if I can.

SNITCH.    He can't Mr Craggs: he can't do it sir. She dotes on Mr Alfred.

WARD.    Does she?

SNITCH.    Mr Craggs: she dotes on him, Sir.                                      80

WARD.    I didn't live six weeks in the doctor's house for nothing: and I doubted that
soon. She would have doted on him, if her sister could have brought it about: but I
watched them. Marion avoided his name, avoided the subject: shrunk from the
least allusion to it with evident distress.

SNITCH.    Why should she, Mr Craggs, you know? Why should she sir.             85

WARD.    Pshaw! She was very young when she made the engagement: it's three years
ago and more—and has perhaps repented it. So perhaps—it seems a foppish thing
to say, but upon my soul I don't mean it in that light, she may have fallen in love
with me as I have fallen in love with her.

SNITCH.    He! he! Mr Alfred, her old play-fellow too, you remember Mr Craggs, 90
knew her almost from a baby. And yet (*to himself*) there's something in what he
says. He's a dangerous sort of libertine to seem to catch the spark, the match from a
young lady's eyes.

WARD.    (*rises and holds* SNITCHEY *and* CRAGGS *by their button-holes*) Now observe,
Snitchey, Craggs. I don't ask you for any advice. I will review in two words my posi- 95
tion and intentions, leaving you to do the best for me, in money matters, that
you can.

SNITCH.    I think it will be best not to hear this, Mr Craggs.

CRAGGS.    *I* think not, too, Mr Snitchey.

WARD.    Well—do as you like about that. If anything in the world is true, it is true 100
that Marion dreads the return of her old lover. Nobody is injured so far. I am so
harried and worried here just now that I lead the life of a flying fish: but my house
and grounds and many a broad acre beside will some day come back to me, and

---

77 *if I can*: 1847 abbreviates the scene from this point, cutting from '...if I can.' to the beginning of
Warden's speech below, 'Now observe, Snitchey...' cutting 'I will review...that you can.' and their
responses, running on his next speech from 'If anything...' and proceeding as here to the end of the scene.
102 *harried*: MS has 'hurried' for 'harried'.
103 *any many...beside*: MS omits 'any many...beside'.

then Marion will be richer as my wife, than as the wife of Alfred Heathfield whose
105      return she dreads. Mind that. Who is injured yet? Now you know my purpose.
When must I leave here?
SNITCH.      Immediately.
WARD.      I shall wait some days.
SNITCH.      You ought not to: but let it be. Are you going? Good night, sir.
110   WARD.      (*shakes hands with them*) Good night. You'll live to see me making a good
use of riches yet. Henceforth the star of my destiny is Marion.
SNITCH.      That star don't shine on the stairs, sir. Take care how you go down. (*light-
ing him*) Good night.
WARD.      (*exit at door*) Good night.
115   SNITCH.      What do you think of all this, Mr Craggs?
CRAGGS.      I don't know.
SNITCH.      (*getting his great coat and gloves*) I thought, too, that pretty face was very
true. Our friend Alfred talks about the battle of life. I hope he mayn't be cut down
early in the day. Have you got your hat, Mr Craggs?
120   CRAGGS.      Here it is.
SNITCH.      Very well—I'm going to put the candle out.

(*He puts the candle out and they grope their way to the door.*

*Chairs and tables to be carried off. Lights down*)


# SCENE 2

DR JEDDLER's *study. A snug old fashioned room, filled up with books, maps etc. A fire
burning in the old fireplace. A table, as if there had been supper on it, glasses etc.*

*The* DOCTOR *in his slippers and dressing gown, in an easy chair.* GRACE *sitting at work.*
MARION *reading a book.*

1   MARION.      (*reading*) And being in her own home: her home made exquisitely dear
by those remembrances, she now began to know that the great trial of her heart
must soon come on and could not be delayed. Oh Home, our comforter and
friend when others fall away, to part with whom, at any step between the cradle and
5      the grave—(*she falters as she reads the last few lines*)
GRACE.      Marion, my love!
DR J.      Why, Puss: what's the matter?
GRACE.      Dear Marion: read no more tonight.
MARION.      (*shutting the book*) I cannot: the words seem all on fire!

---

121   *I'm going to put the candle out*: 1847 omits 'I'm going to put the candle out.'

3   *her home made . . . not be delayed*: 1847 omits 'her home made . . . not be delayed'.

DR J. (*laughing*) What! Overcome by a story-book: Print and paper! Well, well, it's 10
all one. It's as rational to make a serious matter of print and paper as of anything
else. But dry your eyes, love; dry your eye. I dare say the heroine has got home again
long ago, and made it up all round—and if she hasn't, a real home is only four walls:
and a fictional one, mere rags and ink. What's the matter now?

CLEM. (*putting her head in at the door*) It's only me, mister. 15

DR J. And what's the matter with *you*?

CLEM. Oh! Bless you, nothing an't the matter with me. I've bin and grazed my
unlucky elbows again: but it's the better to have them chafed than my temper.
Nothing an't the matter with me but—(*entering*) come a little closer, mister.

DR J. What does she mean? (*he rises and approaches her*) 20

CLEM. (*in a low tone*) You said I wasn't to give you one before them you know.

DR J. One what? Bless me! What does she mean—not a chaste salute! I'm almost
alarmed.

CLEM. (*hunting in her pockets*) No—I don't mean nothing. Britain was riding by on
an errand and see the mail come in, and waited for it. There's 'AH' in the cor- 25
ner. (*gives the* DOCTOR *a letter*) Mr Alfred's on his journey home, I bet. We shall
have a wedding in the house—there was two spoons in my saucer this morning. Oh
lauk, how slow he opens it!

DR J. Here girls—I can't help it: I never could keep a secret in my life. There are not
many secrets indeed worth being kept in such a—well! Never mind that. Alfred's 30
coming home, my dears, directly.

MARION. Directly!

DR J. What! The story-book is soon forgotten—I thought the news would dry those
tears. Yes—'let it be a surprise,' he says, here. But I can't let it be a surprise—he must
have welcome. 35

MARION. Directly!

DR J. Why, perhaps not what your impatience calls directly—but pretty soon, too.
Let us see—let us see—He will be here on Thursday.

MARION. On Thursday!

GRACE. A gay day and a holiday for us. (*to* MARION) Long looked forward to, 40
dearest, and come at last.

DR J. (*resuming his seat*) Ah! Well, he's coming. The day was, when you and he,
Grace, used to trot about arm in arm in his holiday time like a couple of walking
dolls. You remember?

GRACE. I remember. (*going on with her work*) 45

DR J. On Thursday, indeed. That hardly seems a twelvemonth ago. And where was
my little Marion then?

MARION. Never far from her sister, however little. Grace was everything to me,
even when she was a young child herself.

---

14 *I dare say … rags and ink*: 1847 omits 'I dare say … rags and ink'.

24 *I don't mean nothing*: 1847 omits 'I don't mean nothing'.

30 *There are not … Never mind that*: 1847 omits 'There are not … Never mind that.'

35 *What! … must have welcome*: MS omits this speech and therefore Marion's repetition.

50  DR J.    And nothing would serve you, Grace, but you must be called Alfred's wife—so
we called you Alfred's wife—and you liked it better I believe (odd as it seems now)
than being called a duchess, if we could have made you one.

GRACE.    Indeed.

DR J.    Why, don't you remember it?

55  GRACE.    I think I remember something of it, but not much. It's so long ago; Alfred
will find a real wife soon and that will be a happy time indeed for all of us. My three
years trust is nearly at an end, Marion. It has been a very easy one. I shall tell Alfred,
when I give you back to him, that you have loved him dearly all the time, and that
he has never once needed my good services. May I tell him so, love?

60  MARION.    Tell him, dear Grace, that there never was a trust so generously, nobly,
steadfastly discharged, and that I have loved *you*, all the time, dearer and dearer
every day, and oh! how dearly now!

DR J.    Well well, girls: there are many trifles in this trifling world: but yours are agreeable ones enough. It's getting late though: and it is time to go to bed, for we shall have

65  plenty to do tomorrow—making ready for Alfred's return and inviting our friends to
meet him. There's good girls! Good night. Heaven bless you, my darlings.

(*He kisses them, and they go off*)

DR J.    Clemency Newcome.

CLEM.    Yes, mister.

DR J.    You and Britain may finish what is left on the table: you can sit here if you like

70  until the fire's out. It's warmer tonight here than in the kitchen. Good night.

CLEM.    Good night, mister. (DR JEDDLER *goes out*) Britain's in the kitchen all
among the dinner covers and pot-lids, looking at his likeness in them. I'll ring him
up. (*rings*) Lor! how I should like to be a missus. Perhaps I shall be some day.

BRITAIN *enters with a dinner-cover which he has been polishing.*

BRIT.    (*looking round*) Who rung?

75  CLEM.    Me, Benjamin. Doctor Jeddler says we may finish the supper here, and let
the kitchen fire out.

BRIT.    Oh—very good. (*looks at the cover*) It don't improve a man, it don't, not
having his portrait taken in this style. How it alters one, too! There's a long face: and
now, that's an uncommon jolly one. Ha! ha! there's a mouth!

80  CLEM.    I say, Benjamin, are you a-coming.

BRIT.    Oh yes: I'm a coming. I say, Clem: do you think I might have my pipe here?

CLEM.    Well—Dr Jeddler smokes here, sometimes: so I suppose it an't no crime. I'll
put the windows open in the morning.

51  *so we…wife*: MS omits 'so we…wife'.

71  *DR JEDDLER goes out*: 1847 omits Dr J's instruction to Clemency and her response to him, having him
exit with the girls. It then has 'rubbing up' for 'all among'.

77  *it don't, not*: MS omits 'it don't, not'.

82  *no crime*: MS has a deletion: 'sit by the fireplace and then the smoke'll go up the chimney'.

BRIT. (*as they sit down*) Well, Clemmy: how are you by this time? and what's the news?

CLEM. Mr Alfred's coming home directly: there! 85

BRIT. Coming home! that's good! There'll be another job for Snitchey and Craggs, I suppose. More witnessing for you and me perhaps, Clemmy.

CLEM. Lor! I wish it was me, Britain.

BRIT. Wish what as you?

CLEM. A going to be married. 90

BRIT. (*laughing*) Yes! You're a likely subject for that. Poor Clem!

CLEM. (*laughs*) Yes: I'm a likely subject for that: an't I!

BRIT. (*shakes his head*) Not a chance of it.

CLEM. Pretty much! Well, I suppose you mean to, Britain, one of these days: don't you? 95

BRIT. (*smokes*) I ain't altogether clear about it: but—ye-es—I think, perhaps, I may come to that, at last.

CLEM. I wish her joy, whoever she may be.

BRIT. Oh! She'll have that, safe enough.

CLEM. But she wouldn't have had quite such a joyful life as she will lead, and 100 wouldn't have had quite such a sociable sort of a husband as she will have, if it hadn't been for me—not that I went to do it, for it was accidental to be sure—if it hadn't been for me, now would she, Britain?

BRIT. Certainly not. Oh I'm greatly beholden to you, Clem.

CLEM. (*greasing her elbows*) Lor! How nice that is to think of. 105

BRIT. You see, I've made a good many investigations of one sort and another in my time, having been always of an enquiring turn of mind. And I've read a good many books about the general Rights of things and Wrongs of things, for I went into the literary line myself, when I began life.

CLEM. Did you though? 110

BRIT. Yes. I was hid for the best part of two years behind a bookstall, ready to fly out if anybody pocketed a volume. And after that I was light porter to a stay and man-tua maker, in which capacity I was employed to carry about deceptions in oilskin baskets: nothing but deceptions: which soured my spirits and disturbed my confidence in human nature. Then I heard a world of discussions in this house which 115 soured my spirits fresh: and my opinion, after all, is that as a safe and comfortable sweetener of the same, and as a pleasant guide through life, there's nothing like a nutmeg grater—

CLEM. That's just what—

BRIT. Com-bined with a thimble. 120

CLEM. Do as you would, you know, and cetrer, eh? Such a short cut, an't it? (*patting her elbows*)

---

91 *Poor Clem*: 1847 omits 'Poor Clem' here and has Britain call her 'Clemency' throughout.

94 *Pretty much!*: 1847 has 'Only think!' for 'Pretty much!'

102 *to be sure*: 1847 has 'I am sure' for 'to be sure'.     107 *having…mind*: 1847 omits 'having…mind.'

BRIT.    I'm not sure that it's what would be considered good philosophy. I've my
         doubts about that—but it wears well, and saves a quantity of snarling, which the
         genuine article don't, always.

125 CLEM.   See, how you used to go on once yourself, you know.

BRIT.    Ah! But the most extraordinary thing, Clemmy, is that I should live to be
         brought round through you. That's the strange part of it. Through you! Why I sup-
         pose you haven't as much as half an idea in your head.

CLEM.    No: I don't suppose I have.

130 BRIT.   I'm pretty sure of it.

CLEM.    Oh, I dare say you're right. I don't pretend to none. I don't want any.

BRIT.    (*laughing*) What a natural you are, Clemmy. But I can't help liking you—
         you're a regular good creature in your way—so shake hands, Clem. What ever hap-
         pens I'll always take notice of you and be a friend to you.

135 CLEM.   Will you? Well, that's very good of you.

BRIT.    (*gives her his pipe to knock the ashes out of*) Yes, yes: I'll stand by you. (*a noise
         without*) Hark! That's a curious noise!

CLEM.    Noise!

BRIT.    A footstep outside. Somebody dropping from the wall, it sounded like. Are
140      they all abed up-stairs?

CLEM.    Yes, all abed by this time.

BRIT.    Didn't you hear anything?

CLEM.    No. (*they listen*)

BRIT.    (*taking a lantern from a closet*) I tell you what: here's the Doctor's lantern. I'll
145      have a look round before I go to bed, for satisfaction's sake. Undo the door into the
         garden whilst I light this, Clemmy.

CLEM.    Well—I'll light it (*lights it*) but it's all your fancy: you'll only have a walk for
         your pains. There's the candle blown out. (*lights down*)

BRIT.    (*taking the lantern*) Ah! Very likely. Never mind. (*takes the poker*) This'll do.
150      Now I'm ready for it, whatever it is. (*Exit*)

CLEM.    (*looking out through the door*) It's as quiet as a churchyard, and almost as
         ghostly too. Ha! what's that?

(MARION *appears in the study, cautiously*)

MARION.    (*agitated*) Hush! You have always loved me, have you not?

CLEM.    Loved you, child?: you may be sure I have.

155 MARION.   I am sure. And I may trust you: may I not? There is no one else just now,
         on whom I may trust.

CLEM.    Yes.

MARION.    There is someone out there, whom I must see and speak with
         tonight. (MICHAEL WARDEN *appears in the doorway*) Michael Warden: for heaven's
160      sake retire. Not now. In another moment you may be discovered. Wait if you can, in

---

124 *I'm not sure... always*: 1847 omits Britain's speech.

some concealment. I will come, presently. (*she closes the door, as he waves his hand and retires*)

CLEM.   What does all this mean?

MARION.   Don't go to bed. Wait here for me. I have been seeking to speak to you for an hour past. Oh! be true to me!

CLEM.   Here's Britain coming.   165

(*The light of the lantern is seen through the window blind, with the shadows of the panes.* BRITAIN *returns as* MARION *runs off*)

BRIT.   All still and peaceable. Nothing there. Fancy, I suppose. (*he shuts the door*) One of the effects of having a lively imagination. Halloa, why what's the matter?

CLEM.   Matter! (*rubbing her elbows*) That's good in you, Britain, that is! After going and frightening one out of one's life, with noises, and lanterns, and I don't know   170 what all. Matter! Oh, yes.

BRIT.   If you're frightened out of your life by a lantern, Clemmy, that apparition's very soon got rid of. (*blowing it out, after lighting the other candle*) But you're bold as brass in general, and were, after the noise and lantern too. What have you taken into your head—not an idea, eh?   175

CLEM.   No: good night, Britain: good night. I'm sure you must be tired. I'll put everything away: good night.

BRIT.   You seem precious glad to get rid of me—it's impossible to account for a woman's whims.

CLEM.   (*half pushing him away*) No—I'm not but—you know you've got to be up   180 early—good night. (*Exit* BRITAIN)

Well—I'm glad that I haven't got no ideas, for I'm sure I should have lost them! What can all this be about? Oh dear! oh dear! I'm afraid there's something bad going on.

MARION *enters cautiously.*

MARION.   Open the door, Clemency, and stand there close beside me, while I speak   185 to him outside.

CLEM.   (*crying, and embracing* MARION) It's little I know, my dear: very little: but I know that this should not be. Think of what you do.

MARION.   I have thought of it, many times.

CLEM.   Once more: till tomorrow. (MARION *shakes her head*) For Mr Alfred's sake.   190 Him that you used to love so dearly once.

MARION.   (*hiding her face in her hands*) Once!

CLEM.   Let me go out. I'll tell him what you like. Don't cross the doorstep tonight. I'm sure no good will come of it. Oh! It was an unhappy day when Mr Warden was ever brought here! Think of your good father, darling—of your sister.   195

MARION.   I have. You don't know what I do. I *must* speak to him. You are the best and truest friend in all the world for what you have said to me, but I must take this step. Will you go with me, Clemency, or shall I go alone?

CLEM.    I will go with you. But oh! Miss Marion for all our sakes, think of your father,
200    and your home. Think of Mr Alfred—think of the morning he went away.

*Music.* CLEMENCY *leads* MARION *through the door mistrustfully.* WARDEN *appears and receives* MARION. *The door closes.*


## SCENE 3

SNITCHEY *and* CRAGGS *office, as before.*

SNITCHEY *comes in with a candle, and goes to desk.*

1  SNITCH.    There—I believe that is the last indenture and now all is right. Craggs will
   have it, still, that we've made it all too easy. I don't think it will be found so. (*he rubs his
   hands and leaves the table, looking out of window*) B-r-r-r! this is a winter's night with
   a vengeance. Just a night for the hall though, and I hear the Doctor has beaten up all his
5  friends to welcome Alfred Heathfield home. Welcome! Ha! ha! ha! Eh? Who's there?

CRAGGS *enters in full dress.*

CRAGGS.    It's me. Are you coming?
SNITCH.    No: not yet. I must wait, you know.
CRAGGS.    I wish you were.
SNITCH.    Why?
10  CRAGGS.    Because the women are getting impatient and suspicious. I'm afraid we're
   too easy with them.
SNITCH.    It's natural and proper for them to be so. Did you ever know a woman that
   didn't suspect her husband's partner? Mrs Snitchey is suspicious of you on principle: and Mrs Craggs suspects me by the same reason. A pinch of snuff, Mr Craggs.
15  Thank you. (*he sneezes*)

MRS SNITCHEY *and* MRS CRAGGS *enter, extravagantly dressed.*

MRS C.    That's right. Sneeze again Mr Snitchey: sneeze again, sir, what else can you
   expect to do in this abominable office: a regular blue chamber, where I've no doubt
   you'd cut our heads off if you could. Mr Craggs!
CRAGGS.    My love!
20  MRS C.    Don't love me sir; do you know what time it is?
CRAGGS.    (*looks at watch*) It want two minutes and a half to eight, my love.
MRS C.    And is it not time to be off sir? Instead of which you are poking about here
   in the cold, after all kinds of evil deeds.

---

200 *Think of Mr ... he went away*: MS omits 'Think of Mr ... he went away.' And the sd 'WARDEN *appears
and receives* MARION'.

0.1 SNITCHEY *and* CRAGGS *office, as before*: 1847 has 'without the desk, stools, or chairs etc' instead of
'as before'.

CRAGGS.   My dear, Mr Snitchey—

MRS C.   Your Snitcheys indeed! I don't see what you want with your Snitcheys for 25
my part. You trust a good deal too much to your Snitcheys, *I* think: and I hope you
may never find my words come true.

SNITCH.   Mrs Craggs: for self and Craggs: you are uttering a libel.

MRS S.   Who do you mean, madam, by 'your Snitcheys' speaking of Mr Snitchey in
that imaginative plural!                                                        30

SNITCH.   Oh dear: now they're at it.

MRS S.   Your Snitcheys indeed! Just as if you spoke disparagement of an objectionable pair of pantaloons, or other articles not possessed of a singular number.

MRS C.   I intended no offence madam. I merely wished to support our common
cause against the office.                                                       35

MRS S.   Then you do so unpleasantly, madam. Mr Snitchey!

SNITCH.   My dear!

MRS S.   If you ever have been led away by man, you were led away by that man.

SNITCH.   Mr Craggs is my trustworthy partner.

MRS S.   Trustworthy fiddlestick, sir. If ever I read a double purpose in anybody's 40
eye, I read that in Craggs' eye.

MRS C.   What are you insinuating, madam?

CRAGGS.   Dear! Dear! Something very dreadful will happen I know. Come; my
dear: Mrs Snitchey, it's quite time we should be thinking of going.

MRS C.   Of course it is, sir: and ought to have been an hour ago: but your Snitcheys 45
there, has determined to keep us—dying with cold, sir: dying with cold.

SNITCH.   I will follow you immediately, ladies. But I have a little more honey to collect into our hive here. It's all for ourselves you know, my love: for self and Craggs:
and their private partners.

MRS S.   And how long shall you be, sir?                                        50

SNITCH.   Perhaps an hour, my dear: perhaps more.

MRS S.   Then you may go by yourself, sir: for *I* am not going to wait. Go, sir, alone:
or with your bosom friend there, Mr Craggs. (*bounces out of the room*)

SNITCH.   Mrs Snitchey—my love—here—here! (*Exit after her*)

MRS C.   Well, sir.                                                             55

CRAGGS.   Well, my dove?

MRS C.   Are you going to wait here, with your Snitcheys? Are you coming, or am *I*
to go alone, also.

CRAGGS.   My dear, I'm coming.

MRS C.   Then come, sir; immediately : and if you'd only place a little of that confi- 60
dence in your wife, which you do in your Snitcheys there, it would be much more
creditable. Now, sir: I am waiting.

(MRS CRAGGS *seizes the candle with one hand, and drags* CRAGGS *off with the other*)

---

54 *Mrs Snitchey…Exit after her*: MS omits this speech and exit.

## SCENE 4

*The Hall, or dancing room, in* DR JEDDLER's *house, prepared for the ball. The scene must be so constructed as to clear away in an instant. The walls are decorated with holly and evergreens: and lighted by branches, as well as lamps from the ceiling and on the table.*

BRITAIN *is nailing up some flowers against the walls: and* CLEMENCY *is lighting up the candles, as the scene draws. The musicians are seated at the end of the room and are tuning their instruments.* DR JEDDLER *is watching the preparations: and* GRACE *as adjusting* MARION's *hair, who is sitting on an ottoman.*

1   GRACE.    There, dear Marion: Alfred's favourite flowers. The next wreath I adjust on this fair head, will be a marriage wreath: or I am no true prophet, dear.

    MARION.    A moment, Grace, don't leave me yet. Are you sure that I want nothing more?

5   GRACE.    My art can go no further, dear girl: nor your beauty. I never saw you look so beautiful as now.

    MARION.    I never was so happy.

    GRACE.    Aye; but there is greater happiness in store. In such another home—as cheerful as bright as this looks now, Alfred and his young wife will soon be living.

10   DR J.    Well. Here we are, all ready for Alfred, eh?

    CLEM.    More than ready, mister. He won't be here till pretty late. (*aside*) I'm sure I wish he was come. I'm all of a totter.

    DR J.    Ah, an hour or so before midnight. There'll be plenty of time for making merry before he comes. He'll not find us with the ice unbroken. Pile up the fire here,

15   Britain.

    BRIT.    I'll make it blaze sir: and shine upon the holly until it winks again.

    DR J.    It's all a world of nonsense, Puss—true lovers and all the rest of it—all nonsense: but we'll be nonsensical with the rest of them and give our true lover a mad welcome. Upon my word: (*looking at his girls*) I'm not very clear tonight, among

20   other absurdities, but that I'm the father of two handsome girls.

    MARION.    All that one of them has ever done, or may do—*or may do*—dearest father, to cause you pain or grief, forgive her: forgive her now, when her heart is full.

    DR J.    Why my love: why, Puss: what do you mean?

    MARION.    Say you forgive her. That you *will* forgive her. That she shall always share

25   our love. (*hides her face on the* DOCTOR's *shoulder*)

    DR J.    Tut—tut—tut: forgive! What have I to forgive? Heyday, if our true lovers come back to flurry us like this, we must send express to stop 'em on the road and bring 'em a mile or two a day, until we're properly prepared to meet them. Kiss me Puss. Forgive! Forgive what: why what a silly child you are. (*noise of carriages without*)

---

    10   DR J: 1847 begins the scene here, with only Dr Jeddler, Clemency, and Britain on, also curtailing the preceding sd from 'BRITAIN is nailing…'.

    16   *winks again*: 1847 has Marion and Grace enter here.

CLEM. All the candles are lighted, mister, just in time. There's some people. 30

DR J. Come Britain: bustle: and let them in. (*Exit* BRITAIN) Now, darling: cheer up: here are our guests coming. Don't freeze the people on this bleak December night. Let us be light, and warm, and merry, or I'll not forgive some of you!

*Music: through which the guests arrive,* BRITAIN *introducing them.*

BRIT. If you please sir, this is Mr and Mrs Saunders and Miss Laura Saunders!

(*The* DOCTOR *receives them, with his daughters*)

BRIT. And there's a whole lot more down stairs. There's plenty of room (*out at* 35 *door*) up *here*, ladies and gentlemen. (*more guests arrive*) What's your name sir. Thankee—Mr Straggles! I don't know who he's got with him, sir: but I reckon they're his friends. Here's Mr Hall a-coming, sir: and Miss Clifford: walk in. Here's a party.

CLEM. (*to* BRITAIN) I say, Britain—

BRIT. Well, Clemmy: be quick: you mustn't interfere with me now. 40

CLEM. What a lot they will all eat and drink!

BRIT. Well—there's enough for them. Mrs Snitchey!

(MRS SNITCHEY *enters*)

DR J. How d'ye do—how dy'e do, Mrs Snitchey. But what's become of your good husband?

MRS S. I'm sure I don't know. 45

BRIT. Mr and Mrs Craggs!

(MR *and* MRS CRAGGS *enter*)

MRS S. I've no doubt Mr Craggs can tell you, Dr Jeddler.

MRS C. That nasty office.

MRS S. I wish it was burnt down.

CRAGGS. (*hesitating*) He's—he's—there's a little matter of business that keeps my 50 partner rather late.

MRS S. Oh—h! Business. Don't tell me.

MRS C. *We* know what business means.

(*During this short dialogue, more guests have been arriving, whom the* DOCTOR *receives*)

MRS C. I wonder *you* could come away, Mr Craggs.

MRS S. Mr Craggs is fortunate, I'm sure. 55

MRS C. That office so engrosses 'em.

MRS S. A person with an office has no business to be married at all.

CRAGGS. (*to* GRACE) Good evening, Ma'am. You look charmingly. Your—Miss— your sister Miss Marion: is she—

GRACE. Oh she's quite well, Mr Craggs. 60

CRAGGS. Yes—I—is she here?

GRACE. Here! Don't you see her yonder? Going to dance.

(CRAGGS *puts on his spectacles*)

DR J.   Now, fiddlers: strike up. Gentlemen, lead out your partners. Come. (*clapping his hands*) A dance! A dance! Mrs Snitchey may I have the honour? Mr Brandram—
65   Mrs Craggs.

*Dance—Cotillion—during which* SNITCHEY *arrives, and touches* CRAGGS, *who is looking on, on the arm. He starts.*

CRAGGS.   Is he gone?
SNITCH.   Hush! He has been with me for three hours and more. He went over everything. He looked into all our arrangements for him, and was very particular indeed: He—humph: presently.

(*The dance finishes. As it concludes* MARION *leaves her partner: looks anxiously about the room, and then quits it by the door.* SNITCHEY *and* CRAGGS *watching her*)

70  CRAGGS.   You see! All safe and well. He did not recur to that subject I suppose?
SNITCH.   Not a word.
CRAGGS.   And is he really gone: is he safe away?
SNITCH.   He keeps his word. He drops down the river with the tide, in that shell of a boat of his and so goes out to sea on this dark night—a dare-devil he is—before
75   the wind. There's no such lonely road anywhere else—that's one thing... The tide flows, he says, an hour before midnight—about this time. I'm glad it's all over. (*wipes his forehead anxiously*)
CRAGGS.   What do you think—
SNITCH.   Hush! I understand you. Don't mention names; and don't let us seem to be talking secrets. I don't know what to think: and to tell you the truth I don't care now.
80   His self-love deceived him, I suppose. Perhaps the young lady coquetted a little. The evidence would seem to point that way. Alfred not arrived?
CRAGGS.   Not yet: expected every minute.
SNITCH.   Good. It's a great relief. I haven't been so nervous since we've been in partnership. I intend to spend the evening now, Mr Craggs.
85  MRS S.   (*advancing*) It has been the theme of general comment Mr Snitchey. I hope the office is satisfied.
SNITCH.   Satisfied with what, my dear?
MRS S.   With the exposure of a defenceless woman to ridicule and remark. That is quite in the way of the office—*that* is.
90  MRS C.   I really myself have been so long accustomed to connect the office with everything opposed to domesticity that I am glad to know it as the avowed enemy of my peace. There is something honest in that at all events.
CRAGGS.   My dear: your good opinion is invaluable, but *I* never avowed that the office was the enemy of your peace.

67  *for three hours and more*: 1847 omits 'for three hours and more'.
75  *and so goes... that's one thing*: 1847 omits 'and so goes... that's one thing'.
79  *Hush!... don't care now*: 1847 begins the speech 'Hush! His self-love...'.

MRS C.    No, not you indeed. You wouldn't be worth of the office if you had the can-  95
dour to.

SNITCH.    (*to* MRS S) As to my having been away tonight my dear, the deprivation
has been mine, I'm sure: but as Mrs Craggs knows—

MRS S.    (*pulling him away and pointing to* CRAGGS) Look at that man—do me the
favour to look at that man.  100

SNITCH.    At which man, my dear?

MRS S.    Your chosen companion. I'm no companion to you, Mr Snitchey.

SNITCH.    Yes yes, you are my dear.

MRS S.    No no! I'm not. If you can look at that man, and not know that you are
deluded—practised upon—all I can say is—I pity you. (*draws him away*)  105

MRS C.    Is it possible you are so blind to your Snitcheys as not to feel your true
position?

CRAGGS.    My true position, my dear?

MRS C.    Yes sir. Could you see your Snitcheys come into that room, with [out] perceiving the reservation, cunning, and treachery of that man—  110

CRAGGS.    I must confess I did not.

MRS C.    You never do. Does anybody but your Snitcheys come to a festive entertainment like a burglar?

CRAGGS.    My dear—he walked in very mildly by the door.

MRS C.    Pugh! and, here, you assert to me at noonday—  115

CRAGGS.    Noonday, my love—it's nearly midnight.

MRS C.    (*fiercely*) Mr Craggs—you'd provoke an angel.

DR J.    (*advancing*) Come friends: another dance. Mr Snitchey: come here, my friend.
You must dance with Mrs Craggs.

SNITCH.    Sir—I—shall be most happy.  120

MRS C.    You'll be glad I know if I decline. I wonder you can dance out of the
office. (*takes his arm*)

DR J.    And Mr Craggs—Mrs Snitchey.

MRS S.    I wish you would ask somebody else. (*takes his arm*)

*Another short dance, during which*

DR J.    Anything been seen, Britain? Anything been heard?  125

BRIT.    Too dark to see far sir, too much noise inside the house to hear.

DR J.    That's right. The gayer welcome for him. How goes the time?

BRIT.    Just twelve, sir. He can't be long, sir.

DR J.    Stir up the fire and throw another log on it. Let him see his welcome blazing
out upon the night—good boy—as he comes along.  130

(*The dance continues: during it, all the seats and tables, etc must be removed, to prepare
for the change. When it finishes*)

117 *angel*: 1847 omits a long passage here, from Mrs C. 'No, not you' to this point, 'provoke an angel'.

DR J.    (*to* BRITAIN) Tell them where they will find refreshments.

BRIT.    (*aloud*) There's lots to eat and drink in the study, ladies and gentlemen: and I should think you wanted some. This way, now's your time. (*they go out*) Don't be in a hurry. Plenty of room for everybody.

(*The guests exeunt as quickly as possible; the instant they are gone, the scene changes with a sink and fly, and discovers the orchard and house as in first scene, but with a deep snow upon the ground. The windows of the house are transparent, and shadows pass backwards and forwards. The lights must be down. The snow is falling heavily*)

ALFRED *enters hastily, as if from his travels.*

135  ALF.    I couldn't wait an instant longer. I caught the light from the chaise as I turned the corner by the church, and I knew the room from which it shone thro' the old trees—I know, too, that one of them rustles musically in the summer time, at the window of Marion's chamber. I can hardly bear my happiness! Dear Marion: how often I have thought of this time: feared that it might never come: yearned and
140  wearied for it, far away. How I shall surprise them!

(*Goes towards the porch, and meets* CLEMENCY)

CLEM.    (*startled*) Don't go there. Keep back! Keep back.

ALF.    Clemency: don't you know me?

CLEM.    Don't come in. Go away (*pushing him back*) don't ask me why. Don't come in.

145  ALF.    What is the matter?

CLEM.    I don't know. I—I am afraid to think. Go back—hark!

(*A scream heard in the house: and* GRACE *rushes out*)

ALF.    Grace! (*catches her in his arms. She looks at him: shudders: and falls as if fainting upon the ground. He kneels by her*) What is it? Is she dead?

(*Confusion. A crowd of people come from the house, with candles in their hands.* DR JEDDLER *amongst them*)

ALF.    What is it! (*agonized*) Will no one look at me? Will no one speak to me? Does
150  no one know me? Is there no voice among you all to tell me what it is?

DR J.    She is gone!

ALF.    Gone! (*starting up*)

DR J.    Fled, my dear Alfred. Gone from her home and us, tonight. She writes that she made her innocent and blameless choice—entreats that we will forgive her—prays
155  that we will not forget her—and is gone!

---

134 1847 omits the exchange between Dr J. and Britain, and is more technical in the sd: '*when the dancers lead off their partners the third time, R.F.E. Pull below, and ring above.*'

138 *I caught the light … Marion's chamber*: MS omits 'I caught the light … Marion's chamber.'

155 *and is gone*: 1847 omits Clemency's move and all further dialogue except 'Marion!' from Alfred before he kneels.

(CLEMENCY *in the meantime raises* GRACE's *head*)

ALF.   With whom? Where?

DR J.   Here—(*to his friends*) Disperse yourselves along the road: take my horses out: get lights: follow any and every trace that you can see—

ALF.   The snow is falling fast and thick: the white ashes strewn upon my hopes and misery suit them well. What traces can be found: for the footprints are hushed 160 and covered up! Marion! Marion! where are you. Why have you thus so utterly crushed me!

(*He kneels down by the side of* GRACE, *and takes one of her hands into his own, hiding his face with the other as he bursts into tears. The others form a picture. The curtain falls: the snow still descending heavily*)

End of Act II

162.2 *picture*: The illustration is on p. 55 of the volume, at the start of the second part, anticipating its denouement. The fallen girl, the kneeling man, the outstretched arms, the hurry, form an archetypal melodramatic picture.

# ACT III

*A lapse of six years.*

## SCENE 1

*The bar of the 'Nutmeg Grater' Inn, with a window looking out over the country on a bright autumnal afternoon, through which can be seen the sign 'The Nutmeg Grater by Benjamin Britain.' Measures, glasses, spirit tubs etc. A table and chairs, R. Small table and one chair, L.*

*As the curtain rises* BRITAIN *is leaning in the doorway, smoking.*

1 BRIT.    The shower of rain's done a deal of good, and not left anything thirsty. Them dahlias has swilled as much as they can carry—perhaps a trifle more—and may have been the worse for liquor: but the others is all right. Mrs B. is rather late: and it's tea time: she hadn't much to do, I think: there was a few little matters of business
5 after market, but not many. Oh! Here we are at last!

*Music. A chaise heard, and* CLEMENCY *is also heard stopping the horse. She enters, followed by her boy carrying several parcels and baskets.*

BRIT.    You're late, Clemmy!

CLEM.    Why, you see Ben: I've had a deal to do: eight: nine: ten: where's eleven? (*counting the packages*) oh: my basket's eleven: it's all right. Put the horse up, Harry: and if he coughs again give him a warm mash tonight. How's the children, Ben?

10 BRIT.    Hearty, Clemmy, hearty.

CLEM.    Bless their precious faces. Give us a kiss old man.

(BRITAIN *kisses her*)

I think (*drawing all sorts of papers from her pocket*) I've done everything. Bills all settled—turnips sold—brewer's account looked into and paid—'bacco pipes ordered—seventeen pound four paid into the Bank—Doctor Heathfield's charge for
15 little Clem. You'll guess what that is. Doctor Heathfield won't take nothing again, Ben.

BRIT.    I thought he wouldn't.

CLEM.    No: he says whatever family you was to have, Ben, he'd never put you to the cost of a halfpenny. Not if you was to have twenty. Ain't it kind of him?

BRIT.    Very—it's the sort of kindness I wouldn't presume upon, on any account.

20 CLEM.    No—of course not. Then there's the pony: he fetched eight pound two: and that an't bad—is it?

BEN.    It's very good.

CLEM.   I'm glad you're pleased. I thought you would be: and I think that's all, and so, no more at present from yours et cetrer, C. Britain. Ha! ha! ha! there! Take all the papers, and lock 'em. Oh! wait a minute: there's a printed bill to stick on the wall.  25 Wet from the printers: how nice it smells.

BRIT.   What's this, 'To be sold by auction, unless previously disposed of by private contract'—

CLEM.   They always put that.

BRIT.   Yes, but they don't always put this look here, 'Mansion' etc.—'offices' etc.—  30 'shrubberies' etc.—'ring fence' etc. 'Messrs Snitchey and Craggs' etc. 'ornamental portion of the unencumbered freehold property of Michael Warden, Esquire, intending to continue to reside abroad!'

CLEM.   Intending to continue to reside abroad.

BRIT.   Here it is. Look.  35

CLEM.   And it was only this very day that I heard it whispered at the old house that better and plainer news had been half promised of her soon! (*shakes her head as she unconsciously pats her elbows*) Dear, dear, dear; there'll be heavy hearts, Ben, yonder. But it won't bear to think about. Come: you must be ready for tea. (*she has been getting the tea things ready during this speech. She then seats herself*) It's the first  40 time I've sat down quietly today. (*hands* BRITAIN *his tea*) How that bill does set me thinking of old times.

BRIT.   Ah! (*drinks his tea from the saucer*)

CLEM.   That same Mr Michael Warden lost me my old place.

BRIT.   And got you your husband.  45

CLEM.   Well—so he did, and many thanks to him.

BRIT.   Man's the creature of habit. I had somehow got used to you, Clem: and found I shouldn't be able to get on without you. So we went and got made man and wife. Ha! ha! Well! Who'd have thought it!

CLEM.   Who indeed. It was very good of you, Ben.  50

BRIT.   No—no—no. Nothing worth mentioning.

CLEM.   Oh yes it was, Ben: I'm sure I think so, and I'm very much obliged to you. Ah, when she was known to be gone, and out of reach, dear girl, I couldn't help telling— for her sake quite as much as theirs, what I knew, could I?

BRIT.   You told it, anyhow.  55

CLEM.   And Dr Jeddler, in his grief and passion, turned me out of house and home. How often he has sat in this room, and told me over and over again how sorry he was for it! The last time only yesterday when you were out. It was all for the sake of the days that were gone away, and because he knows she used to like me, Ben.

BRIT.   Why, how did you ever come to catch a glimpse of that, Clem?  60

CLEM.   (*blowing her tea, to cool it*) Bless you, I couldn't tell you, not if you was to offer me a reward of a hundred pound. My heart, Ben, who's here?

MICHAEL WARDEN *appears at the door, cloaked and booted, as if from a journey.*
BRITAIN *and* CLEMENCY *rise.*

BRIT.   Will you please to walk upstairs sir. There's a very nice room up stairs, sir.

MICH.  Thank you. May I come in here?

65 CLEM.  Oh, surely, if you like, sir: and what would you please to want, sir?

(*The* STRANGER *looks at the bill*)

BRIT.  Excellent property that, sir.

MICH.  (*to* CLEMENCY) You were asking me—

CLEM.  What you would please to take, sir.

MICH.  If you will let me have a draught of ale, and let me have it here without being

70  any interruption to your meal, I shall be much obliged to you.  (*sits at table, L.*)

BRITAIN *bustles about and gets the beer: then pours out a glass.*

MICH.  It's a new house, is it not?

BRIT.  Not particularly new, sir.

CLEM.  Between six and seven years old.

MICH.  I think I heard you mention Dr Jeddler's name as I came in. Is the old

75  man living?

CLEM.  Yes, he's living, sir.

MICH.  Much changed?

CLEM.  Since when, sir?

MICH.  Since his daughter (*hesitating*) went away.

80 CLEM.  Yes! he's greatly changed since then. He's grey and old, and hasn't the same
way with him at all: but I think he's happy now. He has taken on with his sister since
then and goes to see her very often. That did him good directly. At first he was sadly
broken down, and it was enough to make one's heart bleed to see him wandering
about, railing at the world: but a great change for the better came over him after a

85  year or two: and then he began to talk about his lost daughter and to praise her, aye,
and the world too! And was never tired of saying, with tears in his poor eyes, how
beautiful and good she was. He'd forgiven her then. That was about the same time
as Miss Grace's marriage.

MICH.  The sister *is* married then? To whom?

90 CLEM.  Did *you* never hear?

MICH.  I should like to hear.

CLEM.  Ah! it would be a long story if it was properly told.

MICH.  But told as a short one.

CLEM.  Told as a short one (*musing*) what would there be to tell? That they grieved

95  together and remembered her together like a person dead: that they were so tender
of her, never would reproach her, called her back to one another, as she used to be,
and formed excuses for her. Every one knows that. I'm sure *I* do. No one better.  (*she
wipes her eyes*)

MICH.  And so—

---

70  *sits at table, L.*: MS omits sd, having also left the small table on the left out of its headnote.

82  *He has taken... very often*: 1847 omits this important sentence, 'He has taken... very often.'

CLEM.   And so they were at last married. They were married on her birth-day—it
comes round again tomorrow—very quiet—very humble-like—but very happy.   100
MICH.   And they have lived happily together?
CLEM.   Aye. No two people ever more so. They have had no sorrow but this.

(*The* STRANGER *turns to the window and gazes out.* CLEMENCY *attracts* BRITAIN'S
*notice and tries with the motion of her lips to say 'Michael Warden' which* BRITAIN *cannot understand*)

BRIT.   What's she up to   (*imitates the action*) I haven't the least idea. Milk and water?
No: monthly warning? Mice and walnuts? No—it's no go.
MICH.   And what is the history of the young lady that went away? They know it, I   105
suppose.
CLEM.   (*shaking her head*) I've heard that Dr Jeddler is thought to know more about
it than he tells. But there's only one person can explain the mystery.
MICH.   And who may that be?
CLEM.   (*earnestly*) Mr Michael Warden! You remember me sir. I saw just now you   110
did. You remember me that night in the garden. I was with her.
MICH.   Yes—you were.
CLEM.   Yes sir: yes, to be sure. This is my husband if you please sir. Ben—my dear
Ben—run to Miss Grace—run to Mr Alfred—run somewhere, Ben—bring somebody here directly.   115
MICH.   Stay! What would you do?
CLEM.   (*clapping her hands agitatedly*) Let them know you are here, sir. Let them
know that they may hear of her from your own lips: let them know that she is not
quite lost to them, but that she will come home again yet, to bless her father and her
loving sister—even her old servant—even me, with a sight of her sweet face. Run,   120
Ben, run.
MICH.   Stop! I must beg of you to stop.
CLEM.   Or perhaps she's here now: perhaps she's close by. I think from your manner
she is. Let me see her sir, if you please. I waited on her when she was a little child.
I saw her grow to be the pride of all this place. I knew her when she was Mr Alfred's   125
promised wife. I tried to warn her when you tempted her away. I knew what her old
home was when she was like the soul of it: and how it changed when she was gone
and lost. Let me speak to her, if you please. Is she with you?
MICH.   (*shaking his head*) She is not.
CLEM.   Not with him! He is in mourning, too! Stay—(*faltering*) tell me: she is not   130
here. He doesn't contradict me. I shall never see her again: she is dead—dead, and
gone for ever!

(*She bursts into tears, and hides her face on the table.* BRITAIN *goes to her*)

MR SNITCHEY *enters breathless.*

---

114 *run to Miss Grace…run somewhere, Ben*: MS omits 'run to Miss Grace…run somewhere, Ben'.

SNITCH.    Good heavens, Mr Warden! What wind has blown—phew, I'm so blown my self I can hardly get on—what wind has blown you here?

135   MICH.    An ill one I'm afraid, if you could see what confusion and affliction I carry with me.

SNITCH.    I can guess it all, but why did you ever come here, my good sir?

MICH.    Come! I wanted to know what people would say to me. I see by your manner you can tell me. If it were not for your confounded caution I should have been pos-
140   sessed of everything long ago.

SNITCH.    Our caution! Speaking for self and Craggs—deceased. (*points to his hat-band*) Caution! When Mr Craggs, sir, went down to his respected grave, in the full belief—

MICH.    I had given a solemn promise of silence until I should return, whenever that
145   might be; and I have kept it.

SNITCH.    Well, sir: and we were bound to silence too. I was only apprised, six months since, that you had lost her.

MICH.    By whom?

SNITCH.    By Dr Jeddler himself sir, who at last reposed this confidence in me volun-
150   tarily. He—and only he—has known the whole matter for years.

MICH.    And you know it?

SNITCH.    I do sir: and I know that it will be broken to her sister tomorrow evening. In the meantime let us dine here. It's a very good place to dine at. Self and Craggs—deceased—took a chop here sometimes, and had it very comfortably served. Mr
155   Craggs sir, was struck off the role of life too soon.

MICH.    Heaven forgive me for not condoling with you, but I'm like a man in a dream at present. I seem to want my wits. Mr Craggs—yes, I am very sorry we have lost Mr Craggs.

SNITCH.    Mr Craggs, sir, didn't find life so easy to have and to hold as his theory
160   made it out, or he would have been amongst us now. It's a great loss to me. He was my right arm, my right leg, my right ear, my right eye, was Mr Craggs. I am para-lytic without him.

MICH.    But his name remains in the firm.

SNITCH.    Yes: I try in a childish sort of way, to believe, sometimes, that he's alive. You
165   may observe that I speak for self and Craggs: deceased—sir—deceased.

(MICHAEL *draws his attention to* CLEMENCY)

---

138  *Come!*: 1847 cuts from midway in Warden's previous speech to here, 'if you could see...Come!' but leaves in a redundant speech ascription to him, suggesting changes after the printed version was set up.

143  *Caution! When...full belief*: 1847 omits the second sentence, 'Caution! When...full belief'.

147  *were...her*: MS has 'are' for 'were' and 'all' for 'her', and 1847 'assured' for 'apprised'.

158  *Mr Craggs*: 1847 cuts this response and again fails to remove an unnecessary speech ascription as Snitchey continues.

165  *I try in...deceased*: 1847 omits 'I try in...deceased'.

SNITCH.    Ah, poor thing! Yes: she was always very faithful to Marion. She was always very fond of her pretty Marion: poor Marion! Cheer up, mistress: you *are* married, now, you know, Clemency.

CLEM.    (*sighing*) Yes—I know.

SNITCH.    Well—well: wait till tomorrow.                                    170

CLEM.    Tomorrow can't bring back the dead to life, Mister.

SNITCH.    No: it can't do that, or it would bring back Mr Craggs, deceased. But it may bring some comfort: wait till tomorrow.

MICH.    Come, Clemency: see what you can give us to eat. It may be better than you think for after all. Can we have anything?                                    175

CLEM.    (*sobbing*) Oh yes: you can have anything: everything. Ben: come and help me, in the larder. I can scarcely see out of my eyes.

(BEN *and* CLEMENCY *go off*, CLEMENCY *crying*)

SNITCH.    And, in the meantime, Mr Warden, we will take a turn or two in the garden. Mr Craggs Sir, deceased, liked the green: everything green, sir: it showed his taste. Come, sir: this way. (*Exeunt by door*)                                    180


## SCENE 2 AND LAST

*The house and orchard as in Act 1.*

GRACE *and* ALFRED *are sitting beneath one of the trees with a little child at their feet.*

ALF.    The time has flown, dear Grace, since that night: and yet is seems a long, long   1
time ago. We count by changes and events within us, not by years.

GRACE.    Yet we have years to count by, too, since Marion was with us. Six times, dear husband, counting tonight as one, we have sat here on her birthday, and spoken together of that happy return—so eagerly expected, and so long deferred. Oh!   5
When will it be?

ALF.    Marion told you in that farewell letter which she left for you upon the table, love, and which you read so often, that years must pass away before it *could* be. Did she not?

GRACE.    (*takes a letter from her bosom and kisses it*) Yes.                                    10

ALF.    And that when you met all would be made clear. The letter runs so, does it not my dear?

---

167 *She was…Marion!*: 1847 repunctuates to the original, which changes the sense: 'She was always very fond of her. Pretty Marion! Poor Marion!'

179 *in the garden*: 1847 has 'on the green' for 'in the garden'.

0.2 *little child at their feet*: MS omits the child.

GRACE.    Yes, Alfred: but but there is something else in it that I have never told you.
But tonight dear husband, with the sunset drawing near, and all our life seeming to
15    soften, and become hushed with the departing day, I cannot keep it secret.

ALF.    What is it love?

GRACE.    When Marion went away, she wrote me, here, that you once left her a
sacred trust to me, as I loved her, and as I loved you, not to reject the affection she
believed  (she knew, she said) you would transfer to me when the new wound were
20    healed, but to encourage and return it.

ALF.    And make me a proud and happy man again, Grace. Did she say so?

GRACE.    She meant to make myself so blest and honoured in your love.

ALF.    Now I know why I have never heard this passage in the letter until now—I
know why no trace of it ever shewed itself in any word or look of yours at that
25    time—I know, now, why Grace, although so true a friend to me, was hard to win to
be my wife—and knowing it, my own, I know the priceless value of the heart I gird
within my arms, and thank Heaven for the rich possession!

GRACE.    But see: the sun is going down. You have not forgotten what I am to know
before it sets?

30  ALF.    You are to know the truth of Marion's history. But tell me, Grace, have you
present fortitude to bear the trial, a surprise—a shock: if so, the messenger is waiting at the gate.

GRACE.    What messenger? And what intelligence does he bring?

ALF.    I am pledged to say no more. Do you think you understand me?

35  GRACE.    I am afraid to think. What do you mean? (*agitated*). Stop—Alfred: pause a
minute.

ALF.    Courage, love. The sun is setting on Marion's birthday. Courage, Grace, courage. (*he takes up the child and exits hastily*)

GRACE.    I know not what to dread: or what to hope. The emotion in his face has
40    frightened me. What can the message be? Ah! (*looking to the house*) What is that
coming to the threshold: my father and a figure with him, with its head laid on his
breast. (DR JEDDLER *and* MARION *appear at the porch*. GRACE *screams*) Marion!
Marion! My sister! My heart's dear love!

MARION.    (*rushing towards her*) Oh: joy unutterable, so to meet again! (*they fall
45    into each other's arms*) When this was my dear home, Grace, as it will be now again—

GRACE.    Stay! Stay my sweet love! A moment. I can scarcely bear the voice I love so
well. Oh! Marion, to hear you speak again!

MARION.    When this was my dear home, Grace: as it will be now again, I loved him
from my soul—devotedly—and would have died for him, though I was so young. I
50    never loved him better than I did that night when I left here. But he had gained
unconsciously another heart, before I knew that I had one to give him: that heart
was yours. Alfred had said that there were victories gained every day in struggling
hearts to which these fields of battle were as nothing. Thinking upon that great
endurance cheerfully sustained, but never known or cared for, of which he spoke,

27 *Now I know…rich possession*: MS omits this speech.

my trial grew light and easy: and I resolved that I never would be Alfred's wife. 55
Grace! I then loved him dearly, dearly.

GRACE.  Oh Marion: Marion!

MARION.  I tried to let you know my resolution: but was never understood: and the
time was drawing near for his return. I knew that one great pang, undergone at that
time, would save a lengthened agony for all of us. I knew that if I went away then, 60
that end must follow which *has* followed, and which has made us so happy, Grace. I
wrote to good Aunt Martha for a refuge in her house: and just then, Mr Warden
became our companion.

GRACE.  I have sometimes feared that you married him in your self-sacrifice to me.

MARION.  Stay dearest: listen. I saw Mr Warden, and confided in his honour: 65
charged him with my secret on the eve of his, and my departure. He kept it. Do you
understand me, dear?

GRACE.  Marion, I know not what to think.

MARION.  My love: my sister: do not look so strangely on me. There are countries
dearest, where those who have striven against some cherished, but misplaced feeling 70
of the heart, abjure all worldly loves and hopes, and retire into a hopeless solitude.
When women do this, they call each other *sisters*. But there may be sisters, Grace, in
the broad world out of doors, in crowded places and busy life, still trying to assist and
cheer each other. And such a one am I. Grace, dear Grace: as I left here so I have
returned: my heart has known no other love. I am still your maiden sister: unmarried, 75
unbetrothed: your own loving Marion, in whose affection you exist alone.

DR J.  I'm a converted man: I'm a converted man. I own it  (with some feeling). It's a
world full of hearts with all its folly: even with mine, which was enough to have
swamped the whole globe. Heaven bless you, darlings: heaven bless you.

BOTH.  Dear father! (ALFRED *comes in, as they embrace*)                    80

DR J.  It is a world in which the sun never rises, but it looks upon a thousand blood-
less battles, that are some sort of set off against the miseries and wretchedness of
battle-fields: and a world we should be careful how we libel.

SNITCHEY *and* MRS SNITCHEY *appear at the gate followed by* MICHAEL.

SNITCH.  I beg your pardon Doctor: but have I liberty to come in?

DR J.  Certainly: my dear sir: certainly!                                    85

SNITCH.  (*to* MARION) If Mr Craggs had been alive, my dear Miss Marion, he would
have had great interest on this occasion. It would have suggested to him, Mr Alfred,
that life is not too easy. For Mr Craggs was always open to conviction. If he were
open to conviction now, I—pshaw—Mrs Snitchey, my dear: you are among old
friends.                                                                    90

(MRS SNITCHEY *curtsies to the company*)

55 *Alfred had said...light and easy: and*: 1847 cuts 'Alfred had said...light and easy: and'.

74 *There are countries...such a one am I*: 1847 cuts 'There are countries...such a one am I'.

83 DR J. *I'm a converted man...how we libel*: 1847 cuts three speeches, 'DR J. I'm a converted man...how
we libel', which are Smith's attempt to encapsulate Dickens's message, substituting an empty exclamation for
him: 'Heyday! What's the matter?'

MRS S.   One moment, Mr Snitchey. It is not in my nature to rake up the ashes of the departed.

SNITCH.   No, my dear.

MRS S.   Mr Craggs is—

95 SNITCH.   Yes, my dear: he is deceased.

MRS S.   But I ask you if you recollect that evening of the ball. I only ask you that: if you are not absolutely in your dotage. How I begged and prayed you, upon my knees—

SNITCH.   Upon your *knees*, my dear!

MRS S.   Yes—and you know it—to beware of that man, and be sure that he knew

100 secrets which he didn't choose to tell. I observed it in his eye.

SNITCH.   Mrs Snitchey: Madam: did you ever observe anything in *my* eye?

MRS S.   (*sharply*) No. Don't flatter yourself.

SNITCH.   Because, Ma'am, that night we *both* knew secrets we didn't choose to tell. So the less said the better, Mrs Snitchey: and take this as a warning to have wiser

105 and more charitable eyes another time. But stop. Miss Marion, I brought a friend of yours along with me. Here, Mistress!

(CLEMENCY *comes slowly in; followed by* BRITAIN. *She is still weeping.* MARION *is about to run towards her.* SNITCHEY *checks her*)

SNITCH.   (*to* CLEM) Now Mistress: what's the matter with *you*?

CLEM.   The matter. (*looks up and sees* MARION) The matter: ah! Why—what is it? Real—real flesh and blood. Marion come back alive!: my own darling beauti-

110 ful (*embraces her*) young Miss Marion! Oh dear! Oh dear! I can't bear to be so happy: I can't indeed. (*bursts into tears: clings to* MARION: *lets her go: clings to her again*) Heaven bless you! And you too, master! (*embraces the* DOCTOR) I don't now what to do. Will somebody tell me what to do not to be so happy. And Heaven bless *you* sir. (*to* SNITCHEY *whom she embraces*) My head's going round: and Miss

115 Marion's come back. Britain, Ben: come here. She's come back again Ha! ha! ha! (*she laughs, cries, and then going into hysterics throws her apron over her head, and falls on her husband's shoulder*)

SNITCH.   Mr Britain: don't be affected. I congratulate you. You are now (*he takes a paper from his pocket*) the whole and sole proprietor of that freehold tenement, at present occupied and held by yourself, as a licensed tavern, or house of public entertainment, and commonly called, and known by the sign of 'the Nutmeg

120 Grater.'

BRIT.   Here! Hi! Hulloa: Clemmy: do you hear that? There's news!

CLEM.   (*sobbing*) Yes I hear: don't Ben: it's too much.

SNITCH.   Your wife lost one house, through my client Mr Michael Warden, and now gains another. I shall have the pleasure of canvassing you for the country, one of

125 these fine mornings.

BRIT.   Would it make any difference to the vote if the sign was altered, sir?

---

106 *If he were open...Here, Mistress!*: 1847 cuts the entire exchange between Snitchey and his wife here, from 'If he were open to conviction now' to his summons to Clemency. 'Here, Mistress!'

SNITCH.   Not in the least.

BRIT.   (*handing him back the conveyance*) Then just clap in the words 'and thimble' will you be so good. The Nutmeg-grater and Thimble: and I'll have the two mottoes painted up in the parlour, instead of my wife's portrait.                    130

(MICHAEL WARDEN *comes down*)

MICH.   And let me claim the benefit of those inscriptions. Mr Heathfield and Dr Jeddler, I might have deeply wronged you both. That I did not, is no virtue of my own. I will not say that I am six years wiser than I was, or better: but I have known, at any rate, that term of self-reproach. I can urge no reason why you should deal gently with me. I abjured the hospitality of the house, and learnt my own demerits,  135 with a shame I never have forgotten: yet with some prospect too, I would fain hope, from one to whom I make humble supplication for forgiveness, when I knew her merit, and my deep unworthiness. (*takes* MARION's *hand*)

DR J.   (*aside*) He's much improved: quite another man: and seems to be serious in his intentions, if anything can be serious in—pshaw!                    140

MICH.   Dr Jeddler—let me call your attention to Clemency's library. 'Do as you would be done by.' 'Forget and forgive.'

DR J.   Well: there's my hand: but I've nothing to forgive: and I don't want to forget.

MICH.   Marion: will you extend the same feeling towards me?

(MARION *places her hand in his and retires back*)


136 *I can urge…some prospect too*: 1847 cuts 'I can urge…some prospect too' which obscures the sense of the speech.

141 *let me call*: 1847 substitutes 'give me the benefit of' for 'let me call your attention to'.

144.1 *retires back*: 1847 has a different version of the ending from this point, incorporating the message cut from earlier in the scene and dispensing with the traditional final dance, and also incorporating a plain double meaning about the joint management of the theatre:

> DR J.   I'm a converted man—'tis a world full of hearts, after all!
> ALF.   It is a world full of hearts, on which the sun never rises but it looks upon a thousand bloodless battles, that are some set off against the miseries and wickedness of battle fields, and a world we need be careful how we libel.
> CLEM.   (*pulling* BRITAIN *to her*) Ben!
> BRIT.   Clemency!
> CLEM.   I say, if there should be any more.
> BRIT.   More what? What are you talking about?
> CLEM.   More people any where's with their dispositions a little soured as yours was once, you know—by anything that may have gone wrong, there's nothing as a sweetner like a—
> BRIT.   Thimble!
> CLEM.   Combined with a—
> BOTH.   (*speaking very loud and fast together*) Nutmeg Grater!
> BRIT.   (*to audience*) She hasn't an idea in her head!
> CLEM.   No, no, I don't want none, you know?
> BRIT.   But she's nearly right—so while I keep the Nutmeg Grater, if you'll be so good as to do what you can for the good of the house, I'll do my best to provide good entertainment.

145 BRIT.    Hooray! I don't mean to take liberties: but upon my soul I can't help it. Come, Clemmy: be yourself again. Here's our old friends all upon the road, that have heard the news, and are coming to welcome Miss Marion. And look there—there's the young ladies' good aunt Martha—go and help her in. (CLEMENCY *goes out, and returns whilst* BRITAIN *is speaking with* AUNT MARTHA; *followed by* NEIGHBOURS, SERVANTS *etc.*) And if you please sir  (*to* DR JEDDLER) if I might make so bold, just
150    to suggest a bit of a dance, to shake every body's feelings which have been so upset, down to their proper state, I think it would benefit us all.

DR J.    Oh, my good Britain: do as you please. But we have no music.

BRIT.    Yes there is. The identical old'uns, that were going to the identical fair tomor-row, when Mr Alfred stopped 'em nine years back. They're a little the worse for
155    wear, but here they are.

DR J.    Well: as you please, I say. Come, Clemency: you must dance.

CLEM.    If you please I don't know if I haven't forgotten: but I'll try.

DR J.    Of course: and this shall be a happy night for everybody.

CLEM.    Yes: happy for *everybody*:  (*to the audience*) A least: you alone have the power
160    of ordaining whether it shall be so.

*The Music strikes up and they form into couples.*

*An Old English Country Dance*

THE END

# NINE

Mark Lemon, *The Haunted Man*, Adelphi, December 1848

## INTRODUCTION

*T*HE HAUNTED MAN was the last of the individually published and produced Christmas story/dramas; it appeared in 1848, after a year without an annual tale. This was the year of the presentation of the People's Charter and of revolutions across Europe, a culmination therefore of the kinds of Radical concerns that had powered these little books; and it was also the year Dickens first spoke to his future biographer Forster of his own early life, the memory of the blacking factory that haunted him.[1] The novel of 1849 was to be *David Copperfield*, the closest of his books to a Bildungs-roman. So *The Haunted Man*'s bringing together of social concern and the pain of personal memory embodies its moment. It was not well received.

The work was subject to immediate attack in the press, probably, as the *Era* reviewer said in Dickens's defence, out of envy; this reviewer asserts that '[p]eople expect too much of him' when he is only 'a comic writer of a peculiar class', full of good intentions and fine ideas, even if they are 'vaguely embodied'. The review goes on to contradict this somewhat back-handed compliment with a much more important observation: 'He gives us creations of his own; characters that will last with the reader's life, and others long after that; therefore is he a man of genius.'[2] In *The Haunted Man*, however, there is no new creation of this order, perhaps partly because the writer's theatrical collaborators and inspiration had already moved on. Proof sheets went to Mark Lemon as dramaturg this time, a less sharp, more sentimental writer than Smith, and while the official production was again at the Adelphi, the management there had been taken over by Benjamin Webster; it was operating under the executive manage-ment of his partner Celine Celeste. The venue was on its way to fame as the home of certain peculiarly Victorian dramatic forms: 'screaming' domestic farce and highly wrought sensational melodrama. So this time there were no Keeleys to charge the comic roles with life. The low comedian Edward Wright took on Tetterby, but it was not a role suited to his uproarious, rather blue style of audience interaction. The Ghost was played by O. Smith, Dickens's least favourite member of the old company.

Despite this lack of distinction, the play had an averagely good run, and was even-tually revived in the summer of 1863 as a vehicle for the first West End stage use of Pepper's ghost illusion, whereby the figure of the ghost was projected up on to the

---

[1] Tomalin, 212.    [2] *Era*, 24 December 1848.

stage by a mirroring arrangement of slanted glass. The staging of the initial form of the play is also worth noting: accomplished use is made of the conventions by then established for the stage reflection of modern life. There are punctuating moments of tableau taken from the illustrations in the book, but that static visual emphasis is balanced by the rapid succession of action and scenes. It is especially obvious through the second act, where the scenes shift between Tetterby's house downstairs and up, the exterior of the lodge, a railway arch, a slum street and a room there, and back to Redlaw's chamber with, in some cases, only a line or two spoken in each place. This momentum is achieved by the flexible rapidity of groove and shutter scenery, which closes in or opens to reveal without the need for exits, blackouts, or a drop curtain, but can still show painted views of the modern world; it anticipates much later forms of dramatization, on film.

## THE TEXT

The play was not printed, and only survives in the Lord Chamberlain's collection, Add. MS 43015 ff. 558–96, from which this edition is taken. It is annotated as having been received from Webster on 12 December 1848 for presentation on 19 December.

## Characters and cast of the first production

| | |
|---|---|
| Mr Redlaw | [Henry] Hughes |
| The Phantom | O. Smith |
| Old Philip Swidger | Lambert |
| William Swidger | [James H.] Munyard |
| The Boy | Miss Ellen Chaplin |
| Tetterby | [Edward R.] Wright |
| Edmund Longford | Boyce |
| Longford | Worrell |
| George Swidger | [Christopher] J. Smith |
| Adolphus Tetterby | Master Sydney |
| Johnny Tetterby | Master Woodward |
| Phillip Tetterby | Master Robins |
| Benjamin Tetterby | Master Clark |
| Edward Tetterby | Master Hamilton |
| Samuel Tetterby | Master Jones |
| Thomas Tetterby | Master Hardy |
| Milly | Miss [Sarah J.] Woolgar |
| Mrs Tetterby | Mrs Frank Matthews |
| Miss Thornton | Miss LeLacheur |
| Sally Tetterby | Unk[3] |

[3] First night cast list, derived from *The Adelphi Calendar*.

**9.** Mark Lemon, who dramatized *The Haunted Man* for Dickens and also, with Gilbert Abbott A'Beckett, *The Chimes*. An engraving by A.G. Downing.

# ACT I

## SCENE 1

*An Elizabethan building; Chamber.*

REDLAW *and* PHANTOM *discovered.*

REDLAW.   Who's there?                                                              1

(*Enter* WILLIAM SWIDGER)

WILLIAM.   I'm humbly fearful sir that it's a good bit past the time tonight. But Mrs
William has been taken off her legs so often—
REDLAW.   By the wind? Aye! I heard it rising.
WILLIAM.   By the wind sir—that it's a mercy she got home at all. Oh dear yes. Yes. It   5
was by the wind Mr Redlaw. By the wind. Mrs William is of course subject at any
time, to be taken off her balance by the elements. She is not formed superior to *that*.
REDLAW.   No.
WILLIAM.   No, sir, Mrs William may be taken off her balance by earth, as for example, last Sunday week when sloppy and greasy, and she going out to tea with her   10
newest sister-in-law, and having a pride in herself, and wishing to appear perfectly
spotless though pedestrian. Mrs William may be taken off her balance by air—as
being once over-persuaded by a friend to try a swing at Peckham Fair, which acted
on her constitution instantly like a steam boat. Mrs William may be taken off her
balance by fire, as on a false alarm of engines at her mother's when she went two   15
mile in her nightcap. Mrs William may be taken off her balance by water, as at
Battersea, when rowed into the piers by her young nephew, Charlie Swidger, junior,
aged twelve, which had no idea of boats whatever. But these are elements—Mrs
William must be taken out of elements for the strength of *her* character to come
into play.                                                                          20
REDLAW.   Yes.
WILLIAM.   Yes sir. Oh dear yes! That's where it is sir. That's what I always say to
myself sir, such a many of us Swidgers—Pepper!—why there's my father; sir, super-
annuated keeper and custodian of this Institution eighty-seven year old. He's a
Swidger—spoon!                                                                      25
REDLAW.   True.
WILLIAM.   Yes sir. That's what I always say, sir, you may call him the trunk of the
tree! Bread! Then you come to his successor, my unworthy self! Salt! And Mrs
William—Swidgers both! Knife and fork. Then you come to all my brothers and
their families. Swidgers man and woman, boy and girl! Why, what with cousins,   30
uncles, aunts and relationships of this, that and t'other degree, and whatnot degree,
and marriages, and lyings in, the Swidgers—tumbler! Might take hold of hands and

make a ring round England. Yes sir! That's just what I say myself sir, Mrs William
and me have often said so. There's Swidgers enough without our voluntary contribu-
35 tions—butter! In fact, sir, my father is a family in himself—castors—to take care of
and it happens all for the best. Quite ready for the fowl and mashed potatoes sir?
Mrs William said she'd dish in ten minutes when I left the lodge.

REDLAW.     I'm quite ready.

WILLIAM.     Mrs William has been at it again sir! What I always say myself sir. She will
40 do it! There's a motherly feeling in Mrs William's breast that must and will have vent.

REDLAW.     What has she done?

WILLIAM.     Why sir, not satisfied with being a sort of mother to all the young gentlemen that come up from a variety of paths to attend your courses of lectures at this
ancient foundation—(it's surprising how stone chaney catches the heat this frosty
45 weather to be sure)—

REDLAW.     Well?

WILLIAM.     That's just what I say myself, sir, that's exactly where it is, sir! There ain't
one of our students but appears to regard Mrs William in that light. Every day right
through the course, they put their heads into the lodge, one after another, and have
50 all got something to tell her, or something to ask her. Swidge is the appellation by
which they speak of Mrs William in general, among themselves I'm told; but that's
what I say, sir, better be called ever so far out of your name, if it is done in real liking,
than have it made very so much of and not cared about! What's a name for? To know
a person by. If Mrs William is known by something better than her name—I allude
55 to Mrs William's qualities and disposition—never mind her name though it is
Swidger by rights. Let 'em call her Swidge—Widge—Bridge—lord! London Bridge,
Blackfriars, Chelsea, Putney, Waterloo or Hammersmith Suspension if they like—

(*Enter* MILLY *and* PHILIP)

WILLIAM.     Punctual of course Milly. Here's Mrs William sir! (*aside*) he looks lone-
lier than ever tonight, and ghostlier altogether.

60 REDLAW.     What is that the old man has in his arms?

MRS S.     Holly, sir.

SWIDGER.     That's what I say myself sir, berries is so seasonable to the time of year!
Brown gravy.

REDLAW.     Another Christmas come, another year gone, more figures in the length-
65 ening sum of recollection that we work and work at to our torment, till death idly
jumbles all together and rubs all out. So Philip—

PHILIP.     My duty to you, sir, should have spoken before sir, but I know your ways
Mr Redlaw—proud to say so—and wait till spoken to! Merry Christmas, sir, and
happy new year, and many of 'em. Have had a pretty many of 'em myself—Ha! Ha!
70 And may take the liberty of wishing 'em. I'm eighty-seven!

REDLAW.     Have you had so many that you are happy and merry?

PHILIP.     Aye, sir, ever so many.

REDLAW.     It recalls the time when many of those years were old and new then?
Does it?

PHILIP.    Oh many, many, I'm eighty-seven.                                75

REDLAW.    Merry and happy was it? Merry and happy old man?

PHILIP.    May be as high as that; no higher when I first remember 'em! Cold sunshiny
day it was, out a-walking, when some one—it was my mother as sure as you stand
there, though I don't know what her blessed face was like, for she took ill and died
that Christmas time—told me they were food for birds. The pretty little fellow    80
thought—that's me, you understand—that birds eyes were so bright, perhaps
because the berries that they lived on in winter were so bright, I recollect that, and
I'm eighty-seven.

REDLAW.    Merry and happy! Merry and happy—and remember well?

PHILIP.    Ay, ay, ay! I remember 'em well in my school time, year after year, and all the    85
merry-making that used to come along with them.

WILLIAM.    That's what I always say, father! You *are* a Swidger, if ever there was one
of the family—

PHILIP.    Dear! His mother—my son William's my youngest son—and I have sat
among 'em all, boys and girls, little children, and babies, many a year when the ber-    90
ries like these were not shining half so bright all round us, as their bright faces.
Many of 'em are gone—she's gone—and my son George (our eldest, who was her
pride more than all the rest!) is fallen very low; but I can see them, when I look here,
alive and healthy as they used to be in those days, and I can see him, thank God in
his innocence. It's a blessed thing to me at eighty-seven, when I first come here to    95
be custodian, which was upwards of fifty years ago—where's my son William? More
than half a century ago, William!

WILLIAM.    That's what I say, father, that's exactly were it is. Two times ought's an
ought, and twice five ten, and there's a hundred of 'em.

PHILIP.    It was quite a pleasure to know that one of the founders or one of the    100
learned gentlemen that helped endow us in Queen Elizabeth's time, for we were
founded afore her time—left in his will, among the other bequests he made us, so
much to buy holly, for garnishing the walls and windows, come Christmas. There
was something homely and friendly in it. Being but strange here, then, and coming
at Christmas time, we took a liking to his very pictur' that hangs in what used to be    105
anciently (afore our ten poor gentlemen commuted for an annual stipend in
money) our great Dinner Hall—a sedate gentleman in a peaked beard, with a ruff
round his neck, and a scroll below him in Old English letters. 'Lord! Keep my memory green!' You know all about him, Mr Redlaw.

REDLAW.    I know the portrait hangs there, Philip.                        110

PHILIP.    Yes sure, it's the second on the right above the panelling—I was going to
say—he has helped to keep my memory green; I thank him; for going round the
building every year, as I am doing now, and freshening up the bare rooms with
these branches and berries, freshens up my bare old brain. One year brings back
another; and that year another, and those others, numbers! At last it seems to me as    115
if Xmas time was the birth time of all I ever had affection for, or mourned for or
delighted in—and they're a pretty many, for I'm eighty-seven!

REDLAW.    Merry and happy.

PHILIP.    Now where's my quiet mouse? Chattering's the sin of any time of life, and
120    there's half the building to do yet, if the cold don't freeze us first, or the wind don't
blow us away, or the darkness don't swallow us up. Come away, my dear, Mr Redlaw
won't settle to his dinner, otherwise, till it's cold as the winter. I hope you'll excuse
me rambling on, sir, I wish you good night, and once again a merry—
REDLAW.    Stay! Spare me another moment, Philip, William, you were going to tell
125    me something to your excellent wife's honour, it will not be disagreeable to her to
hear you praise her. What was it?
WILLIAM.    Why that's where it is, you see, sir. Mrs William's got her eye on me.
REDLAW.    But you're not afraid of Mrs William's eye?
WILLIAM.    Why no, sir, sir, that's what I say myself. It wasn't made to be afraid of. It
130    wouldn't have been made so mild if that was the intention. But I wouldn't like to—
Milly—him, you know, down in the buildings. Him, you know, my love, down in
the Buildings, tell, my dear! You're the works of Shakespeare in comparison with
myself. Down in the buildings, you know my love, student.
REDLAW.    Student?
135 WILLIAM.    That's what I say, sir, if it wasn't the poor student down in the buildings, why
should you wish to hear it from Mrs William's lips, Mrs Williams my dear—Buildings.
MRS S.    I didn't know that William had said anything about it, or I wouldn't have
come. I asked him not to. It's a sick young gentleman, sir,—and very poor I'm afraid—
who is too ill to go home this holiday-time, and lives, unknown to any one, in but a
140    common kind of lodging for a gentleman, down in Jerusalem Buildings. That's all sir.
REDLAW.    Why have I never heard of him? Why has he not made his situation
known to me? Sick! Give me my hat and cloak. Poor! What house? What number?
MRS S.    Oh, you mustn't go there, sir.
REDLAW.    Not go there?
145 MRS S.    Oh dear me! It couldn't be thought of.
REDLAW.    What do you mean? Why not?
WILLIAM.    Why you see sir. That's what I say. Depend upon it, the young gentleman
would never have made his situation known to one of his own sex. Mrs William has
got into his confidence, but that's quite different, they all confide in Mrs William;
150    they all trust her. A man, sir, couldn't have got a whisper out of him; but woman, sir,
and Mrs William combined!
REDLAW.    There is good sense and delicacy in what you say William.
MRS S.    Oh dear no, sir! Worse and worse! Couldn't be dreamed of! Oh dear, no sir!
He said that of all the world he would not be known to you or receive help from
155    you—though he is a student in your class. I have made no terms of secrecy with
you, but I trust to your honour completely.
REDLAW.    Why did he say so?
MRS S.    Indeed I can't tell, sir, I wanted to be useful to him in making things com-
fortable, but I know he is poor and lonely—how dark it is!
160 REDLAW.    What more about him?
MRS S.    He is engaged to be married when he can afford it. I have seen a long time
that he has studied hard and denied himself much. How *very* dark it is!

PHILIP.   It's turned colder too—there's a chill and dismal feeling in the room—
William, my boy, turn the lamp and rouse the fire!

MRS S.   He muttered in his broken sleep yesterday afternoon about some one dead,   165
and some great wrong done, that could never be forgotten, but whether to him or
to another person I don't know. Not *by* him, I am sure.

WILLIAM.   And in short Mrs William you see—has done him worlds of good—Mrs
William's apparently never out of the way, Mrs William sir, backwards and forwards, up and down—a mother to him! Not content with this Mrs William goes   170
and finds this very night a creature more like a wild young beast than a young child,
shivering upon a doorstep. What does Mrs William do but brings him home to dry
and feed and keep it till our bounty of food and flannel is given away on Christmas
morning. If it ever felt a fire before it's as much as it did; for its sitting in the old
lodge-chimney, staring at ours as if its ravenous eyes would never shut again. It's sit-   175
ting there, unless it's bolted.

REDLAW.   Heaven keep her happy, and you too Philip! And you William. I must
consider what to do—I may desire to see this student—good night.

PHILIP.   I thank ee sir—for mouse and my son William, and for myself—where's my
son William? William take the lantern and go on first, through them long dark pas-   180
sages, as you did last year and the year afore! Though I'm eighty-seven! Lord keep
my memory green! It's a very good prayer, Mr Redlaw, that of the learned gentleman in the peaked beard, with a ruff round his neck—Lord keep my memory
green! It's very good and pious sir, amen! Amen!

(*Exit all but* REDLAW)
*Enter* PHANTOM.

REDLAW.   Here again?   185
PHAN.   Here again.
REDLAW.   I see you in the fire, I hear you in music, in the wind, in the dead stillness
of the night—evil spirit of myself, why do you come to haunt me thus?
PHAN.   I come as I am called.
REDLAW.   No—unbidden.   190
PHAN.   Unbidden be it. It is enough; I am here! Look upon me! I am he neglected in
my youth, and miserably poor, who strove and suffered, until I hewed out knowledge from the mine where it was buried and made rugged steps thereof, for my
worn feet to rest upon.
REDLAW.   I am that man!   195
PHAN.   No mother's self-denying love, no father's counsel aided me. A stranger came
into my father's place when I was but a child, and I was easily an alien from my
mother's heart—my parents at the best, were of that sort whose care soon ends, and
whose duty is soon done; who cast their offspring loose, early, as birds do theirs;
and if they do well, claim the merit, and if ill, the pity—I am he who in the struggle   200
upward found a friend.
REDLAW.   I am he!

PHAN.     Made him—won him—bound him to me. We worked together side by side.
All the love and confidence that in earlier youth had had no outlet, and found no
205     expression, I bestowed on him.
REDLAW.     Not all.
PHAN.     No, not all, I had a sister.
REDLAW.     I had.
PHAN.     Such glimpses of the light of home as I had ever known, had streamed from
210     her—how young she was, how fair, how loving. I took her to the first poor roof that
I was master of and made it rich. She came into the darkness of life, and made it
bright. She is before me.
REDLAW.     I saw her in the fire but now, I hear her in music, in the wind, in the dead
stillness of the night.
215 PHAN.     Did he love her? I think he did once. I am sure he did. Better had she loved
him less.
REDLAW.     Let me forget it. Let me blot it from my memory.
PHAN.     A dream, like hers, stole upon my own life.
REDLAW.     Ah! It did!
220 PHAN.     A love as like hers, as my inferior nature might cherish arose in my own
heart, I was too poor to bind its object to my fortune then, by any thread of promise
or entreaty—I loved her far too well to seek to do it. But, more than ever I have
striven in my life, I strove to climb. Only an inch gained brought me something
nearer to the height. I toiled up! When day was breaking what pictures of the future
225     did I see!
REDLAW.     I saw them in the fire but now. They come back to me in music, in the
wind, in the dead stillness of the night, in the revolving years.
PHAN.     Pictures of my own domestic life in after time, with her who was the inspiration of my toil—pictures of my sister, made the wife of my dear friend, on equal
230     terms.
REDLAW.     Why is it my doom to remember them too well?
PHAN.     Delusions! For my friend (in whose breast my confidence was locked as in
my own) won Agnes to himself and shattered my frail universe. My sister doubly
dear, doubly devoted, doubly cheerful in my home, lived on to see me famous, and
235     my old ambition so rewarded when its spring was broken and then—
REDLAW.     Then died; died gentle as happy, and with no concern but for her brother.
PHAN.     Thus I bear within me a sorrow and a wrong—thus I prey upon myself. Thus
memory is my curse; and if I could forget my sorrow and my wrong I would!
REDLAW.     Mocker! Why have I always that taunt in my ears?
240 PHAN.     —Forbear—lay a hand on me and die—if I could forget my sorrow and my
wrong I would! If I could forget my sorrow and my wrong I would!
REDLAW.     Evil spirit of myself, my life is darkened by that incessant whisper.
PHAN.     It is an echo.
REDLAW.     If it be an echo of my thoughts—as now indeed, I know it is—why should
245     I therefore be tormented? It is not a selfish thought. I suffer it to range beyond
myself. All men and women have their sorrows—most of them their wrongs—

ingratitude, and sordid jealousy, and interest, besetting all degrees of life. Who would not forget their sorrow and their wrongs?

PHAN.    Who would not, truly, and the happier and better for it. Hear what I offer! forget the sorrow, wrong and trouble you have known.                                    250

REDLAW.    Forget them!

PHAN.    I have the power to cancel their remembrance—say! Is it done?

REDLAW.    Stay! I tremble with distrust and doubt of you; and the dim fear you cast upon me deepens into a nameless horror I can hardly bear. What shall I lose if I assent to this? What else will pass from my remembrance?                                    255

PHAN.    No knowledge; no result of study, nothing but the intertwisted chain of feelings and associations each in its turn dependent on, and nourished by the banished recollections. Those will go.

REDLAW.    Are they so many?

PHAN.    Decide! Before the opportunity is lost.                                    260

REDLAW.    A moment! I call heaven to witness, that I have never been a hater of my kind—never morose, indifferent, or hard to anything around me. If there be poison in my mind, and through this fearful shadow I can cast it out, shall I not cast it out?

PHAN.    Say, is it done?

REDLAW.    A moment longer! I would forget it if I could! Have I thought that, alone?   265
Or has it been the thought of thousands upon thousands, generation after generation? All human memory is fraught with sorrow and trouble. My memory is as the memory of other men, but other men have not this choice. Yes I will close the bargain, yes! I will forget, my sorrow, worry and trouble.

PHAN.    Say—is it done?                                    270

REDLAW.    It is!

PHAN.    It is—and take this with you, man whom I here renounce! The gift that I have given, you shall give again, go where you will. Without recovering yourself the power that you have yielded up, you shall henceforth destroy its like in all whom you approach. Your wisdom has discovered that the memory of sorrow, wrong and   275
trouble is the lot of all mankind, and that mankind would be the happier in its other memories without it. Go! Be its benefactor. Go! Be happy in the good you have won and in the good you do! (PHANTOM *vanishes*)

REDLAW.    Destroy its like in all whom you approach—holloa! Holloa! This way! Come to the light. (*enter* BOY) What is it?                                    280

BOY.    I'll bite if you hit me! Where's the woman? I want to find the woman.

REDLAW.    Who?

BOY.    The woman—her that brought me here, and set me by the large fire. She was so long gone that I went to look for her, and lost myself. I don't want you, I want the woman.                                    285

REDLAW.    That is not the way. There is a nearer one. What is your name?

BOY.    Got none.

REDLAW.    Where do you live?

BOY.    Live! What's that? You let me go, will you? I want to find the woman.

REDLAW.    This way. I'll take you to her.                                    290

BOY.   Give me some of that!

REDLAW.    Has she not fed you?

BOY.    I shall be hungry again tomorrow, shan't I? Aint I hungry every day? There!
Now take me to the woman.

295 REDLAW.    The gift that I have given, you shall give again, go where you will—I'll not
go there tonight. I'll go nowhere tonight. Boy, straight down this long arched passage and past the great dark door into the yard; you will see the fire shining on a
window there.

BOY.   The woman's fire!

REDLAW *bows assent—the* BOY *bounds out of the chamber.*

*End of Act 1*

# ACT II

## SCENE 1

*A small shop parlour.*

TETTERBY, JOHNNY, *and* CHILDREN *discovered.*

JOHN.    There never was such a baby as our baby—everybody knows it as well as the  1
postman or the potboy, there ain't such another baby in the world.

TETT.    You bad boy haven't you any feeling for your poor father after the fatigues of
a hard winter's day since five o'clock in the morning, but you must make a wilderness of home, and maniacs of your parents? Must you Johnny?  5

JOHN.    Oh father when I was taking care of Sally and getting her to sleep! oh father!

TETT.    I wish my little woman would come home! I an't fit to deal with 'em. Isn't it
enough that your dear mother has provided you with that sweet sister, but you must
so behave yourself as to make my head swim—your brother 'Dolphus is late tonight,
Johnny, and will come home like a lump of ice.  10

JOHN.    Here's mother and Dolphus too father I think.

TETT.    You're right! Yes that's the footstep of my little woman. (MRS TETTERBY
*enters with* ADOLPHUS)

MRS T.    Johnny, bring me the baby.

TETT.    Are you wet Dolphus my boy? Come and take a chair and dry yourself.

ADOLPHUS.    No father thank'ee.  15

TETT.    A wonderful boy is Adolphus, he is not above ten years old and his little voice
is as well known at the railway station as the locomotive as runs in and out, which
enables him to come home cheerful.

MRS T.    Ah dear me! That's the way the world goes.

TETT.    Which is the way the world goes?  20

MRS T.    Oh, nothing.

TETT.    My little woman, what has put you out?

MRS T.    I'm sure I don't know.

TETT.    Your supper will be ready in a minute 'Dolphus—*you* shall get some supper
too Johnny—your mother went out in the wet to buy it. It was very good of your  25
mother to do so.

MRS T.    Oh Dolphus, how could I go and behave so—I hadn't no idea of being cross
when I came home—but somehow, Dolphus—

TETT.    I see! I understand! My little woman was put out—hard times, and hard
weather and hard work, make it trying now and then—Dolph my man here's your  30
mother been and bought a whole knuckle of a lovely roast leg of pork, hand in your
plate my boy, while it is simmering—now Johnny here's yours upon a piece of bread,
and put your pudding in your pocket—why are you swallowing there in gluttony

27 *Dolphus*: Tetterby senior is addressed here: he has the same first name as his eldest son.

and idleness instead of coming forward with the baby that the sight of her may
35    revive your mother?

MRS T.    I am better now.

TETT.    My little woman are you quite sure you're better? Or are you Sophia about to
break out in a fresh direction?

MRS T.    No Dolphus no, I'm quite myself—come nearer Dolphus, let me tell you all
40    about it—you know, Dolphus my dear, that when I was single, I might have given
myself away in several directions. At one time four after me at once; two of 'em were
sons of Mars.

TETT.    We're all sons of Ma's, my dear, jointly with Pa's.

MRS T.    I don't mean that—I mean soldiers—sergeants.

45    TETT.    Oh!

MRS T.    Well, Dolphus, I'm sure I never think of such things now, to regret them;
and I'm sure I've got as good a husband, and would do as much to prove that I was
fond of him, as—

TETT.    As any little woman in the world—very good—*very* good.

50    MRS T.    But you see Dolphus, this being Christmas time, when all people who can
make holiday, and when all people who have got money, like to spend some, before
durst lay out a sixpence for the commonest thing; and the basket was so large, and
wanted so much in it; and my stock of money was so small, and will go such a little
way—you hate me Dolphus?

55    TETT.    Not quite, as yet.

MRS T.    Well! I'll tell you the truth and then perhaps you will. I felt all this, and began
to think whether I mightn't have done better, and been happier—if—if I hadn't—

TETT.    If you hadn't married at all, or if you had married somebody else?

MRS T.    Yes—that's really what I thought, do you hate me now Dolphus?

60    TETT.    Why no, I don't find that I do, as yet. Well, my dear, we *are* poor, and there *are*
a number of mouths at home here—

MRS T.    Ah! But Dolf! Dolf! My good kind patient fellow, when I had been at home
a very little while—how different! Then the cheap enjoyments that I could have
trodden on so cruelly, got to be so precious to me—oh so priceless, and dear!—that
65    I couldn't bear to think how much I had wronged them; and I said, and say again a
hundred times, how could I ever behave so, Dolphus how could I ever have the
heart to do it. (*they embrace*)

*Enter* REDLAW.

MRS T.    Look at that man! Look there! What does he want?

TETT.    My dear—I'll ask him, if you'll let me go. What's the matter? How you shake!

---

52 *commonest thing*: The manuscript reads thus, but the sense is lost, perhaps through a copying omission. Dickens's original has '…to spend some, and I did, somehow, get a little out of sorts when I was in the
streets just now. There were so many things to be sold—such delicious things to eat, such fine things to look
at, such delightful things to have—and there was so much calculating and calculating necessary, before I
durst…' *A Christmas Carol and Other Christmas Books*, ed. Robert Douglas-Fairhurst (Oxford: Oxford
University Press, 2006), 358.

MRS T.    I saw him in the street, when I was out just now. He looked at me, and stood  70
near me. I am afraid of him.

TETT.    Afraid of him! Why?

MRS T.    I don't know why—I—stop! Husband!

TETT.    Are you ill my dear?

MRS T.    What is it that is going from me again? What *is* this that is going away? Ill?  75
No, I am quite well.

TETT.    What may be your pleasure, sir, with us!

REDLAW.    I fear that my coming in unperceived, has alarmed you, but you were
talking and did not hear me.

TETT.    My little woman says—perhaps you heard her say it—that it's not the first  80
time you have alarmed her tonight.

REDLAW.    I am sorry for it. I remember to have observed her in the street for a few
moments only. I had no intention of frightening her. My name is Redlaw, I come
from the old college hard by. A young gentleman who is a student there, lodges in
your house, does he not?  85

TETT.    Mr Denham?

REDLAW.    Yes.

TETT.    The gentleman's room is upstairs, sir, there's a more convenient private
entrance; but as you have come in here, it will save your going out in the cold, if
you'll take this little staircase, and go up to him that way if you wish to see him.  90

REDLAW.    Yes, I wish to see him, can you spare a light?

TETT.    I'll light you, sir, if you'll follow me.

REDLAW.    No, I don't wish to be attended, or announced to him. He does not expect
me. I would rather go alone. Please to give me light, if you can spare it, and I'll find
the way.  95

TETT.    Come! There's enough of this. Get to bed there.

MRS T.    The place is inconvenient and small enough, without you, get to bed.

*Scene closes.*


## SCENE 2

*A door leading into the chamber of the student.*

REDLAW.    What have I done? What am I going to do? To be the benefactor of  1
mankind—it is only since last night that I have remained shut up, and yet all things
are strange to me. I am strange to myself. I am here, as in a dream, what interest
have I in this place, or in any place that I can bring to my remembrance? My mind is
going blind!  5

EDMUND.    Come in! Is that my kind muse? But I need not ask her. There is no one
else to come here. The cinders chink when they shoot out here, so according to the
gossips, they are not coffins, but purses. Mr Redlaw—

REDLAW.    Don't come nearer to me. I will sit here. Remain you where you are!
10      I heard, by an accident, by what accident is no matter, that one of my class was ill
and solitary. I received no other description of him, than that he lived in this street.
Beginning my inquiries at the first house in it, I have found him.

EDMUND.    I have been ill sir, but am greatly better. An attack of fever—of the brain,
I believe, has weakened me, but I am much better. I cannot say I have been solitary,
15      in my illness, or I should forget the ministering hand that has been near me.

REDLAW.    You are speaking of the keeper's wife?

EDMUND.    Yes.

REDLAW.    I remembered your name, when it was mentioned to me downstairs, just
now; and I recollect your face. We have held but very little personal communication
20      together.

EDMUND.    Very little.

REDLAW.    You have retired and withdrawn from me more than any of the rest, I
think? And why? Why? How comes it that you have sought to keep especially from
me, the knowledge of your remaining here, at this season, when all the rest have
25      dispersed, and of your being ill? I want to know why this is.

EDMUND.    Mr Redlaw ! you have discovered me. You know my secret!

REDLAW.    Secret? I know?

EDMUND.    Yes! Your manner, so different from the interest and sympathy which
endear you to so many hearts, your altered voice, the constraint there is in every-
30      thing you say, and in your looks warn me that you know me. That you would conceal it, even now, is but a proof to me  (God knows I need none) of your material
kindness and of the bar there is between us. But Mr Redlaw—as a just and a good
man, think how innocent I am—except in name and descent, of participation in
any wrong inflicted on you, or in any sorrow you have borne.

35   REDLAW.    Sorrow! Wrong! What are those to me?

EDMUND.    For heaven's sake, do not let the mere interchange of a few words with me
change you like this, sir! Let me pass again from your knowledge and notice. Let me
occupy my old reserved and distant place among those whom you instruct. Know
me only by the name I have assumed, and not by that of Longford.

40   REDLAW.    Longford?

EDMUND.    The name my mother bears, sir, the name she took, when she might have
taken one more honoured.

REDLAW.    I believe I know that history.

EDMUND.    When my information halts, my guesses at what is wanting may supply
45      something not remote from the truth. I am the child of a marriage that has not
proved itself a well-assorted or a happy one. From infancy, I have heard you spoken of with honour and respect. Our ages and positions are so different, sir, and
I am so accustomed to regard you from a distance, that I wonder at my own
presumption when I touch, however lightly, on that theme. But to one who—I may
50      say who felt no common interest in my mother once—it may be something to
hear, now that is all past, with what indescribable feelings of affection I have, in my
obscurity, regarded him; with what pain and reluctance I have kept aloof from his

encouragement, when a word of it would have made me rich: yet how I felt it fit that I should hold my course, content to know him, and to be unknown. Mr Redlaw, what I would have said, I have said, for my strength is strange to me as yet; 55 but for anything unworthy in this fraud of mine, forgive me, and for all the rest forget me!

REDLAW.    Don't come nearer to me!—the time is past, it dies like the brutes. Who talks to me of its traces in my life? He raves or lies. If you want money, here it is. I came to offer it; and that is all I came for. There *can* be nothing else, and yet— 60

EDMUND.    Take it back, sir, I wish you could take from me with it remembrance of your words and offer.

REDLAW.    You do? You do?

EDMUND.    I do.

REDLAW.    There is sorrow and trouble in sickness, is there not? 65

EDMUND.    Yes!

REDLAW.    All best forgotten are they not?

MILLY.    (*without*) I can very well see now. Thank you Dolf. A gentleman with him, is there!

REDLAW.    I have feared from the first moment to meet her. I may be the murderer of 70 what is tenderest and best within her bosom. Shall I dismiss it as an idle foreboding, or still avoid her? Of all the visitors who could come here, this is the one I should desire most to avoid. Hide me! (*Exit*)

(*Enter* MILLY)

MILLY.    Dear Mr Edmund, they told me there was a gentleman here.

EDMUND.    There is no one here but I— 75

MILLY.    There has been someone come?

EDMUND.    Yes, yes there has been someone.

MILLY.    Are you quite as well tonight? Your head is not so cool as in the afternoon.

EDMUND.    Tut! Very little ails me.

MILLY.    It's the new muslin curtain for the window, Mr Edmund. It will look very 80 clean and nice, though it costs very little. My William says the room should not be too light just now, when you are recovering so well, or the glare might make you giddy. The pillows are not comfortable. I will soon put them right.

EDMUND.    They are very well—leave them alone, pray—you make so much of everything. 85

MILLY.    I have been thinking, Mr Edmund, that *you* have been often thinking of late, when I have been sitting by, how true the saying is, that adversity is a good teacher. Health will be more precious to you, after this illness, than it has ever been. Now isn't that a good, true thing? Ah, even so, and I have read in your face, as plain as if it was a book, that but for some trouble and sorrow we should never know half the 90 good there is about us.

EDMUND.    We needn't magnify the merit, Mrs William—I can't be made to feel more obliged by your exaggerating the case. I am sensible that you have been interested in me, and I say again, I am much obliged to you. Why weaken my sense of

95    what is your due in obligation, by preferring enormous claims upon me? One might
      suppose I had been dying a score of deaths here.
      MILLY.    Do you believe Mr Edmund, that I spoke of the poor people of the house,
      with any reference to myself? To me?
      EDMUND.    Oh I think nothing about it, my good creature. I have had an indisposi-
100   tion—which your solicitude—observe! I say solicitude—makes a great deal more
      of, than it merits; and it's over, and we can't perpetuate it.
      MILLY.    Mr Edmund, would you rather be alone.
      EDMUND.    There is no reason why I should detain you here.
      MILLY.    Except—
105   EDMUND.    Oh! The curtain—that's not worth staying for.
      MILLY.    If you should want me, I will come back willingly. When you did want me
      I was quite happy to come: there was no merit in it; and if you suspect me of meanly
      making much of the little I have tried to do to comfort your sick room, you
      do yourself more wrong than ever you can do me. That is why I am very sorry.
      (*Exit*)

*Enter* REDLAW.

110   REDLAW.    When sickness lays its hand on you again—may it soon be! Die here!
      Rot here!
      EDMUND.    What have you done? Give me back myself!
      REDLAW.    Give me back *myself*! I am infected! I am infectious! I am only so much
      less base than the wretches whom I make so, that in the moment of their transfor-
115   mation I can hate them. The gift that I have given, you shall give again, go where
      you will. (*Exit*)


# SCENE 3

*Exterior of the lodge.*

*Enter* REDLAW.

1     REDLAW.    The change within me makes the busy street a desert and the multitudes
      around me in their manifold endurances and ways of life a mighty waste of sand,
      which the winds toss into unintelligible heaps. Now that I know what I am, and
      what I make of others, I must be alone—yet one showed no sign of change—the boy
5     who rushed into my room. I will seek him out and prove if it be really so. This is the
      lodge where the boy sought shelter—(*Exit and returns with* BOY)
      Get up! You have not forgotten me?
      BOY.    You let me alone! This is the woman's house—not yours.
      REDLAW.    Who washed them, and put those bandages where they were bruised and
10    cracked?
      BOY.    The woman did.

REDLAW.   And is it she who has made you cleaner in the face too?

BOY.   Yes, the woman.

REDLAW.   Where are they?

BOY.   The woman's out.                                                                          15

REDLAW.   I know she is—where is the old man with the white hair, and his son? Aye, where are those two?

BOY.   Out. Something's the matter, somewhere—they were fetched out in a hurry and told me to stop here.

REDLAW.   Come with me and I'll give you money.                                                  20

BOY.   Come where? And how much will you give?

REDLAW.   I'll give you more shillings than you ever saw, and bring you back soon. Do you know your way to where you came from?

BOY.   You let me go, I'm not agoing to take you there. Let me be, or I'll heave something at you.                                                                                               25

REDLAW.   Listen boy! You shall take me where the people are very miserable or very wicked. I want to do them good and not to harm them. You shall have money, as I have told you, and I will bring you back—get up! Come quickly!

BOY.   Will you let me walk by myself, and never hold me, nor yet touch me?

REDLAW.   I will.                                                                                30

BOY.   And let me go before? Behind? Or any ways I like?

REDLAW.   I will.

BOY.   Give me some money first then, and I'll go.

*Exeunt*

# SCENE 4

*A ruinous street.*

*Enter* REDLAW *followed by* BOY.

REDLAW.   Three times have we been side by side. The first time in the old church-     1
yard among the graves—the second time when I looked up at the heavens and saw the moon in glory surrounded by her stars—I knew the name and histories science had appended to them. The third time when I listened to a plaintive strain of music, but could only hear a tune made manifest by the dry mechanism of the instrument,   5
with no address to any mystery within me, without a whisper of the past or of the future, powerless as the sound of last year's running water or the rushing of last year's wind—each time I felt the expression on that boy's face was the expression on my own.

BOY.   In there—I'll wait.                                                                       10

REDLAW.   Will they let me in?

BOY.   Say you're a doctor, there's plenty ill there.

REDLAW.    Sorrow, wrong and trouble, at least haunt this place, darkly; he can do no harm, who brings forgetfulness of such things here.

PHILIP *appears at door.*

15 PHILIP.    Mr Redlaw this is like you, sir, you have heard of it, and have come after us to render any help you can. Ah, too late—too late. (*Exeunt* REDLAW *and* PHILIP)


# SCENE 5

*A mean apartment.*

GEORGE SWIDGER *discovered on bed,* WILLIAM *and* LONGFORD *standing beside.*
*Enter* PHILIP *and* REDLAW.

1 PHILIP.    Too late—you have come too late.
WILLIAM.    That's what I say father—you're right father!
REDLAW.    Who is this?
PHILIP.    My son George, Mr Redlaw—my eldest son George, who was more his
5    mother's pride than all the rest!
REDLAW.    William—who is that man! (*indicating* LONGFORD)
WILLIAM.    Why you see, sir, why should a man ever go and gamble, and the like of that, and let himself down inch by inch till he can't let himself down any lower.
REDLAW.    Has he done so?
10 WILLIAM.    Just exactly that, sir, as I am told. He knows a little about medicine, sir, it seems—and having been way-faring towards London with my unhappy brother, and being lodged upstairs for the night—he looked in to attend upon him, and came for us at his request. It's enough to kill my father!
REDLAW.    Was it only yesterday when I observed the memory of this old man to be
15    a tissue of sorrow and trouble? Are such remembrances as I can drive away, so precious to this dying man that I need fear for *him*? No! I'll stay here.
GEORGE.    Father!
PHILIP.    My boy! My son George!
GEORGE.    You spoke just now, of my being mother's favourite, long ago. It's a dread-
20    ful thing to think now, of long ago.
PHILIP.    No, no, no, think of it. It's not dreadful to me, my son.
GEORGE.    It eats you to the heart, your tears are falling on me.
PHILIP.    Yes—yes—so it does; but it does me good. Where's my son William? William, my boy, your mother loved him dearly to the last, and with her latest
25    breath said—tell him I forgave him, blessed him, and prayed for him. Those were her words to me. I have never forgotten them and I'm eighty-seven.
GEORGE.    Father! I am dying, I know, I am so far gone, that I can hardly speak, even of what my mind most runs on. Is there any hope for me, beyond this bed?

PHILIP.    There is hope for all who are softened and penitent. There is hope for all such—I was thankful only yesterday that I could remember this unhappy son when 30 he was an innocent child. But what a comfort it is, now, to think that even heaven has that remembrance of him.

GEORGE.    Ah! The waste since then, the waste of life since then.

PHILIP.    But he was a child once, before he lay down on his bed at night he said his prayers at his poor mother's knee, sorrowful as it was to her, and me, to think of 35 this, when he went so wrong, and when our hopes and plans for him were all broken, this gave him still a hold upon us, that nothing else could have given.

REDLAW.    The gift that I have given, you must give again—it must come.

GEORGE.    My time is very short, my breath is short, and I remember there is something on my mind concerning the man who was here just now. Father and 40 William—wait!—is there really anything in black, out there?

PHILIP.    Yes, yes, it is real.

GEORGE.    Is it a man?

WILLIAM.    What I say myself, George, it's Mr Redlaw.

GEORGE.    I thought I had dreamed of him. Ask him to come here—it has been so 45 ripped up tonight, sir, by the sight of my poor old father, and the thought of all the trouble I have been the cause of, and all the wrong and sorrow lying at my door, that—

REDLAW.    It is coming fast. (*aside*)

GEORGE.    That what I *can* do right, with my mind running on so much, so fast, I'll try to do. There was another man here. Did you see him? He is penniless, hungry 50 and destitute. He is completely beaten down, and has no resources at all. Look after him! Lose no time! I know he has it in his mind to kill himself.

REDLAW.    It is working. It is on his face. His face is changing, hardening, deepening in all its shades, and losing all its sorrow.

GEORGE.    Why d-n you, what have you been doing to me here! I have lived bold, and 55 I mean to die bold. To the devil with you.

PHILIP.    Where's my boy William? William come away from here. We'll go home—

WILLIAM.    Home, father! Are you going to leave your own son?

PHILIP.    Where's my own son?

WILLIAM.    Where? Why there! 60

PHILIP.    That's no son of mine—no such wretch as that, has any claim on me—my children are useful to me—I've a right to it, I'm eighty-seven.

WILLIAM.    You're old enough to be no older—I don't know what good you are myself. We could have a deal more pleasure without you.

PHILIP.    *My* son, Mr Redlaw! *My* son, too! The boy talking to me of *my* son! Why, 65 what has he ever done to give me any pleasure, I should like to know.

WILLIAM.    I don't know what you have done to give *me* any pleasure.

PHILIP.    For how many Xmas times running have I sat in my warm place and never had to come out in the cold night—is it twenty William?

WILLIAM.    Nigher forty, it seems. Why when I look at my father sir, and come to 70 think of it, I'm whipped if I can see anything in him, but a calendar of ever so many years of eating and drinking, and making himself comfortable, over and over again.

PHILIP.    I'm eighty-seven—and I don't know as I ever was much put out by anything. I'm not agoing to begin now, because of what he calls my son, he's not my
75    son—but I don't know, and I don't care a bit. Berries, eh? Ah! It's a pity they're not
good to eat—berries, eh? There's good cheer when there's berries. Well, I ought to
have my share of it; for I'm eighty-seven and a poor old man. I'm eighty-seven.

# SCENE 6

*The ruined street.*

*The* BOY *crawls from the arch.*

1  BOY.    Back to the woman's?
REDLAW.    Back, quickly! Stop nowhere on the way. (*they hurry off*)

# SCENE 7

REDLAW's *Chamber.*

*Enter* REDLAW *and* BOY.

1  BOY.    Come, don't you touch me! You've not brought me here to take my money
away—
REDLAW.    And this is the only one companion I have left on earth!
BOY.    Here's the woman coming—let me go to her—will you?
5  REDLAW.    Not now. Stay here—nobody must pass in or out of the room now—who's
there?
MILLY.    It is I, sir, pray let me in.
REDLAW.    No, not for the world.
MILLY.    Mr Redlaw, pray sir, let me in.
10  REDLAW.    What is the matter?
MILLY.    The miserable man you saw is worse, and nothing I can say will wake him
from his terrible infatuation. William's father has turned childish in a moment.
William himself is changed. The shock has been too sudden for him. Oh Mr Redlaw,
pray advise me. Help me!
15  REDLAW.    No, no, no!
MILLY.    Mr Redlaw, dear sir! George has been muttering, in his doze, about the man
you saw there, who he fears will kill himself.
REDLAW.    Better he should do it than come near me.
MILLY.    He says in his wandering, that you know him; that he was your friend once,
20    long ago; that he is the ruined father of a student here. What is to be done?—How
is he to be saved? Mr Redlaw, pray, oh pray advise me! Help me!

REDLAW.   Phantoms! Punishers of impious thoughts! Look upon me! From the darkness of my mind, let the glimmering of contrition that I know is there, shine up, and show my misery! Pity me! And relieve me!

MILLY.   Help me! Help me, let me in!                                               25

REDLAW.   Shadows of myself! Spirit of my darker hours! Come back and haunt me day and night, but take this gift away! Or if it must still rest with me, deprive me of the dreadful power of giving it to others. Undo what I have done. Leave me benighted, but restore the day to those whom I have cursed. As I have spared this woman from the first, and as I never will go forth again, but will die here, with no   30 hand to touch me, save this creature's who is proof against me—hear me!

MILLY.   Help! Let me in. He was your friend once—how shall he be followed, how shall he be saved? They are all changed, there is no one else to help me, pray, pray let me in!

BOY *struggling to get to her*

*Picture*

End of Act II

# ACT III

## SCENE 1

*The chemist's room. Dimly lighted—on the ground lies the* BOY—REDLAW *seated in his chair. Music.*

*Enter the* PHANTOM—*with it the* SHADE OF MILLY.

1 REDLAW.   Spectre! I have not been stubborn or presumptuous in respect of her. Oh, do not bring her here. Spare me that!

PHAN.   This is but a shadow, when the morning shines, seek out the reality whose image I present before you.

5 REDLAW.   Is it my inexorable doom to do so?

PHAN.   It is.

REDLAW.   To destroy her peace, her goodness; to make her what I am myself, and what I have made of others!

PHAN.   I have said seek her out, I have said no more.

10 REDLAW.   Oh, tell me, can I undo what I have done?

PHAN.   No.

REDLAW.   I do not ask for restoration to myself; what I abandoned of my own will, I have justly lost. But for those to whom I have transferred the fatal gift; who never sought it; who unknowingly received a curse of which they had no warning, and

15 which they had no power to shun; can I do nothing?

PHAN.   Nothing.

REDLAW.   If I cannot, can anyone?—ah, can she?—stay for a moment! As an act of mercy! I know that some change fell upon me, when those sounds were in the air just now. Tell me, have I lost the power of harming her? May I go near her without

20 dread? Oh, let her give me any sign of hope! At least say this—has she henceforth, the consciousness of any power to set right what I have done?

PHAN.   She has not.

REDLAW.   Has she the power bestowed on her without the consciousness?

PHAN.   (*bows*) Seek her out.

(MILLY'S *shadow vanishes*)

25 REDLAW.   Terrible instructor, by whom I was renounced, but by whom I am revisited, in which, and in whose milder aspect, I would feign believe I have a gleam of hope, I will obey without enquiry, praying that the cry I have sent up in the anguish of my soul has been, or will be, heard, on behalf of those whom I have injured beyond human reparation. But there is one thing—

30 PHAN.   You speak of what is lying here.

REDLAW.    I do; you know what I would ask. Why has this child alone been proof
against my influence, and why, why have I detected in its thoughts a terrible companionship with mine?

PHAN.    This is the last, completest illustration of a human creature utterly bereft of
such remembrances as you have yielded up. No softening memory of sorrow,  35
wrong, or trouble enters here, because this wretched mortal from his birth has been
abandoned to a worse condition than the beasts, and has, within his knowledge, no
one contrast, no humanising touch to make a grain of such a memory spring up in
his hardened breast. All within this desolate creature is barren wilderness. All
within the man bereft of what you have resigned, is the same barren wilderness.  40
Woe to such a man! Woe, tenfold, to the nation that shall count its monsters such
as this, lying here, by hundreds and thousands. There is not one of these—not
one—but sows a harvest that mankind *must* reap. Open and unpunished murder in
a city's streets would be less guilty in its daily toleration, than one such spectacle as
this. There is not a father by whose side in his daily or his nightly walk, these crea-  45
tures pass; there is not a mother among all the ranks of loving mothers in this land;
there is no one risen from the state of childhood, but shall be responsible in his or
her degree for this enormity. Behold, I say, the perfect type of what it was your
choice to be. Your influence is powerless here, because from this child's bosom you
can banish nothing. His thoughts have been in 'terrible companionship' with yours,  50
because you have gone down to his unnatural level. He is the growth of man's indif-
ference; you are the growth of man's presumption. The beneficent design of heaven,
is, in each case, overthrown, and from the two poles of the immaterial world you
come together.

*Scene closed in*

## SCENE 2

*Outside of* TETTERBY's *shop.*

TETTERBY *looks out from door as he takes in one of the shutters—encounters* JOHNNY
*and the baby.*

TETT.    Now then stupid boy where are you coming to?                              1
JOHN.    It's baby—(*baby cries*)
TETT.    What's the matter with it? Eh?
JOHN.    I don't know—I 'spose its teeth.
TETT.    Its teeth! There's a peculiarity about that baby—its always cutting its teeth—it  5
has certainly cut enough, if Mrs Tetterby's to be believed, to make a handsome sign
for the Bull and Mouth. I don't believe it cut any though everything's been done for it;
it's got a bone ring as big as a little boy's hoop—beside having the use of knife handles,
umbrella tops, cruets and nutmeg graters, handles of doors, knobs of pokers, besides

10    the fingers of the family in general and of Johnny in particular. The amount of elec-
tricity rubbed out of that child in a week is not to be calculated, Mrs T's always
saying it's coming through and then the child will be herself; but it never does come
through and the child continues to be somebody else. (JOHNNY *gives baby a poke*)

*Enter* MRS TETTERBY.

MRS T.    You brute, you murdering little boy, had you the heart to do it?
15  JOHN.    Why don't her teeth come through then, instead of bothering me. How
would you like it yourself?
MRS T.    Like it sir! (*takes baby*)
JOHN.    Yes, like it, how would you? Not at all. If you was me, you'd go for a soldier.
I will, too. There ain't no babies in the army.
20  MRS T.    I wish I was in the army myself, if the child's in the right, for I have no peace
of my life here. I'm a slave, a Virginia slave: how you stand there, 'Dolphus—why
don't you do something?
TETT.    Because I don't care about doing anything.
MRS T.    I'm sure I don't.
25  TETT.    I'll take my oath I don't.
MRS T.    You had better read your paper than do nothing at all.
TETT.    What's there to be read in a paper?
MRS T.    What? 'Police'.
TETT.    It's nothing to me, what do I care what people do, or are done to.
30  MRS T.    Suicides?
TETT.    No business of mine.
MRS T.    Births, deaths, and marriages, are those nothing to you?
TETT.    If the births were all over for good, and all today; and the deaths were all to
begin to come off tomorrow; I don't see why it should interest me, till I thought it
35    was a-coming to my turn. As to marriages, I've done it myself. I know quite enough
about them. (*Exit*)
MRS T.    So do I Tetterby—so do I—I never have a holiday or any pleasure at all from
year's end to year's end—why lord bless and save the child, what's the matter with
her now? (*Exit shaking child*)


## SCENE 3

*Interior of* TETTERBY'S.

TETTERBY *discovered seated.*

*Enter* MRS TETTERBY.

1  MRS T.    Oh you're a consistent man, a'nt you? You, with the screen of your own
making there, made of nothing else but bits of newspapers, which you sit and read
to the children by the half hour together!

TETT.     Say used to, if you please, you won't find me doing it any more, I'm wiser now.

MRS T.    Bah! Wiser, indeed! Are you better?                                                    5

TETT.     Better! I don't know as any of us are better, or happier either; better, is
it? (*finds a paragraph on screen*) This used to be one of the family favourites, I recollect, and used to draw tears from the children, and make 'em good, if there was
any little bickering or discontent among them, next to the story of the robin red-
breasts in the wood: 'melancholy case of destitution. Yesterday a small man with a    10
baby in his arms, and surrounded by half a dozen ragged little ones, of various ages
between ten and two, the whole of whom were evidently in a famishing condition,
appeared before the worthy magistrate, and made the following recital': Ha! I don't
understand it, I'm sure, I don't see what it has got to do with us.

MRS T.    How old and shabby he looks, I never saw such a change in a man. Ah! Dear   15
me, dear me, dear me, it was a sacrifice.

TETT.     What was a sacrifice? If you mean your marriage was a sacrifice, my good
woman—

MRS T.    I *do* mean it.

TETT.     Why, then I need to say, that there are two sides to that affair; and that *I* was   20
the sacrifice; and that I wish the sacrifice hadn't been accepted.

MRS T.    I wish it hadn't, Tetterby, with all my heart and soul I do assure you. You
can't wish it more than I do, Tetterby.

TETT.     I don't know what I saw in her, I'm sure, certainly, if I saw anything it's not
there now. I was thinking so, last night, after supper, by the fire. She's fat, she's aging,   25
she won't bear comparison with most other women.

MRS T.    He's common looking, he has no air with him, he's small, he's beginning to
stoop, and he's getting bald.

TETT.     I must have been out of my mind when I did it.

MRS T.    My senses must have forsook me. That's the only way in which I can explain   30
it to myself. (*they begin breakfast*)

MRS T.    These children will be the death of me at last! And the sooner the better I think.

TETT.     Poor people ought not to have children at all. They give *us* no pleasure.

JOHN.     Here! Mother! Father (*running in*) here's Mrs William coming down the street!

TETT.     Why lord forgive me, what evil tempers have I been giving way to? What has   35
been the matter here?

MRS T.    How could I ever treat him ill again, after all I said and felt last night!

TETT.     Am I a brute, or is there any good in me at all. Sophia! My little woman!

MRS T.    'Dolphus dear.

TETT.     I—I've been in a state of mind, that I can't abear to think of, Sophie.          40

MRS T.    Oh, it's nothing to what I've been in 'Dolph.

TETT.     My Sophia, don't take on, I shall never forgive myself. I must have nearly
broke your heart, I know.

MRS T.    No, Dolph, no, it was me! Me!

TETT.     My little woman, don't. You make me reproach myself dreadful, when you   45
show such a noble spirit. Sophia, my dear, you don't know what I thought. I showed
it bad enough, no doubt; but what I thought, my little woman!—

MRS T.    Oh, dear 'Dolph, don't! don't!

TETT.    Sophia, I must reveal it. I couldn't rest in my conscience unless I mentioned
50    it. My little woman—

JOHN.    Mrs William's very nearly here.

TETT.    My little woman I wondered how, I wondered how I had ever admired you—I
forgot the precious children you have brought about me, and thought you didn't look
as slim as I could wish. I—I never gave a recollection, to the cares you've had as my
55    wife, and along of me and mine, when you might have had hardly any with another
man, who got on better and was luckier than me  (anybody might have found such a
man easily I am sure); and I quarrelled with you for having aged a little in the rough
years you've lightened for me. Can you believe it, my little woman? I hardly can myself.

MRS T.    Oh, 'Dolph! I am so happy that you thought so; I am so grateful that you
60    thought so! For I thought you were common looking, Dolph; and so you are, my
dear, and may you be the commonest of all sights in my eyes, till you close them
with your own good hands. I thought that you were small; and so you are, and I'll
make much of you because you are, and more of you because I love my husband.
I thought that you began to stoop; and so you do, and you shall lean on me and I'll
65    do all I can to keep you up. I thought there was no air about you; but there is, and
it's the pure air of home—and that's the purest and best there is, and God bless
home once more, and all belonging to it, 'Dolph!

JOHN.    Hurrah! Here's Mrs William!

*Enter* MILLY.

MILLY.    What! Are *you* also glad to see me, too, this bright Christmas morning! Oh
70    dear how delightful this is! Oh dear! What delicious tears you make me shed. How
can I ever have deserved this! What have I done to be so loved!

TETT.    Who can help it!

MRS T.    Who can help it!

CHILDREN.    Who can help it!

75  MILLY.    I was never so moved. I must tell you, as soon as I can speak—Mr Redlaw
came to me at sunrise, and with a tenderness in his manner, more as if I had been
his darling daughter than myself, implored me to go with him to where William's
brother George is lying ill. We went together, and all the way along he was so kind,
and so subdued, and seemed to put such trust and hope in me, that I could not help
80    crying with pleasure.

TETT.    He was right.

MRS T.    He was right.

ALL.    He was right.

MILLY.    Ah, but there's more than that, when we got upstairs, into the room, the sick
85    who had laid for hours in a state from which no effort could rouse him, rose up in
his bed, and, bursting into tears, stretched out his arms to me, and said that he had
led a mis-spent life, but that he was truly repentant now, in his sorrow for the past
which was all as plain to him as a great prospect, from which a dense black cloud
had cleared away, and that he entreated me to ask his poor old father for his pardon

and his blessing, and to say a prayer beside his bed. And when I did so, Mr Redlaw  90
joined in it so fervently, and then so thanked and thanked me, and thanked Heaven,
that my heart quite overflowed, and I could have done nothing but sob and cry, if
the sick man had not begged me to sit down by him—which made me quiet of
course. As I sat there, he held my hand in his until he sunk in a doze and even then,
when I withdrew my hand to leave him to come here (which Mr Redlaw was very  95
earnest indeed in wishing me to do) his hand felt for mine so that someone else was
obliged to take my place and make believe to give him my hand back. Oh dear, oh
dear, how thankful and how happy I should feel, and do feel, for all this!

(*Enter* EDMUND)

EDMUND.    Kind nurse, gentlest, best of creatures, forgive my cruel ingratitude.
MILLY.    Oh dear, oh dear! Here's another of them! Oh dear, here's somebody else  100
who likes me! What shall I ever do!
EDMUND.    I was not myself, I don't know what it was—it was some consequence of
my disorder; perhaps I was mad. But I am so no longer, almost as I speak, I am
restored. I heard the children crying out your name, and the shade passed from me
at the very sound of it. Oh don't weep! Dear Milly, if you could read my heart, and  105
only know with what affection and what grateful homage it is glowing, you would
not let me see you weep. It is such deep reproach.
MILLY.    No, no, it's not that. It's not indeed. It's joy. It's wonder that you should think
it necessary to ask me to forgive so little, and yet it's pleasure that you do.
EDMUND.    And will you come again? And will you finish the little curtain?  110
MILLY.    No, you won't care for *my* needlework now.
EDMUND.    Is it forgiving me to say that?
MILLY.    There is news from your home, Mr Edmund.
EDMUND.    News? How?
MILLY.    Either your not writing when you were very ill, or the change in your hand-  115
writing when you began to be better, created some suspicion of the truth; however
that is—but you're sure you'll not be the worse for any news, if it's not bad news?
EDMUND.    Sure.
MILLY.    Then there's someone come.
EDMUND.    My mother?  120
MILLY.    Hush! No.
EDMUND.    It can be no one else.
MILLY.    Indeed? Are you sure?
EDMUND.    It is not—
MILLY.    Yes it is! The young lady (she is very like the miniature, Mr Edmund, but  125
she is prettier) was too unhappy to rest without satisfying her doubts, and came up,
last night, with a little servant maid. As you always dated your letter from the col-
lege, she came there; and before I saw Mr Redlaw, this morning, I saw her—*she* likes
me too! Oh dear that's another!
EDMUND.    This morning! Where is she now?  130

MILLY.   Why, she is now in my little parlour in the lodge, and waiting to see you; and
Mr Redlaw is much altered, and has told me this morning, that his memory is
impaired. Be very considerate to him, Mr Edmund; he needs that from us all. (*Exit*)

MILLY.   Shall we go home now Mr Redlaw?

135 REDLAW.   Yes.


# SCENE 4

*Interior.*

1 MILLY.   Oh dear, dear, dear, they are pleased to see me like the rest! Here are two
more. (*Enter* PHILIP *and* SWIDGER)

PHILIP.   Why, where has my quiet mouse been all this time? She has been a long
while away. I find that it's impossible for me to get on without mouse. I—where's my
5 son William?—I fancy I have been dreaming, William.

SWIDGER.   That's what I say myself, father, *I* have been in an ugly sort of dream, I
think—how are you, father? Are you pretty well?

PHILIP.   Strong and brave, my boy.

SWIDGER.   What a wonderful man you are, father!—how are you father? Are you
10 really pretty hearty, though?

PHILIP.   I never was fresher or stouter in my life, my boy.

SWIDGER.   What a wonderful man you are, father! But that's exactly where it is, (*with
enthusiasm*) when I think of all that my father's gone through, and all the chances
and changes, and sorrows and troubles, that have happened to him in the course of
15 his long life, and under which his head has grown grey, and years upon years have
gathered on it, I feel as if you couldn't do enough to honour the old gentleman, and
make his old age easy—how are you, father? Are you really pretty well, though?

PHILIP.   I ask your pardon, Mr Redlaw, but didn't know you were here, sir, or should
have made less free. It reminds me, Mr Redlaw, seeing you here on a Christmas
20 morning, of the time when you was a student yourself, and worked so hard, that
you was backwards and forwards in our library even at Christmas time. Ha! Ha! I'm
old enough to remember that; and I remember it right well, I do, though I'm eighty-
seven. It was after you left here that my poor wife died. You remember my poor
wife, Mr Redlaw?

25 REDLAW.   Yes.

PHILIP.   Yes. She was a dear creature—I recollect you come here one Christmas
morning with a young lady—I ask your pardon, Mr Redlaw, but I think it was a
sister you was very much attached to?

---

135 *Yes*: Lemon as not made clear how Redlaw is present in this scene, with no entry for him. Dickens
had him appear at the door during Milly's long speech beginning 'Ah, but there's more than that' and then
has silent interactions between him and Edmund, before he goes off humbly with Milly as if he realized 'he
knew nothing, and she all' (Douglas-Fairhurst, *A Christmas Carol*, 399).

REDLAW.    I had a sister—

PHILIP.    One Christmas morning, that you came here with her—and it began to 30
snow, and my wife invited the young lady to walk in, and sit by the fire that is always
a-burning on Christmas day, in what used to be, before our ten poor gentlemen
commuted, our great Dinner Hall, I was there; and I recollect, as I was stirring up
the blaze for the young lady to warm her pretty feet by, she read the scroll out loud,
that is underneath that picture 'Lord Keep my Memory Green'! She and my poor 35
wife fell a-talking about it; and it's a strange thing to think of, now, that they both
said (both being so unlike to die) that it was a good prayer, and that it was one they
would put up very earnestly, if they were called away young, with reference to those
who were dearest to them. My brother, says the young lady—my husband says my
poor wife—lord keep his memory of me, green, and do not let me be forgotten!      40

REDLAW.    Philip! I am a stricken man, on whom the hand of Providence has fallen
heavily, although deservedly. You speak to me, my friend, of what I cannot follow;
my memory is gone.

PHILIP.    Merciful power!

REDLAW.    I have lost my memory of sorrow, wrong, and trouble, and with that I 45
have lost all, man would remember!

*Enter* BOY.

BOY.    Here's the man, in the other room. I don't want *him*.

SWIDGER.    What does he mean?

MILLY.    Hush!

BOY.    I like the woman best.                                                      50

REDLAW.    You are right, but you needn't fear to come to me. I am gentler than I was.
Of all the world, to you, poor boy.

MILLY.    Mr Redlaw, may I speak to you?

REDLAW.    Yes—your voice and music are the same to me.

MILLY.    May I ask you something?                                                 55

REDLAW.    What you will.

MILLY.    Do you remember what I said, when I knocked at your door last night?
About one who was your friend once, and who stood on the verge of destruction?

REDLAW.    Yes. I remember.

MILLY.    Do you understand it? This person I found soon afterwards. I went back to 60
the house, and with heaven's help, traced him. I was not too soon. A very little, and
I should have been too late. He *is* the father of Mr Edmund, the young man we saw
just now. His real name is Longford—you recollect the name?

REDLAW.    I recollect the name.

MILLY.    And the man?                                                             65

REDLAW.    No, not the man. Did he ever wrong me?

MILLY.    Yes!

REDLAW.    Ah! Then it's hopeless—hopeless.

MILLY.    I did not go to Mr Edmund last night—you will listen to me just the same as
if you did remember all?                                                           70

REDLAW.    To every syllable you say.

MILLY.    Both, because I did not know, then, that this really was his father, and because I was fearful of the effect of such intelligence upon him, after his illness, if it should be. Since I have known who this person is I have not gone either; but that
75      is for another reason. He has long been separated from his wife and son—has been a stranger to his home almost from his son's infancy, I learn from him—and has abandoned and deserted what he should have held most dear. In all that time, he has been falling from the state of a gentleman more and more, until—

REDLAW.    Do you know me?

80  LONGFORD.    I should be glad, and that is an unwonted word for me to use, if I could answer no.

MILLY.    See how low he is sunk, how lost he is! If you could remember all that is connected with him, do you not think it would move your pity to reflect that one you ever loved (do not let us mind how long ago, or in what belief that he has for-
85      feited) should come to this?

REDLAW.    I hope it would, I believe it would.

MILLY.    I have no learning, and you have much. I am not used to think and you are always thinking. May I tell you why it seems to me a great thing for us, to remember wrong that has been us?

90  REDLAW.    Yes.

MILLY.    That we may forgive it.

REDLAW.    Pardon me Great Heaven! For having thrown away thine own high attribute!

MILLY.    And if, if your memory should one day be restored, as we will hope and pray
95      it may be, would it not be a blessing to you to recall at once a wrong and its forgive-ness. He cannot go to his abandoned home. He does not seek to go there. He knows that he could only carry shame and trouble to those he has so cruelly neglected; and that the best reparation he can make them now, is to avoid them. A very little money carefully bestowed, would remove him to some distant place, where he might live
100     and do no wrong, and make such atonement as is left within his power for the wrong he has done. To the unfortunately lady who is his wife, and to his son, this would be the best and kindest boon that their best friend could give them—one too, that they need never know of; and to him, shattered in reputation, mind, and body, it might be salvation.

105  REDLAW.    It shall be done. I trust to you to do it for me, now and secretly; and to tell him that I would forgive him, if I were so happy as to know for what.

LONGFORD.    You are so generous, you ever were—that you will try to banish your rising sense of retribution in the spectacle that is before you. I do not try to banish it from myself, Redlaw. If you can believe me. I am too decayed a wretch to make
110     professions; I recollect my own career too well, to array any such before you. But from the day on which I made my first step downward, in dealing falsely by you,

---

79 *Do you know me?*: Lemon inserts no entry for Longford. Dickens had Milly rush out and bring him in at this point, and presumably that is intended here.

I have gone down with a certain, steady, doomed progression. That, I say. I might have been another man, my life might have been another life, if I had avoided that first fatal step. I don't know that it would have been. I claim nothing for the possibility. Your sister is at rest, and better than she could have been with me, if I had con- 115 tinued even what you thought me: even what I once supposed myself to be. I speak like a man taken from the grave. I should have made my own grave, last night, had it not been for this blessed hand.

MILLY.    Oh dear, he likes me too! That's another!

LONGFORD.    I could not have put myself in your way, last night, even for bread. But, 120 today, my recollection of what has been between us is so strongly stirred, and is presented to me, I don't know how, so vividly, that I have dared to come at her suggestion, and to take your bounty, and to thank you for it, and to beg you, Redlaw, in your dying hour, to be as merciful to me in your thoughts, as you are in your deeds. I hope my son may interest you, for his mother's sake. I hope he may deserve to do 125 so. Unless my life should be preserved a long time, and I should know that I have not misused your aid, I shall never look upon him more—(*Exit*)

SWIDGER.    That's exactly where it is. That's what I always say, father! There's a motherly feeling in Mrs William's breast, that must and will have went.

PHILIP.    Aye, aye, you're right. My son William's right!                                    130

SWIDGER.    It happens all for the best Milly, dear, no doubt, that we have no children of our own; and yet I sometimes wish you had one to love and cherish. Our little dead child that you built such hopes upon, and that never breathed the breath of life—it has made you quiet-like, Milly.

MILLY.    I am very happy in the recollection of it, William dear, I think of it every day. 135

SWIDGER.    I was afraid you thought of it a good deal.

MILLY.    Don't say, afraid; it is a comfort to me; it speaks to me in so many ways. The innocent thing that never lived on earth, is like an angel to me, William.

SWIDGER.    You are like an angel to father and me, I know that.

MILLY.    When I think of all those hopes I built upon it, and the many times I sat and 140 pictured to myself the little smiling face upon my bosom that never lay there, and the sweet eyes turned up to mine that never opened to the light, I can feel a greater tenderness, I think, for all the disappointed hopes in which there is no harm. When I see a beautiful child in its fond mother's arms, I love it all the better, thinking that my child might have been like that, and might have made my heart as proud and happy. 145 All through life, it seems by me, to tell me something. For the poor neglected children, my little child pleads as if it were alive, and had a voice I knew, with which to speak to me. When I hear of youth in suffering or shame, I think that my child might have come to that, perhaps, and that God took it from me in his mercy. Even in age and grey hair, such as father's, it is present: saying that it too might have lived to be old, 150 long and long after you and I were gone, and to have needed the respect and love of younger people. Children love me so, that sometimes I half fancy—it's a silly fancy,

---

128 *SWIDGER*: Lemon offers no sds to explain that Milly takes Longford away and then re-enters, here, and tends the prostrate Boy, leaving Redlaw in his chair, head in hands.

William—they have some way I don't know of, of feeling for my little child, and me,
and understanding why their love is precious to me, if I have been quiet since, I have
155    been more happy, William, in a hundred ways. Not least happy, dear, in this—that
even when my little child was born and dead but a few days, and I was weak and sorrowful, and could not help grieving a little, the thought arose, that if I tried to lead a
good life, I should meet in heaven a bright creature, who would call me mother!

REDLAW.    Oh! receive my thanks and bless her—

160    MILLY.    He is come back to himself! He likes me very much indeed, too! Oh dear,
dear, dear me, here's another!

*Enter* EDMUND.

REDLAW.    Edmund Longford, the same gentle influence which restored you has
restored me. One lesson of the past which is interest in you and in your choice, be
happy! Be my children!

165    EDMUND.    Generous Mr Redlaw!

REDLAW.    And as Christmas is a time in which of all times in the year the memory
of all our remediable sorrow, wrong, and trouble, in the world round us should be
active with us not less than our own experiences, for all good, witness you and all
here that I vow to protect this forlorn creature; to teach him and reclaim him.

170    BOY.    You'll let me see the woman sometimes though?

REDLAW.    Else I should have learned and suffered to poor purpose, child! Philip,
your hand! How many Swidgers did you tell me there were, William? As many as
would make a ring around England if they joined hands, was it not?

SWIDGER.    Why it's what I *did* say, sir. That's exactly where it was.

175    REDLAW.    Then let us have as many of that good stock here, Philip, to a Christmas
dinner in this hall as you have already bidden to your own fire-side and as many
more as can be assembled on so short a notice.

SWIDGER.    Why lord bless you sir, here's a regiment of Swidgers ready now, and
there's the Tetterbys down to the very baby can be got in half a minute, and there's
180    George who has been removed to the little bed up stairs, I will have *him* down to
gladden my old father's heart. What a wonderful old man he is—(*Exit*)

*Enter* GUESTS—GEORGE—WILLIAM, *the* TETTERBYS *etc.*

MRS T.    (*in alarm*) Ah! Where's the baby?

*Enter* JOHNNY with BABY.

JOHN.    Mother! Mother! It's come through—a double tooth!

REDLAW.    Stay! Philip! There's a good grace worthy of the day upon the wall.

185    SWIDGER.    Aye, aye, Mr Redlaw it's a good prayer Sir—and a pious prayer. It's very
good and pious Mr Redlaw—lord keep

ALL.    Lord keep my memory green.

---

161.1 *Enter* EDMUND: Dickens has Edmund's beloved enter with him here, and Lemon's speech (con-
cluding 'Be my children!') for Redlaw suggests he is addressing both of them.

# FURTHER READING

Bolton, H. Philip. *Dickens Dramatized* (Boston, Mass.: G.K. Hall & Co., 1987).

Fawcett, F. Dubrez. *Dickens the Dramatist* (London: W.H. Allen, 1952).

Fitzgerald, S.J. Adair. *Dickens and the Drama* (London: Chapman & Hall, 1910).

Glavin, John. *After Dickens: Reading, Adaptation and Performance* (Cambridge: Cambridge University Press, 1999).

John, Juliet. *Dickens's Villains: Melodrama, Character, Popular Culture* (Oxford: Oxford University Press, 2001).

John, Juliet. *Dickens and Mass Culture* (Oxford: Oxford University Press, 2010).

MacKay, Carol Hanbery, ed. *Dramatic Dickens* (Basingstoke: Macmillan, 1989).

Pearson, Richard. *Victorian Writers and the Stage: The Plays of Dickens, Browning, Collins and Tennyson* (Basingstoke: Palgrave Macmillan, 2015).

Pemberton, T.E. *Dickens and the Stage* (London: George Redway, 1888).

Schlicke, Paul. *Dickens and Popular Entertainment* (London: Allen and Unwin, 1985).

Slater, Michael. *Charles Dickens* (London and New Haven: Yale University Press, 2009).

Tomalin, Claire. *Charles Dickens, a Life* (London: Viking, 2011).

## OTHER WORKS CITED IN THIS VOLUME

*The Adelphi Theatre Calendar: A Record of Dramatic Performances at a Leading Victorian Theatre*. http://www.umass.edu/AdelphiTheatreCalendar/index.htm.

Anon. *The Universal Songster* (London: John Fairburn, 1826).

Bratton, Jacky. *New Readings in Theatre History* (Cambridge: Cambridge University Press, 2003).

Bratton, Jacky. *The Making of the West End Stage: Marriage, Management and the Mapping of Gender in London, 1830–1870* (Cambridge: Cambridge University Press, 2011).

Dickens, Mamie and Hogarth, Georgina, eds. *The Letters of Charles Dickens* (London: Chapman and Hall, 1880), 2 vols.

Douglas-Fairhurst, Robert, ed. *A Christmas Carol and Other Christmas Books* (Oxford: Oxford University Press, 2006).

Fielding, K.J. 'Thackeray and the "Dignity of literature"' parts 1 and 2', *TLS*, 19 September 1958, 536, and September 1958, 552.

Fitzsimons, Raymund. *The Baron of Piccadilly: The Travels and Entertainments of Albert Smith, 1816–1860* (London: Geoffrey Bles, 1967).

Hatton, Thomas and Cleaver, Arthur H. *A Bibliography of the Periodical Works of Charles Dickens* (London: Chapman and Hall, 1933).

House, Madeleine, Storey, Graham, Tillotson, Kathleen, and Burgis, Nina, eds. *The Letters of Charles Dickens*, Pilgrim edn (Oxford: Clarendon Press, 1965, 1969, 1974, 1977), 12 vols.

McGowan, Mary Teresa. 'Pickwick and the pirates: a study of some early imitations, dramatizations and plagiarisms of *Pickwick Papers*', unpublished PhD thesis, University of London 1975.

Meisel, Martin. *Realizations: Narrative, Pictorial, and Theatrical Arts in Nineteenth-Century England* (Princeton: Princeton University Press, 1983).

Morley, Malcolm. 'Ring up *The Chimes*', *Dickensian*, vol. 47, 1950, 202–6.

Morley, Malcolm. '*Martin Chuzzlewit* in the theatre', *Dickensian*, vol. 47, 1950–1, 98–102.

Morley, Malcolm. ' "*The Cricket*" on the stage', *Dickensian*, vol. 48, 1951–2, 17–24.

Morley, Malcolm. '*The Battle of Life* in the theatre', *Dickensian*, vol. 48, 1951–2, 76–81.

Newman, Walter. *The Keeleys on Stage and at Home* (London: Bentley and Son, 1895).

*Oxford Dictionary of National Biography* http://www.oxforddnb.com.

*Oxford English Dictionary* http://www.oed.com.

Slater, Michael. *Douglas Jerrold, 1803–1857* (London: Duckworth, 2002).

Spielmann, M.H. *The History of Punch* (London: Cassell and Co., 1895).

Stirling, Edward. *Old Drury Lane: Fifty Years' Recollections of Author, Actor, and Manager* (London: Chatto and Windus, 1881), 2 vols.

Trewin, J.C. ed. *The Journal of William Charles Macready 1832–1851* (London: Longmans, 1967).

Wilson, Edmund. *The Wound and the Bow* (Cambridge: Houghton Mifflin, 1941).